Praise for *THE MAIN ENEMY*

Winner of the Cornelius Ryan Award for best nonfiction book on international affairs

"Some study war from an armchair; others through field glasses. The best go into the firing line. Milt Bearden of the CIA was one of those. For those of us who recall the Cold War, this is fascinating stuff. For those who are too young, read and learn."

—FREDERICK FORSYTH, author of *The Day of the Jackal* and *The Dogs of War*

"A new classic of intelligence literature . . . The Bearden/Risen story is a gripping tale of magnificent sweep and significance. In putting it together, Bearden and Risen have produced for us a work of the first distinction."

—RICHARD SALE, United Press International

"This torrid story of spies and counterspies [is] the real thing. . . . [Bearden and Risen] provide interviews and recollections of CIA agents and KGB operatives chronicling the desperate and internecine spy war."

—SEAN FITZPATRICK, *The Virginia Gazette*

Also by Milt Bearden

THE BLACK TULIP

Also by James Risen

WRATH OF ANGELS (with Judy Thomas)
STATE OF WAR

THE MAIN ENEMY

The Inside Story of the CIA's Final Showdown with the KGB

MILT BEARDEN
AND JAMES RISEN

BALLANTINE BOOKS • NEW YORK

A Presidio Press Book
Published by The Random House Publishing Group

Published in the United States by Presidio Press, an imprint of The Random House Publishing Group, a division of Random House, Inc., New York, and simultaneously in Canada by Random House of Canada Limited, Toronto.

www.presidiopress.com

A Library of Congress Control Number can be obtained from the publisher upon request.

ISBN 0-345-47250-0

This work was originally published in hardcover by Random House, an imprint of The Random House Publishing Group, a division of Random House, Inc., in 2003.

Manufactured in the United States of America

First Presidio Press Mass Market Edition: September 2004

OPM 19 18 17 16 15 14 13 12 11 10

To Marie-Catherine
To Penny

FOREWORD

The Main Enemy is the first comprehensive history of the climactic secret battles between the CIA and the KGB in the closing days of the Cold War, when the Berlin Wall fell and the Soviet Union imploded. Beginning with the watershed "Year of the Spy" in 1985 and following through to the collapse of the Soviet Union, the book chronicles the major espionage engagements between the CIA and KGB through the eyes of the spies who fought them.

This is the story of the lives and careers of the generation trained as spies in the shadow of the Cuban missile crisis, who took charge at the CIA and KGB just as Ronald Reagan and Mikhail Gorbachev rose to power in the 1980s and then suddenly found themselves at the center of a maelstrom of historic change. Many of the CIA and KGB officers who faced off in the Cold War have returned to civilian life. And like their fathers, the combat veterans of Normandy and Stalingrad, they have much to remember.

The Main Enemy is the product of a unique experiment, an effort by a CIA insider and an outside journalist to combine forces to write a more revealing and human narrative than either could on his own. This truly was a collaborative project, but the authors also adhered to a strict division of labor in order to abide by certain rules imposed by the CIA on its former officers. As required under CIA regulations, Milt Bearden submitted his portion of the manuscript to the CIA for prepublication review, and then he made redactions requested by the agency. Those redactions were modest and did not affect the story being told.

James Risen did not submit his portion of the book to the CIA for prepublication review. In order to provide a consistent narrative tone, Milt Bearden is referred to in the first person throughout the book, even in those sections of the book written by James Risen.

The book is based on hundreds of interviews conducted over the course of three years with dozens of CIA and KGB officers on either side of the divide. Where there is dialogue in the book, it corresponds to the specific recollections of one or more of the people present in the room. Beyond this, we have taken the liberty of reconstructing several CIA cables. With the exception of an excerpt from one, these are not actual cables but are reconstructions by Milt Bearden based on his thirty years of reading and writing CIA cables; they are similar in tone and language to the real cables sent in each instance.

ACKNOWLEDGMENTS

To all of the men and women who fought the battles described in these pages, we are in your debt. Many of you could not be named because the job is not yet done; others wished not to be named, and we have honored that wish. But your anonymity does not diminish your contribution.

We also owe an enormous debt to our editor at Random House, the matchless Joy de Menil. *The Main Enemy* is infused with her energy and vision.

And one of our greatest advocates has been Tina Bennett, our literary agent at Janklow & Nesbit, whose enthusiasm for our project never wavered.

We wish to thank Jill Abramson, the Washington bureau chief of *The New York Times,* who has been a steadfast friend throughout the years of work on *The Main Enemy.*

We are also grateful for the research assistance of Barclay Walsh, research supervisor in the Washington bureau of *The New York Times.*

CONTENTS

Foreword / vii
Acknowledgments / ix

PART ONE
The Year of the Spy / 1

PART TWO
The Cold War Turns Hot in Afghanistan / 199

PART THREE
Endgame / 359

Epilogue / 513
A Note on Sources / 527
Select Bibliography / 529
Index / 535

PART ONE

THE YEAR OF THE SPY

1

Washington, D.C., 1830 Hours, June 13, 1985

There was nothing more he could do, Burton Gerber told himself again. The run had been choreographed like a ballet, of this he was certain. He had imposed his own iron discipline on the night's operation and had personally signed off on every detail, every gesture. Now that the route had been selected, he could close his eyes and visualize each intersection.

Gerber knew Moscow as well as any American, and from the Central Intelligence Agency's headquarters half a world away, he routinely insisted on approving each turn to be followed on the operational run from Moscow's city center through the bleak outer neighborhoods. Night after night during his own years in Moscow, he had taken his wife, Rosalie, to obscure Russian theaters in distant parts of town rarely frequented by foreigners. His knowledge of Russian and his reputation as a movie buff had served him well. A good case officer has to learn his city, he told himself.

From his office in Langley, Virginia, Gerber had approved the script for the conversation that was to take place at the end of tonight's run, during the ten-minute meeting in the shadows of the Stalinist apartment blocks on Kastanayevskaya Street that was the sole object of the operation. Finally, Gerber had demanded that rigorous rehearsals be conducted inside the cramped working spaces on the fifth floor of the U.S. embassy in Moscow before the run was launched.

A wraith-thin Midwesterner, Jesuitical in his approach to his work, Gerber was one of the most demanding spymasters the CIA had ever sent against its main enemy, the Soviet Union's KGB. As chief of the CIA's Soviet/East European Division for the past year, he had made his mark. His exacting attention to the details of espionage tradecraft and his impatience with those who failed to meet his standards were legendary. Some critics called him a screamer who berated subordinates, but most respected his single-minded devotion to his job and, in an old-fashioned sense, to duty. Gerber was a complex man who evoked a jumble of emotions from those who worked for him. Longtime Soviet/East European hands studied him with the same intensity they brought to their analysis of the Soviet leaders in the Kremlin. What were they to make of a man whose greatest avocation was for the care, feeding, and preservation of wild wolves?

The truth was that Burton Gerber was a deeply spiritual man, a Roman Catholic who felt a moral obligation to the Russian agents he and his case officers were running. He lit a candle at Mass for each one of his agents unmasked and arrested by the KGB. He had come home from serving as station chief in Moscow three years earlier, so he understood the dangers of operating inside the Soviet bloc better than most at CIA headquarters. He believed that nothing less than perfection was owed to America's Russian agents, and if he yelled at case officers who failed to meet his standards, so be it. Cable traffic between Langley and Moscow was frequently dominated by a tense running debate between Gerber and his Moscow station chief, Murat Natirboff, over the minutiae of operations. There were some in SE Division who whispered that Natirboff was miscast as Moscow station chief, and it was increasingly clear that Gerber didn't trust him to get things done right. He seemed to believe he had to run Moscow operations himself—so much so that to some within SE Division, it sometimes felt as if Burton Gerber had never left Moscow.

But at some level, beneath the rigorous precision so necessary to a successful spy, Gerber also believed in both faith and fate. And so, after he signed off on the night's run, he closed the door to his fifth-floor office at CIA headquarters and smoothly turned his mind to other duties.

It was almost perfect late spring weather in Washington. The day was ending quietly as Gerber left for his home in a graceful old apartment building in Washington's Kalorama neighborhood. He had planned a modest dinner that night, after which he had promised to join a night training exercise.

At the very moment one of his officers would be winding his way through Moscow to meet the CIA's most valuable Soviet spy, Gerber would be watching green trainees playacting espionage on the streets of Washington. Better, he thought, that he devote his time to making certain that the next crop of officers be properly schooled than waste his energy fretting over details of a run he could no longer control. Gerber willed himself to stop worrying, to move on.

This was no routine training course, to be sure. Like the Navy's famed Top Gun school for fighter pilots, the CIA's "Internal Operations" course was the most arduous training program the agency had to offer. It was restricted to a handpicked elite—case officers slated for assignments in Moscow, Warsaw, Prague, and other capital cities in the Soviet empire. These were among the most difficult jobs in the CIA. The physical and mental stresses that came with the constant surveillance, the threat of exposure and arrest, meant that "inside work" was a young case officer's game.

After searching for some time for new tactics to defeat the KGB's suffocating surveillance in Moscow, the agency hit upon the idea of adding some green officers to the Moscow pipeline, recruits who wouldn't be easily recognized from other tours of duty. The decision to send rookies to Moscow placed an added burden on the IO course. It had to provide the most realistic training possible for officers who had never before faced a hostile opposition, much less the professional spy catchers of the KGB's Second and Seventh Chief Directorates.

Run by Jack Platt, a gruff ex-Marine and longtime Soviet targets officer, the six-week course simulated "Moscow Rules." The new case officers had to pass messages and receive documents from "spies" even as they were being trailed through Washington by teams of FBI agents playing the part of a hostile counterintelligence service. The FBI agents played hard—because the course kept them sharp for following real Soviet spies. Still, the best-trained CIA officers in the course could defeat the FBI, often through the use of sophisticated electronic devices, such as burst transmission equipment, that allowed them to pass messages without face-to-face contact.

But the FBI always had a lesson in store. The trainees—often with their spouses in tow—would go out on what they thought was an ordinary operation and walk into an explosive surprise arrest. They'd be roughed up and charged with drug dealing by FBI agents who were totally convincing in making it seem as though the bust had nothing to do with the IO course. After a few hours of questioning, only the most controlled students had the will to hold back their CIA connections. Invariably, some would try to talk their way out by explaining that there had been some horrible mistake: *You see, Officer, I was loitering on a deserted street corner late at night with this woman, who happens to be my wife, as part of a CIA training exercise, not to sell drugs.*

Gerber had invited Jim Olson, who had served with him in Moscow, to join him for dinner before they both went and played their parts in the training exercise. Olson, chief of internal operations for the Soviet Division, had amassed a remarkable record in Moscow and was now one of Gerber's most trusted lieutenants. But when he arrived at Gerber's apartment, Olson brought devastating news: Paul Stombaugh had been arrested in Moscow.

Olson's words hit Gerber like a gut shot. He knew instinctively what Stombaugh's arrest meant: The CIA's most important spy in twenty-five years had been rolled up by the KGB. It meant that Adolf Tolkachev, the billion-dollar agent, code-named GTVANQUISH, the man Stombaugh was supposed to meet, had been fatally compromised.

Typically, when an operation was carried off successfully in the heart of Moscow, right in the middle of a rolling sea of KGB surveillance, Langley wouldn't hear about it until the next morning. To keep the KGB from guessing that an important operation was under way, case officers returning from a late-night run would simply "get black," disappear into the city, and wait until the next morning to reinsert themselves into their cover jobs at the embassy. So only when the officer reported to work the next day would he go through a thorough debriefing, while the tape recordings of his brief encounter with the agent were transcribed.

That was when a flurry of messages would come pulsing into Langley, providing the details of how the run had unfolded the night before. Adrenaline would be pumping across the cable traffic, and well into the next day it would infect the small circle in the SE Division managing the case. Days later, the tape recordings of the agent meeting would arrive by diplomatic pouch, allowing senior SE Division managers to hear the tense voices and feel the strained emotions of the Moscow street encounter for themselves. They could then try to gauge the state of mind of an agent most of them had never met, as well as the performance of a case officer trying to ask all the right questions while constantly scanning his surroundings for signs of the KGB.

Success took a while to percolate through the system. But word of failure came quickly. It would originate in Moscow in the middle of the night, a clipped cable chasing the sun and arriving in Washington in the early evening. The first sign of trouble might come from the wife of a Moscow officer, signaling that her husband had failed to return home on schedule. A few hours later, confirmation would come that the officer had been arrested and that a consular officer from the embassy had been dispatched to secure his release from the KGB's Lubyanka Center at #2 Dzerzhinsky. Tonight's message, Gerber knew, meant that Stombaugh, a young former FBI agent now on his first CIA tour, had been ambushed while tracing the run that he had choreographed so carefully.

Gerber made a few quick calls back to headquarters, to make sure that Clair George, Deputy Director for Operations, and others on the seventh floor knew what was going on. After that, he sat down for dinner, determined to go through with his plans to participate in the IO exercises. But even the steel-willed Gerber couldn't keep his mind from wandering back to Stombaugh and to Tolkachev.

He could only imagine how the night's drama had played out eight time zones away in Moscow.

2

Moscow, 2010 Hours, June 13, 1985

The headset crackled with a one-word message: *"Narziss."*

In the darkened rear compartment of an unmarked, windowless KGB van, Major General Rem Sergeyevich Krassilnikov, white haired and imperturbable, shifted slightly in his seat. Krassilnikov knew that the young CIA officer code-named *Narziss*—the pretty one—was about to fall into his trap.

The CIA had tried to fool him, to lull his watchers, Krassilnikov thought. They had wanted him to believe that this was down time for the Main Enemy. The CIA's Moscow chief had just departed the capital with great operational clatter on a trip to the North Caucasus. He had applied well in advance for permission to travel and had provided a thorough itinerary to the Foreign Ministry, who passed it to #2 Dzerzhinsky. He had also "talked to the walls" in his apartment, giving his KGB monitors the clear impression that mid-June, with the chief away, was going to be a slow period for CIA watchers in Moscow. Was this trip to the Caucasus another trick? Krassilnikov could only wonder what kind of a special services chief left his post at such a time. A clever one, possibly.

But Krassilnikov was confident that the bait for tonight's trap would be irresistible. The KGB had found a ringer for Adolf Grigoryevitch Tolkachev, and his job tonight was to walk a few dozen yards carrying a book with a white cover, a mere fifty paces, in Tolkachev's shoes. Nothing complicated. From a hundred feet away, his CIA contact would catch a glimpse of a man he would conclude was Adolf Tolkachev being arrested and dragged into a van. It would be just enough for him to report back to Langley that Tolkachev had been free until that awful moment, sowing seeds of doubt as to when and how the KGB had discovered the spy.

Adolf Tolkachev had been a devastating spy, but he hardly looked the part. A slightly built scientist in his late fifties, Tolkachev worked quietly at a top-secret aviation design bureau in the heart of Moscow. He had been spying for the CIA for the past six years, long enough to have accumulated two code names, CKSPHERE and GTVANQUISH. (GT was a CIA digraph, two successive letters placed before a code name to identify the geographic region of an agent or operation. GT had only recently replaced an earlier Soviet digraph, CK.) Tolkachev had eluded the KGB long enough to deliver tens of thousands of pages of secret documents to the CIA, looting his design bureau's classified library.

But now he was in the Lefortovo investigative and pretrial prison, undergoing enforced "cooperation" with KGB interrogators while he awaited the inevitable—trial, conviction, and certain execution. The KGB had patiently pieced together Tolkachev's communications plan—how he would signal for meetings with the CIA or, conversely, warn his American handlers of trouble. Krassilnikov and his Second Chief Directorate, the KGB's counterintelligence watchdogs, had carefully triggered the communications plan calling the CIA out for tonight's scheduled meeting. As Stombaugh approached the meeting site, Krassilnikov was certain the CIA didn't have a clue that its prized agent was in prison.

Tolkachev's capture some two months earlier had been brutally efficient. A team from the KGB's Seventh Chief Directorate, led by the short fireplug Vladimir Sharavatov and backed up by the elite Group Alfa special commando unit, had arrested the scientist on the lonely Rogachevskoye Shosse near his dacha twenty-five kilometers outside Moscow.

There had been no resistance. The CIA's superagent had gone limp, his knees buckling under him. In those first seconds, Tolkachev's arms were pinned to his sides and Sharavatov deftly forced a thick rope between his teeth to prevent him from swallowing or biting down, in case he had a suicide pill hidden in his mouth. His jacket and shirt were roughly stripped from his shoulders, in case a poison pill had been sewn into his collar. He was then dragged to a windowless bus, where he was expertly stripped, with gloved hands probing his body cavities, and dressed in a blue KGB running suit.

The KGB's fear of the CIA's "special preparations," as the suicide pills were darkly known, had its roots in a case that had gone bad eight years earlier. Alexander Ogorodnik had been a fast-rising young diplomat, an assistant to the Soviet ambassador to Colombia, when he began a secret affair with a Spanish woman living in Bogotá. Thanks to a well-placed wiretap at the Soviet embassy, the CIA was able to eavesdrop on conversations between Ogorodnik, who was married, and his Spanish lover. The CIA's Bogotá chief approached the woman, and she agreed to work with the agency to win Ogorodnik over. She even showed the CIA a secret journal he had entrusted to her, his "testament," which revealed his hatred of the Soviet system. The woman was willing to cooperate because she hoped that if her lover began to spy for the CIA, he would stay with her in the West. But the CIA had other plans.

Ogorodnik agreed to switch sides. Before long, he was allowing the Americans to photograph documents shipped by diplomatic pouch between the embassy in Bogotá and the Foreign Ministry in Moscow. At the CIA's urging, Ogorodnik, now code-named TRIGON, accepted a transfer to the Foreign Ministry's operations center. He received secret training in Bogotá on how to use dead drops to communicate with the CIA in Moscow.

Before leaving Bogotá, Ogorodnik demanded to meet the CIA officer who would be handling him in Moscow. Jack Downing, who was slated to be the next deputy chief in Moscow, flew down to Colombia in the summer of 1974 to reassure him. The two men, both in their thirties, developed a quick rapport, and Ogorodnik soon trusted Downing enough to tell him that he wanted the CIA to give him the means to end his life on his own terms if he was captured. In dramatic meetings, Ogorodnik told Downing that he wouldn't go back to Moscow unless he was "treated like a man" and given suicide pills. The CIA reluctantly complied, and Ogorodnik returned home. He divorced his wife after returning to Moscow, but he never saw his Spanish lover again.

From 1974 until 1977, Ogorodnik served as one of the CIA's most valuable spies in Moscow. He gained access to much of the Soviet Foreign Ministry's overseas cable traffic and was able to hand over top-secret Soviet diplomatic documents that gave the United States unprecedented insights into Moscow's negotiating positions during the strategic arms talks of the 1970s. But he was remembered within the KGB mostly for what happened during his arrest. While the precise details of the incident remain murky, it is clear that soon after his arrest, Ogorodnik took the modified Montblanc pen Downing had given him in Bogotá and used the suicide pill hidden inside. He must have slipped the pen into his mouth and, while cupping his hands over his face, bit down through the stress-weakened barrel and into the cyanide capsule concealed inside it. Still cupping his hands over his nose and mouth, he would have taken three quick breaths, as Downing had instructed him. Before his stunned KGB captors could react, TRIGON was dead.

Near panic broke out in the Second Chief Directorate, and careers were very nearly ruined as a result. From that moment forward, new arrest procedures were put into effect.

Krassilnikov's radio crackled again. "*Narziss* is in the operational area. He made a quick pass by Olga and is now on a bench five hundred yards away." Olga was the name the CIA's "poets"—the men and women in Langley who carefully prepared the instructions in Russian for Tolkachev—had used for tonight's meeting site on Kastanayevskaya Street. Now, their own communications plan was being used for a KGB ambush.

Moscow, 2010 Hours, June 13, 1985

Paul Stombaugh sat alone on a bench in the dark, trash-strewn courtyard of a concrete apartment block. The smell of dog feces assaulted him. He had stopped his final run a few hundred yards short of the site where he was to rendezvous with Tolkachev for a brief encounter, known inside the CIA as a "bren." Unfamiliar with the lay of the land in this area of Moscow, Stombaugh had come to the quiet residential street twenty minutes early. He made one quick pass, saw everything was normal and as described in the casing report, and left the area to stage for the meeting. The only thing that seemed unusual was a large trailer parked on Kastanayevskaya Street about fifty yards from the meeting point, its hitch propped up on cinder blocks. He thought the trailer seemed out of place in a residential neighborhood, but he decided to go ahead with the meeting anyway and settled on the bench to prepare himself.

Killing time without attracting attention was a challenge in a Moscow neighborhood. Stombaugh leaned back and sipped water from a vodka bottle, hoping he looked like just another tired Russian worker escaping reality on a summer evening. He ran through a mental inventory of what he had to accomplish in the next half hour. He quickly checked his miniature tape recorder—all meetings with Tolkachev were recorded, so that every tidbit of the conversation could later be mined by the CIA—and found it was working properly.

In one large, double-lined plastic shopping bag, Stombaugh carried cash bundles totaling 125,000 rubles in small notes, equivalent to almost $150,000. The bag also contained five new compact subminiature cameras concealed in key chain fobs, all preloaded with microfilm, sealed, and set to a precise focal length. The cameras and their settings had received extra attention for this meeting, after the last series of documents failed to develop properly. The problem with the last batch raised the tension for tonight's meeting considerably.

The second shopping bag was packed with American medicine and glasses for Tolkachev and his wife, English-language tapes for their son, books with concealed messages, "intelligence-reporting requirements"—Soviet secrets the CIA wanted Tolkachev to try to steal—and communications plans, printed on water-soluble paper for added security. The bags were so heavy that the plastic handles had started to stretch during Stombaugh's long run, and he was beginning to worry about them. Everything he carried was compromising—fatally so for the man he was to meet.

Stombaugh thought his SDR—surveillance detection route—had gone well. Neither he nor his wife, Betsy, had seen anything threatening during their run. After Betsy dropped him off, he continued on his long SDR. By the time he arrived, Stombaugh was confident that he was now "black"—free of surveillance: Moscow was his.

Moscow, 2025 Hours, June 13, 1985

Five minutes, Krassilnikov thought. And then, with lights suddenly blazing, the KGB's Second Chief Directorate would once again capture an American spy trawling Moscow's streets, gravely threatening the security of the USSR. Another in a remarkable string of successes for Soviet counterintelligence.

Krassilnikov had never been a man of doubts, not about himself, not about the Soviet Union. He was the son of an NKVD general, a true believer in Lenin's dream. Flush with revolutionary zeal in the 1920s, his parents had named him Rem, an acronym for the Russian phrase *Revolutsky Mir*—the Soviet system's loftiest goal, World Revolution. Rem Krassilnikov had proudly followed his father's footsteps into the NKVD's successor organization, the KGB. After training in English and in the crafts of Soviet intelligence, he had been sent abroad as an officer in the KGB's First Chief Directorate, responsible for the KGB's foreign intelligence operations.

Along the way he had married a woman of stout Communist Party pedigree, whose parents had named her Ninel—a popular name in the 1920s, fashioned by spelling Lenin backward. Krassilnikov was moving up in the KGB after stints in Ottawa and Beirut. In Beirut, he had been aggressive enough to try a "cold pitch" recruitment of a rising CIA star, John MacGaffin, who dismissed the attempt. But Krassilnikov eventually came home to Moscow and the world of counterintelligence in the KGB's Second Chief Directorate. By the mid-1980s, he had established himself as a legend, a man of exquisite patience, adept at the hidden art of blunting the attacks from *Glavniy Protivnik,* the Main Enemy, the KGB's term for the United States and the CIA. Within the KGB, Krassilnikov was now called, with some reverence, the "professor of counterintelligence."

Krassilnikov had for a time been chief of the Second Chief Directorate's Second Department, which investigated the activities of British intelligence in the USSR. He had become close to two of Britain's most notorious spies who had defected to Moscow, the legendary Kim Philby and the lesser-known but nearly equally damaging George Blake. His contacts with

Philby and Blake gave him a new understanding of his adversaries; lessons he learned from them would serve him well when he moved up to head the Second Chief Directorate's First Department, the counterintelligence arm responsible for thwarting American operations against the USSR.

For the past six years, Krassilnikov had been engaged in a laborious chess match with American intelligence. But over the past few months, the battle had intensified, and Krassilnikov felt he had begun to clear his opponent's board. Suddenly the Second Chief Directorate was marching from victory to victory, and there was a new excitement in counterintelligence.

Krassilnikov believed, with all his heart and soul, that these successes were due largely to the brilliant investigative techniques of the Second Chief Directorate along Moscow's streets. His men had the CIA in Moscow on the run.

Of course, he admitted grudgingly, they had received some help from the First Chief Directorate. The foreign intelligence boys at Yasenevo seemed to have lately come into some remarkably accurate information. He never questioned the First Chief Directorate about the source of its information—such things could be learned only over time from the "wall talkers" lined up at the urinals used by senior KGB officers—but it seemed obvious to him that the KGB had a mole somewhere inside the CIA's inner sanctum. And a good one. Maybe even more than one.

But even the best tips from foreign spies had to be run to ground, and fully investigated, by the men of the Second Chief Directorate. Only then could an American spy be caught. Krassilnikov was painfully aware of the fact that the Second Chief Directorate never got the credit it deserved.

The First Chief Directorate's insufferably smug attitude soon evaporated as stories about betrayals within its own ranks began to circulate. In May, the acting *Rezident* of the KGB's London *Rezidentura,* Colonel Oleg Gordievsky, came under suspicion of being a spy for the British Secret Intelligence Service. He was lured back to Moscow by an elaborate ruse and was undergoing interrogation at a KGB safe house. The KGB rumor mill had it that Gordievsky's interrogators were using drugs to get him to admit his treachery, but so far without success.

Within days of the Gordievsky compromise, a GRU colonel, Sergei Bokhan, in the military intelligence *Rezidentura* in the Soviet embassy in Athens, came under suspicion of spying for the CIA. He, too, was asked to return to Moscow on an elaborate ruse, but he sensed he was in danger and made a run for it.

Vladimir Sharavatov tapped lightly and opened the sliding door of the van. "*Narziss* is moving."

"It's time to take the walk we practiced this morning," Krassilnikov softly lectured his companion in the van.

Washington, D.C., 1230 Hours, June 13, 1985

At almost the exact moment that Rem Krassilnikov was waiting to spring his trap on the streets of Moscow, Aldrich Ames walked into Chadwicks restaurant, a smoky, down-home hamburger and beer joint crammed into an old storefront on the Georgetown waterfront, hidden under the shadows of the Whitehurst Freeway overpass.

Ames was carrying with him a bag filled with classified documents. He had come to meet Sergey D. Chuvakhin, a Soviet diplomat whom Ames was supposedly trying to recruit as a spy for the CIA. In fact, their relationship was very much the other way around. Chuvakhin was now an intermediary between Ames and the KGB, a convenient cutout since Ames had CIA authorization to meet with him. Over lunch in one of Chadwicks's long and darkly wooded booths, the two chatted quietly, and, when their meal was finished, Ames handed Chuvakhin his bag, which contained, among other things, a list of nearly every Russian agent working for the CIA and FBI. In exchange, Chuvakhin gave Ames a shopping bag filled with cash. It was at that moment that Aldrich Ames irretrievably crossed the line into a life of espionage.

This was the third time Ames had contacted the Russians since he had decided to become a spy. On April 16, he had walked straight into the Soviet embassy in Washington and volunteered his services, and then he met Chuvakhin on May 17 for lunch. Ames later insisted that he hadn't given the

Soviets much of any value until this lunch at Chadwicks. At first, he said, he had tried to scam the Russians, feeding them information about their own double agents.

But on May 19, the FBI arrested John Walker, the longtime leader of a Soviet spy ring in the U.S. Navy, throwing a scare into Ames. Ames didn't buy the FBI's story that Walker's ex-wife had turned him in; he figured somebody inside the KGB had fingered him. So, to avoid Walker's fate, he decided he had to wipe out anyone who might betray him. He turned over to the Soviets the identities of virtually every Russian spy in the American inventory. Of course, he also betrayed agents who could never have endangered him, including Adolf Tolkachev.

What Ames could not know as he walked out of Chadwicks with a bag full of cash was that the KGB already knew about Tolkachev; he was already in a Soviet jail. Paul Stombaugh was just about to spring Krassilnikov's trap, and Ames's decision to compromise the CIA's most important spy had been irrelevant. Still, the KGB would soon begin to exploit the cache of secrets Ames had handed over.

Moscow, 2030 Hours, June 13, 1985

Stombaugh took in the street scene with a sweep of his eyes as he rounded the corner of the apartment block and stepped out on Kastanayevskaya Street. Fifteen yards ahead and on his left, an attractive young woman with dyed red hair was waving her hands in animated conversation in a telephone booth that had been marked as a "taxi phone" on the diagram of the meeting site. Tolkachev's car, with its familiar registration number, was parked on the far side of the street. The parked car was the reassuring "safe, ready to meet" signal he was looking for.

Stombaugh began to walk briskly now, covering the last few yards toward a bench on the far side of the street. Tolkachev was not yet in sight. The pretty redhead in the phone booth ignored him as he approached and kept talking. He was running over in his mind the inventory of actions he had planned for the next few moments when Tolkachev would step out, give the verbal parole, then walk with him into the recesses of a wooded area. There, he would quickly take the used cameras, still sealed with their microfilm inside, stash them in his jacket, and hand over the two shopping bags. If both men sensed it was safe, they could move to Tolkachev's car, where there might be some time for the small talk that had always been so reassuring to Tolkachev during these dangerous meetings over the last six years. Then they would part, heading in opposite directions, each left to deal on his own with the adrenaline rush of clandestine espionage.

As he passed the phone booth and turned toward the meeting point a few yards away, Moscow exploded around Paul Stombaugh. At least five men burst from the cover of trees and brush. Two grabbed his arms from behind as two others snatched the heavy shopping bags from his grip. A fifth man forced his head down as the men holding his arms lifted them high above his head in what had become known as the "chicken wing" seizure, a characteristic modus operandi of KGB arrests. He heard the tailgate of the parked trailer slam to the ground. The night air filled with voices of the men who had been hiding inside, waiting for the trap to be sprung.

Stombaugh almost blacked out from the pain in his shoulders. When he was allowed to stand again and look around, he found the immediate area bathed in light, cameras rolling and flash bulbs popping. Across the street, Stombaugh saw a small group of men quietly observing the arrest scene. Among them was Rem Krassilnikov.

As he was loaded into a KGB van, Stombaugh glanced back to see the redhead in the phone booth, still talking, still showing no signs of having noticed the events taking place across the street. Two KGB men held Stombaugh's arms over the back of the seat in the van for the long ride to Dzerzhinsky Square and the Lubyanka; by now the pain in his shoulders was almost blinding.

Stombaugh never saw the man being roughly led off in the distance, the man carrying a book with a white cover.

Langley, 1700 Hours, June 13, 1985

COPS—the SE Division's chief of operations—was the first senior officer to read the cable from Moscow.

IMMEDIATE DIRECTOR
WNINTEL

1. CASE OFFICER PLIMPTON ARRESTED 2130 HOURS EVENING OF 13 JUNE WHILE ON OPERATIONAL RUN TO MEET GTSPHERE. HE DETAINED AND INTERROGATED FOR FOUR HOURS AT KGB CENTER AT LUBYANKA; CONSULAR ACCESS GRANTED 0230 HOURS AND PLIMPTON RELEASED AT 0430 HOURS. DETAILS WILL FOLLOW WHEN WE REGROUP AFTER OPENING OF BUSINESS 14 JUNE.
2. NO FILE. END OF MESSAGE.

3

Washington, D.C., 0700 Hours, June 14, 1985

Burton Gerber took deep personal pride in the fact that the CIA was running more highly placed agents inside the Soviet Union than at any other time in its history. Better than anyone else at Langley, Gerber knew just how far both he and the agency had come.

Life had never been particularly easy for Burton Gerber. He often told the story of how, as a young boy growing up in Columbus, Ohio, during World War II, he would track the progress of the Allied armies through the military maps in the local newspaper that he delivered to his neighbors. He became fascinated with world events and yearned to earn his stripes in the next war. But since major wars seemed to be spaced about a generation apart, he calculated that he'd come of age in a time of peace. A career in the CIA, clandestinely fighting the Cold War and rolling back the Soviet threat, became an attractive alternative.

Gerber helped put himself through Michigan State by working the night shift at an auto plant, racing back across Lansing to campus every night to study for the next day's tests. After college, he served a stint in the Army before moving on to the CIA. Married but childless, he'd been supported in his steady rise up the American intelligence bureaucracy by his wife, who had been a CIA employee herself and thus understood the demands of the job. Like many other CIA wives, she often got involved in secret operations in support of her husband and his agents.

During his formative years as a case officer in Eastern Europe, Gerber had witnessed the agency's early, amateurish, and often bungled attempts at spying against the Soviet Union, the fleeting successes invariably ending in deadly failure. He had also endured the destructive "sick-think" of the CIA's notorious counterintelligence chief, James Jesus Angleton. Fortunately, he had been overseas as the worst of the Angleton paranoia played out in the 1960s. He'd heard the rumors, of course, the hushed whispers that made the rounds from one outpost to another, about Soviet cases going bad. But when he finally got back to headquarters in the summer of 1970, he got a heavy dose of the ugly truth.

The whole awful story was there, laid out before him in file folders that he could spread neatly across his desk. As he read, page after page seemed to explode with another bombshell, another scandal. The story was fascinating, terrifying, astonishing. Lives had been ruined, and the story had the power to claim more. As he read on, Burton Gerber was forced to doubt what he thought he knew about the institution he loved, almost above all else.

Gerber was a leading member of a new generation just beginning to transform the CIA into a professional intelligence service, the first to be tempered by long, hard, operational experience, much of it behind the Iron Curtain. Gerber and other young CIA officers like him had already logged more time operating against the Soviets and their Eastern European surrogates than any of their older bosses, who were veterans of the Office of Strategic Services—the wartime predecessor to the CIA. That generation had come of age in a less complicated era, blowing up German trains during World War II.

As they rose through the ranks, Gerber and his generation were bringing back an up-close-and-personal feel for the

KGB and its Eastern European proxies, a streetwise know-how that had been lacking in the early CIA. Middle American graduates of state universities and the military, they brought a more democratic face and a sense of professionalism to a service that for years had lived off the amateurish enthusiasm of its elitist founding fathers, whose notions of secret keeping or secret stealing had been shaped by Yale and Skull and Bones.

Gerber was a driven man who was fascinated by the intricacies of espionage. By 1970, he had risen to the middle ranks in the CIA's Soviet Division, joining the cultlike world of Soviet counterintelligence. He was one of the very few people with access to information about the agency's most sensitive operations against Moscow, including the sordid tale of a KGB officer who had defected to the United States, only to be held incommunicado for three years, including more than two years in a nightmarish prison custom-built by the CIA. Never arrested or charged with any crime, he was kept in solitary confinement, not allowed to read or write. For a time, lights in his ten-foot-by-ten-foot cell were kept on twenty-four hours a day, to disorient him and prevent him from developing a regular sleeping pattern. The defector's name was Yuri Nosenko, and his case became enmeshed in a witch-hunt within the upper echelons of the CIA that had not yet run its course as Gerber read the files.

Nosenko began meeting with CIA officers in 1962, defected in 1964, and brought with him the answer to the most pressing question facing the CIA at the time. Was Moscow behind the assassination of President John F. Kennedy? The Warren Commission had concluded that Lee Harvey Oswald had acted alone, but inside the CIA, officials still brooded over his Soviet connections. Oswald had defected to the Soviet Union after serving in the Marines, including a stint at an intelligence-gathering post in Japan, and then, in a bizarre twist, had returned to the United States with a Russian wife shortly before shooting the President. The CIA had not made public its doubts about Oswald—in fact, it had shared few of its concerns with the Warren Commission—but the truth was that the agency had been unable to determine one way or another whether Oswald had been working for the KGB. The question hung in the air at Langley, and when Yuri Nosenko finally came to the United States, the agency was still trying to figure out whether Lee Harvey Oswald was a real-life Manchurian Candidate.

Nosenko said he had the answer. The KGB wasn't behind Kennedy's assassination. In fact, the KGB had been so concerned about Oswald's past and the appearance of Soviet ties that it had searched its own records and couldn't find any evidence that he was working for them.

Yet by the time Nosenko told the CIA what he knew, the agency had already decided he had been sent across to lie. Angleton was convinced Nosenko was a double agent and persuaded others at the CIA that he'd been sent by Moscow to tie them in knots about Oswald and dozens of other sensitive cases. He was encouraged in his paranoia by an earlier KGB defector, Anatoliy Golitsyn, who had told Angleton that every defector after him would be a double agent. It was the perfect story for Golitsyn to tell—it ensured his continued influence, even after he had run out of secrets to reveal. But to believe Golitsyn was to descend willingly into a swamp of paranoia and confusion. For years, Nosenko was locked away in his specially constructed prison at "the Farm," the agency's training center at Camp Peary, near Williamsburg, Virginia, quarantined like a deadly virus.

With his power base secure thanks to his close relationship with CIA Director Richard Helms, Angleton had managed to co-opt key officials in the Soviet Division, convincing them that virtually all of the spies they were running were double agents sent against them by the KGB. Soon, case officers trying to recruit agents from behind the Iron Curtain had to jump through hoops to convince Angleton and his acolytes that their cases were worth pursuing. Those who persisted or challenged the prevailing paranoia were in danger of coming under suspicion of being Soviet agents themselves.

Angleton was certain that the Soviets had penetrated the CIA and launched a mole hunt that lasted for years, ruining one career after another. Ultimately, the investigation turned on its own, and Angleton himself came under scrutiny as a possible Soviet spy. The Salem witch trials had come to CIA headquarters.

The end result of these mind games was virtual paralysis in

the CIA's operations against the Soviet Union throughout much of the 1960s. The last great Soviet agent to work for the CIA without facing Angleton's paranoid scrutiny was Colonel Oleg Penkovsky, a top aide on the Red Army general staff who spied from 1960 until his arrest in 1962. One of the most important spies in CIA history, Penkovsky was the first to pull back the shroud on the Soviet high command and reveal that the Kremlin was operating on bluster and hollow threats. He helped show the West that the supposed missile gap was a myth and that the Soviet Union's nuclear capability was woefully inadequate to challenge the United States. Penkovsky's information helped give President Kennedy the edge over Soviet Premier Nikita Khrushchev during the Cuban missile crisis in 1962.

Yet many of the major cases in the years after Penkovsky were challenged by Angleton. The counterintelligence chief set the bar so high that CIA officers around the world simply stopped targeting Soviets, knowing that these cases would ultimately go nowhere. Worse, recruiting a Russian might bring them under suspicion. Developing a Soviet as a recruitment target would inevitably lead to a confrontation with Angleton's people. The clear implication was always that the case officer in the field couldn't know what part the case played in the broader KGB "monster plot" to deceive the CIA.

By the time Gerber read the files, the agency was in the process of trying to forget, even cover up, the whole sordid Nosenko affair. But Gerber could see the broader effects of the Angleton excesses. Not only had case officers largely stopped trying to target Soviets, the Soviet Division had also been turning away dozens of "volunteers," Soviets and Eastern Europeans who had contacted American officials with offers to work for the United States. The Golitsyn-fed paranoia had convinced the CIA that these volunteers were in fact KGB provocateurs seeking to turn the agency inside out.

Gerber analyzed the files, going back over fifteen years, files specifically on Soviets who had volunteered in Moscow or elsewhere in the Soviet Union, to test Angleton's theories. Was there any evidence to support Angleton's fears? No one had ever dared sift through the CIA's records to challenge the spy hunter's assumptions in such a methodical way. The simple but powerful answer was that the sick-think theories didn't stand up to scrutiny. To Gerber, the facts strongly suggested that the CIA had been turning away one genuine volunteer in Moscow after another, simply out of fear of contamination. The result was that the agency had probably missed out on a gold mine of secrets from citizens of the Soviet empire who had sought to change sides. There would always be dangles and provocations sent against the CIA by the KGB, but that was the cost of doing business. If the CIA was afraid to talk to Soviets, Gerber reasoned, then it might as well close up shop.

Gerber wrote an exhaustive report detailing his findings, concluding that the CIA was killing its chances for success by turning away so many Soviet volunteers. The overwhelming majority of them appeared to be legitimate, and Gerber offered sensible guidelines to ferret out the few who might be dangles. Above all, Gerber concluded, there was no evidence that the Soviets had ever allowed a serving KGB staff officer to approach the CIA as a double agent. Moscow simply didn't trust them enough. KGB officers who volunteered were almost certainly genuine.

Gerber was proud of his work, which he finished in the spring of 1971, just as Angleton's power over Soviet operations was about to be tested by an unlikely outsider.

By 1971, Helms had finally recognized that the CIA's Soviet Division needed shaking up. He turned to David Blee, an old Middle East hand, to fix it. Blee had made his mark in the Third World; in Delhi, he had orchestrated the 1967 defection and flight to freedom of Josef Stalin's daughter, Svetlana. Blee didn't want to leave his job as chief of the CIA's Near East Division and protested that he had no experience in Soviet affairs, but Helms told him that was exactly why he wanted him. Soviet operations had to have fresh blood, and Blee, a careful bureaucrat but an outsider, was being given the cover by Helms to take on Angleton.

When Blee arrived in his new office on the CIA's fifth floor, he found a note from Angleton waiting for him, inviting him down for a chat. Angleton, still chief of the CIA's Counterintelligence Staff, had been stunned that an outsider was taking over Soviet operations, and when Blee arrived in his darkened office, Angleton told him that he had no business whatsoever in his new job.

Blee's years in the Middle East had given him a pragmatic sense of how to run spy cases, and he could tell instinctively that the Soviet Division had lost its way. To steer the division out of its dark corner, he cleaned house, moving out longtime managers who defended the old methods and replacing them with officers who were new to the division and had not been infected by the Angleton paranoia. Blee was careful never to directly confront the counterintelligence chief; he just went his own way without asking permission.

Soon, Gerber's report on volunteers found its way to Blee's desk. Blee thought its analysis made perfect sense and promptly decided to change the agency's policies on Soviet volunteers. They were to be vetted professionally and then welcomed, not shunned. Wherever possible, they were to be persuaded to remain in place and spy from behind the Iron Curtain.

Blee named Barry Kelly, a red-haired, freckled Irishman who had served with him in the Middle East, to take over as Moscow chief and gave him orders to dust off the old files and air the place out. He was given a list of Soviets who had previously offered to collaborate with the CIA but had been dismissed or ignored for years. Kelly was told to try to resume contact, and before long he was transforming Moscow operations as dramatically as Blee was changing SE Division as a whole.

Blee also sent Havilland Smith, one of his key aides, on a whirlwind tour of the CIA's overseas stations to convince skeptical case officers around the world that sanity had returned to Soviet operations and that it was safe once again to go after Russians. Blee's new open-door policy quickly bore fruit, and within a few years the CIA had developed a remarkable stable of agents behind the Iron Curtain, virtually all of them volunteers.

The CIA's paralysis during the 1960s had masked the fact that, just below the radar screen of upper management, young case officers had been busy modernizing espionage techniques, improvising new means to communicate safely and securely with spies behind the Iron Curtain. They had been frustrated that they hadn't been able to put much of this new "tradecraft" to use during the previous decade, but now Blee's revolution meant that their tactics could be put to the test.

Havilland Smith was one of them. Among the first CIA case officers to be stationed permanently behind the Iron Curtain in the late 1950s, Smith had returned from Prague and Berlin determined to take advantage of the opposition's greatest weakness, rigid orthodoxy. Given high-level approval in the early 1960s to develop new tricks for case officers working inside the Soviet bloc, Smith began consulting magicians to learn about techniques of misdirection and practiced the new tactics on the streets of Washington. He folded what he learned into the newly developing concept of operational tradecraft, perfecting what became one of the CIA's standard methods for passing messages, the so-called brush pass.

Smith's greatest contribution was a concept that came to be known among CIA officers as "moving through the gap." He realized that by carefully planning a surveillance detection route in a hostile city, a well-trained case officer walking a meticulously timed route, turning street corners successively, could create a lengthening gap between himself and the trailing surveillance. Eventually, he would be out of sight of the surveillance teams for a few brief moments. Messages or packages could then be laid down or picked up undetected from dead drops at carefully predetermined points on an operational run. The gap might last only a few brief seconds, but for a well-trained case officer, that might be long enough.

Certainly the tradecraft was never foolproof, and when an operation went sour, the CIA always worried that a street-level slipup was to blame. It was easier to blame bad tradecraft than to hunt for a betrayal from within, particularly among CIA officers who had been so disgusted by Angleton's witch-hunts.

In fact, for years after Ogorodnik committed suicide and his last case officer, Marty Peterson, was ambushed in a knockdown melee beside the Moscow River, the CIA believed that some tradecraft mistake—not a KGB penetration of the CIA—was responsible. A series of unexplained incidents in 1977 actually convinced CIA Director Stansfield Turner that the agency's Moscow operations were fatally flawed by poor tradecraft. Ogorodnik and Peterson's explosive arrests were followed by the exposure of GRU Colonel Anatoli Filatov, GTBLIP, who had spied for the CIA while stationed in Algiers. He was arrested after he returned to Moscow, where he was caught trying to load a dead drop. His CIA case officer, Vincent Crockett, was eventually rolled up as well.

In the midst of these losses, a disastrous and suspicious fire broke out in the U.S. embassy. Soviet firemen, probably sent by the KGB, arrived to put out the flames. They were blocked from gaining access to the most sensitive sections of the embassy, including the CIA's station—but it was a close call.

Newly appointed to run the CIA by President Carter, Turner became convinced that the rewards from running operations in Moscow weren't worth the risks. He ordered a total stand-down of the station. The action forced the CIA to break contact with a series of newly recruited agents, some of whom were permanently lost as a result. Just five years after David Blee had brought the SE Division out of the Angleton sick-think, Moscow operations were once again plunged into paralysis.

Turner's stand-down lasted a year and a half. From 1977 through the fall of 1978, frustrated case officers in Moscow Station did little besides identify new clandestine sites they could use for future meetings with agents—if they were ever allowed to meet agents again. The stand-down would not be lifted until the most persistent Soviet volunteer of the decade—Adolf Tolkachev, the CIA's most valuable spy since the legendary Penkovsky—made his fourth approach to the CIA, offering the Americans the keys to defeating the Soviet Union in the air wars of the future.

CIA Headquarters, Langley, Virginia,
0845 Hours, June 14, 1985

Paul Redmond walked unannounced into Burton Gerber's corner office. Gerber was writing on a yellow legal pad. Without looking up, he handed Redmond a stack of Moscow cable traffic and continued writing.

Redmond glanced quickly over Gerber's shoulder at the small child's blackboard on which Gerber wrote in white chalk each morning his four- or five-word thought for the day. The board was still clean. As he sat in the chair opposite Gerber's desk, Redmond began to read the cables. He had seen the initial cable reporting Stombaugh's arrest the night before. But in the cold light of day, as more detailed cables arrived from Moscow Station, the enormity of the loss sank in.

IMMEDIATE DIRECTOR
WNINTEL
MOSCOW 2199

1. FURTHER TO REF, CASE OFFICER PLIMPTON WAS ARRESTED 2130–2135 HOURS EVENING OF 13 JUNE WHILE ON THREE HOUR OPERATIONAL RUN TO MEET VANQUISH. NO SURVEILLANCE DETECTED AT ANY TIME DURING RUN. PLIMPTON DETAINED AND INTERROGATED FOR FOUR HOURS AT KGB CENTER AT LUBYANKA UNTIL CONSULAR ACCESS GRANTED 0230 HOURS AND PLIMPTON RELEASED AT 0430 HOURS.
2. ARREST OF PLIMPTON APPEARED CHOREOGRAPHED WITH CAMERA ELEMENTS ALREADY IN PLACE, SUGGESTING COMPROMISE OF VANQUISH PROBABLY OCCURRED FAR ENOUGH IN RECENT PAST TO GIVE KGB AMPLE TIME TO SET UP AMBUSH. PLIMPTON DID NOT SEE VANQUISH AT THE SITE OF THE AMBUSH, THOUGH WHAT APPEARED TO BE VANQUISH'S CAR WITH MOSCOW LICENSE TAGS WAS PARKED NEARBY AS SAFETY SIGNAL.
3. ANTICIPATE PLIMPTON AND SPOUSE WILL BE GIVEN USUAL FORTY-EIGHT HOURS TO DEPART THE USSR. WILL ADVISE TRAVEL DETAILS WHEN KNOWN.
4. AMBASSADOR HAS BEEN BRIEFED. HE EXPECTS SUMMONS FROM FOREIGN MINISTRY LATER THIS MORNING TO BE ADVISED OF PNG ACTION AGAINST PLIMPTON AND SPOUSE.
5. PLIMPTON SPOUSE REMAINED AT RENDEVOUZ SITE WAITING FOR PLIMPTON UNTIL 0115 HOURS. AT 0005 HOURS SHE NOTED GROUPS OF PEOPLE IN PARK OBVIOUSLY SEARCHING FOR SOMETHING OR SOMEONE. AT 0105 HOURS A SOVIET FEMALE APPROACHED PLIMPTON SPOUSE AND ASKED HER FOR DIRECTIONS TO LOCAL LIBRARY. PLIMPTON SPOUSE CORRECTLY DEDUCED THAT WOMAN WAS KGB AND THAT PLIMPTON HIMSELF HAD PROBABLY

BEEN ARRESTED. SHE RETURNED HOME AT THAT TIME TO AWAIT PLIMPTON'S RETURN AT 0530 HOURS.

6. DEBRIEFING OF PLIMPTON AND SPOUSE CONTINUES. WILL ADVISE BY SEPARATE CABLES ADDITIONAL OPERATION DETAILS PLUS INVENTORY OF CASH (RUBLES), CAMERAS, OPERATIONAL MATERIALS AND MEDICATIONS PLIMPTON CARRIED, ALL OF WHICH RETAINED BY KGB. END OF MESSAGE.

Gerber was still writing, and Redmond chose not to interrupt his train of thought. He glanced at the teak end table beside him. On it sat a farewell gift fashioned for Gerber by a CIA technical officer at the end of his stint as Moscow chief. A black steel tube bent into an elbow shape was mounted on a wooden base. Suspended by a beaded chain from the elevated end of the elbow was a black glass sphere. Redmond knew the message behind the odd creation: The outline of the steel elbow and dangling chain was suggestive of a taw, the twenty-third letter of the Hebrew alphabet.

GTTAW was the code name for the CIA's cable-tapping operation on the outskirts of Moscow, an operation that had harnessed the best in American technical and human intelligence. The tap had been placed on an underground communications line between Moscow and Krasnaya Pakhra, the location of a nuclear weapons research institute southwest of the Soviet capital. For years, the United States had listened to communications between the scientists working at the complex and defense officials back in Moscow by intercepting signals beamed through the air by microwave; but by the late 1970s, the Soviets had wised up and buried land lines underground. When American listening posts went silent, U.S. spy satellites began to search for clues of a new land-based communications system. It took them a while, but they finally detected telltale signs of construction alongside the main road between the complex and Moscow. Satellite photos soon revealed a series of manholes along the route, sites where maintenance workers could access the underground cable lines for repairs. Working with the National Security Agency, the supersecret eavesdropping and code-breaking arm of the U.S. government, the CIA hatched a plan to tap the lines and began training case officers at the Farm for the physically demanding operation.

In 1979, Jim Olson had been the first CIA case officer to go down into a manhole, and he planted the first listening device. It worked; the CIA and NSA had developed a unique "collar" that could eavesdrop on the cable without requiring a physical tap into the line. Soon, CIA officers were making regular runs out to the rural road where the tap was located to retrieve the tapes, which were constantly recording everything going over the line. It was a reprise of the CIA's famous Berlin Tunnel of the 1950s and in many ways a landlocked version of the U.S. Navy's equally secret operations to tap the Soviet Navy's offshore communications cables.

It ran like clockwork for five years, but in the spring of 1985, when one of Stombaugh's colleagues in Moscow Station had gone to retrieve its tapes, a secret alarm warned him that the device had been tampered with, and the officer aborted. After a lengthy debate between Moscow and Langley, the decision was made to send in another case officer, one who was at the end of his tour, thus making the risk of his walking into an ambush slightly more acceptable. When the officer returned successfully with the recording device, the celebration was short-lived. The tapes were blank. It was unclear whether there had been a malfunction or the KGB had tampered with them, so TAW remained on a list of unsolved "anomalies."

Scratch TAW, Redmond thought. First TAW, and then there was the problem with Bokhan two weeks ago.

Sergei Bokhan, a colonel in the GRU—Soviet military intelligence—code-named GTBLIZZARD, had been spying for the CIA for ten years. In 1978, during his first tour in Greece, Bokhan told the CIA that a young American had walked into the Soviet embassy in Athens offering to sell the secret manual for the KH-11 spy satellite. His information led to the arrest of former CIA employee William Kampiles, who sold the manual for just $3,000. In 1984, during a second tour in Athens following a stint back home in Moscow, Bokhan revealed that a Greek agent with access to defense contractors had given the GRU technical data for the U.S. Army's advanced Stinger antiaircraft missile. The loss of the Stinger was especially troubling for the Pentagon, since the Stinger was considered the most advanced shoulder-launched antiaircraft weapon in the world. As the GRU's deputy *Rezident* in Athens, Bokhan was moving up in the Soviet espionage bureaucracy and promised to become an increasingly valuable mole.

Then on May 21, Bokhan received a call from GRU headquarters, instructing him to return to Moscow within a few days instead of waiting for his August home leave. His senses sharpened. He was told he had to return home because his eighteen-year-old son, Alex, was "having problems" at Kiev Military Academy. But it didn't tally. Bokhan had spoken by phone to his brother-in-law in Kiev just a few days earlier and knew there was no problem with his son at that time. Were his bosses finally on to him? Bokhan became convinced that something was wrong when the GRU *Rezident* in Athens began nagging him about the matter, insisting that he return home by the end of the week. He tried to stall for time and called for an emergency meeting with his CIA case officer, Dick Reiser.

Bokhan hurriedly laid out for Reiser what had happened, and both Athens chief David Forden, who happened to be back in Washington at the time, and Burton Gerber agreed that the sudden interest in Bokhan's swift return was ominous. Gerber sent word to Athens to tell Bokhan not to go home. The CIA quickly set in motion Bokhan's emergency exfiltration plan, and a few days later he was in a CIA safe house in the Virginia countryside.

TAW, BLIZZARD—and now scratch VANQUISH. One, two, three. Coincidence? Not fucking likely, Redmond thought.

Redmond was chief of the branch of the Soviet/East European Division responsible for all clandestine operations inside the Soviet Union. At forty-four he was an irascible, irreverent, Boston Irish Harvard man who some said owned just two shirts, both faded plaids with the sleeves permanently rolled above his elbows. On what his subordinates considered his good days, he wore a bow tie.

Redmond had served overseas in Zagreb, Kuala Lumpur, Athens, and Cyprus, but he and his wife, Kathy, had decided in 1984 not to venture overseas again until their two children were grown. Tethered to a headquarters job, Redmond, like Rem Krassilnikov, had found his niche.

His philosophy of U.S. intelligence was that given half a chance, Americans wouldn't get into the spy business at all. And if forced into it, they wouldn't be particularly good at it. He didn't consider this a negative quality of the American psyche; it was just a condition to be factored into the way he did his job. Even though he was now on offense—running operations against the Soviets—Redmond had a natural inclination to the defense, counterintelligence. He believed that sooner or later the CIA would be penetrated by the KGB. Not a small-time penetration like Kampiles. No, America had not yet found its Kim Philby.

Maybe James Jesus Angleton hadn't been as crazy as people thought. He had been convinced there was a mole inside the CIA. He had just been wrong about who, what, when, and where.

4

Moscow, June 13, 1985

Early on the morning of the Stombaugh ambush, Krassilnikov had visited Adolf Tolkachev at Lefortovo Prison. He sat patiently with the tired and defeated man in a second-floor interrogation room of the converted seventeenth-century czarist fortress, going over for a final time the procedures the scientist had used to arrange meetings with the Americans.

Tolkachev had been in total isolation since his arrest, and under Krassilnikov's relentless interrogation, he had confessed—haltingly at first, then almost eagerly. Inevitably, he told everything as he formed a strange bond with the aging spy hunter. Krassilnikov gradually began to understand the narcotic rush, the exquisite excitement, that Tolkachev had found in his new calling. He didn't spend time fretting over the harm Tolkachev had done to the Soviet Union. That could be left to those doing the damage assessment. Nor did he allow himself to loathe the traitor. Tolkachev was a counterintelligence challenge, a testimony to the professionalism of the men of the Second Chief Directorate who had tracked him. All that was left now was to tie it all together, and Adolf was being helpful on that score.

Adolf Tolkachev had lived with his secret for six years. He had never shared it with anyone, not even his wife or son. The operational discipline imposed on him by his CIA handlers had been sobering, but Tolkachev had always been fatalistic about the risks he was running. He had asked the CIA for a suicide pill in case of arrest, and after three refusals—the CIA's self-imposed requirement—he had been given a cyanide capsule concealed, like the one given Ogorodnik, in a fountain pen.

A thin, stooped man who stood just five feet five inches tall, Tolkachev was still in his fifties, but he looked ten years older. Born in 1927 in Kazakhstan, he grew up in Moscow, where he and his wife, Natalia, both worked at the same research institute while raising their son, Oleg. They shared a life of relative comfort as part of the Soviet *nomenklatura* and made their home in #1 Ploshchad Vosstaniya, one of the city's "Seven Sisters," a Stalinist wedding-cake apartment building reserved for the pampered Soviet elite on Moscow's Garden Ring.

Yet even as he rose through the system, Tolkachev brooded in silence. He harbored a deep hatred for the Soviet system, fueled in part by the ruthlessness with which the state had dealt with his wife's family. Natalia's mother had been executed during Stalin's reign of terror in 1938, and her father had been imprisoned in a Soviet labor camp for years and died shortly after his release in 1955. Eventually, some relatives had emigrated from Russia to Israel, but Tolkachev never told his CIA handlers whether he or his wife was Jewish.

All Tolkachev had in life was his wife and son. By the mid-1970s, he had become obsessed with somehow reaching beyond himself and dealing the system a heavy blow. He envied the dissidents who were beginning to challenge the Soviet system. Perhaps, he mused, if he had been a writer, he could have published *samizdat,* the underground dissident literature that had emerged in Moscow in the 1970s. But he was a scientist at a secret military design facility; with his security clearances, he could never attend a meeting of dissidents. The KGB would immediately discover him and he would be fired from his job—and perhaps arrested. He didn't dare tell anyone he knew about his attitudes toward the government, for fear that he would be denounced. For years, he admired the dissidents from afar but took no steps to join their cause.

Finally, he settled upon a simple solution. He would become a silent dissident. He would become a spy for the United States. But how could an unassuming, middle-aged scientist with no intelligence background get in touch with the CIA in the heart of Moscow? Tolkachev's zeal for his new task overcame his natural caution, and he decided that the simple and direct approach was best.

He was just turning fifty when he took the plunge in January 1977. At a gas station reserved for foreign diplomats near the U.S. embassy, he walked up to a car with diplomatic license plates and asked the driver if he was an American. When the man said yes, Tolkachev dropped a note through the car window and walked away.

By coincidence, the American happened to be Robert Fulton, the CIA's Moscow station chief, who hurried back to the embassy to examine the note. Tolkachev had written vaguely that he had information that would be of interest and wanted to talk to someone about providing it to the United States. He didn't identify himself in the letter and gave no indication of what that information might be.

It was the kind of "volunteer" approach that happened periodically in Moscow, perhaps half a dozen times a year, and that usually turned out to be either a KGB provocation or the product of a Russian's overheated imagination. Once, for instance, the CIA had received a letter from a man living in Kaluga, Russia, who said he was in "electronics" and wanted to help. A CIA officer went to extraordinary lengths to break free of surveillance so as to call him from a pay phone; it turned out he was in home electronics, and the joke became that the CIA had found its own toaster repairman. In the endless stream of volunteers there was always, it seemed, someone with information on how the KGB was controlling the minds of Russians through dental implants, using the electric power grid to transmit their orders. So Moscow Station was skeptical when Tolkachev first made contact, and Fulton did not respond to his note.

But Tolkachev refused to accept this silent rejection. He watched for Fulton's car and left a second note. The CIA again chose not to respond, and Tolkachev tried yet again with a third note. Through his insistent notes, the CIA began to realize that he was a serious volunteer. The frustrated scientist wrote in one message that he could understand why the CIA was not responding, that they might fear he was a KGB provocateur. But he added that he was not willing to say more about who he was or what he knew for fear the information would fall into Soviet hands.

By the time Fulton left Moscow for home, Tolkachev had dropped three notes, none of which had been answered. When Gardner "Gus" Hathaway took over as Moscow chief in mid-1977, Tolkachev was continuing to leave notes and was still being ignored by the CIA.

Stansfield Turner had imposed his Moscow stand-down, preventing Hathaway from responding, but the station chief soon began to plead with Washington to let him contact the anonymous volunteer. Jack Downing, now back in Washington from Moscow and serving as Turner's special assistant, also lobbied his boss to lift the ban on Moscow operations.

Meanwhile, Tolkachev was growing bolder. He gave a note to Hathaway that included a portion of his telephone number. He said that if the Americans came to a certain bus stop at a certain time, they would see him holding an object that had the last two digits of his phone number on it. The CIA sent an officer out, and sure enough, he got the complete telephone number. By now, Turner had relented. He decided to let Hathaway contact the mysterious volunteer. But when an officer, briefly free of surveillance, called the number from a pay phone, Tolkachev's wife answered, and the CIA officer hung up.

The two sides continued to miss each other for months. Unaware that the CIA had tried to phone him, Tolkachev left another note for Hathaway, and when that failed to prompt a response, he finally approached the Italian majordomo of Spaso House, the U.S. ambassador's residence. As the man stepped out of a car with American diplomatic license plates and walked into a Moscow market, Tolkachev sidled up to him. He asked if he could get a message to an American diplomat. When the man said yes, Tolkachev handed him another note.

Tolkachev had by then made half a dozen approaches, and the CIA was increasingly convinced that not only was he a genuine volunteer, but he was gambling with his life in his reckless bids to reach out to them. It was time for them to seize control and create a secure means of communications with their eager volunteer. Still, Hathaway had to move gingerly; any foul-up with this operation might convince Turner to shut things down in Moscow for good.

Ducking out during an intermission in a performance of the Bolshoi Ballet, Hathaway's deputy, John Guilsher, managed to stay free of surveillance long enough to call Tolkachev from a pay phone. This time he found him home. He immediately told him that the United States had received his messages and that it was time for him to stop his approaches. For his own safety, he would have to be patient from now on.

The next time Guilsher called, he was at a pay phone near Tolkachev's apartment. Come out to the pay phone, Guilsher told Tolkachev, and pick up the dirty glove you'll find in the booth. Inside the glove, Tolkachev found a message from the CIA along with secret writing materials and questions for him to answer to prove that he had the kind of access to Sovict technology he had claimed in his notes.

When Tolkachev mailed his answers to an accommodation address in Germany, the agency's experts immediately realized that he was the real thing: a scientist with incredible access to Soviet secrets. They concluded he was not a double agent; there was no way the Soviet government would dangle a man who actually handled such vital military information. After the CIA had pored over his answers, Guilsher was told to recontact Tolkachev in January 1979.

This time, Guilsher called from a pay phone near Moscow's Gorky Park and asked Tolkachev to come out immediately to meet him. The two men walked around the park and began laying out a plan for Tolkachev's espionage career.

It soon became clear that Tolkachev could not be handled through the traditional and impersonal methods the CIA preferred to use in Moscow. He was prepared to provide several dozen rolls of film at a time, far too much material to be left at a dead drop in an alleyway. He would have to be met in person, regularly, by a case officer in Moscow. To arrange the meetings, the CIA would communicate with Tolkachev through sophisticated short-range burst transmission devices, including a new system called Discus, which could send messages of up to 2,300 characters as far as a mile away.

After that first meeting, Tolkachev and Guilsher met about once every three months. At first, Tolkachev provided long, handwritten notes on the advanced "look-down, shoot-down" radar systems for Soviet fighter aircraft that he was helping to design. Before long he was given a 35 mm camera and film, and he began handing over bags filled with rolls of photographs of classified documents from his institute. Tolkachev amazed his handlers with his prolific production; at one meeting alone, he turned over 174 rolls of film, with 36 exposures apiece. Tolkachev didn't have a private office at his design bureau, but he was willing to take huge risks, photographing documents at his desk with co-workers nearby. He learned to pile stacks of books around him so that he could photograph documents without being observed. Inside the office, he used miniature cameras provided by the CIA; at first, he was given a "molly," a camera the size of a matchbox. Later, the CIA replaced it with a T-100, a slender cylinder about 1½ inches long, followed by the more advanced T-50. But he preferred the more reliable 35 mm camera and would often take documents home at lunchtime or overnight and photograph them in his apartment before returning them to the design bureau's library.

His production astonished the CIA and made him a secret superstar inside the American national security apparatus. At Langley, insiders liked to say that Tolkachev "paid the rent" for the agency, justifying the CIA's budget virtually by himself. His intelligence allowed the U.S. Air Force to see what the Soviets were planning for their next generation of fighter aircraft, and that meant that new American planes could be engineered to defeat them before the Soviet fighters ever flew.

Among the many secrets Tolkachev handed over during his six years as a spy were the designs for the avionics, radar, missiles, and other weapons systems for the MiG-23; the missile and radar capabilities of the MiG-25; and the existence of the new Su-27 fighter and the MiG-29 and its advanced radar. Tolkachev's information also frequently showed the Pentagon how its research to counter Soviet systems had been heading down the wrong track, and several American defense programs were revised or scrapped as a result. In December 1979, the Air Force completely reversed direction on a $70 million electronics package for the F-15 fighter aircraft. In a 1979 memo to CIA Director Stansfield Turner, Air Force Chief of Staff General Lew Allen Jr. stated simply that Tolkachev's intelligence "was of incalculable value." In May 1979, the CIA hosted a three-day seminar for a small group of officials from the Defense Intelligence Agency, the Air Force, and other agencies to review Tolkachev's work. The consensus was that Tolkachev had saved the U.S. military "billions of dollars and up to five years of R&D time."

Tolkachev never told his wife or son about his espionage, to protect them if he was ever arrested. This sometimes led to communications glitches. His apartment was only five hundred meters or so down the Garden Ring Road from the U.S. embassy, and his signal that he was ready to meet with the agency was to open a *fortochka,* a small ventilating window common in Soviet apartments. A CIA officer would check his ninth-floor window on his way to work, or his wife could pass by on a shopping run. But at least once, after Tolkachev left the window open to signal for a meeting, his wife closed it before anyone from the CIA had a chance to check it; Tolkachev was left waiting at the meeting site alone.

Tolkachev did not ask for money in his initial messages to the CIA, and after he began to meet with Guilsher he made it clear that he was motivated by a deep hatred of the Soviet system. Still, he told Guilsher he wanted the CIA to pay him so he could be certain that the agency took him seriously and that the Americans valued his information. The CIA obliged, handing over hundreds of thousands of rubles bought on the black market in Germany and setting aside far more in a reserve account he could use if he ever defected.

Tolkachev was smart enough not to spend his cash lavishly. He bought a car for the first time in his life, but it was a simple

Zhiguli, a Soviet-built Fiat. He also found a small dacha for his family. Still, he began to feel uncomfortable with the huge sums of money he was receiving from the CIA, money he couldn't spend without drawing suspicion. Eventually he asked his handler to give some of his money to the families of jailed Soviet dissidents. The CIA never did meet that demand, but the request convinced the agency that he was driven by deeper motives than cash.

He did, however, make requests of a more personal nature. He asked for medicine and books for himself, including Aleksandr Solzhenitsyn's *Gulag Archipelago,* which was banned in the Soviet Union; the memoirs of Israeli Prime Minister Golda Meir; novels of Russian masters like Turgenev and Pushkin; and, incongruously, Hitler's *Mein Kampf.* (The KGB would later have a field day when they discovered this; they would play on Tolkachev's first name, Adolf, and smear him by alleging that he was a closet fascist.)

He also wanted to give a few small things to his family. He asked for supplies that were hard to come by in Moscow for his son's studies in architecture, and Western rock and roll for the boy's music collection, from Led Zeppelin to Uriah Heep and the Beatles. The CIA worried that he would have a hard time explaining how he'd come by new American records, so the agency's technicians bought the records, rerecorded the music on cassettes, and packaged them so they looked like cheap knockoffs from Eastern Europe.

In the fall of 1980, David Rolph, a young Russian-speaking case officer, took over from Guilsher and became Tolkachev's lifeline to the CIA for the next two years. Rolph was part of a new generation of highly educated case officers who would make their mark in the coming decade. Before joining the agency, he had been a country lawyer in southern Indiana, married with small children and increasingly fearful that his dreams of seeing the world were passing him by. An Army brat, Rolph had grown up on a series of military bases, but mostly at Fort Knox, Kentucky. After graduating from the University of Kentucky, where he studied Russian history, he enlisted in the Army one step ahead of the draft in the midst of the Vietnam War. The Army sent him to Russian-language training in Monterey, California, and before long, Rolph found himself in training for Army intelligence. A quick promotion to officer followed, and by 1971 he was serving as an Army intelligence officer in the Berlin Brigade. The end of the Vietnam War meant an early discharge, and Rolph returned to school, this time to Indiana University, for a master's degree in Russian studies. He was hoping to become a college professor. But the academic job market in the mid-1970s was abysmal, so he switched to IU's law school in search of a more marketable degree and paid his family's bills by working as a flight instructor at Bloomington's airport. After law school, he worked one year as an attorney at a small practice in Spencer, Indiana, but the work was simply too boring to keep his interest, and he sent off an application to the CIA.

When he took over the Tolkachev case, Rolph became the front man for what had become a veritable industry within the American intelligence establishment, one that was built upon Tolkachev and his secret documents. In the days leading up to a meeting with Tolkachev, Rolph could feel the anticipation and tension build across the cable traffic from headquarters. He knew how much was riding on each meeting; yet he also knew that he couldn't let the pressure from Langley push him into taking unacceptable risks. He had little difficulty reminding himself that Tolkachev's life mattered more than the secrets he might pass at the next meeting. Rolph stayed with his personal rule—if he ever felt he wasn't absolutely free of surveillance, he would abort the meeting.

But Rolph never had to cancel a meeting, thanks to Moscow Station's ingenious use of disguises and identity transfer techniques, which allowed him to break free of surveillance on a regular basis.

Before some of these meetings, Rolph and his wife would make an obvious show of visiting the apartment of the station's deputy technical officer, a man the KGB knew did not conduct clandestine operations. In the apartment, Rolph would switch into a disguise that made him look like the tech officer, and then he would leave the compound with the station's chief technical officer—the boss of the man he was imitating. After driving around Moscow in a VW van for an hour to make certain they weren't being followed, Rolph would switch into a second disguise so that he could pass for an average Russian worker. He would walk an elaborate surveillance detection route through the streets of Moscow for the next two hours before finally heading to the meeting site. The whole process was reversed on the way back. All the while, his wife and the deputy tech officer would have to sit perfectly still in the apartment, so that the KGB's eavesdroppers wouldn't detect that the tech officer was still home.

By early 1981, Tolkachev had bought his little Zhiguli, and he and Rolph began to hold their meetings inside the car, parked on the street. Rolph worried endlessly about the security of these car meetings. In winter, the Zhiguli's windows would steam up while they talked; Rolph worried that a local militiaman would pound on the door and wonder why two men—rather than a man and a woman locked in a passionate embrace—were inside.

Rolph was soon struck by Tolkachev's fatalistic attitude toward his work as an American spy. He seemed resigned to the fact that he would eventually be arrested and appeared driven to steal as many secrets as possible before the inevitable end. Rolph was handling the case when Tolkachev began demanding a suicide pill. When his request was initially rebuffed, Tolkachev started handing notes to Rolph to deliver straight to the CIA Director and the President. He wanted them to know that it was his personal wish to receive such a pill and was not an idea forced on him by Rolph or anyone else. Finally, after nine months of begging, Rolph gave him one cyanide capsule. Once he bit down on the capsule, Rolph instructed Tolkachev, death would come in three to five seconds.

Tolkachev was always eager to find new ways to increase the number of documents he could copy for the CIA. Early on in his espionage career, he found that he could check classified materials out of the library at his design bureau and take them home at lunch to photograph before handing them back in. But then the library began tightening up its security procedures and eventually required that an employee leave a security badge—a *propusk,* in Russian—before checking out materials. All employees had to show their ID cards to enter or leave the building, so the new regulation meant that Tolkachev could no longer take documents home to photograph.

Tolkachev told Rolph that if the CIA could forge a *propusk* for him, he could leave his original ID card with the library when checking out classified materials and flash his fake one to go in and out of the facility. Tolkachev gave photographs of his *propusk* to the CIA, which finally fabricated a copy after months of trying to match its exact colors and design.

By late 1982, Tolkachev had produced so much and was calling for meetings with the CIA so frequently that the agency decided to tell him to slow down. He was taking too many risks.

There was no sign of trouble at the regularly scheduled meeting in April 1983, but soon after that, Tolkachev panicked and broke off contact for several months. He'd heard that an investigation was under way at his institute. The word in the office was that some sensitive information had apparently leaked from the design bureau, and security officials were launching a probe. For a time, Tolkachev became so convinced that the KGB was closing in on him that he would go to work with his cyanide pill tucked carefully in his mouth. He even went into a meeting with his supervisor with the "L-pill" between his teeth, in case his boss was about to denounce him as a spy. A little pressure on the capsule, a few deep breaths, and he would escape. But after ten minutes of innocuous talk about a technical matter, the meeting ended, and Tolkachev returned to his cubicle, cyanide pill still in his mouth, hands clammy, adrenaline coursing through his system.

Tolkachev took everything linking him with the CIA to his dacha, itself bought with CIA money, and burned it in his wood stove—communications plans, intelligence collection requirements, everything, including a bag of cash. He watched over 200,000 rubles go up in smoke.

But in the end, Tolkachev's craving for excitement won out. After skipping three meetings with the CIA (his case officers had to abort two attempts to meet him during the same period), Tolkachev reestablished contact in November 1983. He told the CIA about the security probe at his institute, but by then he was confident that the investigation was over.

Once again Tolkachev began photographing secret documents. This time, his production was reduced—he had already copied most of the key documents related to his field of expertise. Now he was mostly providing updated information to supplement material he had given the Americans in previous years. The CIA held only two meetings with Tolkachev in 1984; the case had peaked.

Tolkachev's last meeting with the CIA came in January 1985, when two anomalies occurred that would later raise questions at Langley. He opened a different *fortochka* in his apartment from the one he had used in the past to signal for meetings. And when he handed over his film at the meeting, it turned out to be out of focus. The CIA knew that the KGB sometimes had agents it had brought under control hand over out-of-focus photography of top-secret documents, in order to convince the Americans that their agent was still safe and working without actually revealing any sensitive information. During their brief January meeting, Tolkachev warned his new case officer that he was worried about the film. He said he'd photographed the documents in a darkened bathroom at the design bureau but wasn't sure the pictures would come out.

Still, when Tolkachev failed to show up for a scheduled meeting in April, there was no great sense of alarm. After all, it had happened before. The CIA went to a backup plan, calling for an emergency, out-of-sequence meeting, using one of the prearranged signaling options. But by then Tolkachev was under arrest, and he had revealed his communications plans to the KGB. Paul Stombaugh's emergency contact signal to Tolkachev—his car, with American diplomatic tags, parked in front of a fruit and vegetable store on Tchaikovsky Street, a Moscow city street map tossed casually on the dashboard—was spotted by Krassilnikov's stakeout.

Krassilnikov let the CIA request pass without response. Having Tolkachev miss an emergency meeting might sharpen his adversary's senses, but it wouldn't be enough to convince the Americans that there had been a serious security breach. The CIA's agents in Moscow frequently missed meetings for any one of a dozen reasons. He would toy with the Americans a little longer.

On June 5, the CIA aborted an attempt to meet with Tolkachev after a case officer detected KGB surveillance. Finally,

Krassilnikov decided to end the game. At exactly 12:10 P.M. on June 13, a time set in the CIA communications plan months earlier, he opened the small *fortochka* at the top of the large set of windows facing Tchaikovsky Street in Tolkachev's apartment.

Krassilnikov closed the little ventilation window exactly one-half hour later, as the communications plan called for. A CIA officer "read" the window signal in a routine drive-by, and by late afternoon of the next day, two CIA officers—Paul Stombaugh, whose KGB code name was *Narziss,* and a second officer given the KGB code name *Lark*—were both on the move. The Americans had taken the bait. Even the Moscow weather was cooperating; the skies had abruptly cleared after three days of thunderstorms.

Shortly after 5:00 P.M., Paul and Betsy Stombaugh were "called out" by static surveillance: The KGB was alerted that the couple had left home and were moving around the city. For the next three hours, they appeared to be on a routine shopping expedition. The Stombaughs made three stops at shops in various parts of Moscow, all frequented by diplomats. Their car was lost by surveillance on two occasions, but each time it was picked up by another static team in a different part of town and reported back to Krassilnikov's command post. Krassilnikov had ordered the surveillance teams following both Stombaugh and the other officer to stay back as far as possible. He didn't need close-in trailing surveillance, since the ultimate destination on this pleasant June evening was under his complete control. The CIA officers could make their runs as elaborate and as long as they liked, but eventually one of them would come to him and spring his trap.

By 8:00 P.M. Sharavatov began to feel it was Stombaugh making the run to meet Tolkachev. After their third stop, the Stombaughs were lost again for seven minutes, until Betsy Stombaugh was picked up shortly after 8:00 P.M. pulling into the parking lot of the Ukraine Hotel on the banks of the Moscow River. She was alone.

5

Moscow, 1901 Hours, June 18, 1985

Colonel Oleg Antonovich Gordievsky, until four weeks earlier the acting *Rezident* of the KGB station in London, was at this moment trying to will himself into invisibility to everyone save the British Secret Intelligence Service in Moscow. Sweat beaded on his face as he stood stiffly in his gray raincoat, the shiny toes of his rubber boots evenly aligned just inches from the curb of Kutuzovsky Prospekt in busy central Moscow. He stared blankly out at the traffic whirring by him, wondering whether the perspiration was driven by the deep pit-of-the-stomach fear that had been his constant companion for the past four weeks or the Cuban rum he drank late into almost every night. Probably both, he decided.

He knew that his attempt to look like just another Muscovite struggling to get home at the end of a rainy day was futile. His peaked leather cap, an acquisition from his posting in Denmark, was out of place with his drab Russian raingear; and the newspaper-stuffed Safeway supermarket shopping bag he gripped in his left hand was, he was certain, a gigantic red flag fluttering in the faces of pedestrians hurrying toward the Kievsky metro station and the limousines filled with Party seniors whirring past him in the center lane of the wide boulevard. He was terrified that his appearance somehow screamed out, "He's here, the runaway British agent, catch him before he gets away!"

But both the hat and the Safeway shopping bag were Oleg Gordievsky's only links to those who might save him from the faceless executioner he knew would be waiting for him in that special dark corridor in the basement of Lefortovo Prison.

Counting the seconds as he trembled at the curb, exposed and vulnerable, Gordievsky prayed that someone from the SIS station would perform the promised nightly drive-by of this tiny pinpoint on the Moscow city map and see him as prescribed in his emergency instructions. If a British officer did spot him, that would set in motion an SIS plan to rescue him and get him out of the country.

The nightmare had begun shortly after Gordievsky's summons from London to KGB Center in Moscow a month earlier. It was certainly not a development he thought menacing, though all sudden recalls are unsettling to Soviet intelligence officers who have "turned." In this case, Gordievsky had been expecting a recall at some point so that headquarters could confirm his formal appointment as *Rezident* of the KGB's London Station.

Through a series of well-choreographed expulsions of KGB officers in London, Gordievsky's handlers had maneuvered their star agent into position to take over the top job in the United Kingdom. The previous acting KGB chief in London, the brilliant counterintelligence careerist Leonid Nikitenko, had weeks earlier been ordered out of Britain in the escalating spy wars between London and Moscow.

Since the time he had first volunteered to spy for the British while serving in Denmark more than a decade earlier, Gordievsky had provided London with a wealth of information. His most sensitive piece of intelligence came when he warned London that the aging KGB leadership believed that the new American President, Ronald Reagan, was preparing to launch a nuclear war. In 1981, KGB Chairman Yuri Andropov had told a KGB conference that the United States was preparing for a nuclear strike against the USSR. Moscow Center took the threat seriously and soon sent out orders to KGB residencies in NATO countries to look for signs of a pending attack. Code-named RYAN—a Russian acronym for a nuclear missile attack—the operation reportedly became the KGB's top intelligence priority by 1982. (It was also known as VRYAN, for *Vnezapnoe Raketno-Yadernoe Nazpadenie*—surprise missile attack.)

RYAN was the product of Moscow's paranoia about Reagan. Andropov, with little exposure to the West, seemed convinced that Reagan was such an extremist that he was willing to destroy the world in the name of his right-wing ideology. Gordievsky told the British about RYAN and Moscow's exaggerated fears of Reagan. Prime Minister Margaret Thatcher personally briefed Reagan on RYAN and its implications.

Still, NATO went ahead with "Able Archer," a nuclear launch exercise, in November 1983, simulating the actual procedures the NATO allies would use at the start of a nuclear war. Only later did the United States learn how badly Able Archer had shaken the Soviets. The KGB reported back to Moscow that NATO was on actual alert, and Soviet forces were placed on alert status as well. The volatile combination of Able Archer and RYAN had created one of the worst nuclear scares since the Cuban missile crisis—and Washington didn't even know it until after it was over.

The British decided to hide Gordievsky's identity from the Americans, but that didn't stop the CIA from trying to figure out where London was getting its information. Burton Gerber was determined to identify the British source and assigned the SE Division's chief of counterintelligence, Aldrich Ames, to puzzle it out. By March 1985, Ames thought he had the answer—Gordievsky. Ames sent a cable to the CIA's London Station asking whether Gordievsky fit the profile. The answer was yes, and the CIA concluded—without being officially told—that Gordievsky was a British mole.

When Gordievsky arrived in Moscow in mid-May, his confidence evaporated. He immediately discovered that his apartment on Leninsky Prospekt in southwest Moscow had been surreptitiously searched. Were it not for a few subtle traps he had laid out, he might never have known it had been entered.

A few days later, he was taken to a KGB dacha a few kilometers from the First Chief Directorate's headquarters, where he was fed drug-laced brandy and interrogated by KGB counterintelligence specialist General Sergei M. Golubev, the KGB officer who by the end of the Cold War would be the man most identified with Moscow's use of drugs and poisons against the enemies of socialism. Then, without further explanation, Gordievsky had been told that while he could continue his service in the KGB, his London posting had been terminated. He was free to take a month's leave.

Within days he had spotted the first surveillance. Gordievsky was convinced he was followed to a health spa in Semyenovskoya, about a hundred kilometers south of Moscow. He had apparently held his own in the interrogations, although he still had no recollection of the details. KGB counterintelligence didn't seem to have the goods on him, not just yet, but the noose was tightening. The KGB had to be acting on a well-founded suspicion, and it would only be a matter of time before they had what they needed for the perversely legalistic Soviet system to charge him with espionage. What had gone wrong? The question had eaten away at him since he had returned to Moscow. Had the displaced Nikitenko become suspicious?

After what seemed like an eternity, but in reality was no more than three or four minutes, Gordievsky eased back from the curb and fell into the flow of pedestrians heading toward the Kievsky metro station. His only thought was a fervent hope that the British had seen him. He would not know for three more weeks that he had left a minute too early.

CIA Headquarters, Langley, Virginia,
1330 Hours, June 18, 1985

Paul Stombaugh had managed to dodge the Washington press corps since his expulsion from Moscow and arrival in Washington two days earlier. CIA security officers had escorted Paul and Betsy and Rusty, their seven-year-old son, around the reporters waiting at Dulles International Airport and registered them under an assumed name at a Washington hotel. Burton Gerber visited the Stombaughs in their hotel room that first night and said all the right things. He assured them he shared their sense of personal and professional loss in the Tolkachev operation and he knew they had done their best to keep Adolf Tolkachev alive. It was just another reminder of the risks associated with the business, he told them soothingly. Both Paul and Betsy Stombaugh could see in his eyes that Gerber meant every word, that he felt the loss as a human tragedy as well as an intelligence setback.

Now, two days later, Stombaugh was sitting in Gerber's fifth-floor corner office undergoing his first real debriefing. On the couch next to him sat Paul Redmond, chief of USSR operations, a notepad in his lap. Jim Olson, the taciturn chief of the SE Division's operations group, which oversaw all activities inside the Soviet Union and the Warsaw Pact countries, sat in the corner. Gerber sat below a framed pencil etching of a pack of wolves in the wild on the wall behind him. It was sparingly entitled *Wolves*.

Gerber listened intently as Stombaugh finished his account of the ambush and arrest in Moscow four days earlier.

"After we arrived at Dzerzhinsky I was trundled up the elevator and shoved into a holding room with the two KGB men who had ridden with me in the van. They still held on to my arms, even while we went up the elevator." Gerber had learned from the CIA medics that Stombaugh's shoulders had been severely stressed. Full recovery might take up to a year. "They only let go a couple of minutes while they had me strip to my undershorts. After that they sat on either side of me and held my arms again while we waited, I guess, for the others to set the cameras up in the adjoining room."

"Anyone else come in to talk to you?" asked Redmond.

"Nobody. I finally told the two goons that they really didn't need to hold on to my arms anymore. I wasn't going anywhere and they could relax."

Gerber said nothing, but there was an intensity in his eyes that told Stombaugh he was taking in every word.

"The two guys looked at each other for a second, and then just shrugged and let go of my arms. And that was that. Then after a while another one I hadn't seen before came in from the adjoining room and told me to put my pants and shirt on and come with him."

"Any name?" Redmond asked.

"No. No names. I didn't exactly feel like I was in a position to ask." Stombaugh quickly regretted his last comment and hoped he didn't sound flip. He glanced over at Gerber but read nothing in the man's face.

"We'll take a look at the mug books and see if you can make any of them out," Redmond said, making a note on his pad.

"At any rate," Stombaugh continued, "when I went next door they had everything I'd been carrying laid out on tables. It was all there, the rubles, stacked, but no longer banded—they must have counted—the cameras, the books, medicines, eyeglasses, the tape recorder. Photographers were snapping away at me and the materials I was carrying until an older man with white hair told me to sit down while he stood across the desk from me. He was the senior man. Everybody deferred to him. He looked at me for a second or two without saying anything, for dramatic effect, I think, then quietly asked me to explain what I was doing with all that stuff.

"I told him I was an American diplomat and that I wasn't required to answer any of his questions. I said I wanted my embassy notified of my whereabouts immediately, and that he knew the rules."

"And his response?" Gerber asked.

"He went on a tirade. Threw the word *diplomat* back in my face and asked me if all the spy gear laid out on the table was what American diplomats carried around these days."

Redmond broke in. "He did this in English?"

"No. We only spoke Russian. But his tirade seemed pro forma, rehearsed, maybe played to the others in the room. There was a lot of sound and fury and what was supposed to pass for anger, but I never saw anything like that in his eyes. He was kind of sad looking, actually, like he knew something I didn't."

Gerber shifted his weight, but his eyes held Stombaugh's. "You can finish all this downstairs, Paul. Now tell me about Father Roman."

Stombaugh was taken aback by Gerber's abrupt switch from Tolkachev to the bizarre affair of Father Roman Potemkin. Since he had returned to Washington, no one at the CIA had asked him the most obvious question—not Gerber, not even the famously spooky Paul Redmond. Nobody had asked him if the KGB had tried to "pitch" him, to "turn" him while they had him under their control. And now Gerber had just signaled an end to the debriefing on his arrest by changing the subject to the strange case of Father Roman. Stombaugh knew only the most recent twists in the convoluted case, one whose peculiar beginning went back four years, long before Stombaugh had arrived in Moscow.

In 1981, an unidentified Soviet scientist approached an American journalist in Moscow and handed him a mysterious package. Some time later, the package found its way from the journalist to the CIA. The journalist asked for and received a pledge of secrecy from the agency, which tucked the affair away in a compartment that would remain closed for decades.

The package was an intelligence windfall. Analysts at the CIA's Office of Scientific and Weapons Research examining the 250 pages contained in the package found data on the Soviet strategic weapons program that had until then been the subject of only the most speculative analysis. The level of detail and precision in the documentation could redraw American assessments of Soviet nuclear weapons development, but only if crucial additional data could be acquired. The Soviet weapons experts inside the U.S. intelligence community were unanimous: The information included in the package was simply too sensitive, too revealing, to be disinformation designed to confuse the West. The information was so good, in fact, that the anonymous volunteer held the promise of being one of the most highly prized sources the CIA might ever obtain on the Soviet nuclear target. There were already whispers that the source could do for Soviet nuclear programs what Adolf Tolkachev had done for aviation research and development.

Yet the anonymous source had taken care to omit key details that completed the picture. Those could be gathered only through sustained, clandestine contact with him in Moscow. He had to be recontacted, at almost any cost.

The excitement in the analytical community translated into dismay inside the Directorate of Operations, which was given the seemingly impossible task of finding the mysterious volunteer. The handwritten letter included in the package laid out in imaginative detail how the CIA could meet its author in Moscow, but the date was more than six months past by the time the CIA received the packet. The letter bore neither a signature nor other identifying markers. While the CIA could develop a kind of mental image of the scientist from clues in the package—one hint came from a poem—the agency had no way to track him down. By the time Paul Stombaugh arrived in Moscow in 1984, the case that had held the promise of a second Tolkachev had turned into a frustrating dead end.

But in early 1985, a new letter breathed life into the mystery.

On January 24, 1985, Nicholas Daniloff, Moscow correspondent for *U.S. News & World Report,* arrived in his office at 9:30 A.M. and, as part of his morning routine, opened the yellow mailbox hanging on his door. Inside, he found an unstamped envelope, addressed to him in Russian handwriting with no return address. When he ripped open the envelope, Daniloff found a second envelope, this one addressed to U.S. Ambassador Arthur Hartman. A savvy and seasoned Moscow journalist, Daniloff weighed the probabilities and quickly suspected that the letter was part of a classic KGB ruse to entrap him. After all, there were ample precedents for such provocations, designed to justify leveling charges of espionage against members of the foreign press corps in Moscow. He made a quick decision and set in motion events that would explode onto the front pages a year and a half later.

Daniloff and Ruth, his wife, left the *U.S. News* office immediately by car for the American embassy. Checking constantly for the telltale beige or white Ladas or Zhigulis of the KGB Seventh Directorate, they drove along the Garden Ring Road and through Smolensk Square, pulling up at the U.S. embassy on Tchaikovsky Street. When they had made it past the Soviet militiamen posted at the entrance and arrived safely inside the chancery, they let out a sigh of relief and went to the office of the senior press and cultural affairs officer, Ray Benson. Daniloff turned the package over to Benson, who quickly opened the second envelope while Daniloff stood by. They found a third envelope inside, this one addressed to CIA Director William Casey. Inside was a letter, six or seven pages in length, with dense handwriting in an odd and difficult-to-decipher script. Neither Daniloff nor Benson could make much sense of the letter except that it appeared to relate to weapons research. The word *raketa*—rocket—appeared repeatedly in the text.

Daniloff felt uneasy as he left the embassy; he sensed the letter spelled trouble. He had told Benson that he assumed the envelope had been left in his mailbox by Father Roman Potemkin, a curious young man who claimed to be a religious activist. Father Roman had suddenly appeared in Daniloff's life a month earlier, when he came to the *U.S. News* bureau just before Christmas claiming that he wanted to talk to an American reporter about antireligious oppression in the Soviet Union. Daniloff, fearful of KGB listening devices in his own office, steered Father Roman outside and listened to his story while walking down Kosygin Street through a light snowfall. Father Roman talked about the antireligious campaign the government was mounting during the run up to the one thousandth anniversary of the introduction of Christianity to Russia in 1988. He said he was a member of something called the Association of Russian Orthodox Youth, an activist organization that worried, by his account, the cautious leaders of the establishment Russian Orthodox Church. He also told Daniloff he had been arrested and sentenced to two years of "corrective" labor for purportedly being involved with stolen church icons.

Daniloff took Father Roman's phone number and came away from the meeting intrigued—yet also very suspicious. The son of Russian émigrés, Daniloff understood the Russian mind and soul far better than did most American correspondents. Even Father Roman's name raised red flags—phony Potemkin villages had been created centuries earlier as illusions to trick Catherine the Great. Daniloff knew it wasn't easy for Russians to obtain the telephone numbers of foreign correspondents in Moscow. But Father Roman said he had asked a friend who knew a secretary in the Foreign Ministry's press section to provide the name and number of an American correspondent who could speak Russian. Daniloff's suspicions deepened. It sounded like a lame cover story for someone who had been sent by the KGB. After their December meeting, Daniloff decided to keep his guard up if Father Roman reappeared.

On January 22, Father Roman phoned Daniloff. This time he told him he was sending him information concerning Russian Christian youth. Two days later, the unstamped envelope appeared in his mailbox. Daniloff assumed it was from Father Roman—no one else had told him to expect mail. The letter's appearance only deepened Daniloff's suspicions about him and his possible ties to the KGB.

At the embassy he told Benson all he knew about Father Roman, in part to protect himself if he was walking into a Soviet trap.

Sitting in Gerber's office at CIA headquarters, the SE Division chief again prodded Stombaugh to walk back through the Father Roman story. "Go on, Paul. Let's start with exactly what happened in March."

Stombaugh leaned forward and began to tell the part of the story he knew best.

Moscow, 1415 Hours, March 23, 1985

Stombaugh knew he was clean as he negotiated the narrow path through hurriedly shoveled snow in the northeast Moscow suburb. The sky was a brilliant, cloudless cobalt blue, but at ground level, the fresh snow was already turning a dirty gray. A heavy spring snowfall the night before had tied Moscow traffic in knots, giving an edge to the American as he carefully engineered his escape from KGB surveillance. Stombaugh had been on his surveillance detection run since 11:00 A.M. and was convinced he'd been surveillance free from the start and had blended into the flow of Muscovites braving the cold on a brilliant Saturday afternoon. He was dressed in Russian winter clothing, with a fur hat and heavy woolen coat. Stombaugh had learned during the first cold snap after his arrival in Moscow that a case officer seeking anonymity never went out in the cold without a warm hat. The first time he went out bareheaded in the winter, he was stopped three times by helpful babushkas scolding him for not wearing a hat.

His task that bone cold afternoon was a mix of high risk and high gain—he was trying to deliver a letter from the CIA to Father Roman. As he struck out for a public telephone booth, Stombaugh concentrated on the elements of his operational outing.

He had carefully handled the letter for Father Roman, keeping it free of fingerprints or other contaminants that might lead the KGB back to the CIA. The letter's text was the carefully crafted product of a lengthy debate at CIA headquarters and at Moscow, all of which had been triggered by Nicholas Daniloff's visit to the U.S. embassy eight weeks earlier.

Daniloff's decision in January to go the American embassy with his envelope had quickly caught the CIA's attention. Inside the CIA's secure enclosure on the fifth floor of the embassy building, station chief Murat Natirboff and CIA case officer Michael Sellers spread the pages of Daniloff's letter across a table and began a rough initial translation.

At first, the densely written pages seemed to be filled with breathless rantings—there was a slightly crazed quality to them. But as they read on, the two CIA officers realized that the letter also contained some tantalizing information. Was this a message from a verbose—yet very real—volunteer? Hard to tell, but after Tolkachev, Moscow could no longer dismiss the possibility. Natirboff decided to send the letter on to Langley, thinking it might be the last they would hear of it.

But the response from headquarters was instantaneous and explosive. The handwriting, along with many of the themes touched on in the letter, had convinced Langley that it had been written by the same mysterious volunteer who had provided the tantalizing strategic material four years earlier. Natirboff was told that reestablishing clandestine contact with the author was now a top priority. He was authorized to meet with the man who had brought the letter to the embassy, Nicholas Daniloff. While the CIA was prohibited by presidential order from using American journalists in their intelligence operations, the agency just wanted to ask Daniloff a simple question: How can we find the person who gave you this letter?

In March, Natirboff asked Curt Kamman, the embassy's deputy chief of mission, to invite Daniloff to the embassy. By then, Daniloff was busy covering the rise of Mikhail Gorbachev, but he agreed to stop by. When he arrived, Kamman steered him to an acoustic conference room, the soundproof "bubble" in the embassy's political section. Just as Daniloff was explaining to Kamman what he remembered about Father Roman and the letter, repeating what he had told Benson the first time he had come to the embassy, Natirboff joined them. Daniloff recognized him only as an obscure embassy counselor for regional affairs, but the reporter quickly surmised from his questions that the swarthy man with thick black hair combed straight back and a deeply lined face was CIA. Only later did he learn that Natirboff was the CIA's Moscow station chief.

The conversation was unsettling for Daniloff. Natirboff focused on the letter he had received in January. It appeared, Natirboff explained, to be a letter from a dissident scientist trying to contact the CIA. Daniloff said he found that hard to believe. He was convinced Father Roman was working for the

KGB, and he assumed that the letter had come from him. Natirboff asked the reporter to tell him everything he knew about the apparent courier, and Daniloff ended up giving him a physical description of the young Russian, along with his telephone number. The CIA turned Father Roman's telephone number over to the National Security Agency, the secret code-breaking and eavesdropping arm of the U.S. intelligence community. The NSA matched a likely address in Moscow with the telephone number.

Stombaugh was sent out to try to track Father Roman down and, through him, to establish contact with the elusive scientist.

Stombaugh located a public telephone booth not far from the address Langley had provided for Father Roman. Convinced he was still surveillance free, he quickly slipped an induction loop over the telephone's earpiece to record the conversation on his body-worn miniature cassette tape recorder. He dropped his kopek coins into the slot and dialed Father Roman's telephone number. He dialed slowly, so that the rickety Moscow telephone switching system would route the call through on the first attempt.

A woman answered on the third ring. *"Allo . . ."*

"Is this the home of Roman Potemkin?" Stombaugh asked in practiced Russian.

"I am his mother. Roman is not here." The woman's tone of voice sounded natural and unrehearsed.

"Do you know when he might return?"

"In about an hour."

"Thank you. I'll call back then."

Stombaugh gathered his thoughts. He had established that the telephone number was, in fact, that of Roman Potemkin, but he knew there was still plenty of danger. If Father Roman was a KGB provocateur, a real possibility, the telephone could be a KGB-controlled "answering service." He'd have felt better if Father Roman himself had answered rather than a woman claiming to be his mother with the message that Potemkin would return in an hour. That could give the KGB time to get Father Roman to the phone, but again, only if the operation was under their control. The risks hadn't really increased, Stombaugh thought. He decided to wait the hour and then make the second call. He set off on foot to keep moving while he searched for a second public telephone.

Just over an hour later, Stombaugh dialed Roman Potemkin's number for a second time. A man picked up after the second ring.

"Allo."

"Are you Father Roman?" Stombaugh said in accented Russian.

"Da . . ."

"I have information from our mutual friend, Nikolai. I have something for you. Can you confirm your address is as follows?" Stombaugh read the address he had been given.

"No, that's wrong."

"Can you tell me your correct address? Please speak slowly."

The man repeated the address, and Stombaugh wrote it down carefully, the wire loop leading from the earpiece to the recorder in his coat pocket serving as a backup.

"Thank you, I hope to be in touch soon." Stombaugh put the phone back in the cradle and quickly replayed the recording of the conversation and confirmed the address. Checking the map, he calculated that it was a forty-five-minute walk from where he had made the call. Stombaugh weighed the variables in his mind. He had now made two phone calls to a religious activist who had contacted an American journalist, just the type of person who would attract KGB attention, even if he wasn't already under their control. If the phone was tapped, it would be clear to the monitors that a foreigner had called Father Roman twice, but thus far nothing more incriminating than that. And it was unlikely, Stombaugh thought, that Father Roman's phone would be live-monitored in a city where routine telephone taps numbered in the tens of thousands. He concluded that if he moved quickly, he could get to Father Roman's address and deliver his letter without walking into KGB surveillance. All bets were off, of course, if Father Roman was already under KGB control.

In what the CIA called "light disguise"—mustache, glasses, hat, and Russian clothing—Stombaugh walked for nearly an hour before arriving at Father Roman's apartment block. He entered the building and located the apartment number Father Roman had given him. His knock was answered by a young man in his late twenties or thirties, with long hair and what Stombaugh would later describe as a "soft look."

"Are you Father Roman, and did you deliver an envelope to someone?" Stombaugh asked.

"Da," the man answered, but Stombaugh could not read deeper meaning into his positive response to the key question. Nevertheless, he slipped the letter into his gloved hand and handed it to Father Roman. He then nodded a good-bye and quickly left the apartment.

As he made his way back home by foot and public transport, Stombaugh took inventory of what had been given up so far. He had probably exposed himself as a CIA officer, though he'd been in disguise and had been careful not to leave fingerprints on the letter. And he had identified "Nikolai" as an intermediary in his call to Father Roman. There had been no mention of the word *journalist* in conjunction with Nikolai. This had all been discussed with Washington before the operation was undertaken and considered an acceptable risk. If the letter fell into the wrong hands, there would be no easy way to link Nikolai with Nicholas Daniloff—unless, of course, Father Roman had been under the control of the KGB from the start. But that would give the KGB nothing beyond the confirmation that the package they had prepared for William Casey had actually been delivered by Daniloff, according to their own plan. Stombaugh arrived at his apartment just as darkness fell over Moscow, drained but still convinced that he had been "black" for the entire day.

The letter Stombaugh handed to Father Roman had included instructions on how the scientist could contact the CIA. Those instructions included directions on how to arrange a meeting with a CIA officer that could be fully understood only by the person who had written the original 1981 letter to the CIA. Stombaugh began waiting each Thursday at the meeting site, located near the Kiev station not far from Moscow's city center. But no one appeared to make contact.

On April 5, Father Roman called Daniloff again and gave him a curious message: The March 26 meeting had not been possible. The message to Daniloff was, "Your guys behaved in such a way as to prejudice the meeting." Sensing danger, Daniloff immediately told Father Roman he didn't know what he was talking about—and hoped that the KGB eavesdroppers on his telephone line had picked up his response.

Six days later, at a press conference held by visiting House Speaker Tip O'Neill at the U.S. ambassador's residence, Spaso House, Daniloff once again met Kamman. As they walked through the grounds of the ostentatious villa just one mile west of the Kremlin, Daniloff told the American diplomat about the latest message from Father Roman. The journalist stressed again to Kamman that he wanted to be kept out of whatever was going on.

Each Thursday, meanwhile, Stombaugh made his pass by the meeting site near the Kiev station, searching in vain for the scientist who would never appear, until word came from a new and unexpected quarter that the Father Roman operation had gone awry.

On April 18, Michael Sellers made contact with a KGB officer who had offered to spy for the CIA a few months earlier by dropping a sheaf of documents through the car window of a political officer assigned to the American embassy. While the Americans didn't know the KGB officer's identity—he insisted on anonymity—it was clear from the information he had supplied in his initial drop that he was a KGB officer, possibly from the counterintelligence directorate, although there was debate over whether he was from the Second Chief Directorate or from a Moscow district office. The CIA encrypted him GTCOWL and set in motion the means to try to handle him in Moscow.

Sellers was the second CIA officer to meet COWL. The first meeting had gone poorly because the case officer who'd been sent couldn't understand COWL's rough Russian dialect.

During his meeting with Sellers, COWL provided confirmation that the KGB was using a special tracking substance against American case officers in Moscow. COWL told Sellers that chemicals were being used against them and sprayed a sample of the chemical into a plastic bag. Sellers, whose Russian language was at the high end of CIA fluency ratings, had an easier time with COWL than the first officer, but even he found it hard to understand his guttural Russian. COWL turned out to be a hard-bitten, streetwise officer in the local Moscow branch of the KGB. He had little patience for an American who couldn't catch his colloquialisms.

Having shaken KGB surveillance during his long run before the meeting, the six-foot-five-inch Sellers spent hours walking the streets with COWL during that first contact. COWL surprised him by revealing that the KGB knew about the CIA's letter to Father Roman. As they wound through alleys and side streets, with the Russian looking continually over his shoulder to check for KGB surveillance, he explained to Sellers that the CIA had given the letter to "the wrong guy." Eventually, Sellers came to understand that the person Stombaugh had given the letter to was working for the KGB and had turned the letter over to the authorities. COWL did not suggest that the Daniloff affair had been a frame-up from the beginning. COWL made it sound as though the CIA had simply assumed too much by accepting Daniloff's guess that Father Roman was the one who had left him the anonymous package. By handing the letter to Father Roman, the CIA had handed it to the KGB.

The meeting with COWL effectively shut down the mystery-shrouded Father Roman operation, setting in motion the beginnings of finger-pointing that would not play out until more than a year later. After COWL told the CIA that Father Roman was working for the KGB, there was a plan within the CIA to warn Daniloff that he had stumbled onto a KGB provocateur. But Daniloff never received the warning.

CIA Headquarters, 1345 Hours, June 18, 1985

Stombaugh sensed Gerber's agitation as he finished the account of his March 23 run. In fact, Gerber was furious with Stombaugh. He felt that Stombaugh had violated his orders to keep Daniloff's name out of the operation by using the name "Nikolai." Within days of Stombaugh's March meeting with Father Roman, Gerber had cabled a sharply worded reprimand to Moscow, upbraiding Stombaugh for identifying "Nikolai." But this was Gerber's first chance to meet with Stombaugh and hear his explanation in person.

Gerber had been Moscow chief when the original package from the anonymous scientist had been handed over to the CIA, so he had lived with the case for years. He was convinced that the original package had contained some of the most important material the CIA had ever obtained from the Soviet Union and had immediately recognized the importance of Daniloff's letter. As with all Moscow operations, he had tried to choreograph the efforts to contact Father Roman. The letter Stombaugh had handed over—which Gerber insisted did not include the name "Nikolai" or any reference to Daniloff—had been written to his specifications.

This case was so important—and Stombaugh's actions so troubling to him—that Gerber focused on the Father Roman affair even as Stombaugh and the rest of the SE Division were trying to deal with the final collapse of the Tolkachev case. For Gerber, Stombaugh had committed an unpardonable sin by placing Daniloff at risk; Stombaugh, on his end, felt that Gerber was trying to shift the blame. He believed that by mentioning Nikolai, he had done nothing more than use a reference that was already included in the CIA's letter to Father Roman. Stombaugh disputed Gerber's assertion that there was no reference to a Nikolai in the letter that Gerber had approved.

It soon became clear that the Father Roman affair would make it difficult for Gerber and Stombaugh to work together in the future. The dispute with Gerber never hampered Stombaugh's career, however; he was a rising young star within the Directorate of Operations and would find plenty of opportunities outside of Gerber's orbit.

6

Langley, 0830 Hours, July 10, 1985

Furnished with a by-the-book faithfulness to the rank and seniority of its long string of occupants, the office of the deputy chief of the Soviet/East European Division was dominated by a scuffed Federalist-style wooden desk and matching credenza. A pair of ancient straight-backed leather chairs were lined up against one wall, and a sofa and a side chair in tired blue fabric were propped up against the other. The office seemed to declare that it had just been vacated, possibly in a hurry.

It was my first day on the job, and I was still wondering how I had ended up as deputy in SE Division, the most insular subculture in the CIA's Directorate of Operations. I had received a terse one-paragraph cable in Khartoum, my last post, advising me that upon arrival at headquarters in July, I would report in as deputy chief of the Soviet/East European Division. I knew the decision had been made by Clair George, the Deputy Director for Operations, with Bill Casey's hand in there somewhere.

Clair George liked to say that he had plucked me out of obscurity in Texas, where I was running the CIA Dallas office, and sent me off to ride the whirlwinds of Africa, first in Nigeria and then, more significantly, in the Sudan, shepherding the Ethiopian Falasha Jews on their long trek to Israel and then protecting a team of Mossad agents on the run in Khartoum. The operation to spirit the Israelis out of Khartoum just as the new Sudanese government was closing in had caught Bill Casey's imagination. But it was Clair's deputy, Ed Juchniewicz, who was really my mentor. Juchniewicz had pushed for my new assignment as a way of stirring things up in Burton Gerber's SE fiefdom.

Juchniewicz knew that Gerber and I were as different in temperament, experience, and skills as any two officers in the Directorate of Operations. I had a reputation for working in crisis situations in remote corners of the world. To some back at Langley, in fact, I was considered too much of a Third World cowboy, better suited to dusty covert operations than quiet "denied-area" spy cases.

By contrast, Burton Gerber was, in CIA parlance, a "sticks and bricks" man—the master of carefully plotted clandestine operations behind the Iron Curtain. There was a foreboding in his eyes that conjured up the Cold War—the glare of floodlights on the Berlin Wall on a cold January night. Gerber was the closest thing the CIA had to George Smiley. Between us, we seemed to embody the two archetypes of the DO: the Third

World operator who toppled governments and ran covert wars, and the clandestine intelligence collector who moved softly through the Soviet empire, meeting agents and unloading dead drops. The best CIA officers could do both, but Khartoum and Lagos required a different set of skills and a different personality type from Moscow. So when I was teamed up with Burton Gerber, a culture clash of sorts was inevitable.

When I first arrived at Langley in 1964, the CIA was still at the low end of its learning curve. The young men and handful of women who came to Washington that fall to become part of the class of OC-19 were a new generation of CIA officers, most born just before the Japanese attack on Pearl Harbor. Many of their fathers had gone to college on the GI Bill after the war, some the first members of their families to climb that once tightly restricted ladder. OC-19, to be sure, had its share of graduates from Harvard, Yale, and Princeton, but most of its members came from dots on the map spread farther afield. They came to serve as officers of the CIA's elite clandestine service—the DDP, as the spying side of the agency was then known. It stood for Deputy Directorate for Plans, an enchantingly vague name that could apply either to the organization or to its chief.

I'd served four years in the Air Force and spoke both Chinese and German when I first reported for duty at Langley. After a year of training, my first field assignment was in Bonn. By then, the most active arena for the Soviet-U.S. contest had shifted quietly from Germany to the Third World. The Berlin Wall had made it far more difficult to conduct espionage operations along the front lines in the divided city. Berlin was now a training ground for newly minted case officers, rather than the hub of espionage operations that it had been in the early days of the Cold War. Old German hands had taken to sarcastically calling Berlin "Brandenburg's school for boys" and longed for the old days.

I was transferred to Hong Kong in 1968 for a tour of China watching, then rotated back to Europe in 1971 for four years in Switzerland. Intelligence collection requirements during this period had made a subtle shift from gathering information that might help win the war in Vietnam to gathering information on the Paris peace talks and parallel deliberations in

Geneva that would help the United States cut its losses and get out of Vietnam. While in Switzerland I saw us lose our cockiness as a nation and as an agency; it seemed a short journey from the hopeful early 1960s to America's withdrawal from Vietnam without victory, the self-destruction of Richard Nixon's presidency, and the fall of Saigon.

My arrival back in Washington in the summer of 1975 coincided with new attacks on the agency by a post-Watergate Congress. The CIA in 1975 was anything but the self-assured organization with an unchallenged mission I had joined. The DDP had been renamed, this time in plain vanilla, as the Directorate of Operations. It was awash with men and women who'd been run out of Southeast Asia by the North Vietnamese Army and were walking the halls looking for jobs.

After one year at headquarters, I was sent back to Hong Kong—mercifully, I thought at the time. President Carter's new DCI, Admiral Stansfield Turner, brought the President's moralistic sensibilities to Langley with him, and soon field case officers were tasked with transforming the often ugly business of espionage into a "morally uplifting experience" for both case officers and their foreign agents. The President thought that America had an "inordinate fear of Communism," and his DCI agreed. Within a few years, Turner had dismantled many of the capabilities the CIA had built up over the decades, dismissing them as Cold War relics. By the time Iranian revolutionaries took sixty-six Americans hostage in Teheran in November 1979, there was precious little the CIA could do about it with the resources it had in place at the time. To add insult to injury, the U.S. embassy in Islamabad was sacked and burned by a howling Pakistani crowd the same month. As 1979 closed out, the United States seemed on the run across the globe, and the Soviet Politburo apparently decided that it could tidy things up south of its border without much trouble from a besieged America. On Christmas Eve in 1979, the USSR took the plunge into Afghanistan and within a month seemed in full control of the cities.

The year 1980 was no kinder to the United States or the CIA. The humiliation in Teheran was compounded by the disaster of Desert One, when eight Americans died in the ill-fated attempt to rescue the American hostages who were still held in Teheran. The year ended with the election of Ronald Reagan as President, and moments after his inauguration, the American hostages were released by Teheran.

Before Reagan's new Director of Central Intelligence, William J. Casey, arrived at Langley, I was off for what would turn out to be a four-year interlude in Africa. By 1985, Casey decided he wanted me back in Washington, either running his pet project in Central America or working on the Soviet Union. After four years on the job, the DCI had decided that the CIA had to deal aggressively with the "Evil Empire," Ronald Reagan's term for the Soviet Union. Casey had taken a demoralized agency and pumped it up with people, money, and, most important, a mission. I thought things were beginning to look bright again at Langley.

But even then, few insiders knew what the old man was really up to. People seemed to think he had a hand in every action that might put pressure on the Soviet Union, forcing the already visible cracks to open a little wider. There were rumors about his discreet meetings in the Vatican with the Polish pope, his deals with the Saudis to keep oil prices down so that the Soviets couldn't reap windfall profits from their oil sales, and his efforts to block a proposed Soviet oil pipeline to Western Europe. And to be certain, Casey had discovered the Soviet Union's Achilles' heel in Afghanistan. Far from having the situation cleared up in a few months, the Soviets, by 1985, had become bogged down in Afghanistan. Their casualties were mounting, and now there seemed no end in sight for their 120,000-strong army. What had begun as a short-term operation in 1979 had exploded in their faces. They were paying for their adventure on a grand scale, not in small part because of Bill Casey's CIA. It seemed it was the Soviet Union's turn to be on the run. I was settling in at Langley to be part of what Bill Casey thought was the endgame.

I eased back in my recliner and examined my desk. It had three stacked wooden document trays, all empty, a large cut-glass ashtray, and a gallon-size, clear plastic container with the word *BURN* emblazoned in bold red on either side. When I slid open the top drawer, I found two pencils, both freshly sharpened, two government-issue ballpoint pens, and a dozen paper clips. There was nothing else, at least at first glance. But as I pulled out the drawer a little farther, I saw what must have been my predecessor's tools for coping with the job of being Burton Gerber's deputy: three empty Excedrin bottles and a bulbous rubber thimble that slips over the thumb, enabling a conscientious reader to flip quickly through large stacks of documents. Examining the rubber thumb closely, I noted that it was worn and blackened by ink. Some job, I thought as I tossed the Excedrin bottles in the trash can and put the rubber thumb back in the drawer.

"The last guy almost wore that out," said a voice from the open door. I looked up to see a man of medium height with a slight paunch and brown hair just beginning to gray at the temples. His complexion was flushed and offset by deep blue eyes that betrayed little of what was going on behind them. He was coatless, the sleeves of his shirt rolled above his elbows, and he wore a neatly tied bow tie.

"Paul Redmond," the man said, confirming the earlier suggestion of a Boston accent. "I run USSR operations.

"I meant it about the rubber thumb," he added. "You'll wear it out working your way through all the cable traffic here each morning."

"Everybody reads everything?" I asked.

"Everybody reads everything he reads, if they can get their hands on it." Redmond gestured to Gerber's corner office just beyond the adjoining wall. "And he starts an hour earlier than the rest of us."

I leaned back in my chair. "One of those, huh? Is there a test at the end of the day?"

"Yeah, but it's multiple choice, so a cowboy from Africa Division can probably just pass it." No smile yet—Redmond was still sizing me up. "Let me know if I can help you settle in."

"How 'bout we start with you telling me what you're doing in the USSR, say, in an hour?"

"Easy," Redmond said, "our branch runs the division's spies in Moscow."

"How's business?"

"Getting a little slack. Everybody's getting rolled up. This whole place is falling apart. And not just Moscow. You heard the bureau just arrested a secretary in Africa Division for spying for the Ghanaians? For chrissakes, the Ghanaians can penetrate this place!"

Redmond was gone before I could respond or even make up my mind if I was going to like the guy or not. I thought I would.

7

Viborg, USSR, 1450 Hours, July 20, 1985

Oleg Gordievsky pressed his face into the underbrush as a military bus carrying female dependents from a nearby army base passed the spot where he was hiding a few dozen yards off the narrow road. He had spent the last two nightmarish days traveling by train, bus, and truck from Moscow to the rendezvous point his SIS handlers had chosen near the village of Viborg, not far from the Soviet-Finnish border. And at this moment the fear of being caught had been temporarily displaced by a relentless attack of mosquitoes infesting the marshy wood where he was awaiting his rescue.

Checking his watch for what must have been the hundredth time in less than forty minutes, he heard the whine of an engine. Looking up, he saw two cars pull to a halt just opposite his hiding place. Two men jumped out and looked around expectantly. Gordievsky's spirits soared as he recognized one of the men as the officer from the SIS station who had confirmed to him in a brush contact in Moscow a week earlier that the exfiltration plan had been set in motion. Much later, Gordievsky would learn that the second man was Raymond Lord Asquith, grandson of Britain's legendary Prime Minister and a promising Russian specialist in the British SIS.

In a matter of seconds, Gordievsky was curled up in the trunk of one of the cars, a thermal blanket pulled tightly around him, a mild sedative already beginning to work at his raw nerves. Beside him was a flask of cool water and an empty bottle in case he needed to urinate. There was nothing more for him to do now but wait calmly for success or failure. As his body began to surrender to the sedative, he heard the strains of pop music filtering from the car's sound system into his hiding place. It was not his kind of music, Gordievsky thought, but it was his link to those who controlled his fate.

The Soviet-Finnish Border, 1530 Hours, July 20, 1985

Gordievsky had calmed considerably since he had taken his place in the trunk of the car. For the first time in three days he could no longer hear his own fear-driven heartbeat. Though the heat was stifling in the cramped quarters, he was thankful that the mosquitoes had been left behind in the marsh. Counting off each stop the car made at the Soviet border checkpoints, he controlled his breathing and hoped that the thermal blanket would effectively conceal his body heat from prying KGB sensors. As the car pulled to a halt for the fifth and what he thought would be the final time on the Soviet side of the border, he heard the voices of a couple of Russian women and assumed that he had cleared the KGB checkpoints and that the car was now passing through Soviet customs. Gordievsky held his breath as he heard the whining and sniffing of dogs near the car. From inside the car's trunk he couldn't know that the wife of one of the British SIS officers was busily popping potato chips into the drooling mouth of the customs dog, keeping it away from the rear of the car.

After two minutes that seemed like an eternity, the car began to move, and the pop music from the tape deck once again filtered into Gordievsky's cramped quarters. As the car accelerated, the pop music stopped abruptly, replaced a moment later by the strains of Sibelius's *Finlandia,* the signal that the car had crossed over the Finnish frontier.

The KGB later suspected that the CIA had played a role in Gordievsky's exfiltration, but it was entirely a British-run operation. Thanks to analysis conducted by Aldrich Ames, the CIA had learned on its own that Gordievsky was spying for the British, but London didn't officially tell the CIA that

Gordievsky was a British agent until well after he was safely across the Soviet border.

Sheremetyevo Airport, Moscow, 1000 Hours, July 24, 1985

Vitaly Sergeyevich Yurchenko struggled to calm himself as he stood before the passport control booth while the young KGB border guard on the other side of the glass flipped through the pages of his freshly issued Soviet diplomatic passport. He doesn't look more than seventeen, Yurchenko thought, fighting off the urge to bang on the window and tell him to get a move on. He'd done that enough times in the past, but this time leaving the USSR was different.

The border guard looked up at Yurchenko. The KGB colonel was a tall, athletically built man with blond hair, deeply set slate gray eyes, and a broad Slavic face offset by a blond, scraggly mustache curving below the corners of his mouth.

"Let's not take all day, young man. I've got a flight to catch." Yurchenko hoped he sounded cool and on the friendly side of authoritative. But inside he was in turmoil. He kept telling himself he was absolutely safe—there was nothing anyone could know. Only he, Vitaly Sergeyevich Yurchenko, senior colonel, soon to be general in the First Department, First Chief Directorate of the KGB, could possibly know what demons had been raging inside his head in the weeks since cancer had taken his mother in May. No one could know he had been quietly engineering an opening to travel abroad. No one could know what he was planning. Breathe deeply and calm down, Yurchenko told himself. Nobody can possibly know.

Finally the border guard reached for the telephone, talked for a few seconds, then stamped Yurchenko's passport and slid it back to him without comment. Yurchenko snapped it up and turned toward the international departures lounge for his flight to Rome.

South of Rome, 1030 Hours, July 28, 1985

The man's demeanor raised a red flag. Here was Thomas Hayden, a U.S. Navy radioman with a top-secret clearance, sitting with two KGB officers in the woods near a secluded beach south of Rome, drinking Pilsner Urquell. The gathering itself was no less than an act of high treason for Hayden, yet he was hardly sweating. At least not any more than he was, thought Vitaly Yurchenko.

Yurchenko had been interrogating the man, in the breezy way that intelligence officers like to chat up agents, with a patter of sometimes linked and sometimes disjointed questions designed to pin him down, ferret out a detail, or simply knock him off balance. But Hayden handled the probes well, occasionally breaking the pace by holding out his empty glass for a refill of the cool Czech beer. At the end of the opening round of vetting, Yurchenko threw the voice analysis scam at Hayden, asking him if he could record his responses to his questions for later screening in the KGB's technical lab. A kind of voice polygraph, Yurchenko explained.

With no other choice, Hayden easily agreed, and Yurchenko reached into his shopping bag filled with picnic supplies and pretended to switch on a recorder. There was none, but Hayden couldn't know that.

Yurchenko's KGB colleague, Aleksandr Chepil, watched the visitor from Moscow center probe his trophy agent with some apprehension. Personally, Chepil had no doubts about Hayden—he was the prize of his career, the kind of agent an enterprising intelligence officer could easily parlay into an Order of Lenin, if he made certain to share the "success" up the ladder.

What's more, Hayden had taken on new urgency for the KGB. Just two months earlier, John Walker, head of the KGB's Navy spy ring, had finally been arrested after an espionage career that dated back eighteen years. The Walker ring, which included Walker's brother Arthur, his son Michael, and his old Navy friend Jerry Whitworth, had provided the Soviets with an invaluable window into the U.S. Navy's communications and codes since the Vietnam War. Moscow was desperate to find a replacement, and Hayden was a promising candidate. Chepil felt good about his agent, but he knew that others at Moscow Center were beginning to question Hayden's bona fides. The best that could happen here today was that Yurchenko would declare the case a good one and then take some credit for getting it on track. Chepil had no problem with that. It was the way things worked in the KGB.

What Chepil and the others in the Rome *Rezidentura* didn't know was that Yurchenko had been the one who had seeded doubts about the Hayden case back in Moscow. It was his gambit to set up this trip to Italy. Yurchenko had made it clear back in Moscow that he had to go vet Hayden and make sure Rome wasn't being taken for a ride.

Now, here in the secluded picnic area near the beach, Yurchenko was convinced that he'd called the case right. Hayden was, his instincts told him, quite probably a dangle. After he'd gone over his list of questions, Yurchenko slipped his hand back into the picnic basket, ostensibly switching off the recorder.

Glancing up, he caught Hayden studying him, probably for his report to his counterintelligence case officers, he concluded. He saw the American's eyes return a couple of times to his right hand, looking at the missing joints on his middle and ring fingers, scars left by a winch accident when Yurchenko was an ensign in the Soviet Navy. That will be enough for his Office of Naval Investigation handlers, Yurchenko thought. They'll have plenty of clues when they try to identify me. But by the time they put it all together, they'll be coping with a bigger surprise. Yurchenko smiled to himself and saw that *that* seemed to unsettle Hayden just a little.

Yurchenko told Hayden that after cooling off for a few months—enough time to let the Walker thing die down—they would pick up contact again. Then they could get down to the job of prying secrets out of the U.S. Navy communications center in Naples, where Hayden worked.

As Hayden prepared to leave, Yurchenko looked him in the eye and said, "Tom, you are very clever, and I admire your bravery and courage."

Chepil left the meeting with a sense of relief that his agent had passed muster. Hayden left wondering what Yurchenko's last words really meant. Whatever doubts he may have had about Hayden, Yurchenko kept them to himself. No sense in making extra work for himself by declaring Hayden a dangle—he had plenty to do in Rome over the next few days without another distraction.

During his stay in Rome, Yurchenko grilled the officers in

the *Rezidentura* on their knowledge of the rank-and-file CIA officers in Rome. He found varying degrees of understanding of the nature of the adversary, along with more than the usual inflation of the CIA's numbers in Italy. Checking the *Rezidentura*'s diagram of the CIA presence in Rome, Yurchenko skipped over the name of the CIA's Rome chief, Alan D. Wolfe. The diminutive but legendary Wolfe was well known in Middle Eastern intelligence circles, where he had earned the nickname "the Golden Wog"—a name he owed as much to his flamboyance as to his thick mane of blond hair. In his days as the CIA's Near East Division chief, he had once famously declared that he ruled an espionage empire "from Bangladesh to Marrakech."

Yurchenko scanned the list for a name that he might recognize from his own experiences in Washington or Moscow. He knew that the list was liberally sprinkled with the names of Americans who weren't spies at all, just energetic political or economic officers working the diplomatic circuit who the local KGB *Rezidentura* mistakenly believed were in the CIA. Finally, his eyes settled on the name of David Shorer.

Shorer had been arrested in Leningrad almost ten years earlier, along with an agent the CIA had been running in the Soviet defense industries. The roll-up of the operation, in itself significant enough, took on even greater significance because of the severe physical abuse inflicted on Shorer when he was seized at a dead drop site under a Leningrad overpass. The Second and Seventh Chief Directorate officers had been instructed to play it extra hard in retaliation for a rough-and-tumble arrest by the FBI of a Soviet intelligence officer in New York two months earlier.

As he flipped through the *Rezidentura*'s files on the CIA office in Rome, Yurchenko took note of Shorer's office telephone number. He had a surprise in store for Mr. David Shorer.

Rome, 1430 Hours, August 1, 1985

Yurchenko had left the Villa Abamelek, the Soviet embassy staff compound in the western suburbs of Rome, early, explaining to his colleagues that he would check in at the embassy near the Vatican, spend a couple of hours at the *Rezidentura,* and then take the rest of the day off. He muttered something about wanting to take in the sights in Vatican City and suggested to the *Rezident* that he had a special contact planned, something sensitive and outside the purview of the Rome *Rezidentura*. Mysterious activities by visiting seniors from Moscow Center were not all that unusual in Rome, not since the days when Boris Solomatin was KGB *Rezident* in Rome and, as rumor had it, was running a very high level agent right in the heart of the Vatican. Any senior visitor from Moscow Center who dropped a hint that he might be up to something spooky at the Holy See was given a wide berth by the *Rezidentura*. The offer of the *Rezident* to have one of his officers accompany him had been tepid; rebuffing it had been easy. Yurchenko said he would return to the compound for a dinner planned for him that evening.

He spent the rest of the morning making the tourist rounds of the Vatican. He stopped a couple of times while wandering around St. Peter's Square, ostensibly to rest and watch the flow of tourists on holiday in Rome. But in reality, he was conducting an extensive dry-cleaning run, becoming a part of his surroundings while looking for telltale patterns and repeaters among the milling tourists. By early afternoon he knew he was surveillance free and hailed a cab. His instructions to the driver were terse: "Hotel Ambasciatore, Via Veneto."

Among the things Yurchenko carried with him was a bag filled with Russian herbs and traditional home remedies for the stomach ailment the KGB officer was convinced was a cancer that would soon kill him.

Rome, 1435 Hours, August 1, 1985

David Shorer stared at the telephone on his desk, willing it to ring. He had just been alerted that a call had come in for "Mr. David Shorer, who served in Leningrad," from a man speaking English with a heavy Slavic accent and describing himself as a Soviet official who wanted to "come over to your side." The man hadn't sounded like a crackpot, the colleague had said.

After a ten-minute wait the phone rang. Shorer picked it up on the third ring.

"Shorer."

Yurchenko began with his explanation. "Mr. David Shorer, I am a Soviet official who is interested—"

Shorer cut him off. "Where are you now?"

"Across the street from the entrance to your embassy."

"Hang up the phone and walk across the street to the American embassy now. I will meet you at the main entrance."

Yurchenko put down the receiver in the public telephone booth in the Ambasciatore Hotel and began to walk the last few hundred yards of his long journey. Shorer made his way to Post One, the main entrance of the majestic nineteenth-century Palazzo Margherita on Rome's stylish, tree-lined Via Veneto that served as the American embassy. A colleague was already positioned in the small office where Shorer would take his Soviet visitor. The concealed tape and video recorders were being loaded and checked, and the Soviet defector kit was being put in place. Shorer arrived at Post One just as the tall KGB colonel pushed through the door.

Shorer intercepted Yurchenko before anyone else could get to him. "Do you have any identification?"

"I am Vitaly Sergeyevich Yurchenko," he said, handing over his Soviet diplomatic passport. "I am a colonel in the KGB, Department One, First Chief Directorate."

Shorer had spent his career in the Soviet/East European Division and knew in an instant that the biggest counterintelligence catch in the history of the CIA had just dropped in his lap. He hastily ushered Yurchenko to the "walk-in room" and asked him to sit in a straight-backed chair on one side of a table. Shorer took the other chair and pressed a button under the table, activating the video recorder concealed in a bookcase behind him. On the table before him lay a folder containing all the documents he would need in the next crucial hours with the man who now sat before him.

"Please state precisely who you are and why you have come to us," Shorer said as he hit the record button of the tape player on the table and began arranging the forms in both Russian and English for Yurchenko to read and sign.

Yurchenko faced the bookcase squarely, assuming correctly the location of the concealed videocamera, and began to speak in heavily accented English. His head was almost spinning. He had so much to say and had planned this moment in his mind over and over again since his mother had died. But now he didn't know where to begin. Then a sense of calm came over him, and he began, "I am Vitaly Sergeyevich Yurchenko. I am a colonel, soon to be a general, in the KGB. . . ." Dave Shorer was furiously scribbling notes on a yellow legal pad.

Langley, 1230 Hours, August 1, 1985

The handful of senior officers at Langley aware of the drama unfolding in Rome had been in high spirits ever since the arrival of the first cable from Dave Shorer summarizing Yurchenko's defection. Burton Gerber notified Clair George and his deputy, Ed Juchniewicz, and raised the question of informing the FBI. George decided that Gerber should tell the FBI about Yurchenko later that same morning at a farewell luncheon for Edward O'Malley, the outgoing chief of the FBI's Intelligence Division. Ultimately, the FBI would have a high interest in what Yurchenko had to say, particularly since he had been posted to Washington, D.C., a few years back.

As visiting FBI officials and their CIA counterparts, about two dozen in all, gathered in the posh seventh-floor executive dining room a few doors down from Bill Casey's suite, Gerber and counterintelligence chief Gus Hathaway took Ed O'Malley aside and gave him the news. Yurchenko's name meant nothing to the CIA seniors or their FBI counterparts, so the full impact of the defection was not yet clear. No mention of the defection was made to the broader audience at the luncheon.

**CIA Headquarters, Langley, Virginia,
1620 Hours, August 1, 1985**

Something close to an animal scream in the adjoining office brought me out of my chair. I quickly stepped around the corner into Burton Gerber's office, where I found my new boss engrossed in an immediate-precedence, restricted handling cable. Gerber tore off a copy and handed it to me without comment as he continued to read. I was halfway through the first page when he glanced at his watch, wondering how long it would take Clair George and Ed Juchniewicz, two floors up, to call. They were the only other recipients of messages transmitted in this restricted channel and would probably be reading their copies at this moment.

CITE: ROME 22345 011405Z AUG 85
IMMEDIATE HEADQUARTERS SECRET/
RESTRICTED HANDLING
WNINTEL
REF: ROME 22340

1. FURTHER TO DEBRIEFING OF KGB COLONEL VITALY SERGEYEVICH YURCHENKO DPOB 2 MAY 1936, SMOLENSK, USSR. DEBRIEFING CONTINUES IN WALK-IN ROOM, BUT FOLLOWING SALIENT, POSSIBLY ACTIONABLE TAKE FROM INITIAL DEBRIEF OF YURCHENKO WILL BE OF SPECIAL INTEREST:
   A. THERE NO IMMINENT SOVIET PLANS TO ATTACK U.S.
   B. YURCHENKO KNOWS OF U.S. VOLUNTEER TO KGB, CODE-NAMED "MR. ROBERT," WHO DESCRIBED AS FORMER CIA OFFICER PIPELINED FOR ASSIGNMENT TO MOSCOW BUT FIRED FOR UNSUITABILITY ISSUES AND POLYGRAPH PROBLEMS IN 1983–84. YURCHENKO ADVISES THAT "MR. ROBERT" PROVIDED IDENTIFYING DATA ON SOVIET DEFENSE INDUSTRY SCIENTIST ADOLF TOLKACHEV RECENTLY ARRESTED IN MOSCOW IN JUNE THIS YEAR FOR ESPIONAGE ON BEHALF OF CIA, AS WELL AS CIA ASSET IN BUDAPEST DESCRIBED AS SOVIET COLONEL, POSSIBLY INTELLIGENCE OFFICER, KNOWN WITHIN CIA CIRCLES AS "THE ANGRY COLONEL." KGB COUNTERINTELLIGENCE IS CONDUCTING EXHAUSTIVE SEARCH FOR ANGRY COLONEL BUT WITHOUT SUCCESS TO DATE.
   C. YURCHENKO ALSO CLAIMS "MR. ROBERT" HAS COMPROMISED CIA TECHNICAL OPERATION IN MOSCOW, AND POSSIBLY ONE OTHER TECHNICAL OPERATION CIA RUNNING AGAINST USSR.
   D. "MR. ROBERT" REPORTEDLY MET SECRETLY WITH KGB IN VIENNA WITHIN LAST FEW WEEKS.
   E. YURCHENKO ALSO REPORTS KGB HAS RECRUITED NSA EMPLOYEE WHO PROVIDED DETAILS ON SENSI-

TIVE NSA MARITIME OPERATIONS AGAINST SOVIET NORTH SEA SUBMARINE FLEET. YURCHENKO CANNOT RECALL NAME OF NSA EMPLOYEE, BUT MET THE VOLUNTEER PERSONALLY WHILE HE SERVED AT SOVIET EMBASSY WDC.

F. YURCHENKO REPORTS THAT KGB DEPUTY REZIDENT LONDON—HE CANNOT REMEMBER NAME—RECALLED IN MAY UNDER COVER COUNTERINTELLIGENCE INTERROGATION/INVESTIGATION. YURCHENKO HAS HEARD KGB USING "TRUTH DRUGS" ON THIS MAN AT REMOTE LOCATION. NO FURTHER DETAILS.

2. YURCHENKO HAS SIGNED FORMAL REQUEST FOR ASYLUM. SEPARATE MESSAGES WILL FOLLOW BY IMMEDIATE NIACT PRECEDENCE AS DEBRIEFING PROGRESSES.
3. BELIEVE IT MOST PRUDENT TO MOVE YURCHENKO DIRECTLY TO CONUS ASAP. HE BELIEVES IT ONLY MATTER OF THREE-FOUR HOURS BEFORE KGB ROME REZIDENTURA PEOPLE WILL START LOOKING FOR HIM, POSSIBLY REQUESTING ASSISTANCE OF ITALIAN SECURITY. IF WE CAN HAVE HIM AIRBORNE BEFORE THAT HAPPENS SO MUCH THE BETTER. PLEASE ADVISE.
4. FILE: DEFER. E2IMPDET.

"It's Howard. 'Mr. Robert' is Edward Lee Howard," Gerber said with what I thought was a strange calmness in his voice. "Edward Lee Howard has betrayed us."

I was about to ask who Howard was when the phone rang. Gerber picked it up, paused, and said, "Yes, Clair. I've just read it." He listened to the DDO for a moment, then said quietly, "Yes. There's no question. It's Howard."

Looking behind Gerber at his little blackboard, I saw the single word written in white chalk: *Resolve!*

Later, in my office, I went over the first trace memo providing background on one Vitaly S. Yurchenko. It contained the standard biographical information, the usual boilerplate memoranda from the FBI, but one entry caught my eye. Yurchenko was the hapless Soviet embassy security officer who in 1976 had turned over to the D.C. police a packet tossed into the embassy compound by former CIA officer Edwin G. Moore. Moore had been trying unsuccessfully to volunteer his services to the KGB by dropping notes in the mailbox of Dimitri Yakushkin, the KGB Washington *Rezident.* When the KGB failed to contact him—they mistakenly feared an FBI provocation—he had taken the desperate step of tossing a package of secrets over the fence. Vitaly Yurchenko, the report stated, thought the package might have been a terrorist bomb and called the police. Moore ended up with a fifteen-year federal jail sentence, and Yurchenko got the bungler of the year award at Lubyanka.

Interesting guy, I thought. I was looking forward to meeting our new prize the next morning.

8

Andrews Air Force Base, Maryland,
0700 Hours, August 2, 1985

Chuck Medanich scanned the milling crowd of CIA and FBI officers in the VIP lounge at Flight Operations at Andrews Air Force Base. Medanich, a stocky southerner with a broad and open face, could have passed for a linebacker or a security guard. But he was actually the chief psychologist for the CIA's Defector Resettlement Staff, and it was his job to move defectors through the flow of the intelligence community while keeping an eye on their mental health. He had been up past midnight the previous night, laying in supplies at the Oakton, Virginia, safe house reserved for Yurchenko's initial debriefing. Gerber had called Medanich in for a meeting and personally asked that he "see to things." Gerber had also assigned Aldrich Ames, chief of counterintelligence inside SE Division, to help Medanich get things ready for the debriefing. Ames would be one of Yurchenko's initial debriefers.

Medanich and Ames had stocked the safe house with the

usual defector fare: juices, Coca-Cola, milk, bottled water, coffee, tea, bread, eggs, bacon, cold cuts, fruit and vegetables, a few six-packs of beer, a bottle of vodka, and one of bourbon. They worked into the early morning getting the town house ready, then agreed to meet outside the CIA headquarters building a few hours later, at 6:00 A.M., for the drive out to Andrews Air Force Base. There they would greet the C-141 bringing Yurchenko and his escorts, flying in from Rome via Frankfurt, Germany. But Ames didn't show up on time, so an impatient Medanich called up to the SE Division office to see if anyone knew where he was. A secretary answered that they hadn't heard from him. After a few minutes, Medanich headed out to Andrews without him. As Medanich waited for the plane in the spartan VIP lounge at Andrews, he was beginning to wonder if Ames, the man who was supposed to debrief Yurchenko, would ever arrive at all.

As the plane landed and taxied to a stop, Customs and Immigration officers clambered aboard to process Yurchenko's paperwork. Medanich saw Ames arrive at the VIP lounge just as Yurchenko was being brought off the plane and into a milling crowd of FBI agents, CIA officers, and other government officials.

Ames thrust himself into the crowd and approached Yurchenko with a line that prompted Medanich to roll his eyes.

"Colonel Yurchenko, I welcome you to the United States on behalf of the President of the United States."

Medanich glanced at Ames. His introduction was awfully pompous, especially for a guy who had nearly overslept and missed the whole thing. The group quickly formed into a motorcade led by armed CIA security officers in rented sedans, followed by the FBI contingent in their official cars and a van. Ames left his old Volkswagen at Andrews. It would remain illegally parked in front of Flight Operations for three days.

If Aldrich Ames's behavior at Andrews seemed somewhat odd and contrived, there was a good reason for it. Ames wasn't certain whether Yurchenko knew he was a Soviet mole. Ames was one of the CIA's most knowledgeable students of the KGB, and from Yurchenko's initial debriefing in Rome and a quick reading of the CIA's files, he had tried to gauge whether

Yurchenko had been in a position inside the KGB to have access to his case. Ames believed the answer was no, but he wasn't quite sure.

Ames was being handled by Directorate K, the counterintelligence division inside the KGB's First Chief Directorate. Yurchenko had left Directorate K under a cloud in January 1985, at least three months before Ames had volunteered, and had since been named one of several deputies in the American Department in the First Chief Directorate, responsible for Canada and U.S. reserves. But Ames knew the KGB bureaucracy was filled with dozens of "deputies" with small areas of responsibility, and few ever knew what their bosses were doing.

Ames was pretty confident that if anyone in the American Department of the First Chief Directorate knew about his case, it would only be the chief and his most trusted aides. Yurchenko was likely out of the loop. But Ames couldn't be sure, since he knew that Yurchenko could have heard "corridor gossip" about his case. He hadn't mentioned anything about the case during his initial debriefing in Rome, but he could be saving the bombshell for after his arrival in Washington.

Ames decided he had to test Yurchenko as soon as possible. So in the back of the car as they drove away from Andrews, he broke off their conversation long enough to hand him a note that he had prepared earlier. "If you have any particularly important information which you wish to provide only to the Director or another senior U.S. official, tell me, and I will take you to him."

Yurchenko grinned at Ames and said he had no message that required such special care. The confirmation came as a relief.

But then Yurchenko passed on some KGB gossip that sent a chill through Ames. It was, Ames would later recall, "one piece of corridor gossip of great relevance to me, despite the tight compartmentation the KGB used." It seems likely that Yurchenko told Ames that he had heard of a sudden and unexplained trip home to Moscow by the KGB's Washington *Rezident,* Stanislov Androsov. Androsov (along with his counterintelligence chief, Viktor Cherkashin) had turned up in Moscow in April or May, so the speculation along the corridors in the First Chief Directorate's headquarters was that something big had happened in Washington at about that time.

Ames quickly calculated how best to handle this nugget of information. It was the sort of thing, he later recalled, that he could put into his debriefing report with confidence that no one would notice it for some time. Perhaps no one would ever pay much attention to it, if he buried it deep enough.

The tip went into the Yurchenko file without anyone connecting the Androsov trip with the CIA's 1985 losses. In part, that was because Yurchenko's identification of Mr. Robert—Edward Lee Howard—seemed to answer the problems the CIA knew about at the time, particularly the loss of Adolf Tolkachev.

It felt a little ridiculous, but the CIA driver had his orders: Instead of heading straight from Andrews to the safe house, he began a countersurveillance run, zigzagging around Washington for at least a half hour to make sure that the KGB wasn't on their tail. When they arrived at the town house, followed by other government vehicles, there was no way to hide from the neighbors the fact that something strange was going on.

Oakton, Virginia, 1000 Hours, August 2, 1985

The scene at the Oakton safe house, a modest town house on Shawn Leigh Drive, was anything but discreet. A line of government cars awkwardly disgorged a dozen passengers at the door while Medanich fumbled with the keys. I arrived just as the group was ushered inside. Yurchenko stood out among the group.

"Colonel Yurchenko, I am Thomas Fannin, representing Mr. William Casey, the Director of Central Intelligence," I said. "He has asked that I personally convey to you his compliments, and tell you that if there is anything you need, just ask."

Yurchenko seemed pleased that Casey had sent a personal envoy to welcome him.

"Thank you, Mr. Fountain," he said, getting my alias wrong. "Please tell Director Casey that I have no special needs at this moment, and that your boys have taken wonderful care of me from the moment I met them in Rome. Our KGB boys would still be trying to figure out what to do with someone like me, and yours already have me in Virginia." Yurchenko's English was heavily accented, and he was clearly running on adrenaline, but he struck me as genuinely grateful for the treatment he had received so far.

"Colonel, Mr. Casey asked me to assure you that he is available at any time if you have information that you would prefer to share only with him. Do you have any such information?"

Yurchenko shook his head, while pointing to Ames. "I have already told that one, that colleague, that I have no such information. But I have much, very much, to tell you and the boys."

Before I could respond, Ames was at my side, having seen Yurchenko point in his direction. "Need any help, Tom?" he asked, using my alias.

"No. No help needed." I looked at Ames, whom I had just met for the first time the previous afternoon, and thought, I don't even know what alias this guy's using. Maybe we ought to try to get this thing a little more organized.

McLean, Virginia, 0900 Hours, August 3, 1985

Burton Gerber pulled his gray Toyota into the slot next to my car in the parking lot of Charley's, a popular happy hour meeting spot off Virginia's Route 123, a short drive from CIA headquarters. Both of us were a few minutes early for a hastily called Saturday morning meeting with the FBI. It was the second day after Yurchenko's defection. Gerber got into my car to wait for the FBI.

"You said you knew Jim Geer," Gerber said, directing the air-conditioning vent away from himself. Geer, the newly appointed chief of the FBI's intelligence division, was one of the men we'd come to meet. He had just wound up his duties as director of the FBI laboratory and hadn't yet reported for his first day on the new job—that would take place on Monday. Geer's predecessor, Ed O'Malley, had retired the day before, and the whole affair—the Yurchenko defection and the Mr. Robert investigation—was suddenly in Geer's lap.

"Yeah, he was ASAC in Dallas when I was down there about five years ago. He's a big, easygoing guy. Tennessee. Smart, professional. Didn't seem too caught up in the turf battles. At least not back then." I motioned to the envelope in Gerber's hand. "That it?" He nodded. "Does the bureau know anything about him?"

"OS sent a memo over to the bureau yesterday, but they didn't identify Howard as Mr. Robert."

Gerber had, in fact, been frustrated the day before when the CIA's Office of Security officials had hedged on the message they sent to the FBI concerning Yurchenko's revelation about a Mr. Robert. Gerber had said he was convinced that Yurchenko was referring to Edward Lee Howard; he was the only person who could possibly fit the description offered by the Soviet defector. Gerber had lived with the Howard case ever since he took over SE Division a year earlier, and he knew far too much about Edward Lee Howard's messy divorce from the CIA to think that it could be anyone else. But the Office of Security had not told the FBI of the almost certain match between Howard and "Mr. Robert," costing the bureau a day in their investigation. Gerber had decided to bring the bureau into the loop on Saturday morning, two days after Yurchenko walked into the U.S. embassy in Rome. And that's why we were here in Charley's parking lot.

When he first applied to become a CIA case officer in 1980, Ed Howard had seemed like an ideal candidate, with an interesting mix of government and private-sector experiences in Latin America. An Air Force brat, he had served in the Peace Corps and the U.S. Agency for International Development in Latin America and later held a management job at a company in Chicago before his natural restlessness led him to think about working for the CIA. It was the mystique of the agency, the notion of a secret life on the edge, that had attracted him.

Howard easily admitted to past drug and alcohol use while undergoing the required polygraph test for new applicants. The CIA's standards had recently been relaxed—the Office of Security had been forced by the realities of the 1970s to be more flexible in approving new employees who acknowledged past casual drug use, so Howard passed through the first screens of the system. Questions would later be raised, however, about whether Howard's drug use—even the incidents he acknowledged on his polygraph—should ever have been defined as casual.

After operational training at the Farm, Howard was chosen, in early 1982, for assignment to Moscow. His wife, Mary, whom he had met in Colombia while they were both in the Peace Corps in the early 1970s, would also be trained by the CIA so she could help him in his Moscow operations. David Forden, chief of the SE Division at the time, was told by the division's security officer that Howard had a past record of drug use, but Forden was assured that it was not significant enough to prevent Howard from being offered a sensitive post. At the time, CIA rules prohibited a division chief from examining an employee's security and medical records himself, so Forden had to rely on the security and medical staff to tell him what was in the files.

After language school and training in Jack Platt's Internal Operations course, Howard was assigned as a deep cover officer in Moscow. He would be given a "clean slot"—an obscure job in the embassy that had never before been used as cover by the CIA. The clean slot postings were given only to young case officers like Howard who had never served overseas before and thus would never have been identified by the KGB as agency officers.

With a well-planned and low-key arrival on the Moscow scene, KGB surveillance would pay cursory attention to clean slot officers like Howard, while concentrating on already identified American intelligence officers assigned to known cover slots. The agency had started placing deep cover officers in clean slot jobs while Gerber was Moscow chief in the early 1980s; one of Gerber's first clean slot officers had been Dennis McMahon, a first-tour officer who had successfully handled Adolf Tolkachev. Now that Gerber was division chief, he was strongly committed to the practice of relying heavily on clean slot officers—even if they were untested rookies, like Howard.

While studying the Russian language in preparation for his Moscow assignment, Howard shared an office with Michael Sellers, another Moscow-bound case officer. During their year or so in the pipeline, Howard and Sellers spent one day a week and weekends "reading in" on the CIA's Moscow operations. While most of the case files revealed only the cryptonyms of the Soviets working for the CIA in Moscow, Howard could have gained access to files with their true names. The Tolkachev file was enormous, enough to fill several cabinet drawers, and even if Howard did not know SPHERE's true name, there was more than enough operational detail for the KGB to pinpoint Tolkachev, including his address.

In April 1983, just before his final clearance for assignment to Moscow, Howard was asked to take another polygraph test, a standard requirement for officers about to be assigned to a sensitive area. This time, the polygraph told a different story. Howard's personal failings weren't passed over. There was evidence of ongoing drug and alcohol use and an instance of petty theft—Howard acknowledged that he had stolen cash from the purse of a woman on an airplane. Under questioning on one of the polygraphs, he also revealed that he had cheated during a training exercise designed to test his ability to work on GTTAW, the Moscow cable-tapping operation. During the exercise at the Farm, Howard was supposed to carry a weighted backpack while climbing into a manhole, a mock-up of the TAW site. Instead, he had stuffed his backpack with cardboard to make it easier to get into the hole. Howard failed the polygraph, and a second, a third, and a fourth, before the CIA's Office of Security recommended a personnel evaluation board be convened to review his suitability for employment. After an extensive review by the panel of senior CIA officials, including Forden, Howard was fired in early May 1983.

On the day he was told to leave the CIA, electronic entry and exit records would later show that he had gone in and out of the building several times in quick succession before turning in his CIA badge for the last time. Howard left the CIA with nothing to show for his time except bitterness, a knowledge of Russian, and a head full of some of the agency's most closely guarded secrets.

Suddenly out on the street, with a wife and a new baby to support, Howard was stunned and humiliated. It didn't take long for him to start drinking again. He moved back to New Mexico, where he had been born, and took a job with the state legislature as an economic analyst. But he never stopped seething about the treatment he had received from the CIA.

The first signs of trouble came quickly after his firing. Howard began to make bizarre late-night telephone calls from his home to the special Washington tie-line to the U.S. embassy in Moscow, in one instance leaving a message with the Marine guard for Moscow station chief Carl Gebhardt, telling him that he wouldn't be showing up for his physical.

His telephone calls to Moscow were reported back to CIA headquarters, and they began to trouble Forden. He went to the Office of Security to see if the agency could monitor Howard's telephone. In the spring of 1984, after he was told that the CIA didn't have the legal power to tap Howard's phone, Forden went to David Blee, then the CIA's counterintelligence chief, to tell him about the phone calls to Moscow and to warn him that Howard might be a security risk. Forden later recalled bitterly that Blee had simply smiled and done nothing.

Back in Santa Fe, Howard's mood was darkening. His drinking was getting steadily worse. In February 1984, he was arrested for assault after he fired a gun during a street fight with some local kids he followed from a bar in Santa Fe. Only his white-collar background and his job at the state legislature saved him from jail.

In May 1984, Howard showed up one night on the Washington doorstep of Tom Mills, one of his former supervisors in the SE Division. Howard had been drinking heavily, and he complained to Mills that he had been "fucked" by the agency. Troubled by the episode, Burton Gerber, who was just taking over SE Division from Forden, sent a psychologist with Mills to New Mexico to talk with Howard and gauge his mental condition.

Howard admitted to them that on his trip back to Washington, he had loitered outside the Soviet consulate, debating whether to walk in to the KGB. He had gone to the consulate, rather than the embassy, because he knew from his CIA training that the FBI didn't monitor the consular affairs section as carefully, he told them. He insisted that he hadn't actually gone inside; he said he had resisted the temptation once he thought about what becoming a spy for the Soviet Union would do to his son, Lee.

The psychologist brought another bit of news that Gerber found equally unsettling—Howard no longer seemed such a mess. He seemed in control of himself and in much better shape. It was as if he had made an important decision to change his life.

Gerber passed along the news to the CIA's security office and arranged for the agency to pay for psychological treatment for Howard. But the CIA had still not warned the FBI that Edward Howard now might be a threat to national security. Later, FBI officials would tell Gerber that they wouldn't have been able to take action against Howard at that time, since there was no proof that he had committed espionage. But Gerber and other CIA officials still paid dearly later for their failure to notify the FBI.

Even though there still wasn't enough evidence yet to prove conclusively that Howard had become a spy, it was long past time to break the news to the FBI. With Yurchenko's warning, everyone who had been involved with the Howard case began to realize just what a mistake it had been to throw him out onto the street.

Gerber looked out his window just as two FBI sedans pulled in beside him. "Here they are," he said flatly.

Afterward, the FBI would omit any mention of this Saturday meeting when it gave its account of the Howard case. Instead, FBI officials would insist that the CIA waited much longer to inform them that they knew Howard was the spy Yurchenko had described.

But in fact, Gerber also warned the FBI about one of Howard's hidden skills. The fired CIA officer had taken the CIA's most advanced training—Jack Platt's Internal Operations course—so Gerber wanted the bureau to be aware of Howard's ability to evade surveillance.

Oakton, Virginia, 1030 Hours, August 3, 1985

The air in the Oakton town house was blue from cigarette smoke when Chuck Medanich arrived the morning after Yurchenko's arrival on U.S. soil. Up the short staircase from the foyer, Yurchenko was sitting at the dining room table peering over a list of names with FBI agents Michael Rochford and Reid Broce.

Yurchenko stood up when Medanich walked in. He's restless, Medanich thought. Nervous energy.

"Good morning, Alex." Medanich used the operational alias Yurchenko had chosen until his new identity was developed.

"I have no need of sleep," Yurchenko said excitedly. "Too much work to do. Each time I close my eyes I stand again up in bed and think of one more thing to tell the boys. I now must sleep always with a pen and paper. Sometimes things I have not remembered for years just pop into my head and I have to write them down before they leave again."

Medanich turned to the FBI agents. "You guys want to take a break? I'd like a couple of minutes alone with Alex."

Medanich led Yurchenko into the small kitchen off the dining room. "Can I get you anything to drink, Alex? How about a Coke?"

The tall KGB colonel took a half-full two-liter bottle of Coke from the countertop and began to pour a glass. "Ice?" Medanich asked.

"No ice. Americans like everything with ice. It makes them sick. Never should use ice!"

"Alex," Medanich said, "I'm going to be with you almost constantly in these early weeks and months of settling in. You're a man who has much of great value to give our side, but I want you to know that my job is to see to it that your needs are understood. I want you to know that you can turn to me anytime something is bothering you, or even when nothing is bothering you. And if you ever have anything you want to discuss with someone other than the colleagues here, anything that you want to bring directly to the attention of Mr. Casey, just tell me. Mr. Casey is deeply interested in your welfare, and he wants you to know that."

Yurchenko nodded in understanding. "These boys are fine, and I have much to tell them. But I have been here more than one day already, and I thought I would by this time hear from Mr. Casey. . . ." He let his sentence trail off without transforming his statement into a request.

Medanich put his hand reassuringly on the defector's shoulder. "Mr. Casey sent me here this morning to tell you personally that he is briefing the President on the courageous decision you have made," he said, "and he will call you personally to welcome you to the United States on Monday."

"He should tell President Reagan that I have come to him to help him in the struggle," Yurchenko replied, perking up.

"That's precisely what he is telling the President." So that's where the agitation is coming from, Medanich thought. His sense of self-importance. "Is there anything I can do to help you in these first few days? Do you need rest, some time to gather your thoughts?"

Yurchenko shook his head vigorously. "I need no rest. I have had a lifetime to gather my thoughts for this. And I must work fast because my own time may not be long."

Medanich decided to let Yurchenko's statement pass, at least for the moment. He would bore in on that one later. There were too many people involved in this operation, he thought. The FBI and CIA were crawling all over the place. Word of Yurchenko's arrival had spread rapidly through the intelligence world, and Medanich worried that everyone would want to be a part of the espionage freak show in Oakton.

Yurchenko had been brought to this town house in a congested suburb only because the agency's stock of available safe houses had been so low at the time. But it was clear the CIA needed to find a better place to stash its defectors outside of the twenty-five-mile zone around Washington, D.C., in which Soviet diplomats were allowed to travel. Taking in the scene at the town house, Medanich grimaced and thought to himself that this resettlement, one of the biggest in CIA history, was being conducted with all the subtlety of a goat-fuck.

Over the next few days, as Medanich had feared, the safe house became a tourist stop for intelligence officers. What was worse, the debriefings were badly organized; too many different agencies were clamoring to grill Yurchenko on their pet issues.

At first, Yurchenko didn't seem to mind, since he had so much he wanted to get off his chest. He was so eager to talk that one day he pulled out a large sheaf of paper and spread it across the kitchen table so he could diagram the KGB's organization. But even as he and Medanich were hunched happily over the table, an FBI official who was not involved in the case arrived unannounced and invited Yurchenko to dinner. Yurchenko turned to Medanich and asked, "Do I have to go with him?" Medanich, furious at the interloper, said no. Yurchenko declined the dinner invitation and quickly returned to his organizational chart. Medanich had a feeling Yurchenko wouldn't remain so tolerant if this kind of chaos wasn't brought under control soon.

CIA Headquarters, Langley, Virginia, 1410 Hours, August 5, 1985

Bill Casey was leaning so far back in his chair that I thought he might actually topple over. Gerber and I were sitting in two straight-backed chairs in front of Casey's desk in the DCI's birch-paneled seventh-floor office. Behind us, through floor-to-ceiling windows, lay the lush, wooded panorama of the Virginia side of the Potomac. On the corner of Casey's desk was a stack of books with titles ranging from Middle East oil politics to history and the stock market. Casey was a voracious reader. He would devour books all weekend, returning on Monday to tell his closest aides which ones they should read, perhaps even how to read them.

Gerber and I were in Casey's office to brief the DCI on the initial counterintelligence take from Yurchenko. Gerber confirmed that he was convinced Yurchenko's Mr. Robert, a dismissed CIA employee who had turned to the KGB, was Edward Lee Howard.

"What do you think about the Howard thing, Milt?" Casey asked.

"Sometimes we get what we deserve," I said.

I felt, more than saw, Gerber bristle beside me. "I can't imagine anyone thinking we deserve this kind of treachery," Gerber said tensely.

"What I mean is that Howard's firing and the way it was handled is driving his revenge. The agency can't say it was uninvolved in pushing him over the edge. I'm not saying that minimizes in any way what he's done, Burton."

Casey stopped the exchange with one of his standard throwaway lines. "Hey, so we make mistakes." Turning back to the subject of Yurchenko, he was almost gleeful. "How's it goin' with him?" Casey had almost given up on trying to pronounce Yurchenko's name.

"He's running on nervous energy," I said. "But Chuck Medanich, our psychologist, doesn't think he's in a higher than usual state of agitation for someone who's done what he's just done."

"So you want me to call him?" Casey asked, looking at the typed note in front of him.

"Just call him and welcome him aboard," I said, handing Casey the suggested talking points on a pair of three-by-five cards. "Here's some language that will go a long way with him right now."

Casey glanced at the cards as he dialed the number himself, waiting until Yurchenko came on the line.

"Alex"—Casey tilted his head back and peered through his bifocals at the three-by-five cards—"this is Bill Casey." He paused to listen to the stream of words from Yurchenko. "Yeah, sure. I couldn't agree more. I just wanted to welcome you personally to the United States. Together we can accomplish much."

Casey listened to Yurchenko for a few moments, then added, "Alex, when you've rested a little and talked to our colleagues, you and I can get together for a quiet dinner. In the meantime, you can always get a message to me through Tom Fannin. . . . Yeah. . . . Yeah. . . . And thank you again for coming to us to help with the struggle."

Casey flipped the three-by-five cards on his desk and winked at me.

Vienna, Austria, August 9, 1985

Edward Lee Howard flew from Albuquerque to Zurich on August 7 and on to Vienna two days later. He had arranged for a hurried leave from his job at the New Mexico state capitol. He told his boss that his grandmother, who had been ill, had suddenly died.

Howard would spend only two days in Vienna, returning to Santa Fe on August 12. It would later be learned that Howard's grandmother was neither dead nor living in Austria or Switzerland. It was not his first trip to Austria, either. He had traveled there in September 1984, when he first met his KGB contacts. It was either during that meeting or at a subsequent one that he betrayed Adolf Tolkachev. He probably also compromised the TAW operation at about the same time.

Whether he knew Tolkachev's real name or not, Howard certainly provided the key information the KGB needed to identify him. Rem Krassilnikov later insisted that the KGB's Second Chief Directorate was already investigating Tolkachev before the First Chief Directorate provided information about Tolkachev from a source. But while the Second Chief Directorate had conducted a security probe of Tolkachev's institute in 1983—before receiving Howard's information—the KGB had not focused on Tolkachev specifically until Howard betrayed him.

9

Lefortovo District, Moscow, 0930 Hours, August 10, 1985

The white Volga sedan wound its way through the Lefortovo district of old Moscow, a once elegant section of the city built on the Yauza River. Named after Franz Lefort, its Swiss planner, who had been a confidant of Peter the Great, it had once been a posh residential district of cobblestone streets reserved for foreigners. The original Lefortovo Palace, which had dominated the district, had been designed with three intersecting wings forming a letter *K,* a tribute by its architect, so the story went, to his demanding and fleeting lover Catherine the Great.

By now, however, the palace's name had become synonymous with the mystery and despair of what it had become—the Lefortovo pretrial and investigation prison. Lefortovo and its blood-soaked history had long since tempered the Russian soul. It is not known precisely how many of the Soviet Union's elite died inside the prison in the late 1930s, giving Lefortovo the dubious honor of being Stalin's premier "shooting prison."

The long cell-block corridors of the old palace had been painted an eerie flat black, and scuppers had been cut deep along the seams of walls and floors in some spots for quick pressure-hose cleanups after a busy night of shooting. In addition to the long line of Soviet officials purged after falling from Stalin's grace, Lefortovo had also held Raoul Wallenberg, the Swedish savior of thousands of Hungarian Jews in the 1940s, and, more recently, Natan Sharansky, the irrepressible Jewish dissident who had eventually been allowed to immigrate to Israel as part of a spy trade.

Rem Krassilnikov's Volga pulled to a halt before the high brown metal gate in front of an ocher building marked 3A.

Krassilnikov knew Lefortovo's history but thought it unrelated to his honorable work of catching spies. Krassilnikov was a true believer in the Soviet system and couldn't understand the questioning attitude of the younger generations. To his mind, the job of extracting confessions from traitors could not be compared to the purges of the past. The only shootings that took place in Lefortovo now were by judicial decree. It just so happened that business was booming these days.

Krassilnikov currently had two "guests" in separate isolation cells. One, the now resigned and courteous Adolf Tolkachev, had come to terms with the irreversibility of his situation. He was being most helpful, Krassilnikov thought.

But this new one that Sharavatov's men had netted was still in the indignant, tough-guy defensive stage. He was still searching desperately for that single snappy answer that would turn the game against his tormentors and make his awful problem vanish in a burst of overwhelming logic. But finding a harmless explanation for why he had been caught in the act of unloading an American dead drop full of cash was turning out to be more than even Lieutenant Colonel Leonid Georgiyevich Polyshchuk could handle.

Polyshchuk was a KGB counterintelligence colonel in Moscow on leave from his posting in Lagos, Nigeria. When Sharavatov's men had arrested him three days earlier, he had put a patchy, theatrical defense on the spot. He said he'd come to meet a woman at the Severyanin station and that he'd stepped into the field only to relieve himself and had been mistakenly arrested. While pissing on the stones around the electric pylon, he said, he'd suddenly remembered he ought to get a substantial rock to place under the rear wheel of his car to keep it from rolling down the sloping street where he had parked it. His parking brake was faulty, he explained, expecting that to clear up the little "misunderstanding" on the spot. But when pressed, Polyshchuk couldn't remember the woman's name, and when he led Sharavatov, who by this time had arrived on the scene, to his parked car, Sharavatov found two wooden chock blocks in the car's trunk. Why didn't he use these? Sharavatov asked. All Polyshchuk could conjure up was that he had forgotten he had them. He'd been off on a diplomatic assignment for a long time and hadn't inventoried the contents of his car trunk.

Later that night, a thorough search of Polyshchuk and his car sealed the KGB colonel's fate. The hand-drawn sketch of the field where the dead drop was located contained an error in a street name, one of several Krassilnikov knew appeared in an American-produced Moscow city plan used by the CIA. Polyshchuk also carried with him another map with a spot marked on Gorky Street where he was to leave his "have unloaded dead drop" signal, so that the American special services would know their package had been safely retrieved. And as the methodical search continued, a detailed communications plan printed on water-soluble paper was found sealed inside the lining of his glasses case.

Krassilnikov knew he had his man. Just two days earlier, he'd brought the KGB colonel before the KGB Chairman, Viktor Chebrikov, who had made a simple demand of the haggard prisoner. "Remember your officer's honor," Chebrikov had demanded. "Do the right thing." Krassilnikov had then left Polyshchuk with his own thoughts for a few days. He'd become helpful sooner or later, Krassilnikov thought. They all did, eventually—and there was plenty of time.

Now, in the cold light of day, Krassilnikov waited in the second-floor interrogation room of Lefortovo's newer wing. The time for a cover story defense has passed, he thought as he rose to answer the knock on the door that signaled Polyshchuk's arrival. Krassilnikov carefully signed the jailer's receipt for his ward, flipped a switch at the door that lit a red light in the hallway to signal an interrogation in progress, and let Polyshchuk into the sparsely furnished interrogation room. The KGB colonel had showered but not shaved. He would get a visit from the Lefortovo barber in a few days. His eyes still had traces of red from either the alcohol of the night before or a sleepless night with his thoughts. The ill-fitting blue Lefortovo running suit, and the shoes with the laces removed, further diminished his presence.

Laid out on a conference table jutting off at right angles from Krassilnikov's desk were the materials Sharavatov's men had seized the night before. The effect was shattering. There could be no denial when faced with the maps, the money, the secret messages, the high-tech concealment, and all the incriminating evidence Polyshchuk had carried on his person. Krassilnikov let the enormity of the display sink in for a few minutes. He knew that once again he had his man cold.

Colonel Leonid Georgiyevich Polyshchuk's life as a CIA spy had actually begun eleven years earlier. He had come to the CIA's attention in 1974 during the first years of détente; under more relaxed rules of engagement, Soviet intelligence officers were allowed to have greater contact with American diplomats and even CIA officers. Polyshchuk, taking advantage of the new opportunities, had started to cruise the watering holes of his backwater posting in Katmandu, Nepal. He quickly popped up on the radar screen of the CIA's chief in Katmandu, who picked up on the man's taste for liquor and the local casino. He soon learned that Polyshchuk had worked himself into a classic fix—he'd run through his KGB cash by trying to make a killing at the tables. Polyshchuk desperately needed cash to balance his books before his bosses discovered the money was missing. Polyshchuk agreed to take a "personal loan" from the American, and the transition from their personal agreement to the next step was easy. Polyshchuk would become a spy and cancel his debt.

As Polyshchuk's tour in Katmandu came to an end, he agreed to be trained in clandestine communications for "internal handling" by the CIA in Moscow. SE Division officer Sandy Grimes traveled to Katmandu and trained him in the skills needed for secure internal operations. With clandestine communications materials, Polyshchuk was sent on his way to

Moscow. He was told not to do anything for the CIA for the next year, to cool off, and to work his way into a job with the most interesting access. In a year, Polyshchuk would give a "sign of life" in Moscow, standing at a specific corner wearing a fur hat he had bought in Katmandu, with a special leather bag over his shoulder. A CIA drive-by would spot him and confirm that he was alive. Then the operation would resume.

There were alternate dates for the sign of life, plus a few preaddressed postcards Polyshchuk could mail as backups to signal that he was ready to begin receiving his encrypted radio broadcasts. The CIA knew that Polyshchuk could perform all these tasks and still be under KGB control. But that was one of the risks of running a spy in Moscow.

Polyshchuk was a no-show at all of his sign of life sites in Moscow, and not one of his postcards was ever received by the CIA.

Back home, Polyshchuk had destroyed the incriminating equipment given him by the CIA and hoped his relationship with the Americans would be dropped and forgotten. He burned everything that would burn and buried the rest, thinking that no one would ever know.

SE Division assumed he got cold feet. It was possible he had been compromised, but there was no evidence of that. At the CIA, he was listed as "INACTIVE/WATCHLISTED." The agency would be watching for the next time that Polyshchuk was posted overseas.

The operation came back to life eleven years later, in February 1985, when Polyshchuk was assigned to Nigeria as the Line KR counterintelligence officer in the Soviet *Rezidentura*. Before long, he was back in business. Most of the CIA's contacts with Polyshchuk in Lagos were brief "car pickups," where the CIA officers would talk to him on the run, but the Americans also arranged a few more lengthy debriefings in one of their local safe houses.

As in Katmandu, Polyshchuk's information on the KGB's local operations in Lagos was not of great interest to the Americans. Still, the CIA once again hoped that their agent could be convinced to spy from inside Moscow.

The opportunity came in April 1985. Polyshchuk reported that he had received a letter from his parents telling him of a stroke of luck. A condominium apartment near their home in Moscow had come onto the market, and Polyshchuk could buy it for 20,000 rubles. Polyshchuk told the CIA that he had been looking for just such an apartment near his parents for years and had asked his parents to keep up the search while he was away in Africa. Concerned that he had to move fast or lose the apartment, Polyshchuk said that he had already requested leave to go home to Moscow to close the deal. He explained that this was commonplace for KGB or Foreign Ministry officers living abroad; the difficulties of finding and purchasing apartments in overcrowded Moscow were shared by many of his colleagues. His request was approved by Moscow Center, but only on condition that he take his full annual home leave, to save travel costs and time away from the job. Again, Polyshchuk told his CIA case officers that such an arrangement was routine. The only problem was that he didn't have the 20,000 rubles.

The CIA could give him the money, he said, and he'd carry it with him to Moscow. He would never be searched.

SE Division accepted Polyshchuk's explanation with few reservations. The story made sense. For the CIA, there seemed to be an added benefit; here was another chance to coax Polyshchuk into working in Moscow. He had given a variety of excuses about why he had failed to reestablish contact after he had returned to Moscow from Katmandu. But it was clear that he had been afraid of the risks.

This time, the CIA believed it had a great way to convince Polyshchuk to unload a dead drop in Moscow and, in effect, get his operational feet wet. To get his 20,000 rubles, then worth about $30,000, Polyshchuk would have to get it at a Moscow dead drop.

The CIA officers persuaded Polyshchuk that it would be too risky to carry the cash through customs at Moscow's Sheremetyevo Airport. He'd be much safer picking it up after he arrived clean in Moscow. Polyshchuk finally agreed, and by May 10, the CIA had identified a dead drop site in Moscow that could be used in the operation.

Polyshchuk left his last meeting with his handlers in Lagos in high spirits.

* * *

Krassilnikov thought back over Polyshchuk's arrest. He recalled how officers of the Seventh Chief Directorate, acting under the direction of the Second Directorate, had arrested Polyshchuk while he was picking up the money-filled rock at the Moscow dead drop site. The Americans must be second-guessing the decision to have him pick up his money in Moscow. They would be wondering what went wrong for quite some time.

Krassilnikov would forever insist that the men of the Second and Seventh Directorates deserved the credit. One of his subordinates had come to him and said that his men could feel that the Americans were about to go operational. Krassilnikov had agreed to put whatever resources were necessary on the Americans and deferred to his number two, Valentin Klimenko, to manage those resources.

On the night that a CIA officer had placed a rock full of rubles near a pylon, leaving it there for Polyshchuk to pick up later, Klimenko had more than twenty surveillance vehicles and forty surveillance personnel following him. With so many resources, the men of the Second and Seventh Directorates were able to stand off more than five hundred meters at all times. After watching the CIA officer leave the cash-filled rock, it was just a matter of waiting and watching at the dead drop site to see who showed up.

The KGB would make certain that the CIA got the message that Polyshchuk had been unmasked thanks solely to solid legwork by the Second and Seventh Chief Directorates. In Washington and Bonn, and perhaps elsewhere in the West, KGB officers were told that a drunken KGB colonel had been arrested after he was followed and watched, and the news soon got to the CIA from its agents inside those KGB *Rezidenturas*.

But the CIA never quite believed it. Was the story KGB disinformation? What about the fact that Polyshchuk's long-sought apartment in Moscow had suddenly become available? Had it been a ruse to lure him back to Moscow?

10

Coventry, Virginia, August 15, 1985

Moving Yurchenko to a secluded safe house near Fredericksburg, Virginia, well outside the twenty-five-mile travel limit for Soviet diplomats posted in Washington, brought a sense of order to his debriefings. The large, single-family house, isolated on several waterfront acres, offered an ideal setting for the case. In Oakton, Medanich had grown frustrated with the espionage tourists, but they were unlikely to make the long drive to Fredericksburg. Now, only the intelligence officials who had real business with Yurchenko would show up.

The KGB colonel had settled into something of a routine, and the debriefings had eased into the steady pace known in the trade as "counterintelligence production." Yurchenko was living up to his early promise. The flurry of activity over his identification of Edward Lee Howard as a probable KGB agent had calmed after the FBI was finally brought in on the case. Though the bureau had still not arrested—or even interviewed—the troubled former CIA officer, he was now under surveillance.

The second KGB agent Yurchenko had mentioned, an NSA employee who had volunteered to the KGB in Washington in 1980, was still unidentified. But it was clear that the NSA source had betrayed the U.S. Navy's supersensitive undersea cable tap of Soviet submarine command communications—Operation Ivy Bells, an enormously expensive operation. The revelation that Ivy Bells had been compromised prompted an intensive and exhaustive effort to find the spy. Yurchenko underwent a series of debriefings and also pored through mug books of NSA employees in order to help. He'd been in on the initial meeting with the NSA volunteer—he thought it had taken place between 1977 and 1979—and had helped smuggle the man out of the Soviet embassy disguised as a Soviet worker after shaving his beard. But he still hadn't seen his photo in any of the mug books.

Meanwhile, Yurchenko had backpedaled from his initial reporting on Navy chief Thomas Hayden, the supposed American spy he'd met on a secluded beach south of Rome. He was now telling his debriefers that he had known Hayden was a provocation all along. Sensing the CIA's lack of urgency in pursuing the lead, he concluded, correctly, that Hayden had been a dangle. Yurchenko shifted gears smoothly and began saying he had smelled a bad operation even before he left Moscow. But, he explained to his debriefers, he had needed a reason to travel out of the Soviet Union. The loss of the John Walker spy ring, and the possibility that Hayden represented a replacement for Walker, meant that the Soviets couldn't pass up the Navy communications specialist. He shrugged off as a joke his earlier admonition to the FBI not to shoot Hayden, whom he described as a dangerous spy but still a good man.

The debriefings eventually moved away from the CIA's immediate interest in identifying American traitors and shifted into the esoteric world of KGB counterintelligence efforts in Moscow. Yurchenko then began to talk about the chemicals that the KGB used to try to track CIA officers in Moscow.

Since the late 1950s, the CIA had known that KGB technical laboratories had been developing a variety of synthesized chemical agents that would enable them to track CIA officers and their Soviet agents inside the USSR. The stories ranged from the ingenious to the ribald, including rumors of KGB experiments with chemical substances—pheromones—associated with female dogs in heat. The procedure was simple. The KGB sprayed the pheromones where they might be transferred to a Moscow case officer's shoes—the floor mats of a car, for example. When the case officer was known to have "gone operational," the KGB would set male dogs on his trail. Bingo! One had no difficulty conjuring the image of the hapless CIA case officer in Gorky Park with a pack of amorous hounds in ardent pursuit.

Stories of KGB tracking techniques had come from a variety of sources and defectors, and in the early 1980s one CIA case officer, a young woman assigned to Leningrad, had found the inside of her gloves coated with a yellowish chemical. A year after the Leningrad discovery, CIA covertly received another sample of the chemical substance directly from GTCOWL—the anonymous KGB officer in Moscow who had handed over a sample of the substance to his Moscow case officer. COWL had warned that the KGB was using the substance to "keep track of your people."

Laboratory tests of the glove from the female officer in Leningrad had revealed the presence of a compound identified as nitrophenylpentadienal, NPPD for short. The second sample, provided by COWL, was also the odorless organic compound NPPD. U.S. government scientists examining the chemical could find no NPPD in lists of tens of thousands of toxic chemicals. A review of journals by the American Chemical Society turned up seven articles on NPPD and related compounds, six of which had been written by Soviet scientists. Using a screening method developed by Bruce Ames, a Berkeley biochemist, researchers determined that NPPD could be mutagenic—that is, if absorbed by humans in an unaltered form, it could cause alterations in cell structure. In humans, mutagens can be carcinogenic but are not always so. But the early tests set off alarm bells at the CIA.

By the time Yurchenko confirmed the use of tracking agents, the CIA was facing a growing problem. At what point would the agency have to tell its employees, the State Department, and the rest of the world what it knew about NPPD? By the third week of August 1985, it was clear that the time for hedging on NPPD had run out. Gerber assigned me the task of coordinating how the CIA should go public with its concerns about NPPD, now known within the agency as "spy dust."

Moscow, 1830 Hours, August 21, 1985

I was sitting alone at the back of the auditorium in Spaso House, the prerevolution mansion that served as the residence of the U.S. ambassador to the Soviet Union. The American community of Moscow had gathered for a briefing by a State Department team on the potential health effects of spy dust, a subject of intense controversy in the international media over the last few days. James Brodine, a State Department medical officer, was on the stage explaining to a skeptical audience that it had been known for some time that the Soviets were employing chemical agents. Until recently, the United States believed the Soviets used them only sporadically. But during the spring and summer of 1985, Brodine explained, the Soviets had apparently increased their use. What's more, recent laboratory tests had tentatively classified the spy dust as a mutagenic compound, prompting the State Department to inform the American community about it and to protest its use to the Soviet authorities.

The reaction in the Spaso House auditorium was a mixture of resignation and irritation. Embassy employees had little comment; there was nothing new about aggressive Soviet actions against U.S. personnel in Moscow. Some in the audience remembered how the KGB had flooded the U.S. embassy with microwave transmissions, for reasons that were never completely clear. At least a few Americans were still being monitored for possible long-term health effects from the exposure.

But the press corps was more alarmed, and American reporters based in Moscow began to grill Brodine about the health threats stemming from the spy dust. Their questions suggested that they felt like innocent victims in a U.S.-Soviet spy game.

As Brodine fielded questions from reporters, the CIA's Moscow chief took a seat in the empty row behind me. "Welcome to Moscow," he said quietly.

I glanced over my shoulder and nodded without comment. Both of us listened as Brodine and other members of the team tried to maintain a delicate balance between their duty to alert the assembled Americans to a potential health hazard and the need to avoid generating panic. Mutagens, Brodine explained, are not always carcinogenic and include some of the most common compounds people expose themselves to on a daily basis, such as coffee. The team ended its formal presentation with the announcement that an expanded technical team from Washington would arrive in Moscow within days to begin collecting environmental samples in the homes, offices, and automobiles of all Americans wishing to be sampled, including private citizens residing in Moscow.

As the crowd filed out of the auditorium, the CIA officer fell in step with me long enough to whisper a brief message. "Nine o'clock tomorrow at Post One. You'll be met."

The next morning, I sat with the Moscow chief in the cramped quarters of the "yellow submarine," the custom-built enclosure that served as the CIA work area. It was a three-hundred-square-foot, hermetically sealed metallic box floating on cushions of air with a self-contained power supply. No electronic devices were allowed inside. Even manual typewriters had been forbidden, ever since a successful KGB attack on thirteen IBM Selectric typewriters in the Moscow embassy. In an ingenious operation discovered by the CIA in 1984, the KGB had managed to place the typewriters in secure areas of the embassy used by State Department personnel. The typewriters had fallen into Soviet hands while being shipped to the U.S. embassy, and tiny transmitters had been installed by the KGB, sending every word typed on the machines to a KGB electronic listening post outside the embassy. Typewriters used in the CIA area had not been compromised, but Burton Gerber didn't want to take any chances.

Even inside the secure enclosure, we spoke in whispers and half sentences as we discussed the anomalies Moscow had been experiencing over the past year. In the midst of our conversation, he paused and wrote out a message on a single sheet of paper from a yellow legal pad. He pushed it across to me.

"Sometimes I think they're in here with me," the note read.

I took his pencil and scribbled out a reply: "How long?"

"All of 1985."

I left Moscow the next day.

11

Santa Fe, New Mexico, August 25, 1985

Edward Lee Howard had been trained to spot surveillance in the CIA's operational pressure cooker—the Internal Operations course—and by the end of August he was convinced he was being followed. Howard began to notice every jogger and repairman on his isolated street. He was convinced that he had been tracked by a circling aircraft while driving into the desert.

Howard was right that he was being followed, but he was also seeing ghosts, believing the surveillance to be far more extensive than it was. Of course, he had good reason to be paranoid. Howard knew this was not a game. It wasn't going to end in a friendly after-action critique. He began to review his options.

Lisbon, 1630 Hours, August 27, 1985

Like most of the CIA's clandestine meetings with GRU Lieutenant Colonel Gennady Smetanin, this one was rushed. Smetanin had called the out-of-sequence meeting on the outskirts of Lisbon to advise his CIA case officer that he had been asked to begin his home leave in the next two days, so he could be back on the job in Lisbon in late September. As the meeting ended, it was agreed that the next scheduled meeting would take place on October 4, at another prearranged meeting site on the outskirts of Lisbon. Smetanin told his case officer he didn't think there was anything out of the ordinary about the accelerated vacation schedule. In fact, he and his wife were looking forward to getting back to Moscow and taking care of personal matters, including their purchase of an apartment.

CIA Headquarters, 1530 Hours, August 27, 1985

"He's been compromised." Paul Redmond was matter-of-fact as he read the Lisbon cable in my office.

"What makes you think that?" I asked, looking for some sign of bad news in the routine cable from Portugal advising that GTMILLION was returning to Moscow early on home leave.

"I just know. It's like Bokhan."

"How'd he get compromised?" I was trying to understand whether Redmond actually knew something or his darkening view of counterintelligence had taken over.

"Somebody told them about him. Maybe someone in here."

"You think the problem's in here?" I waved my hand to indicate the inner sanctum of SE Division.

Redmond nodded. "Either they're reading our cables or they've got someone talking to them. One or the other. Take your choice."

"What can we do about MILLION?"

"It's too late. He's gone. I'm just saying we'll never see him again, and there isn't a damn thing we can do about it. I'll be happy if I'm wrong. But I'm not."

Redmond left my office, and then, under the watchful eye of Gerber's secretary, I went to Gerber's four-drawer safe in his outer office and retrieved a small two-ring notebook with a thick red stripe running diagonally across the black cover. I was one of five people in the division with access to the notebook, which contained the case histories of all SE Division operations going back more than a dozen years. Turning to the page for GTMILLION, I found in cold summary language the story of Gennady Smetanin.

In 1983, GRU officer Gennady Smetanin had secretly sent a letter to an officer in the Defense Attaché's office of the U.S. embassy in Lisbon. Smetanin offered his services to American intelligence, in return for which he said he would expect certain considerations. If there was interest, he wrote, a personal ad should be placed in a certain Lisbon paper. I flipped the page but couldn't find the language of the ad in the summary.

The CIA chief in Lisbon reported that same day that he was convinced the volunteer was a provocation. He suggested that the package from Smetanin be turned over to Portuguese counterintelligence. But the SE Division chief at the time was a survivor of the Angleton era and had fought such paranoid fears throughout his entire career. He strongly believed that if CIA officers didn't pursue potential recruits, there was no reason for them to be in the field. He sent a cable back to Lisbon not to do anything until they received instructions from SE Division on how to handle the volunteer.

In the summary of the operation in the notebook, there were references to the first clandestine meetings with Smetanin. He said he had stolen almost $400,000 from his GRU *Rezidentura* and needed immediate help in replacing it before an upcoming audit that could expose him. He said that was why he had approached the Americans.

My eyes ran to the next entry in the notebook, one summarizing a grueling polygraph examination that had been administered to Smetanin in Lisbon. It showed that he had not been truthful about embezzling the funds. I recognized the name of the polygraph operator, an old German American professional most in the DO knew simply as "Hans." During the interrogation, Smetanin had admitted to lying about the money. He figured the CIA would give him the money if they wanted the operation to continue. Smetanin was actually proud of the way he had handled his business dealings with the CIA. In the end, he got a good part of his money, and the CIA got its penetration of Soviet military intelligence.

As I returned the notebook to Gerber's safe, I wondered if Redmond's fears would mark the final entry for GTMILLION.

Back in my office, I took stock of what I had witnessed in my first five weeks as Gerber's deputy in SE Division. By now the initial furor over Edward Howard's betrayal had subsided. Though few discussed it openly, the outrage over Howard's treachery was now mixed with an odd sense of relief. There was a feeling that Howard had never really been a member of the DO brotherhood; the system had culled him before he ever made it through the probationary period. To be sure, the rationalizations couldn't bring back Adolf Tolkachev. But at least the integrity of the DO remained somehow intact, or so the thinking went.

Only Paul Redmond was having none of it.

Langley, 0815 Hours, September 16, 1985

Every time I laid eyes on the angular features of Rod Carlson, I saw the face of Abraham Lincoln. Carlson was chief of the SE Division's counterintelligence group, a rail-thin man who had spent his career in operations against the Soviet Union. Carlson first traveled to the USSR as a student "legal traveler" under a CIA program in the late 1950s. He was a meticulous man, some thought humorless, who never displayed doubts about his life's work against the USSR. Carlson was approaching the end of his career—he had announced plans to retire in a few months—and was planning to spend his time restoring old houses. His attention to detail would fit nicely with his new pursuit.

In Gerber's office, Carlson briefed the SE chief, Redmond, and me on his meeting two nights earlier with a human penetration of the Washington *Rezidentura,* a KGB Line X officer responsible for scientific and technical intelligence in the United States. The Soviet agent was known as PIMENTA within the FBI and as GTGENTILE within the CIA.

"We met on Saturday night at a prearranged site near the walking path along the C and O Canal. The bureau provided countersurveillance. It was a clean meeting and lasted about eight minutes. The take on the *Rezidentura*'s activities since our last joint meeting was modest." Carlson's briefings were always dry and stuck to the essentials.

"At the end of the meeting, PIMENTA said that Androsov called the line chiefs separately over the last few days—he'd returned from Moscow earlier in the week—and briefed them on the gossip at Center. The biggest nugget was that Androsov said a First Directorate officer had been arrested unloading a dead drop in early August." Carlson glanced down at his notes. "The officer was a little drunk at the time he was arrested . . . no name was given . . . Androsov told one of the line chiefs that would probably come later and that anyone who knew the man would be asked to write the usual report on him. Androsov said the arrest was the result of the vigilance of the Second Directorate." Carlson paused and checked his notes again.

"Androsov made it clear it was the Second Directorate and

the surveillance guys in the Seventh Directorate that caught the Americans putting the dead drop down about two weeks earlier. They ran a stakeout on the drop site until the guy came around to pick it up. The dead drop was loaded with rubles."

"It's WEIGH." Gerber's voice was soft, without drama.

"It's WEIGH," Paul Redmond said in agreement.

"What did he say, Rod?" Gerber asked. "The part about them catching the drop being loaded."

Carlson repeated what PIMENTA had told him, that the American special services officer had been spotted by a surveillance team of the Seventh Directorate while laying down the dead drop, probably sometime in late July.

"It was the casuals under the bridge," Gerber said.

Gerber had been worried ever since the July operation in Moscow, which called for Moscow to put down a rock loaded with cash for GTWEIGH in a field near a power pylon. In a follow-up report, the Moscow case officer who had left the rock had said he had seen "casuals"—men or women who seemed to be in the area on their own business—about two hundred yards from the dead drop site. The case officer had decided to go through with the operation despite the casuals, and Gerber had wondered ever since whether that had been the right decision. The casuals could have been part of a KGB surveillance team or Soviet citizens who reported what they saw to the KGB.

"It was the casuals," he repeated. "They spotted him wandering around in the field." The warning from PIMENTA was the first hard evidence of an agent actually being arrested since Tolkachev.

I glanced over at Redmond, whose demeanor offered no clues as to what he was making of all of this. After the meeting broke up, I took Redmond into my office.

"What do you think?"

"Three possibilities. One, the casuals did their socialist duty and snitched on our guy, and the KGB eventually found the rock and staked it out. Two, they weren't casuals at all, but KGB surveillance, and they found the rock and staked it out. Three, we've got a bigger problem. Take your choice." Redmond's manner telegraphed his growing conviction that there was a cancer at the heart of the CIA.

"What's your choice?" I asked, already sensing his answer.

"Three. We've got a problem."

"Tell me why."

"Too many fucking problems all at once. It never happens this way. We lose operations, but not like this. TAW goes dead. Bokhan gets an elaborate but phony recall. Stombaugh gets busted with VANQUISH. MILLION gets called home early from Lisbon, and now WEIGH gets rolled up in Moscow. Add to that the fact that the British ran Gordievsky for years without any problem, we figure it out in March, and then he gets called back to Moscow. The KGB's got too much good luck all of a sudden. Life doesn't work that way. You tell me if we've got a fucking problem."

12

Washington, D.C., September 18, 1985

The decision was finally reached at FBI headquarters on Wednesday, September 18, to close in on Edward Howard the next day. Over the previous three weeks, the FBI had maintained discreet surveillance and had tapped his home telephone. They had established a post near Howard's house, where one agent could keep watch and alert other agents whenever Howard left home.

Jack Platt, Howard's old instructor in the Internal Operations course, was worried. No one had officially told him that Howard was under investigation, but the signs were all around him. Security officers had come to ask him if he could list all of the trainees who had taken the IO course, been slated for Moscow, and later been fired. Platt said there was only one—Edward Howard. He figured out that Howard was the target of the spy probe launched after Yurchenko's defection and went to see Burton Gerber.

Platt told Gerber he wanted to warn the FBI about Howard's countersurveillance training, so the bureau would send its best watchers—nicknamed "the Gs"—out to Santa Fe. The Gs were the only FBI surveillance agents who could keep up with a trained CIA officer, Platt believed. If the FBI used local agents against him, Howard would play them like fools.

But Gerber had never liked Platt, and he had little time for him. The last thing he wanted now was to have Platt freelancing, and he didn't bother telling Platt he'd already warned the FBI that Howard had taken the IO course.

Irritated at getting the brush-off from Gerber, Platt used his personal contacts at the bureau to arrange for the agents handling the Howard investigation to officially request an interview with him. On September 9, he briefed FBI Special Agents Bob Noonan and Mike Anderson on Howard's training. He told them that he'd evaluated Howard as an above-average student and that Howard had gone up against the FBI's best surveillance teams and done well. By now, both Gerber and Platt had warned the FBI that Howard was a man with a dangerous combination of skills and cunning.

At the same time, the FBI was taking an interest in another former CIA employee, William Bosch. After a disastrous tour as a case officer in Bolivia, Bosch had been fired by the agency. In February 1984, Bosch and Howard met in New Orleans to commiserate, and Howard suggested that he and Bosch join forces to get even with the agency that had dismissed them. Why not go to Mexico City and volunteer to the Soviets? Bosch stared at him. Was he kidding? Later, Bosch claimed he had serious doubts about Howard from that time on.

Bosch was living on South Padre Island off the Texas coast when two FBI agents began to ask about him at a nearby apartment complex where he had once lived. Bosch, who by coincidence was in the management office at the time, overheard them and told them who he was. The two FBI agents were not prepared to deal with him directly and waved him off, claiming they were looking for someone who spelled his name differently.

But Bosch wasn't buying that story, and he called Howard

in Santa Fe to complain. He told his friend he thought the CIA was snooping around him, using phony FBI credentials. Howard, by now convinced that his telephone was tapped, didn't say much during Bosch's phone call. But he realized that the FBI was looking for Bosch because of him. And he knew he'd said some incriminating things to Bosch. The most revealing conversation had occurred just two and a half months earlier, on South Padre Island. Howard had told Bosch that he had taken the final step against the CIA. "I did it," Howard had told Bosch. "I'm *really* playing hardball. What do you want, five, ten, fifteen thousand dollars?"

Howard would later tell Bosch that he was only joking, but Bosch came away from the outing convinced his friend's life had become very complicated indeed.

The FBI would not learn this until September 21, almost seventy-two hours later.

Santa Fe, 1330 Hours, September 19, 1985

The call came at 1:30 on Thursday afternoon. Special CIA Security Agent Jerry Brown told Howard there was an important matter he needed to discuss with the FBI. As David Wise wrote in his 1988 book on the Howard case, the FBI wanted Howard to meet them at the Santa Fe Hilton, a short walk from Howard's office in the state capitol. Howard agreed.

Jerry Brown's partner in the planned initial confrontation was Special Agent Michael Waguespack, who was widely recognized as one of the most effective interviewers in the bureau. Phil Parker, one of the key FBI officials running the Howard investigation, had handpicked Waguespack for the interview. Brown was there to provide depth and continuity; he was the "sound man," the agent most familiar with the telephone tap coverage of the Howard home and thus most familiar with Howard's state of mind.

Howard arrived at the Hilton to find Brown and Waguespack and his former CIA supervisor, Tom Mills, whom he had not seen in over a year. Mills's role was to nudge Howard into talking openly to the two FBI agents. After he had given his words of encouragement, Mills left the hotel room. And Edward Howard's life began to crumble.

Waguespack opened the interview by showing Howard a copy of a *Washington Post* story on the defection of Oleg Gordievsky to Britain. Waguespack told Howard that Gordievsky had identified Howard as a Soviet agent. That was a lie, a cover story dreamed up by the FBI to protect Yurchenko, whose defection had not yet been publicly reported.

Howard denied the accusation, and Waguespack asked him if he would take a polygraph. Howard said bitterly he would never take another polygraph; that was what had destroyed his career at the CIA. He said he wanted to get a lawyer, and Waguespack told him he had twenty-four hours.

Back at his office, Howard called his wife, Mary, and hurriedly told her that the FBI was accusing him of being a Soviet agent. Howard then drove home, and now the FBI surveillance was open and obvious all the way to his neighborhood. As he drove up to his house, Howard saw two FBI agents trying to talk to his wife. Howard went into his house and immediately called his lawyer, Mort Simon, and told him what was going on. Simon told him not to talk, and Howard went out to get Mary and pulled her away from the agents.

Within an hour, Howard's psychiatrist, Dr. Michael Dudelcyzk, called to say that the FBI had been asking about him. Howard tried to explain and asked Dudelcyzk for a prescription of tranquilizers so he could calm down.

That night, Howard called Bosch and revealed that the FBI was after him, not Bosch. Finally, before going to bed, he walked around his neighborhood to check out the surveillance. He spotted a utility van not far from his home.

South Padre Island, Texas, 0600 Hours, September 20, 1985

An insistent knock at the door of his beachfront condominium rousted Bill Bosch out of bed. Two men identifying themselves as FBI agents said they wanted to talk to him about his relationship with Edward Lee Howard. Bosch talked briefly with the agents and agreed to meet them again the next day for a polygraph examination.

In Santa Fe, meanwhile, Howard was acting cool. His boss in the state legislature, Phil Baca, had been interviewed by the FBI and knew Howard was in trouble, but he was surprised at how calm Howard seemed. In a formal presentation that morning, Howard didn't appear to be a man under intense pressure. After lunch, Howard told Baca he needed to take the rest of the afternoon off before a business trip to Austin, Texas, scheduled for Monday. Howard then told Baca that he might be contacted by federal officials, who might ask him questions about him and his travels. It was no big deal, Howard assured him.

After he left the capitol. Howard withdrew $300 from his bank account, stopped by Mort Simon's office to get the name of an Albuquerque attorney who specialized in federal criminal law, and then drove home to pick up Mary to go shopping. As he and Mary pushed their basket through the aisles of the Santa Fe Safeway, Howard recognized and approached a member of the FBI surveillance team and said he wanted another meeting. The rattled FBI agent made a quick call and then told Howard that Jerry Brown would be waiting for him at the Santa Fe Hilton.

In a brief meeting with Brown and Waguespack, Howard said he would have a criminal attorney by Monday and that he was canceling his Austin trip. They could get together on Monday. By the end of the day on Friday, the FBI believed it had matters under control in Santa Fe.

Moscow, September 20, 1985

In what was to become a recurring nightmare for the CIA, the press release summed up the disaster in clinical language:

> Tass is authorized to announce:
>
> The USSR State Committee for Security has uncovered and arrested an agent of the U.S. special services—A. G. Tolkachev, a worker in a Moscow research institute. The spy was caught in the act of passing secret materials of a defense nature to Paul M. Stombaugh, an officer of the American CIA, who acted under the cover of second secretary of the U.S. embassy in Moscow.
>
> It has been established that the American special services provided Tolkachev with specially designed min-

iature cameras with which he photographed secret documents, as well as with the means of codes, ciphers, and rapid acting two-way communications radio sets, and other materials for espionage work. Potent poisons which had been given to the spy by the Americans were also seized.

The contents, along with instructions from the U.S. Central Intelligence Agency, discovered at Tolkachev's residence, indicate that his use as a spy was linked with the CIA's plans to conduct large-scale subversive activities against the Soviet Union. The investigation continues.

It was no surprise. Still, the Tass announcement darkened the mood at Langley.

Santa Fe, 0900 Hours, September 21, 1985

Edward Lee Howard was moving methodically. He had stalled the FBI until Monday, but that meant he had to make his move now. His training began to kick in. At about 9:00 A.M., Howard and his wife left their house, and for more than two hours they drove around town looking for places that he could use to elude his FBI surveillance. He was planning to employ a tactic he had learned in the IO course: He would jump from a moving car while his wife drove around a corner. It was the old CIA trick of moving through the gap, taking advantage of the few seconds when they would be out of sight of surveillance. But Howard's plan came with a twist: As soon as he jumped out of the car, his wife would activate a pop-up dummy to take his place. By the time the surveillance picked them up again, they would still see two people sitting in the car. The dummy ("JIB" in CIA parlance, for "jack-in-the-box") was crude, but at night and from behind, it could fool them long enough for Howard to make his escape.

Back home, Howard made a tape recording for his wife to use of a call to his psychiatrist, so that it would seem as if he wanted to set up an appointment later that week. That afternoon, a baby-sitter came to take care of their toddler, Lee. Howard and his wife told the sitter they were going out to dinner in Santa Fe. After saying good-bye to his son at about 4:30 P.M., Howard drove off with Mary.

Somehow, the FBI surveillance team missed them and didn't realize that Howard had left his home. Although the bureau had a trailer parked a few hundred feet away with television monitors scanning the area and a clear line of sight of the route out of the neighborhood, the rookie agent inside the trailer didn't see the couple drive away. Phillip Parker, then the top deputy in the FBI's counterintelligence division, recalls that the FBI had surveillance units nearby, ready to follow Howard. But they had to be told when Howard left his house, so they could get into place to follow him. And since the rookie in the trailer never told them he was out of pocket, they didn't know it was time to start tracking him.

"The choke point was thc man watching from the trailer, and the big mistake was to put a first-office agent there," says Parker.

Of course, Howard didn't know he wasn't being followed, so he and Mary went through with their elaborate plans to evade the FBI. They ate dinner at a Santa Fe restaurant, and Howard called home to talk to their baby-sitter, thinking that would lull the FBI's monitors, reassuring them that they knew exactly where Howard was. But again the FBI missed the signal; no one picked up on the fact that Howard was at a restaurant calling home, not inside his house making an outgoing call.

Howard drove away from the restaurant at about 7:00 P.M., with his wife behind the wheel. At the turn he had identified that morning, he popped up the Jib and then jumped out of the car into some bushes. Mary drove on, and Edward Lee Howard was "black" in the Santa Fe night.

When Mary arrived back home, the FBI agent in the trailer was stunned; he didn't know the couple had ever left the house. But with the Jib in the front seat beside her, the agent breathed a sigh of relief. At least they were both back now.

The FBI was having greater success that day with William Bosch on South Padre Island. The former CIA officer had agreed to take a polygraph examination and told the FBI about his conversations with Howard. He told the FBI how Howard had suggested they get back at the CIA by going to Mexico City to volunteer to the Soviets. Most ominously, he told the agents how Howard had said to him, "I did it." With Bosch's statements, the FBI seemed on the verge of obtaining the probable cause needed for an arrest. But that could come Monday.

Meanwhile, Howard made his way to his empty office at the state capitol, typed a letter to Phil Baca, and caught a hotel shuttle van for the Albuquerque airport. Ironically, the shuttle made a stop in front of the Santa Fe Hilton—where the FBI agents waiting to interrogate Howard were staying. But again the FBI missed him, and Howard's trip to Albuquerque was uneventful. He hopped on the first flight available, to Tucson, Arizona, and soon was gone, having successfully made the FBI's surveillance agents look like a bunch of Keystone Kops.

After spending the night at an airport motel, Howard got on an early-morning flight for St. Louis and New York. He sat next to movie star Lee Marvin on the first leg of the trip. They chatted about the book Howard was reading—Tom Clancy's *The Hunt for Red October*. Howard changed planes again in New York and was on his way to Europe by Sunday night, just as the FBI was finally discovering that he was gone.

13

Montreal, September 24, 1985

Chuck Medanich, playing the role of father confessor, had been bracing for the worst all the way up from Washington. Medanich had a gift for reading people, for understanding the human heart, and he knew that this CIA-sponsored hunt for the love of Vitaly Yurchenko's life was a long shot at best.

Yurchenko had come to America two months earlier without his wife or daughter or his adopted son, and, in truth, he showed no great remorse about leaving them behind in Moscow. To be sure, he had made it clear to the first CIA officer he met when he walked into the U.S. embassy in Rome that he wanted his defection kept quiet, in the hope that the Soviet authorities would not feel compelled by bad publicity to punish his family. Having cast his lot without them, Yurchenko felt a responsibility to ensure that they were treated correctly by the Soviet authorities. Without proof that he had defected, the legalistic Soviets would have to move cautiously against his family.

Yurchenko's dream of a new life in the West did not include his wife. It revolved instead around his secret love, Valentina Yereskovsky. Vitaly and Valentina—they had fallen in love years earlier when they had been thrown together in the Soviet diplomatic community in Washington. From 1975 until 1980, Yurchenko had served as the security officer in the KGB's Washington *Rezidentura,* while Valentina, the wife of a Soviet diplomat, had been working as the pediatrician for the Soviet community. Yurchenko fell in love, and he yearned to someday, somehow, escape with her for a life far away from the complications of marriage and KGB security.

Sitting in a safe house in Virginia, Yurchenko fondly recalled the romantic Washington that he and Valentina had shared so briefly. The two had parted when Yurchenko was transferred back to Moscow, leaving the KGB officer to build dreams of a new world around his love for Valentina. Eventually he came to believe that Valentina would be ready to fly away with him on a moment's notice. All he needed to do was show up.

The CIA agreed to arrange a dramatic reunion between Vitaly and Valentina in Montreal, where her husband was now posted. The risks for the CIA and for Yurchenko were high, but perhaps Valentina would indeed come away with her lover and Yurchenko's outlook on his new life would brighten. Yurchenko had come to trust Medanich, so the plainspoken Texan would travel with the Russian and help him through the trauma of this reunion.

For his part, Medanich had come to respect Yurchenko; he seemed a cut above the other Soviet defectors he had handled during his career. Yurchenko had a puritanical streak and adhered to a spartan (if very odd) diet. He enjoyed cooking beef tongue and other Russian specialties he believed would soothe his ailing stomach. He never expressed interest in having the CIA procure women for him or in indulging himself in other vices. The recent death of his mother from stomach cancer had convinced Yurchenko that he was living on borrowed time, and while the loss seemed to have spurred him on to his impulsive decision to defect, it didn't mean he was a man of uncontrollable urges. He was, Medanich concluded, a man of honor. He had been happily telling the CIA everything he knew about KGB operations, had provided the tip that had led the CIA and FBI to Howard, and now all he hoped for was a reunion with the woman he loved and a fresh life on the American side of the Cold War.

For Yurchenko, the night before the trip to Montreal was like the night before the junior prom. Medanich arranged for a haircut and a new suit so he would look his best for his girl.

Yurchenko flew from Washington with Medanich and a CIA security detail to a military base near Plattsburgh, New York. The small group then drove across the border to rendezvous with the CIA's station chief in Canada and one of Yurchenko's main CIA debriefers, Colin Thompson, a Soviet Division officer in charge of Eastern European counterintelligence. The Canadian government provided security and logistical support for the visit, to make sure the KGB didn't try to grab Yurchenko while he was out of the United States.

Yurchenko and his entourage spent one night in a Montreal hotel under the watchful eyes of the Canadian security personnel. The Canadians didn't want Yurchenko to go out on the streets during the evening, but Medanich realized that he was so nervous, endlessly pacing in his room, that he needed to get out. Medanich finally overruled the Canadians and took him out for a walk, while a tense Canadian security detail followed close on their heels.

Valentina had returned from home leave in Moscow just before Yurchenko and his CIA detail arrived in Montreal. The

CIA tried to arrange for Yurchenko to approach her as soon as she returned, just in case the Soviets knew about their relationship. The CIA figured that if they moved quickly, the Soviets wouldn't have enough time to plan an ambush.

The plan was simple: Yurchenko would go to Valentina's apartment at lunchtime, while her husband was at the office and when she would most likely be one of the few people in the building. Canadian security personnel had the site covered, with lookouts across the street radioing back to a makeshift command post and undercover personnel posing as maintenance workers just down the hall. They were poised to move in quickly at the first sign of trouble.

When Yurchenko knocked on the apartment door, Valentina seemed to be expecting him. But his dreams were quickly shattered. When he asked her to come with him, she sternly said no. Later, Yurchenko confided to Medanich what she had said. She told him that she had loved a KGB colonel, not a traitor.

I have loved two men in my life, she told him. My father and you. My father is dead, and now you are dead in my eyes. You are nothing but a traitor.

The rejection was very dramatic, very Russian, and absolutely devastating. Valentina never let Yurchenko inside her apartment; the entire exchange took place at her door and lasted just two or three minutes. His head spinning, Yurchenko found his way back downstairs, back to the car and Medanich, back to a life now empty of dreams.

Colin Thompson left Montreal uncertain whether Valentina had ever really shared Yurchenko's dream of a life together. Thompson never warmed to Yurchenko, at least not the way Medanich did, and he wondered if Yurchenko's idea of having Valentina run away with him was merely a fantasy to avoid a lonely existence as a Russian defector in the United States.

After a brief countersurveillance run to make sure they weren't being followed, Yurchenko's driver headed for the border. The Canadians made the exit from downtown Montreal easier by blocking off traffic.

Yurchenko said little in the car as they sped away from the scene of his heartbreak. Matter-of-factly, he told Medanich what Valentina had said but added little about his own thoughts. Yurchenko, ever the KGB officer, didn't want to say much in front of a driver he didn't know well. And Medanich didn't pry; the pain was evident.

It was raining hard by the time they got back to Plattsburgh; the remnants of a tropical storm were pounding the Northeast. The weather fit Yurchenko's foul mood. While he was in Montreal, the story about his defection had broken in *The Washington Times,* and the rest of the Washington press corps was chasing the story. Some CIA officers had an awful feeling that the leaks might have come directly from CIA Director William Casey, who was eager for some positive press now that controversy was mounting over the CIA's aggressive activities in Central America, particularly the mining of Nicaraguan harbors.

Yurchenko had discovered the leaks in the worst possible way: He picked up a Montreal newspaper and saw a story about himself, just as he was being rejected by Valentina. He lost his love and his anonymity at the same time, and his bitterness about his fate deepened.

That night, at the officers club, Yurchenko had a drink; it was the only time he did so in front of Medanich. Even then, he stopped at one.

The weather cleared the next morning, and they boarded their plane for Washington in brilliant sunshine. Yurchenko's spirits seemed to lift briefly as he stood in the door of the plane, breathing in the morning air. But on the flight back to Washington, he seemed to be wrestling with his fate. He was convinced that the KGB had brainwashed Valentina, that they had turned her against him. Now, for the first time, he had to think about life without her.

He turned to Medanich. You are single, Yurchenko observed. What is it like to be a bachelor?

"I've been married and I've been single," Medanich said carefully, not knowing what answer Yurchenko wanted. "There are advantages both ways."

Back in Washington, Yurchenko's mood grew worse. Without Valentina, he found it harder to accept the slights he perceived. His anger over the media leaks mounted, and he felt his handlers were showing him off to the world—and cutting off his options.

By mid-October, Medanich and others at the CIA realized that Yurchenko needed a break. Maybe a trip out west would take his mind off his troubles, off Valentina. This time, Medanich would not be along to help soothe Yurchenko's nerves. Colin Thompson took his place, joining Yurchenko and the rest of his detail on a tour of the West. Thompson and Yurchenko didn't get along, which doomed the trip almost from the start.

After flying to Phoenix, Yurchenko and his escorts drove to the Grand Canyon, Las Vegas, and Bryce Canyon, Utah. The idea was to let him relax and see the country, but the trip only reconfirmed his fear that he didn't fit into this strange culture. Far from Washington, Yurchenko found it harder to make himself understood by Americans unfamiliar with his heavily accented English. Coached to ask for oatmeal instead of porridge for breakfast, he was embarrassed when a waitress was puzzled by his request for "houtmeal." It was his first exposure to life outside his CIA-created bubble, and he found it bewildering. He later confessed to Medanich that he felt like a baby, a proud KGB officer now unable to do things for himself.

In Las Vegas, Yurchenko was put off when his minders offered to find him a prostitute. It was clear that the pleasures of Las Vegas—gambling, sex, and liquor—were lost on Yurchenko.

The highlight of the trip came when the group was flagged down in rural Arizona and met by an FBI agent carrying a book of mug shots for Yurchenko to plow through. The FBI was anxious to track down the NSA spy, since he had told the Soviets about one of the most costly eavesdropping operations in American history. Yurchenko had already gone through a series of other mug books of NSA employees and had come up dry. But this time, the FBI widened the net to include a photo of a former NSA employee. It didn't take long for Yurchenko to identify Ronald Pelton, who had left the NSA before he began spying, as the man who had visited the Soviet embassy.

But as soon as Yurchenko picked Pelton out of the mug book, Thompson saw a change in him. Suddenly, Yurchenko realized that by fingering Pelton, he might have to testify in court, and he would thus publicly confirm the fact that he had defected. Such an open display would almost certainly prompt the Soviet authorities to move against his family and make it impossible for him to ever return home. Thompson later believed it was at that moment that Yurchenko began to think about finding a way out of his new life.

Medanich could see after Yurchenko returned from the trip that it had done nothing to improve his outlook. By late October, he was concerned that Yurchenko was slipping away mentally and emotionally. Medanich was an instinctive man, and his gut had been warning him about the Yurchenko case for some time. He had always had a slightly spooky feeling whenever he drove down to the Coventry safe house near Fredericksburg to visit Yurchenko. He could never quite put his finger on it, but during their walks by the beaver pond on the property, he sometimes felt as if they were being watched. There were minor incidents—strangers driving down the lane leading up to the safe house, for instance—that heightened his suspicions. There was never any evidence that the strangers were there to watch Yurchenko, but Medanich just didn't like so many coincidences.

Now, Yurchenko's mood was changing rapidly. Medanich finally wrote a memo detailing his fears, warning that unless something was done and done fast, Yurchenko would end his cooperation with the United States government. The memo was sitting on Burton Gerber's desk by the beginning of November. Later, Medanich wished he had used stronger language in his memo and had warned that Yurchenko might redefect.

Even before Gerber saw Medanich's memo, he had also begun to see signs of trouble. In mid-October, Gerber went to see Yurchenko at the Coventry safe house. Gerber was accompanied by Murat Natirboff, who happened to be in Washington and had asked to meet Yurchenko. Natirboff told Gerber that he was interested in talking to Yurchenko about KGB operations in Moscow.

Leaving Natirboff behind, Gerber and Yurchenko took a walk on the grounds of the safe house by themselves, and Yurchenko calmly but firmly told Gerber how he felt about the leaks, which by then had reached flood stage. "Mr. Gerber, how can I trust your service when everything I tell you ends up in the newspaper?"

The next day, Gerber told his colleagues what Yurchenko had asked him, and Gerber said that he had no answer. The Russian was right: The CIA had failed him. Gerber wrote a memo for his superiors, warning that Yurchenko's mood had darkened and that the case could be in trouble.

14

Alexandria, Virginia, October 4, 1985

As he went through his mail at home, Viktor M. Degtyar, a Line PR officer in the KGB's Washington *Rezidentura,* found an intriguing letter addressed to him and postmarked "Oct. 1, Prince George's County, Md." Inside was a second envelope, marked "DO NOT OPEN. TAKE THIS ENVELOPE UNOPENED TO VICTOR I. CHERKASHIN." There was no name or return address on either envelope, but whoever had sent this letter knew something about KGB operations in Washington. Mailing a letter to the home of a KGB officer bypassed the dangers of a more direct means of approaching Soviet intelligence officers under the watchful eyes of the FBI. And the very fact that the sender knew the name and home address of a KGB officer—and knew the name of the man in charge of counterintelligence for the *Rezidentura*—strongly suggested that this letter was to be taken seriously.

Once the letter was delivered to the *Rezidentura,* opened, and read, any doubts that the KGB might have had about its significance evaporated:

> Dear Mr. Cherkashin:
>
> Soon, I will send a box of documents to Mr. Degtyar. They arc from certain of the most sensitive and highly compartmented projects of the U.S. intelligence commu-

> nity. All are originals to aid in verifying their authenticity. Please recognize for our long-term interests that there are a limited number of persons with this array of clearances. As a collection they point to me. I trust that an officer of your experience will handle them appropriately. I believe they are sufficient to justify a $100,000 payment to me.
>
> I must warn of certain risks to my security of which you may not be aware. Your service has recently suffered some setbacks. I warn that Mr. Boris Yuzhin (Line PR, SF), Mr. Sergey Motorin (Line PR, Wash.), and Mr. Valeriy Martynov (Line X, Wash.) have been recruited by our "special services."
>
> . . . Details regarding payment and future contact will be sent to you personally. My identity and actual position in the community must be left unstated to ensure my security. I am open to commo suggestions but want no specialized tradecraft. I will add 6 (you subtract 6) from stated months, days and times in both directions of our future communications.

As if his letter wasn't already intriguing enough, the volunteer also passed on information about recent Soviet defectors to the United States, as well as some of the government's most sensitive technical operations targeting Soviet intelligence activities in the United States.

Stanislov Androsov, the KGB *Rezident,* and Viktor Cherkashin, chief of counterintelligence in the *Rezidentura,* knew immediately that this volunteer was genuine. The letter corroborated some of the information that Cherkashin had received from Aldrich Ames a few months earlier, and the KGB was already quite satisfied that Ames was not a double agent. He had provided too much information to be a double. Like this new volunteer, Ames had also fingered Martynov, Motorin, and Yuzhin, and as a result they were all already under suspicion. To be sure, Martynov had been allowed to take his summer home leave—and then return to the United States—after Ames had identified him as a spy, perhaps because the Soviets were not yet certain what to make of Ames or his information. But this new source was providing corroboration.

The letter writer did not reveal his identity, but to an experienced counterintelligence officer like Cherkashin, the letter offered plenty of clues about where he worked. From Ames, the KGB knew that the Russian spies inside the Washington *Rezidentura* and other stations in the United States were handled jointly by the CIA and the FBI. But a CIA officer like Ames with broad access to the agency's Soviet programs might also be aware of Russian agents in Moscow and other locations overseas. An FBI agent would not. By contrast, an FBI agent involved in counterintelligence would have greater detailed knowledge of collection operations targeted against the Soviets in the United States. "I think it would have taken Cherkashin about thirty seconds to figure out that the letter was from an FBI agent," Paul Redmond would later observe.

The letter writer was smart enough to realize that the secrets he was planning to hand over to the Soviets could finger him, even if he never gave the KGB his name. He acknowledged in his letter that the "box of documents" he planned to send to Degtyar would "as a collection . . . point to me."

Androsov and Cherkashin knew how to protect this volunteer. Earlier in the year, both had flown back to Moscow, rather than send a cable, to inform Center about Ames. Now, the KGB code-named this new volunteer B and slowly created an operational environment in which he could begin to thrive. On October 15, Degtyar received a package at his home containing a large number of classified documents from B. Androsov and Cherkashin could hardly believe their luck; just five months after Ames, this new, anonymous volunteer was providing equally astounding material from the heart of the U.S. intelligence community. The KGB's Washington *Rezidentura,* knocked off balance by John Walker's arrest earlier in the year, was now tapping into the mother lode.

At 8:35 A.M. on October 16, FBI surveillance personnel routinely monitoring the Soviet embassy watched Degtyar arrive for work with a large black canvas bag that he didn't normally carry. They duly noted that detail in their logs, and that tiny shard of information lay in the FBI surveillance files for years afterward, unexplained and seemingly unimportant.

Meanwhile, Viktor Cherkashin began thinking of ways to

convince Valeriy Martynov to return to Moscow without making him suspicious.

New York, Early October 1985

He had done it. He had mailed the letter on his way back to Washington for a meeting at FBI headquarters. Even if the KGB concluded that it came from someone in the bureau, it would be difficult to trace back to a supervisory agent in the New York Field Office. Mailing it to Degtyar at his home had added another layer of protection; Robert Hanssen knew that the FBI didn't routinely go through personal mail addressed to KGB officers at their homes. After all, the only people who knew where KGB officers lived were a few CIA officers and FBI agents. No reason to cover their personal mail.

Hanssen had been transferred to New York ten days earlier. This would be his second tour of duty in New York—and his second stint as a Soviet spy. In 1979, a few months after he was first assigned to counterintelligence in New York, Hanssen had walked into the New York office of AMTORG, a Soviet trade organization that served as a front for the GRU, and offered his services as a spy. As a junior FBI special agent, Hanssen had limited access to the bureau's secrets. Still, he was able to reveal to the Soviets the identity of one of the most important and longest-surviving spies within the Soviet hierarchy, a source known inside the FBI as TOP HAT—and at the CIA as BOURBON. TOP HAT was GRU General Dmitri Polyakov, who had first been recruited by the FBI while he was in New York in the early 1960s. Hanssen also handed over the FBI's classified listing of Soviet diplomats believed to be intelligence officers, letting the Soviets know how much the FBI knew about its intelligence operations in the United States—and which of its officers had so far eluded detection.

The Soviets reacted in an odd manner to Hanssen's information about Polyakov. At the time Hanssen betrayed him, Polyakov was serving in India. He was recalled to Moscow by the GRU in 1980 and apparently retired soon after that—the CIA lost contact with him in Moscow. Polyakov was not arrested until 1986, years after his retirement, by which time he had also been identified by Aldrich Ames. The Soviets felt they needed corroboration before arresting a general.

Hanssen spied for the GRU until his wife discovered his espionage in 1980. When she walked in on him in the basement of their home in Scarsdale, New York, he suddenly began to cover up what he was doing. Afraid that he was having an affair, she began to grill him, and he finally told her that no, there was no other woman—he was handing over information to the Soviet Union. He convinced her that he was tricking the Russians, giving them worthless information in exchange for cash.

Bonnie Hanssen, a devout Catholic who was then pregnant with their fourth child, was stunned. She believed her husband when he said that he was "tricking" the Russians, but she still understood that Bob was playing an extremely dangerous game. She told him she thought that what he was doing was "insane" and that it might get him fired from the FBI.

Fearful for her family's future, Bonnie convinced her husband to go with her to talk to their priest. Bob and Bonnie were members of a small conservative Catholic organization called Opus Dei and went to see their priest at Opus Dei's center in Westchester County, Reverend Robert Bucciarelli. Father Bucciarelli initially told Hanssen that he had to turn himself in to the FBI. That night, Bonnie cried herself to sleep, fearful of what was to become of their family. But the next morning, the priest called the Hanssens back and asked them to come see him once again. This time he suggested a way out—if Bob would give the money he had received from the Soviets to charity and agree not to spy further, he didn't need to surrender to the authorities. Relieved, the Hanssens went home. Bob promised Bonnie he wouldn't deal with the Russians again and would send his Soviet money to Mother Teresa.

Bob Hanssen had one problem—he had already spent some of the money the Soviets had paid him. Bonnie was determined to fulfill their commitment to Father Bucciarelli and insisted that Bob repay the entire amount—about $30,000—and not just the cash that remained. Bob Hanssen realized that meant he would have to make installment payments to Mother

Teresa for years to come. The family teetered on the verge of bankruptcy as a result.

Bonnie tried to make sure that he was making the payments—and staying clean. She would regularly ask her husband if he was sending money to Mother Teresa and would also archly grill him about whether he had started up again with the Russians. Yes, Bob would say, I am still making the payments. No, he would say, I am not dealing with the Russians. Bob would act hurt each time she questioned him about his vow never again to work with the Soviets. Marriage is built on trust, after all.

The Hanssens moved back to Washington when Bob was transferred to headquarters for a senior post in counterintelligence, and by 1985 he was able to tell his wife that he had finally paid off their debt to Mother Teresa. After years of barely scraping by, the Hanssens no longer had a secret financial obligation hanging over their heads.

In October 1985, Bob was transferred back to New York, and this time Bonnie was determined to maintain a modest lifestyle so her husband wouldn't be tempted to go back to the dirty but lucrative game of playing with the Russians. During their first tour in New York, the Hanssens had lived in Scarsdale, one of New York's most expensive suburbs. This time, Bonnie insisted that they find a cheaper place to live, so they settled in a modest three-bedroom house in Yorktown Heights, a small town about ninety minutes north of New York City. There was no reason now that the Hanssens couldn't make it on Bob's FBI salary.

But Bob Hanssen found the pull of espionage too strong to resist. So just as he was transferring back to New York he volunteered again, this time anonymously, and to the KGB in Washington rather than the GRU in New York. The Soviets never connected their new volunteer with the earlier agent working for the GRU in New York. Hanssen didn't want any more slipups.

At the time he sent his letter to Degtyar, Hanssen was about to take on a job with much broader access to the FBI's counterintelligence secrets than he had had during his earlier stint as a spy. He had just been named a supervisor in a foreign counterintelligence squad in the New York Field Office, handling technical operations against Soviets operating at the United Nations and in the Soviet consulate in Manhattan.

But more important, he had just completed an assignment as chief of the unit that analyzed information collected by the FBI on Soviet intelligence operations in the United States. He had also served on a special committee that was in charge of coordinating the FBI's technical intelligence projects against the Soviets. So when Bob Hanssen volunteered to spy for the Soviets a second time, his head was filled with secrets, including many that the FBI had received from the Central Intelligence Agency.

Perhaps the most explosive secret that Hanssen betrayed to the Soviets was the fact that the FBI and the National Security Agency had jointly built a tunnel underneath the new Soviet embassy complex in Washington. The new embassy complex wasn't fully occupied yet, but the FBI and NSA had already constructed the tunnel in order to eavesdrop on conversations among Russian diplomats and intelligence officers. What's more, the American contractors working on the embassy compound had been infiltrated with FBI agents, who had worked hard to ensure that the compound was built as one big megaphone. They'd even made sure that a special sound-conducting paint had been used in the embassy, including on internal pipes, so that sound would travel more readily and be easier to pick up from the FBI tunnel.

Hanssen betrayed so many secrets shared jointly by the FBI and CIA, in fact, that years later, when counterintelligence investigators began to hunt down the source of the leaks, they were convinced the betrayal had occurred in Langley, not at the FBI. One innocent CIA officer, who by coincidence was both involved in a case Hanssen betrayed and happened to jog in a suburban Virginia park where Hanssen made some of his dead drops, would come under intense and prolonged scrutiny.

Even Bob Hanssen may not have been quite sure why he had decided to become a spy. He was hardly a classic case. Unlike others who had turned to espionage as a form of revenge against a system that had denied them advancement, Hanssen was not stalled in his career. He volunteered to the Soviets just as he was being given a promotion. Ideology didn't explain it: Hanssen was a devout Catholic and avowed anti-Communist. He lived modestly with his wife and children and carpooled to work, even after he took the Soviets' cash. The money was nice, but there was something more. Perhaps the only explanation was that Bob Hanssen had an addictive personality, and espionage somehow fed his cravings.

A native of Chicago and graduate of Knox College, a small liberal arts school in Illinois, Hanssen took a few years to find his footing. After majoring in chemistry and studying Russian at Knox, he switched to dentistry at Northwestern, later shifting to business and accounting. Married to Bonnie by 1968, he received an MBA from Northwestern in 1971, and by 1973 he was a certified public accountant, working briefly as an accountant in Chicago and then as a financial investigator for the Chicago Police Department. By the time Hanssen finally joined the FBI in 1976, he was nearly thirty-two.

Following a stint in a white-collar crime squad in Gary, Indiana, he was transferred to New York in 1978 to work on accounting-related matters, but the next year he volunteered to join the New York Field Office's intelligence division. With his business and accounting background, he was assigned to help create an automated counterintelligence database for the New York office. The database would help the FBI keep track of Russian intelligence officers operating in the United States.

In 1981, just after he had broken with the GRU, he was transferred to FBI headquarters and began to move up through the ranks. He became a supervisory special agent in the intelligence division and later moved into the budget unit there, helping to prepare the FBI's classified intelligence budget requests to Congress. Finally, in 1983, he moved into the Soviet analytical unit. The KGB could not have asked for a more knowledgeable or better-placed spy. Years later, American investigators would discover that the KGB came to consider their anonymous new spy, B, to be more valuable than Aldrich Ames.

The trick would be to keep him producing secrets. But Bob Hanssen had his own inner clock that would tell him when to spy and when to lie low.

15

Langley, October 1985

Edward Lee Howard had been on the run for over a week when the first solid clues of his whereabouts began to surface. The FBI had traced his travel from Albuquerque to Tucson to Helsinki, but the trail ended there. Some at the FBI thought he had linked up with the KGB in Finland, then traveled into the Soviet Union under their protection. Others in the bureau felt he had traveled to Finland to throw off his pursuers, hoping they'd believe he'd defected to the Soviets and give up the hunt, thus allowing him to travel under a false name to one of his more familiar Latin American haunts. The CIA was convinced that once in Finland, Howard would head straight to the USSR.

In early October, a clandestine CIA source in the Soviet embassy in Helsinki reported that over a period of two days at the end of September, there had been a flurry of activity at the KGB *Rezidentura.* It was whispered that a very important person was secretly spirited out of Finland and across the USSR border to Leningrad in a Soviet embassy vehicle.

There was little doubt at the CIA that the mysterious visitor in Helsinki was Howard, though it would take the FBI a little more time to believe that Howard had actually crossed over to Leningrad. In his own book—written years later from Moscow, almost certainly with the cooperation of the KGB—Howard claimed that he had wandered the world before settling down in Moscow. He insisted that he had even spent time in the United States. But the CIA remained convinced that he was taken across the border into the Soviet Union soon after his arrival in Helsinki.

Coventry, Virginia, 1530 Hours, October 25, 1985

Yurchenko seemed somehow more settled. Maybe it was his recent trip to Nevada. We were outside now, walking in the cool October sunshine down to the lake that the Coventry property fronted. He was mildly animated about a beaver lodge he had been watching over the last few months, and during lunch he had insisted we walk down to take a look. Lunch had been another of Yurchenko's quirky boiled-chicken-breast-and-carrot affairs. He still cooked for himself as if he were suffering from a terminal disease, and he still couldn't seem to get beyond chicken breast and veal tongue. An American doctor had given him a clean bill of health; much to his astonishment, he did not have stomach cancer and was not about to die and rejoin his mother.

Over lunch Yurchenko told me the story about Vladimir Vetrov, a KGB Line X (Science and Technology collection) officer who had volunteered to spy for the French five years earlier, only to be arrested a year and a half into his new career for a senseless murder in a Moscow park. A few years into his twelve-year prison sentence, it had been discovered that Vetrov was not only a murderer, but also a spy who had been working for the French under the code name FAREWELL. Yurchenko said he thought Vetrov had been betrayed by his letters to his wife, or perhaps by a prison informant. He wasn't sure which story was accurate—he'd heard both at different times.

Once Vetrov had been exposed as a spy, he was ordered to write a complete confession. When he handed the notepad containing his "confession" back to his KGB interrogators at Lefortovo, it was completely filled with a tight script that, upon close inspection by General Sergei Golubev, first deputy head of Directorate K, counterintelligence, turned out to be one of the most virulent attacks on the KGB establishment that had ever been produced inside the organization itself. Golubev, according to Yurchenko, reread Vetrov's indictment a few times and decided just to lock it away. Yurchenko said that in addition to brutalizing the KGB, Vetrov devoted much of his statement to lionizing the French and the West. The hardcore Golubev—he'd headed the team that had interrogated

Gordievsky a few months earlier and six years before that had been implicated in the infamous poisoned umbrella murder of Georgi Markov, the Bulgarian émigré writer—decided the confession should never see the light of day. Word nevertheless spread about the confession and about how Vetrov had walked to his execution without showing the slightest hint of remorse. Or fear.

Now, proceeding down to the lake with walking sticks Yurchenko had fashioned from saplings, I decided to tell the KGB defector why I had dropped in on him unannounced. "Alex, I told you before I'd let you know if there was any unpleasantness coming in the press."

Yurchenko cocked an eye. "You have more unpleasantness, Tom?"

"Yes, Alex, I have more unpleasantness. It is about Artamonov."

At that moment a glistening beaver broke the water's surface beside the lodge at the point where the lake fed into a small stream. "There, Tom! See him!"

Then, as suddenly as he had become excited at spotting his beaver, the KGB colonel became quiet again. After a moment he asked, "What is the unpleasantness about Artamonov, Tom?"

"I said before that we would try to keep what we learned from you about Artamonov's death out of the newspapers. But I've just learned that it's going to be published within a week."

There was no expression on Yurchenko's face as he listened. "Why?"

"Because of our laws. There is a lawsuit by Artamonov's widow against the United States, and we have no choice but to share with her and her attorney what you have told us."

"When will you do this?"

I was struck by the calmness with which Yurchenko was taking the news—I'd expected a much more dramatic response. "I met with the Defense Department and the FBI yesterday at the Pentagon. The lawyers there representing all three agencies agreed that now that we have the full details from you, we must pass them on to Artamonov's wife and her attorney. It has to be done now. There's no choice."

"What do I have to do about it?" Yurchenko's question seemed odd, out of context.

"I don't follow, Alex."

"Do I have to go to your courts and speak on Artamonov?"

"Not yet. We're looking at our options for dealing with that problem. Nothing's been decided as of now."

I hoped I sounded convincing, since the question of Yurchenko ultimately having to testify in court was far from resolved. What was certain was that within a matter of days the press would explode with the whole sordid story, the kidnapping in Vienna, the chloroforming and hefty injection of sedatives for the drive to the Czech border. Then the panic when the KGB got Artamonov on "friendly" Czech soil and discovered he had stopped breathing. The futile attempts at CPR, the brandy poured down his throat by a panicky KGB officer, the injection of adrenaline by another. Then the understanding that Nikolai F. Artamonov was dead. Finally, the details of a cover-up that included enlisting the General Secretary of the USSR to lie to two U.S. Presidents. All of that would start appearing in the newspapers in a matter of days, and the man in the hot seat, Vitaly Yurchenko, seemed calm and appeared to be taking it all in stride.

"Will you tell me when they tell his wife?"

"I'll call you myself."

Yurchenko's face lit up again. "Look, Tom. The beaver!"

Driving back to Washington that evening, I thought I should be feeling pretty good about Yurchenko taking the news about going public with thc Artamonov case so well. But somehow I didn't.

In 1959, at thirty-one, Nikolai Artamonov was the youngest torpedo-destroyer commander in the Soviet Baltic Fleet. While his ship was on station near the Polish port of Gdansk, he met a beautiful Polish dental student named Blanka Ewa Gora. Nikolai and Ewa decided to escape together and ultimately set their sights on defecting to the United States. Artamonov decided to commandeer a motor launch from his destroyer, and then he and Ewa took off for Sweden across the Baltic. They made it to Sweden and never looked back. Artamonov had left a wife and son in Leningrad.

After his defection, Artamonov was debriefed by the CIA and given a new identity as Nicholas George Shadrin and a job serving the Defense Intelligence Agency as an analyst of Soviet naval developments. While Artamonov had been convicted of treason and sentenced to death back home in the Soviet Union, Shadrin soon blended into suburban life in the United States.

That all changed in 1966, when the KGB counterintelligence group responsible for tracking the Soviet Union's traitors spotted Shadrin on the lecture circuit in Washington, where his reputation as an analyst of Soviet military power was growing. The KGB decided to mount an intricate operation to turn Shadrin back against the CIA and ultimately bring him back to the USSR to denounce the agency and the decadent West. KGB Colonel Igor Kochnov was assigned the task of approaching Shadrin and carried two personal letters from Shadrin's ex-wife and his son to win him over. Kochnov approached Shadrin in a Virginia supermarket, and Shadrin feigned interest but then promptly reported the contact to the CIA. The agency told him to convince the Soviets that he was willing to spy for them. Shadrin would now be a triple agent.

The case only became more confused when Igor Kochnov, the KGB colonel who had approached Shadrin, volunteered to spy for the CIA.

The case became so complex that the FBI, CIA, and DIA all became involved, and there were competing theories within the U.S. intelligence community about Shadrin's true loyalties, even though he and his new wife eventually became naturalized U.S. citizens.

By the mid-1970s, the KGB had lost interest in running Shadrin as a double agent. Instead, they wanted to kidnap him and spirit him back to the USSR as a prisoner of the espionage wars. For their snatch operation, the KGB decided on the European city where they felt most at home, Vienna. Shadrin would be kidnapped in Vienna, drugged, and driven across the border into Czechoslovakia.

On December 18, 1975, Shadrin was sent to meet the KGB in Vienna. Shadrin agreed to a second meeting with the KGB two days later, on December 20. Then, he simply vanished.

The U.S. government initially asked Ewa Shadrin to cover for her husband's absence and to remain quiet while efforts were made to secure his release. She was told at one point that Henry Kissinger, then Secretary of State, would raise the issue with the Soviet ambassador, Anatoly Dobrynin.

At first, Ewa cooperated with the government's requests. But eventually it became clear to her that her husband had been sent to Vienna without adequate protection, and her attempts to get answers to her questions were met with cold silence.

In 1976, a few months after Shadrin's disappearance, his case began to get presidential attention, when President Gerald Ford asked Soviet General Secretary Leonid Brezhnev about Shadrin's whereabouts. Brezhnev responded that Shadrin had indeed met with representatives of the Committee for State Security in Vienna on December 18, 1975, to discuss his repatriation to the Soviet Union, but he said he had failed to show for a second scheduled meeting. Brezhnev said he had no further information about Shadrin but could assure the American President that he was not in the Soviet Union. President Carter raised the Shadrin case again with Brezhnev but got the same answer.

Shadrin's fate had remained a mystery until Yurchenko had arrived with the answer. He told the CIA that Shadrin had died in a botched kidnapping by the KGB. Thrown into the trunk of a car for the drive across the Austrian border, Shadrin had been drugged to keep him quiet. But the KGB had mistakenly given him an overdose, and when the KGB men stopped their car and opened the trunk to check on their prisoner, they found that he was dead.

When Yurchenko told the CIA about Shadrin's death, he warned his debriefers that this was one of the darkest secrets of the KGB. Brezhnev had lied to two American Presidents about Shadrin, so the credibility of the head of state was on the line. Yurchenko made it clear to the CIA that if Moscow ever found out that he had revealed the truth about Shadrin, the KGB would go after Yurchenko's family and property. Yurchenko, like Shadrin before him, would be sentenced to death in absentia. It was no wonder he was afraid he might have to testify in court. Perhaps the CIA was trying to ensure that Yurchenko could never go home again.

Santa Fe, 1530 Hours, October 28, 1985

Jack Platt sat across from Mary Howard in a room at the La Quinta motel in Santa Fe. Of those in the intelligence world who knew her at all, Platt probably knew her best. He'd assessed Mary as a hard worker, but Ed's dominance over her was total. But he wasn't a marriage counselor. Platt's job was to get the young Americans up to speed in a matter of a few months and then to send them into the Moscow grinder. It was true, however, that many of the spouses bonded with him and came to look on the gruff ex-Marine as a father figure. Mary was one of those, and he liked her no-nonsense approach to a difficult job.

He recalled how well she had handled herself when she and Howard had been arrested in an elaborately staged drug bust in Washington. The couple had been given the task of recovering a dead-dropped half-pint milk carton, ostensibly loaded with microfilm from a site near the Maine Avenue marina. Just as Howard unloaded the dead drop, both he and Mary were arrested with the violence typical of a drug bust. They were immediately separated. Mary was thrown into the back of a car with one of the FBI's "Gs" who had become famous for his ability to play the role of a drug addict/dealer. On the ride to the FBI's Washington Field Office, the G in the car with Mary Howard kept her in a state of near terror as he moaned and complained loudly to the driver that he would vomit if he wasn't let out of the car immediately. Through all this, Mary remained tearful but silent, even when the FBI agent came into the interrogation room with the "results" of the lab tests on the milk carton she and Howard had retrieved: #3 heroin.

Meanwhile, in a separate WFO interrogation room, Howard had quickly broken cover with the FBI agent playing the role of his attorney. Almost immediately, Howard was ready to shrug off the bust as a joke, while his wife was hanging tough in another room. The arrest was not graded in a formal sense, but Howard had a hard time accepting that Mary had performed more stoically. Platt had come to like and respect the mild-mannered young woman, perhaps more than her husband. But in the end, Howard had done well enough to get Platt's clearance to enter the Moscow pipeline.

Now, sitting here in the aftermath of Howard's escape, Mary Howard was attempting to deal with her nightmare, and with the truth. The FBI had maintained full coverage on Mary Howard, including a much belated dispatch of the Gs to Santa Fe, to watch Mary in case she, too, decided to make a break for it. Platt had been asked by the FBI to go to Santa Fe to hold Mary's hand and nudge her into full cooperation.

Mary knew she was in over her head. After Howard's escape, in which she had played a supporting role, the FBI told her that her son's future depended on how she responded to the bureau's request for a full account of what she knew about her husband's involvement with the Soviets. Mary came to fear that her son might not only be without a father, but could be without a mother if she didn't cooperate. So she began to talk, and she sat for two difficult polygraph sessions. Before the polygrapher strapped her to the machine, Platt told Mary Howard, "Just tell the truth."

After the polygraph sessions, the FBI was satisfied that Mary was not guilty of any criminal acts, since no warrant had been issued for her husband's arrest at the time she helped him escape. The bureau was convinced that Mary was not involved in her husband's suspected espionage, although she provided valuable insights into Howard's actions. Platt saw a new strength developing in Mary.

Before Platt left Santa Fe, Mary Howard received a phone call from a Russian, who told her that her husband was safe and well. The call was probably from Moscow, routed via Switzerland, which was as far as the FBI could trace it.

Washington, D.C., October 31, 1985

The Shadrin story broke in the press as fast as I had predicted, and Yurchenko's name was mentioned prominently as the source of the new information about Shadrin's death at the hands of the KGB. Now, Yurchenko felt he could no longer trust the CIA.

Burton Gerber had issued a standing order that Yurchenko should not be brought inside the twenty-five-mile radius around Washington unless he had a business or medical appointment, or unless Gerber had given prior approval to the trip. The point of moving him out to Coventry had been to put him outside the zone in which Russian intelligence officers from the Washington *Rezidentura* could legally operate; bringing him back downtown placed him at risk of exposure to the Soviets, Gerber believed. But on Halloween, with Yurchenko's mood worsening, Medanich and a CIA security officer took Yurchenko down to watch the wild Halloween parade and street festival in the city's Georgetown neighborhood. Yurchenko and his watchers mingled with thousands of partyers along the jammed streets.

Gerber didn't authorize the trip. He didn't even hear about the Halloween outing until two nights later, after Yurchenko and one CIA security guard went back to Georgetown one more time.

16

Coventry, November 2, 1985

Yurchenko waited until there was just one CIA security officer on duty and then said he was restless and wanted to go for a drive. In violation of standing orders requiring that he be accompanied by more than one security officer when out in public, the young officer, Tom Hannah, agreed to take him for a ride. Yurchenko told Hannah that he wanted to go shopping, so the two headed up Interstate 95 toward Washington and stopped at a mall in Manassas, Virginia. Yurchenko went into Hecht's, where he'd been once before with his CIA handlers, and ducked into the dressing room to try on some clothes. Later, after his escape, CIA officers noticed that there was a pay phone by the dressing room. Was it possible, they wondered, that he had noticed the pay phone on his earlier shopping trip and maneuvered his security guard back to the store so he could place a call to the Soviets?

After the side trip to Hecht's, Yurchenko told Hannah he wanted to try French food for dinner and suggested they drive into Georgetown. Hannah knew that Yurchenko and his escorts had been to Georgetown just two nights before, so he figured it was okay to go back again.

After ordering at the Georgetown restaurant Au Pied de Cochon, Yurchenko quietly made his move. He told the inexperienced Hannah that if he didn't come back, it wasn't his fault, and then he simply walked out the door. Inexplicably, Hannah sat and waited for a time before calling to notify anyone that the biggest defector in CIA history had walked out on him.

Hannah finally called Colin Thompson at his home, just as Thompson was on his way out the door to meet a date. Thompson told Hannah to call him back at his date's home if Yurchenko didn't come back in the next few minutes. By the time Thompson arrived at the woman's home, Hannah called again in a panic, and Thompson finally agreed to come down to Georgetown to help look for the Russian. He was soon joined by others from the CIA and FBI, all of whom began to search through Georgetown's streets. Thompson hoped at first that Yurchenko might have ducked in to see a Russian film playing at a nearby theater, and both the CIA and FBI kept up the search through the night.

As soon as he was notified of Yurchenko's disappearance, Burton Gerber thought: He's gone back. He knew that the street-by-street search in Georgetown would be fruitless, and he grew increasingly angry and frustrated by the sloppy way his officers had handled Yurchenko that night. He blew up during a rancorous telephone conversation with Thompson, who seemed far too casual and unapologetic about the whole affair. Yurchenko's disappearance effectively ended Thompson's career in the Soviet Division and any hope he had for advancement at the CIA. He spent his last years at the agency in the defector program, trying to prove that he could, in fact, work well with them.

Soviet Embassy, Washington, D.C., November 2, 1985

It was late when Viktor Cherkashin was summoned to the Soviet embassy. He met KGB *Rezident* Stanislov Androsov in the parking lot. Standing in the parking lot, where no one could hear their conversation, Androsov told Cherkashin that Yurchenko was back.

Cherkashin was stunned. He blurted out a few well-chosen Russian words to express his feelings about this increasingly bizarre situation. Then he went up to the apartment where Yurchenko was being kept under the watchful eye of a security guard. Cherkashin assumed his best stage presence to convince Yurchenko that he was happy to see him. He hugged him and welcomed him back into the fold.

Cherkashin didn't believe Yurchenko's story—that he had been drugged and kidnapped and forced to reveal secrets. But he and Androsov immediately saw the opportunity presented by Yurchenko's change of heart.

Reston, Virginia, 0330 Hours, November 3, 1985

The first call came from Burton Gerber.

"Milton, when did you last see Yurchenko?"

I thought for a moment. "About a week ago. Maybe a little longer. It was when I told him about the Shadrin business. Why?"

"You haven't heard?" Gerber was incredulous. "He walked away from his security officer last night in Georgetown. Didn't anyone call you?"

"Not until you just called."

"He's redefected."

My mind was racing, thinking back on my last meeting with Yurchenko.

"I'm not so sure. Maybe he's just kicking back and telling us to ease off him." I wasn't convinced by my own argument, but I felt I had to throw something in the mix.

"He's redefected." Gerber paused and then added, "Get in touch with Colin."

I had barely hung up the phone when the second call came in, this one from Ed Juchniewicz, the number two man in the Directorate of Operations.

"Did you fuck up the Yurchenko thing?"

"Ed, I'm not even convinced Yurchenko's redefected."

"What the fuck you think he did, run off to get laid?"

"Maybe something not far from that. He might have just decided he needed to write himself a three-day pass."

Juchniewicz was silent for a moment. "Don't try taking that to the bank. Your buddy's gone." Then the phone went dead.

The mystery of Yurchenko's whereabouts was solved Monday afternoon. Beginning at around 3:00 P.M., the press officer at the Soviet embassy started alerting select members of the Washington press corps that there would be a press conference at 5:30 that afternoon, at which time they would be able to put some questions to Colonel Vitaly Yurchenko. The State Department didn't find out what was going on until 4:00 P.M., when it received an official protest delivered by the Soviet embassy, complaining of the "criminal act committed against V. S. Yurchenko."

At the press conference, Yurchenko, flanked by Minister Viktor Isakov, the interpreter Vitaly Churkin, and a third Soviet official, Vladimir Kulagin, sat at a green felt–covered table in the reception room of the Soviet embassy. The room was filled with American and foreign reporters, as well as a large number of Soviet embassy officials. Yurchenko, clearly breaking with what was supposed to have been a more scripted session, switched erratically from Russian to English, often leaving his interpreter in midsentence. But the story he told was one that fit neatly with the Soviet view of how America's "special services" operated against Russian intelligence officers. He wove a tale of kidnapping and incarceration.

"I was forcibly abducted in Rome by some unknown persons. . . . Unconscious, I was brought from Italy to the U.S.A. . . . Here I was kept in isolation . . . forced to take drugs, and denied the possibility to get in touch with official Soviet representatives."

Back at CIA headquarters, senior officers in the SE Division watched the press conference in Gerber's office. We were largely silent until Yurchenko began to rail against his CIA tormentors. Then Redmond broke the silence.

"He's using the Bitov defense," he said. He was referring to Oleg Bitov, who'd defected to the British in 1983 and after one year had changed his mind and redefected to the Soviet Union. Bitov had claimed that he'd been kidnapped and controlled by mind-altering drugs for the entire year, during which he had made a series of public appearances denouncing the Soviet Union. The Soviets welcomed Bitov back in the fold, using his redefection for propaganda purposes. It bolstered the KGB claim that Western special services often resorted to the use of kidnapping and drugs.

During his CIA debriefings, Yurchenko had provided an insider's view of the Bitov hoax, which he had said was just another case in which the KGB could knock the Western intelligence services off balance with a lie. But now, on the television screen, Yurchenko was saying that he'd been in a fog most of the time during his CIA captivity and that his CIA minders had used the drugs as a means to "deceive the government, including Mr. Casey," into thinking that he was a willing defector. The KGB colonel described in detail the "contract" the CIA had forced him to sign, wherein he would receive $1 million as a bonus, with an annual stipend of $62,500 with inflation adjustment, plus $48,000 to pay for furnishings.

"The price of doing business just went up," I said. "Now everybody is going to want the Yurchenko deal."

The press conference lasted a little over an hour, with Yurchenko generally holding his own through the questions about Howard and Shadrin. Each time he would say, often through his slick interpreter, that the first he had heard any of these names was when he read them in the American press. He would go on to say that he was able to resist the questioning, except when he was drugged. Then he would be presented with signed "confessions," written in his own hand and revealing what he thought must have been state secrets. Similarly, his CIA interrogators would play tape recordings of him giving up state secrets, he said, but always when he was under the influence of the CIA's drugs.

By the end of the press conference, the Soviets had scored propaganda points. And the CIA was quickly faced with a flood of accusations that Yurchenko's redefection was the result of poor handling by the agency.

The timing could not have been worse. It coincided with two other high-profile cases of botched defections from the Soviet Union. In Kabul, Afghanistan, a Soviet soldier had walked into the American embassy and requested asylum.

Over a period of several weeks, the Americans had rebuffed Moscow's demands that the young soldier be handed back, until the soldier himself had changed his mind and returned to the Soviet fold.

The second incident was the attempted defection of a sailor from a Soviet merchant ship in New Orleans. Twice he jumped aboard an American Coast Guard cutter, and twice he was returned to his ship by the Americans. Both incidents were so recent that the Yurchenko case seemed to provide final proof that there was something fundamentally wrong with the way the United States was handling would-be defectors.

Yurchenko's face again filled the television screen. This time his rambling answer to a question about Shadrin directly touched the small group assembled in the CIA office. "Mr. Gaihrber," Yurchenko said in his heavy accent, "aren't you ashamed?"

I looked for a reaction in Gerber's face. He had already anticipated taking a hit for the Ed Howard affair . . . and now this.

U.S. Department of State, 1800 Hours, November 5, 1985

I slipped by the press and television crews gathered at the C Street entrance of the State Department. The media was already staked out for Yurchenko's arrival at Foggy Bottom for the 6:00 P.M. "confrontation," a scripted protocol to determine whether Yurchenko was freely returning to the Soviet Union. When a Soviet official defected to the United States, the Soviets would request an interview with the defector to ask if he or she had made the choice without coercion. In most cases, Soviet defectors refused to meet the Soviet authorities because they felt such meetings were incriminating. The United States was under no obligation to make the defectors available to the Soviets. But on the rare occasions when a Soviet redefected, the United States insisted on a meeting at the State Department to give the Soviet one last chance to change his mind. Yurchenko had refused the Soviet request for a confrontation in August, hoping that he could simply fade from the scene. Tonight, the Soviets were coming with apparent relish for this reverse confrontation. I planned to be at the meeting on the outside chance that Yurchenko would see me and change his mind. It was a long shot—nobody was banking on it.

The Soviet delegation entered the plush reception room and quickly took their seats. Yurchenko, dressed in a new gray suit and matching tie, was accompanied by the embassy minister, Viktor Isakov; press counselor Boris Malakhov; and Vitaly Churkin, their interpreter. The American side was represented by Deputy Secretary of State John Whitehead, Assistant Secretary of State for Europe Rosalyn Ridgeway, and two officers from the European bureau. Yurchenko glanced around the room for a familiar face. When he saw me seated across the room, he held my gaze for a split second's recognition.

Whitehead dispensed with the formalities and quickly got down to business. "The purpose of our meeting here tonight is to determine whether Mr. Vitaly Yurchenko has chosen of his own free will to return to the Soviet Union."

Isakov, barely waiting for Whitehead to finish his opening remarks, responded in his annoying, almost cloying, manner of speech. "Mr. Yoorchinka is for the first time exercising his free will in your country. His decision to return to his home has certainly been freely made. Mr. *Yoorchinka*"—Isakov again stressing his own pronunciation of the defector's name—"was never in the United States of his own free will—"

Cutting Isakov off, Whitehead said, "We're here to determine only that Mr. Vitaly Yurchenko desires to leave the United States. We have more than ample evidence of Mr. Yurchenko's freely made decision to come to the United States in August this year. We'd like to hear directly from Mr. Yurchenko."

Yurchenko seemed agitated and energized, much as he had been the first time I had seen him. He spoke in English. "I am returning to the Soviet Union after more than three months that American special services have taken me in Rome. I escaped from your special services after they have drugged me." Turning toward me, he said, "This man, Tom Fountain, is from your special services, but I don't think Tom knows they used drugs with me. But now I am going home."

I said nothing, and Whitehead ended the meeting as quickly as he began it. "Then it is clear that Mr. Yurchenko has chosen to return to the Soviet Union," he said. "We will respect that decision, regardless of how it was reached. Thank you, gentlemen, for coming here tonight."

Dulles Airport, 1615 Hours, November 6, 1985

The cameras followed Yurchenko in his Burberry raincoat as he climbed the stairs to the chartered Aeroflot jet, paused for a moment, then turned and waved, more in defiance than as a farewell. FBI agents Rochford and Broce were conspicuously present with the ground maintenance staff at the foot of the stairs, but again, there was no turning back for Yurchenko. He spotted both agents with whom he had become close over the last three months and broke his stride for a second to greet them with a smile. He seemed to be contemplating extending his hand, but he checked himself and then continued up the stairs without a halt.

Back at CIA headquarters, while all eyes were locked on the departing Yurchenko, Rod Carlson was looking intently at the "honor escort." He turned to Paul Redmond.

"There's PIMENTA."

"Which one?" Redmond asked. He had been with Carlson the night before when PIMENTA had telephoned to say he'd be doing "escort duty" to Moscow for a week.

"The second one, the young-looking one."

Later, in Gerber's office, Redmond had a sense of foreboding about the presence of yet another spy for the American side taking an unexpected trip back to Moscow.

"I'm worried," Redmond said. "PIMENTA going back bothers me."

"Did Howard know about the PIMENTA operation?" Gerber's question was directed at Redmond.

"PIMENTA wasn't being geared up for internal handling. I'll check for paper, something Howard could have seen, but that won't tell us much. You know how secrets work their way around this place."

"What about our debriefing of Yurchenko?" I asked. "Did we spend too much time on Line X?" Was it possible that Yurchenko had gleaned from the questions he was asked by the CIA and FBI that the Americans had a source in Line X, which conducted scientific and technical espionage? PIMENTA was a Line X officer in the KGB's Washington *Rezidentura*.

"Always possible," Redmond answered. "Rod can run it by

Ames and the others and see what they think. But none of this is going to make much difference. We've got another compromise."

"I'll check it out," said Carlson, who was the supervisor of the two men assigned to debrief Yurchenko. "Ames checks in on Fridays from language school."

During his debriefings, Yurchenko had said that Edward Howard had told the KGB that there was an "angry colonel" who had volunteered to the CIA in Budapest. That had to be GTACCORD.

In mid-September, Moscow reported that GTACCORD had signaled that he had information to pass. But now the SE Division was worried that the KGB had identified GTACCORD as GRU Colonel Vladimir Mikhailovich Vasilliev. There was a good chance of an ambush if the CIA responded to GTACCORD's request for a meeting in Moscow.

So before Moscow was given the green light to meet with GTACCORD, I was asked to talk with Yurchenko to try to determine how much progress the KGB had made in identifying the "angry colonel" whom Howard had mentioned.

"What can you tell me about the angry colonel Edward Howard betrayed?" I had asked him during a meeting at the Coventry safe house.

Yurchenko bristled for a moment. "Tom, I have told the story of the angry colonel many times. It is always the same."

"I know, but this is important now."

"You are meeting him now?" Yurchenko became more interested.

"We are trying to decide what to do. And you can help. I want you to tell me again how far you think the investigation of the angry colonel had gone when you came to us in August."

Yurchenko was thoughtful. "We were looking at every KGB colonel in Hungary, including every KGB colonel assigned to the Southern Group of Forces of the Red Army. But we had no leads. It was very slow. But they will find him, with patience."

I focused again on the fact that Yurchenko had assumed that GTACCORD was a KGB colonel, not the military intelligence colonel he in fact was. Howard must have misidentified GTACCORD to the KGB, sending them off in the wrong direction, screening the KGB in Hungary, not the army.

"If they had found the colonel, and brought him under control, do you think they would set up an ambush this soon?"

"Maybe. It's Dzerzhinsky politics. A colonel is important. But I think they have not found him. I think you can meet him. I would do that."

The next day, Moscow was told to unload GTACCORD's dead drop. The operation was pulled off without a hitch a week later, with operatives at the dead drop site finding valuable photographs of Soviet military documents wrapped in plastic and then again in dirty rags to look like trash. There was relief in SE when Moscow's report of the successful outing was received. But it was short-lived.

Langley, 1000 Hours, November 19, 1985

"The other shoe dropped on PIMENTA."

Paul Redmond was standing in the doorway to my office.

"What!"

"The bureau just let us know that PIMENTA's wife got a call from Moscow—they're not sure who called—saying that he'd hurt his leg, some sort of a deep cut when he arrived in Moscow with Yurchenko, and that it required some very tricky surgery to repair some nerve damage. The caller said it was serious enough for her to pack up the children and come home. She's getting ready to go now."

"Shit!" was all that I could muster.

17

Langley, 0830 Hours, November 20, 1985

The cable from Bonn was a routine notification of a "no show." Under normal circumstances, it would have generated only mild concern. But circumstances in SE Division were by now no longer normal. There was an unshakable foreboding hanging over the division, and the loss of contact with any agent added to the dread.

Bonn reported that KGB Lieutenant Colonel Gennady Varennik, working under Tass cover in the Soviet embassy in Germany, had failed to show for his last scheduled meeting and had also failed to signal for an alternate. Varennik, encrypted as GTFITNESS, had last been met in a Bonn safe house on November 4, at which time he'd reported that he'd been asked to take part in an unscheduled planning session in Karlshorst, the KGB's regional headquarters in East Berlin. The purpose of the Karlshorst meeting, Varennik assumed, would be to refine a KGB plan to sow terror among U.S. Army troops and their families through coordinated attacks against targets frequented by U.S. personnel in Germany. The aim behind the terror campaign, Varennik had reported earlier, was to throw the U.S.-German relationship into turmoil by making it look as though the bombings were the work of domestic German terrorist cells—the aging remnants of the Baader Meinhof gang or the more modern and active Red Army Faction.

Varennik's previous reports on the KGB's proposed terror campaign had generated an intense debate in both the operational and the analytical sides of the CIA. Some discounted them as outright fabrication or at a minimum the product of an overactive imagination. Others, and that group included Bill Casey, zealously believed the KGB was capable of such atrocities. Casey and the hard-liners were convinced that the Soviets had been behind the assassination attempt against Pope John Paul II, so what would stop them from this? The debate was inflamed by the fact that there had recently been terrorist attacks in Germany that had taken three American lives. Those attacks seemed to fit the MO described by Varennik, so Varennik's reporting captured the attention of the highest levels of Washington readership, including President Reagan. His disappearance would draw a similar level of interest.

Paul Redmond wasn't particularly interested in the debate over how evil the "Evil Empire" was or wasn't. He'd leave that to others. His focus was down in the trenches, the hand-to-hand combat of the spy business, not where it all fit in the grand scheme of things. He just wanted to find out what had happened to Gennady Varennik, who seemed to have just fallen down the same hole that had swallowed up so many of SE Division's Soviet agents over the last six months. Redmond's mood was foul as he briefed me on the operation.

"He came to us in April this year. That's important," Redmond said. "That was after Ed Howard left the division and the agency . . . and even after Mary Howard left, for those who want to believe Howard was still getting pillow talk stuff from Mary. Whatever happens, we can't pin this one on Howard."

"How'd we get him?"

"He got us. Called one of our guys in Vienna, someone he knew when he was posted there, said he needed to talk to him right away."

"All this on the phone?" I was surprised that a KGB officer would go operational on the phone in Austria, where the KGB's ability to monitor CIA activities was extremely good.

"Yeah, I know. But if FITNESS is in trouble, it's not because of that phone call. Anyway, after that first contact, we shifted this out of sight right away. We had Chuck Leven get in touch with him in Bonn—safe house meetings, full controls. Chuck was in Moscow with Burton, he can run a tight op."

"What was the motivation?" I asked.

"Mixed. Said he was in trouble with money. Not much money, less than ten grand, but the usual story—he needed to get it back in his cash box right away. New baby, tough time with the expense of living in Germany. But he told Leven he was more interested in warning us, and maybe the world, about the wacky plot Moscow and Karlshorst were hatching to blow up targets in Germany, kill some Americans, and drive a wedge between the U.S. and the Germans. Maybe start World War Three in the process."

"You believe it?"

"Doesn't matter what I believe. Everybody's trying to pin everything on the Sovs. You know who the believers are. Your buddy—" Redmond motioned toward the ceiling, a shorthand gesture to Casey's office on the seventh floor. Casey did take the darkest stories of the Soviets at face value. Arguing against him could be dangerous for a CIA officer's career. "Besides," he said, "that buffoon Gennady Titov is running things at Karlshorst these days, and he's capable of anything—even this dumb idea."

I nodded, wondering why every time Titov's name came up it set Redmond off. A streetwise KGB officer, Titov had been expelled from Scandinavia in an infamous spy scandal involving Norwegian Labor Party leader Arne Treholt. He was now directing KGB activities in East Germany, and the involvement of a man called "the Crocodile" within the halls of Lubyanka in German operations lent some credence to Varennik's reports.

"What else did he give us?"

"Some stuff on KGB penetrations of the Germans. Hasn't checked out yet." He added darkly that a KGB officer working for the CIA had to have a death wish. Especially these days.

Our conversation lingered in my mind after he left. Redmond had captured one of the cardinal truths of the spy business, that it took a special personality to commit high treason against the USSR. Trouble was, there weren't many old Soviet agents in "retired" status to run a behavioral theory against. And the CIA's meetings with agents were so brief and intense that there was almost never time to ask the Russian spies why they did it. Some never wanted to talk about it. Others expressed a hatred of the Soviet system, saying they wanted to damage it as much as possible. Those agents required special handling to ensure that they didn't become overeager and wind up in prison. Some called it a kind of patriotism—for Russia instead of the Soviet Union.

A few defectors who'd jumped ship after a short stint emptying a safe here or there in a KGB *Rezidentura* were still around, living comfortably in America. But the members of that special breed who stood their ground, determined to make a difference by working against the system from the inside, were increasingly lying in unmarked graves. Penkovsky, Popov, Ogorodnik, and Filatov headed that list. And now new names were being added at a dizzying rate: Tolkachev, Polyshchuk, Smetanin, Martynov . . . and possibly Varennik. There should be a special section fenced off and set aside at Arlington Cemetery for all these men, I thought. Maybe then they could get the recognition they deserved.

Two days later, a follow-up report came in from Bonn. Varennik's wife had been called from Moscow and told that her husband had slipped on ice and injured himself badly. She and the children would have to return to Moscow immediately.

Langley, December 1985

Clair George kicked off the special briefing in the Director's large, birch-paneled office on the seventh floor. Edward Lee Howard had now been gone for ten weeks, and six weeks had passed since Yurchenko had made his dramatic exit. Outwardly, Casey seemed to have put the deep personal embarrassment of both events behind him. The investigations were still under way, and a couple of seniors sitting around the table would take hits, but they would survive.

"Bill, we have some unexplained losses in Moscow," George said. "More than we ought to expect, even from Moscow operations."

"How many?" The old white-haired DCI looked deceptively disinterested. He was taking in every word.

"Burton will give you the details." George turned to Gerber, seated next to him at Casey's conference table.

Gerber began to brief Casey. "Last May we had a sudden recall of an asset from Athens to Moscow," Gerber said. "GTBLIZZARD, a GRU colonel. The agent was convinced the recall was contrived, a trap, and we decided to pull him out. He's here now, but that's not how it worked out for some others."

Casey stared at Gerber without comment. Out of the corner

of my eye, I caught Juchniewicz glancing at the ceiling, willing Gerber to get on with it.

"Then in June we had the arrest of Paul Stombaugh and the loss of our aviation engineer, GTSPHERE. That was followed by the arrest, probably in August, of a Line KR officer we were handling in Lagos, GTWEIGH. He was in Moscow on home leave, and we believe he was arrested unloading a drop of rubles we put down for him.

"Then another GRU colonel was recalled from Lisbon unexpectedly in late August—GTMILLION. He hasn't returned. On November 6, one of our assets in the KGB *Rezidentura* in Washington, GTGENTILE—the bureau calls him PIMENTA—went home unexpectedly on the same plane as Yurchenko. And he's vanished. His family was recalled a week later with the story that he'd had an accident and they should join him immediately."

Casey's drooping eyelids flickered at the mention of Yurchenko, but he said nothing as Gerber continued.

"Then later last month an asset in Germany, a KGB lieutenant colonel, GTFITNESS—the source of the reporting on KGB plans to bomb American targets in West Germany—was suddenly called to East Berlin. He's disappeared, and his family has been brought home. Again, they said he'd had a serious accident."

"How many's that?" Casey asked gruffly.

"Six."

"Over how long?"

"Six or seven months," Gerber said quickly.

"Jesus! How many you got left?"

Gerber paused for a second as he mentally ran through the remaining inventory of Soviet assets, then he tentatively answered, "We've got two active cases in Moscow. Two or three more outside. And some inactive cases on ice, maybe three of those."

I ran the numbers mentally and tried to figure out whom Gerber had in mind. I came up with GTCOWL, the man who had provided the spy dust. Then there was GTEASTBOUND, a scientific source who worked at an institute far to the east of Moscow. The outside cases he was referring to probably included some scattered around Asia. The cases on ice must have included GRU General Polyakov and a few others who had been off the air for a year or more.

Casey scowled and looked around the table. "What are you doing about this?"

Clair George picked up from Gerber. "We're looking at either a technical penetration or a human penetration."

"Technical? You think they're reading our mail?"

"Maybe," George answered. "We'll run some traps to see if it's our commo. And we'll run some more traps to see if they've technically penetrated our Moscow setup."

"What about the human penetration? You think there's a spy in here?"

"That's the other possibility," George said. "There's only two, human or technical."

"Whacha gonna do about that?" Casey grumbled.

"Run some tests to see if the people on the bigot list for these kinds of operations might be the problem," George responded.

"How big's the list?"

"Don't know yet. We're looking at it. Certainly all of us in this room, plus a lot more."

Casey grinned. "You got me on the list?"

"Right at the top," Clair George shot back.

"It's easy enough," Redmond said. "We create an agent someplace and begin reporting on him by cable. We create another phony agent and send someone to Moscow to talk it up." Gerber had called Redmond into his office to work out a strategy for running the traps to try to detect a penetration somewhere along the line. He asked me to join them. "Then we wait to see if anything happens. If either one gets rolled up, we've got a problem on the line we're testing. If they don't, we're no better or worse off than we are now. It's a long shot, but it's worth it."

Gerber agreed and told Redmond to start setting things up. He would create two Soviet spies who never were.

•

Nairobi, Kenya, December 1985

I flew to Kenya under an alias and took a room opening onto an inner garden at the venerable Norfolk Hotel in Nairobi. An hour after my arrival, there was a light knock at the door and I quickly ushered in the CIA chief in Nairobi, the agency's preeminent Africa hand, Bill Moseby, and his deputy, Dave Lameroux. Moseby had been alerted through a back channel that I would be "passing through" Nairobi and that I'd be staying at the Norfolk under an alias. He'd been told to contact me there.

A descendant of the Confederate cavalryman who led Moseby's Raiders in the Civil War, Bill Moseby had spent most of his career in Africa. With his tailored safari suits and his waxed and twirled mustache, he looked more like a colonial plantation owner than one of the most accomplished CIA managers on the continent. Blind in one eye and deaf in one ear from two different accidents, Moseby was nevertheless an avid hunter, and he often sported a faint half-moon indentation on his forehead, caused by the kick from a recoiling telescopic sight lined up awkwardly with his good eye.

"What can I do for you, bwana?" Moseby said, using the greeting he reserved for fellow veterans of the CIA's African operations, of which I was one.

I silently shook hands with Lameroux, a former Air Force navigator with whom I'd entered on duty two decades earlier, and turned up the volume on my television set. After pulling chairs together, we leaned in close and I began my whispered briefing.

"I'll give you the facts. We've been losing assets in Moscow, and Soviet assets around the world, one by one for the last seven or eight months. It can't be natural attrition. It's got to be something else."

"What's Nairobi got to do with it?" Moseby asked.

"Nothing really, except that you've got an obnoxious colonel running the GRU *Rezidentura*. And we'd like to use him for a little test."

Moseby and Lameroux looked at each other quizzically. "That jerk? He's all yours. But how?"

"You've had enough casual contact with the colonel for it to be common knowledge both here and back at Moscow Center. You and I are going to create an operation over the next few days that will make it look like he's decided to work for us. When we're finished, it will look like he's a CIA asset.

"We're going to kick this off with a restricted handling cable, reporting that you arranged for me to contact the colonel. We'll say in the cable that he approached you and wanted to talk to someone from Langley. You accommodated him. I came out here to make the pitch. Then we send the next RH cable reporting the pitch, saying he accepts. From that point on we start a tightly controlled and graduated operation using special communications channels to test for a penetration at key points along the line back to Gerber and SE."

"How will you know when your trap's been sprung?" Moseby asked.

"When they throw your colonel on an Aeroflot flight to Moscow with his hands tied behind his back."

"How many people are going to read the traffic on this?"

"Not too many at first. A handful. We'll start with the short list. Then we'll broaden it out."

"Maybe we'll get lucky."

"Yes, bwana"—Moseby smiled—"if you get lucky, the colonel's luck runs out."

"That's right," I said. "But if you tell us he's been dragged back home, we'll start moving pretty fast on our end. We'll find our problem before they do anything permanent. If we find our penetration, we'll tell 'em. Gerber and Hathaway will go see the KGB and say, 'Oh, by the way, your GRU colonel from Nairobi is actually an okay guy. We just had to set him up for this little experiment.' "

"Will they buy that?" Lameroux asked.

"Probably. They're picky about those things. We're assuming that your buddy wouldn't confess. And without a confession they don't move all that fast. This isn't going to be a career enhancement for him, but he'll be okay."

"When do we start?" Moseby asked.

"How about now?" I said, taking a legal pad from my suitcase.

Langley, Mid-December 1985

Paul Redmond read the cable from Nairobi carefully. It was a three-page account of the meeting Moseby had ostensibly arranged for me with the GRU *Rezident* in Nairobi. The cable arrived at the special communications center just before the opening of business, and two copies had been couriered to Gerber's office. Redmond had been called to the front office to read one of the two copies reserved for the chief of the SE Division. Beyond that, only two other copies of the cable from Nairobi had been couriered to the seventh-floor office of the DDO, where they would be read by the DDO and his two executive officers. The total count of people with access to the cable traffic this first go-round would be limited to seven, including Gerber's secretary. Then Redmond would slowly begin casting the net wider.

18

Moscow, Early January 1986

Rem Krassilnikov had another "guest" in Lefortovo Prison, a KGB major from a local Moscow city district. The lead to this new spy had been handed down from above, providing Krassilnikov with just enough information to allow him to launch a methodical search that ultimately led him to Major Sergey Vorontsov, a tough KGB officer working in Moscow's Lenin Hills district. Vorontsov hadn't been cooperative at first, but like the others, he came around. Krassilnikov had the full story, but neither he nor his superiors were eager to take the next step and reel in an American to close the case. That could wait a little longer. Patience.

In the meantime, Krassilnikov was on another exciting hunt. He had been alerted, again discreetly from above, that the Americans were planning a technical probe of some sort across the entire expanse of the USSR, from the port of Nakhodka in the Far East.

Technical sensing equipment would be concealed in a custom-rigged shipping container loaded aboard a freighter in Japan and delivered to Nakhodka. From there it would be transferred onto the trans-Siberian railroad for the long journey to Leningrad, a route that was becoming increasingly attractive for the export of goods from Asia to Western Europe. Krassilnikov hadn't questioned the source of the tip when he received it. He cast his net wide for the technical probe and knew that the officers of the Second Chief Directorate would reel it in as soon as the equipment entered Soviet territory.

Embassy of the USSR, Washington, D.C., January 1986

Colonel Viktor Cherkashin suppressed his rage as he sat in his tiny cubicle in the KGB's cramped, windowless *Rezidentura* on the fourth floor of the Soviet embassy in Washington, D.C. He's going to get him killed, Cherkashin told himself. Kryuchkov is going to get our man killed. He can't resist wrapping up the American spies in Moscow, and the CIA is going to figure out something's wrong, that someone has talked.

Cherkashin had been at his post as chief of counterintelligence in the KGB's Washington *Rezidentura* when Aldrich Ames had downed a few extra drinks at the Mayflower Hotel and walked into the Soviet embassy to volunteer to become a spy. He knew he had a real catch—and he'd taken extreme measures to protect his new spy. Fearful of leaks, he decided against sending a cable back to Moscow Center. Instead, he flew back to deliver his message personally to Vladimir Kryuchkov, head of the KGB's First Chief Directorate, which handled foreign intelligence operations.

Cherkashin circumvented his entire chain of command, including Dimitri Yakushkin, chief of American operations, and Vitaly Yurchenko, a top security officer in the American section. Both men had served at the Soviet embassy in Washington, and both would most likely have been on the distribution list for any cables he might have sent from Washington. But the KGB, like most professional services, had a standing procedure allowing officers to go directly to the top whenever they learned the identities of traitors within the ranks. Ames had handed over the names of KGB moles. Cherkashin told no one in Moscow about his new recruit except Kryuchkov and his immediate circle of lieutenants.

But Kryuchkov had broken one of the cardinal rules of counterintelligence. He was moving quickly—and stupidly, in Cherkashin's view—to roll up agents identified by their new volunteer. Kryuchkov had been feeling increasingly insecure about his position since his longtime mentor, Yuri Andropov, had died. Whatever political infighting was going on back in Moscow, Cherkashin worried that the Americans would realize their security had been breached and would launch a mole hunt.

Now, sitting in the *Rezidentura,* with electronic white noise whirring silently between the double walls specially constructed by KGB technicians, Cherkashin knew that the most valuable agent the KGB had ever had inside the CIA was at grave risk. He was not at risk because of any mistake they had made in Washington. He was at risk because Vladimir Kryuchkov wanted to knock KGB Chairman Viktor Chebrikov off balance and steal his job.

Langley, January 1986

Bill Casey's secretary smiled up at John Stein as he entered the DCI's outer office. "You can go right in, Mr. Stein. Mr. George is already with him."

Pushing through the heavy, soundproof door to the DCI's office, Stein saw Casey and the DDO seated at the conference table at the far end of the room.

A burly man in his mid-fifties with salt-and-pepper hair, John Stein had risen through the ranks of the clandestine service. After a stint in the early 1970s as deputy chief in the SE Division, he had survived the bureaucratic chaos of Casey's first year as CIA Director, when Casey made the disastrous decision to appoint Max Hugel, one of his Republican fundraising pals, as DDO. Stein emerged as DDO himself after Hugel was forced to resign amid a scandal following a few months at the CIA. Two years later, Casey moved Stein out, replacing him with Clair George. Stein became inspector general. He was just leaving that post for language school and was on his way to becoming chief in South Korea when he was called into the meeting in Casey's office.

Bill Casey spoke first. "John, we've got a problem," he said. "Clair can lay it out for you."

Stein glanced over at Clair George and realized his somber mood was genuine, not one of the theatrical plays for which the DDO was famous.

"We're losing Soviet assets, a lot of them. You still know all the big cases, don't you?"

"Sure. I was DDO during a lot of them. Howard?"

"Howard accounts for some of the losses, but not all. We think there's still a problem. Maybe technical—something to do with communications—maybe human. Could be here, or maybe Moscow. We want you to take a look. A fresh look. Don't count anything in or out. And keep it between us. No one else is to know you're doing this. Understood?"

Stein hesitated a moment. "I'll need someone in SE to help me, to get me the files. Is Redmond okay?"

"Okay," Clair George said. "Just keep it quiet."

Later that day, Stein called Redmond. The two men had worked together in the past, and Stein was pretty sure Redmond could be counted on to take the problem seriously and keep his mouth shut. Redmond knew his way around the SE file system and wouldn't have to ask anyone where to find what he needed. He could check out the files without drawing attention to himself, pass them to Stein, and take them back for safekeeping.

With Redmond's help, Stein spent the following six weeks poring over the division's secret files. He was looking for any pattern, any clue that might connect the losses to a single weakness—human or technical—somewhere in the system. At the end of his review, Stein wrote a précis of each case and then a final paper for Casey. He concluded that the CIA had a leak of some kind.

In March, Stein took the paper to Casey and briefed the Director in person on his findings. He told Casey that he believed there could be a communications breach somewhere—"and that is between you and NSA to find out." Then he said the other possibility was that there was a mole inside the CIA. "And that we can do something about," he said. "I would recommend that you start by looking at Moscow, which is smaller and a more manageable place to start an investigation, and then look at headquarters. But I would try to make sure it's not in Moscow first." The bottom line was that it was time for the Director to "put some people together to work on the problem." When Stein raised the possibility that there was a spy inside the CIA, Casey was less than forthcoming in his response.

"Hmm," he said noncommittally. "We got to put people on it."

Stein left for South Korea without ever hearing whether the DCI had followed up and actually launched a mole hunt. He never saw Casey again. Later, Stein would learn that Casey never launched a major mole hunt. Stein would also conclude that Casey didn't tell anyone about his final briefing.

By the time Stein was secretly recommending to Casey that he should start looking for a mole, Burton Gerber had already taken a series of defensive measures to make certain that the 1985 losses couldn't happen again. He ordered a dramatic change in the way the SE Division handled its most sensitive cases. Gerber realized that the controls had become too lax. SE Division had been running more Soviet agents than ever before, and as a result more people were involved in handling them. He was determined to reduce the numbers. To do so, he created what he called the "back room." It was a new system with special handling procedures for cables and other files on Soviet agents. Sandy Grimes and Diana Worthen, two trusted and experienced SE Division officials, were put in charge of making the new system work in early 1986.

Initially, that meant handling agents without any cable correspondence between Langley and the field. When a new agent was identified and recruited, CIA officers would fly back and forth to Washington to discuss the case. The word went out to senior officers in the field that if they got a potentially important Soviet intelligence source, they were not to send any cables about the case: They should get on a plane and tell Gerber in person.

Before resuming cable traffic on sensitive cases, Gerber insisted on adding a new layer of encryption. Normally, cables were decoded in the CIA's communications center and then routed up to the division. But now, all cable traffic about Soviet cases was encrypted twice. The CIA officer handling the case would encrypt a message before turning it over to a CIA communicator, who then encrypted it again before sending the cable. At headquarters, the communications center would decipher the code added by the communicator, but that would reveal only the second layer of encryption. Just a small handful of top officials in SE Division had the keys to decipher that second code. In the field, often the only person with the code was the chief. Field stations were not allowed to keep paper files on the new cases, and they were not to be discussed within the station. Meetings between headquarters personnel and field officers involved in the cases were treated as if they were being held behind the Iron Curtain—Moscow Rules applied. The officers would meet in safe houses for the debrief or at CIA stations in the field.

By February 1986, Gerber could see that the new system was working; the CIA developed two new Soviet agents, and they were not compromised or arrested by the KGB. Gerber still didn't know what had caused the 1985 losses, but he knew that he had stopped the hemorrhaging.

Moscow, January 1986

Barry Royden, the CIA's deputy chief of counterintelligence, sat across from the Moscow chief; his mission was straightforward enough. He was going to brief the Moscow chief and his deputy on a new operational success against the KGB in Bangkok. Only there was no operation in Bangkok. The name of the new KGB recruit was real enough, but the rest of the story was a carefully crafted fabrication scripted for delivery to whatever technical penetration the KGB may have been able to set up inside the yellow submarine that served as the Moscow work spaces. The Moscow chief was slightly uncomfortable with Royden's direct verbal briefing. He'd been worried for months about the possibility that his enclosure had somehow been penetrated and had scribbled his haunting note to me just five months earlier: "Sometimes I think they're in here with me."

Royden was now testing that suspicion.

19

Moscow, February 21, 1986

Rem Krassilnikov was shocked at what the KGB had found when the vessel *Siberia Maru* docked in Nakhodka with container #CTIV-1317221 aboard. The container was scheduled to be loaded onto the first available freight train bound for Leningrad, on a journey that would cross all eleven of the USSR's time zones over a period of three to four weeks. According to the shipping manifest, the container was packed with a cargo of handicrafts bound for Leningrad, where it would be forwarded to an address in West Germany.

When KGB investigators opened the container, they found stacks of cardboard boxes carefully packed with ceramic flower pots, all innocent enough. But after removing the first two rows of cardboard boxes, they came upon a wooden partition. When they pulled that back, they found what Krassilnikov would describe to his superiors as a "miracle laboratory." Concealed cameras were trained through narrow slits disguised as ventilation ports on either side of the container. These fed into computers attached to a sophisticated collection of scientific sensors. An arduous KGB analysis of the equipment would reveal its high-tech Cold War mission—to sense sources of radioactivity across the vast expanse of the USSR. The KGB found that the equipment could register the intensity, spectral composition, and total dose of neutron and gamma radiation; establish the location of the reading, the atmospheric pressure, and the temperature at the time of the sampling; and link this data to panoramic photography taken simultaneously through the ventilation slits. The KGB concluded that the "miracle laboratory" had the capability of mapping the geographic locations of nuclear weapons production, storage, and transport points across the expanse of the Soviet Union. The sensors were found to be capable of identifying a nuclear warhead with one kilo of plutonium within a radius of ten meters. The KGB scientists estimated that the system could function for up to three months on its own power sources and that there could be only one possible intelligence service behind container #CTIV-1317221—the American Central Intelligence Agency.

Krassilnikov, convinced that the discovery in Nakhodka could be used to great advantage in the battle against the American special services, recommended a major propaganda exposé. To his surprise, the suggestion was received with a cool silence, a disappointment he attributed to the fact that Eduard Shevardnadze was Foreign Minister at the time and earnestly engaged in "new thinking." But Krassilnikov was not willing to give up quite so easily on his discovery.

Langley, Late February 1986

I read the cable from Tokyo and wondered how long it would take for the SE world to come unstuck again. I had my answer when I saw Paul Redmond at my door.

"They got ABSORB," Redmond said without emotion, the way a man does when he no longer has any doubts.

"Yeah," I said, tossing the Tokyo cable into my out box. "Was Howard read in on the operation?"

"Shouldn't have been. But who the hell keeps secrets around this place anymore?"

"Can we find out?" I asked.

"We're looking at it."

"What are you thinking?"

Redmond paused. "You know what I'm thinking."

Moscow, March 10, 1986

Michael Sellers had met GTCOWL only once, almost exactly one year earlier. During that first meeting, a two-hour-long walking conversation as the two men furtively navigated Moscow's back streets and alleys, the KGB man never revealed his identity. He said he knew how closely the KGB tracked American CIA officers in Moscow and didn't want to take any chances with his own security. Sellers knew him only by the name they'd agreed to use—"Stas."

Stas had first volunteered in 1984, when he dropped an envelope through the open window of the car of an American embassy official as he walked by. The CIA eventually sent an officer to contact him, but the officer who managed to break free of surveillance that night couldn't understand the volunteer's Russian, and the meeting had been a bust. The failure of that first meeting fueled a debate back at CIA headquarters about whether the Soviet was a real volunteer.

COWL was gruff, and even an excellent Russian speaker like Sellers found him difficult to understand. Sellers took him to be from the Second Chief Directorate's local counterintelligence forces in Moscow. He was the Moscow version of a New York cop, a Soviet Popeye Doyle. He made no bones about what he wanted. It was money, and he wasn't shy about the cynicism of his approach. He grew impatient whenever Sellers, who was wearing a tape recorder, asked him to repeat or clarify something.

But the man knew plenty about the KGB's tracking of CIA operations in Moscow, and as the two spies cautiously made their way through the city's darkened streets, COWL warned Sellers that he wouldn't provide the CIA with documents that could be traced back to him, and he demanded that any money passed to him come from "clean" sources outside the Soviet Union and be placed in packages that were never opened by CIA officers in Moscow.

Sellers and COWL had worked out a careful communications plan to set up future meetings. COWL gave Sellers a phone number to call at prearranged times, with ten-minute windows he declared as "safe." The CIA later concluded it was a KGB duty phone line, one that couldn't be traced to any specific individual in the KGB. COWL would arrange to be the only officer at that number at the prescheduled times, and the CIA would call with prearranged, innocuous-sounding messages.

After one meeting, COWL dropped out of sight for several months. He failed to respond to one call but eventually responded to another call-out in March 1986. Sellers was sent out to meet him.

On the night of March 10, Sellers thought he had broken free of surveillance for his late-night run by pulling off an identity transfer with another embassy employee. Later, when he was "black" on Moscow's icy streets, he quickly changed into Russian street clothes and melted into the flow of Muscovites on their way home.

The meeting site was an alleyway between two Stalinist apartment blocks not far from Moscow's Lenin Hills district. Sellers arrived at the meeting site at 10:30 P.M., and as he got to within twenty feet of COWL, he could sense something was very wrong. COWL had lost weight and, it seemed to Sellers, his tough-guy swagger. When he began to speak, he could only stammer. The man was a ghost of his former self, and in that instant Sellers braced himself for what he knew was about to happen.

Oh, shit, Sellers said to himself. Here it comes.

Suddenly, glaring lights lit up the street, and men came running from all directions. The arrest, Sellers thought, was straight out of the movies. He was thrown into the back of a van by a small army of KGB security men, and GTCOWL disappeared in the blur.

In the back of the van, the KGB men, talking among themselves in Russian—perhaps not realizing how well Sellers could understand them—appeared confused as to whom they had just arrested. Finally, one of the security men reached over to Sellers, and as he pulled off his fake mustache, a look of recognition flashed across his face.

"Ah, Misha!" the man exclaimed, using the Russian diminutive of Michael. The CIA disguise was better than they had anticipated. The security men noticed the mud on Sellers's shoes, and they began debating in Russian how he could possibly have gotten out of the embassy and disguised himself as a Russian worker without anyone on the surveillance stakeout team noticing him.

The van drove Sellers and his minders to an annex of Lubyanka Prison—the interrogation office at #2 Dzerzhinsky.

Sellers spent only a few hours in interrogation. By 2:30 A.M., Stuart Parker, a counselor officer in the American embassy, had arrived to take him home. But during those few hours, Sellers had sparred with Rem Krassilnikov, trying to parry each question from the KGB's gray ghost. Normally, CIA officers were told to say nothing while under arrest, except to declare diplomatic immunity and ask to see a counselor officer from the embassy. Sellers knew the game, but he couldn't resist giving a few jabs, especially since he could speak Russian with his captors. When Krassilnikov told Sellers that his arrest would damage his career with the CIA, Sellers told him he was wrong; it wouldn't hurt his career at the agency. Perhaps to encourage Sellers to keep talking, Krassilnikov tried to switch to small talk, describing the little details of his life known to the KGB. He was the goaltender on the American embassy's broom ball team—what did he think about American hockey versus Russian hockey? But in trying to keep Sellers engaged, Krassilnikov revealed some interesting facts. It became clear to Sellers that the KGB didn't know how he had gotten out of his apartment for his meeting. The KGB still didn't have a good understanding of the CIA's identity transfer techniques, and finding Sellers at the arrest scene had puzzled them; his watchers thought he was still in his apartment.

It wasn't until long after his arrest that Sellers learned COWL's real identity: Sergey Vorontsov.

Langley, March 11, 1986

The "mornings of compromise" were becoming an unsettling routine. The notification of the COWL ambush had arrived the previous evening, and everyone at the staff meeting was aware of what had happened in Moscow the night before. Redmond poked his head in my office on the way to Gerber's office for yet another briefing on a compromise in Moscow.

"Let's go to the morning miseries," I finally told him.

Yasenevo, USSR, March 12, 1986

Valentin Aksilenko sat in his fifth-floor office in the First Chief Directorate's American Department, pondering a string of strange occurrences. Since he'd left the Washington *Rezidentura* three years earlier, he had been the headquarters branch chief watching over the KGB's foreign intelligence operations in Washington. And watching Washington was getting more curious for Val Aksilenko, a big, thoughtful man with thinning red hair. At forty-five, he had done well for himself and for the KGB, and during his five-year tour in Washington he had been promoted to colonel in the KGB's Line PR—political intelligence. But now it seemed that the familiar world he had taken for granted had slipped its axis. He felt increasingly uneasy, but he couldn't put his finger on the source of his discomfort. Probably it was his own problems, he thought. His marriage was falling apart. Maybe it was a combination of things. Even the job he thought he understood so well was becoming increasingly opaque. Things were happening that he couldn't account for or understand.

The anomalies had begun last June, when the American was arrested. Contradictory reports began to surface regarding the identity of the Soviet traitor he had been trying to meet, but the only common thread in the competing stories was the spy's first name—Adolf. It seemed that people at the top wanted the name to stick out. Maybe it was because this Adolf was arrested a month after the celebrations commemorating the end of the Great Patriotic War. But there was another message in the dogged use of the spy's name, which some thought might even be a phony name cooked up by the KGB leadership. But why?

Then, in September 1985, stories began making the rounds at Yasenevo that a fellow First Directorate officer had been caught red-handed by the boys in the Second and Seventh Directorates unloading a dead drop in Moscow—a rock full of rubles was what they were saying. It took a while for the man's name to surface, but eventually the rumor mill pointed to a Line KR officer on leave from Lagos.

Then there was the story of the incredible escape of Gordievsky while under active investigation. Contradictory facts were still being leaked out on that case, too, mostly in the form of finger-pointing between the intelligence and the counterintelligence directorates. Speculation as to how he had escaped and who had helped him was rampant. Some were convinced that the American special services must have been in on it with the British. Others thought Dzerzhinsky Square—KGB headquarters—had been part of the conspiracy.

But there was nothing official on any of this from the top. They were staying very quiet.

On top of that, there was the lingering problem of Vitaly Yurchenko, who had come home to Moscow a hero, complete with an honor guard. The trouble was that nobody believed his story.

The Yurchenko affair was an affront to most officers in the First Directorate, who knew that his story of heroic resistance, single-minded determination, and valiant escape was a fantasy dreamed up by Yurchenko to save himself from execution. They knew the yarns, carefully repeated and spun by Kryuchkov and his deputy, Vadim Kirpichenko, were nonsense. Aksilenko could understand the leadership's desire to sweep Yurchenko's treason under the rug, but he couldn't understand turning him into an institutional icon. Nobody who'd worked in the West seriously believed the nonsense that the CIA had drugged Yurchenko. The rank and file were beginning to write off the whole affair as just another sign of the corrupt KGB leadership protecting itself. Yurchenko had been promoted to flag rank just as he defected. That made him one of the boys. It wasn't the same when a lieutenant colonel jumped ship. The grumbling grew.

Even comments filtering down about former CIA officer Edward Lee Howard made no sense. No formal acknowledgments had been made that Howard had been working for the KGB, but there were leaks that he might be responsible for the recent successes in rolling up American assets in Moscow. Aksilenko had read the coverage of the Howard affair in the American press as it crossed his desk, but it never quite tallied with the leaks he heard inside the KGB.

And now on his desk before him was a scripted report advising "Tass was authorized to announce" that an American diplomat had been arrested the previous night committing an act of espionage. No further details.

Something was going on, Aksilenko thought; so many of these strange incidents seemed to have their origins in Washington. And here he was, the KGB's foreign intelligence branch chief responsible for Washington, and he didn't have a clue what was happening. Maybe he could pick up something from Valeriy Martynov, who had been part of the "honor guard" escorting Yurchenko back to Moscow. Martynov was still around, Aksilenko had heard, but he'd taken a fall and was recovering from surgery.

20

Langley, Late March 1986

Sometime in early March, the CIA chief in Bonn sent a cable by special courier to Langley. A letter dropped anonymously into the mailbox of a Bonn case officer had informed him that KGB officer Gennady Varennik had been uncovered as a CIA agent. To establish his bona fides, the letter's author gave the name of Varennik's CIA handler, Chuck Leven, and promised to reveal why and how Varennik had been caught. Further details would be made available to the CIA if a package containing $50,000 was placed in a dead drop site in East Berlin, the letter writer said. The money should be cached in waterproof packaging and left under a particular flagstone on a walking path. Instructions were all carefully detailed in the letter. Finally, the author asked that a signal be transmitted on an HF frequency from the American embassy's backup transmitter. That signal would confirm receipt of the letter and that it was being acted upon.

The letter sent a shock through the leadership of SE Division, in part because it offered ammunition to support all of the major theories then in play about the cause of the lost agents. The statement that Gennady Varennik had been compromised was a confirmation of what was already known, but the promise of details was enough to encourage the CIA to agree to the letter writer's conditions. There was a debate about whether the letter was a KGB ruse, but no one counseled against going along with the writer's demands.

Bonn was instructed to make the broadcast, and East Berlin was authorized to make the drop of $50,000 in a park. Some in SE Division were puzzled by the coincidence that the operation was taking place in East Berlin. An operational backwater because of its smothering Stasi surveillance, East Berlin was beginning to heat up.

It all began with the setup of the CIA chief in East Berlin, a female case officer who had previously served in Austria. A Hungarian contact had invited her to dinner at a quiet East Berlin restaurant, but they were quickly joined at their table by a Soviet with a heavy briefcase. The Hungarian politely excused himself on cue, leaving the field to the Soviet, whose intentions became clear immediately.

Unloading a videocassette player from his briefcase, the Soviet, a senior KGB American targets officer, explained to the East Berlin chief that he had prepared a little video story of the last several years of her career. He switched on the machine and turned the screen to face his quarry, while the KGB production of *This Is Your Life* rolled across the screen.

There were outside shots of her apartment in Vienna, along with recordings of conversations that seemed to have been picked up by KGB microphones planted in her walls. The Vienna story line bluntly suggested that the conversations captured by KGB microphones in her apartment had led directly to the compromise of CIA operations in Austria. This would all be bad for her career, would it not?

As the television drama cut to East Berlin, the scripting became more provocative. More candid shots followed, obviously taken by concealed Stasi cameras shooting through pinholes in her apartment walls and ceiling. These were accompanied by similar shots of at least one of her fellow East Berlin officers, also female, dramatically fading to black. As the KGB officer added his own narrative voice-over to the video, he began to insinuate that the unmarried East Berlin chief might be involved in a lesbian relationship, something she would certainly not want known in Langley. As the tape played out and the KGB officer switched it off and stowed away his player, he turned to the CIA chief and made his pitch. She could come across and assist the KGB, or she would soon begin to suffer the consequences of all her "mistakes."

The CIA chief thanked the KGB man for the evening's entertainment and told him he was barking up the wrong tree. She said she would report the evening's events in great detail to Washington and told him he could do whatever he wanted with his video. The next morning, Langley had a full cabled account of the attempted recruitment.

I was dispatched within twenty-four hours to West Berlin to see if there was anything she felt more comfortable expanding on in person. We had a long talk about the incident in a corner niche at the Kempinski Hotel in West Berlin, and I concluded there was nothing more to be added to the report, beyond some color and atmospherics about the meeting and the heavy-handed pitch. The East Berlin chief could provide a more detailed account when she next visited Langley.

The incident might have been filed away had it not been for a similar occurrence just a few weeks later in Brazzaville, the capital of the Congo, another Soviet client-state where the KGB had free rein. There was no video game this time, just an out-of-the-blue recruitment pitch by a visiting KGB officer appearing at the female CIA chief's home. She was cold-pitched on the spot to commit treason. Like the East Berlin chief, she flatly turned down the KGB and reported the incident in detail to headquarters. Gerber thought the isolated officer in Brazzaville might welcome some assistance and sent Sandy Grimes, a longtime SE Division officer, to Africa to do the debrief.

As it turned out, there was no more substance to the Brazzaville episode than there had been to the pitch in East Berlin. The CIA was unable to make much sense of these approaches to its female officers. Some wrote it off as another ploy by the KGB, a brainstorm similar to the one a few years back that had the KGB mounting crude recruitment approaches to black CIA officers. The KGB had hoped that they would be bitter about CIA racism and thus receptive to their overtures. That ploy hadn't worked any better than the approach to the two women. Others wondered if the new tactic was aimed at sowing distrust within the CIA of its female officers. The theory was that if two had turned down and reported KGB pitches, might there not be another one out there who had not rejected Moscow's overtures?

None of these theories was particularly compelling, but on the heels of the anonymous letter from Bonn, yet another mystery was added to the strange occurrences of the last year. No one had a clear idea of what was happening to the CIA's Soviet sources. The only thing on which everyone could agree was that there had been a cataclysmic failure somewhere in the system. By the spring of 1986, a new, whispered term had entered the lexicon of the inner circle of SE Division—"the 1985 losses."

Langley, May 8, 1986

Looking down at the Moscow cable on my desk, I read again the spare language reporting that a Moscow case officer had been arrested the previous evening while on an operational run to meet EASTBOUND. The cable read exactly like the others following the arrests of SPHERE and COWL. But then what else was there to report beyond the fact that a Moscow officer had walked into an ambush, had been taken to #2 Dzerzhinsky, and then had been released a couple of hours later? The cables always ended with the promise that details would follow.

I flipped through the stack of follow-up cables, pausing to look over the final one, where the Moscow officer requested that his father be asked to reserve rooms for him and his wife at their club in Maryland. That one would set Gerber off again. Gerber had taken a dark view of this case officer's operational judgment after he'd been detained some weeks earlier on a nighttime run in the far suburbs of Moscow. The officer became disoriented and took a wrong turn, ending up at the main gate to the KGB's First Chief Directorate headquarters at Yasenevo. He was detained for a few minutes, questioned, and then released.

When the cable reporting the incident arrived the next morning, Gerber exploded. He had a simple rule: A case officer should know his city. If he could get lost and end up driving through the main gate of the enemy's foreign intelligence headquarters, what other mistakes might he make?

Now, reading the cable asking for comfortable accommodations at his father's club in suburban Maryland, I wondered what was going through Gerber's mind. Gerber was not a clubby man and didn't have much patience for those who were.

KGB Headquarters, Moscow, May 8, 1986

Krassilnikov was quite pleased with the way the last ambush had worked out. The Second Chief Directorate had been given a tip about a radar scientist and had ultimately identified the man. Rather than simply arresting the scientist, however, Krassilnikov had taken pains to turn the spy operation back against the Americans. He'd planted a story in the man's design bureau that the American special services were suspected of having penetrated the establishment and that the subject could enjoy a "certain amnesty" by turning himself in. It worked. The man came forward and cooperated fully, up to the point of setting up the ambush of the American special services officer in a courtyard in an apartment block on Moscow's Malaya Pirogovskaya Street.

Krassilnikov's men watched from a distance as the case officer left for home at the end of the day and began his long and laborious surveillance detection run. When he was convinced that he was black, he began an elaborate foot run. He walked straight into Krassilnikov's trap.

Later, in the holding room at Dzerzhinsky, a pale and subdued CIA officer watched without comment as the contents of his bag were laid out on the table. There was a "Kharkov" razor concealing a subminiature camera and a number of prewritten letters, ostensibly from American tourists to relatives and friends back in the United States. The scientist was to use these to correspond with his handlers, using secret writing on the backs of the letters. Concealed inside a notebook were the intelligence requirements—the CIA's questions—about the spy's defense design bureau. Krassilnikov was very pleased with himself. He had caught his spy without jeopardizing the sources of the tips that were coming his way.

Langley, 1600 Hours, May 16, 1986

I pushed through the blue door of the DDO's seventh-floor office, wondering again whose idea it had been to paint all the doors at Langley in garish electric blues, canary yellows, and forest greens. It happened while I was assigned to Hong Kong in the 1960s. Upon my return one summer, I found the old battleship gray motif of CIA headquarters gone, replaced by off-white walls and brightly colored doors. It was supposed to be good for morale. When I walked into his office, Clair George went right to the point.

"It's Friday. I want you to think about it over the weekend, but I'm planning to send you out to Islamabad to take over the Afghan program."

In the months since I'd returned to Langley from Africa, I'd become aware that our covert action program with the Afghan resistance had taken a new turn and that Reagan had rewritten the ground rules. I had also heard that the chief in Islamabad running the Afghan program had fallen afoul of Clair's deputy, Ed Juchniewicz, and that Clair and Casey were deciding on a change of leadership in Islamabad. What I had not heard a hint of was that I was being tipped for the job.

"You really want to wait until Monday for an answer?"

"Talk to your wife. Get her input."

"She'll be ready to go. When do you want me out there?"

"Go out and take a look this month, and then get out there by July."

Marie-Catherine, my wife, was indeed ready to move to Pakistan. A French *pied-noir,* born in Morocco, she had spent most of her life shifting between France and Africa, where we had met while she was teaching at the French School in Lagos. She had moved across the continent to join me in Khartoum in 1983, and we were married there in 1984. Bill Casey's "wedding gift" had been telescoping Marie-Catherine's naturalization process from seven years to about ten days. Pakistan would be no problem for her.

Langley, 1015 Hours, May 19, 1986

Out of the corner of my eye I spotted Jack Platt staking out my office, waiting for an opening to slip in on me as soon as I finished my conversation on the secure green telephone, an unambiguous signal for privacy that even Platt would hesitate to violate. But as soon as the handset was in its cradle, he slipped by the gatekeeper and dropped a handful of papers on my desk.

"I need these signed pretty quick, chief. A real rush job." Platt's usual laid-back attitude seemed a little forced. I started looking for the flimflam, knowing instinctively that it was probably no accident that Platt was in need of some rush action just as Burton Gerber was away and I was acting division chief.

"Sit down, Jack. You've got a minute for me, don't you?"

"Sure. But this is moving fast, and I saw you were pretty busy, and—"

"It's okay, Jack," I said, picking up the sheaf of papers, "I'm not pressed."

The top document was a standard agency travel order for "operational travel" to Guyana using any mode of transport from "sea to air to surface." It already had the requisite Latin American Division signatures, and I signed it without particular hesitation. After flipping to the second signature flag, I glanced at the document and set down my pen.

"What the hell is this, Jack?"

"It's a requisition order for a Winchester thirty-caliber semiautomatic hunting rifle, with four-by-forty scope sight attached, with felt-lined carrying case and fifty rounds of match ammunition." Platt recited the nomenclature on the requisition form in the stilted monotone of a mentally challenged government supply clerk.

"I know it's a gun, Jack, but you're just going to have to tell me who you're going to kill before I sign off."

"It's for MONOLITE. Rankin and I are going down to Guyana to work on him again. Nice gun might soften him up. Guy's a big hunter."

"Is this thing going anywhere? Or are you and Rankin just jerking each other off?"

"Who the fuck knows? You do what you can. And you really can sign that, so just go ahead and do it. Trust me."

I knew that MONOLITE had been a long-term joint developmental target of the FBI and CIA ever since he'd been assigned to the Soviet embassy in Washington in the late 1970s. Platt had been a street case officer then, and a good one, until his drinking problem had sent him to rehab. Sober for five years now, he hadn't lost his need to continually test the system and those in charge of it.

"And are you going to tell me why this is such a rush?"

"I gotta go out and buy the gun and get it on its way to Guyana today. That's the rush. MONOLITE pitched up there last year, and Rankin and I thought we'd go down and see if he's had a change of heart."

"And you just discovered you needed to get a rifle into this operation this morning? Or maybe it's because Burton Gerber took off this morning and you thought I'd be an easier touch?"

"What do you think?" Platt cracked a smile for the first time.

"I think you waited until Burton was out of here to bring this in. What is it? The gun, the operation, or the fact that you personally drive Gerber nuts with all your bullshit?"

"Yes."

"Yes, what?"

"It's the gun and the operation and me and all the fucking weird hangups our leader has. But this is worth doing."

"How long have you been trying to get this guy?"

"Who? Gerber?"

"Goddammit, Jack, quit dicking with me!"

"We've been working this guy pretty steady for about six or seven years. I musta pitched him a hundred times."

"Did he give you anything?"

"He still loves me."

"What the hell does that mean?"

"It means that he doesn't run for cover like every other asshole in the KGB who sees me coming."

"He ever pitch you back?"

"Once, maybe. Asked me how I'd feel if he asked me to come over to his side. I said, What for? To spend the rest of my life in a fucking breadline? And he never asked me again."

"What does Gerber think of the operation?"

"Probably hates it."

"Why? Because of the operation or because it's your operation?"

"Five years ago he ordered me to pitch the guy—give him his last chance to come to the promised land—when he was out in San Diego at a volleyball tournament. Did you know he's an Olympic-grade volleyball player? Once when we were both a little drunk, he told me volleyball got him into the KGB. Said some guys recruited him out of the university to play for a team at Dynamo Sports Complex in Moscow. He didn't know who the hell they were until they told him he was playing for team KGB! After a while he stopped playing volleyball and started playing spy. He likes to say he's the only guy who went to the First Chief Directorate on an athletic scholarship. Anyway, I didn't pitch the guy like Gerber told me, but I kept the thing alive. Introduced the FBI guys to him, but he still told us to fuck off every time we hit him. The FBI wants to keep trying, and Gerber can't stop it now with the bureau on board."

"How long have you been planning this trip?"

"About a month."

"What does Gerber know about it?"

"Nothing."

"How long have you known about Gerber's travel plans?"

"About a month." Platt smiled again.

I signed the requisition for the Winchester and handed the papers back to Platt. "Don't go down there and get him killed."

"Like everybody else around here?"

"Yeah, like everybody else around here. Might ask him what he's hearing about that."

I watched Platt, wearing faded frayed blue jeans and beat-up cowboy boots, walk out of the front office area carrying his papers. Platt was the kind of guy the CIA wouldn't touch today. And I thought that was too bad.

First Chief Directorate Headquarters, Yasenevo, July 1986

Val Aksilenko no longer had any doubts that something very strange was going on. The latest round began with whispers of the arrests of Valeriy Martynov and Sergey Motorin, who had both served with him in Washington.

Martynov, a Line X officer responsible for scientific and technical collection in the Washington *Rezidentura,* had come back to Moscow with Vitaly Yurchenko as part of the defector's "honor guard." He never reported in at Yasenevo. At first, the word was that he'd suffered a serious accident that required surgery. He'd been taken to a sanitarium outside Moscow to recuperate. They'd even brought his family back from Washington to be by his side, the stories went.

Aksilenko hadn't seen Martynov since his return, and he had no idea what had happened to him until rumors of his arrest began to circulate in June. Similar stories started circulating about Sergey Motorin, another former officer in the Washington *Rezidentura,* now working in Directorate A, the active measures department responsible for black propaganda against the United States and its allies. Aksilenko's boss in the American Department, Anatoly Slavnov, told him in confidence that Motorin had been arrested for working for the Americans.

Aksilenko was incredulous. Two officers from the same *Rezidentura*! He was never close to Martynov, but Motorin had worked for him, and it pained him to see the young maverick officer in such trouble. Motorin was a rule breaker, a free spirit, but Aksilenko liked him. He'd sparred with Dmitri Yakushkin, the Washington *Rezident* at the time. Yakushkin plainly detested Motorin and did everything in his power to make his life miserable while he served under him in Washington. A Line PR officer, Motorin was miscast in intelligence work, but he was not the disaster Yakushkin believed. The *Rezident* saw him as just another privileged troublemaker, the son of a senior Party official from Archangel. Motorin had reinforced his political position even further by marrying the daughter of another senior Party man. Yakushkin thought he traded on that, too, and despised him all the more.

It was no secret inside the *Rezidentura* that Motorin had girls on the side and that he had cut corners. But most of his transgressions were dismissed as small stuff, all acceptable enough within the context of the "new realities." Toward the end of his Washington tour, when he seemed to be producing better political intelligence, Aksilenko had gone to bat for him with Yakushkin, telling the skeptical *Rezident* that Motorin was finally catching fire. It didn't work. If anything, Yakushkin was even more negative, and Aksilenko found himself in an unpleasant tug-of-war over the young officer. In the end, he concluded that Yakushkin disliked Motorin so much that it was useless—and perhaps dangerous—to continue to defend him. Only later would Aksilenko learn that Motorin's improved performance in Washington had come about because he was being fed intelligence by the FBI and CIA in order to improve his standing with his superiors.

When Motorin was transferred from Washington back to Moscow, Yakushkin tried to bar him from serving in a sensitive post. He wanted him shunted off to a job where he could do no real harm. So he was assigned to Department A, responsible for black propaganda operations against the United States and its allies.

Motorin's arrest, coming on the heels of the arrest of Martynov, sparked a frenzy of rumors and gossip throughout the First Chief Directorate. Motorin simply disappeared, and for months no one knew where he was. During this period, he was forced to call a woman he'd had an affair with in Washington to tell her he "was fine and thinking of her often." The call was intended to reassure the FBI.

There was a grand deception game under way at Yasenevo, and the pieces of the game that were visible to Val Aksilenko were sharpening his senses. From the First Chief Directorate, there had been four cases in the last year of officers crossing over—the acting *Rezident* in London, the counterintelligence officer in Lagos, and now the two officers from the Washington *Rezidentura.* Add to the mix the peculiar case of Vitaly Yurchenko, and you had five. As Val Aksilenko struggled with his thoughts, he thought maybe the number could go even one higher, to six. Yes, he'd add the convoluted case of Vladimir Mikhailovich Vetrov, the Line T guy executed for spying for the French two years ago. That was a case of clever misdirection if he ever saw one.

Vladimir Vetrov was a wild man by First Chief Directorate standards. He was strong and physical, with a quick temper. Some thought him abusive—he'd been reprimanded in the past for his outbursts, one time for beating one of his bosses almost to a pulp. In addition to his abusive side, Vetrov was an unabashed Francophile who made no attempt to hide his admiration for almost all things French. It was an appreciation he'd picked up during his Paris posting in the late 1960s, and he still carried a case of French champagne in the trunk of his car, "just in case," he always said.

So it was no real surprise, at least at first, when in February 1982 word shot through Yasenevo that Vetrov had been arrested for the murder of a homeless vagabond in a Moscow park where he was having a "French liaison" with a woman described as Vetrov's mistress. According to the initial story, Vetrov and his mistress were happened upon by a park denizen, who attempted to shake down the KGB officer. In a burst of temper, Vetrov set upon the man and killed him with a knife. Then, possibly fearing that his mistress would betray him to the police, he stabbed her and left her for dead. Then, incredibly, he returned to the scene of the crime an hour later and was spotted by his mistress, who was not seriously wounded after all. He was arrested on the spot, and in a particularly swift case of Soviet justice, he was tried and sentenced to twelve years in prison. Later, nobody would ever recall hearing the actual name of the vagabond Vetrov had murdered.

Then the story began to change. The supposed mistress turned out to be a notorious First Directorate sex groupie who had bedded down as many KGB foreign intelligence officers as she could chalk up in the few years she had been hanging around the gates of Yasenevo. Then the murdered "vagabond" was transformed into another KGB officer, a jealous lover who happened upon the couple locked in an embrace and fought with Vetrov. But neither was available to tell her or his own story—the woman disappeared, and the man Vetrov killed was never named. Then in 1984, the other shoe dropped when the story of Vetrov's arrest and execution for spying for the French flashed through the First Directorate.

Whispers and speculation began immediately. In the end, Aksilenko began to doubt the entire Vetrov legend, with the notable exception of his execution. He already dismissed the murder in the park as contrived, and the idea of Vetrov betraying his treason in letters to his wife or to a prison snitch didn't pass the most basic test of logic. No KGB man would have poured his heart out in a letter. He would have toughed it out in prison for ten or twelve years; it was long, but nowadays there were worse places to be. Something else must have happened to Vetrov—of this, Val Aksilenko was now convinced.

Now, against the backdrop of all the other revelations of

treason in Yasenevo over the last year, it finally seemed to fit. The Vetrov story was part of the grand deceptions, the elaborate smoke screens, surrounding the betrayals of so many Yasenevo officers in the last two years.

What the hell was going on? Aksilenko asked himself. What were they hiding?

Then came the biggest shock of the year.

Walking into Dmitri Yakushkin's office in mid-July, Aksilenko found the KGB general engrossed in a report. He could see from across the desk that it was top secret. Aksilenko muttered a familiar greeting, but Yakushkin didn't respond, and he sat in awkward silence until Yakushkin finally lifted his eyes. After staring vacantly at Aksilenko for a moment, Yakushkin handed the paper across his desk.

Aksilenko began to read a summary of the arrest of GRU General Dmitri Polyakov. As he read, Aksilenko glanced self-consciously over the top of the paper at Yakushkin, who seemed to be disoriented and devastated by the report of Polyakov's treachery. Finally, his voice shaking, Yakushkin spoke.

"This man is a general, like me, Valentin. Who are we to trust? If we can't trust a general, who can we trust?"

Aksilenko had no answer—the question didn't demand one. He felt uncomfortable, not only because of Yakushkin's strange demeanor, but because the document he had been handed was so clearly restricted to a level of access high above his own.

New York, August 23, 1986

There were two unique characteristics to the FBI's operation that led to the arrest of Soviet scientist Gennady Zakharov on espionage charges during the dog days of August 1986. The first was that the entire operation had, from the outset, been a sting designed to entrap Zakharov, a physicist assigned to the United Nations in New York, into committing acts that would get him arrested. The second was that Gennady Zakharov was living and working in the United States as a UN employee *without* diplomatic immunity.

The KGB interpreted this operation as a profound breach of etiquette. There would have to be payback. It wouldn't take the

Soviets long to identify an American living in Moscow without diplomatic immunity who could serve their purposes.

Moscow, 1220 Hours, August 30, 1986

Nicholas Daniloff, Moscow correspondent for *U.S. News & World Report,* had just left his last meeting with Mikhail Luzin, his "Misha from Frunze," a young Russian who in the past had provided insights into the heavy toll that the war in Afghanistan was taking on the Russian boys who were being sent out to the front. After five years as the newsmagazine's Moscow bureau chief, Daniloff was closing out his tour in the Soviet Union and was about to head home to Washington. His successor, Jeff Trimble, was already in Moscow.

On the embankment near the Moscow River, Daniloff gave Misha a package of Stephen King novels—works by the master of horror were hard to come by in the Soviet Union. In return, Misha handed Daniloff a tightly wrapped package that he said included photographs taken in Afghanistan. Misha had given Daniloff photographs taken by Russian soldiers fighting in Afghanistan before, and though the pictures had been of such poor quality that they'd been of little use for the magazine, Daniloff still felt that Misha had helped him understand the terrors that were haunting Russian soldiers being sent off to fight the Afghan rebels.

Daniloff was walking back to his apartment in Leninsky Prospekt, with the package of photographs from Misha in a white plastic bag dangling at his side, when a van suddenly pulled up next to him and a group of men in civilian clothes quickly enveloped him. Without a word, two of the men grabbed him, forced his arms behind his back, handcuffed him, and pushed him into the van. As the van sped off, Nicholas Daniloff felt like a disembodied observer who had just witnessed his own arrest. He was still trying to sort through the fog of what was happening to him as the KGB van pulled into the gate of Lefortovo Prison.

Daniloff's arrest immediately generated international headlines as the Western press corps railed against the Soviet decision to hold a foreign correspondent. The incident ballooned into a diplomatic crisis, one that threatened an upcoming summit between President Reagan and Soviet leader Mikhail Gorbachev. The Soviets quickly made it clear to the Americans that the Daniloff and Zakharov cases were linked, further complicating the Reagan administration's efforts to free the journalist. Public diplomacy was set in motion: U.S. Secretary of State George Shultz and Soviet Foreign Minister Eduard Shevardnadze met to try to reach a compromise in time to save the summit.

Meanwhile, Daniloff, in jail and facing repeated interrogations, soon realized that "Misha from Frunze" wasn't the KGB's only concern. Before long, the Soviets began to ask him about Father Roman Potemkin—and the CIA.

Knowing that it had left Daniloff exposed as a result of the botched Father Roman affair from the year before, the CIA secretly contacted the KGB while Daniloff was in prison and set up a quiet meeting in Vienna to talk about the case. To contact the Soviets, Burton Gerber activated the "Gavrilov channel," a secret communications line first established between the CIA and KGB in 1983.

The Gavrilov channel, named after a nineteenth-century Russian poet, had been the KGB's idea. The Soviets had approached the Americans in the most straightforward way possible: They knocked on the apartment door of Carl Gebhardt, the CIA's Moscow chief in 1983. But Gebhardt wouldn't open the door, so the KGB's message initially went unanswered.

When Gebhardt reported the contact to Langley, however, the KGB's proposal reached Bill Casey. Burton Gerber, who'd returned from Moscow the year before and was then serving as deputy in the European Division, was called into a meeting with Casey and others to decide whether to respond. Gerber told Casey that he thought they should meet with the KGB. The agency had nothing to lose by hearing what the Soviets wanted to talk about. Casey came around and asked Gerber to go do it himself.

Gerber wanted another CIA officer as a witness, so Gus Hathaway, the head of counterintelligence, went along, too.

The first meeting took place at the Soviet embassy in Vienna and opened with a scene straight out of the movies. As Gerber and Hathaway walked up to the entrance, the front gate to the embassy compound slowly swung open, before they'd even had a chance to ring the bell.

Soon, Gerber and other CIA officials were meeting on a semiregular basis with their KGB counterparts, usually in Vienna, a city where the Soviets felt particularly comfortable. The two sides used the Gavrilov line to tamp down potential crises between the two intelligence services, as well as to discuss ways they might actually find some common ground. One area the CIA pursued was counterterrorism: The Americans asked the Soviets for help in trying to find out what had happened to William Buckley, the CIA chief in Beirut who had been kidnapped and tortured. Buckley eventually died in captivity, and the Soviets never provided any help on the matter.

The Gavrilov channel remained open until the Reagan White House tried to exploit it for political and diplomatic purposes, over Burton Gerber's strong objections. When Gerber was told to activate the Gavrilov channel to talk to the Soviets about a particularly sensitive diplomatic issue, he at first refused, arguing that Gavrilov had been established purely for the two professional intelligence services to hash things out. He knew that the KGB would object to its use as a diplomatic back channel. But he was told that the National Security Council had issued orders for him to do it anyway. In the end, he went to the meeting with the KGB in Vienna and passed on the message as he was directed. But just as he had predicted, the Soviets responded badly, and the Gavrilov channel was suspended for years afterward.

Before that breakdown, however, Gerber was able to use the Gavrilov channel to arrange a meeting in Vienna with Anatoly Tikhonevich Kireyev, the formidable chief of counterintelligence for the KGB's First Chief Directorate. Gerber needed to talk with Kireyev about the Daniloff mess.

Gerber's message to Kireyev was simple: Daniloff was not a spy and had nothing to do with the CIA. At the end of the meeting, Kireyev casually asked Gerber a telling question.

"Did you ever meet Father Roman?"

"No."

"You're lucky." Kireyev sighed. "He was a pain in the ass."

It was just one more confirmation that Father Roman had been a KGB agent.

Eventually, the logjam in the Daniloff case broke. On September 12, the two governments agreed to arrange for both Daniloff and Zakharov to be released from prison and held in the custody of their own embassies. Finally, on September 29, Daniloff was allowed to leave the Soviet Union without facing trial. He quickly left for Frankfurt and then the United States. Zakharov was released by the United States the next day. The Reagan administration faced a brief spate of criticism for allowing the Soviets to link the two cases, but the crisis had been defused.

With tensions rising in the wake of the Daniloff-Zakharov showdown, the intelligence war between Washington and Moscow finally burst into the open and took on a diplomatic life of its own. On September 17, the United States ordered twenty-five Soviet diplomats at the Soviet Mission to the United Nations to leave the country; the Reagan administration said they were intelligence officers. On October 19, the Soviets ordered five American diplomats out of Moscow in retaliation. The tit-for-tat expulsions and declarations that spies were persona non grata soon escalated into what became known inside the CIA as the "PNG war." By the end of October, fifty-five Soviet diplomats had been ordered out of Washington. Since the CIA presence in Moscow and Leningrad was so much smaller than the KGB's staff in Washington, New York, and San Francisco, the Soviets had a hard time retaliating in kind.

But they finally responded by pulling out the 260 Soviet employees who handled cleaning, cooking, and other day-to-day chores at the U.S. embassy in Moscow. The KGB's move was inspired; it virtually paralyzed the embassy. Even though the Americans knew their local employees reported back to the KGB, they still relied on their Russian servants to help them navigate the nightmarish Moscow bureaucracy and keep the embassy functioning.

The retaliatory expulsions had a dramatic effect on the CIA's ability to conduct operations in Moscow. With the departure of Murat Natirboff, Gerber asked Jack Downing to return to Moscow as the new chief. Downing had been deputy chief in the late 1970s and had handled the TRIGON case, and Gerber wanted someone with extensive experience in Moscow to help rebuild after the 1985 losses. Downing had already served as Beijing chief, so he would now become the first man in CIA history to run CIA operations in the two capitals of world Communism.

The PNG war forced Downing to delay his transfer; the CIA didn't want him to arrive just in time to be expelled. After months waiting out the battle at headquarters, Downing finally moved to Moscow in November, only to find that the withdrawal of the embassy's Russian staff made it nearly impossible to get anything done. Before long, Downing was spending his days washing the ambassador's car and handling other cleaning chores rather than spying on the KGB. With virtually all of its agents rolled up and the CIA chief running errands for the ambassador, the CIA's Moscow operation was all but out of business.

First Chief Directorate Headquarters, Yasenevo, Late August 1986

The hall talkers out at Yasenevo agreed on one thing about their chief, Vladimir Kryuchkov: He had "grown taller" in the last few months. And he had grown bolder. Kryuchkov seemed to have new confidence in his stewardship at Yasenevo. And his growing relationship with the new General Secretary, Mikhail Gorbachev, was also part of the buzz. The lackluster First Directorate chief of the last several years was beginning to look to some like a new force.

Evidence of Kryuchkov's new operational energy began to manifest itself in small but important ways. For as long as he had been engaged in intelligence operations against Americans, Val Aksilenko had known that there was a hard-and-fast rule of thumb inside the KGB. If your American agent was polygraphed by the CIA or FBI, you could write him off. He could never be trusted again, because chances were he'd been broken and then doubled back against you. This view had been unyielding dogma for decades. Now, word was filtering down from above—Aksilenko first heard it from his boss in the American Department, Anatoly Slavnov—that the polygraph policy was no longer hard and fast. It had evolved to the point where under the "right conditions," an American could go through the polygraph grinder and still be trusted by Moscow

Center. Aksilenko was taken aback by the course change on the polygraph. What had prompted the change? he wondered. Had the technical people come up with a way to beat the polygraph? Had someone actually beaten the machine?

KGB Headquarters, Lubyanka, August 30, 1986

From the moment of his arrest on July 6, 1985, Dmitri Fedorovich Polyakov had instantly understood that his long journey was finally over. There was no more need for evasion, no need to worry about the next knock on the door.

The original investigation of Polyakov was triggered by the first tip to the GRU from Robert Hanssen in 1979. Polyakov had been recalled and had been forced to retire, but a KGB counterintelligence general had intervened, arguing that a general in the Red Army simply could not be a spy. A proposal devised by Rem Krassilnikov to unmask Polyakov as a traitor had been turned down, and the investigation was put on ice.

The general went into retirement. And while questions lingered, the case gradually receded into the background. Polyakov settled into his new life puttering around his dacha, tending to his grandchildren, and engaging in one of his passions, woodworking and cabinetmaking.

Five years later, the last missing piece snapped into place. The KGB finally had the goods on the GRU general, straight from its new source in Langley, Virginia.

Polyakov had known instinctively that he was being called in for his final reckoning when he received a summons on July 4 to attend a retirement ceremony at GRU headquarters in Moscow two days later. He was suspicious of the pretext, and his son, Peter, now an officer in the GRU, heightened that suspicion when he told his father he thought he'd spotted stakeout surveillance on the narrow road near their dacha. Polyakov told his son to keep his concerns to himself. He didn't want to spoil the weekend gathering of his family for his sixty-fifth birthday.

The arrest on Monday morning was full of well-practiced fury. As he entered GRU headquarters in full dress uniform, decorations arranged neatly across his breast, he was seized by five men. One held his head in a hammerlock while the other four stripped his tunic and shirt from his chest in case he'd hidden a suicide pill in a seam. Dmitri Polyakov put up no resistance. He simply stood there, leaning his weight against the men who held him in their viselike grip. Polyakov was stripped naked and quickly examined for concealed "special preparations." He was then dressed in a blue KGB running suit, handcuffed, and advised of the charges against him. His sole request was that his wife and sons be spared any suspicion or indignity.

As the interrogations began, Polyakov offered no apologies. He declared that he'd had ample opportunity to leave the USSR, but he'd never considered that an option. Everything he had done had been *for* the Russian people, not against them. Whatever was to become of him, he told his interrogators without emotion, was his own cross to bear. And he would bear it with honor. That, too, would be part of his contribution to bringing about a revolution in thinking in the USSR. He was a social democrat of the European sort, he said. That had been the reason for his struggle over the decades. Now his death would be another part of his struggle.

Polyakov's story came out smoothly and without reservation. He told it all, in great detail, and with an element of pride that unsettled his interrogators. Never wavering from his conviction that he had done the right thing, he repeatedly said he would do it again, faced with the same choices.

Born in the Ukraine in 1921, Polyakov graduated from the Soviet Military Academy at Frunze in time to see combat as an artillery officer in World War II, an experience burned into his consciousness and which defined him as one of the generation that held back the Third Reich. After World War II, Polyakov shifted into military intelligence, serving an early posting to the GRU *Rezidentura* in New York in the 1950s. After a tour of duty at GRU headquarters in Moscow, Polyakov returned to New York in 1961 for a second stretch as a GRU spy. By this time he had concluded that the suffering and sacrifice of the Russian people during the Great Patriotic War had been betrayed by the corruption and sheer evil of the Soviet system. It was during this time that he crossed the line and volunteered his services to the FBI, launching a dual life that would span almost three decades—that of a rising star in the GRU and that of a man the FBI and CIA called TOP HAT, ROAM, BOURBON, and BEEP.

The CIA became the primary agency handling Dmitri Polyakov during his assignment to Burma in 1966. As with so many before him, his decision to take a stand against the Soviet system would ultimately bring him before the executioner in a darkened Moscow subbasement.

Polyakov was promoted to the rank of general in 1974, an upward move that gave him access to a wealth of information on everything from long-range military planning to nuclear strategy to research and production of chemical and biological warfare agents. By the time he dropped from sight in 1980, Dmitri Polyakov had provided American intelligence with the most voluminous and detailed reporting on the Red Army of the entire Cold War.

Polyakov gave his interrogators details of his work as a spy without signs of regret, and his demeanor soon became a source of discomfort for some within the KGB's inner circle. He had not been motivated by greed. Polyakov had accepted only small gifts from the Americans—a few shotguns and rifles, some woodworking tools, and what amounted to little more than pocket money. He hadn't done it for revenge, either. He had done his part, he maintained to the end, because he could not allow the USSR to win its war against the Russian people.

21

Moscow, 1500 Hours, October 22, 1986

The announcement was in the standard language of the Soviet apparatus:

> Tass is authorized to announce that as already had been reported, the USSR State Security Committee exposed

Adolf Tolkachev, an employee of a Moscow research institute, as an agent of U.S. intelligence and started criminal proceedings against him.

It was established during the course of the investigation that Tolkachev, in pursuit of selfish ends and on account of his hostile attitude to the Soviet state, had maintained espionage contacts with U.S. intelligence agents who had been in Moscow under the guise of U.S. embassy personnel.

The military collegium of the USSR Supreme Court, which examined the criminal case filed against Tolkachev, found him guilty of high treason in the form of espionage, and, considering the gravity of his crime, sentenced him to the exceptional measure of punishment, death.

The presidium of the USSR Supreme Soviet rejected Tolkachev's appeal for clemency.

The sentence has been carried out.

Langley, 1530 Hours, October 30, 1986

It was anticlimactic, Paul Redmond thought as he read the report confirming what he had known all along. Valeriy Martynov and Sergey Motorin had been arrested, the report said. They had been tried and convicted and were to be executed for espionage. The report stated that the men had been arrested in 1985, almost a full year earlier. The FBI told Redmond a few months back that Motorin had called his girlfriend in Washington to let her know he was fine. That had knocked Redmond off balance momentarily, but now he was more convinced than ever that an elaborate deception was under way designed for just one purpose—to protect a valuable source.

In the last eight months, the strange case of "Mr. X," the KGB volunteer who had dropped a letter in a Bonn case officer's mailbox in March, had played out without leading to any firm answers. Langley reacted quickly to his initial approach, and the $50,000 he had demanded was laid down for him in a German dead drop. The possibility that the CIA's communications had been compromised—Mr. X had suggested just such a technical penetration in his first letter—had been thoroughly checked out, without results. In his subsequent letters, Mr. X had attempted to raise suspicions about one CIA case officer, Chuck Leven, who had been handling Gennady Varennik. Leven was fabricating his financial dealings with Varennik, skimming, the author of the mysterious letters had charged.

Redmond thought the ploy was too cute by half. Of all the case officers on the street, Leven would be the last to start fooling around with his cash box. Feeding the CIA disinformation about its case officers was an old KGB trick, and Redmond wasn't falling for it. Clair George also thought the operation was bad from the start, and when Redmond had the handwriting on the Mr. X letters carefully examined, it seemed there was a faint resemblance to the handwriting in the communications plans the KGB had provided John Walker over the years.

The information Mr. X provided about how Gennady Varennik had been compromised still bothered Redmond. In his second letter, Mr. X said that Varennik's father had come across some material evidence of his son's betrayal, and as a good and loyal former counterintelligence officer of the KGB during the Great Patriotic War, he had turned his son in to the authorities. The father was convinced that his son would ultimately be set free, after having served some jail time.

With the arrival of Mr. X's sixth letter a few weeks earlier, Redmond became convinced that the whole case was a ruse. But what kind of ruse? Either Mr. X was involved in a scam—he'd gotten a bundle of money from the CIA—or the KGB was running an elaborate deception game. But for what purpose? They had a spy to protect, Redmond concluded. A big one.

The inventory of lost agents and operations over the last fifteen months was devastating. Now there were rumors of more damage, that two more assets had been rolled up. One, a KGB officer last seen in Indonesia, Vladimir Piguzov, code-named GTJOGGER, had reportedly been arrested during the summer. Vladimir Potashov, an officer in the Institute of the USA and Canada, encrypted GTMEDIAN, had been arrested about the same time, according to the latest reports. Nothing made sense these days, Redmond thought, except his conclusion that there was probably a spy somewhere.

The phony recruitments in Nairobi and Moscow had been painstakingly played out for months without any sign of the bait being taken. Both Soviet intelligence officers set up in the fake operations remained in place, and Redmond concluded that the two probes had failed. But why? he wondered.

Frustrated, he decided it was time to put all his thoughts on paper.

Vienna, Austria, 2000 Hours, December 14, 1986

Ambassador Ron Lauder's Christmas party for the American embassy staff was an elegant affair. Lauder had a knack for combining the old-world grace of Vienna with the new money chic of his mother, who had transformed beauty into big business. The eggnog and *glühwein* had flowed, the Christmas carols had been sung in English and German, and a sense of camaraderie and celebrity had flowed throughout the ambassador's residence.

Jim Olson, the CIA chief in Vienna, was circulating from group to group along with his wife, Meredith, exchanging Christmas greetings, fulfilling the function that fell to senior members of Lauder's country team. An old SE Division hand who'd done battle with the KGB in Moscow a few years earlier, Olson had been the first man "down the hole" in the CIA's cable tap outside Moscow, and he knew his craft. He'd just arrived in Vienna, having lived through the nightmare of the last eighteen months in SE Division, and he harbored lingering doubts about the 1985 losses. Now, as he worked the ambassador's Christmas party, Olson began to notice one of the Marine security guards hanging back slightly but following him from group to group. As the party began to break up, the Marine intercepted Olson and self-consciously said he needed to talk to him. His voice quavered as he spoke. Olson saw fear verging on panic in the man's eyes.

"I'm Clayton Lonetree. I know who you are, Mr. Olson. They told me when I got here."

"They told you?"

"I served in the embassy in Moscow as a Marine security

guard and got into something with the KGB. I'm in over my head." The Marine was stiff. He spoke in stilted bursts, as if he were reciting lines he had carefully written for this moment of confrontation. To Olson, the young man appeared barely under control, almost psychotic. He took the Marine by the elbow and led him to a quiet corner where they could talk in private.

"Did you give up classified information in Moscow?" he asked, trying to gain control of the conversation in the short time he knew they would have before the guests began to file out.

"No, sir," Lonetree responded.

As he looked at the Marine, Olson suspected that he was lying. "Did they give you money?"

"No, sir."

"Were you involved with a woman?" Watching Lonetree closely, Olson wondered if he might break down right there. "Are you meeting the KGB here in Vienna?"

"Yes, sir. They were the ones who told me about you."

"Who do you see here?"

"George. That's all I know."

"When is your next meeting?"

Lonetree hesitated only a moment. "December 27."

"Where?"

"At a church not far from here."

Olson quickly wrote a number on a piece of paper and handed it to the terrified Marine. "I want you to keep all of this to yourself," he said. "You are to tell no one else that we have spoken. Do you understand?"

"Yes, sir."

"When do you get off duty tomorrow?"

"At noon, sir."

"Tomorrow, after you are off work, leave the embassy and call this number from a pay telephone. I'll answer. Don't identify yourself. Just be friendly and tell me what time we can meet. The meeting place will be the McDonald's on Spätenplatz. You know the place?" Olson kept the instructions simple. He doubted Lonetree's ability to handle anything more complicated, more secure, in a city like Vienna, which the KGB still felt was their operational preserve.

"Yes, sir. I know McDonald's."

"We'll meet there at the time we've agreed to on the phone. Then we'll go somewhere to talk."

"Yes, sir," Clayton Lonetree said.

Olson saw that the panic was still in his eyes. "You'll tell no one about our talk. Understood?"

"Yes, sir."

Olson left the Christmas party and went to cable CIA headquarters, outlining his account of the encounter with Clayton Lonetree. By early the next morning, he had received instructions from Langley to debrief Lonetree on the nature of his relationship with the KGB in Moscow. He was told to stay alert for the possibility of running Lonetree in place for a while, until the CIA could determine how much damage he had done. But Olson was convinced that Lonetree was too close to an emotional breakdown, too panicked, to function as a double agent and reported that observation to Langley as he prepared for the meeting with the Marine.

Shortly after noon, the telephone rang. Olson picked it up before the third ring.

"Sir, I could meet at two-thirty."

"Two-thirty is fine," Olson responded. "I'm looking forward to seeing you."

Jim Olson selected a young counterintelligence officer with a good background on the KGB to accompany him to the initial debriefing. He hoped that the young officer would help calm Lonetree down and ease his fears.

Lonetree was waiting at the McDonald's on Spätenplatz when Olson and his colleague arrived. Quickly taking the Marine in tow, they drove him to a safe site, where they conducted their initial debrief. The instructions from CIA headquarters had been specific—Olson was to determine how much damage had been done.

Langley, 1330 Hours, December 22, 1986

Paul Redmond read the latest wrap-up from Vienna on Lonetree. Olson was not only a seasoned intelligence officer, he was also a lawyer, and his summary of the debriefing sessions with the Marine guard concluded that this was no longer a counterintelligence operation. It should now be a criminal case.

As Clayton Lonetree talked, it became clear to Olson that he had fallen into the oldest KGB trap in the business. While serving as a Marine guard at the U.S. embassy in Moscow, Lonetree, a lonely young Native American, had met a beautiful Soviet embassy employee, Violetta Seina. Their affair was in violation of the embassy's policy forbidding fraternization between Marine guards and Soviet women, so the two kept their relationship secret. But as the relationship with Violetta deepened, her "uncle Sasha" suddenly appeared, completing the classic honey trap. Lonetree began passing information to Violetta's kindly uncle and responded to his directions to serve as his eyes and ears in the U.S. embassy.

After his transfer to Vienna, Uncle Sasha appeared in the Austrian capital and introduced Lonetree to "George," his KGB colleague in Vienna. Lonetree continued providing information to the KGB in Vienna and received occasional payments for his services, until he could no longer live with himself.

Olson recommended in his summary report that the case be turned over to the prosecutors. He concluded that the CIA had reached the end of its proper involvement.

Redmond didn't like the idea, but he knew Olson was right. Clayton Lonetree was spirited out of Vienna on Christmas morning by a team of officers from the Naval Investigative Service, just eleven days after he approached Jim Olson at the ambassador's residence.

To assess the damage, Redmond decided he'd have to order a comprehensive review of all documents sent to Moscow in any way related to the agents who had been lost in the last eighteen months. If the KGB had a Marine guard on their payroll in Moscow, they might have gotten into the CIA area—and the agency's files. Someone would have to look through every cable in Moscow's files that mentioned the agents who had been arrested to see if a KGB break-in—possibly facilitated by Clayton Lonetree—could explain the 1985 losses. Redmond would ask Sandy Grimes and Diana Worthen to handle the investigation.

Moscow, 1940 Hours, December 22, 1986

The waitress brought two more tumblers of gin to the two men at the corner table and took away the four empty glasses. As an afterthought, she dumped the overflowing ashtray on her serving tray and sullenly walked away. Aleksandr "Sasha" Zhomov and his boss, Valentin Klimenko, were seated at a low table in the bar of the Press Club at the Soviet Foreign Ministry near Moscow's Old Arbat. They had been there, drinking imported English gin and smoking Marlboro filters, for about an hour before Klimenko dropped the bomb on his subordinate.

"Sasha, I have a job for you."

Zhomov watched his boss expectantly. With thick, dark hair, the blue-eyed Klimenko was a small, wiry man in his early forties. Both men were American specialists in the KGB's Second Chief Directorate, and both knew as much about the Americans in Moscow as anyone in Soviet counterintelligence. Valentin Klimenko was Rem Krassilnikov's deputy, and Aleksandr Zhomov directly supervised the people who watched the Americans twenty-four hours a day, seven days a week. Zhomov's people put their American charges to bed in the evening and woke them up each morning. Sometimes, depending on the particular American, they had the means to "watch" them while they slept.

"You have one month," Klimenko continued, "to come to me with a plan for something special for our American special services boys. One month."

"Something special?"

"Yes. Something that will get us deep inside them, give us a window we've never had, something that will tell us what they're doing to us, how they do it, maybe even how they smuggle their agents out."

Zhomov fell silent as he contemplated what Klimenko might be asking of him. Just thirty-two, Aleksandr Zhomov had spent most of the last ten years following the Americans in Moscow. Along the way, he had learned English well enough to converse in it with almost native fluency, even though he had never met any of his American targets. But he felt he knew them all. He had listened carefully to what they said to one another when they felt they were alone in their apartments. He knew when and how often they made love to their wives, or maybe even the wives of other men. He knew what problems they were having on the job in Moscow or back home when they received telephone calls on the Moscow-Washington tie-line. Zhomov and his people knew almost everything you'd want to know about the Americans, except what they might do next. And now Klimenko was asking him to come up with a way to deal with that.

"How many people will I have on this?" Zhomov asked.

"Just you." Klimenko held up a single finger, and his expression, a sort of half smile, didn't change. "You'll be all alone."

"Rem Sergeyevich?" Zhomov's question was clear. Was their boss Krassilnikov in on this?

"You won't need to discuss this with Rem Sergeyevich. He doesn't need to be bothered."

Klimenko's answer spoke most loudly in what it did not say. Zhomov took the answer at face value, unable to decide whether Krassilnikov was in or out. Klimenko helped him understand.

"You'll report to me and I'll report to the Chairman."

"So that's it. You, me, and Viktor Mikhailovich."

"That's it, Sasha. You, me and Chairman Chebrikov." Klimenko finally smiled, flashing Russian gold.

Later that night when he was alone, Sasha Zhomov thought deeply about the new requirement Klimenko had levied on him. He could do it. But it would have to be something bold, something that broke all the old rules. He poured himself another drink, this time Georgian brandy, and thought some more about his plan. Yes, he thought, it could work. The first thing he would have to do was start a few quiet interrogations of the traitors, the ones who had not been dispatched by a bullet. That would be a good place to start.

PART TWO

THE COLD WAR TURNS HOT IN AFGHANISTAN

1

Islamabad, June 1, 1986

Two weeks after Clair George told me I was being assigned to Islamabad to run the Afghan covert action program, I made a quick visit to Pakistan for briefings and to take the lay of the land. The visit gave me a chance to meet the CIA's man in charge, Bill Piekney, and to get his view on how the war was going, both politically and on the battlefield.

Slender but not tall, well groomed and soft-spoken, Bill Piekney was a consummate CIA man who had enjoyed a rapid rise up through the CIA's Directorate of Operations. The former Navy officer knew the rules, did as he was told, and did it well, and for two years running the covert action program in Pakistan, Piekney had played by the rules. Steady as she goes, had been the order. Don't let things get out of control.

He'd worked well with the Pakistanis to keep the supplies moving and to keep the cost of the occupation of Afghanistan high for the Soviets. But a shift in Soviet tactics from broad rural pacification efforts to more sharply focused helicopter-borne special operations against resistance infiltration routes and strongholds had paid off for the Soviets. The war was going badly for the resistance, and for Bill Piekney.

Now, with a change in ground rules in Washington, Piekney was caught in a political bait-and-switch game among congressional hawks, the Pakistani government, and the CIA's seventh floor.

Rawalpindi, Pakistan, January 1986

Piekney could feel his jaw dropping as the words that Senator Orrin Hatch had flown halfway around the world to hear came tumbling out of the mouth of Mohammed Zia ul-Haq, the soft-spoken president of Pakistan. Why, of course, yes, certainly, Pakistan will permit the United States to ship Stinger missiles to the Afghan rebels through our territory, Piekney heard the ever adaptable Zia tell the anti-Communist Republican from Utah. Yes, certainly, we will train the mujahideen in their use. Yes, I agree, it is time to turn the heat up on the Soviet Army.

Zia, now in his seventh year as Pakistan's self-appointed leader, had entered politics as had so many of the leaders in the Third World, wearing khaki. He had been made Army chief in 1976 by Zulfiqar Ali Bhutto, Pakistan's charismatic Prime Minister, in the fatally mistaken belief that he was controllable, perhaps even a little slow out of the starting blocks. A fervent Islamist, Zia would be either at the mosque or out on the golf course, Bhutto had thought, and was not likely to become a threat to his own leadership.

A year later, Zia was running Pakistan and Bhutto was sitting in jail waiting for the hangman. In the face of almost universal outcry and condemnation from the West, Zia had Bhutto tried on a variety of still controversial charges and sentenced to death. To everyone's surprise, the death sentence was actually carried out in April 1979, eight months before the Soviets launched their Afghan adventure. Washington turned a cold shoulder to the generals in Islamabad after Bhutto's execution, but the estrangement would be brief. After one look at the map of Central Asia, President Jimmy Carter understood that if he was to oppose the Soviet grab in Afghanistan, it would have to be in partnership with Zia ul-Haq.

Carter moved quickly. In early 1980, he sent his national security adviser, Zbigniew Brzezinski, to Islamabad for consultations with the new leader of Pakistan. The two agreed to join forces, and the United States quietly began to assemble the wherewithal to mount a sustained effort to support the Afghan resistance, and to do it in secret. But on a not-so-secret side trip, Brzezinski traveled the length of the Khyber Pass to the Pakistani outpost at Michni Point, where he was photographed squinting along the sights of a Soviet AK-47 assault rifle, its muzzle elevated and pointing into Afghanistan. In that moment, the President's national security adviser became the symbol of the impending U.S. involvement in Afghanistan's endless martial history.

Zia, from the outset, believed his generals could work with the CIA, whose history in Pakistan dated back to the 1950s, when it flew high-altitude U-2 surveillance flights over the Soviet Union from northwest Pakistan. The massive hangar at the military side of the Peshawar airport was still nostalgically called the "CIA hangar" a quarter century after CIA pilot Francis Gary Powers was brought down by Soviet air defenses over Sverdlovsk. There was a record of cooperation with the CIA, and the Pakistanis felt comfortable with it.

But Zia drew the line at allowing the American hand to show. Keep it covert, he had insisted. The Pakistani leader had come to associate the introduction of American-made weapons, especially antiaircraft missiles, as a first step toward bringing in the Pentagon. He was concerned, possibly rightly, that if the Pentagon got its nose under the tent, it would be only a short time before the American involvement in the war had slipped from his control.

Though Zia admired the United States, he knew that no Pakistani leader should invest too deeply in the American relationship. The good times were very good for Pakistan, but they were always followed by estrangement. When Ronald Reagan was elected in 1980, Zia calculated that with the conservative, anti-Soviet Republican in the White House, he might expect a consistent American policy toward Pakistan as long as the Soviets remained in Afghanistan. When Reagan was reelected four years later, the Pakistani president rightly decided that the U.S.-Pakistani relationship might actually carry through to the end of the Soviet adventure. But even as he deepened Pakistan's involvement with the United States in Afghanistan, he always kept a finger to the wind and a sharp eye on the mood of the American Congress.

The United States had entered the fray for a combination of moral and geopolitical reasons for what seemed like the long haul. Some in Congress thought that the war could happily last forever, that the Soviets could be bled the way the United States had been for over a decade in Vietnam. Others, by the sixth year of the war, were less comfortable with what seemed to them a cynical strategy of fighting the Soviets down to the last Afghan. Still other lawmakers saw the Afghan adventure as the Soviet Union's fatal weakness. These hawks no longer wanted just to mire the Soviets in the Afghan bog; they wanted to defeat them and believed they could if the United States would only stop pulling its punches. Thus, an alliance of congressional hawks and moralists formed in early 1985, the bloodiest year of the Soviet occupation, and together they would force a change in the rules.

Until 1985, the Soviets had focused their efforts on attempting to eliminate popular support of the mujahideen in the countryside; it was a scorched-earth policy that accomplished nothing beyond forcing millions of Afghans to seek refuge in Pakistan and Iran. The mujahideen still owned the countryside. After 1985, when Gorbachev signaled his tacit agreement to give the Army its head for one more year, Soviet tactics shifted to the use of helicopter-borne special operations troops—Spetsnaz—against resistance strongholds and infiltration routes. The casualties mounted on both sides, but the advantage seemed to have shifted to the Soviets.

Reagan responded to the pressures from Congress and the Soviet escalations by signing National Security Decision Directive 166, a presidential order that redefined U.S. goals in Afghanistan in unambiguous terms—push the Soviets back across the Amu Dar'ya, the river that marked the border between the Soviet Republic of Uzbekistan and Afghanistan. The CIA's covert action role in Afghanistan dating back to the Carter administration called for "harassing" the Soviets, not driving them out. Reagan was upping the ante, and now he actually believed he could win. But the question of the Stinger, which many saw as vital to this new phase of the war, had yet to be resolved. The CIA consistently reported to Congress that the Pakistani president simply wouldn't countenance the escalation that was sure to follow the introduction of American missile systems. Piekney was the third in a line of Islamabad chiefs to be shackled by Zia's policy since 1979, and he had never thought the Pakistani president would waver from that course.

Now, as he sat stunned in Zia's private office, tucked away at the rear of the old colonial governor's residence, Piekney felt as if he had been the victim of a political ambush—which, of course, was exactly what he was.

Orrin Hatch had come to Rawalpindi to test Zia one more time and to hear his objections for himself. Accompanying the senator was Michael Pillsbury, a policy provocateur who bounced between congressional staff jobs and political positions in the Pentagon and who had persuaded Hatch to push for Stingers. At the CIA, Pillsbury was seen as a noisome gadfly, a persistent pest who inserted himself into policy debates without really understanding the nature of intelligence or the ground rules for covert action. But people like Pillsbury might not have mattered if the Stinger issue had been receiving high-level attention at the White House or State Department. It was precisely because top-level Reagan administration officials weren't focusing much attention on Afghanistan that midlevel bureaucrats like Pillsbury were able to step into the policy vacuum. Tensions between the CIA and Pillsbury provided much of the drama behind Hatch's meeting with Zia.

As he traveled to Pakistan, Pillsbury had a problem: CIA Director Bill Casey was determined to prevent him from sitting in on Hatch's meeting with Zia to discuss the CIA's covert action program in Afghanistan. Days before the congressional delegation arrived in the country, Piekney had received a cable from Langley passing on an order from Casey blocking Pillsbury from attending the meetings with Zia. Piekney was told Pillsbury lacked the appropriate clearances for the meetings concerning the CIA's Afghan covert action program. Before Hatch's delegation arrived, Piekney called back to CIA headquarters and asked Near East Division Chief Bert Dunn to reaffirm the order.

"Let me make sure I have this straight. I should tell Hatch that he can't bring Pillsbury in, right, Bert?"

"That's right."

After greeting the congressional delegation, Piekney found himself standing with Hatch, and the senator soon asked Piekney the question he had been dreading. Was it all right if Pillsbury sat in on the meetings with Zia? Cautiously, Piekney told Hatch that, actually, he had received orders to keep Pillsbury out.

"Well, do you mind if I call Bill Casey and talk to him about it?" Hatch asked.

"Of course not," Piekney said.

Hatch was escorted to a telephone, where he placed a call directly to Casey back at CIA headquarters.

After some persuading from Hatch, Casey backed down and agreed to let Pillsbury attend the meetings. But Piekney later heard from a colleague who was in the room with Casey that as soon as he hung up, he became angry with himself for caving in to the senator's demands. That evening the Americans, with Pillsbury in attendance and various other members of Hatch's delegation, all crowded into Zia's private office. And it was there that Piekney heard Zia suddenly, and without warning, change six years of Pakistani policy in an instant.

Hatch's meeting with Zia turned out to be a watershed event in American support for the Afghan rebels. With Zia's approval, opposition within the Reagan administration to the direct infusion of American arms collapsed. The United States would be turning up the heat on the Soviet 40th Army in Afghanistan, and Bill Piekney could only shake his head as he thought about how rapidly the political ground had shifted in both the United States and Pakistan.

Langley, July 12, 1986

Back in Washington, I began to close up shop and prepare for my transfer to Islamabad in early August. It was a standing tradition for a DO chief on his way to the field to have a private talk with the DCI before heading out, and my checkout talk with Casey took place three weeks before my departure. Any ambiguities in the job description that may have plagued Piekney had all but evaporated by the time I received my marching orders from Bill Casey.

I'd known Casey since he took his first trip abroad as DCI in 1981 when I was chief in Lagos, Nigeria. I had been on the ground in the oil-rich, rough-and-tumble West African country for about six months when I found myself standing on the steaming tarmac of Murtala Muhammad Airport, waiting for the arrival of a USAF C-141 carrying Ronald Reagan's new DCI, the old OSS man and Wall Street operator who had already begun to breathe new life into an agency adrift for the last half dozen years. As soon as the black Starlifter pulled to a whining halt, two of Casey's bodyguards whisked their charge down the short ladder from the paratroop jump door. Within moments I was in the back of a limousine with the white-haired DCI and caught up in one of Lagos's infamous "go-slows," the unique Nigerian version of gridlock.

We were traveling in a tight, three-car convoy, and at one point when we were at a dead standstill, an unsuspecting Nigerian motorist broke into our motorcade, briefly separating us from the lead car. A Nigerian security officer riding shotgun with us calmly stepped out of the car and shouted through the closed window to the offending driver. The man ignored him until the officer took his heavy, handheld Motorola, smashed out the side window, and repeated his demand. The man quickly pulled to the side of the road.

Casey, taking all this in, seemed about to comment when there was an insistent knock at his window. Looking over, I saw a Nigerian youth about twelve years old holding up a twenty-five-foot green garden hose, still in factory packaging, and gesturing animatedly to Casey.

"What's he want?" Casey mumbled, bemused by the frantic Lagos scene.

"Wants to sell you a garden hose," I answered. "It's a hot item on the black market. Pirates take the stuff off the ships backed up in port. This week it's garden hoses."

Casey flashed his toothy smile for the first time. "Not really an impulse buy, is it?"

"Welcome to Nigeria, Mr. Director." We both laughed, and over the next two days the beginnings of a personal friendship with Casey developed, one that would last until his death. He stayed two days as my houseguest in Lagos. Under the watchful eye of his personal physician, who traveled with him, I poured Casey's rum and tonics in the evening—he'd quip that he liked tonic water, but the taste was so bad that he could drink it only with a shot of rum in it. And in the morning I fried his bacon and scrambled his eggs. From that point on, he took a personal interest in where my career was heading and was eager for me to move across the continent to Khartoum two years later, another spot he had visited in his first foray to Africa in 1981.

So here we were five years later about to set off on what was becoming Casey's endgame vision for the Soviet Union. The DCI tilted back in his recliner and peered over his glasses at me as I took one of the wingback chairs in front of his desk. With his soup-stained tie, Casey looked his usual disheveled self. I glanced at the stack of books on the corner of his desk to see if I could make out the titles for his weekend reading.

"Headin' out?" Casey asked before I could get a good look.

"Early next month, but this is the only hole you had in your schedule for another guy on his way to the field. They're stacking up outside your door."

"Everybody's turning over this year. Don't know why Clair lets it happen that way . . . all that turnover. Seems dumb to me. Never mind. Watcha gonna do out there, Milt?"

"What do you want me to do?" I threw his probe back at him.

"I want you to go out there and win. That's what the President wants. He put it in writing. We've been screwin' around long enough with this steady-as-she-goes approach. Zia's always telling me to turn up the heat a little but not to let the pot boil over . . . you know, that kind of stuff."

"That's what he's been telling everybody these days from what I hear, except the earful he gave Hatch."

Casey rolled his eyes at the mention of Senator Hatch. He'd had enough of the so-called 4H Club—Senators Orrin Hatch, Jesse Helms, Chic Hecht, and Gordon Humphrey—who, along with their staffers, had been demanding bolder CIA action in Afghanistan.

"Old Zia's still pretty smart, and you want to listen to him when you get out there. Whenever you want him to do something that's above your pay scale, tell him and General Akhtar I said I wanted it done. It'll make a difference."

"You really want to give me that kind of a blank check?" I said, leaning forward to make sure he meant it. "I'll use it, you know."

Casey had developed a close relationship with both Zia and his intelligence chief, General Akhtar. Zia had shrewdly calculated that Casey would stand with Pakistan as long as Reagan was in the White House, and Akhtar, also shrewdly, bought into any policy that Zia had embraced. That all three men clearly liked one another just added to the relationship. Allowing me to trade on that relationship was no small matter.

"You do whatever it takes to win out there. I want to win the whole thing. Afghanistan is only part of it. I'll give you everything you'll need. Fight's finally done on the Stingers, and you got all the money you'll need. A billion enough for ya?" The old man slipped into the mumbled half sentences that told me his mind was racing around some great vision that I had only a small part of.

"Yeah, a billion ought to do it," I said.

"When are the Stingers going in?" he asked.

"They're training some guys now. Ought to be deployed in early September."

"What about the broadcasts?"

Clair had told me that Casey had been promoting a plan to broadcast propaganda into the Soviet Central Asian republics, an idea no one else thought was a good one. Casey was convinced that he could push the Soviets against the wall, but almost everyone else at Langley and in Foggy Bottom was convinced that if pushed too far, the Soviets might overreact and strike back at Pakistan. Clair had told me to watch for anything that looked as if it was going to spill over the Amu Dar'ya into the USSR. I'd taken that to mean anything on the ground or on the airwaves.

"I'm still reading in on that," I said, choosing to dodge the question, "but everything's pretty much on track as I understand it. When're you planning to come out and check the traps?"

Casey peered over his glasses at me for a moment without answering. I could only guess where his thoughts were carrying him. I knew he liked nothing better than flying around in his VIP module, lashed inside a black C-141 and checking things out in the field, but I also knew that he was under growing attack from the Hill for his other pet project—the Central American Task Force, whose mission was to get the Sandinistas out of power in Nicaragua. "God, soon as I can—getting out of here right now is no easy task. Maybe before the end of the year."

"I'll scramble your eggs when you come."

That brought a smile from Casey and the meeting to an end. "You go on out there and do what it takes, Milt," he said. "Tell Akhtar and Zia that I'll be out as soon as I can get away from here. And tell Zia I'm still watching his pot. I won't let it boil over."

Casey gripped my hand as I rose to leave his office. I didn't know it then, but this would be the last time I'd see the old man.

2

Islamabad, Pakistan, August 1986

The summer monsoon was winding down in Pakistan's Punjab province, leaving behind a rich, verdant haze over the capital city of Islamabad, whose tranquillity belied the existence of a brutal, earth-scorching war a little more than a hundred miles to the west. As I made my way through Islamabad's light traffic to my office each morning, I was struck by the city's extraordinary setting. To the west of the main government and diplomatic enclave lay the graceful slopes of the Margalla Hills, mere foothills, but rich in geological promise as they forced their way northward, twisting, pushing ever higher. In a stunningly beautiful stretch of Pakistan's Northern Territories, they fused together with the great ranges that would become the towering Karakorums driving northward into China, the Himalayas stretching eastward across the rooftop of the world into India and Nepal, and the Hindu Kush, reaching skyward above the battles in neighboring Afghanistan. There were peaks topping twenty thousand feet that no one had even bothered to name.

Down country and closer to home was the sprawling city of

Rawalpindi, its nineteenth-century army cantonment an ever so faintly glowing ember of the old British empire. In the past, it was the city of Kipling and serious-minded Englishmen in khaki serving the queen on the playing fields of Central Asia. If Islamabad was too sterile, too new and ordered, for an old South Asia hand, there was always the option of disappearing into the labyrinthine alleyways and roiling sea of humanity that was Rawalpindi a few miles to the east and escape backward in time. Kipling was gone, but other serious-minded men in khaki remained, still struggling with the modern variation of the same old game.

It all came together here in the western reaches of Pakistan's Punjab province, the past, the present, and the future, all the tectonic forces of nature and of politics. In Afghanistan the Soviets were in their sixth year of occupation, still struggling against an undiminished rebellion. Though it would be another few years before the toll was known, casualties among the Afghan population were approaching one million killed. There were no firm estimates as to the numbers of injured, other than the reasonable guess that they outnumbered the dead. Another five million had been driven from their homes into exile either in Iran or Pakistan, and millions more were refugees in their own country, displaced by the Soviet invaders. The Soviets were on their way to losing almost fifteen thousand men, triple that wounded, and hundreds of thousands incapacitated by disease. And there seemed no end in sight.

The bitter Washington debate over our Afghan policy that took up much of 1985 and early 1986 had ended by the time I arrived on the scene in Pakistan. There was no more dispute over our mission. The congressional hawks had been calmed and the moralists assuaged. We were in it to win. Those had been my instructions from Bill Casey and, he'd assured me, from the President.

In 1986, there were few in the Congress or the administration who believed the Soviets were seriously seeking an exit strategy. Soviet Foreign Minister Shevardnadze had told U.S. Secretary of State George Shultz the previous year that Gorbachev wanted to get out of Afghanistan, but there was no evidence on the ground to back up that view; nor was there any evidence that the Georgian Foreign Minister's comments represented a consensus in the Politburo. On the contrary, it still looked as though the war might just go on indefinitely or that the Soviets might even be on the verge of winning it. In the summer of 1986, there was no talk of going easy on the Soviets to give them a breather so they could get out. The talk, instead, was of going full tilt and making sure that the loose coalition of countries supporting the resistance didn't wobble.

Allied with the United States in the effort to assist the Afghan people in their struggle were China, Saudi Arabia, the United Kingdom, and Egypt, all major players and all, like the United States, with their own national agendas for entering the fight. For the first six years of the struggle, those complex agendas were more or less in concert. They wouldn't always be that way.

China, characteristically, took the long-term view. Beijing wanted to prevent the USSR from expanding its empire into Afghanistan, within easy reach of the Gulf of Oman, where it could serve as anvil to India's hammer on Pakistan, wedged uncomfortably in between. China had fought one brief war with India a quarter century earlier and still had unresolved border disputes with the Soviet Union that on more than one occasion had come close to serious eruption in the far northeast. China's relationship with Pakistan had been one of the few constants in the ever shifting alliances of the region. So from the start, China was in it to win, but it was also patient.

Saudi Arabia, in particular its Wahhabi clerical structure, was distracted at the time of the Soviet invasion of Afghanistan by the Iranian revolution and the rise of Ayatollah Khomeini and Shia militancy. The Saudis were more than bystanders in the Iran-Iraq war in the early 1980s, and thus their involvement in Afghanistan and Pakistan was just another important facet of Saudi policy in the region. They had been independently supporting the Afghan resistance in the period just before the Soviet invasion, and the decision to join with the United States after the invasion was a rational extension of their consuming concern with Iran's spreading influence. And not a few in the royal family thought lending a hand to the Afghan resistance gave the powerful Wahhabi clerics something important to do farther from home. Pakistan's leader,

Mohammed Zia ul-Haq, was a pious man who had opened up Pakistan to the Wahhabis, who were establishing Koranic schools, *madrassas,* in growing numbers. And at that time, with oil prices in the $40-a-barrel range, the costs of working with the Americans seemed manageable.

The United Kingdom, under Margaret Thatcher, was never far from the United States in dealing head-on with Soviet expansionism. And with an inside track on the rules of "the great game," the British were a natural ally, though there was always an underlying prickliness about the come-lately Americans taking the lead in their old backyard.

Egypt was a well-compensated quartermaster and armorer, supplying tens of thousands of tons of Soviet/Warsaw Pact–design weapons to the Afghans and in the process fulfilling its duty to the jihad. Later in the conflict, Egypt and many other Islamic nations found Afghanistan a convenient dumping ground for homegrown troublemakers. Egypt quietly emptied its prisons of its political activists and psychotics and sent them off to the war in Afghanistan, with the fondest hopes that they might never return.

The CIA program had grown over the last six years, from a few tens of millions of dollars under President Carter to hundreds of millions in the early 1980s. Carter's national security adviser, Zbigniew Brzezinski, had in 1980 secured an agreement from the Saudi king to match American contributions to the Afghan effort dollar for dollar, and Bill Casey kept that agreement going over the years. Thus, the budget for the new fiscal year beginning on October 1, 1986, would approach half a billion from Riyadh and half a billion from U.S public coffers. These funds would be spent on everything from Chinese- and Egyptian-made small arms, mortars, and rockets to recoilless rifles and the thousands of Japanese trucks and Chinese mules required to carry it all across zero line, as the border between Pakistan and Afghanistan was called.

It seemed to me, as I took stock of the war a month after I'd arrived, that the stage was set. Now all we needed was a little luck.

The Kremlin, August 1986

Anatoly Chernyaev had one of the most daunting tasks in the Kremlin. As foreign policy aide to General Secretary Mikhail Gorbachev, his job was to guide the new Soviet leader through the political mine field blocking a speedy and graceful exit of Soviet forces from Afghanistan. The durable and imperturbable foreign policy expert knew the job had to be done, not only for his boss, but for the good of the USSR. From the day he signed on as Gorbachev's foreign policy adviser a year earlier, he began to apply the common sense and political savvy he had developed over the last two decades in the Central Committee's International Department to the USSR's most consuming foreign policy issue—Afghanistan.

He knew the main obstacle to quitting Afghanistan was ideological—how to get out without looking beaten, as the Americans had in running away from Vietnam. Perhaps the Americans had the resilience to survive the loss of prestige, but the USSR didn't. That was a fact. Chernyaev also knew that Gorbachev didn't have the option of blaming the disaster of the Afghan enterprise on a string of dead predecessors. He couldn't simply cut his losses and declare it had been a mistake from the beginning. Things weren't done that way in the USSR. Maybe Khrushchev had pulled off attacking Josef Stalin's years of tyranny in his "secret speech" a generation ago, but that had been an internal matter, not one that involved an issue as fundamental to Soviet policy as dismantling the Brezhnev Doctrine of never abandoning a fraternal socialist nation. Gorbachev would have to sidestep the issue of the decisions made seven years ago and chart a new course. Never mind that those decisions were colossal errors, based at least in part on intelligence from the KGB that bore scant resemblance to the truth. It wasn't that the KGB didn't know the realities, Chernyaev decided, it was that they reported what they thought Moscow wanted to hear.

During the course of 1979, KGB Chairman Yuri Andropov and Defense Minister Dmitri Ustinov had come to two disturbing conclusions on Afghanistan. First, they had decided that the United States planned to establish military bases in Afghanistan to replace their listening posts in Iran, which they had lost when the shah was overthrown. Such a move, Andropov and Ustinov insisted, would forge yet another link in the chain of America's encirclement of the Soviet Union. Their second conclusion was that Hafizullah Amin, Afghanistan's foreign minister at the time, was maneuvering to displace Moscow's own handpicked man in Kabul, Nur Muhammad Taraki, who had seized the presidency and the premiership in the April Revolution just a year earlier.

The threat to Taraki from Amin was viewed as all the more sinister by some in the Politburo because of a KGB black propaganda effort to malign Amin by portraying him as an agent of the CIA. The logic was compelling—after four years at Columbia University, Amin had to be a CIA agent. Once in power, the reasoning went, he would change camps, abandoning Afghanistan's ties to the USSR and aligning with the United States. How long would it then be before U.S. intermediate-range Pershing missiles were aimed at the USSR from American bases in Afghanistan?

As was sometimes the case with propaganda efforts, the KGB operation against Amin backfired. About all it accomplished was to stir up more trouble in an already deeply divided People's Democratic Party of Afghanistan and give the Moscow leadership one more bogus reason to complete the slide toward military intervention. In the end, the Politburo hard-liners swallowed the story of Amin being a CIA agent and added it to the growing list of reasons to take the plunge into Afghanistan. The fact that Amin was no friend of the United States, and even nursed a lifelong grudge against Columbia University for twice failing him in his doctoral thesis, was never factored into the equation. Amin was a central part of the problem, and that was that.

The mounting crisis had been brought home to the Politburo in monthly installments throughout 1979. In February, the American ambassador in Kabul, Adolph Dubs, was murdered during a failed rescue attempt after he'd been kidnapped by terrorists and held in the Hotel Kabul. The Soviet (and KGB) hand was visible in the cover-up—the three captured terrorists were summarily executed before American authorities could interrogate them. The autopsy showed that Dubs was shot several times in the head from a distance of about six inches, but the United States was able to do nothing beyond protest the use of force in freeing Dubs and cut off the remaining aid to Afghanistan, which it had intended to do anyway.

Then in March, Afghan warlord Isma'il Khan butchered a number of Soviet officers, soldiers, and their families in the ancient southwest Afghan city of Herat. After the Herat incident, Taraki pleaded for the USSR to send in a contingent of troops to put down the growing rebellion. That same month, Amin quietly took one of Taraki's posts, appointing himself premier. The "CIA's man in Kabul" was on the move, or so the advocates of intervention in the Politburo concluded.

Through the spring, Taraki's pleas for Soviet military intervention were repeatedly rejected by the Kremlin, but the Politburo opened debate over Afghanistan in earnest after the Herat slaughter. Foreign Minister Andrei Gromyko initially declared that "under no circumstances" could the Soviet Union "lose" Afghanistan, a position he almost immediately reversed when he decided that if the USSR intervened in Afghanistan, the world would brand it the aggressor, détente with the West would collapse, and the USSR's actions would be declared in violation of the tenets of the UN. Alexei Kosygin, the ailing seventy-five-year-old Premier, allied with Central Committee Secretary Andrei Kirilenko, led the opposition in the Politburo to any military intervention. They would not waver from that position throughout the debate.

But Taraki persisted. Send in your Central Asians, he said, nobody will even notice. Thus the Soviet military adventure in Afghanistan began incrementally. First there was the deployment in June of a battalion of Soviet Central Asians dispatched in to "guard Soviet installations." They were followed by another detachment of airborne troops in July. Then Andropov sent in a unit of KGB special operations troops the same month.

KGB reporting during the summer of 1979 grew increasingly alarmist, with declarations that the military situation was out of control. There was always the suggestion that the American hand was behind the troubles, particularly after Amin succeeded in his widely predicted move against Taraki. After surviving two attempts on his life and brutally consolidating his power within the Kabul structure, Amin ordered Taraki killed in October. The KGB concluded that America's man was now fully in charge in Kabul, and by the time the first snows had fallen in 1979, the analysis of a looming, American-fomented disaster on the USSR's vulnerable underbelly had seized the imagination of the Politburo. GRU reporting from the Afghan capital countered the gloomy KGB dispatches in those critical months, but it was ignored.

Leonid Brezhnev was outraged by Taraki's murder just days after his warm reception in Moscow, during which Brezhnev had assured Taraki that he would "take care of him." Taking the assassination as a personal insult, the ailing Soviet leader shifted his position in favor of a military response. Andropov, whose KGB had worked behind the scenes to remove Amin over the summer, including the two failed attempts on his life, also took Taraki's murder personally, and with Brezhnev coming on board, the course for intervention was set.

Events began to move rapidly in the fall. In late October, the KGB sent specialist teams throughout Afghanistan to conduct Operation Zenith, a polling effort to determine popular reaction to a Soviet military intervention. KGB reporting now focused on the proposition that Hafizullah Amin was sliding into the Western camp, adding a new spin that a bridgehead in Afghanistan would give the United States a much needed base for the ultimate invasion of Iran as punishment for the hostage taking by the ayatollahs. The encirclement of the USSR by American missiles would be complete, and Afghanistan's "loss" would spark similar problems for the USSR among the "fraternal" nations of the Warsaw Pact. The fact that none of this was true was simply no longer in consideration.

On December 12, 1979, the Politburo met and formally ratified the proposal to send in the Army. Defense Minister Ustinov, KGB Chairman Andropov, and Foreign Minister Gromyko signed the order to dispatch a "limited contingent." Brezhnev's close confidant Konstantin Chernenko wrote out by hand a short protocol endorsing the proposal to intervene, entitling it "Concerning the Situation in 'A' "; he then asked all Politburo members present to sign diagonally across the text. Brezhnev, who joined the meeting late, was the last to pen his shaky signature across the document.

Operations Oak and Storm were launched on Christmas Eve, and there would be no turning back. Amin was killed, and the new Soviet "emir of Afghanistan," Babrak Karmal, was installed in a military operation that went like clockwork even though it was devised on the fly, as grand entrances by foreign armies into Afghanistan have generally been over the centuries. Going into Afghanistan had been a breeze, but then it always happened that way.

That was how it had all started almost seven years ago. Gorbachev had given the Army leeway to do what it had to to get the job done militarily in 1985, but even that hadn't translated into measurable gains on the ground—just a more costly stalemate. Now it was time to get out, and Chernyaev had to manage the road map for a clean exit and to keep his job in the process. He had his work cut out for him.

Gorbachev had made his first move in the fall of 1985 at a Politburo meeting, when he read moving passages from emotion-filled letters from mothers who had lost sons in Afghanistan. Chernyaev noted in his diary that Gorbachev raised the emotional pitch while sidestepping the underlying question of whether the entire venture had been a mistake from the start. He first questioned the Afghan policy publicly in February 1986, at the Twenty-seventh Party Congress, and would raise the stakes again the following week in a speech in Vladivostok, when he described Afghanistan as a "bleeding wound."

There would be no turning back after that.

First Chief Directorate Headquarters, Yasenevo, August 1986

For the last two years, Leonid Vladimirovich Shebarshin had had the taxing job of making sense of a badly managed war. As deputy chief of the First Chief Directorate's Analytical Department, and as the KGB's most experienced general officer in South and Central Asia, Shebarshin was doing his best to inject a small dose of something not much in evidence when the Politburo had decided to invade Afghanistan seven years earlier—reality. His mission was to help get the Army out of Afghanistan while leaving behind a friendly government. It was a tall order, Shebarshin concluded, a political challenge rather than a military objective.

Handsome at just over six feet, with thick black hair and piercing eyes, Shebarshin, at fifty, had spent most of his professional life in Asia. After graduating from the Oriental faculty of the Institute of Foreign Relations at Moscow University in 1958, he took a Foreign Ministry posting to Pakistan. He returned to Moscow four years later, making the shift so many of the Foreign Ministry's most capable young diplomats seemed to be making in those days—into the KGB. He joined their foreign intelligence arm, the First Chief Directorate. After two years of training, Shebarshin was off on an unbroken thirteen-year run in South Asia, alternating between the KGB *Rezidenturas* in Pakistan and India. After a stint at Moscow Center, he was posted as KGB *Rezident* in Iran, arriving in Teheran just as the tortured decision-making process leading to the Soviet invasion of Afghanistan was gathering speed in the Kremlin and as the Iranian revolution was about to engulf Teheran.

The first indications that Afghanistan might not be good news were driven home to Shebarshin on New Year's Day 1980, when the Iranians demonstrated against the Soviet embassy. The demonstrators did little damage, but they had finally been distracted from their dawn-to-dusk outrages at the American embassy some two thousand yards away. Some Soviet analysts thought that the anti-American mood in Iran would translate into a pro-Soviet policy with the ayatollahs, but Shebarshin dismissed such musings as wishful thinking. From the moment of the takeover of the American embassy by the "students" in 1979, the KGB *Rezident* was convinced that sooner or later the same outrages would be played out against the Soviet Union. According to the Iranians, the USSR was still the "small Satan," just one level of evil down from the American "great Satan," at least in the view of Iran's revolutionaries. Imam Khomeini had made this point to the Soviet ambassador shortly after the intervention in Afghanistan—he had said to Moscow's envoy that the military intervention was a grave mistake for which the USSR would pay dearly.

To reinforce their disapproval of events in Afghanistan, the Iranians turned on the Soviets briefly, then ratcheted up the pressure in January 1982, when they sacked the Soviet embassy, the same historic building in which the Teheran Conference of 1943 had been convened. Shebarshin did not miss the irony of the destruction of some of the remaining icons of World War II cooperation among Stalin, Churchill, and Roosevelt at the hands of the Iranians four decades later.

He returned to First Chief Directorate headquarters at Yasenevo 1983 and had been the First Directorate's man on Afghanistan ever since. Witnessing the humiliation of the United States at the hands of Iranian revolutionaries had sobered him, but nothing he saw of the USSR's management of its adventure in Afghanistan gave him confidence that a second superpower could not be brought to its knees by Islamic militants in Central Asia. On the contrary, he was convinced Moscow had misread events in Afghanistan at most important points since before the first dispatch of the "limited contingent" in 1979. The Afghan war was not an action to eradicate "bandits," as the Afghan leadership and the Soviet Politburo contended, but a fight against committed Afghan Muslims and an Afghan populace that overwhelmingly supported them. It was a war that couldn't be won, at least in the way it was being fought.

Now, in 1986, a few bold men inside the system were beginning to address the question of how the Soviet Union was to climb out of the Afghan pit. KGB Chairman Yuri Andropov had been one of the hawks in 1979 whose signatures could be found on the Politburo order to send in the troops, and he had kept his commitment to the end, remaining a hawk after he took over as General Secretary when Leonid Brezhnev died in 1982. Now Andropov was history, and it was with great irony that many Kremlin and Lubyanka insiders came to believe that he was ultimately brought down by a mysterious ailment he'd picked up in Kabul during a visit in February 1982. By March 1983 Andropov was on dialysis, and a year later, despite heroic efforts by his physicians, he was dead.

Andropov was succeeded by the man he had outmaneuvered when Brezhnev died, Konstantin Chernenko, Brezhnev's loyal aide who had ramrodded the decision to intervene in Afghanistan through the Politburo in December 1979. Chernenko's luck was no better than Andropov's. A dying man when he took over from Andropov, he himself was gone thirteen months later. It was with the passing of Chernenko that the chain of the old guard was finally broken. Succeeding him was the fifty-four-year-old Mikhail Gorbachev, who took over at the Kremlin with little experience in foreign affairs but with powerful doubts about the Soviet Union's Afghan adventure. Gorbachev had not been a member of the Politburo until a year after the intervention in Afghanistan—his signature was not among those on the order to send in the Army in 1979. Though it was not known at the time, Gorbachev took over in the Kremlin with a single, unencumbered goal in Afghanistan: to get out. But he also knew that getting out would be far more difficult than going in—the one immutable truth about Afghanistan.

Now it fell to Leonid Shebarshin to bring a dose of reality to the KGB's handling of Afghanistan. His work was cut out for him. He knew the Americans had no intention of making the Red Army's exit from Afghanistan easy. According to all accounts, they were going to do everything in their power to make it as difficult as possible. The level and quality of American assistance to the bandits had increased dramatically, according to reports reaching Shebarshin's desk.

3

Kabul, Afghanistan, 1700 Hours, August 26, 1986

The corrosive acid in the brass barrel of a time pencil, a device specially developed in the laboratories of the CIA's Office of Technical Services, ate through the thin wire restraining a spring-loaded firing plunger at almost precisely 1700 hours. At that instant, the cylinder slammed forward, completing an electrical circuit and sending a succession of high-speed impulses from a pack of E cell batteries through wires leading to a dozen rockets propped up and aimed at the puppet Afghan

8th Army's ammunition dump at Kharga, outside of Kabul, the capital of Afghanistan. The Chinese-made 107 mm rockets ignited in sequence, and within a few tenths of a second they were off, in flight toward their target some six kilometers away. The mujahideen who had set up the delayed-action launch were by now even farther away.

In what would later be described variously as the vengeance of God, superb planning and execution, or just plain dumb luck, there followed that evening and into the night a signal event in a war that had been going very badly for the Afghan resistance. At least one of the white phosphorus rockets flew into a storage warehouse containing a supply of surface-to-air missiles (SAMs) that had been delivered by the Soviets to the Afghan Army to protect them against air attacks from Pakistan. The rocket's explosion ignited the fuel tanks of the SAMs, setting off a chain reaction of secondary explosions that radiated and spread from storage area to storage area within the giant Kharga facility, which at that moment was packed with about forty thousand tons of ammunition. Tens of thousands of mortar rounds, mountains of stacked rockets, and the SAMs themselves began to cook off one after the other as the chain reaction spun out of control. The firefighting teams never had a chance—the fire was out of control the minute the first white phosphorus rocket struck its target.

All through the night, the diplomatic corps in Kabul was treated to a fireworks display that grew in magnitude as the secondary explosions worked their way from bunker to bunker. A BBC camera team on the roof of the British embassy captured the devastation of the strike, and soon the footage was being relayed around the world. Watching the pyrotechnics on Pakistani television that night in Islamabad, I wondered how many mujahideen commanders would take credit for the attack, even before the fires had begun to burn out at Kharga. The answer was quick in coming.

Peshawar, Pakistan, 0930 Hours, August 27, 1986

Three press conferences were called almost simultaneously the next morning by the press offices of the Peshawar-based Afghan resistance parties. By ten o'clock, Commander Abdul

Haq and General Rahim Wardak, two of the most press-conscious of the mujahideen commanders based in Peshawar, had claimed credit for the attack. A similar announcement followed from Gulbuddin Hekmatyar's press office, and the other resistance parties would quickly follow suit. Rahim Wardak, derisively called the "Gucci commander" because of his camouflage fatigues, impeccably tailored to conceal an unmilitary girth, presented the most comprehensive operational plan, complete with maps and diagrams. But the flamboyant Abdul Haq, who had received the attention and much of the devotion of the mostly American press corps in Peshawar, ended up getting credit from the media for the operation. I never did find out who launched the attack—a dozen commanders insisted they were responsible—so I just decided to believe all or none of their claims. Kharga was smoking, and the mujahideen had a hundred new heroes. That was enough for me.

Langley, August 28, 1986

Jack Devine played the video of the Kharga blast a second time and knew it was just what he needed. A career officer in the Latin America Division of the Directorate of Operations, Devine had worked his way through some serious mine fields in South America, serving in Chile during Salvador Allende's bloody overthrow and later as chief in Buenos Aires in the years of the disappearances during the military regime. He had earned a reputation for having sharp political instincts and a keen sense of how to navigate through treacherous times. At six feet five, Devine was hard to miss in his new fiefdom—he'd taken over the headquarters end of the Afghan project in June, just as it had been elevated from a country branch activity to a full-fledged task force, a change that cut the number of people looking over his shoulder to just two, the DDO and his deputy. Devine was exactly the right man to deal with the crosscurrents on Capitol Hill, within the Reagan administration, and on the CIA's own seventh floor.

When Clair George had asked him to take over the task force that spring, there wasn't much going right in the war. Reports from the field were an unbroken string of dismal accounts of the Afghan resistance's inability to get their supplies from Pakistan through the hundreds of infiltration routes into eastern Afghanistan. It wasn't clear to Devine whether that was because of the increasingly successful Soviet helicopter assaults along the supply routes or because of the growing fatalism of the Afghan fighters. That fatalism had been picked up by the media—those who were still interested in Afghanistan—and most pundits were about to call the match to the Soviets. Important pockets of Capitol Hill were still supportive, but countering the staunchest advocates of American support to the Afghan resistance was a growing cadre of members of Congress and their staffers who were beginning to question the morality of bleeding the Soviets down to the last Afghan. Even at Langley there was a sharp divide as to whether it made sense over the long haul to keep up the pressure on the Soviets in Afghanistan. Analysts of the USSR tended to dismiss as futile the efforts of primitive tribesmen taking on a superpower. The Near East analysts saw it differently, and there was a tension between the two schools that would remain throughout the war.

By August, Devine had figured that something had to give—and soon—or the fatalists would want to back off and try a new approach. The Soviets were beginning to talk about "an Afghan problem," but they were still banking on a political agreement that would give them most of what they wanted—a friendly, neutral Afghanistan with their chosen people in charge. They wanted no erosion of the Brezhnev Doctrine—even though Brezhnev himself was long gone. As a result, there was no movement in any direction, and it appeared to Devine that the current stalemate would ultimately lead to a loss of commitment in Washington, unless something big happened and soon. Looking at the footage of the brilliant secondary explosions lighting up the night sky around Kabul, he had what he needed, at least for now.

Over the next week, Jack Devine would play the video a few dozen times for key members of Congress and the CIA, and Bill Casey would arrange a private showing for Reagan. If we get a few more lucky shots like this, Devine started thinking, we might just get the worm to turn.

Islamabad, September 3, 1986

The reverberations of the Kharga attack were still being felt a week after the strike, partly thanks to the media, who'd had a chance to watch the fireworks from the rooftops in Kabul, and partly because the CIA managed to show the resistance the fruits of their work in the form of satellite imagery couriered to Pakistan a few days later. Within the week, I briefed the Pakistanis and a few Afghan commanders using the satellite photos of the attack.

The first set of images showed the 8th Army ammunition dump at Kharga five days before the attack, the storage bunkers full of neatly stacked ammunition and equipment. A careful inspection of the one-meter resolution imagery would enable us to distinguish stacked boxes of mortar rounds from the larger wooden boxes containing rockets. The site was jam-packed and waiting to blow.

The next set of photos were of the morning after the attack. When they were held up to the earlier shots, the effect was dramatic. Every bunker and revetment in the earlier photo seemed to have been torched, leaving behind an empty, blackened scar. Wispy smoke trails, still drifting up in corkscrews, were frozen reminders of the seething devastation.

Early assessments led our analysts to conclude that the Soviets would have trouble replacing the losses. With unstable ammunition cooking off unpredictably for weeks, Kharga was out of commission indefinitely. And resupply would challenge an already strained Soviet logistics system, all of which meant that operations would have to be seriously curtailed. This break couldn't have come at a better time. It wouldn't be long before the snows started filling the high passes and the war would settle down again to its dormant winter mode. When the fighting season kicked off the next spring, the mujahideen would have at least one advantage.

And for dramatic effect we calculated the cost-effectiveness of the attack, sharing the results with Pakistan's intelligence service and the resistance leaders. The price of the rockets used in the attack was $110 each, for a total of less than $1,500. The cost to the Soviet patrons of the Afghan Army must have been about $250 million, not counting the even greater cost of their morale.

So as I finished my first month in Islamabad, I decided that with everything else in place, a little bit of extra luck would indeed help. Never mind that Kharga was a fluke; you take what you can get. It had given a new energy to the resistance and had taught me how even the smallest of breaks could be parlayed into events that could alter the course of a war.

First Chief Directorate Headquarters, Yasenevo, September 3, 1986

Leonid Shebarshin had read the reports. There was no hard evidence on the cause of the explosions, but speculation in Kabul pointed to two possibilities—a lucky rocket strike or an accident. He had learned that there were rarely clear-cut answers to any questions in Afghanistan, that truth and reality were always mixed with myth and, often enough, with sheer fantasy. The possible explanations for any occurrence were never separated by mere degrees; they were always poles apart.

The first of his Afghan reality lessons was driven home during his trip in the spring of 1984, just after what had been touted in the 40th Army command as the heaviest and most successful joint strike in the war by the Soviet and allied Democratic Republic of Afghanistan (DRA) forces against the stronghold of Ahmad Shah Massoud in the Panjshir Valley. Deputy Defense Minister Marshal S. L. Sokolov, a rugged old-line tank officer, wanted to look over the battleground himself. He choppered the sixty miles north from Kabul with Shebarshin as part of his inspection team.

The team found nothing, absolutely nothing, to observe. There was no populace to be won over by propaganda teams in the valley, no opposing forces to fight, just ripened, unharvested wheat fields dotted with Soviet and Afghan tanks. The optimistic Soviet generals welcoming Sokolov had provided a splendid, perfectly ordered briefing on the battle for the Panjshir Valley and the current security situation. As Shebarshin listened to the briefing, he wondered how any army could lose a war when it had such a meticulous battle plan as was shown there on the maps all covered with colored triangles, squares, and circles. Victory seemed very much in reach.

But in the course of the briefing, Shebarshin spotted signs of concern on the face of Marshal Sokolov. "Where is the enemy?" the chain-smoking Sokolov—he preferred American More kings—asked in his calm, fatherly manner. "Is he hiding in the nearby gorges?"

"Yes, Comrade Marshal of the Soviet Union," the briefing officer responded confidently. "We have outposts, patrols, and choppers to follow his movements."

Shebarshin found the briefing incomprehensible, but not because he lacked a military background. It just didn't pass the logic test. The briefing officer stated with cool detachment that of the three thousand enemy bandits in the operation, seventeen hundred had been killed. The remainder withdrew from the battle, taking with them their dead and their weapons. "How can thirteen hundred rebels carry off seventeen hundred of their dead—and their weapons?" Shebarshin asked naively. "And can such a force represent a threat again after such a defeat?"

The briefer chose to ignore his question, but Shebarshin would soon have an answer from his own sources. There had been almost no enemy casualties in the battle—perhaps fifteen had been killed. Ahmad Shah Massoud had been forewarned of the Soviet thrust into the Panjshir Valley and had pulled out his troops and much of the population of the valley ahead of the attack. Shebarshin would never know for certain who had tipped off Massoud to the assault, but his suspicions pointed to senior officers within the DRA Defense Ministry in Kabul. At any rate, the Soviet sweep into the Panjshir Valley in 1984 created the myth of Ahmad Shah Massoud, the invincible "Lion of the Panjshir." The myth would take on a life of its own as Massoud became the idol of the French and the odds-on darling of the British press, who followed events closely in their old empire.

But Leonid Shebarshin would come to know another side—and there were many—of Massoud. For one thing, he knew about Massoud's secret contacts with Soviet military intelligence through a GRU officer operating under the pseudonym "Adviser." Over the last three years of the Soviet occupation,

Massoud's back channel to the Soviets would serve him well. Always just one step away from a final agreement to cease hostilities, the 40th Army command held back from launching major assaults into Massoud's stronghold until the final stages of their withdrawal from Afghanistan in 1989.

Shebarshin learned another lesson on that first trip to Afghanistan—the Soviet Army's formula for determining enemy casualties. The calculation was derived from a mathematical equation in which the total number of rounds fired at the enemy was divided by a predetermined factor provided by Defense Ministry analysts. The resulting quotient was the official enemy body, regardless of whether any dead were actually found on the battlefield. It was this formula that produced the number of thirty thousand bandits killed in action each year for the last four years. Simple and structured, Shebarshin thought back in 1984. But with absolutely no relationship to reality.

Islamabad, September 1986

The air conditioner in the teak-paneled reception room whirred softly in the background, its gentle hum a welcome damper to the tension generated by the silence in the room. The room was sterile, void of decoration, save for the elegant, framed calligraphy from the Koran hanging in all four corners where the paneled walls met the ceiling. We were in Islamabad, in the inner sanctum of Pakistan's secret intelligence services.

I studied the leaders of the seven resistance parties sitting impassively, even sullenly, in the awkward silence. Their appearance was as varied as their personalities, ranging from unkempt mullah to radical Islamic chic. Sitting there in silence, the seven Afghan leaders cast sidelong glances in my direction, sizing me up one by one as they waited. We were all waiting for Major General Akhtar Abdur Rahman Khan, director general of Pakistan's Inter-Services Intelligence Directorate, known universally as ISI. There had been no introductions—they would have to wait for Akhtar's grand entrance.

My view of the war, after two months on the scene, was uncomplicated. It was clear that of all the confrontations in the mountains, valleys, and deserts of that tortured country over the millennia, few were ever about Afghanistan itself or its people. Whether it was Alexander the Great, or a string of Mogul emperors, or imperial Britain and Russia jockeying for advantage in the great game, the clashing of armies in Afghanistan was always a derivative of some larger campaign of conquest. The people living between the Oxus and the Indus Rivers were secondary, almost incidental, to the goals of the great empires as their armies marched into or passed through Afghanistan.

This latest round of conflict was no exception. Regardless of the moral underpinnings of Jimmy Carter's initial stand on the Soviet invasion, American goals had moved beyond Carter's early vision of right and wrong. Our effort in Afghanistan had now become a central component of the endgame of the Cold War. Driving the Soviets out of Afghanistan was the goal; the welfare of the people of Afghanistan would be improved along the way, it was hoped, but that was not essential.

These Afghan leaders, too, knew how secondary their aspirations and sufferings were to our seemingly common goal of fighting the Soviet 40th Army. While the Afghan people might have reason to respect or possibly even like their fleeting American allies, their leaders would never trust our motives, nor would they expect us to trust theirs. We might share a few goals, but only a fool would think we shared real values. All in all, I thought it was an honest enough way to do business.

Akhtar breezed into the room with his interpreter, a Pashto-speaking colonel known by the camp name "Bacha." The general shook hands around the room and immediately launched into an opening monologue, enlightening the assembled Afghan leaders on the importance of America's new contribution to the war and the courage of the Pakistani president for raising the struggle against the Soviets to a new level. Somewhere in the middle of his more than a little imperious opening he introduced me as the new American in charge of the arms pipeline to the fighters. Overdone, I thought, but good theater.

Akhtar, Zia's point man on Afghanistan, was the only serving general officer in the Pakistani Army other than the president himself, who had begun his career in the British Indian Army almost four decades earlier. At sixty-one he was slim and fit, an image he worked hard to maintain. His khakis were crisply starched, and his eyes were clear and commanding, but with a secretive cast that left me wondering where the truth might be found, or even if it could be found. In the official pecking order of the Pakistani Army, Akhtar ranked below the generals who commanded the key army corps garrisoned throughout Pakistan and below the service chiefs. But in real terms, Akhtar was as close to Zia as any general in the Army, and he made a point of reminding all who might have questioned his authority that he was quartered in Rawalpindi Cantonment practically next door to his friend. A man of unquestioned loyalty to Zia, Akhtar had been running his Afghan effort since its inception. His approach to the Afghan leaders swung between patronizing and paternal.

To my right was Sibghatullah Mojaddedi, leader of the "moderate" Front for the Rescue of Afghanistan. A small man with a medium-cropped beard mostly gone gray, Mojaddedi was a revered leader of the Naqshbandi Sufi sect and the head of a family of religious leaders with long involvement in modern Afghan politics. He had been imprisoned in Kabul a number of times, once for plotting to assassinate Khrushchev in the early 1960s on a state visit to Afghanistan. His party had a reputation for corruption and ineffectiveness on the battlefield. Mojaddedi himself hadn't been inside Afghanistan in three years, perhaps longer, and his party's only real strength was its gift for public relations. In that department it was near the top. The diminutive leader caught me studying him and flashed a faint smile, perhaps welcoming me to the fight. I held his gaze for just a second, knowing I was being scrutinized by the others, always on the lookout for signs of threatening alliances.

Next to Mojaddedi was Professor Burhanuddin Rabbani, the lone Tajik among the "Peshawar Seven"—the other six were from the Pashtun majority that made up over 40 percent of the Afghan population. A former professor of Islamic law at Kabul University, Rabbani bore some resemblance to the diminutive Sufi sitting by his side on the couch. He had the same salt-and-pepper beard, the same gentle eyes, and the same impassive demeanor. But all similarity stopped there. Rabbani was a tough infighter who at forty-six had built a large and effective resistance party from his northern base in Badakhshan, in the process luring away large numbers of able commanders from other resistance parties. The most famous commander in Rabbani's Jamiat Islami, which translates loosely as "Community of Islam," was the fabled Ahmad Shah Massoud, whose stronghold was in the Panjshir Valley north of Kabul. Rabbani was a cipher. I could read nothing in his face as he stared at the floor. He didn't scan the room and appeared to have no interest in making eye contact with me.

Gulbuddin Hekmatyar, on Mojaddedi's other side, leaned forward slightly in his seat and took a long look at me. He was a commanding presence, and his movements drew the others involuntarily into following his gaze. Hekmatyar was the darkest of the Afghan leaders, the most Stalinist of the Peshawar Seven, insofar as he thought nothing of ordering an execution for a slight breach of party discipline. He was the single leader who stirred controversy in both Moscow and Washington, where his brand of paranoid fundamentalism was equally understood and feared. The KGB had a special *disinformation* team tasked with sowing discord among the Peshawar Seven, and Gulbuddin Hekmatyar, as Pakistan's favorite, was its central target. The line from Moscow blended known facts with classic KGB fantasy. There was the story of Gulbuddin the Kabul University radical throwing acid in the faces of young Afghan women who refused to wear the veil; the cool murderer, killing with his own hands fighters who violated his code of loyalty. And there was in furtive circulation a KGB-forged order from Gulbuddin to one of his lieutenants for the murder of one or more of the other Afghan leaders.

Gulbuddin Hekmatyar was forty, of medium height and build, with clear, olive skin and a coal black beard to match his black eyes. He wore a light gray wool *shalwar kameez* under an open black vest and a tightly wound black turban. A former classmate of Ahmad Shah Massoud's, Gulbuddin was now the Panjshir commander's mortal enemy. Colliding ambitions would have been enough to keep them at sword point, but their ethnic difference—Massoud was Tajik, Hekmatyar Pashtun—added tribal distrust as a multiplier of their hatred. Though convenient battlefield alliances had been forged from time to time, they had long since torpedoed any existing common ground. Their rivalry would become a preoccupation for the remainder of the war, setting the stage for more brutal competition in the years ahead.

I watched Gulbuddin as he fingered his agate prayer beads and waited for him to speak. But he said nothing, and the moment was again commandeered by General Akhtar, who had watched closely the silent interplay between us and now drew the attention of those in the room back to himself.

"To ensure that this new weapons program is an unqualified success, I will ask that each of you take personal responsibility for the monitoring and control of these new antiaircraft missiles. If any of these weapons fall into enemy hands, or if I hear of any of these missiles being sold to others, I will hold each of you personally responsible. Anything less than your complete commitment to these measures will be a serious betrayal of the jihad." Akhtar's admonition was stilted and overly officious, but he had laid out the new procedures neatly for my benefit. Invoking Islam and the sanctity of the jihad had been a flourish for his audience.

Gulbuddin was the first to pick up the signal from Akhtar that the discussion period had opened. Speaking in Pashto, in a controlled tone, he was a few seconds into his presentation when Akhtar cut him off.

"Engineer Gulbuddin, please speak English," Akhtar said, barely concealing his irritation. "Your English is perfectly good."

"Of course, General," Gulbuddin replied, and he picked up where he had left off, this time in precise, uninflected English.

"I wish to take this opportunity to reiterate the gratitude of the people of Afghanistan to President Zia and to you, General Akhtar, for the steadfast support you and your countrymen have given to us in our time of need. I also thank our friend for the assistance his government has provided us through Pakistan in the past. That assistance has allowed us to stand up to the Russian invaders, and now to stop them—"

"Thank you, Engineer Gulbuddin," said Akhtar, cutting him off again. "I think we can move on from here."

Akhtar's abrupt intervention came as a surprise, and not only to me. Even Rabbani lifted his eyes from the floor. Gulbuddin was the Pakistanis' favorite—Zia and the powerful Islamic parties saw him as Pakistan's "solution" in postwar Afghanistan—yet he was being put down here in front of me and the others. I decided later that Akhtar thought he might be building up to an attack on the United States and decided not to give him enough rope to hang himself on our first encounter.

Another voice broke in, bringing the tension down a notch. I glanced to my left and caught sight of Pir Sayed Ahmad Gailani, the only leader among the seven who'd come to the meeting in a silk-and-cashmere suit instead of a *shalwar kameez*.

"I have no reservations as to the requirements for accountability," he said, "and can guarantee that the fighters of the National Islamic Front for Afghanistan will do their duty to provide complete protection for the missiles entrusted to them." As he spoke in his cultured English accent, I took stock of the dapper Gailani. A small, well-trimmed goatee, an affectation of the old Kabul elite, European tailor, Italian cobbler, a Patek Philippe peeking out from under the cuff of his $2,000 suit. No wonder his men were called "Gucci commanders," I thought. Gailani was a true holy man, a hereditary *pir* of the Qadiriya Sufi sect, with which most Pashtun Afghans are associated. He came from a wealthy family broadly associated with prerevolutionary leaders of Afghanistan. He rarely, if ever, strayed into Afghanistan, preferring instead to spend much of his time in London, and he was Europe's most popular moderate Afghan leader.

The third so-called moderate, Nabi Mohammedi, neither spoke English nor understood it. A religious leader and former Afghan parliamentarian, Nabi simply nodded in agreement with whatever Ahktar was saying through Colonel Bacha. He looked bored, and every so often he'd open his small snuff can and snort a pinch of the powdered tobacco. Among the three moderates, Nabi's party, the Movement for the Islamic Revolution of Afghanistan, was the least public relations oriented, the least corrupt, and the most effective in the field.

Across the room from me were the other two hard-liners, Abdul Rasul Sayyaf, a great barrel of a man and an ardent member of the Muslim Brotherhood, and Maulvi Yunis Khales, the red-bearded mullah from Nangarhar. Khales spoke no English. Sayyaf claimed not to, either, but he betrayed himself with a look of understanding as Gulbuddin and Gailani spoke.

A Cairo-educated professor of Islam, Sayyaf wore a perpetual half smile, as if he were sharing a secret with whomever he happened to have locked in his gaze. He formed a party jointly with Gulbuddin Hekmatyar in the early 1980s, after he was released from prison, but the union was short-lived. They shared common origins in the Muslim Brotherhood and solid connections to Saudi money, but little else. Sayyaf spoke fluent Arabic and was particularly popular among the Arabs who were arriving in Pakistan and Afghanistan in increasing numbers from Egypt, Saudi Arabia, and the Persian Gulf.

The last of the Peshawar Seven was a unique character of the Afghan War, Maulvi Yunis Khales, the mullah from Nangarhar. In his mid-sixties, Khales looked severe and forbidding, but behind the long, scraggly beard tinted red with henna was a face with a hint of kindness and a constant look of bewilderment as he contemplated so many things that seemed beyond his control. Khales was a regional leader, without pretense to national stature like some of the others in the room. His operations were generally limited to the eastern provinces of Nangarhar and Paktia, but where many of the other leaders stayed put in Pakistan, Khales, even at his age, went into Afghanistan regularly with his men to lead the fight.

Khales was the least politically complicated of the seven. He was committed to fighting the Russians until they left his country. After that, he would most likely disappear from the political scene and return to his chores as the head of a *madrassa,* an Islamic school where he had once taught his students lessons from the Koran. Word had it that the old Koranic teacher had enough energy left over to pour into his new bride, who was said to be about a quarter his age and who was rumored to be carrying a new descendant in an already long line of Nangarhari holy men.

Khales spoke in Pashto at some length, then waited for Colonel Bacha to translate. I caught a brief exchange of glances between Akhtar and Bacha, nothing more than an almost imperceptible shake of the head and a corresponding nod from Bacha. When Khales finished, the colonel translated in just a few sentences what had taken him much longer to say.

"Maulvi Khales says that what President Zia has decided and what the American President has promised will be good for the jihad," said Bacha. "He says that he will do his part to ensure that the special weapons are controlled."

Akhtar finished up quickly and invited us into the dining room for lunch, effectively closing out any further discussion.

The centerpiece of the luncheon that followed was roasted quail served with crisp efficiency by the military stewards in khaki uniforms with red Afridi tribal headgear. The lunch itself was uneventful, with a minimum of small talk. The Afghans were in a great rush to finish in time for the noonday call to prayers, and they ate their lunch hurriedly. The only drama I witnessed at the table was the specter of Sayyaf, wedged between Mojaddedi and Gailani, struggling to make sense of the Western dining setting. First he ate Gailani's salad, then Mojaddedi's, then he took bread from both. There must be symbolism in this, I thought. Mojaddedi looked across the table at me with an expression that seemed to say, *See what I have to put up with?*

Despite the theater, these seven leaders were there for a reason: They served as the conduits for as many as a quarter million full- and part-time fighters in the field. There were more parties, notably the Shia Hazaras, who'd been cut out of the usual pipeline. Try as we might, we couldn't seem to bring the number down below seven—and if all the parties claiming a right to a seat at the table in Peshawar had actually been included, it would have grown to many more. The lion's share of the logistical and financial support we provided through the Pakistanis went to the three so-called fundamentalist parties, led by Rabbani, Hekmatyar, and Khales. Sayyaf came in a close fourth, and the three moderates pulled up the rear.

I would have to deal with the Washington fan clubs of the three moderate parties for the rest of the war, and with the recurring suggestion that if we would only funnel more supplies to the moderates, not only would the war end sooner, but nice guys would be in charge at the finish. But the reality was that Islam, in its unique Afghan incarnation, was the one thing that held the fighters together. Trying to socially engineer Afghanistan through our distribution of weapons while the Soviets still had 120,000 troops on the ground was, I thought, a recipe for disaster, though the case would be made later that the war itself had done its own social reengineering.

4

Ojhri Camp, Rawalpindi, Pakistan, September 1986

The only illumination in the primitive classroom emanated from a pinpoint light source projecting from behind a white sheet draped across the front of the room. I stood in the back, watching as a group of mujahideen from Gulbuddin Hekmatyar's party sat stiffly on benches and listened as a Pakistani officer drilled them one more time on the firing sequence of the Stinger. A handful of Pakistani officers had been taught how to use the missile in the United States a few months earlier, and they were now training the Afghans. Standing there taking in the scene, I mused about the cost differential between the massive multimillion-dollar Stinger training dome in Ft. Bliss, Texas, and this little classroom with its white bedsheet scrawled with a hand-painted scene of Afghan terrain. Behind the sheet, a Pakistani noncommissioned officer slowly moved a penlight whose light source the students would track and eventually "kill" with their Stinger training units. Primitive, but it did the job for about a hundred bucks.

Tight screening of candidates for training had been one of the conditions we set down in introducing the Stinger. The Afghan trainees in this and all subsequent groups would be vetted both for skill and reliability. Leading candidates were drawn from the pool of mujahideen gunners who had already brought down Soviet or DRA aircraft with SA-7 missiles, an inferior Soviet copy of a much older American missile that had been in the mujahideen arsenal for a few years but used with little success. The need for skill was obvious, but reliability was equally important: There was still a great deal of concern that the Afghans might turn around and sell their Stingers. And with Iran and the Soviet Union bordering Afghanistan, there would be no shortage of bidders. Like all other programs in which we were involved, only Afghan fighters were to be trained. No foreign volunteers would be included in the program; they were a motley lot, increasingly the dredges of the prison populations of the Arab world.

At one time, the CIA had mulled over the idea of training volunteer Arab legions to take part in the war, but the idea was immediately scrapped as unwise and unworkable. Contrary to what people have come to imagine, the CIA never recruited, trained, or otherwise used Arab volunteers. The Afghans were more than happy to do their own fighting—we saw no reason not to satisfy them on this point.

"Lights!" the chief instructor said in Dari from the rear of the room, and the classroom quickly lit up, revealing a collection of a dozen mujahideen. In their midst was Engineer Ghaffar, a heavily bearded man clearly in charge of the group. I had been fully briefed on the fighters being trained—including Ghaffar, who had two confirmed kills using SA-7s. The fighters, to a man, wore regulation full-length beards. All wore gray or beige *shalwar kameez* and rolled Chitrali hats.

"Ready for a final two-man drill?" the officer asked his unconventional students.

Ghaffar, Stinger training unit in hand, was now joined by his second gunner. He nodded without comment.

"Lights out! Procedure drill!" the instructor barked, handing a second Stinger training unit to the second gunner. He shouted a few orders to his assistants behind the sheet, alternating between Dari and English for my benefit. It appeared the group had been prepared well for my visit. Having undergone inspections myself back when I was in uniform, I had no reason to expect the game would be played differently here.

"Give us two targets. High left and center right!"

"Ready?"

"Ready," answered the two gunners in unison.

"First step?"

"Stinger on the shoulder!" came the instant reply.

"Second step?"

"Knock off the front cover and pop up the sight!"

"Third?"

"Screw the battery cooling unit into the well, start the gyro motor with the thumb switch," Ghaffar announced without hesitation. I got a running translation from the Pakistani brigadier escorting me through the camp.

"Start tracking! Ghaffar high left target, Gul the right target!" the Pakistani officer ordered.

The gyro motor noise grew louder as the two units tracked their targets and the cheek-to-bone vibrators began to kick in, reverberating against the gunners' cheeks. Each time the training units locked on to the infrared target, the room was enveloped by the shrill screech of the "identification friend or foe" alarm. There had been some debate as to whether the Stingers issued to the mujahideen should even have the IFF feature, since there were no friends in the skies of Afghanistan. In the end, the IFF stayed—and the fighters simply considered it another part of the sound-and-light show they valued so highly. Cheek-to-bone vibrators were a useful complement to the shrill siren of the IFF, in that they sent a physical confirmation that the gunner was on target when he might not be able to hear the IFF in the din of battle.

"What's next?" the instructor shouted.

"Uncage!" came the instant response from both commanders as both men hit the black rubber-covered "uncage" button on the left side and at the forward end of the grip stock.

A loud siren filled the room, and the vibration told both gunners that they were ready to fire.

"What's next?"

"Superelevate. Place the target in the sight. Pull the trigger." Two voices spoke as one.

"Your targets are MI-24Ds. Which of the three sights do you use?"

"Center sight!"

"Fire! Shut down! Two kills," the instructor said with a smile, relaxing now, clearly pleased with his little demonstration. If the gunners could replicate this precise sequence in the field, they'd bring down their targets every time.

"Engineer Ghaffar, why do you superelevate before you fire?"

"Because the rocket launches out six meters and drops

slightly as the main rocket motor kicks in, sir. Superelevating keeps it lined up on the target it has acquired. If you don't superelevate, the rocket might drop too low to pick up its target once the motor kicks in."

I left the classroom more impressed by the makeshift nature of the training facilities than by the scripted performance arranged for my benefit. Nevertheless, I was convinced that the fighters would be able to use the Stinger successfully. Unlike the British-made Blowpipe that had been introduced almost a year earlier in small numbers, the Stinger was what the Afghans desperately needed—a "fire and forget" missile that allowed a gunner to live and tell of his encounter with Soviet gunships. With a Blowpipe the gunner had to acquire his target optically, fire the missile, and then stand his ground, usually upright and in the open, while he guided the missile with a toggle all the way to the target. The predictable result was an uneven duel between the MI-24D and the lone gunner, with the gunner more often than not ending up a martyr. The Soviet-designed SAM-7, widely available on the gray and black arms markets, was no more effective, but for a different reason. It was reliable, and even then just marginally so, only when it was "looking at" the hot tailpipes of an enemy aircraft. It could rarely acquire an incoming aircraft head-on. So the Afghans would usually have to wait until the enemy aircraft, either a helicopter or a fast mover, came in, dropped its bombs or fired its rockets, and then turned tail, at which time the SAM-7 gunner could pop up and let his missile fly—that is, if he was still alive. In every sense the Stinger was a revolutionary weapon, and even before it was first fired in combat, a belief began to spread through the highly superstitious ranks of the resistance that it possessed certain magical powers. They would eventually come to value the Stinger as their American amulet, their talisman for victory.

Though I hadn't been part of the early political debate in Washington on the wisdom of giving the Afghans the Stinger, I had been brought in peripherally, so I knew something about the furor it had caused on Capitol Hill. Clair George asked me to brief Senator Sam Nunn of the Senate Armed Services Committee on the fact that Stinger technology had already been lost to the Soviets. The GRU officer who'd bought the system from an agent inside NATO was none other than Colonel Sergei Bokhan, the CIA's man in Athens. Now, I thought as I left the training classroom in Ojhri camp, let's hope after all the sound and fury over getting this little baby into the war that it really works.

The Soviets were deeply concerned about the new technology behind the Stinger, and they'd had a couple of years to develop countermeasures. I would soon find out if they had been successful.

Northeast of Jalalabad Airfield, 1505 Hours, September 25, 1986

Engineer Ghaffar and his three dozen fighters had been moving constantly since they had crossed over zero line into Afghanistan one week earlier. Now, on the afternoon of September 25, they were settling into a concealed position about a mile northeast of Jalalabad airfield, some two miles southeast of the city. A thriving trading town that had hosted supply caravans and garrisoned armies for two millennia going back to Alexander the Great, Jalalabad had been the hinge of the bloodiest of Afghanistan's wars going back to antiquity. It was the destination of the ill-fated British garrison that in 1842 set off in retreat from Kabul with 16,500 British and Indian troops. After constant ambush along the ninety-mile line of retreat, only one British officer arrived at Jalalabad safely.

The Soviet garrison at Jalalabad was ideally situated near the point where the Kabul and Konar Rivers joined up and began to wind their way, skirting the Khyber Pass, into Pakistan to join the mighty Indus in its search for the sea. There had been a few Soviet combat air patrols over the last two days as Ghaffar and his men jockeyed into their final firing position, but they had been fast-moving MiGs or Sukhois, flying too high for a sure shot. Ghaffar had let them pass through the area without firing. He was hoping for fresh targets today, possibly MI-24D gunships, the dreaded, heavily armored attack helicopters that had swept over his country with impunity since the invasion. They would usually come home to Jalalabad late in the afternoon, after completing the day's mission. He and his men could wait, hidden in the scrub grass and large boulders on a slight rise in the terrain. That afternoon the wind was blowing from the northwest; landing aircraft, even helicopters, would probably approach from downwind.

Ghaffar and his men sat quietly in their hidden position, fitting the three grip stocks with missiles, checking and rechecking their work, and monitoring enemy troop activity nearby through their binoculars. As the men settled down to wait, a few of the fighters quietly prayed for strength and wisdom in battle. They sought help and guidance from the Creator of Death, the Avenger. Ghaffar himself recited Ya-Rashid, the Guide to the Right Path, to ensure that he would be steered according to His eternal plan.

Ghaffar would later tell me that he had uttered Ya-Rashid for exactly the one thousandth time when his targets came into view, eight beautiful MI-24D gunships. Quickly Ghaffar ordered his other two gunners to their positions. Both perched their weapons on their shoulders, poised like hunters stalking their prey.

"Wait until I give the order to begin the procedures," Ghaffar told his gunners as he shouldered his own weapon. The other fighters took their positions, two of them shouldering their Stingers and preparing for the launch sequence on the order from Ghaffar.

"Knock off your front covers and pop up your sights!"

"Cover off! Sight up!" two voices answered in quick succession.

"Hold your battery cooling units until I give you the order to screw them into the wells!" Ghaffar instructed, excitement building in his voice.

"Altitude one thousand meters, range twenty-five hundred," one of Ghaffar's men called out, giving the others the range of the approaching aircraft.

"Engage BCUs!" Ghaffar shouted, and screwed his battery cooling unit into the well.

"BCU engaged!"

"BCU engaged!"

"Begin tracking!" All three gunners flipped the thumb switch in unison. The sound of the gyro motors gained strength as the Stinger trackers picked up the heat from the approaching helicopters, each gunner sighting in on a prearranged section of the helicopters' formation to avoid wasting a precious missile. By now all three gunners were getting a strong cheek-to-bone vibration, indicating that they had acquired their targets. The IFF signals kicked in, filling the air with a shrill, piercing sound that seemed only to increase the excitement of the team. The gunships had dropped to about one thousand feet as they made their final approach to the Jalalabad airfield.

"Uncage!" Ghaffar ordered. The acknowledgments came almost instantly as the other two gunners hit the rubberized rectangular buttons, fully arming their Stinger missiles.

At this point, each gunner was on his own, relying only on the training he had received at Ojhri camp as he followed the pinpoint of light behind the white sheet. In less than two seconds, the three gunners had superelevated their missile tubes and fired. The first Stinger shot out of Ghaffar's tube, traveled the prescribed six meters on its launch charge, and then failed to ignite. The missile fell to the ground, clattering among the rocks until its momentum was spent. A dud!

But before the impact of that failed launch set in, the second and third gunners had fired their missiles, and the slender arrows shot toward their targets at twice the speed of sound, leaving widening white trails arching across the blue skies above Jalalabad. Ghaffar had reloaded his grip stock with a second tube when the first missile struck its target. The first helicopter exploded in midair and fell like a rock off the end of the runway just as the second missile found its target, sending the second MI-24D into a wild spiral caused by the loss of two of its rotor blades in the explosion. By the time the second gunship hit the ground about six hundred yards from the burning wreckage of the first kill, Ghaffar had reloaded and acquired his second target, zeroing in on one of the five remaining choppers now taking wild evasive actions to avoid whatever was stalking them.

Ghaffar picked his second target carefully. He wanted to kill the lead helicopter in the flight and already had solid cheek-to-bone vibration signaling target acquisition when his target turned toward him and came screaming directly at his position. Ghaffar superelevated his Stinger and fired his second shot of the day while holding his target in the sight. The missile shot out of its tube, ignited its rocket motor instantly, and flew true and straight toward the lead MI-24D as the chopper lay over almost on its side and began dropping right toward him. As the gap closed to less than a thousand meters, Ghaffar saw bright flashes coming from the 23 mm Gatling gun slung under the Hind. The cannon rounds flew wide of their target, kicking up rock as they hit and exploded. The missile closed the remaining gap and exploded on contact with the hot turbine engine.

"Allah hu Akhbar!" came the cries of the fighters all around him. The explosion of the fuel tanks tore the helicopter apart in midair, showering the area with debris. Ghaffar saw the fighter whose job was to videotape the attack jumping up and down with the others, calling out, "God is great!" the red recording light of the Sony still burning and the lens pointing straight at the ground. Ghaffar only hoped that something had been captured on tape before the cameraman was overcome by the excitement of the kills. I would later view the video and see both the confirmed kills and the wild shots of ground, dusty sandals, and sky as the cameraman jumped about.

"Gather up the equipment and be ready to move out in two minutes!" Ghaffar shouted to his fighters, the excitement now out of his voice, having resumed his authority. Turning to his cameraman, he said, "Move as close to the wreckage as you can and get some pictures." Then to another of his team: "Destroy the Stinger that misfired. Pound the center of the missile with a large rock. Be careful not to strike the warhead!"

The standing order had been clear: Functioning Stingers were under no circumstances to fall into enemy hands. Ghaffar made a decision on the spot to destroy the electronic circuitry of the dud missile rather than try to bring it home, fearing its warhead might explode on the way. Within minutes, Ghaffar and his team had cleared the area and were on their way to motorized transportation waiting for them ten kilometers away. They would travel home to Pakistan that evening to report their success. Ghaffar took the frequency hopper radio from one of his fighters' packs and broke radio silence for the first time since he had deployed one week before.

"Three confirmed kills at southeast end of the target airfield," he reported. "Four missiles fired. One missile failure." The secure transmission from Ghaffar's radio flashed to ISI receivers high in the mountains across zero line in Pakistan, sending the electrifying news of the first major victory against the Soviet helicopter fleet.

Islamabad, 2030 Hours, September 25, 1986

An urgent call had come in from Colonel Riaz, aide to General Akhtar, on the evening of the Jalalabad ambush. His message was brief and to the point: The first team deployed to Nangarhar had brought down three targets late that afternoon. Would I please advise Mr. Casey and ask for some satellite coverage of the scene? I returned to the office and reported the claim of success to Langley, along with the observation that on the heels of the Kharga attack just one month earlier, the events at Jalalabad today might trigger a shift in mood of the Afghan resistance.

When I picked up the cable traffic the next morning, I had two messages on top of the stack from headquarters. The first cable thanked me for my account of the shoot-down reports but cautioned me to take claims of success by the mujahideen with a grain of salt. I was instructed to secure independent confirmation of these and future kills.

The second cable, referring back to the first, was short and to the point. It said, in inimitable Langley cablese:

> BELAY REF, SATELLITE IMAGERY CONFIRMS THREE KILLS AT JALALABAD AS REPORTED. PLEASE PASS OUR CONGRATS FOR JOB WELL DONE!

I watched with deep interest as Soviet air operations stood down in eastern Afghanistan over the next week. When operations resumed, patrolling aircraft were flying much higher than before the ambush.

The war was entering a new stage.

Langley, September 26, 1986

Jack Devine, chief of the Afghan Task Force, flipped through the twelve-by-eighteen sheets of the morning pass of satellite coverage of Jalalabad and decided on the spot that the war had taken the turn he needed. On the heels of the total destruction of the ammo dump at Kharga a month earlier, what he saw before him gave him the crucial ingredient he was looking for—momentum. He picked up the phone and dialed Casey's officc two floors up.

When the DCI's secretary came on the line, he said, "Jack Devine. Can I see him right now? I've got some photos he ought to see."

"Come on up and I'll work you in," said the DCI's secretary.

Devine made a quick call to the DDO's office to inform Clair George and his deputy, Tom Twetten, that he was heading up to Casey's office to show the DCI the satellite photos of the Jalalabad shoot-downs, getting quick clearance to skip the chain of command.

The Jalalabad imagery was a fluke, a lucky hit by a satellite that just happened to be passing over in an orbit that offered cloudless coverage of Jalalabad hours after Engineer Ghaffar brought down the first three helicopters. But it was a fluke that came at the perfect time.

Casey was alone when Devine was ushered into his office. As Devine spread the imagery sheets on the desk, Casey leaned over to get a better look.

"These are the three helicopters brought down in the first deployment," Jack said, pointing to the burned-out hulks clearly visible in the high-resolution satellite photos.

There was a twinkle in Casey's eye as he said, "This changes it all, doesn't it?"

"It does. There hasn't been a day like this in a long time."

"They're gonna lose, aren't they?" Casey mumbled.

"This changes the dynamic. That's for certain," Devine answered, not willing to go as far as Casey seemed to be taking the first Stinger attack.

"Leave 'em with me, Jack. I'll take 'em down to the President."

The meeting was over almost before it started. But Devine left the DCI's office convinced that the old man really believed something new had entered the equation in Afghanistan. Now if only they could keep it up.

Islamabad, September 30, 1986

I hit the rewind button and played the tape again. I could make out Engineer Ghaffar, full black beard and beige rolled-wool Chitrali hat, just as he elevated and fired off his Stinger. Then the shaky picture cut to another gunner firing and to his missile drawing its white condensation trail in a graceful arc across the cloudless sky. The next frames showed the missile closing in on an MI-24D helicopter now centered on the screen. As the missile struck the chopper's engine, the sound of the explosion was drowned out by the cries of Ghaffar's team shouting over and over, *"Allah hu Akhbar!"* The next minute of tape was a collage of jumping feet, earth, sky, and an occasional knee, as the cameraman on Ghaffar's team abandoned his task of recording the ambush, dropped his camera to his side, and joined in the celebration when two more helicopters were brought down in rapid succession.

After another break in the sequence, the twisted hulk of one of the downed helicopters came into focus. Then a crouching mujahideen with a Kalashnikov at his side floated into the field of vision, approaching the crash site on foot. The final ten seconds of the film were a series of gruesome shots of the Soviet crew of the MI-24D, their lifeless bodies strewn about the wreckage. In the background audio were the voices of the Stinger team, their Pashto curses and epithets being hurled at the mutilated crewmen, punctuated by rapid fire from their Kalashnikovs. The body of one of the dead crewmen bounced and rolled a little as the submachine rounds ripped into it. Finally, the camera zoomed in on the face of a dead Soviet soldier. He looked about twenty, his face somehow peaceful in the awful setting. I thought of my own son, a Ranger officer who spent a lot of his time in helicopters, and of these dead soldiers' parents somewhere in the USSR.

I turned to my admin chief. "Make copies of this and get it off to the task force right away. But cut out the last scene at the crash site. I don't want that to go to Washington. Let me see it again when you've edited it."

Kabul, 40th Army Headquarters, September 30, 1986

The reaction in Kabul to the first Stinger ambush outside Jalalabad was mixed. On the one hand, a near total stand-down on flight activity was called within hours of the Jalalabad incident while 40th Army investigation teams surveyed the scene of the ambush, debriefed the surviving aircrews, and drew their conclusions. The instant assessment was that the

American Stinger had finally been deployed, an issue that Soviet intelligence had followed closely while it was debated openly in Washington during the previous year. Within a day, orders were issued to secure "bandit-free areas" in a ten-mile radius from all air bases in Afghanistan. It was an impossible order, and the 40th Army command knew it. But issuing it seemed to demonstrate an ability to deal with the new threat. Additionally, all aircraft landing or taking off were instructed to make spiral descents and climb-outs at the airfields. The new rule of thumb was that twenty thousand feet was the assured safety altitude, about twice the ceiling of the Stinger.

Great efforts were made to assure Soviet and Afghan pilots and aircrews that the Stinger was just another problem that could be dealt with. Soon, they were told, aircraft would be fitted with systems for dispensing high-intensity flares that would draw the infrared-seeking Stingers away from the heat of the aircraft engines by luring them to lock on to the flares falling away from the aircraft.

More quietly, however, 40th Army headquarters began closely documenting the effectiveness of the new American missile, noting how many rebel groups were being equipped with Stingers, how many had been fired, and how many Soviet or DRA aircraft had been struck. Within the first year they calculated the success rate of the Stinger at 20 percent, up from about 3 percent when the rebels used the inferior Soviet SA-7 system.

Langley, Early October 1986

Tensions between the Soviet and Near East analysts on the task force had increased since the first Stinger ambush at Jalalabad. There were reports coming in from all sources—signals, intelligence, human intelligence reporting, and satellite imagery—that put the level of Soviet and DRA aircraft brought down over the last few weeks at about one a day, or one every two to three days if you took the more conservative estimate. The Soviet analysts would not accept the higher number and demanded photographic confirmation of every aircraft shoot-down before it would be counted.

Jack Devine dismissed the debate as senseless and left it to the analysts to argue out. What he did see was the immediate stand-down of air activity following the shoot-down and the change in Soviet air tactics once flights were resumed. The "Stinger effect" wasn't just a matter of numbers; it was also the increase in morale and effectiveness of the resistance forces. There'd been a shift in the tone of reporting from Islamabad, too, in the week following the Jalalabad ambush. No longer were the mujahideen sitting in their camps in Pakistan awaiting their fates. They were pouring into eastern Afghanistan, now that interdiction by Soviet and DRA aircraft of their infiltration routes seemed reduced. Yes, Devine said to himself, September 25 was a turnaround. Let the purists worry about the numbers. He knew what it meant, and so did his team in Islamabad.

Over the next week, Devine would show the dramatic video footage of the downing of the MI-24Ds to selected members of Congress and the Reagan administration. Bill Casey would run the tape himself for President Reagan. The effect in Washington was just as it had been in Afghanistan: A new sense of commitment could be felt to stay the course. And it couldn't have come at a better time. When Casey got out to Pakistan for his next visit, there would be something tangible to celebrate with the men he had supported for the last six years.

5

Islamabad, October 1986

Casey would never make his promised visit to Islamabad—his world was rapidly narrowing to Washington, where he had fallen prey to the growing rumblings of Iran-contra and to a Congress increasingly after his blood. But his deputy, Robert Gates, traveled to the field in late October. His visit got off to a jumpy start.

In the cable exchanges leading up to the DDCI's visit, I had asked that the traveling party stay in a duplex house I controlled in a quiet residential quarter of Islamabad. I thought we could move about more discreetly than if the party stayed in the high-visibility Holiday Inn in Islamabad, with its usual contingent of international media. Gates's administrative staff agreed, until word percolated down to them that the intended quarters were also the location of our temporary storage site for the Soviet weapons systems we had acquired through an elaborate program of battlefield scavenging in Afghanistan. It seems that Gates's security chief couldn't bear the thought of the DDCI sleeping with a Soviet AT-4 antitank guided missile ready to cook off under his bunk. Could we clear out the explosive stuff before bedding down our visitors? I was urgently asked. I assured headquarters that we could.

The Khyber Agency, Pakistan

It was a crystalline, dry season day, dry even for that time of year, when I took Gates and his party to the Khyber Agency training site in a mix of helicopters—two slick French-made Pumas and a rattling American UH1 "Huey." The Pakistani pilots swept low over mud-walled villages tucked into the foothills of the North-West Frontier Province, the scrub pines of the hilltops passing just feet below us as we cleared the ridgelines. Dropping down on the billowing red smoke canister signaling the wind direction at the primitive heliport, Gates mused that much, maybe too much, preparation had gone into his visit. He would later use the term *Potemkin village,* but I preferred to describe what we were seeing as good public relations. I told him to treat it as the best show the Pakistanis and the Afghans could put on for us and judge it on those terms. Military inspections were pretty much the same everywhere—a lot of show and no surprises.

The Pakistani officers handling Gates's visit had been through it before with Casey's visits to the region and the growing traffic from Washington. They knew how to take care of their American visitors with a flashy trip to the North-West Frontier Province, the Wild West tribal area of Pakistan where the mujahideen training sites were set up. The camps, designed to handle up to a hundred Afghan fighters for a week or two at a time, were usually struck after a couple of training cycles and moved to another location. There were endless possibilities for training sites in the rugged northwest, and it seemed that the Soviets and their Afghan intelligence service, Khad, were never able to effectively track our movements. Not one of the camps was successfully attacked by air or by infiltration teams during the years I was involved with the program.

A bunch of small arms had been laid out for review: assault rifles, light and medium machine guns, rocket-propelled grenade launchers (RPG-7)—the hands-down favorite of the mujahideen—and 75 and 82 mm recoilless rifles. Crew-served weapons, 12.7 and 14.5 mm machine guns, 82 mm mortars, and 107 and 122 mm free-flight rockets, were also set up for firing, and the Pakistanis and their trainees put on an incomparable show. They fired everything in their arsenals at targets whitewashed onto the surrounding hillsides at two hundred, three hundred, and one thousand yards, and they put on a damn good show.

One blue-eyed young Afghan gunner—he looked no more than fifteen—snapped up an RPG-7 on command and quickly slipped a round in the muzzle, pulling the safety pin and streamer out of the conical warhead as he laid the launcher on his shoulder. He brought the outline of a Soviet tank two hundred yards away into the optical sight and fired, all in about two seconds. As the round struck the target dead center with a great explosion and a shower of rocks, there were a hundred cries of approval. We saw white rock after white rock "destroyed" by the small arms, prompting Gates to wonder if the gunners might not be Pakistani shills. I thought not. The one thing it had never been necessary to fake in Afghanistan was shooting skill.

After the small-arms demonstrations, we walked a few hundred yards to another area where the mortars, rockets, and recoilless rifles would be fired at targets—large chalked circles—one and two thousand yards down the narrow valley. Along the way, hidden, heavily camouflaged mujahideen would pop up out of rabbit holes or from under scrub bushes just at our feet, shouting menacingly while training their Kalashnikovs on Gates and me. All great theater, at least after the first one had popped up.

The crew-served weapons were demonstrated with the same skill—almost all direct hits on the chalked targets. Gates again wondered aloud how much of what he was seeing was real. I told him I wasn't sure it mattered. The weapons were real, the people were real, and if they ultimately took the guns and their skills to war against the Soviets, that was good enough for our purposes. It would all be just fine as long as the war continued to go our way.

Late on the evening after our visit to the Khyber Agency, I arranged for a close relative of Commander Ahmad Shah Massoud's to visit Bob Gates discreetly in the privacy of the safe house. Massoud's man made the usual pitch to the DDCI, telling him that the Pakistanis were giving the lion's share of the supplies to Massoud's archfoe, Gulbuddin Hekmatyar, and that as proof of the claim of Pakistani favoritism it was a Hekmatyar commander who was given the first issue of Stingers. Would Gates intercede with the Pakistanis and see to it that Massoud got his share of Stingers? Gates said he would and promised also to talk to the Pakistanis about establishing a more equitable share of all the ordnance.

Eager to demonstrate his gratitude, Massoud's man reached inside his *shalwar kameez* and whipped out a Soviet 9 mm Makarov semiautomatic. Would the DDCI accept this small offering as a token of appreciation from Ahmad Shah Massoud?

As he began to explain that the cold, dead fingers of a Soviet colonel had been pried from the weapon by Commander Massoud himself after a great battle in the Panjshir Valley, the DDCI's security detail had their hands on their own weapons in a sort of Mexican standoff and were waiting nervously a few feet away to see what would come next. Nothing did, but for the next three years I would have to brief the security details of high-level visitors to expect a Makarov to pop into the scene at some point during discreet meetings with mujahideen commanders.

Bob Gates left Islamabad with a good understanding of the way things were going at a critical moment in the war. During his meeting with President Zia, he had been told that the heat should be turned up in the war, but that care should be taken so the pot did not boil over. President Zia asked pointedly for intelligence on India's plans for a major military exercise on its border with Pakistan, Operation Brasstacks. The Pakistanis had been concerned for weeks over the training exercise planned by India's new and hawkish Army chief of staff, General Krishnaswami Sundarji. The DDCI responded with the standard "Friends do not discuss friends with friends," but he added another important line to that answer. He said that neither do friends let friends get into trouble. That statement, though vague and noncommittal, seemed to satisfy the Pakistanis for the moment, as they believed that whatever was to happen in Brasstacks, the United States would be watching and would intervene before things got out of control.

First Chief Directorate Headquarters, Yasenevo, October 1986

Leonid Shebarshin had been briefed that all of the technical countermeasures against the Stinger had been put in place. Soviet and DRA aircrews were flying above the ceiling of the American missile and taking intensive defensive precautions when approaching and departing from airfields in Afghanistan, particularly those in the east.

The KGB's point man on Afghanistan had also learned that over the last few days the GRU had successfully acquired two Stinger missiles from their penetrations of Afghan resistance groups. He was unaware of the details of the GRU's previous acquisition of the documentation on the missile from a NATO source, though he did know that the Defense Ministry had a set of countermeasures ready to put into effect almost immediately after the Jalalabad shoot-downs of the three MI-24Ds. With the acquisition of the two Stingers and the development of even more effective tactical and technical countermeasures, the impact of the Americans' new missile might be reduced.

Much ado about nothing, Shebarshin had concluded. The military would manage to carry out its mission, but the real challenge in Afghanistan remained unchanged.

The Kremlin, November 13, 1986

A sense of fatalism could be felt among the men gathered at the special session of the Politburo to discuss Afghanistan. It had been known for over a year that Gorbachev was determined to quit Afghanistan—he said as much at the Party Congress in February—but it was also known that he had given the Army a year to win, or at least create the illusion of winning, and then get out. Today's meeting was believed by some to signal the end of the waffling. Much of it was there in the restricted minutes of the meeting that Anatoly Chernyaev filed away for his boss:

"Have all comrades familiarized themselves with the memoranda from Comrades Chebrikov, Shevardnadze, Sokolov, and Dobrynin?" Gorbachev opened the meeting with a reference to the documents that had been provided each Politburo member before the meeting.

The handful of men who ran the Soviet Union answered in the expected affirmative.

"Then let us exchange opinions. My intuition is that we not waste time. We have been fighting in Afghanistan already for six years. If our approach is not changed, we will fight for another twenty to thirty years. Our military must be told that they are learning badly from this war. Are we going to fight on endlessly, making a testimony that our troops are incapable of dealing with the matter? We need to finish this process as soon as possible."

Following the rigid protocol of the Politburo, the first member to respond to Gorbachev's opening remarks was the redoubtable Andrei Gromyko, until the previous year the longest-serving Soviet Foreign Minister—twenty-eight years—and now chairman of the Presidium of the Supreme Soviet. It was Gromyko who, a year earlier, had made the speech nominating the new Soviet leader as General Secretary.

"It is necessary that we establish a strategic goal. Too long ago we spoke of the necessity of sealing the borders of Afghanistan with Pakistan and Iran. Experience has shown that we have been unable to do this because of the difficult terrain and the existence of hundreds of passes in the mountains. Today, the necessity is to set the strategic goal of ending the war."

Gorbachev broke in at this point to reinforce Gromyko's point. "It is necessary to include in the resolution the importance of ending the war in the course of one year—at maximum two years," he said.

Gromyko picked up where he left off. "On our part there

was an underestimation of the difficulties when we agreed to give the Afghan government military support. The social conditions in Afghanistan made quick resolution of the problem impossible. There was no support among the population—in the Afghan Army the number of conscripts equals the number of deserters. Just now a more concrete discussion with [Afghan President Muhammad] Najibullah is needed. A certain plan of action is necessary. Here, it seems, our participation is needed, in particular, in contacts with Pakistan. Concerning the Americans, they are not interested in a settlement in Afghanistan. On the contrary, it is to their benefit for the war to drag out."

Gorbachev nodded in agreement and said, "That's right," but this time he did not intervene.

"Right now the situation is worse than half a year ago," Gromyko continued. "In a word, it is necessary for us to pursue more actively a political settlement. Our people will breathe a deep sigh if we undertake steps in that direction. Our strategic goal is to make Afghanistan neutral, not to allow it to go over to the enemy camp. But most important, our goal is ending the war. I would agree that it is necessary to limit this to a period of one to two years."

There was no clear indication in the minutes of how this was received. KGB Chairman Viktor Chebrikov spoke next, in keeping with his rank. "On this question many decisions have been made," he said. "Much energy has been expended. But unfortunately, the situation both in Afghanistan and the region remains difficult. I support the proposal of Mikhail Sergeyevich that it is necessary to push the problem to a logical conclusion. Indeed, we posed the question of sealing the border. Andrei Andreyevich [Gromyko] is partly right, speaking about the difficulties of such an operation, due to geographic and other conditions. But partly the failure in sealing the border was also tied to the fact that not everything was done that could have been. Right now the enemy is changing his tactics. He is going underground. It is necessary to look for the means to a political solution of the problem. The military path for the past six years has not given us a solution. We need to invite Najib to Moscow for frank talks. He has never been here, and it is time for frank talks."

At this point, Foreign Minister Eduard Shevardnadze, the white-haired Georgian who had rapidly gained influence within Gorbachev's foreign policy team, weighed in. "Right now we are reaping the fruit of the hasty decisions of the past. Recently, much has been done to settle the situation in Afghanistan and the region. Najib has assumed the mantle of leadership. He needs practical support, otherwise we will bear the political costs. We must state precisely the period of withdrawal of Soviet troops from Afghanistan. You, Mikhail Sergeyevich, said it correctly—two years. But neither we nor our Afghan comrades have solved the problem of creating an Afghan government that can function without the support of our troops. There is dispute as to who must accomplish the sealing of the borders—the Army or state security organs. I support the proposition of Viktor Mikhailovich [Chebrikov] on the importance of meeting with Najib."

"We can give these instructions to Comrade Kryuchkov, who is now in Kabul," Gorbachev interjected.

"Both Comrade Kryuchkov and Comrade [Yuli] Vorontsov [a senior Foreign Ministry official] are good people," Shevardnadze said, "but their discussions with Najib cannot replace a meeting between Najib and the General Secretary."

"The concept of settlement exists," Gorbachev interjected. "We have established that—but the practicalities remain unresolved." Turning to Deputy Defense Minister Sergei Akhromeyev, he then said, "Sergei Fedorovich, perhaps you will solve it?"

Akhromeyev seemed to sense this was too big a burden for him to take on. "No," he said flatly, "it will not be possible to solve it."

Anatoly Dobrynin, head of the International Department of the Communist Party's Secretariat, and before that the USSR's ambassador to Washington through every U.S. administration from Kennedy to Reagan, stepped into the discussion. "I come out in favor of receiving Najib in Moscow. Right now a message could be sent to Comrade Kryuchkov about the meeting with Najib."

"Military actions in Afghanistan will soon be seven years old," Akhromeyev interjected. "There is no single piece of land in this country that has not been occupied by a Soviet soldier. Nevertheless, the majority of the territory remains in the hands of rebels. The government of Afghanistan has at its disposal a significant military force: 160,000 men in the Army, 115,000 in Sarandoy militia, and 20,000 in state security organs. There is no single military problem that has arisen and that has not been solved, and yet there are still no results. The whole problem lies in the fact that military results are not followed up by political actions. At the center there is authority; in the provinces there is not. We control Kabul and the provincial centers, but on occupied territory we cannot establish authority. We have lost the battle for the Afghan people—the government is supported by a minority of the population. Our Army has fought for five years and is in a position to maintain the situation at its present level. But under such conditions the war will continue for a long time. Fifty thousand Soviet soldiers are stationed to seal off the border, but they are not in a position to close off all passages where cargo is transferred across the border. We have the capacity to maintain the situation at its current level, as I said, but we need to look for a way out and to resolve this question, as Andrei Andreyevich [Gromyko] has said, once and for all. We must go to Pakistan."

"Why do you hinder Najib?" Gorbachev asked his deputy defense minister.

Akhromeyev seemed defensive. "He should not be building headquarters, but a state committee on defense. We allow him to make cadre changes."

Veteran diplomat Yuli Vorontsov, the man tasked with translating the musings of the Politburo into negotiating positions with the Americans and Pakistanis, politely interjected at this point. "A few words, if I may, to continue the thought just expressed by Comrade Deputy Defense Minister. Afghanistan is a peasant country. But it is the peasants who have least benefited from the revolution. There are only five million out of a population of eighteen million under the control of the government. To the question of how this can be explained, I have been told that the regions under the control of the counterrevolution are better supplied with essential goods shipped there as contraband from Pakistan. Urgent measures are needed to improve the situation of peasants in the government zone. Many members of PDPA leadership are without initiative and have gotten used to waiting for recommendations from our advisers. Such is not the case with Comrade Najib. He creates the impression of a talented and decisive person. He must be given the opportunity to make decisions himself, without allowing himself to become distracted by secondary details. And he must have the opportunity to create his own team himself."

Gorbachev waited for Vorontsov to conclude his remarks, and then he spoke again. "In October of last year in a Politburo meeting we set a course of resolving the Afghan question," he said. "The goal we raised was to expedite the withdrawal of our forces from Afghanistan and simultaneously to ensure the emergence of a friendly Afghanistan for us. It was projected that this should be realized through a combination of military and political measures. But there is no movement in either of these directions. The strengthening of the military position of the Afghan government has not taken place. National consolidation has not been ensured, mainly because Comrade Karmal hoped to continue in power in Kabul with our assistance. It was also said that we fettered the actions of the Afghan government. All in all, up until now the projected concept has been poorly realized. The problem is not in the concept itself, but in its realization. We must operate more actively, and with this guide ourselves with two questions. First of all, in the course of two years, we must effect the withdrawal of our troops from Afghanistan. Fifty percent by 1987, and in the following year another fifty percent. Second of all, we must pursue a widening of the social base of the regime, taking into account the arrangement of political forces. In connection with this, we should meet with Comrade Najib and possibly even with other members of the Central Committee of PDPA Politburo. We must start talks with Pakistan. Most important, we must make sure that the Americans don't get into Afghanistan. But I think that Americans will not go into Afghanistan militarily."

Akhromeyev agreed. "They are not going to go into Afghanistan with the armed forces," he said.

Dobrynin added his assent. "One can reach an agreement with the Americans on this question."

"We must give instructions to Comrade Kryuchkov to meet with Najib and invite him to visit the Soviet Union in December," Gorbachev said in conclusion. "It will also be necessary to tell Comrade Najib that he should make key decisions himself. Entrust the comrades, taking into account the discussion that took place in Politburo meetings, to coordinate, make operative decisions, and make necessary proposals on solving the Afghan question and settling the problem of Afghanistan."

The men who ran the USSR announced in a single voice, "We agree."

And the resolution was passed.

6

Washington, December 1986

Casey's luck had begun to run out. It all started in November, when the Republicans lost the Senate and the Iran-contra scandal burst onto the front pages of the world press. By early December, the DCI was beginning to show the effects of what would later be diagnosed as a brain tumor. His security detail had reluctantly shared their concerns with Bob Gates, and a number of Casey's close associates had seen him lose his train of thought, bump into things, and even fall. Nevertheless, Casey continued to keep his schedule of ever rougher congressional hearings on Iran-contra through early December. Congress had begun circling in earnest.

Even eleven time zones away in Islamabad we were beginning to feel the effects of the Iran-contra investigations. Our covert action program in Afghanistan had offered many involved in congressional oversight of CIA programs, staffers and members alike, a balance in an otherwise prickly relationship with the agency. Some hard-core opponents of CIA activities in Central America enthusiastically supported the covert action in Afghanistan. It was clean and neat, while Central America, to them, was cloaked in ambiguities. Supporting our efforts in Afghanistan beefed up their anti-Communist credentials, giving them the leeway to stand firm in their opposition to the contras.

Smelling blood in Iran-contra, some members and their staffs were now looking for a link between the Afghan covert action program and the efforts of Bill Casey and Oliver North to end-run congressional mandates on activities in Central America. No evidence was ever found because there was no link. But that didn't deter those who were digging from thinking that we were stopping ships loaded with ordnance at Karachi and sending them off to Nicaragua and Honduras.

This fresh interest prompted me to open up new areas of inspection for our congressional overseers, to bring them more directly into the nuts and bolts of the program than was required by law or previously allowed by agency management. I quietly began taking the occasional delegations out to the training camps, off to ammunition dumps, to let them see the things they were paying for. The effort had returns—perhaps even to the point of backfiring. It wouldn't be long before everyone on Capitol Hill seemed to want a testosterone-pumping tour of a mujahideen training camp. It was a difficult balancing act, but in the end, the Afghan program succeeded largely because Congress was united behind it. The U.S. funding for the program was congressionally mandated—and Congress came to see it as their program as much as it was the CIA's. It seemed to me that it was better to have Congress inside the tent pissing out than outside the tent pissing in. It worked, especially when there were occasional setbacks and I could turn to the oversight committees as partners rather than adversaries.

But back in Washington, things were going from bad to worse for Bill Casey. He was deteriorating visibly day by day. Concerns over his condition had finally reached the point that the senior agency physician, Arvel Tharpe, insisted on looking in on him in his office on the morning of December 15. During his examination, the DCI had a seizure with violent muscle spasms. Dr. Tharpe gave Casey an injection of Valium to control the muscle spasms and set in motion the emergency procedures that had long been in effect for a DCI falling ill in his office. Within minutes Casey was on his way to Georgetown University Hospital.

Lahore, Pakistan, 2130 Hours, December 17, 1986

General Akhtar's aide asked me to hold the line, he would put the general on in just a second. I was sitting in my room at the Pearl Continental Hotel in Lahore, having a nightcap with Marie-Catherine, when the call came through, and instinctively I knew it would not be good news. Akhtar's voice confirmed my hunch.

"Milton, you've got to get word to Mr. Casey that the Indians are becoming dangerously provocative with their buildup on the border."

"I'll see what I can do," I said, thinking it wouldn't be much till I got back to Islamabad.

"Mr. Casey should know right away that the situation is dangerous," Akhtar repeated, as he often did when the subject was Indian machinations.

There was little I could say. Not only was I out of pocket in Lahore and away from my secure communications, and not only did I have absolutely no new details on the level of alert on the Indo-Pak border, but I had learned the previous day that Casey had "come down with something" at Langley two days earlier and was in a Washington hospital undergoing tests. No further information was available. Apparently, news of Casey's health hadn't yet reached Pakistan. I decided not to say anything at the time for fear of exciting an already excited General Akhtar. Bill Casey seemed to be the general's personal talisman.

"I'll be back in Islamabad first thing tomorrow, General, and I'll get in touch as soon as I arrive."

"I'll send a car," he offered.

"I'll call as soon as I get back," I repeated.

"It's tomorrow, then," Ahktar said, and rang off.

Islamabad, December 18, 1986

The next morning, Akhtar was all business. He had maps out on his table and ran through positions and troop deployments as he gave me the Pakistani assessment of General Sundarji's training exercise on the border.

"They're using this as an excuse to crack down on Sikh separatists," Akhtar said. "The Indians, particularly General Sundarji, are always accusing us of creating problems with the Sikhs. But everybody knows it was Sundarji himself who caused all the problems—he was behind the incident at the Sikh temple, you know."

I did indeed know that two years earlier General Sundarji had stormed the Sikhs' holiest shrine in Amritsar, the Golden Temple, setting off one of the bloodiest Sikh uprisings in a decade of uprisings. And I knew that the Indians, like the Pakistanis, always saw their neighbor's hand in their internal problems.

As if on cue, Akhtar added, "The Indians are mucking around in the Sindh, stirring up trouble for us there. I'm certain they're going to do something dangerous—you have to pass that along to Casey. We need his help. We need to know if the Indians are planning to move up to the border."

"I'll pass your concerns along," I said noncommittally. I was seeing firsthand the depth of distrust between the Indians and Pakistanis. There was no limit to what one side was willing to believe of the other. The intensity verged on the psychotic, and it would not be the last time that I would be drawn into escalating tensions between the two countries. The split between India and Pakistan was like a bad divorce, all the more acrimonious because of their long bond and cohabitation.

As I prepared to leave, I decided to tell Akhtar that Casey wasn't well. There was still no official word on his condition, but I wanted Akhtar to hear it from me rather than from the press or from his attaché in Washington.

"General," I said, turning back to him at the door, "I've just heard that Mr. Casey was taken ill three days ago. They're running some tests in the hospital. Bob Gates is acting DCI now, and I'll pass your concerns directly on to him. It's a good thing that he was just out here for a visit. He'll have a leg up on the situation."

Akhtar was suspicious. "You're sure it's just some tests?"

"So far as I know," I answered.

I could see Akhtar had his doubts about Casey's tests being routine. The pessimist in him was taking hold—he seemed to sense that he was losing his good-luck charm.

"Please call if there's any news at all."

"I will," I said, leaving a troubled General Akhtar behind to deal with the Indians on the border and the possible loss of his man in Washington.

Later that morning, I notified Langley of the level of tension building in Pakistan as the new Indian exercise got under way. I didn't know at the time that the tension would almost spin out of control in a matter of weeks. Nor did I have a feel for just how serious Bill Casey's situation was at that time, physically and politically.

First Chief Directorate Headquarters, Yasenevo, January 1986

Leonid Shebarshin had been following the drama unfolding on India's border with Pakistan with special attention. He knew that the Pakistanis would see a massive conspiracy behind the Indian exercises, that they would become convinced the exercise had been mounted to draw their attention, and that of their American friends, from the ongoing war on their western border to a possible flare-up on the eastern front. He knew the Pakistanis would also conclude that the plot to destabilize Pakistan had been hatched in Moscow and that everything would evolve according to some grand plan.

But the KGB general also knew that South Asia had a way of getting mired all by itself, without the master hand of the Kremlin behind every plot, real or imagined. The truth of the matter was that the Indians were carrying out their Brasstacks exercise on their own and that Moscow had no hand in pushing them to create a diversion to ease the pressures in Afghanistan. Never mind that it might be working out that way; it just wasn't part of a grand plan.

Nevertheless, Shebarshin would have to follow Brasstacks closely. That old South Asian bugaboo—miscalculation and overreaction—could always pop up. And that could heat things up, probably more than anyone would like.

Islamabad, January 29, 1987

I sat alone in the ISI reception room, waiting for Akhtar to join me for the "urgent" meeting he had called to discuss "events on the border." He was referring to Brasstacks and to Pakistan's response. General Sundarji and Zia had made a series of troop moves and countermoves that by mid-January had escalated tensions to the point at which the slightest movement could have sparked a war.

On January 19, the New Delhi press screamed, PAK MASSING TROOPS ALL ALONG BORDER, and Indian Prime Minister Gandhi expressed "tremendous concern" about the Pakistani buildup at a press conference the next day. Over the next week, both Indian and Pakistani intelligence fed their respective press corps a steady stream of inflammatory rumors of the other side's preparations for war. The Indians became convinced that Zia had stealthily maneuvered an armored corps into position for a lightning strike into India's Punjab, with the goal of separating Kashmir from the rest of India. As tensions grew, there were press reports of Pakistani Army engineers mining the bridges around Lahore as a means of stopping the Indian advance that was now so sure to come. On January 23, India mobilized its forces, and Pakistan followed suit. The stage for another war between the two South Asian neighbors was set. That same evening, Zia directed his prime minister, Mohammed Khan Junejo, to call his counterpart in New Delhi to open a dialogue to deescalate. Then, against the counsel of his advisers, Zia announced he planned to attend a cricket match in New Delhi. And almost as quickly as it had arisen, the tension dissipated.

Akhtar strode into the reception room with his note taker, Colonel Riaz, trailing two steps behind him. He was talking as he entered.

"The president pulled it off," Akhtar said, beaming.

"Pulled it off?" I was a little taken aback by Akhtar's smug sense of triumph.

Akhtar frowned. "Yes. It was close, but Zia's nerves were steel. He held back his troops from their forward deployed positions right up until the last minute. And he made sure the Indians knew what he was doing by letting them intercept his communications! It was masterful."

"Sure it was masterful," I said, "but I still haven't found the logic in why it almost came to war. What was that all about?"

Akhtar motioned to Riaz to stop taking notes and leave the room. When we were alone, he lowered his voice and leaned toward me as he spoke.

"Rajiv Gandhi," Akhtar said after Riaz had left, "is a playboy, a joker who lost control of his Army chief of staff. The president signaled to New Delhi as far back as October that the Brasstacks exercise was provocative, and would be responded to in kind if they didn't back things down. But Sundarji must have thought he could ignore our concerns, and Gandhi wasn't paying attention until two weeks ago when his own press started talking of war. Then he tried to catch up."

"Yeah," I said, "and almost too late. Was it just provocation gone wild, or was there something else going on?"

"It was Sundarji," Akhtar said as if sharing a profound confidence. "He wanted a war. He thought he could provoke President Zia into taking the first step, making the first mistake. He thought he could roll into Pakistan and have it all cleaned up in a week. Then Zia moved his forces around a bit in Bahawalpur, particularly his armor, and Sundarji got a different picture. It was Pakistan who might have things tidied up in a week!"

"This heated up so fast and cooled down so fast that we still haven't figured out how close you came to war. How close was it?"

Akhtar held up his hand, forming a trigger finger. "It was that close," he said, pulling the imaginary trigger. "All it would have taken was some junior commissioned officer along the border—their JCO or ours—getting nervous, pulling his trigger, and setting it all off. Zia knew that, and he knows the Indian mind. He backed them down."

"It's a hell of a way for a couple of potential nuclear powers to deal with each other," I said.

Akhtar bristled at the word *nuclear*. "But Pakistan isn't a nuclear power, and you, more than most, know that."

The subject, and the atmosphere, had changed. The most serious point of friction between the United States and Pakistan centered on Pakistan's nuclear weapons program, a secret arms race with its neighbor that had been under way since India detonated its first test device in 1974. There were a handful of congressional mandates sanctioning Pakistan for developing nuclear weapons, but most were subject to a presidential waiver. And up until now, Reagan had been able to certify that Pakistan had not crossed the proliferation threshold. So any mention of Pakistan and nuclear development to Zia's intelligence chief was likely to set him on edge. I'd asked the question to see if Akhtar thought Sundarji might actually have been staging the whole Brasstacks exercise to provide cover for a preemptive strike at Pakistan's nuclear centers near Islamabad. He didn't bite.

"That's encouraging, General," I said, sensing that Akhtar had decided to end the meeting, which he did, as usual, with an abrupt change of subject.

"How is Mr. Casey doing?" he asked. "The president is concerned about him."

Word of Casey's worsening condition was out, and few in the international intelligence club expected the DCI ever to return to Langley. Who might succeed him was the subject of whispered speculation both in Washington and abroad. "He's not doing too well, I'm afraid. But he's alert and knows what's happening in all his favorite places, including Islamabad."

Akhtar softened. "Well, please see that he knows we appreciate all he has done for us over the years. And please pass along our appreciation to Mr. Gates for whatever role he played behind the scenes in defusing the little problem we had here."

"I will, and please pass Mr. Gates's regards to the president for his cool handling of the crisis over the last month. It didn't have to work out as well as it did."

Akhtar rose and escorted me to Riaz, who was standing right outside his door.

The Kremlin, February 27, 1987

It seemed that Gorbachev had his consensus, Anatoly Chernyaev said to himself as he reviewed the minutes of a series of Politburo meetings over the last five weeks on the question of Afghanistan. Muhammad Najibullah had made his visit to Moscow in December, and he had made a good impression. The word in Moscow was that he was a serious-minded man who could take the difficult first steps of preparing for the day when he would not be supported by the Soviet army.

There was no turning back from the decision to withdraw from Afghanistan, though the Kremlin was still reluctant to declare to the world that its policy of intervention had been flawed from the start. Such sentiments had not, however, prevented frank comment among Politburo members on past errors. At sessions held on January 21 and 22, Eduard Shevardnadze had made it clear that the decision to exit was the right one and pulled few punches when it came to where he thought the blame for the Afghan debacle should lie.

"I won't discuss right now whether we did the right thing by going in there," the Foreign Minister declared, easing into exactly the criticism he said he would avoid. "But we did go in there absolutely without knowing the psychology of the people and the real state of affairs in the country. That's a fact! And everything we've done and are doing in Afghanistan is incompatible with the moral character of our country."

"It was incompatible that we went in?" Gromyko asked pointedly.

"Yes, this, too," he said. "The attitude toward us is more negative than it seems. And we're spending a billion rubles a year for this. An enormous sum, and responsibility needs to be taken for it. Let us add up again in every detail how much Afghanistan needs to get by at the present time! Nikolay Ivanovich," he said, referring to Nikolay Ryzhkov, the architect of Gorbachev's economic restructuring program, appointed to the Politburo in 1985 and soon after promoted to head of the Council of Ministers, "doesn't have this data right now, but in the United States they think we'll need two billion a year. And the Japanese think it's three billion. I'm not even talking about the costs in lives."

"We won't talk right now about how this revolution came into being," Gorbachev interjected, "how we reacted and how we vacillated about whether or not to deploy troops."

"Yes, yes," Gromyko assented, nodding in agreement.

"Right now we must address the present and determine what steps need to be taken."

"The report of Eduard Amvrosieyevich [Shevardnadze] provides a realistic picture," said Ryzhkov. "The previous information was not objective. The situation forces us again to approach the problem in a serious way." He spoke of the difficulty of making progress in an illiterate society and of the misery of people's material prospects. "It's better to pay with money and kerosene than with men," he said. "Our people don't understand what we're doing there, or why we've been there for seven years. It's easy to leave, but we can't just throw everything to the whims of fate. Many countries would forsake us. We need to leave a neutral, friendly Afghanistan behind. What steps should be taken? Why not a mercenary army? What will prevent it from deserting? Good money. It's better to hand out arms and ammunition, and to have them fight themselves if they want. Meanwhile we can turn to a parallel political settlement. We need to use all contacts with Pakistan and the U.S."

"We cannot bring them freedom by military means," said Igor Ligachev, Gorbachev's right-hand man. "We have suffered defeat in this area. And what Eduard Amvrosieyevich has said is the first objective analysis we have had. We didn't consider the consequences when we set our hopes on the military route. I think the policy of national reconciliation is the correct one. If the question is put before the people, is it better to let our soldiers die or restrict themselves to every kind of aid, I think that every person to the last will favor the second path. And we have to work on the Pakistani avenue, with India, with China, and with America. But to leave as the Americans did from Vietnam—no, we still have not come to this, as they say."

Marshal Sokolov added his own somber assessment. "The military situation has recently become worse," he said. "The shelling of our garrisons has doubled. They are mainly fighting in the villages, counting on our retaliating against the population centers. It is impossible to win such a war by military means."

"Thus we confirm our firm policy," said Gorbachev in closing. "We will not retreat once we have started. Act in all directions. Analyze where and how our aid is best to be used, start up foreign policy mechanisms through Cordovez and Pakistan, try to do business with the Chinese and, of course, the Americans. When we went into Afghanistan we were wrapped up in ideology and calculated that we could leap ahead three stages right away—from feudalism to socialism. Now we can look at the situation openly and follow a realistic policy. We accepted everything in Poland—the church, the individual peasant farms, the ideology, and the political pluralism. Reality is reality. Comrades, let us speak correctly. It is better to pay with money than with the lives of our people."

With his consensus almost solid in the Politburo, Gorbachev continued to press home the case for an exit from

Afghanistan over the following days and weeks. A month later, on February 23, Gorbachev reinforced his case in another Politburo meeting, at which he declared, "Now we're in, how to get out racks one's brains. We could leave quickly, not thinking about anything and blaming everything on the previous leadership. But we can't do that. India would be concerned, and they would be worried in Africa. They would see this as a blow to the authority of the Soviet Union and to national liberation movements. They would tell us that imperialism would go on the offensive if we leave Afghanistan. But domestic considerations are important, too. A million of our soldiers have been to Afghanistan. And all in vain, it turns out. They will say you've forgotten about the casualties and the authority of the nation. It creates a bitter taste—why did people die? Don't exclude America from an agreement, even as far as making a deal with them. And we need to rub Pakistan's nose in it—let them know the Soviet Union isn't going anywhere. Could Zia ul-Haq possibly be invited to Tashkent to meet with me, even 'pay' him in some way? We need flexibility and resourcefulness, for otherwise there will be a slaughter and Najib will fall. Continue the talks, don't let them be broken off. And possibly we'll have to make concessions about the withdrawal periods. Are there any doubts about what I have said right now?"

The men who ran the Soviet Union answered in one voice: "No, no!"

"Then let us act accordingly."

7

Islamabad, March 1987

Bill Casey died a month before the snows began to melt in the high passes, but not until after he'd been able to see the first signs of the turnaround in Afghanistan he was so certain would come. Negotiations with the Soviets in Geneva were becoming increasingly intense, and there was a growing sense they'd finally concluded they couldn't win. But there were still few in Washington who believed they would just pack up and leave Afghanistan anytime soon. So the war went on.

I never saw the DCI again after my meeting with him in July 1986, but even with all of his luck running out at the same moment, he hadn't forgotten that I was out there trying to carry out what he'd ordered. Just before he collapsed in December, he honored me with distinguished officer rank, a tribute that went to one or two senior officers in each directorate at the end of each year. I never had a chance to thank him.

Bob Gates had been selected by Casey himself to succeed him as DCI, but after a congressional confirmation process marked by bitter accusations against Gates for every misdeed from cooking the books on assessments of the USSR to intentionally keeping himself out of the loop on the Iran-contra affair, Gates withdrew. It would take until May before FBI Director Judge William Webster would be nominated for the Langley job. He would be easily confirmed by a Congress still smarting over missing the chance to bring Bill Casey to heel.

Heading into my second fighting season, I was mercifully far from the politics of Washington and able to concentrate on the war. I was convinced that the now mystical triumph of the Stinger had to be followed by other powerful successes if we were to keep up the fragile momentum we'd established. To achieve this, we needed a succession of "silver bullets" to both sustain the high energy of the Afghan resistance and keep Moscow on the run. If the rebels were seen as growing in strength and determination, the Soviet leader's hand could only be strengthened as he guided the USSR out of Afghanistan. There was no urging from Washington to ease up, as if that might encourage the Soviets to leave the field earlier. Thus, 1987 would be marked by all-out pressure.

Jack Devine had left to take over in Rome and was replaced by Frank Anderson, an officer with broad experience in the Near East. At forty-five, the tall, athletic Anderson had done service in rough-and-tumble Lebanon, where he had also studied Arabic early in his career. Serving in the wilds of Yemen and in a string of countries across the Maghreb, Anderson had come to understand the shifting realities of the world of Islam. But it was in Washington that he had developed his sharpest political skills. He was a natural for the Afghan Task Force, and to my great fortune, the handover from Jack Devine to Frank Anderson was seamless.

By the spring of 1987, the menace from the air had subsided, in large part because of the Soviet and DRA decision to fly above the Stinger's ceiling. Soviet armor had become the new challenge. Though we'd been asked repeatedly over the years to provide something, anything, to give the resistance an edge over Soviet tanks and armored personnel carriers (APCs), nothing had worked. The problem was range. The antiarmor weapons in the mujahideen arsenal—RPG-7s and the 75 mm and 82 mm recoilless rifles—were limited to about a three-hundred-yard killing radius as they were employed by the Afghans. A three-hundred-yard duel usually meant that a mujahideen gunner might get a shot off at a tank or APC, but as often as not he would be killed as soon as he fired.

To turn the tables, Anderson decided to deliver a new weapon, if possible, every few months. He concentrated on antiarmor systems that would foster the same jubilation among the Afghan fighters as the Stinger and cultivate the same sense of dread among the enemy forces. The results were magic. Within a few months, I took delivery of two new antitank weapons that did for armor what the Stinger had done for aviation. Anderson's covert arms procurement team first came up with the French-made Milan antitank missile. The Milan, when fired, trailed behind it a thin copper wire through which the gunner sent electrical, course-correcting commands as the missile flew toward its target. With an effective range of at least three thousand yards, the Milan increased the killing range of the mujahideen tenfold, and soon reports of spectacular successes were flowing back from the battlefront, along with anecdotal reports of excited reactions among Soviet and, especially, DRA armor commanders upon discovering the telltale copper wires strung across the rugged battlefields. In one particularly spirited battle on the Jalalabad plain at the mouth of the Konar Valley, a Milan gunner brought down an MI-24D hovering low over the battlefield, an act that added new verses to the Afghan ballads of war. Eastern Afghanistan, where most of the Milans were deployed, was perfect ambush country, and soon after its deployment we saw fewer tank probes out into the field.

The next silver bullet came directly out of the Warsaw Pact arsenal. Anderson's team acquired a supply of Soviet-designed SPG-9s, 73 mm recoilless rifles, and sent them by air to Pakistan. The SPG-9 had an effective range of about a thousand yards, roughly triple the killing range of the older recoilless rifles in the resistance inventory. As the mujahideen began to train on the new weapon, they couldn't conceal their enthusiasm at being able to reach out to targets at three and four times the range they'd been limited to over the years. I even took a couple of shots myself at a white tank chalked onto a cliff about eleven hundred yards away. I got one bull's-eye and one too close to call—but both worth a resounding *"Allah hu Akhbar!"* from the Afghan trainees gathered around me as I lay on the ground, firing the slender antitank round across the valley of the temporary training camp. All through the next fighting season the mujahideen kept up the pressure with hit-and-run ambushes, and in the major Soviet and DRA assaults of the season, the new systems were crucial.

But the introduction of each new silver bullet brought with it the problem of distribution to the resistance parties. Those who were issued the weapons were winners, and those who did not get the new weapons were the complainers. The new antitank systems were issued to commanders in eastern Afghanistan, where much of the fighting was taking place and where the systems would do the most good. Certainly they were of more use in Paktia and Nangarhar, where the Soviets were still mounting major assaults, than they'd be in the Panjshir Valley, which had settled into a quiet lull. Ahmad Shah Massoud appeared to have established an undeclared cease-fire with the Soviet 40th Army and now spent much of his time shoring up his position politically across the north of Afghanistan.

As negotiators in Geneva inched closer to a political settlement, the Afghan resistance parties began to jockey for position for the post-Soviet period. Ahmad Shah Massoud was far ahead of the other major resistance leaders as he formed his

Supreme Council of the North, a loose union of northern commanders that would one day become known as the Northern Alliance. But Gulbuddin Hekmatyar, Massoud's archenemy, would not be far behind in preparing for a showdown after the Soviet withdrawal, which he believed would soon come. As these and other commanders and party leaders sought their own advantages, I would become increasingly embroiled in the fractious politics of a war drawing to a close.

Islamabad, March 1987

Congressional criticism of the CIA's perceived favoritism of the Afghan fundamentalist parties over the moderates had been manageable as long as successes continued on the battlefield and there was no clear end in sight. But as evidence of a developing Soviet exit strategy grew, Washington's distaste for the fundamentalists mounted, and it was only natural that their attention should focus on the dark and mistrustful favorite of the ISI, Gulbuddin Hekmatyar, and his Hisb-e-Islami.

At least some of the stories about Gulbuddin's idiosyncratic evil deeds were, I knew, traceable to black propaganda originating with the KGB's disinformation teams in Kabul. Others could be traced to Indian intelligence operations or to moderate Afghan party leaders working Capitol Hill. To deal with the growing stream of congressional inquiries on Hekmatyar and our alleged favoritism toward him, I needed a better measure of the man—something more than the "group therapy" observations I had made up until then. I told Akhtar I wanted a meeting with Gulbuddin—just the two of us, I insisted.

A couple of days after my request, Colonel Bacha brought Gulbuddin into a small interview room at ISI headquarters, bare except for three chairs and a low table. On Bacha's heels came a steward with a pot of tea, three cups, and a plate of cookies. As the colonel was about to take a seat, I laid my hand on his shoulder and said that General Akhtar had given me his assurances that the meeting would be a strictly one-on-one affair. Bacha's services would not be needed, as the engineer spoke excellent English. The colonel muttered something to Gulbuddin in Pashto, which I assumed was a reassurance that he'd be standing by outside the door if needed, and grudgingly left the room.

Gulbuddin Hekmatyar's family were Ghilzai Pashtuns of the nomadic Kharotai tribe, who had migrated from Ghazni in the Pashtun east to Kunduz in northern Afghanistan. Gulbuddin studied for two years in the military high school in Kabul, but he left before graduating. He entered the College of Engineering at the University of Kabul but failed to complete his studies there, too, and found his calling instead as a political activist and fervent Islamist, becoming involved in the Kabul campus Islamic Movement's Muslim Youth branch. He took up violent opposition to the Communists, who were by then strengthening their hold on Afghan politics, and was jailed for two years for murdering a Maoist-Communist opponent. It was also during this period that he had his first of many confrontations with another student activist at the university, a young Tajik from the Panjshir Valley, Ahmad Shah Massoud. The two activists would vie for center stage in the Afghan drama for the next thirty years.

After his release from prison in the early 1970s, Hekmatyar fled to Peshawar, where, along with other Afghan Islamists, and with the support of Pakistan, he became a fundamentalist activist against the government of the Afghan Republic. In 1975, after the Islamist-instigated rebellion against the Afghan government failed, Gulbuddin formed his own radical party, the Hisb-e-Islami, the Party of Islam.

Gulbuddin pulled out his agate prayer beads and began to run the beads through his fingers, one at a time. He had come because he had been forced to and appeared in no hurry to open the conversation himself.

"I'd like to thank you, Engineer, for making yourself available to meet with me this morning," I said, eager to get down to business. "I know how pressing matters are with you."

There was the faintest nod, but no response.

I went directly to the point. "Engineer Gulbuddin, you know we're committed to helping your people, but you go out of your way to irritate Americans. Is there something I ought to know, something I'm missing?" Gulbuddin wasn't an engineer, and I knew it. But resistance party leaders came in only two categories—clerics and engineers. If a commander or party head wasn't addressed by the clerical titles of "mullah" or "maulvi," then it had better be "engineer." So Engineer Gulbuddin it would be.

"I can't answer for the irritation of the Americans," he said with clipped impatience. "That would be your concern."

This guy really doesn't like us, I thought. "It started two years ago when you refused to meet with our President Reagan, and it continues. I don't really care what you think of the United States, but your attitude makes it difficult for me to help your commanders in Afghanistan."

"How so?" Gulbuddin heard a threat in what I'd just said. Perhaps I was going to tell him that I would see that his commanders were cut off from the supply lines.

"Because your reputation as a brutal fundamentalist," I said, using the terminology to provoke him, "who hates the United States as much as he hates the Soviet Union is well known in Washington. The story is spread around Washington by your brothers in the jihad, with their complaints that you receive more support from your Pakistani brothers than you deserve. These complaints end up with me. Some in my government say we should provide you with nothing. That distracts me. And it could cause problems for your commanders."

"What is brutal fundamentalism?" Gulbuddin said, clicking his prayer beads.

"You know as well as I do the stories of your throwing acid in the faces of young women at Kabul University for not wearing the veil—"

"Fantasy. That never happened."

"That you personally killed your own party members for disloyalty. That you execute the prisoners your commanders take, particularly Hazaras and Jowzjanis."

"This is more fantasy. It is trivial. My party is disciplined, but—"

"Is it fantasy or is it trivial, Engineer Gulbuddin? There is a difference."

To this he did not respond.

"These things are important to me because my government thinks they're important," I continued. "I wouldn't have taken your time or mine if these matters were either fantasy or trivial."

"I am fighting an enemy that is brutal, and I match their brutality. But the stories are lies, and they are unimportant. It's not important what your government thinks of me. I don't need support from you or your Congress. I can capture enough weapons from the enemy to fight the jihad."

"Stingers, Engineer? Can you capture Stingers?" It was widely known that Engineer Ghaffar, the commander of the Stinger team that brought down the first MI-24Ds at Jalalabad the previous September, was from Gulbuddin's party.

"The means to fight belong to the people of Afghanistan."

This guy is a tough nut, I thought. His world shifts seamlessly between fact and fantasy. "Engineer Gulbuddin, what matter is there of importance that you'd like to discuss?"

"Let's talk about why you plan to kill me. I know what you're planning to do."

"I'm planning to kill you?"

"Yes, maybe even you. Maybe now. You're armed. I can see that." Hekmatyar was looking under my left arm at what he must have thought was a weapon pressing against my jacket. I opened my jacket so that he could see there was no weapon, just a wallet.

Gulbuddin smiled slightly. "They say you are always armed."

"The colonel says this?"

Gulbuddin smiled but did not answer. The truth was I was armed, but the Makarov I usually carried was in the small of my back where he couldn't see it.

"Why would I want to kill you?" I said, and for a fleeting moment thought that Hekmatyar had actually come up with a good idea. I would in later years often wonder how it might have played out if I had dropped him then and there.

"Because the United States has understood that we have now defeated the Soviet Union, a superpower like the United States. And the United States can no longer feel safe with me alive. That's why you feel you must kill me."

"I think the engineer flatters himself," I said.

Gulbuddin fingered his beads and smiled, but his dark eyes showed nothing. "Yes, perhaps I flatter myself."

The meeting ended with the same tension with which it had begun. I accomplished nothing beyond having spent some time alone with the man who would be a problem for the rest of my time in Pakistan. I would have two more such meetings with Hekmatyar, and other officers on my staff would meet with his closest deputies. But of the leaders of the Peshawar Seven, it would be only Gulbuddin Hekmatyar whom I would have to count as an enemy, and a dangerous one. And, ironically, I would never be able to shake the allegations that the CIA had chosen this paranoid radical as its favorite, that we were providing this man who had directly insulted the President of the United States with more than his share of the means to fight the Soviets. Gulbuddin would later claim that at one of our meetings I had tried to buy him off with an offer of several million dollars, which, of course, he claimed he'd turned down.

Islamabad, March 1987

The CIA's covert action program in Afghanistan was congressionally mandated and funded, an arrangement that brought more oversight from Congress than was the case with any other agency activity, with the exception of the covert action in Central America. On balance, congressional interest in the Afghan program was positive. If anything, we at the CIA felt that Congress might just love what we were doing in Afghanistan a little too much. Some members of Congress seemed more determined to drive the Soviets out of Afghanistan than many in the executive branch directly involved with the war. One of these was Congressman Charlie Wilson, the flamboyant Texas Democrat from the rural second district deep in the piney woods northeast of Houston.

A 1956 graduate of the U.S. Naval Academy, Charlie Wilson was elected to the Texas State Legislature while he was still on active duty in the U.S. Navy. Having served aboard a destroyer in his early Navy days, Wilson ended up in the Intelligence Directorate (G-2) on the Joint Staff at the Pentagon. He was elected to the U.S. Congress in 1972, arrived in Washington in 1973, and by the time the Soviets invaded Afghanistan in 1979, he was an established member of the Democratic machine, a man whose personal flair and flashy womanizing masked a deep substance and a steadfast loyalty to the cause he had chosen to champion. Well over six feet tall and rail thin, Charlie would be described by one profiler as a Texan who could "strut while sitting down." He reveled in telling stories of his womanizing, particularly if there was the slightest chance that a prude was within earshot. He told and retold the story of how Bill Casey had noted in wonderment that all the young women working in Charlie's Washington office were uniformly and strikingly attractive. Charlie's response, which he later only mildly regretted, was, "Bill, you can teach 'em how to type, but you can't teach 'em how to grow tits." That comment and others would make Charlie a standing target of opportunity for Washington feminists, but it added panache to a man whose main cause as a congressman would be tormenting the Soviets until they turned around and left Afghanistan.

Charlie made his first trip to Pakistan in 1982 and on that visit struck up a personal relationship with President Zia that would last and deepen until the president's death six years later. That visit would be followed by many more, plus a few cross-border forays into Afghanistan. But it would be in Washington that Charlie Wilson would make the most difference to the CIA's effort in Afghanistan. By the early 1980s, the Texas congressman was a member of the Defense Subcommittee of the House Appropriations Committee, a position that enabled him to identify and generate funding for the CIA's Afghanistan program. More than any other member of either house, Charlie fashioned Congress into the engine that drove the CIA's program for Afghanistan. He understood early on that if he was able to get an assignment to the House Permanent Select Committee on Intelligence (HPSCI), that assignment, linked with work on the House Appropriations Committee, would put him in charge of the congressional component of the CIA effort in Afghanistan.

But House Speaker Jim Wright had problems with Charlie going on the HPSCI; the Democrats on the committee were blocking the maverick Texan because he had voted on the floor for continuing aid to the Nicaraguan contras. That vote had elicited the ire of what Charlie referred to as "the liberals" in his party, in particular Jim Wright, who was deeply committed to cutting off all aid to the contras. Behind the scenes, Dick Cheney lobbied for Wilson's assignment to the HPSCI, and after Charlie gave Wright his assurances that he would concentrate on Afghanistan and, as he would later characterize it, that he "wouldn't fuck around in Central America," he got the HPSCI assignment. From that point on, he was perfectly situated to concentrate on his central political passion—driving the Soviets out of Afghanistan and tormenting them in the process.

A man of his word, Charlie never touched the Central American tar baby again, even when Bill Casey was in desperate need of just such a congressional champion. After Jim Wright fell afoul of the House Ethics Committee and was replaced by Tom Foley, Wilson stayed focused on Afghanistan and left Central America to others.

My first contact with Charlie came in June 1986, just before I went out to Islamabad. Since we were both from Texas, Charlie and I spoke the same language and hit it off immediately. I had come to appreciate greatly what he was doing for us—it seemed that whenever we needed another $20 million urgently for the development of some new system for the Afghan resistance, Charlie would find us $40 million. And so it went. After I arrived in Pakistan, Charlie would be the first of many congressional delegations coming our way, and always my most challenging. The very term *codel* for "congressional delegation" would normally strike something close to fear in the heart of a U.S. mission abroad. But a Codel Wilson would mix delight and confusion with the usual dose of fear.

If Charlie's central political passion was pushing the Soviets out of Afghanistan, the congressman was not without other delights. His constant traveling companion in those days was Annelise Ilschenko, a stunning woman from the Cleveland Ukrainian community who had come to Washington as a member of an Ohio congressman's staff. In the mid-1970s, Annelise had managed to capture the Miss World USA crown, an achievement that qualified her to fit neatly into the dazzling retinue of the colorful congressman from Texas. How she blended into the scheme of the rigidly Islamist North-West Frontier Province, where she was a frequent fixture with Charlie, was another matter. With Annelise often wearing leather pants in the Khyber Agency, I was never sure whether the rugged Afridis in the Khyber Agency thought she was a woman or a boy, or whether it even mattered to them. Annelise, to put it mildly, made an impression in the North-West Frontier Province.

Islamabad, March 1987

Akhtar's aide had called me at the office with a curt request. "A car is on the way," he said. "The general needs to see you right away."

I was escorted past the Pakistan Army guards at the entrance to ISI headquarters and directly into Akhtar's conference room. The normal five-minute wait—engineered, I thought, as a reminder of the general's sense of our pecking order—was cut to less than a minute. Akhtar breezed into the room alone, sat down, and got right to business. He ignored the mess steward who set a pot of black tea and cookies on the table between us. I steeled myself for a possible tirade from the general and imagined any number of possible complaints.

"It's Charlie," Akhtar said. "He's very unhappy."

Leaning back in my chair with a sense of relief that the issue "only" involved the Texas congressman, I scrolled back and considered Charlie's activities over the last few months. He had made a couple of short forays into Afghanistan before I took over the program, and I knew he'd planned another, more grandiose visit a few weeks back. But as he'd reached zero line near Miram Shah, he was stopped by the Pakistani Frontier Forces on the orders of his friend General Akhtar. Charlie had told me he'd been stopped cold at the border, but he'd concealed how disappointed he'd been.

"Charlie is not happy," the general repeated, still trying to prompt a comment from me.

"This is true, I suppose. He told me he was stopped at zero line. Why'd you stop him? It wouldn't have been the first time he'd gone in."

"I stopped him because it wasn't safe. Everybody in the North-West Frontier knew he was going in. What would I do if someone killed him?"

"I can see your point," I said. "But I think you've asked me here because a deeply unhappy Charlie Wilson has more potential for trouble for you than a freshly martyred one."

Akhtar smiled weakly, seeing that I understood his problem. "Exactly," he said. "And the president has also heard of this. So what do we do?"

The mention of the president added a special texture to the

problem. I could only imagine the discussion Akhtar and Zia might have had about Charlie's disappointment.

"Why not arrange a trip for Charlie and his friends?" I said. "Exciting and safe."

"Arrange?" Akhtar pondered.

"Yes. You make sure that everything goes according to a script and that everybody walks away a winner, especially Charlie."

"You'll clear this with your headquarters?" Akhtar asked tentatively.

"Not a chance. This is your show, but I'll be happy to help out in the background."

"You won't tell Washington?" Akhtar seemed incredulous over what he must have thought was a total breach of discipline on my part.

"I can't think of anyone at my headquarters who would want to know in advance about Charlie Wilson going off to war."

Akhtar shrugged. "I think he wants to fire a Stinger."

Jesus, I thought. We've just gone from a grade B movie script to a Cecil B. De Mille production.

"Maybe there could be some Soviet or DRA aircraft activity in the area when Charlie goes in," I said. "With all the talk on the frontier about him going into Paktia, the Soviets will surely hear about it. Maybe they'd like to drop a little ordnance to welcome him."

Akhtar grimaced. "That's precisely why I stopped him last time."

"But there ought to be a few real Stinger teams in the area. Not just Charlie and a Stinger." I ignored Akhtar's temporary retreat.

"And you don't think your headquarters would want to know about this?"

"General," I said, "there's no one at Langley who'd want to have anything to do with this one way or another. Nobody would want to tell me to support it or to prevent it. And I won't burden them with *our* little problem."

Akhtar just shook his head in resignation. "I'll get my people working on it and get back with you," he said. Then he abruptly changed the subject. "Milton, we have to do something about the MiG-21 pilot."

"Do something?" I asked, taken aback by the change of course in the conversation.

"He's not adjusting well," Akhtar said somewhat cryptically.

The MiG-21 pilot to which the general was referring was a young DRA fighter pilot who had flown his jet into Pakistan a few months earlier to accept a standing offer of a cash bounty to any Afghan Air Force pilot who defected with his aircraft. The CIA had standing orders for any and all Soviet aircraft, and my predecessor, Bill Piekney, had been successful in acquiring a flyable MI-25 attack helicopter two years earlier. The jet fighter had been a welcome addition to the growing USAF inventory of Soviet warplanes.

"What do you mean, he's not adjusting well?"

Akhtar fidgeted. "He thought things would be different here. He'd been fed up with the closed-in life in Afghanistan and thought he'd get to celebrate a little more here."

"Celebrate?"

"You know how these young guys are. They want to get leaked." Now Akhtar was actually squirming.

"Leaked?" I asked, thoroughly enjoying the general's discomfort.

"Yes. Maybe you can have your people take the young man to Bangkok or somewhere. It's hard to get a young man leaked here in Islamabad." Akhtar rolled his eyes a little, as if sharing a personal confidence.

"I understand, General. You want us to take this fighter pilot somewhere and get him *laid*?"

A light went on. "Yes, laid! That's what he needs," Akhtar declared.

So I left ISI headquarters with the dual problems of a Texas congressman who, legend had it, never had trouble getting laid and who more than anything else wanted to go to war, and an Afghan fighter pilot who wanted out of his war and more than anything else to go to Bangkok to get laid.

In the end, we'd take care of them both.

Paktia Province, Afghanistan, May 1987

Several weeks later, Charlie Wilson was back in Pakistan. This time he crossed over zero line without mishap. He was accompanied by the Gucci commander, Rahim Wardak, and some very tough fighters from Jalaluddin Haqqani's militias in Paktia Province. The group, with Charlie riding a white stallion, traveled into the Khowst region, mounted a few attacks on the Soviet and DRA garrisons there, and marauded the countryside. Though he never got to fire his Stinger—Haqqani's people had actually dragged chains and tires on the dirt roads in a futile attempt to attract enemy fighter aircraft to the clouds of dust—he did manage to have a memorable combat tour at the front. I stayed hidden in the "long grass" throughout, coordinating as best I could with Akhtar to make sure all went well and all our friends returned home safely.

Charlie would make yet another trip into Afghanistan as the Soviets were in full retreat. But for that visit he would bring a CBS *60 Minutes* crew led by Harry Reasoner and producer George Crile. The whole team—producer, correspondent, rock star Charlie Wilson on a new white stallion, camera- and soundmen, and a gaggle of mujahideen—went off to celebrate the victory over the Soviet garrison at Ali Khel. The CBS show that finally aired ended with Mohammed Zia ul-Haq's lasting three-word assessment of how the war in Afghanistan had been won:

"Charlie did it."

8

Islamabad, Late April 1987

The call from Clair George came through to my secure communications center in Islamabad late in the afternoon. There was none of the usual opening banter; Clair was all business.

"Milt, I want you to think very carefully before you answer the question I am about to ask. Do you understand?"

"I understand, Clair," I said, wondering what the hell and how big the issue was that had prompted the call from the DDO. I had worked for Clair for years, and this was the first time he had ever gone to the bother of calling me directly in the field on the secure line.

"Were you in any way involved in an attack on an industrial site deep inside the Soviet Union . . . in Uzbekistan . . . anytime in the last month?"

There it was. Clair wasn't trying to prompt an answer with his careful, almost lawyerly, question. He was just conveying to me the seriousness of the matter and giving me a chance to forgo a flip answer right off the bat. The fact that this was a secure line without an official record was also not lost on me. As it turned out, the answer was easy.

"No, Clair. If anything like that is going on, we're not involved here. You can say straight out that the agency is not involved."

"Absolutely uninvolved? No foreknowledge?" Clair's voice lightened a little, but he was still insistent. He wanted no room for misunderstanding.

"Clair, I don't know precisely what you're talking about, but I can say I had absolutely no foreknowledge of any attack across the Amu Dar'ya. But if it happened, and if they used weapons we have provided, would that mean involvement? I don't think so. We stand by our position that once the stuff's delivered to the Paks, we lose all control over it."

"Please say again that there was no involvement in the planning or execution of an attack, any attack, on Soviet territory."

"Clair, that's absolutely correct. We have not been involved in any way with planning or carrying out attacks on the Soviet Union."

"That's fine, Milt. You may or may not be getting a cable on this. If you do get one, answer it just the way you answered me."

"Okay, Clair, but how about a question?"

"Sure."

"What the hell is going on?"

"There has been some discussion between Dobrynin and Shultz over certain matters in the USSR last week. I just wanted to be sure to have your input."

What Clair might have said was that he wanted to be sure that I wasn't off freelancing with the Pakistanis and the mujahideen by carrying the war across the Amu Dar'ya into the Soviet Union. Clair never sent the cable, and I never heard from him on the matter again. But I decided to find out what ISI knew about the incident.

Islamabad, Late April 1987

Major General Hamid Gul would have been a tough armor officer in anybody's army. His reputation for boldness and unconventional action had been established during the tense days of the India-Pakistan confrontation five months earlier, when the Indian Army carried out its training exercise on Pakistan's border. Gul, then an armor commander in Multan in southern Punjab, had caused a flurry of concern in the Indian general staff when his division had "gone missing." He had, in fact, quickly and secretly moved his armor out of garrison and kept it away from India's prying eyes for much of the exercise, raising expectations that he might strike into India's Punjab Province from almost any direction.

After the tensions on the Indian border subsided, President Zia made one of his periodic shuffles at the top of his general staff and promoted Akhtar, who was then head of ISI, to lieutenant general and assigned him as chairman of the joint staffs committee. Hamid Gul was transferred from Multan to take over at ISI. In my first meeting with him, Gul told me that he was a "moderate Islamist," a tough disciplinarian, and open-minded. I told him I thought we'd get along fine, if for no other reason than because the job demanded it. After a few meetings, I thought I spotted a side of Hamid Gul that could make the slide from "daring and bold" to plucky or even harebrained, and much later I would find that I was right.

I called on Gul at ISI headquarters shortly after Clair's tense telephone call and found him primed to talk about the incursion across Amu Dar'ya. With him was Brigadier Mohammed Yousaf, his chief of military operations, whom I had come to consider my single greatest adversary in ISI. Yousaf resented the American involvement in his program and made few bones about it. If he could have his way, the United States would simply deliver sixty thousand tons of ordnance each year to Karachi, throw in a few hundred million in cash, and leave the rest to him. He didn't welcome our suggestions and generally ignored anything that looked like a demand. I had decided that one way or another, it would be better for Yousaf to move on, but it would take a while to make that happen.

I took one look at the scene with Yousaf and the note taker and decided I wanted to clear the room. "General, let's dispense with the formalities and go straight into an executive session," I said. I was referring to a protocol for a meeting between just me and the ISI director general. There would be no aides, no note takers, no written record. Gul nodded and dismissed his two officers with a wave of his hand. I glanced at Yousaf as he left the room and got a look in return that convinced me I had at least one enemy in ISI.

"This is about events in the USSR?" Gul said as soon as we were alone.

"It is indeed, General."

"There was an . . . occurrence in the last days, but I have been assured that the order has been sent that put an end to such things."

"How's that possible, General? How can you call back these operations? I've always been told by Yousaf that such things were spontaneous."

Gul fidgeted. I guessed he'd come under pressure from his own government and was improvising his story about the strike across the Amu Dar'ya.

"I have assured the prime minister that I have issued orders that there will be no further incursions into the USSR for the time being."

General Gul still hadn't answered my question on how he could stop the attacks. The prime minister, Mohammed Khan Junejo, a politician from Sindh Province, was now running the parliament in a hybrid democracy that left Zia in power as both president and chief of Army staff. It was my bet that Zia was letting Junejo handle this hot potato and that Gul was feeling the pressure without Zia there to cover his back. Zia might even have been amused to watch the drama from a distance.

"General, there have been representations in Washington, and I have been bluntly asked for assurances that there was no American involvement in the incident. I've given those assurances."

Gul smiled. "I'm sure the representations in Washington and your conversations about them would not have achieved the level of bluntness of the conversation Sahabzada had with the Soviet ambassador two days ago."

A former Army general and wartime hero, Sahabzada Yaqub Khan was Pakistan's flamboyant and able foreign minister. I could only imagine how a conversation between Hamid Gul and the headstrong old warrior Sahabzada Yaqub Khan might have gone. At least it explained the uncertainty I'd seen in Gul since our session began.

"I'm not so sure, General. The Soviet ambassador in Washington had a very frank discussion with George Shultz. I'm sure the messages were about the same."

"The Soviets left the impression that the response to any future attacks would be at their source, meaning here in Pakistan. I doubt the Soviets hinted at attacking the United States." For the first time in our conversation, Hamid Gul smiled, but his smile was full of irony and a little pain.

"I have no idea what was said, General. I can only guarantee you that there was a certain level of excitement."

"Yes, a certain level of excitement." Gul smiled again. "I've ordered it stopped immediately," he repeated, and I thought I detected in his words a hint of an admission that he might not be fully in control.

"Will it stop?" I pressed.

"Yes," he said resolutely. "The effort will be stopped. How quickly is another matter."

Gul was finally opening up. He would, no doubt, follow orders. It was clear that he had inherited a problem, one in which he didn't have a great personal stake. But it was also clear that he had been on the job long enough to have difficulty blaming everything on his predecessor, who, in any case, was very much under the protection of Zia.

"General," I said, "we're going to have to work closely together as we bring this war to some sort of a conclusion. And we'll have to be willing to meet in executive sessions and to be as open with each other as we have been today. If Brigadier

Yousaf had been with us, I doubt that we could have been as frank with each other."

"You're right, Milton," Gul said. "We'll have to keep our eyes on both the war and the politics."

I left that meeting understanding that the armor officer was still at the low end of his learning curve. But I saw something in his eyes that told me he would take to the political side of the job, maybe even come to like it one day.

A day later, I received the first of a series of discreet telephone calls from Gul's predecessor, General Akhtar. Would I be free for a quiet dinner at his quarters in Rawalpindi Cantonment that evening, just the two of us? I said I would.

Rawalpindi, Late April 1987

Akhtar had not moved into the quarters reserved for the chairman of the joint staffs in Rawalpindi Cantonment. He preferred instead to stay put in his old quarters because of their proximity to Zia's residence. He received me in the driveway of his colonial bungalow and accompanied me to his dining room, where we had a working dinner of chicken tikka, creamed spinach qorma, seekh kabob, and dal, along with freshly made chapatis and roghi nan, the flat breads baked in a tandoor. Akhtar, as was his custom, ate sparingly. The meeting wasn't about the dinner; it was about what was going on in the Afghan program since he had left.

I preempted Akhtar's agenda with my own by asking a point-blank question. "General, Bill Casey briefed me fully on his discussions with you about operations across the Amu Dar'ya."

"Casey was always interested in doing something up there," Akhtar said, a note of suspicion in his voice.

"I know, but there were always other voices urging caution," I said. "I'm afraid Bill Casey was impatient with those who didn't appreciate his ideas for the Central Asian republics."

"It all started with Casey's idea to send the Uzbek-language Korans across in numbers. But then your people backed out. I think we took the idea and improved on it."

"I'm sure you did, General. Though your operations might have been more effective than even you might have planned.

There has been much discussion of some events north of Termez. . . ."

Akhtar's defenses were up again. He looked down and fiddled with his food. When he spoke again, there was an edge of irritation in his voice. "I have heard that they may have gone a bit too far. But how can you stop those people? You and I know that they're all the same people . . . north of the Amu Dar'ya or south of it, they're all kin. Any problems there are of the Soviets' own making. They drove their own people down into Afghanistan in the 1920s. Now they're just getting paid back!"

"Of course, General, but you'll agree that this might fall under the category of, how would President Zia put it, boiling the pot over?"

Akhtar caught the note in my voice when Zia's name was mentioned.

"Has the president become involved in this?"

"I haven't heard. I think it has fallen to the prime minister and to Sahabzada. Maybe that is the appropriate level for problems like this."

"Yes," Akhtar said, still waiting, it seemed, for the punch line.

"General, do you think Brigadier Yousaf might be encouraging these cross-border operations because of some mistaken belief that they were what you and the president and Bill Casey wanted . . . that he might be doing this without fully informing Hamid Gul?"

Brigadier Mohammed Yousaf had been involved with the operational side of the Afghan effort for the last four years and was a well-known Akhtar man. He had recently been passed over for promotion to major general and might be on his way out of the program. At least that was the scuttlebutt I'd picked up.

"Yousaf is a good soldier," Akhtar said. "I'm certain that he's keeping Gul advised."

"I'm certainly relieved to hear that, General," I said, and changed the subject to Akhtar's latest fitness program. "How's the treadmill working out?" I asked.

"About three miles a day," he said. "And you, any time for exercise?"

"Just staying ahead of what's happening around here is all I can handle," I answered as I rose to leave.

A few days later, I would learn that Yousaf had retired from the Army, though a connection between his departure and the Uzbek operation was never clear to me. I did subsequently hear from contacts in the Army that Brigadier Yousaf was particularly critical of my stand on incursions across the Amu Dar'ya—just another example of the Americans being weak-kneed, he'd complained. Yousaf, it turned out, had a hand in planning the incursions into the USSR, though the degree of Akhtar's own involvement remained in doubt. Problems in the Soviet Central Asian republics bordering Afghanistan would continue to plague the Soviets, but there would be no repeats of the tensions of April 1987.

9

Aboard the *Red Arrow* Express, May 1987

Jack Downing, a stocky, handsome Texan in his forties, was considered by many inside the CIA to be Hollywood's version of a CIA case officer—a Harvard man and a Marine veteran. His father had been a naval officer who died at the Battle of Salvo Bay in World War II, and his mother had been a buyer for the original Neiman-Marcus in Dallas. Downing had been raised with high expectations and a sense of duty. He was a straightforward, uncomplicated man, a trait that seemed slightly odd inside the byzantine world of intelligence. But he was also an excellent linguist who picked up languages easily, and he was a careful traditionalist about his espionage tradecraft. He had spied in both Beijing and Moscow, was fluent in Chinese and Russian, and knew more about "denied area" work than just about all the instructors at the Farm combined. During his first tour in Moscow in the 1970s, he had handled TRIGON; now, Gerber was calling him back, and Moscow was to be his. Gerber told him his task was to rebuild the Soviet spy networks that had been so devastated by the 1985 losses.

No matter how many times he had taken the overnight train from Moscow to Leningrad, Jack Downing found it difficult to sit still throughout the more than eight-hour journey aboard the jewel of the Soviet Union's railroad system. The *Krasnaya Strelka,* the *Red Arrow,* had pulled out of Moscow's Leningrad station just before midnight, but it wouldn't arrive at Leningrad's Moscow station until nearly 8:30 A.M. It was inevitable that he would, at some point in the long night, desperately need a cigarette.

It was just after dawn when Downing left his wife and daughter behind in their first-class compartment, threw open the doors between the rocking cars, and walked haltingly back to the *Red Arrow*'s caboose. Spring was arriving in the Soviet Union, and it was just warm enough for Downing to grab a quick smoke in the open air.

"Jek?"

Cigarette in hand, Downing turned quickly and saw a dark young Russian man with flashing eyes and a broad smile.

"Yes," Downing replied, instantly sensing that he was talking with a KGB man. The two were alone at the back of the train, with the wind and the noise of the rails masking their meeting, yet the Russian was still too cautious to say anything further. The man pressed an envelope into Downing's hand and hurried away, back into the darkness of the train's corridor. Downing's case officer instincts suddenly kicked in, and he stuffed the envelope into his coat, waited for the Russian to disappear, and returned to his compartment. The incident had taken no more than one minute.

Even in the privacy of his own compartment, Downing didn't dare take out the envelope to examine its contents. He and his family had been assigned the exact same compartment that Downing was always given by the Soviet rail system when he traveled on the *Red Arrow,* and he assumed that meant it was heavily bugged, probably with both audio and video.

It took all of Downing's patience and training to sit with his wife and daughter for the next several hours in the cramped compartment with the envelope hidden away. But it wasn't until the train pulled into Leningrad and Downing was safely inside the CIA's secure Leningrad office that he finally reviewed what the man had furtively passed him.

As he read, Downing could barely contain his excitement. Inside the envelope, he found a grainy surveillance photograph of himself and his wife as they walked into a Moscow subway station. In the photograph, they were heavily bundled up against the cold, and there was snow piled up in the background. He calculated that the picture had been taken the previous winter, soon after his arrival to take over as Moscow chief. He also found a lengthy note from the young Soviet, stating that he was indeed a KGB officer, that he was increasingly angry and frustrated with the Soviet system, and that he wanted someday to leave for America. Until that day, however, he was ready to spy for the CIA. He had included the photograph of Downing and his wife as proof that he was with the KGB and that he had access to information of unique interest to the CIA chief.

While he didn't give his name during this first message, the Russian stated that he held an important position within the American Department of the KGB's Second Chief Directorate, the spy hunters who watched the CIA's officers in Moscow. He was the executive assistant to the chief of the American Department, and he was also personally in charge of monitoring the CIA's Moscow station chief. He was thus Jack Downing's KGB case officer, so he knew everything the KGB knew about Downing: his work, his travel, his family. Most intriguing, he knew when and where the KGB was following Downing around Moscow and what other secret methods the KGB was using to keep track of him.

Since he was Downing's KGB case officer, he said he would know when it was safe to communicate. He wrote that Downing shouldn't try to contact him or schedule meetings. Instead, he gave Downing a brief list of restaurants and theaters around Moscow that he should visit by car on Friday nights. He should park, leave his car unlocked, and then go inside and eat dinner or watch a movie. The Russian would then leave a message in Downing's car—right under the noses of the KGB's surveillance teams. He could do so because of the peculiarities of the KGB's surveillance habits. On Fridays, the KGB knew,

American diplomats received their overseas mail. The KGB was always looking for opportunities to rifle through the mail of key diplomats and CIA officers, looking for anything that would provide a handle on the individual, some hint of vulnerability. So on Friday nights, the Russian could easily explain to the surveillance men with him that he was entering Downing's car to check his briefcase and his mail.

If Downing wanted to send him a message in return, the American could leave a specially marked envelope inside his briefcase in the car. Downing's briefcase, left casually behind in his car, was to be the letter drop, the mailbox for their clandestine communications. The Russian also wrote that he could continue to meet Downing on the *Red Arrow;* he would always know when Downing was scheduled to make another trip to Leningrad.

For Downing, the Russian's sudden appearance couldn't have come at a more opportune moment. Since his return to Moscow in November, Downing had become increasingly worried and depressed by the state of the CIA's operations in Moscow. The 1985 losses had left the CIA with virtually no assets left to run inside the Soviet Union. The PNG war that had erupted following the Daniloff affair had further reduced Moscow's effectiveness, delaying Downing's arrival by several months while several experienced CIA case officers were expelled in the tit-for-tat game with Washington. Meanwhile, Gorbachev's decision to withdraw Soviet administrative and clerical personnel from the U.S. embassy in October in retaliation for President Reagan's decision to oust hundreds of Soviets from the United States had paralyzed the embassy's operations. U.S. embassies, regardless of location, were notoriously more dependent on their local workforce, their so-called foreign service nationals, than were Soviet embassies.

The Clayton Lonetree case in December further shook the CIA; the agency feared that the Marine guard had given the KGB access to Moscow Station. At first, CIA counterintelligence experts believed that Lonetree could not have done much damage by himself; there were always at least two Marine guards on duty at the embassy. But in March, while Downing was in Frankfurt for a meeting with DDO Clair George, the CIA discovered that a second Marine guard,

Arnold Bracy, may also have aided the KGB. If Lonetree and Bracy had been conspiring together for the Soviets, it was quite possible that they had given the KGB access to SE Division's crown jewels.

No wonder, then, that CIA officers in Moscow, suffering through such an extended losing streak, were beginning to second-guess themselves and their methods. In its best days, in the late 1970s and early 1980s, Moscow operations had a certain cachet within the CIA, and Moscow case officers walked with the swagger of those who believe they are the best of the best. They had reason to preen: Moscow was then running the most dazzling inventory of agents in CIA history.

But now, everything that had been built in the late 1970s and early 1980s had been swept away, and with it, the confidence of the case officers in Moscow. Murat Natirboff left Moscow in the summer of 1986, just as the KGB was rolling up the last of the CIA's agents; Gerber wanted him replaced. But for the next five months, while Downing cooled his heels waiting for a truce in the PNG war, Moscow went without a chief, and the drift took its toll. There had been too many arrests, too many blown operations, so CIA officers were beginning to see shadows and ghosts.

The American case officers came to believe that it was no longer possible to break free of the KGB in order to conduct operations. They began to mutter about the mysterious, almost mystical capabilities of the KGB to follow their every movement and began to believe the KGB had developed "ultradiscreet surveillance," a new layer of surveillance that kicked in just when you were certain you were free. You could never see this new surveillance, so there was no way to prove it didn't exist. Case officers began to second-guess their instincts on the streets of Moscow, aborting missions at the slightest sign of casual Soviet interest. The new, unspoken mantra in Moscow was that there was no way to beat the KGB.

Downing was eager to snap Moscow out of the doldrums, but even he was beginning to wonder what was going wrong. After Bracy's revelations, Downing was ordered to put Moscow on a new kind of twenty-four-hour-a-day alert status. A CIA officer would have to be in the office at all times, just to make certain no one could get in. Downing decided that he and two other officers would take turns sleeping in the office at night, so that the secured space was never unattended. For this arduous new duty, he picked officers whose cover had already eroded so badly that the KGB had probably identified them as CIA officers; the fact that they were not going home at night wouldn't suddenly compromise their identities as spies to the KGB.

But even this new precaution wasn't enough. Langley soon ordered that every single piece of paper, every fake rock used in dead drops, every piece of equipment and furniture inside the CIA area, be packed up and shipped back to the United States for examination. So for a time, Moscow was stripped to the bare walls while the CIA tried to determine whether the Marines had given the Soviets access to the office.

A close examination of the security measures in Moscow suggested that the KGB had not gotten in. The main door was a vault with a combination lock, and there were two inner doors with locks as well. The Marine guards didn't have the combinations to any of them. The locks also had special counters that revealed how many times they had been opened, and officers were required to keep a log that noted the count on each lock. Similar locks on safes were logged as well. To be sure, the counters on the locks sometimes skipped, causing slight anomalies in the numbers logged. But those anomalies weren't consistent enough to suggest that the KGB had broken in.

What's more, Moscow was equipped with a hidden camera that revealed who had been inside, and an in-depth review of hours of videotapes never showed any KGB entry into the premises. While there were brief gaps when the camera hadn't been working, those gaps were never deemed significant. Despite the CIA's initial concerns, senior CIA officials were soon convinced that the Marines hadn't let the KGB into the CIA's Moscow office.

In the end, the Marine guard spy scandal died away, as the investigation petered out amid heavy criticism of the way the case had been handled by the Navy and other agencies. Officials were never quite sure what Lonetree and Bracy had done and whether the hysteria surrounding the case had led to exaggerations about the extent of their work for the Soviets. But in the spring of 1987, as Jack Downing was trying to rebuild, the Marine spy case was one more bad headache.

So now, just when Downing was getting desperate for a change in fortunes, here was this young Soviet offering him a look at the other side's playbook.

After notifying CIA headquarters about the potential new KGB agent, Downing scrupulously followed the Russian's instructions. Every Friday without fail, he and his wife went out to dinner at one of the preselected restaurants (a list that, unfortunately, didn't include Downing's favorites in Moscow), and each time he left his briefcase tucked away in his car. Inside, he included an envelope with a message for the Russian, asking him for specific information that the CIA was eager to know about KGB operations.

It turned out that the Russian had a mind-bending story to tell. He said that he had unique access to a major new counterintelligence campaign being planned by the Second Chief Directorate to disrupt and confuse the CIA's Moscow operations even further. Over the next few months, the Second Chief Directorate was planning to dangle a series of double agents in front of the CIA, in order to keep the agency so busy, so tied up trying to vet the volunteers, that it couldn't deal with real spies who might actually volunteer. They would be walk-ins, volunteers selected from segments of the Soviet government that the KGB knew were of special interest to the United States. The KGB was changing the rules of the game in Moscow, becoming both more aggressive and more sophisticated in their methods.

Before long, the *Red Arrow* volunteer gave Downing the identities of at least four of the double agents who he said would appear over the next four months, and, like clockwork, they began to approach the Americans, offering information. Now Downing felt he was inside the KGB's game and hoped he could determine which walk-ins were double agents and which might be the real thing.

The KGB man also provided a list of the CIA agents who had been arrested since 1985 and revealed how many had been executed. Other informants had told the CIA about the arrests of some of the compromised agents, but Downing's new source now provided conclusive evidence of the extent of the security breach. Langley had never told Downing how many agents had been lost. So he was stunned when he read the list prepared by his source, who was soon code-named GT-PROLOGUE.

CIA Headquarters, Langley, Virginia, May 1987

Burton Gerber shared Jack Downing's excitement about the sudden appearance of PROLOGUE. Since his early days in SE Division, fighting the Angleton paranoia about walk-ins and volunteers, Gerber had developed a rule of thumb that had become accepted wisdom within the CIA: The KGB never dangles one of its own staff officers. The Soviets didn't trust their own people enough to let a KGB officer with access to sensitive information walk into the Americans as part of a double agent operation. How could they be certain that he wouldn't simply keep walking across the line and defect? What's more, the Soviets knew that the CIA and FBI wouldn't believe a KGB officer was a genuine volunteer unless he revealed some important secrets. And the KGB had never been willing to part with enough secrets to make such a double agent believable. So Burton Gerber had long argued that when a KGB staff officer volunteers to become a spy, he's not a double agent. Why should PROLOGUE be any different?

But slowly a debate within SE Division's senior leadership began to develop about PROLOGUE. The man from the Second Chief Directorate had come along at just the right moment, just when the CIA was desperate for new sources inside Moscow. And he was handing over information that was bound to entice the CIA. Was he too good to be true?

Gerber and Paul Redmond, the SE Division's most enduring skeptic, wondered what to make of PROLOGUE. Edward Lee Howard, who had defected to Moscow in 1985, certainly could have told the Soviets about Burton Gerber's inviolable rule of thumb. Could it be that, thanks to Howard, the KGB was now turning Gerber's logic back on him?

It was too early to tell. Gerber and Redmond realized that the only way to find out if PROLOGUE was genuine was to run the operation for a while. Paul Redmond had always believed that production was the best measure of an agent; if

PROLOGUE began to hand over secrets that the KGB would never want revealed, then Redmond, the least trustful man in SE Division, would be convinced.

Gerber agreed. What did he have to lose by running PROLOGUE? The KGB already knew Downing's identity as Moscow chief, so he would not be compromised by meeting with PROLOGUE, even if he was a double. What's more, if the Russians were intent on framing Downing and forcing him out of the country, they could do it at almost any time. They wouldn't need such an elaborate ruse.

And what if PROLOGUE was real? Then he might just be able to provide the solution to the mystery surrounding the 1985 losses, and to Burton Gerber, that possibility was worth the gamble.

Moscow, June 1987

The restaurant that Jack Downing had selected as the site for his first exchange was hardly Moscow's best. Jack had brought his wife along with him for a late Friday night dinner, and, following PROLOGUE's instructions, he had left his briefcase in his car, unlocked and parked on the street outside.

Inside, Jack and Suzie did their best to eat the greasy and unpalatable cuisine while marking time for PROLOGUE to check out their car. The restaurant was nearly deserted, and for good reason. Suzie soon found that she had to keep her feet up off the floor in order to avoid the rats scurrying underneath their table.

But enduring the meal had been worth it; the communications plan had worked. Back in his office, Jack Downing found that the package he had left was gone. In its place was a message from PROLOGUE with the list of the CIA's agents who had been arrested and what had become of them. Downing had been away from SE Division in the early 1980s, when many of these cases had been run; now he could see how much had been gained—and now lost—by SE Division during his absence.

PROLOGUE had also handed over copies of the KGB's personnel assessment reports on both Downing and his predecessor, Murat Natirboff. It amused Downing that the KGB's assessment of his performance, including a discussion of his first tour in Moscow, was far more positive and flattering than the report that had been filed by the KGB team that had watched Natirboff.

Moscow, July 1987

Downing began to eat out every Friday night and was always careful to park his unlocked car nearby, where PROLOGUE could easily find it and make a quick exchange. He also tried to find an excuse to take the train to Leningrad as often as possible, although he was worried that if he went too frequently, his travel schedule would draw too much attention from the KGB. He decided not to take the train trip more than once every three months; that meant he would have to rely almost exclusively on his Friday night restaurant excursions for his communications.

But PROLOGUE was maddeningly unpredictable, and Downing was never certain when the KGB man would actually show up for an exchange. Downing and his wife would often return from yet another meal at one of PROLOGUE's handpicked, stomach-churning eateries only to find that the letter he had left for PROLOGUE was still in his briefcase, with no message in return. Downing soon found that PROLOGUE would contact him only about once a month, which meant that three out of four of his grisly meals were for naught.

PROLOGUE's "production"—Paul Redmond's term for the quality and quantity of the secrets he was handing over—was now steady, and events began to prove its accuracy as well. The engineer who PROLOGUE said would be the first dangle to appear flagged down a CIA officer driving through summertime Moscow. The new case presented Downing and Gerber with an unusual headache. The CIA was now convinced, thanks to PROLOGUE, that the new volunteer had been sent by the KGB. But if the CIA rejected the engineer's advances, the KGB might suspect the CIA had been tipped off he was a double agent and begin searching for a mole within its ranks. Burton Gerber had lost too many good agents over the last two years; he wasn't about to take any risks with this one. The CIA would have to handle the engineer as if he were a genuine spy and never give the KGB any reason to doubt that they had fooled the Americans.

Over the next four months, other double agents began to volunteer to the CIA in Moscow, and like the engineer, the CIA assigned case officers to handle each one. Before long, the double agent cases came to dominate the workload in Moscow, and Downing could see that far too much of the time and energy of his case officers was being spent on agents that the CIA knew to be frauds.

Sometimes the KGB got sloppy with these double agents. In one instance, a message from one Soviet agent was left for the CIA in a dead drop site that was being used to communicate with another Soviet agent. The only explanation was that both agents were under KGB control, and the Soviets had mixed up the communication instructions for the two cases.

But the CIA had to look the other way and keep the cases running in order to protect PROLOGUE. At least Moscow was busy. Working on the double agent cases got the CIA's officers out onto the streets, and that was something of an accomplishment for an operation that had had its confidence shaken. By the summer of 1987, in fact, case officers in Moscow were aborting their operational runs so frequently that Burton Gerber and the desk inside SE Division that dealt with internal operations were beginning to despair of any successful operations besides PROLOGUE.

They were seeing ghosts, and even the latest electronic gear designed to detect KGB surveillance didn't help. The CIA sent new, briefcase-size sensors that could pick up hidden transmissions from surveillance teams, and Moscow officers were instructed to lay them on the front seat of their cars while driving through the city. But each time an officer launched on a run, the device would send out an alarm, so the machines seemed to confirm Moscow's worst fears about the KGB's ability to track the Americans. Maybe "ultradiscreet surveillance" really did exist after all. Only later did the CIA discover that the alarms on the sensitive equipment were being triggered by faint electric emissions from the engine of the car, particularly when a CIA officer was making a sharp turn.

10

Islamabad, June 1987

The afternoon sun glinted off the sleek black Cadillac Fleetwood as it cruised through the light traffic of the Pakistani capital. Heavily tinted windows kept prying eyes from seeing if the backseat was occupied, but the presence of the Toyota Crown with two armed bodyguards trailing closely behind was a pretty good indicator that it was. Yet the flag was furled and cased in its fender well, suggesting perhaps to the careful observer that there was nothing official about this outing.

In the air-conditioned coolness of the backseat, Ambassador Arnie Raphel turned to me with an impish grin on his face.

"You know, every time I ride in this car I remember when I was a boy and thought it was every Jewish kid's dream to tool around the Catskills in the backseat of a big black Cadillac Fleetwood."

I glanced over at Raphel, a man three years my junior and a rising star in the foreign service. "Maybe," I said, "but this ain't the Catskills."

"Doesn't matter. It's only the Cadillac that counts." Raphel leaned back in the plush velour and was quiet the rest of the way to the embassy.

Arnie Raphel had taken over from the crusty career ambassador Dean Hinton as ambassador to Islamabad a month earlier. His arrival in Pakistan coincided with a growing but far from universal conviction in Washington that the Soviets were finally moving toward signing an agreement to pull out of Afghanistan. Raphel knew there was much work to be done before a deal would be sealed, but he arrived in Islamabad as the first American ambassador in seven years who would be more challenged by a probable peace in Afghanistan than by a seemingly unending war.

I had just accompanied Raphel to ISI headquarters for an unofficial call on Hamid Gul. We were bantering aimlessly for the benefit of the ambassador's Pakistani driver, an alert man who always had at least one ear tuned to the conversations in the backseat. We would wait until we were in the American compound before discussing our meeting with the ISI chief.

Raphel had extensive prior service in Pakistan and knew the language and the country better than any American on his staff, or probably anyone in the State Department. He had known Zia before the general was named chief of Army staff by Bhutto eleven years earlier, and he easily picked up his old relationship with the president and, by extension, with the president's men, who were aware of Zia's fondness for the ambassador. As a result, the important doors opened easily for Raphel, giving him a leg up on his new job.

Back at his residence, Raphel spoke more freely. "Why do I look at Hamid Gul and see a plucky little general who might one day take over the country?" he asked.

"Because one day he just might do it," I said.

"Seeing him takes me back to when I met Zia for the first time. I thought then that he'd eventually be running the place."

"Bhutto didn't see it, though. He thought Zia was a little dim, right to the end."

"Isn't it always that way. The guy who ought to figure it out never does."

"It sure was with Bhutto and Zia."

"Well, maybe you should add keeping an eye on the PLG to your list of things to do," Raphel said.

"PLG?"

Raphel grinned. "Yeah, plucky little general."

"He's plucky all right." It was curious that military officers who were diminutive in stature were almost always characterized as tough or plucky. Raphel's name for Gul would stick.

"Do you think he really got your message about the raids across the Amu Dar'ya? I'd have liked to talk to him about it, since that was the big thing on Shultz's Soviet-Afghan agenda last month."

"He got the message from Yaqub Khan and, I guess, Zia," I

said. "I don't think he needed another reminder from you or me." I'd asked Raphel not to raise with Gul the raid into Uzbekistan that had caused such a flap a month earlier. I told him the matter had been settled and that he might want to start off with the ISI chief on a positive note rather than opening an old wound at his first meeting.

"We can expect attacks on about everything Gul and ISI do from now on. As long as it was about winning a war, the hill was quiet. But with it looking like the Soviets are quitting, the sharks have already started circling your plucky little general."

"You mean *our* plucky little general, don't you?"

"Yeah," Raphel said. "Our PLG."

Arnie Raphel and I would work together closely during his next fifteen months in Pakistan, with a notable absence of the usual CIA–State Department tensions I'd seen over the years. Our goals were common and concentric, the prime one being getting the Soviets out of Afghanistan. If that actually happened, we'd have to begin thinking of the next steps for a post-Soviet Afghanistan trying to come to grips with peace. That would be a tough task for a country that had known little else but war for a generation.

The Kunjerab Pass, June 1987

The Kunjerab Pass between Pakistan and China is as close to the roof of the world as one can reach in a wheezing Toyota Land Cruiser. At 16,400 feet above sea level, a carburetor-fed, low-compression engine like the Land Cruiser's could go the distance far better than its more high-strung, fuel-injected cousins, but the oxygen-thin air at that altitude still made it tough going on car and driver. My wife and I had made the trip from Islamabad to Kunjerab, a wrenching journey on the Chinese-built Karakoram Highway, in three days, only briefly delayed by a landslide that had to be cleared with a blast of dynamite by Pakistani Army engineers. We reached the Kunjerab, the wide plateau that rolls back down into China's Xinjiang Province, as the first of the old British Bedford and shiny Japanese Hino trucks with their loads of mules crested from the other direction, heading back to Pakistan and to the heavier air below.

I knew from my own shortness of breath and light-headedness that the Pakistani drivers and their cargoes of mules must have been suffering. And sure enough, as the first of the convoy of trucks shifted into low gear for the descent, one of the Bedfords veered off the road and set off on a wobbly course across the tabletop plateau on the top of the world. It had gone no more than a hundred yards before it turned up the gradient and almost lazily flipped over on its side, its wheels still spinning and its load of mules tumbling out on the ice-hard surface. Surprisingly, all of the animals struggled to their feet, checked things out, and then just stood their ground. A groggy driver, also unhurt, and his relief crawled out of the cab of the capsized truck and joined the other Pakistanis trying to get halters on the loose mules, a task they accomplished in less than ten minutes. In another few minutes, the truck was righted by sheer brute force and the animals reloaded for the descent into Pakistan.

Thus began my sideline involvement in the mule trade, one of the more offbeat jobs in the prosecution of an increasingly unconventional war.

Mules, as any mule lover will tell you, are among the best of man's improvements over nature. They combine the strength of the horse with the temperamental coolness, stamina, and low maintenance of the donkey. Put the two together and you get the ideal pack animal for mountain warfare. But you can't just find good mules in the natural way of things. You have to work very hard at it.

Most pack mules are the offspring of a male donkey, a "jack," and a female horse, whose union produces a "horse mule" or a "john." It is possible to reverse the process and breed a male horse and a female donkey to produce a "hinny," but the failure rate of such unions is high and serves to discourage commercial breeders. So most of the pack mules that ended up hauling ordnance into the Hindu Kush and the White Mountains of Afghanistan were johns, sturdy little Chinese johns.

Having been raised in Texas, I was always pretty familiar with horses, but mules were a new experience, and a complicated one, I would soon learn. Though I had long been aware of the vastly different reactions of horses and mules to gunfire and explosions, I had never understood the reason for this. Over the next few months, I would have ample opportunity to learn. The donkey is an energy conserver by nature, a careful assessor of the situation and cautious selector of an appropriate reaction. If startled, a donkey will usually jump a little, check things out, and then hunker down until he sees something that might seriously threaten him. When it comes to gunfire, a well-trained donkey won't even flinch. A horse, on the other hand, under the same circumstances, will often bolt. Training does not always mitigate this trait. When the two animals are mated, the resulting product—the mule—is generally unflappable. Mules have a reputation for being stubborn and cantankerous, but mule aficionados are quick to point out that they may not really be stubborn at all; they just take a little longer to decide whether or not to waste their energy.

As I became embroiled in quartermastering the Afghan War, I discovered that on an annual basis we needed more mules than the world seemed prepared to breed. The weapons and other supplies the CIA was providing the Afghan resistance had grown upward of sixty thousand tons per year—all of which had to be hauled from Pakistan across zero line and over three hundred different infiltration routes to the commanders in the field. Such a daunting task required a combination of five- and ten-ton trucks, smaller pickups, and, finally, pack mules. So for the years I was involved in the Afghan resistance, we moved several thousand mules over the Kunjerab Pass from China and down into Pakistan to training camps, where we matched up mujahideen youngsters with their mules and taught both how to get along and, ultimately, how to survive.

The Chinese mules were never really enough, both in numbers or in size, so we had to turn to other sources for specialty mules. Though I was never less than amazed at the ability of the Afghan Task Force in Langley to come up with precisely what I needed when I needed it, I often thought that my cables back to headquarters on the topic of mules might have tested their patience and credulity.

For much of my time in Islamabad, I had a legend from the CIA's paramilitary past working with me, a gnarly veteran named Dutch Snyder. Dutch was an old hand who knew whatever you needed to know about mules and mule skinners and much beyond that. He had been in and out of combat throughout Southeast Asia, ending up in the CIA's special operations group, where he trained both CIA officers and friendly services around the world in the art of unconventional warfare. If Dutch didn't have an answer for an offbeat problem in a guerrilla war, there probably wasn't one.

Dutch helped me with much of the procurement needs for the war, and occasionally he and I would conspire to slip in a "nonstandard" requirement for the mules the task force was buying for our program just to see if everyone in Langley was paying attention. A typical cable might have read like this:

IMMEDIATE DIRECTOR
WNINTEL—MULE REQUIREMENTS FOR FY 88

1. TASK FORCE SHOULD SEEK ONLY MULES THAT MEET THE FOLLOWING STRINGENT REQUIREMENTS FOR PROGRAM NEEDS:
   A. NO MORE THAN THREE YEARS OF AGE.
   B. IN POSSESSION OF ALL THEIR TEETH.
   C. NO LESS THAN 12 HANDS HIGH NOR MORE THAN 17 HANDS.
   D. VETERINARY PASSED IN EXCELLENT GENERAL HEALTH.
   E. FEMALES PURCHASED BY TASK FORCE SHOULD BE CERTIFIED AS STUMP BROKE.
2. PLEASE ADVISE SOURCES AND DELIVERY DATES WHEN KNOWN.
3. NO FILE.

As every Texas or Tennessee redneck knows, "stump broke" is a ribald characterization of a boy and his female mule and the things they might do with the boy standing behind his mule on a tree stump. Dutch and I thought it would take Langley a while to figure out that point E was a joke, but we were wrong. It wouldn't take the task force long to get beyond its Ivy Leaguers and find someone who knew a little something about mules *and* rednecks, for soon we received a cable that read something like the following:

IMMEDIATE ISLAMABAD
WNINTEL—MULE REQUIREMENTS FOR FY 88
REF: ISLAMABAD 139987

1. YOUR SPECS FORWARDED REF HAVE BEEN FOLDED INTO THE PROCUREMENT PROCESS. REGRET, HOWEVER, THAT OUR MOST RELIABLE SOURCES OF MULES DO NOT REPEAT DO NOT PROVIDE STUMP TRAINING OR STUMP BROKE CERTIFICATES. WE HAVE RUN EXHAUSTIVE IN-HOUSE REVIEW OF PERSONNEL FILES TO LOCATE OFFICERS IN THE AGENCY WHO FAMILIAR WITH COMPLEX CERTIFICATION PROCESS AND HAVE FOUND THAT ONLY TWO ARE SNYDER AND BEARDEN NOW, BY FORTUNATE HAPPENSTANCE, IN ISLAMABAD. (THIS DATA RETRIEVED FROM THEIR MEDICAL RECORDS.) BELIEVE THAT ISLAMABAD WILL THUS BE ABLE TO MAKE CERTIFICATIONS AS NECESSARY IN THE FIELD. HQS WILL HANDLE ALL OTHER SPECS.
2. NO FILE.

Touché.

Islamabad, November 1987

Another silver bullet made its debut late in the year—the 120 mm Spanish mortar. For the first seven years of the conflict, the resistance had only the Warsaw Pact 82 mm mortar in their artillery arsenal. A reliable weapon, the 82 mm mortar was nonetheless limited in range and effectiveness as employed by the mujahideen. Indirect firing tactics were taught to the Afghan gunners but rarely used; instead, the resistance fighters normally fired their mortars at targets within direct sight at ranges of no more than a few thousand yards. The new Spanish mortar, larger and with devastating explosive power, had a range of about ten thousand yards. It came, moreover, with a ranging system worked out by Langley in close cooperation with the U.S. Army that fused the low-tech mortar with the high-tech world of satellite guidance.

It was as simple as it was effective. The mortar team would infiltrate by night to within about eight thousand yards of their target, preselected by screening satellite imagery of Soviet or

DRA garrisons. The mortar men would set up their tubes and then determine their own precise location using a global positioning satellite (GPS) receiver. Once their exact coordinates had been calibrated, the leader of the team would feed the GPS data into a small computer, add the coordinates of the target, and then query the computer for the precise compass direction and elevation to aim their mortars in order to hit their target with the first round.

The gunners would attach a specially designed "north-finding module" to the mortar tube and adjust its azimuth, or compass direction, according to the information provided by the computer so that it would be pointed precisely at the target. Winds aloft could be factored into the calculations to ensure that the first round fired at the target hit it with full surprise. The firing procedures, seemingly complicated to the layman, were quickly picked up by the Afghan gunners selected to head the mortar teams. In theory and in field tests, the new satellite-guided system would be a remarkable breakthrough for the resistance fighters who heretofore relied on "walking" their mortar rounds in on a target and in the process forfeiting the element of surprise. We trained the mortar teams in October and dispatched the first of them into the Konar Valley in late November.

Chagasaray, Afghanistan, 2235 Hours, November 28, 1987

The Konar Valley is among the most picturesque settings in eastern Afghanistan. The fast-flowing Konar River cuts through a series of spectacular gorges and winds its way through valleys with sheer walls rising up thousands of feet to pine-covered plateaus. Along the river are stands of poplar, cherry, and apricot trees; the occasional rope-and-board suspension bridge provides the only means of crossing over the river to the east and to Pakistan's rugged northern territories.

The Spetsnaz battalion garrisoned at Chagasaray about midway down the valley toward the Jalalabad plain had for years had a free hand in running interdiction operations against the infiltration routes from neighboring Pakistan. Tonight, it would have the tables turned on it.

The combined Pakistani-mujahideen team made its way

across the Konar River well after dark, leading pack mules loaded with four Spanish mortar tubes, base plates, assorted ammunition, and thick asbestos blankets for wrapping the still hot tubes and loading them onto the mules after the attack. The caravan made its way undetected to a point eight thousand yards from the Spetsnaz garrison.

After setting up their mortars precisely as trained, the team checked and rechecked the GPS readings and the azimuth and elevation of their mortar tubes. Once satisfied that everything was done exactly right, they loaded the heavy mortar bombs into the tubes. The gunners grasped their lanyards and tensely awaited the order to fire. When it came just after 2230 hours, they pulled their lanyards and all hell broke loose.

Three of the tubes fired as planned, but the fourth exploded, killing two of the crewmen and seriously wounding a third in the jaw with a piece of shrapnel. Uncertain of the cause of the disaster, the officer in charge ordered the mortars dismantled and loaded on the mules, along with the dead and the wounded gunner, for the hurried return to Pakistan.

Ojhri Camp, 1020 Hours, November 29, 1987

I met with my Pakistani counterparts the next day to probe what might have happened. The mood was dark as we searched for answers. The first thought, a long shot, was that the cold temperatures at the higher elevations of the Konar Valley might somehow have acted on a flaw in the metallurgy of the mortar tube, causing the failure. But we dismissed that as unlikely and finally decided to put the mortars on a supply flight that was at the Pakistani military airfield at Chaklala that day and send them back to the United States for testing. We sent the wounded gunner back on the same flight for treatment—his jaw had been nearly blown off, and he had traveled on mule back to Pakistan with it held together by his tightly wound turban. According to the Pakistani officer on the team, the wounded man had never uttered a word of complaint.

Back in the United States, the Army replicated the same cold-weather conditions for its tests of the remaining mortar tubes but failed to duplicate the failure experienced in Konar. Suspicions from the outset pointed to the most logical,

The "taxi phone" on Kastanayevskaya Street in the Moscow suburbs where Paul Stombaugh was ambushed in June 1985.

Paul Stombaugh and his son in Moscow, 1985.

Vladimir Sharavatov, the Seventh Directorate surveillance supervisor who was involved in most of the KGB arrests of American spies depicted in this book.

The U.S. embassy in Moscow (center foreground), with the spires of Adolf Tolkachev's apartment building in the background.

Viktor I. Cherkashin, the Line KR chief in Washington who handled Aldrich Ames's walk-in and the letter in which Robert Hanssen volunteered to spy for the KGB. (Courtesy of Jacqucline Mia Foster, Contact Press Images)

Major General Rem S. Krassilnikov, chief of the First Department of the KGB's Second Chief Directorate, 1985.

Krassilnikov in 1999, at the site where Leonid Polyshchuk (GTWEIGH) was ambushed in August 1985. (Courtesy of Jacqueline Mia Foster, Contact Press Images)

Burton Gerber, chief of the SE Division, 1984–1989.

Valentin Klimenko, Krassilnikov's deputy and later head of the American Department of the FSB. He is now the FSB's representative in Tel Aviv.

Aleksandr "Sasha" Zhomov, aka Phantom, aka PROLOGUE, at home with his spaniel in 2001.

A Moscow signal site being read by a Moscow case officer in a drive-by. Note the "V" mark on the pillar—a signal from a Soviet agent that an operational task has been carried out.

Jack Platt, chief of the SE Internal Operations course, 1987.

Paul Redmond, deputy chief of the SE Division and later deputy chief of counterintelligence, 1995.

Jack Downing, former chief in Moscow and Beijing and Deputy Director for Operations.

Gennady Vasilenko as a young KGB officer.

General Leonid Shebarshin, 1987.

A disabled Soviet tank that became a landmark on the road from Parachinar, Pakistan, to Ali Khel in Afghanistan's Paktia Province.

Milt Bearden and Frank Anderson at Ali Khel shortly after the Soviet garrison fell in 1987. The Soviet major who was adviser to a battalion of Afghan government troops died in the assault. Note the vodka bottle at the lower left.

The redoubtable Chinese mules on the road to Nangarhar.

Aerial shot of a transient mujahideen training camp in North-West Frontier Province, Pakistan.

Chinese-made 107 mm rockets being set up for delayed launch.

Front row, from left: Major General Hamid Gul, director general of Pakistan's Inter-Services Intelligence Directorate (ISI); Director of Central Intelligence William Webster; Deputy Director for Operations Clair George; an ISI colonel; and Milt Bearden at a mujahideen training camp in North-West Frontier Province, 1987.

Afghan resistance leader Sibghatullah Mojaddedi and Milt Bearden in 1988.

From left: Gulbuddin Hekmatyar, Burhanuddin Rabbani, William Webster, Hamid Gul, Ambassador Robert Oakley, Deputy Director of Central Intelligence Richard Kerr, and Milt Bearden at a meeting in Islamabad, 1988.

From left: Gulbuddin Hekmatyar, Richard Kerr, and Maulvi Yunis Khales in Islamabad, 1988.

Milt Bearden and Richard Stolz in Torkham moving supplies into Nangarhar Province, Afghanistan, 1988.

Milt Bearden in Paktia Province with two of Hekmatyar's fighters, 1987.

Milt Bearden and Frank Anderson in Paktia, 1987.

Top Soviet hands at CIA headquarters. From left: Milt Bearden, Gardner "Gus" Hathaway, Steve Weber, Deputy Director for Operations Dick Stolz, Paul Redmond, and Burton Gerber.

Oldrich Cerny, Václav Havel's national security adviser (left).

Polish intelligence chief Andrzej Milczanowski with Milt Bearden in Warsaw.

Milt Bearden, David Rolph, and Rem Krassilnikov in Dzerzhinsky Square with "Iron Felix" still standing in the background, 1991.

From left: Valentin Klimenko, David Rolph, John MacGaffin, Milt Bearden, and Rem Krassilnikov in a KGB safe house in Moscow, 1992.

The Lubyanka headquarters of the KGB defaced by demonstrators sending their message to the international audience in both Russian and English on August 22, 1991. (Courtesy of Bruno Mahlmann III)

The entrance of Lubyanka was defaced with a swastika on the evening of August 22, 1991. (Courtesy of Bruno Mahlmann III)

The pedestal that held the statue of "Iron Felix," Dzerzhinsky Square, August 22, 1991. (Courtesy of Bruno Mahlmann III)

"Iron Felix" being hauled down by a German-built crane on the night of August 22, 1991. (Courtesy of Bruno Mahlmann III)

Boris Yeltsin, captured on film by a CIA officer, at the Russian Parliament in August 1991. (Courtesy of Bruno Mahlmann III)

Paul Redmond in front of a fragment of the Berlin Wall at CIA headquarters.

fundamental error made during the preparations for the attack, what mortar men call a "double feed." Testing that suspicion, Army investigators purposely loaded one mortar tube with two rounds—a double feed—and fired it. As expected, the tube exploded just as the one had in the Konar Valley, leaving no doubt among the investigators that an overanxious gunner had loaded his tube twice that night without realizing it. And he'd paid for his error with his life.

The Army's verdict of a "double feed" in the Chagasaray incident was accepted with relief. The Pakistani officers in charge of the mortar project knew well the realities of both mortars and combat anxieties and had no difficulty accepting the results of the American tests. Instead of brooding, as soon as the 120 mm mortar was cleared for combat, they mounted the operation once again on December 15, aimed against the same target. Despite their misgivings about returning to the same target area, the second time around was a spectacular success.

The gunners again moved under cover of darkness to within about eight thousand yards of the Chagasaray garrison, set up their tubes, queried with the GPS satellites, set their azimuth and elevations, and let loose a barrage of rounds that struck the Spetsnaz battalion garrison with complete surprise. The Soviets never knew what happened to them. They made a futile attempt at counterbattery fire but succeeded only in hitting one of their own outposts. The mujahideen gunners dropped round after round down their tubes, long overstaying their planned time on target, until they had expended their ammunition. Then they rolled their tubes in the asbestos blankets, loaded them aboard their mules, and made their way back to Pakistan in the last hours of darkness.

By the time the sun was high in the sky, a CIA KH-11 satellite looked down on the Spetsnaz garrison at Chagasaray and took a series of photographs of the devastation wreaked by the new weapon. When I showed the imagery boards to the Pakistanis and the Afghan commanders ten days later, the effects of the attack were stark. Just like the before and after imagery boards of the Kharga ammunition dump in August 1986, the boards of Chagasaray before the attack showed the intact wooden barracks buildings, the battalion vehicles neatly parked, and the usual evidence of an active, orderly military installation set along the Konar River. The shots taken after the attack showed the burned-out shells of the buildings, scattered and destroyed vehicles, and a few new, undamaged vehicles that were determined to belong to the Soviet Army team that had arrived on the scene the next day to investigate the attack.

The attack against Chagasaray had a special effect on resistance morale. In a war characterized more by defensive operations and ambushes than by offensive attacks on main-line Soviet units, the devastation of the Chagasaray garrison marked a qualitative change in the way the resistance carried its war to the Soviet 40th Army. Although the success of the strike was never replicated with the same dramatic results, the mortar attack was just one more event that reinforced the Soviet decision to quit Afghanistan. By the end of 1987, even the hard-core doubters in Washington were becoming convinced that Moscow was ready to quit.

11

Nottoway Park, Fairfax County, Virginia, November 23, 1987

Bob Hanssen was back in his element as he walked purposefully down the dirt path to the small footbridge on the quiet edge of the busy county park. He reached down, and in a dark crevice just beneath the footbridge, he could feel the spot. It was one of his favorite dead drop sites, one the KGB had creatively named "Park." The last site they'd recommended, named "AN" and located in a more remote park in the far western suburbs of Fairfax County, had not been satisfactory as far as Hanssen was concerned. It was far from his home in Vienna, Virginia, and it required too much physical effort, too much undignified mess, for the middle-aged FBI agent. With new management responsibilities at work, six children at home, and an increasingly active life in the Catholic Opus Dei religious community, Hanssen was a busy man, and he didn't have time for such cumbersome security arrangements. Using his code name B, he had just written a frosty letter to his KGB handlers about the dead drop issue, urging a switch back to the more convenient Park.

"Recognize that I am dressed in business suit and cannot slog around in inch-deep mud," he wrote in a November 19 letter. "I suggest we use once again original site." He had complained about AN in September, too, writing to the KGB, "I am not a young man, and the commitments on my time prevent using distant drops such as you suggest. I know in this I am moving you out of your set modes of doing business, but my experience tells me we can be actually more secure in easier modes."

So now Hanssen was back at a dead drop site in his own neighborhood, one where he felt far more comfortable. But more important, Bob Hanssen was happy with his new job as supervisor of the FBI's Soviet Analytical Unit, a position that gave him access to virtually all operational and analytical documents related to the Soviet Union produced by the FBI's counterintelligence squads. One interesting document to cross his desk during his first months back in Washington was the summary of an October trip to Guyana by CIA officer Jack Platt to renew his friendship with Gennady Vasilenko. Platt had dutifully sent a copy of his trip report to the FBI, which was working with the CIA on the Vasilenko case—code-named MONOLITE—and it didn't take long for it to pass through Hanssen's office.

That night in Nottoway Park, Hanssen was turning over a copy of Platt's report to his Soviet handlers, along with a package of other secret documents, including a detailed account of the KGB secrets that Vitaly Yurchenko had revealed to the CIA and FBI before his curious redefection to Moscow. He left the package, wrapped tightly in plastic, tucked underneath the footbridge, exactly where he found another package from the KGB waiting for him, one that contained $20,000 in cash and a letter from the KGB telling him that another $100,000 had been deposited on his behalf in a Soviet bank. The letter also contained specific questions about classified information for Hanssen to answer in the next exchange.

Just across the street from Nottoway Park, a few yards away from where Hanssen was stooping in the dark, were tidy subdivisions filled with well-tended houses, home to dozens of CIA, FBI, and Defense Department employees and their families. One senior CIA counterintelligence officer in particular lived just two blocks away, and he jogged almost daily through Nottoway Park along a route that passed close to the Park dead drop site. Like Bob Hanssen, he specialized in Soviet matters, and years later, the eerie similarities in their lives would come to haunt the CIA man and his family and would nearly destroy his career and his life.

Havana, Cuba, January 11, 1988

The hands came out of nowhere, shadows reaching out to clamp Gennady Vasilenko's arms to his sides, even as his body was being roughly dragged down and his head was slammed with a dull thud to the floor of the small Cuban house, opening a bloody gash. The KGB security agents had been hiding inside, waiting for Vasilenko to arrive from the airport on what he believed was a routine trip for KGB business. Instead, he had come to Havana only to find himself crumpled over and suffocating, caught up in a sudden and brutal KGB ambush.

Tall, athletic, and above all fun loving—too much so, perhaps, for his own good—Gennady Vasilenko was the KGB's deputy *Rezident* in the Latin backwater of Georgetown, Guyana, where he was supremely bored, particularly after his last overseas assignment, a far more interesting tour of duty in Washington. He had little to do in Guyana besides think about hunting and women and drinking, not necessarily in that order, while providing some limited support for halfhearted Soviet and Cuban forays into the revolutionary politics of South America. Vasilenko had been ordered to Cuba so that he could use the KGB's secure facility inside the Soviet embassy in Havana, where he was told he was to write the secret "counterintelligence annex" to the annual report for the embassy in Guyana. He figured it wouldn't take long to document a year's worth of desultory operations in Georgetown, where almost nothing of any consequence had happened since the members of the Jonestown cult drank their Kool-Aid and committed mass suicide back in the late 1970s. So he'd have plenty of extra time in Havana, and he hoped it would provide an opportunity to see old friends and catch up on KGB gossip. He had arranged for a KGB colleague to pick him up at the airport, and he was planning to stay at his friend's home for a few days.

At the airport he was met instead by a local KGB security officer, who told him his friend had been suddenly called away. The security officer, thoughtfully, had found him another house to use during his stay. But as soon as he walked into the house, the ambush exploded around him. Vasilenko was given little chance to catch his breath before the interrogations began inside what he now realized was a KGB safe house.

"Do you know Mr. Platt of the CIA?" his questioners demanded.

Vasilenko shuddered quietly.

Jack Platt. So that's what this is all about, he thought as he tried to recover from the brief beating. Yes, of course I know Platt, you bastards. Jack, what have you done?

Jack and Gennady. The American and Russian spies had been friends since 1977, nearly inseparable at times, breaking all the Cold War rules against fraternization with the enemy. Theirs was a friendship that helped put a human face on the Cold War battle between the CIA and KGB and showed that personal bonds of loyalty could overcome the ruthless games played by spies on both sides.

Platt, then a Washington-based officer in the CIA's Soviet Division, was trolling for Russians to recruit when a Soviet defector, a former classmate of Vasilenko's at the KGB's training institute, had identified Gennady as one of the KGB officers working under diplomatic cover in the Soviet embassy in Washington. Gennady had never imagined that he would one day be a KGB spy. He had the soul of a jock, a Russian version of a frat boy with dreams of playing volleyball on the Soviet Olympic team. Born in 1941, he had been an engineering student at the Avtomotora Institute in Moscow and had by the early 1960s emerged as one of the best young volleyball players in the USSR. In 1964, he seemed assured of making the Soviet team that was heading to the Summer Olympic Games in Tokyo, until a shoulder injury kept him off the Olympic squad.

Despite his injury, Vasilenko kept playing volleyball on club squads in the city and eventually caught the eye of Dynamo, the powerful KGB-backed sports association, and was recruited for the Dynamo volleyball team. By the late 1960s, he found his way from the volleyball squad into the real KGB, and after attending the Yuri Andropov Higher KGB School, he was ushered into the KGB's foreign intelligence arm, the First Chief Directorate. In 1976, he was assigned to Line KR, counterintelligence, and was sent to the Washington *Rezidentura.* Later, he would joke to Platt that he was the only Russian who had joined the KGB on an athletic scholarship.

Platt, by contrast, was an American Army brat who had attended a dozen different schools around the United States and Europe and had graduated from Williams College in Massachusetts before becoming a Marine officer in 1959. He left the Marines for the CIA in 1963, spending five years as a case officer in Austria, followed by another three in Laos. He liked to joke that he was transferred from Laos to Paris as a reward for helping the United States "take second place in the Asian war games."

When Platt set his sights on Vasilenko as a potential recruit, he began maneuvering all over Washington in an effort to meet him in a seemingly casual and coincidental way. Platt had an intermediary arrange it so he could bump into the Russian at a Harlem Globetrotters game in Washington, and the two ended up sitting together and chatting throughout the game. By the end of the game, Platt realized, he actually liked Vasilenko. He was completely different from most of the KGB hoods he'd come across in the past—natural and disarming, a man who seemed to love life more than he loved Marx and Engels. But that didn't mean that Gennady Vasilenko was going to be a pushover for a CIA recruitment pitch. Vasilenko may not have been a good Communist, but he was a proud Russian, and he wasn't interested in betraying his country.

For Platt, Vasilenko was an intriguing challenge. The CIA

officer, who was working the recruitment jointly with FBI counterintelligence agents, soon realized that Vasilenko loved the game as much as he did. Gennady seemed to think he could tease the Americans into showing him a good time without having to step across the line into becoming a spy. He could deflect Platt's entreaties—which were sometimes vague, sometimes more explicit—by turning the tables and pitching Platt to work for the KGB.

"What in the hell could you offer me?" Platt chided Vasilenko. "A great new life in the socialist workers paradise?"

The case almost collapsed before Platt could get it going. In September 1979, Platt and an FBI agent working with him took Vasilenko out to drink at the Gangplank restaurant, one of Platt's favorite haunts along Washington's Potomac waterfront. At the time, Platt was a fourteen-to-sixteen-beer-a-day alcoholic, and he was trying to recruit the Soviet through a beery haze. On this night, his FBI colleague got drunk as well, and unlike Platt, he couldn't function well while drinking. As they both sat with Vasilenko at the Gangplank, the FBI agent became loud and sloppy and late that night turned to the customers at the next table and began telling them exactly what was going on at their table.

"Hey, you know what we're doing over here?" the FBI agent said through slurred speech over his shoulder. "I'm in the FBI, he's in the CIA, and we're trying to recruit this Russian."

Unfortunately, the customers drinking at the next table were also CIA analysts from the Directorate of Intelligence, and the next morning they reported the incident to the CIA's Office of Security. The FBI agent was taken off the case and transferred out of Washington, and Platt was confronted by his boss, who told him that he was a drunk who needed help. If he would admit his problem and ask for help, the CIA could arrange treatment for him, his boss told him. If not, it might be time to brush up his CV and start looking for another job.

Platt finally agreed to do something about the drinking and checked into a hospital. When he was admitted, he hadn't had a drink in twelve hours, but his blood alcohol level showed he was still drunk. Released a month later after going cold turkey, a newly sober Platt asked his supervisors to let him renew his contacts with Vasilenko. At first they balked, saying the case had been irretrievably botched by that FBI agent at Gangplank. But Platt persisted, and in January 1980, he reestablished contact. As he expected, Vasilenko was happy to hear from him, and the two picked up where they had left off, except that now Platt didn't drink with the KGB man.

Vasilenko dutifully reported his contacts with the CIA to his supervisors in the KGB *Rezidentura* and explained that he was hoping to turn Platt into a Russian agent. His bosses were not overly happy about the contacts, particularly when it became clear that Vasilenko and Platt were seeing each other quite frequently and there were no signs that Platt was edging closer to betraying the CIA. But Vasilenko argued that he knew what he was doing; besides, if KGB officers weren't allowed to meet CIA officers, how could they ever hope to recruit them as spies? The KGB *Rezident* agreed, but Vasilenko was on notice that he had to tread carefully. Over time, the relationship between Gennady and Jack became a true friendship, over drinks at cafés and restaurants around Washington, over family dinners at their homes. Eventually they worked up the nerve to go out hunting and shooting together in the West Virginia forests. Still, Platt and his FBI colleagues could never move Vasilenko beyond what the CIA called a "developmental"—a target of a recruitment, but not yet a spy. He would sometimes talk about office gossip, but Platt couldn't get him to betray his operations.

In fact, even as Vasilenko and Platt were meeting for drinks and dinner, the Russian was involved in the most important case of his KGB career. In January 1980, Ronald Pelton, a disgruntled former employee of the National Security Agency, had walked into the Soviet embassy in Washington, offering to sell information about the agency's operations against the Soviet Union. Pelton told the KGB about a sensitive operation called "Ivy Bells," in which American submarines had planted taps on undersea telephone cables used by the Soviet Navy in the Sea of Okhotsk on the Soviet Union's Pacific coast.

Vasilenko was the first KGB officer to meet with Pelton. During his first visit to the Soviet embassy, it was Vasilenko's job to spirit him out without being detected by the FBI surveillance teams that staked out the embassy. Vasilenko decided to dress Pelton in a disguise and put him on a bus crowded with Russian embassy employees going home for the evening in order to sneak him out through the back of the embassy building. After that operation, Vasilenko kept meeting with Platt without telling him anything about Pelton. But Vasilenko's bosses gradually became more suspicious of his contacts with Platt and finally ordered him to break it off. Once again Vasilenko grew angry, but this time he didn't try to argue. Instead, he continued to see Platt and simply stopped reporting the contacts to his supervisors.

Platt's bosses, meanwhile, were growing frustrated with his inability to close the deal with Vasilenko. Some at the CIA wanted him to either break off the contact or force the issue by threatening to blackmail Vasilenko. The Soviet was now having unauthorized contacts with a CIA officer; couldn't Platt use the threat of exposure to force Vasilenko to cross the line? Platt angrily refused to use such hardball tactics. It wasn't because he considered Vasilenko a friend—Platt's ultimate goal of recruiting Vasilenko trumped his friendship with the KGB officer—it was because he knew the strategy was doomed to fail. Vasilenko was a roustabout, but he also had a stubborn sense of honor, and trying to blackmail him would only backfire. No, Platt realized, the only way Gennady Vasilenko would ever become an American spy was if he decided to do so on his own. Jack Platt just wanted to keep up the friendship so that he could be there if and when he was ready.

In 1981, Vasilenko was transferred from Washington back to KGB headquarters in Moscow, and Platt realized that there was no way he could maintain contact with him there without putting him at risk. Platt told Vasilenko to have a nice time back in the socialist paradise, secretly hoping that a couple of years back in the drudgery of Moscow would convince him of the merits of working for the United States. He vowed to himself that when Vasilenko reemerged for his next overseas assignment, he would track him down and recruit him once and for all.

In 1984, Vasilenko finally came out again, this time assigned to Guyana. The Soviet ambassador in Guyana had excellent connections back in Moscow and had complained that his embassy deserved a fully staffed KGB *Rezidentura*. That was, after all, a measure of status within the foreign affairs bureaucracy. Vasilenko was sent to Georgetown as deputy *Rezident* to help satisfy the sudden demand. Back in Washington, Platt had moved on to a new assignment, running the CIA's Internal Operations training course, teaching young CIA officers how to work behind the Iron Curtain. But he was also trying to watch for signs that Vasilenko had reemerged from Moscow. It took a while, but eventually Vasilenko was back on the CIA's scope, and Platt started asking for permission to go to Guyana to try to pick up where he had left off in 1981. By October 1987, Platt had finally been given approval to travel to Georgetown and to buy a hunting rifle to take to Vasilenko as a kind of homecoming present. Platt hoped that he could convince Vasilenko to go hunting with him in the wilds of South America as a way to renew their friendship after so many years apart.

It turned out that Vasilenko was just as eager to see Platt, but he did recognize that there were new dangers. It was one thing to go out to dinner in Washington with an adversary; that was part of the business of intelligence. But how could Vasilenko explain to his bosses in Moscow the fact that his CIA friend had flown thousands of miles—bringing along an expensive gift—to renew their friendship? From now on, all of their contacts would be unauthorized, and Vasilenko had to make certain they remained out of view. He had good reason to be more cautious now; KGB Center was swirling with rumors that old colleagues from Washington had been arrested and that other KGB officers had fallen under suspicion as well. There seemed to be a bloodbath under way in Yasenevo, and morale was plunging. Officers walking the corridors felt like hiding their faces, in case another mole might be just around the corner. Paranoia and fear, the birthrights of the KGB, began to climb to pre-détente levels.

But just because Vasilenko wanted to keep his friendship with Platt a secret didn't mean that he was ready to spy for the Americans. He wanted to see Platt mostly because he was bored and wanted some diversion. He was still rebuffing all of Platt's offers to spy, still teasing him with KGB office gossip without crossing the line into espionage. Platt spent a few days in Guyana, meeting Vasilenko each day along the oceanfront seawall, little more than a cement levee erected to protect a military hospital built just beyond the beach in nearby lowlands. The men brought snacks, drinks, and ice so they could picnic each day out of sight of the prying eyes of Soviet personnel at the embassy. During the afternoons, they would have shooting contests, firing pistols at tin cans. While they kept their conversations light, there were small signs of progress along the way that kept Platt interested from a professional standpoint as well. At one point, Vasilenko casually mentioned that a KGB man named Vladimir Tsymbal had been sent from Moscow to visit the Washington *Rezidentura* in 1985 and again in 1987.

Platt was intrigued by this offhand remark. Tsymbal, Platt knew, was a covert communications specialist in the First Chief Directorate's Line KR. The CIA knew from past experience that Tsymbal was used by the KGB to arrange the delicate covert agent communications details for highly sensitive operations. He was one of the KGB's top technical experts, and when Tsymbal showed up somewhere, the CIA's first instincts were to start looking for a spy. So why had Tsymbal been sent to Washington in 1985 and again two years later? What agent operations in Washington were so important that they required Moscow's best covert communications tech? Probing for answers from Vasilenko was no use; even if he wanted to tell Platt, he wouldn't have known the truth. No, Platt would just have to report back to headquarters on what Vasilenko said and see if the counterintelligence analysts in Langley could make sense of Tsymbal's travels.

In October 1987, Platt wrote up a summary of his trip to Georgetown, complete with Vasilenko's mysterious reference to Tysmbal's visits to Washington, and sent a copy along to the FBI, since the MONOLITE case was still considered a joint CIA-FBI operation. Platt retired from the CIA in 1987, but he returned immediately as a contractor in order to try to finish the case. He was planning to return to Georgetown in February to see his old friend once again.

As he tried to compose himself for further interrogations, Gennady Vasilenko could only think again, Jack, Jack, what have you done?

Aboard a Soviet Freighter Bound for Odessa, January 1988

Gennady Vasilenko had said little to his inquisitors in Havana, so they had thrown him on board a freighter headed back to the Soviet Union, where the KGB would have plenty of time to convince him that he should talk. Gennady was not confined on board; the KGB figured he had no place to go. But as he paced the deck, he began to seriously consider jumping overboard in the middle of the Atlantic, ending his life and the pain that he knew was now descending on his family. Yet as the ship trudged through the waves, bearing him back to an unforgiving future, Vasilenko finally rejected suicide. He was not a spy, he shouldn't have been arrested, so he would fight for his life.

Lefortovo Prison, Moscow, June 1988

The interrogations of Gennady Vasilenko had been endless, covering the same ground time and again, focusing on Platt's October trip to Guyana, prompting the same responses from Vasilenko each time. *Yes, I knew Platt. Yes, I continued to see him even though I had been told to break off contact, but I thought I could recruit him. No, I never spied.*

Vasilenko knew just how deadly this game of endless questions and repetitive answers really was. Inside Lefortovo, if a decision was made by a tribunal for the verdict of death, the execution could be carried out right on the premises. Men he knew and had worked with in Washington, Motorin and Martynov, had been shot inside these same prison walls. There would be no public trial, no appeals.

But the KGB was strangely legalistic, and Vasilenko soon realized that the investigators had very little hard evidence against him. They had apparently arrested and jailed him based on reports of Platt's visit to Guyana, but that didn't seem to be enough for a tribunal to order his execution. Fortunately for Vasilenko, Platt had never exaggerated his success with Vasilenko, even in his internal CIA reports. The trip report Hanssen had provided to the KGB showed only that Vasilenko had held an unauthorized meeting with him in Guyana.

But the KGB inquisitors decided to fill in the blanks and skillfully sought to convince Vasilenko that they already had enough evidence with which to convict him. During his first interrogation in Lefortovo, the investigators claimed that Cuban intelligence had discovered a tape recording of his October meeting with Platt in Georgetown. Platt, they said, had left it behind in his hotel. Confess, they said. We have the smoking gun.

But Vasilenko remembered that Platt had promised him he would never tape-record their conversations, and he decided to trust his friend and call the KGB's bluff. He realized that they were lying, trying to frighten him into a false confession, and that realization saved his life. Vasilenko became convinced that the KGB's questioning was so intense only because the investigators needed him to implicate himself.

So he refused to cave in to the pressure, refused to confess to espionage that he had not committed. After each session, his frustrated inquisitors sent him back to his cell, where they relied on informers they had planted as his cellmates to determine whether he would admit to guilt during unguarded moments. From January through June, the KGB sent three different informers in to share a cell with Vasilenko; each came back saying that he had not confessed and did not appear to be a spy.

Complicating the investigation for the KGB was the fact that they couldn't find any of the "spy gear" or communications plans that they typically discovered when they uncovered a CIA mole. Did that mean he was innocent, as he proclaimed? Or did it just mean that he was very clever?

The investigators were running out of time to prove their case. Vasilenko's arrest had touched a raw nerve within the ranks of the KGB's First Chief Directorate, where the psychic wounds from so many arrests, executions, and defections of friends and colleagues over the past three years were beginning to take their toll. First Directorate officers had been stunned at first, but now the arrest of a popular and unpretentious officer wasn't going down well at Yasenevo. In an informal and secret KGB poll of his co-workers in counterintelligence, none of his colleagues said they believed he was a traitor. Vasilenko was also aided by the fact that his wife was from an influential family; so the KGB had to prove that it had an ironclad case before it ordered his execution.

But the KGB lacked convincing evidence, so its secret tribunal decided not to prosecute Vasilenko on espionage charges. Instead, the tribunal ordered Vasilenko cashiered for failing to report unauthorized contacts with the Americans and for illegally smuggling the hunting rifle Platt had given him into the Soviet Union. He was released from jail in June, simultaneously stripped of his rank, and thrown out onto the streets of Moscow without a pension and without a job. Eventually, Vasilenko's contacts in the KGB's old boy network slowly helped him pick up the pieces of his life.

Back in Washington, Jack Platt was distraught. All he knew was that Vasilenko had disappeared, and he had no idea whether his friend was alive or dead. With no sign of life, Platt quit his contract job at the CIA in 1988, quietly simmering over the fact that something had gone wrong on an important case and no one at the agency seemed to be doing anything about it. He bitterly warned friends who were still in the CIA's Soviet/East European Division to "watch their backs." But the truth of the matter was that by 1987, the CIA and the FBI were no longer expending much energy trying to explain why they had lost so many agents. Operations were up and running again in Moscow, and the atmosphere of suspicion that had descended over SE Division was starting to lift.

12

Islamabad, February 2, 1988

Arnie Raphel and I were sitting on my verandah in sweaters, enjoying the bracing coolness of the Islamabad evening. Over the last few months, it had become virtually certain that Gorbachev was ready to quit Afghanistan, his preconditions for a friendly and neutral Afghanistan no longer blocking the negotiations. Discussions in Geneva between the U.S. negotiator,

Undersecretary of State for Political Affairs Mike Armacost, and his Soviet counterpart, Yuli Vorontsov, had reached a critical stage. We expected the final breakthrough at any moment, and Raphel and I were discussing prospects for an interim government in Afghanistan when my steward interrupted our conversation. It was a call for the ambassador, he reported solemnly. Arnie disappeared for five minutes, then returned, tilted his glass to mine, and said, "It was Armacost. It's over. They're going to sign in Geneva. Gorbachev will announce it in a week."

"That's it?" I said, still letting the news sink in. "Now what?"

"The 'now what' part might even be the hard part," Raphel said.

And he was right. The road to a settlement had been full of detours ever since Gorbachev took his first tentative steps just over two years earlier, and Washington was split down the middle on the issue of whether the Soviets would ever really leave. Mike Armacost had declared flatly in mid-1987 that the Soviets would withdraw. Eduard Shevardnadze told George Shultz in September 1987 that they would be out of Afghanistan by 1988, but Shultz held the substance of his conversation with the Soviet Foreign Minister tightly until November of 1987, when he finally shared it with the DCI, Bill Webster.

But the CIA was still doubtful about how Gorbachev would manage the withdrawal politically, pulling it off without looking like the United States at the end of its Vietnam experience. Bob Gates bet Armacost $25 that the Soviets wouldn't be out of Afghanistan by the end of the Reagan administration, though he acknowledged that the decision to get out had been made.

Precisely one week later, Mikhail Gorbachev addressed the Soviet people and declared that Soviet troops would commence their withdrawal from Afghanistan on May 15 and would complete it by March 15 the following year.

Chiang Mai, Thailand, April 10, 1988

As soon as it appeared certain that the Geneva Accords would be signed, I took off for a short break in Thailand with Marie-Catherine. The fight over the agreement had been long, but the

Soviets, against most predictions, had finally bitten the bullet. The formal agreement would be signed in Geneva on April 14 and would go into effect on May 15. The Soviets would thus begin their withdrawal on May 15 and complete it within nine months, by February 15, 1989, almost ten disastrous years after they had invaded Afghanistan.

We arrived in Chiang Mai two days ahead of the Thai New Year and had planned on doing little or nothing for a few days while the lively up-country Thais swept their ancestral graves, cleaned up their houses, and happily doused anyone in town with cleansing water. I checked in with our people in Thailand as a courtesy and to let them know how and where to reach me if someone came looking. When a colleague called the next day and suggested that I come back to the office to read an immediate precedence cable, I tried to double-talk the subject out of him.

"Where's it from?" I asked.

"From the place you work now," came the reluctant, spooky answer.

"What can you tell me about it?" I probed.

"Wait a minute." There was a pause as he scanned the cable again. "It looks like an ammo dump has blown up."

I was relieved that the cable had turned out to be a routine report of another mujahideen success just before the Geneva Accords went into effect. It might reinforce the wisdom of the Soviet decision to throw in the towel. I guessed that Islamabad was probably sending it along as an info copy to me to give me some more good news while I was on break. "Okay," I said. "Thanks. That's great. I'll get all the details when I get back. If you would, just do me a favor and send a short cable back to my people with one word: 'Bravo.' Sign my name to it. Okay?"

"Wait a minute. Your guys are saying that the dump that blew is *your* dump, the one not far from where you live! There's a firestorm at your place."

"Oh, shit. Tell them I'll be back as soon as I can."

By the time Marie-Catherine and I got back to Islamabad, the most dangerous explosions had subsided. But ammunition was still cooking off at Ojhri camp, where thousands of deadly, unstable rounds were strewn about, ready to blow at the slightest jolt. When Ojhri blew, there were close to ten thousand tons of rockets, mortars, small-arms ammunition, plastic explosives, and Stingers in storage. Many of the 107 mm rockets had launched, some causing casualties throughout Rawalpindi and in nearby Islamabad; but since they were not fused, the rockets had not exploded on impact and there had been far less damage and loss of life. A couple of 107 mm rockets hit the American International School in Islamabad, causing an understandable panic among the parents and students but no injuries.

The people of Rawalpindi were less fortunate. The first major explosion flattened a shanty town that had built up outside the walls of Ojhri camp, killing dozens. As the explosions continued through the morning, with black clouds rising above Ojhri and drifting over Rawalpindi, many others were killed by falling ordnance and debris. At day's end, casualties were up to one hundred killed and one thousand injured.

First Chief Directorate Headquarters, Yasenevo, April 10, 1988

Leonid Shebarshin considered the Ojhri camp explosion another good example of the abilities of Najibullah's intelligence and security service, the Khad. He had no doubt that Khad had been behind the operation, but he also had no doubts that they had done it on their own, not in cooperation with the KGB special units in Afghanistan. Shebarshin had a deep respect for the capabilities of the Afghan special services, particularly in the area of "dirty tricks," which is how he classified the destruction of the American and Pakistani supply dump at Ojhri camp. He was not naive enough to think that his Afghan colleagues would share with him everything they planned and felt no disappointment that the massive explosion at Ojhri could not be credited to the Soviet Committee for State Security.

It was a good operation, Shebarshin concluded, and it couldn't have come at a better time, just days before the signing of the Geneva Accords.

Ojhri Camp, April 12, 1988

I was met at the airport and taken directly to Ojhri, where I was given a tour by Brigadier Janjua, the new officer in charge of the military assistance to the Afghans. As we walked carefully through the still smoldering rubble, I asked him how it had happened.

"We're still investigating," Janjua said, "but it looks like one of the porters dropped a box containing one of the new Egyptian rockets, maybe a white phosphorus one. There was an explosion and a fire in the warehouse, and while the workers were moving the wounded to safety, the fire spread out of control. In minutes the whole thing went up."

"The Egyptian ordnance again?" I asked, shaking my head.

"The Egyptian stuff again," Brigadier Janjua answered, anger in his voice.

There had been a history of problems with the Egyptian ordnance. In the early years of the war, the Egyptians seemed to have swept the trash out of their warehouses and packed it up along with their old and unusable ordnance and sent it off to Pakistan for the Afghan resistance. A year or so earlier, there had been a fire in Ojhri involving Egyptian white phosphorus mortar bombs. Only quick action by camp personnel had prevented a similar disaster then. In later years, however, the quality of the Egyptian supplies had improved, and there were fewer complaints. But listening to Brigadier Janjua's initial take on the disaster, I guessed that this would be the first of many versions of what had happened—maybe even the easiest to understand.

"Was there anything anyone could have done?" I asked.

"Maybe. If they'd tried to handle the fire instead of the injured, it might have been different. But probably not. It was out of control very quickly," Janjua answered. "After that, about all anyone could do was get out of the way. And some of our boys couldn't even do that."

I went from Ojhri to the embassy, where Ambassador Raphel, with the help of my deputy Philippe Jones, had coordinated the American response. There had been no American casualties, but a few near misses had unnerved the community. Some embassy employees were asking to be sent home right away.

Arnie Raphel was coolheaded from the first blast, which he'd heard all the way from Rawalpindi. He had dryly asked Philippe Jones at one point while the rockets were still flying, some of them landing near the embassy itself, whether it was really a good idea to have stored so much ammunition so close to Islamabad and Rawalpindi. Phil had answered truthfully that it sure as hell hadn't been such a good idea in view of events, but that was the way the Pakistanis had wanted it.

He never brought up the question of who might be to blame again. Instead, he cabled the Department of Defense to dispatch explosive ordnance disposal (EOD) teams to Pakistan to assist in the cleanup. The EOD teams arrived in a matter of days, and for the next several weeks small explosions would be heard each day as the teams detonated the unstable ordnance they had carefully collected.

Though the ambassador was able to keep a cap on American finger-pointing, the blame game in the government of Pakistan was running rampant. Ojhri was still smoking when the first accusations began to fly. Prime Minister Junejo launched an attack against ISI and the Army. The Army counterattacked with criticism against General Akhtar, who had left ISI almost a year earlier, and Akhtar counterattacked by laying the blame at Hamid Gul's feet for storing too much ordnance at Ojhri. The battle between Junejo's government and Zia's Army escalated almost as quickly as the explosions at Ojhri.

Then the whispering began.

The coincidence of the destruction of ten thousand tons of ordnance at Ojhri and the signing of the Geneva Accords four days later spawned rumors that the KGB had sabotaged Ojhri. Others, adding new spin to the same story, preferred to have the Indians, probably acting on behalf of the KGB, behind the sabotage. There was a flurry of alleged eyewitness sightings of Indian Mirage fighters flying at low level in the area just before the first explosion; one of them, the rumors had it, had fired a particle beam straight into the ordnance stored at Ojhri, setting off the conflagration. A sort of one-upmanship entered the game, with each new version of KGB and Indian perfidy becoming more rococo than the last. And before long, the rumor mill decided to settle on the most delicious culprit of all—the Americans. Soon authoritative reports were circulating that the Americans had blown the Ojhri dump as part of a secret deal with the Soviets. The evil conspiracy of the two superpowers had sprung out of the tortured concept of "negative symmetry"—agreed to by the United States and the Soviet Union as an annex to the memorandum of understanding they had in Geneva. Specifically, the United States had made the following statement:

> The obligations undertaken by the guarantors are symmetrical. In this regard, the United States has advised the Soviet Union that the United States retains the right, consistent with its obligations as guarantor, to provide military assistance to parties in Afghanistan. Should the Soviet Union exercise restraint in providing military assistance to parties in Afghanistan, the United States similarly will exercise restraint.

That was enough for the multitudes already suspicious of our intentions in a post–Geneva Accords world, particularly those who interpreted the statement about symmetry as an American bailout. It was a short trip to the conclusion that the Americans had agreed to blow Ojhri.

Like most storms, the Ojhri story finally died with a heave and a sigh. The heave came after six weeks of attack and counterattack between the Army and the prime minister and culminated with Prime Minister Junejo taking the bold steps of blocking Zia's senior Army promotions and demanding a public airing of the results of an Army inquiry into the Ojhri disaster. On May 29, Zia would respond in the way he knew best for dealing with meddlesome prime ministers.

Islamabad, May 30, 1988

"Can you believe it?" Arnie Raphel said with a tone that matched the dispirited look on his face.

Raphel was referring to the sudden overnight move by Zia, who had fired Prime Minister Junejo for corruption and incompetence and dissolved the national and provincial parliaments. The men in khaki were back in charge in Pakistan.

"Sure I can believe it. At least he didn't throw him in jail."

"Were you picking up anything that would have tipped us off?" Raphel asked a little guardedly.

"Absolutely nothing. My guess is that Zia made up his mind last night and decided to move then. I'm not going to kick myself for missing it. How 'bout you?"

"I was with the president last night," Raphel said softly. "I met with him and then rode around Islamabad with him for an hour. And all we talked about was the endgame in Afghanistan. How things were going pretty well and how we all had to be sure to get a new interim government in place before the Soviets left. He was concerned that we were only interested in kicking the Soviets out and a little cavalier about what happened after that. We could always pack up and go home, but Pakistan would still be next door to Afghanistan. Not the slightest hint that he was about to shut down Junejo."

Listening to the ambassador, I saw the reason for his dark mood. "And you're feeling responsible, because you know Zia so well and he didn't even tell his buddy Arnie Raphel what he was going to do. Right?"

"You know Washington, the whispering will start tomorrow. What the hell kind of a relationship does he have with Zia, for chrissakes! He rides around with him and Zia says nothing much but then goes home and fires his prime minister!" Raphel said.

"Yeah, I know what you mean. But I don't see what you can do about it."

"Take a look." Raphel motioned toward his computer terminal.

I sat at his desk and read the telegram he'd drafted describing his meeting with Zia the previous evening and commenting on the president's actions a few hours later. When I finished I said, "It's too defensive. Don't send it. I'd just get back to work and let the political section deal with the reporting telegram. And think of the positive side. Now you won't have to spend all that time with that jerk Junejo. You can do all your business at Army House."

Raphel smiled, this time without irony. "You didn't report in your channel that you thought something was brewing?" he asked.

"And not run it by you first? Not a chance. I missed it just like you. But I didn't have dinner with the guy the night before. I think I'll rush back and tell my people that if they think

I look bad, take a look at Arnie Raphel. He was tooling around Islamabad with the man while he was planning his move and missed it! That'll take the heat off me."

Arnie Raphel never looked back, at least as far as I could tell, though he did continue to take heat from Foggy Bottom for missing the signs that Zia was making his move.

Islamabad, 1600 Hours, May 15, 1988

I climbed up on the couch in my office and placed the first green magnetic disk on the map of Afghanistan mounted on my wall. It covered Barikot at the north end of the Konar Valley in eastern Afghanistan and represented the first withdrawal of a Soviet 40th Army unit from a combat garrison. I then slapped a green disk over the Soviet garrison at Jalalabad, and over the next few days, the green disks would begin to cover hot spots all over Afghanistan, as the Soviets faithfully executed their pledge to pull out half of their troops in the first six months under the terms of the Geneva Accords.

They were finally on their way out.

Kabul, 0430 Hours, May 16, 1988

Leonid Shebarshin was startled awake by a clap of thunder, then another that seemed just above his head. He looked up through the window to see the first faint light of a summer dawn. The downpour should follow soon, he thought as he closed his eyes again and listened to the next deafening clap, followed by four more at regular intervals. Now that his mind was cleared of sleep, his thoughts of summer rain evaporated, replaced by the understanding that Kabul was under heavy bombardment from the bandits who occupied the high ground surrounding much of the capital. During a short break in the shelling, he caught the sound of the muezzin's plaintiff call to morning prayers.

Two mornings earlier, the first columns of Soviet troops had crossed the Amu Dar'ya, heading for Termez, never again to return to Afghanistan. The ten-year war was finally winding down. The troops were on their way out.

Islamabad, August 4, 1988

I had quit for the evening when the telephone rang. It was an ISI officer from the Afghan cell.

"Mr. Milton," he said, "there has been an aircraft shot down near Parachinar."

"Ours or theirs?" I was never sure when I would learn that someone had brought down a commercial flight along the border where Pakistani Fokkers flew on an irregular schedule.

"It was an Su-25, and it has come down in very good condition. The pilot ejected."

"You're sure it's a Sukhoi-25?"

"We're getting verification. The crash site is under control of one of the militias. They say the aircraft is in excellent condition."

"Stinger get it?"

"No. A lucky burst from triple A."

"That's great, Colonel." I was delighted. A lightly damaged Su-25, a superb ground attack aircraft, would add nicely to the equipment we had been collecting from the Afghan battlefield over the last ten years. We had delivered a mint-condition, flyable MiG-21bis to the USAF for use in its aggressor training squadron a few months back, and my predecessor, Bill Piekney, had gotten his hands on a serviceable MI-25 attack helicopter that he had sent back home for the U.S. Army to play with. We had actually been able to pick up one or two copies of just about everything on the battlefield over the years, and some items, such as flares used by the Soviets to counter heat-seeking missiles, were being bought by the case from Soviet quartermasters through a series of elaborate cutouts.

"Can you get word to the people at the crash site to keep souvenir hunters away from the plane?" I didn't want anyone carrying off the nose cone or the tail cones, where the weapons systems and avionics were located.

"Nobody will touch the aircraft, but you'll have to commit to buy it now. Otherwise they'll put it out for bids."

Sure they would, I thought. This war was great business for the battlefield scavengers and the scrap metal guys. It was tailor-made for the Afghan entrepreneur. Everybody was in the game, from most of NATO to the Chinese. But we often had right of first refusal, and the Afghan traders knew where to go with their first offer. I even knew of some enterprising scrap dealers in Paktia and Nangarhar Provinces who would arrange for mujahideen militias to stage attacks on Soviet garrisons just to get the garrison to counter with an artillery barrage, so that the next day they could wind up the hill in their old Bedfords and offer to buy the scrap brass from the garrison commander (they operated pretty close to the daily fix on the local scrap markets). It was also good business for a Soviet commander in a lonely outpost. For good measure, the wily scrap metal dealers would usually throw in a case of Stolichnaya or tinned caviar or Kamchatka crab wheedled out of another garrison earlier. Everybody ended up happy, and only rarely did anyone get hurt.

"What do they want?"

"Mr. Milton, I am sure that you can get this Sukhoi for less than ten Toyota Hilux pickup trucks. And maybe some BM-12 rocket launchers."

"How many trucks? And how many BM-12s?" I asked, knowing that it would be pretty close to ten.

"Maybe eight each, Mr. Milton. But the trucks should be new and white with red pinstriping. And it would be better if there are some with double cabs—room for five inside the cab."

"Look, Colonel. You find the new trucks from your motor pool, but you can be sure I'll cover you. Same goes for the BM-12s. Do we have a deal?"

"Yes, I think we do."

"Then I'll need your office to get the Sukhoi across zero line; my people will manage it from there. Can you put it under twenty-four-hour guard until I get instructions? I'll have an answer tomorrow. And thanks. This might be a big break. But for God's sake, don't tell those guys we're excited about it. Okay? They'll jack up the price."

"Fine, Mr. Milton. But there's one more thing. They also have the pilot."

"The pilot!"

"Yes. A gray-haired colonel ejected and was captured. He was only very slightly hurt and is in custody of the same militia holding the plane. What are your thoughts on the pilot?"

"Just make sure nothing happens to him," I said.

I had long preached to both the Afghans and the Pakistanis that the mujahideen needed to change their ways when it came to the treatment of Soviet prisoners, in particular downed pilots. Soon after I arrived in Pakistan, I was shown a photograph of a Soviet pilot in a silver flight suit, up to his waist in snow, skin burned by the relentless sun, with a bullet hole in the side of his head. His Tokarev semiautomatic was still clutched in his hand. He had killed himself rather than be captured. Soviet pilots had it particularly rough when captured, hence their extreme caution since the introduction of the Stinger in 1986. The greatest fear was not so much being hit as falling into mujahideen hands.

I had made it clear that American policy was that captured pilots be treated as prisoners of war under the norms of international agreements and that I would even be prepared to offer rewards for pilots repatriated to the USSR or, if they so desired, resettled in the West.

"They will give him to us for two more trucks and perhaps two more BM-12s."

"Let's make the same deal. You pay the militia and I'll cover you. And I'll want to talk to General Gul first thing in the morning."

"I'll send a car, Mr. Milton."

Jalalabad, August 9, 1988

The 40th Army had pulled its forces out of Jalalabad early in their front-loaded withdrawal in mid-May, handing over to the Afghan 2nd Army Corps the city that had once been the old winter residence of Afghan kings. Many in the Soviet limited contingent believed that as soon as the Soviet troops pulled out of Jalalabad, Afghan defenses would collapse and the bandits would take the Nangarhar provincial capital. Some even thought that the local Afghan allies of the Soviets would panic and try to clamber aboard their departing tanks and helicopters, as the South Vietnamese had done when the Americans pulled out of Saigon. But that hadn't happened, and one of the few men on the Soviet side who was convinced that it wouldn't was Leonid Shebarshin, who ninety days after the withdrawal of 40th Army troops from Jalalabad was on an official visit to Kabul with Vladimir Kryuchkov, the new Chairman of the KGB.

There had not been a single Soviet soldier in Jalalabad since the May pullout—it had been determined to be too great a risk. But to Shebarshin's amazement, Kryuchkov, another believer in the durability of the Najibullah regime, decided he would chance a quick run to Jalalabad. He and Shebarshin boarded a blacked-out Antonov AN-26 transport in Kabul after dark for the short flight to Jalalabad. Shebarshin felt self-conscious, awkward, and uncomfortable in the parachute he and the KGB Chairman were told to don, all the more so since he had no idea how the thing worked beyond the quick briefing he'd been given. Just jump out the door and pull the ring there on your chest and you'll be fine, he'd been instructed. Nor did he draw much comfort from the pistol strapped to his side. If he jumped, he thought, he'd probably lose it. Shebarshin decided such thoughts were unworthy of a man, but then again for the sake of objectivity they should at least be noted, he would later say.

As the Antonov lifted off the runway, the pilot put it into a series of steep climbing turns that seemed to take almost twenty minutes before the lumbering turboprop transport was above the effective range of the Stinger gunners. As they leveled off for the short flight along the Kabul River, the historic route of retreat of a doomed British Army almost a century and a half earlier, Shebarshin could see flashes of artillery and small-arms fire like blinking matches twenty thousand feet below. Almost as soon as the Antonov had reached altitude, it began its descent into Jalalabad, using the same gut-wrenching spiraling motion, but this time downward. As soon as they pulled to a grinding halt at the end of the runway, engines still turning, the passengers were whisked out to a waiting car. The Antonov then wheeled around and took off into the night sky; it had been on the ground in Jalalabad for no more than a minute.

Kryuchkov and Shebarshin were put up for the next two nights in the family residence of Pir Sayed Ahmad Gailani, the Afghan resistance leader. The rebel leader's home had been damaged by occupation troops over the years, but the staff still spoke of their old master with a tone of reverence. It wouldn't take much to fix it up after the war was over, Shebarshin decided as he surveyed the elegant old house.

The next day was surreal, sheer make-believe as they toured in and around Jalalabad, meeting with Afghan officials and troops in the field. In the stifling heat of the Jalalabad plain, they pinned medals on rows of khaki chests and heard the same half-believed mantra that everything was okay. Everything was under control. Here and there were fading red posters extolling inevitable victory. Muslim fatalism, thought Shebarshin as he absorbed the scene.

The second night, a blacked-out Antonov dropped into Jalalabad to pick up the two VIPs for the return to Kabul. The two men were rushed aboard and in seconds were in a spiraling ascent above the city to safety and the corridor home. After takeoff, the crew noted in the log that large-caliber tracer fire followed their ascent until they were above the range of any weapons known to be in the bandits' hands. At 2245 hours, they were back on the ground in Kabul.

First Chief Directorate Headquarters, August 15, 1988

Back in Moscow, Leonid Shebarshin mused over another one of the many distractions of a war coming to an end. A freebooting militia commander in Paktia Province near the Pakistan border, a man of constantly shifting allegiances, had captured an Air Force colonel when his Sukhoi-25 was shot down near the Pakistani border about ten days earlier. Negotiations had been under way since the day after the shoot-down for a cash ransom for the release of the colonel. Shebarshin was aware it would cost a tidy sum to secure the freedom of a full colonel, certainly more than might be paid for a lieutenant, but it was worth it to get a brave officer out of captivity. Too many pilots had died at the hands of the bandits over the years, and now it seemed that everybody was willing to make a deal.

The Paktia shoot-down was a case in point. Within hours of the incident, a message had been delivered to the 40th Army and to the KGB that a white-haired colonel was safe and sound and that those holding him were ready for a trade. Now all that had to be done was the haggling over the price. Not a bad way for a pilot to end his own war, particularly considering the alternatives, Shebarshin thought. He scanned the report until he found the colonel's name. He decided he didn't know the man.

Islamabad, August 15, 1988

The operation to extract the downed Su-25 from Paktia had gone well, as had the bargaining over the pilot. The pickup trucks and the rocket launchers were handed over in return for the plane and the pilot. We never sought access to captured Soviet pilots or other troops unless they stated clearly to the Pakistanis that they wanted to defect to us. Memories of Soviet interrogations of U.S. POWs in Vietnam and Korea were fresh enough, and the policy was that there would be no direct American interference with captured Soviet combatants. The previous year, we had assisted in the resettlement of three Soviet soldiers who had been held by the mujahideen for more than a year and finally decided they wanted to resettle in the West. They ended up in Canada, but we helped process them into the resettlement system.

Most of the Soviet soldiers who fell into mujahideen hands were a pretty troubled lot. Hazing in the Soviet Army made for a miserable life in the best of times, but add to that the crushing insanity of the war in Afghanistan, and it was no surprise that a significant number of Soviet troops were sliding into the Afghan drug scene. Many of them were actually captured by the rebels after having been lured away from the safety of their garrisons on drug deals. Once captured, some very quickly found an enthusiasm for Islam and for the Afghan resistance. They had heard enough stories of their comrades being buried alive or becoming the objects of entertainment for primitive men with knives. Even then, their lives with the mujahideen were often a terrorized combination of concubine and beast of burden. By the time they ended up with us on their way to a resettlement in the West, they were in need of more help than we were often able to give.

After being pulled out of Paktia, the Soviet colonel remained the guest of the Pakistanis while arrangements were worked out with the Soviet embassy in Islamabad for his repatriation. Hamid Gul told me that the Soviet airman was a congenial man who had no interests beyond going home to Moscow to fight another day. He gave up no information and didn't take the usual defection bait—the big-chested homecoming queen blonde, the bass boat, and the pickup truck with Arizona plates that I had told Hamid Gul to offer him. Instead, the pilot was handed over to the Soviet embassy in Islamabad, and two weeks later he was in Moscow, where he was regaled and decorated for his heroism and his steadfast commitment to his "internationalist duty."

His rescue was characterized as the result of the gallant efforts of the "competent organs." No mention was ever made of how his release had been arranged; certainly nothing was said of the Toyotas or the BM-12s the CIA had kicked in. Altogether a nice final chapter, I thought. But it wasn't yet the end of the game for the colonel. Years later, the kindly, white-haired colonel would be at center stage in Moscow politics.

13

Rawalpindi, August 13, 1988

Akhtar couldn't let go of Afghan affairs since he had handed over ISI to Hamid Gul six months earlier. Though his move to take over as chairman of the Joint Chiefs of Staff had included a promotion to lieutenant general, he felt left out of the action in the last days of the war. He continued to call me for a quiet dinner talk every month or so; in return, he would update me on what was going on in the Army. A pretty good trade, I thought, and so it was that I joined him for dinner on the evening of August 13.

Akhtar was in good spirits, having survived the scandal of

the Ojhri camp disaster, but just barely, and only because Zia had kicked out Prime Minister Junejo's civilian government. I had kept up these quiet sessions with Akhtar for the last eighteen months partly as a means of keeping tabs on the current thinking among the corps commanders and senior staff chiefs and partly because I had become close to the general. He would invariably probe for information on what Hamid Gul was up to in Afghanistan, sometimes critically, but since the Soviets were well into their withdrawal, and since most of the news was reasonably good, I never felt I was being caught between a suspicious predecessor and an ambitious successor. Toward the end of our dinner, I mentioned the big event of the week.

"I suppose you'll be joining everybody else in Bahawalpur on the seventeenth," I said, referring to the field demonstration in Bahawalpur of the American M1 Abrams tank we were trying to sell the Pakistan Army.

"Bahawalpur? Who's going?" Akhtar was perplexed; he clearly hadn't heard about the demonstration.

Catching his tone, I tried to downplay its importance. "They're showing off the Abrams tank, but you know all about it. It's a technical affair. I understand the president will be going."

"Bahawalpur?" Akhtar said again, clearly irritated at having heard from me about a military gathering that involved President Zia. "Will you be going along?"

"No, I've got nothing to do with the Abrams. I'll leave that to the representational crowd, the ambassador and some of our military brass."

The rest of the dinner was awkward, and I tried to change the subject by briefing the general on the progress CIA technicians were making in salvaging the Su-25, which, it turned out, was as promised in excellent condition. But Akhtar had little interest in this or any other subject, and I ended up leaving for Islamabad a little earlier than usual.

Islamabad, 0830 Hours, August 14, 1988

The next morning, I had barely gotten through my cable traffic before Akhtar was on the line from Rawalpindi:

"Funny thing about the Bahawalpur affair. I found my invitation on my desk when I arrived at the office this morning. It was held up in the mailroom. I'm sending over an invitation for you, as well. You can come with me. It ought to be an interesting day."

"Thanks, General, but I'll have to check my schedule and get back to you."

I didn't believe for a minute that Akhtar's invitation had been on his desk. I was sure that he'd made life unpleasant for anyone around him below three-star rank and that the hastily prepared invitation had been the only way to end the unpleasantness. When my invitation arrived by courier later that day, I tossed it in a burn bag, pausing for only a second or two to contemplate whether I ought to give it to my deputy Jim Morris and have him cover for me. Not worth it, I decided.

Islamabad, 1800 Hours, August 17, 1988

I had just walked into my residence in Islamabad's quiet and shady Shalimar residential quarter when my phone rang. It was my secretary, still at work.

"Milt, it's Susan. We just got an odd call saying that President Zia's plane has crashed."

"Is there any more than that?" I had an instant sinking feeling that what Susan had just reported was true.

"No, they're trying to check it out now."

"I'll be right in," I said.

I was back in the office in ten minutes, by which time there was no longer any doubt about the crash. The reports coming in from Bahawalpur also placed Arnie Raphel on the plane with the president, as well as Brigadier General Herb Wassom, a fine Army officer and a good friend who ran the military cooperation office in the embassy. Fragments of information were coming in by the minute, and the early assessment was that there had been a catastrophic loss of life among senior officers in the Pakistan Army. The first thing I did was send a "Critic" message with worldwide distribution, outlining the facts as we knew them. The Critic message is called for whenever events occur in an area of interest to the United States that might even remotely deteriorate into a military confrontation.

The assassination of a major world leader fell into that category, and there were already whispers, soon to be shouts, that Zia's plane had been brought down by an assassin's hand. This could only add tension to the always tricky standoff between Pakistan and India, particularly if a leadership vacuum in the Pakistan Army was perceived by the Indians as an opening for mischief.

With the ambassador dead, the management of the U.S. embassy fell to the deputy chief of mission, Elizabeth Jones, one of the Department of State's finest foreign service officers. Beth, as everyone called her, had just arrived in Islamabad and had hardly unpacked before the disaster struck. Yet within the first hour after the news came in, she had put in motion a crisis management plan that worked flawlessly until she was replaced by Robert Oakley, who arrived in Islamabad a few days later with Secretary of State George Shultz for President Zia's funeral and to accompany the remains of Ambassador Raphel and Herb Wassom back to the United States.

As the drama unfolded in Bahawalpur, the list of the dead on Zia's plane continued to grow. An hour after I had returned to the embassy, I learned that General Akhtar was among those presumed dead, which now included eight Pakistani general officers, several brigadiers and colonels, and a number of civilians, for a total of thirty-one persons aboard the president's C-130. It was later learned, after the arrival in Chaklala of the second C-130, this one carrying Vice Chief of Army Staff General Mirza Aslam Beg, that Ambassador Raphel and General Wassom had only at the last minute been invited by the president to join him in his VIP compartment inside the C-130 for the flight home. Another American Army officer, Brigadier General Mike Pfister, returned to Islamabad alone in the embassy aircraft. I had assumed Mike had also been killed with the others and was delighted to see him show up late in the day.

The sun had not set on the day of the crash before substance was added to the rumors of foul play. Apparently the president's C-130 had begun diving and climbing in a porpoise fashion immediately after takeoff and continued to fly in this erratic manner until it finally dove straight into the ground, with all engines at full throttle. The impact was tremendous, and the fire was intense. Early evidence of a conspiracy centered on crates of Multan mangoes that had been loaded aboard the aircraft as gifts at the last minute. And, as usual, eyewitness reports had the C-130 exploding in midair before the crash. There had obviously been a bomb in the mango crates, was the conclusion of the day. That story was followed quickly by another suggesting that a gas had been released in the cockpit, incapacitating the crew. Soon began the search for likely plotters of what had already been accepted as the assassination of President Zia.

General Beg, who by sudden default was now the man in charge in Pakistan, was the first name on the short list, if for no other reason than that he was not on the plane with Zia. General Beg paid a condolence call the evening of the crash on the ambassador's wife, Nancy Ely-Raphel, a foreign service officer and attorney who had taken a leave of absence to accompany her husband during his posting to Islamabad. Someone later observed that the general seemed edgy and uncomfortable in her presence. Before the day was over, there were whispers that Beg was behind the crash—certainly he stood to gain the most from the sudden departure of Zia from the scene, and certainly he was a man of ambition. Rumor fed rumor, and as the conspiracy theories thickened, others would soon be added to the short list of probable assassins, including me.

First Chief Directorate Headquarters, Yasenevo, 0800 Hours, August 18, 1988

Leonid Shebarshin wondered how long it would take before fingers began pointing to the KGB as the evil genius behind the crash of Zia's plane. He had already passed up the proper assurances that the KGB's Afghan allies in Khad had nothing to do with the crash, and there had been no real questioning from above as to whether the KGB had a hand in it. But there was, to be sure, interest in determining if there was foul play, and if so, whose.

Shebarshin himself thought that the crash, if not just plain bad luck, was probably the result of internal disputes in Pakistan. He'd lived there long enough to know that old feuds live on forever and that sooner or later someone would seek retribution for the execution of Zulfiqar Ali Bhutto; sooner or later someone would have to pay Zia back. Either way, Shebarshin knew he'd have to keep his eye on the how and why of Zia's death.

Islamabad, 0700 Hours, August 18, 1988

Early the next morning, with the wreckage of Zia's C-130 still smoldering and under guard, I received a cable from Langley suggesting I consider sending the team of technicians salvaging the Su-25 to the crash site to search for clues, before the site became cold and contaminated. The technicians were experienced in the examination of air crashes, the cable had said. I took the suggestion under consideration, and after consulting with my deputy, Jim Morris, and the embassy air attaché, I advised Langley it would be a mistake to use the visiting technicians. Whatever good they might be able to do would be outweighed by the fact that the CIA had people poking around in the rubble of Zia's plane a day after it went down. Questions would linger eternally as to what we were doing at the crash site and what we'd added or removed to cover up our hand in the crash. Langley sent me a short cable seconding that position. Later, I would be glad that our technicians had not been dispatched to the crash site, as more and more people became convinced that the crash had been engineered by the CIA, with me as the executioner.

There was an impeccable South Asian logic in the suggestion that the United States was involved in Zia's death. According to the growing conspiracy theory, the elaborate U.S. endgame in Pakistan and Afghanistan had begun with the destruction of Ojhri camp in the spring, followed by the killing of the president and his generals in August, as they were now "in the way of bigger things." As the story went, the United States wanted to be certain that the mujahideen would not hamper the Soviet withdrawal, and thus the CIA had arranged for the destruction of the ordnance depot at Ojhri. And to be sure that the plans Zia and Akhtar had put in place for a post-Soviet Afghanistan a decade earlier failed, both men had to be liquidated. Then, per secret agreement, the Soviets would be able to withdraw with honor, and the fundamentalist resistance parties would be unable to complete their victory in Afghanistan. The Soviets would be given their "decent interval" from the time of their withdrawal and the collapse of the Najibullah regime. Ambassador Raphel and General Wassom had simply been unexpected and unfortunate collateral damage, but in the end, they were acceptable losses.

It made a wonderful yarn, but it was sheer hallucination. Nevertheless, once the story gained momentum, it would never again be fully discounted, only improved upon.

The sad fact was that the Pakistan Air Force had probably put its president and many of his generals on an aircraft with mechanical problems. But the Pakistan military establishment couldn't accept such a reality and, despite a complete lack of evidence of a conspiracy, stuck to its guns on the assassination theory. General Gul later told me that he was convinced the Indians were behind the crash, and when I said that there was no evidence to support his claim, his response explained it all.

"Milton, you still don't understand the Indians. They would never leave any evidence that they had been involved. *That,* Milton, *is* the evidence of their involvement." Hamid Gul eventually gave up on the Indian plot and would in later years tell anyone who would listen that he was convinced the CIA had killed Zia.

A few days after the crash, I was faced with a macabre problem. A team of pathologists dispatched from Washington to make a positive identification of the remains of Ambassador Raphel and General Wassom had come up with human remains that belonged to neither man. As testimony to the intensity of the fire and the tremendous impact of the crash, positive identification of the men in the VIP module proved challenging for the American team and close to impossible for Pakistani pathologists. The Americans ultimately succeeded in their task, however, and arrangements were made for the remains of the two fine public servants to be flown home on Secretary Shultz's plane. But what to do with the unidentifiable remains?

I contacted friends in the Pakistani Army, and we arranged for a solemn transfer of the remains of the unknown officer resting in a hand-rubbed rosewood chest draped with a Pakistani flag. The handover took place at sundown, and the remains were buried the next morning in the military cemetery, giving a final salute to the unknown *shaheed.*

Secretary of State George Shultz led the American delegation to Pakistan to attend President Zia's funeral and to take Arnie Raphel's and Herb Wassom's remains back home. He was accompanied by Robert Oakley, who at the time was responsible for the region on the National Security Council. Oakley would stay on as ambassador as we wound down this phase of war in Afghanistan and as we stood by and watched the next phase begin.

Charlie Wilson and Annelise Ilschenko also attended Zia's funeral, and Annelise's powder blue floral *shalwar kameez* ended up attracting far more attention in the large American procession than the craggy, solemn face of George Shultz. Before the secretary's delegation departed with the flag-draped coffins, a small ceremony was held in the embassy compound in Islamabad, with taps being played by the teenage son of one of the embassy staff.

Islamabad, October 1988

The snows came early in 1988, drawing down to winter dormancy the last fighting season of the USSR's nine-year war in Afghanistan. The commander of the Soviet Union's 40th Army, General Boris Gromov, had on his way out of Afghanistan finally shown that the Red Army could perform as a superpower should. Six months after the withdrawal began, Gromov had pulled out the bulk of his garrisons without mishaps serious enough to interrupt the process or create a diplomatic crisis. Despite counsel from both Pakistan and the United States to leave the Soviet forces alone as long as they were heading for home, there were a number of harassing attacks by the mujahideen. The hatred ran deep in a country where every family had buried their dead from the brutal war.

A couple of times, Gromov's troops had taken what I thought were dangerous routes of exit, and they ran into trouble passing through some valleys in the center and north of the country. On those occasions where the Soviets took casualties, they would protest. One time after the retreating units came under heavy assault for taking what anyone who knew the mujahideen might have told them was the wrong fork in the road, I was given a gentle warning. I was at the large October 1 Chinese National Day celebration when I was approached by one of the old-style heavies of the Soviet embassy in Islamabad, a minister-counselor named Botshan-Kharchenko.

"Mr. *Buuurdon.*" He made his usual mess of my name. "Perhaps we should speak."

"Why not?" I said, stepping away from what was easily the finest buffet spread in Islamabad's diplomatic community.

"You must understand, Mr. *Buuurdon,* that these attacks against our troops as they withdraw must stop."

"And if they don't?"

"Then perhaps we will halt our withdrawal. Then what will you do?"

"It is not what I will do, Counselor, it is what the Afghans will do. And I think they will simply keep on fighting and killing your soldiers until you finally just go home."

"But you have some control over such matters. . . ."

"No one has control over such matters, Counselor, except the Soviet Union."

"Mr. *Buuurdon,* you must still understand that there will be consequences if these attacks continue."

"I am sure there will be, Counselor."

There would be more such conversations between me and the Soviets, and though the attacks continued sporadically, withdrawal stayed on schedule. But on the whole, the Soviets managed to find their way out of Afghanistan without major disasters slowing them down. By the time Christmas 1988 rolled around, marking with it the ninth anniversary of the Soviet invasion, even the revenge-driven mujahideen commanders were convinced that the Soviet phase of their struggle was all but over. They began moving their forces into position for the next stage of the conflict, the struggle against the Soviet puppet regime of Najibullah in Kabul. And beyond that, the disparate forces that made up the Afghan resistance began jockeying for advantage in the phase that was to come after Najibullah had finally fallen, the fight to see who among the major players would emerge on top of the rubble heap that Afghanistan had become.

Ahmad Shah Massoud had been the first of the major leaders in Afghanistan to see the handwriting on the wall. He became convinced that the Soviets were actually going to honor the commitment signed in Geneva in April 1988, and even before the ink was dry on the accords, Massoud had redirected his energies to forging an alliance for the future struggle against the Pashtun majority. In particular, he was gearing up for his showdown with his nemesis, Gulbuddin Hekmatyar. Across the northern tier of Afghanistan, Massoud cut deal after deal with local commanders and forged what he at that time called the Supreme Council of the North, a non-Pashtun alliance of primarily Tajiks and Uzbeks, thereby positioning himself in the starting blocks for the race to Kabul once the puppet regime began to wobble.

Similarly, several of the Pashtun party leaders such as Gulbuddin and Sayyaf had been stockpiling ordnance for the post-Soviet phase of the fight. As a result, there were constant complaints from all of the party leaders that the United States had abandoned the mujahideen. The resistance leaders always referred to the Ojhri camp disaster as "proof" of U.S.-Soviet connivance, designed to leave the Pashtun parties without the means to carry the fight to Kabul. I had meetings with the Peshawar Seven during those last months of the war, and the theme was always the same: We're out of supplies, and you have left us in the lurch. At one particularly heated session, I took a gamble. Sayyaf had made an eloquent speech complaining that his commanders inside Afghanistan had only captured weapons and ammunition at their disposal since we had cut them off. As his harangue ended, I took the floor, addressing the Peshawar Seven through Colonel Bacha, the interpreter.

"I have heard from all of you about the lack of ordnance. In particular, I have heard from Professor Sayyaf that his stores are empty. I can't understand how that could be possible, when our satellites just yesterday photographed his supply bunkers in Ali Khel and Zhawar Kili, and our estimates are that he is very well supplied."

Sayyaf, who almost always spoke through an interpreter, understood exactly what I had said and responded quickly in English. "I have less than nine hundred tons in Zhawar and about the same in Ali Khel," he said defiantly. But the effect was the opposite of what he had intended.

Mojaddedi broke in. "That's two thousand tons. Professor Sayyaf says he is out of ammunition and he has two thousand tons in Zhawar and Ali Khel alone!"

There was a hubbub among the other party leaders, and Sayyaf grew quiet. It was not the first or the last time that the impartial eye of the KH-11 satellite would intervene to break up a quarrel. It was irrelevant that there had been no overhead imagery of Sayyaf's bunkers in Paktia province—the other six parties believed there had been.

The United States and the Soviet Union would continue to supply their respective clients as the Soviets stuck to their withdrawal schedule over the winter months and into early 1989. The CIA estimated that there was more than enough ordnance in-country to finish the job of dislodging the Najibullah regime and that there would be no shortfalls. Demands for more ordnance were understood as calls for supplies for the future, the post-DRA future, when the Afghans would begin the nasty business of seeing who would end up ruling the roost. And there was little American interest in becoming part of that fight.

As the new year rolled in, Kabul was surrounded by what the Pakistanis called a "ring of steel." Each of the mujahideen parties had groups overlooking the capital from winter camps in the nearby hills, and it was clear that the stage was set for a siege after the last Soviet soldier stepped across Friendship Bridge. The foreign diplomatic community had drawn down to near zero over the last few months, and as the final date for the Soviet withdrawal came—February 15, 1989—the battle lines were drawn.

14

Islamabad, 0700 Hours, February 15, 1989

I had been in my office since 0630 hours, waiting for relayed reports of the last day of the Soviet occupation of Afghanistan. I stood by my wall map, checking and rechecking the pins marking the locations of Soviet garrisons throughout the country, red for units still in-country, green for those already withdrawn. The whole of Afghanistan was now covered with green pins, with only a few red ones left in Kabul, in Mazar-e-Sharif, and along the main withdrawal route to the north, through the Salang tunnel and across the Shomali and Mazar-e-Sharif plains. Today it was over. Boris Gromov would walk out of Afghanistan, thus ending 3,331 days of senseless war.

I had received reports that Gromov had actually been in the Soviet Central Asian Republic of Uzbekistan for the last couple of days and that he would fly down to a point on the road from Mazar to the Friendship Bridge at Termez to link up with the last column of the 40th Army on its way home. It was all to be carefully choreographed by the little general himself.

I waited as the reports came in.

Termez, Uzbekistan, February 15, 1989

General Boris Gromov wanted the arrangements to be just right. The international press had been shuttled from nearby Termez in Uzbekistan to a special media center, complete with a new covered pavilion overlooking Friendship Bridge. The body of a hapless young trooper killed the day before had been furtively carried across the bridge before the press had time to reason that his blanket-wrapped form represented the last Russian soldier killed in the war. The cameras of several dozen news services zoomed in on the center of the bridge, where a lone Soviet tank had pulled to a halt. The figure of General Boris Gromov jumped from the turret, pulled his battle-dress tunic smartly into place, and strode purposefully over the last hundred yards toward the Soviet side of the Oxus. Just before he reached the end of the bridge, his son Maksim, a slim, awkward fourteen-year-old, greeted his father with a stiff embrace and presented him with a bouquet of red carnations. Son and father marched the last fifty yards out of Afghanistan together. At that moment, Gromov became the USSR's "hero of Afghanistan."

I never understood why.

In the almost ten years of war, the Soviet Union admitted to having lost around fifteen thousand troops killed in action, with several hundred thousand wounded or disabled from disease. General Gromov's brilliantly staged exit from Afghanistan would grow rapidly into a national disaster for the USSR, yet he was the hero of Afghanistan. The Soviet adventure ended as it began, with fantasy and make-believe.

Islamabad, February 15, 1989

My telecommunications chief stepped into my office with his report.

"He's out."

I nodded and said, "Send it now."

And with that order we sent an immediate cable to Langley with two words etched out of Xs covering the whole page:

CITE: ISLAMABAD 222487
IMMEDIATE DIRECTOR
WNINTEL INTEL
SUBJECT: SOVIET OCCUPATION OF AFGHANISTAN

```
XX        X        XX     XXXXX
 XX      XX      XX       X
  XX    X X    XX         XXXXX
   XX X    X XX           X
     XX      XX           XXXXX
```

```
XX        X        XX      XXXXX      X     X
 XX      XX      XX      X        X    XX    X
  XX    X X    XX       X        X    X X   X
   XX X    X XX         X        X    X   X X
    XX       XX          XXXXX       X    XX
```

FILE DEFER:

That same night I ended a ritual. My office was about three-quarters of a mile away in a straight line from the Soviet embassy. Since I had arrived in Pakistan in the summer of 1986, I had kept a table lamp lit in my window twenty-four hours a day, covering a period now approaching three years. Word had come back to me from a number of sources that the KGB *Rezident* in the fortresslike Soviet embassy just a rifle shot away had often commented that my office appeared to be occupied at all times of the day or night. On one occasion, a KGB man had even said to me directly that he had noticed I worked late each evening, since the lights in my office were always burning.

As the sun dropped beyond the Margalla Hills on the night of February 15, 1989, I turned off all the lights in my office, including the table lamp that had burned steadily for the last three years.

First Chief Directorate Headquarters, 1230 Hours, February 15, 1989

It was over. Fortieth Army commander General Boris Gromov's staged exit from Afghanistan had profound propaganda value. It added a sense of finality, Shebarshin thought, to the final act of a drama that had turned to a tragedy. Before Gromov had made his dramatic return home as the symbolic last Soviet soldier to walk out of Afghanistan, there had been calls from Najibullah for a "small Soviet force to carry out limited functions." There were additional calls for Soviet air strikes in eastern Afghanistan, in Paktia near Zhawar and Khowst, and at other bandit strongholds. But Shebarshin had been dead set against any more Soviet intervention. There was no stomach for more adventures in Afghanistan.

Leonid Shebarshin was under no illusions that the Soviet Union had acted nobly at the end of its Afghan adventure. On the contrary, he was convinced that Gromov's splendid performance before the world press was just another step in the betrayal of Afghanistan. Betrayal or not, it was irreversible. The USSR would have to live with whatever deal Shevardnadze had cut in backroom meetings with his counterparts, George Shultz and James Baker. And eventually the USSR would have to live with its shame.

Shebarshin had been through it all, the good, what little there was of it, and all of the bad. He had been the KGB man on the spot in Kabul in May 1986, when the Soviet Union decided that its man Babrak Karmal was the source of the failures and had to go. But there was a problem. The old man hadn't quite gotten the message when he passed through Moscow a few weeks earlier, when he'd been told that his time to let go of power had come. Shebarshin was sent to Kabul to help Karmal exit gracefully. He had actually edited the text of Karmal's abdication speech, a most dishonorable task, he thought, one that at times brought bitter outbursts from the Afghan leader: "Who knows Dari, General, you or I?"

Shebarshin knew he had compromised his own conscience and that Karmal's premonitions of "bad times" for both Afghanistan and the Soviet Union were not based on personal hysteria. The old man threatened and cursed, and at no point did he yield to the temptation of pitying his "soulless opponents." If Karmal had been a Russian, Shebarshin thought as he slugged it out verbally with the old man, he'd have simply said, "Fuck you! Do what you want." But Karmal was Afghan, and in the end he did yield, and he made his speech, handing over to Moscow's new "chosen one," Najibullah.

And now it was over. Shebarshin thought he should be recovering from his own sense of dishonor. But he wasn't. The small wound that had been inflicted so long ago by the proud old man had grown into an ulcer. And it would continue to grow. Shebarshin would add the betrayal of Najibullah to that of Babrak Karmal, a disloyalty that had even greater consequences for Afghanistan and the USSR.

Shebarshin, along with the KGB Chairman, Vladimir Kryuchkov, had been the two strongest voices saying that Najib would hold on much longer than the naysayers suggested. The pessimists gave the Afghan leader a month or two before his Army would collapse, mutiny, and then turn on him. But Shebarshin knew Najib well and was convinced that if there was any form of aftercare by the withdrawing superpowers, Najib might even pull off a few deals and survive over the long run.

He had spent enough time with the big bear of a man to appreciate his quick mind and flexibility. He might even make it, Shebarshin thought. But deep down he knew the USSR would let him down. It was one of the reasons he tried to avoid becoming personally involved with the likable Afghan, a thirsty man with a quick wit—he favored Chivas Regal Scotch. Shebarshin had been to Najibullah's home on the grounds of the old palace. He had met Fatan, his dutiful wife, and their three daughters, who always seemed to be giggling about something, maybe just about the KGB man's presence in the family home. Shebarshin steeled himself to resist any instinct of developing a personal friendship with the Afghan president, though they would have been friends under almost any other circumstances. He even decided against asking him to autograph a photograph of the two men together. That might imply a connection he didn't want to have to deal with later. No, Shebarshin decided, he'd keep it strictly business with the Afghan leader. That way it would be easier to betray the man when the time came.

Karmal had made his peace with Afghanistan. Fate had moved him from Kabul to Mazar-e-Sharif and the protection of General Dostum, and finally to Moscow, where he would live out his last years, all but forgotten. Shebarshin would never see him in Moscow. He was too ashamed. And he was deeply ashamed to see the way the Afghan affair would end, with the Soviets betraying their old friends and the Americans pressing for their usual unconditional victory, whatever that would mean. Shebarshin was convinced that the Americans could, if they were realists, make a deal with Najib that would have a better chance than any other approach to peace. But he was also convinced that the Americans would have nothing to do with such a deal. They'd eventually come to regret it, he thought. The only other possible statesman on the Afghan scene, the only other man who might look beyond the dangerous, narrow view of ethnic conflict, was Ahmad Shah Massoud. The Soviet side could live with Massoud, Shebarshin thought, but could the Pakistanis and the Americans? Probably not, he decided. And they'd come to regret that, too.

Islamabad, May 1989

The 40th Army was a fading memory as spring gave way to summer, but Najibullah was hanging tough as ever. Far from collapsing as soon as darkness fell on the Soviet withdrawal, the Soviet puppet leader held on, and the confrontation between the mujahideen and the Najibullah regime was settling into a low-attrition standoff as all sides jockeyed for advantage, none willing to commit to a major engagement.

Pakistan was off on another of its infrequent experiments with democracy, having elected as prime minister Benazir Bhutto, the daughter of the man Zia had hanged a decade earlier. In the late spring, the fledgling government of the Radcliffe- and Oxford-educated Bhutto pushed ISI to mount a major attack on Jalalabad, hoping to seize the city in what was hoped would be the first of a series of victories. The Peshawar Seven had been against it, as had most of the commanders in eastern Afghanistan, but the prime minister was eager for a victory to coincide with her attendance at the Organization of the Islamic Conference meeting that spring. So the assault on the provincial capital went forward.

The battle turned into a fiasco; the failure of the resistance to take the city gave Najibullah a psychological second wind. I made a few trips through the Khyber Agency during the Jalalabad campaign and found the siege a halfhearted effort that senselessly piled up casualties on both sides. Pickup trucks smeared with mud in hand-painted camouflage raced toward Jalalabad, their beds jammed with fighters and weapons. Threading their way back along the old Grand Trunk Road more slowly toward Torkham, the same trucks carried the wounded and the stacks of dead from the stalemated battle.

On one trip to Torkham while Jalalabad was under siege, I took along the visiting DDO, Richard Stolz. While viewing the movement of supplies into Afghanistan and of the wounded out, one of the Pakistani officers traveling with us approached and whispered in my ear, "We've caught a man photographing you and Mr. Stolz! He says he's an American working for *The Washington Post.*"

Though both Stolz and I were dressed in *shalwar kameez,* we were nonetheless obviously foreigners.

"Where is the guy?" I asked.

"Don't worry. We've got his camera. We'll take care of him." The Pakistani officer winked and motioned about twenty yards away to a young man with a scraggly beard and dressed in Afghan garb talking to two of his officers. The colonel's answer was far from reassuring.

"No, Colonel. Let's not just 'take care of him,' " I said. "Give him back his camera and let him go. But first let's get Stolz out of here."

If, by 1989, there was one man working at Langley who most clearly embodied the old-school traditions of the CIA, it was Richard Stolz. He was a throwback to the first crop of Ivy Leaguers who had joined the CIA in the years immediately after World War II. Born in 1925 and raised comfortably in New Jersey, Stolz enlisted in the Army at eighteen and by late 1944 was a combat infantryman with the 100th Division in France. After the war, he graduated from Amherst College and made his way to New York, where a college friend quietly contacted him and asked him if he was bored at work and would like to be part of something interesting going on in Washington. It was, at the time, the typical recruitment pitch at the fledgling CIA, which relied heavily on elite eastern college connections to fill its new officer corps.

Short and slight, and with a quiet, unassuming demeanor, Stolz took to the intelligence business and in the early 1960s was chosen to be the CIA's first chief in Moscow. After just a few months in Moscow, Stolz was kicked out by the Soviets in retaliation for the FBI's aggressive action against a KGB officer in Washington. Yet he continued his smooth rise up the CIA's management ranks until 1981, when he decided he couldn't work for President Ronald Reagan's new CIA director, Bill Casey.

Stolz was London station chief when Casey took over at the CIA. Casey quickly asked him to return to headquarters to serve as one of two deputies to Max Hugel, a Republican crony whom Casey was going to name DDO. Stolz was deeply insulted that he was being asked to nursemaid an amateur and retired rather than accept the assignment.

Hugel was forced out by scandal in just a few months, and Casey ruefully put the professionals back in charge, first naming John Stein to be DDO and later replacing him with Clair George. At first, Stolz probably regretted his decision to leave, since it looked as though he could have been rapidly promoted to DDO if he'd just waited it out.

But in the long run, it turned out to be a blessing in disguise. It meant that he was out of the CIA, and untainted, when the Iran-contra scandal engulfed the DO's leadership in the mid-1980s.

After Casey's death in 1987, William Webster, the highly regarded FBI Director, was asked by President Reagan to take over the CIA and steer it out of the Iran-contra morass. Webster turned to Stolz, whom he had known at Amherst, and asked him to come out of retirement in 1988 and get the DO back on track. The fact that Stolz had been out of the CIA throughout Iran-contra made him a much more attractive candidate for Webster, who was then trying to deal with increasingly aggressive intelligence oversight committees in Congress. It also meant that Dick Stolz, who as a young case officer had experienced the earliest of the CIA's battles against the Soviet Union, would return to lead the DO during the Cold War's final days.

By early 1989, the upheaval in Eastern Europe was just beginning, but Stolz could already see that SE Division needed new leadership. Stolz and his deputy, Tom Twetten, believed that the entire Directorate of Operations had to change, but nowhere was the need for an overhaul more pressing than in the SE Division.

Stolz had run the division himself in the 1970s, when it was called the SB Division (for "Soviet Bloc"). He was old school, but still he recognized that the division had to be aired out to keep up with the accelerating pace of events. He knew that Burton Gerber was one of the best of the CIA's Soviet operations officers, but he had been division chief for five years—far too long, in Stolz's opinion.

Stolz and Twetten knew that the SE Division had to start thinking more broadly to seek out the kind of political intelligence that policy makers in Washington were hungry for as they tried to grapple with the accelerating pace of change in the Soviet empire. But they also worried that SE Division managers were still so focused on obtaining yet another microdot message from a spy inside the KGB that they were missing the big picture. Stolz realized that Burton Gerber and his deputy, Paul Redmond, were both products of the SE Division culture and were not the right people to try to change it. Stolz wasn't certain how rapidly the division should or could be overhauled, but he knew that it had to change.

For his part, Gerber also recognized that he had been in the job too long. He had already quietly gone to Stolz to ask that he be allowed to move on to a new post.

Dick Stolz had come out to Pakistan not only to take a look at the endgame of the war, but to tell me that I would be returning to headquarters in July to take over SE Division from Burton Gerber. It was time for a change, was all that the DDO had said.

Islamabad, June 1989

June brought an end to predictions of a rapid collapse of the Kabul regime. Not only was it holding on, but the resistance had turned to deadly squabbling, splitting sharply along ethnic and regional lines. In the process, the warring parties made it nearly impossible for the international aid agencies to deliver desperately needed humanitarian assistance inside Afghanistan, and the bitter internecine fighting discouraged the millions of refugees piled up in Pakistan and Iran from returning home. The international community tired of the replay of the old Afghan drama and began to disengage.

There were few workable ideas of how to make the place whole again, and absent a major international effort—a waning possibility—Afghanistan would revert to its old unruly ways, this time armed to the teeth with the leftovers of a decade of proxy superpower warfare. Already the Afghan resistance, whose struggle against the overwhelming strength of a superpower had captured the West's imagination, was losing even its most devoted supporters. Yesterday's romantic freedom fighters were today's scruffy thugs.

The Western media closed up shop in neighboring Pakistan to chase new and more dramatic stories in places like Tiananmen Square, where a new hero was born, a Chinese student staring down a People's Liberation Army tank. The media's departure was followed by the so-called Afghan Arabs, who began to trickle back to their homes in the Middle East, filled with a profound sense of accomplishment and with ideas for radical change at home. Among them was the son of a Saudi billionaire, Osama bin Laden, a construction engineer who had built a number of orphanages and homes for the widows of resistance fighters in North-West Frontier Province, as well as tunnels and ordnance depots burrowed into the mountains of Nangarhar and Paktia.

By the mid-1980s, the call to jihad had reached all corners of the Islamic world, attracting Arabs young and old and with a variety of motivations to travel to Pakistan to take up arms against the Soviet invaders. There were the genuine volunteers on missions of humanitarian value; there were the adventure seekers on the paths of glory; and there were the psychopaths. As the war dragged on, a number of Arab states quietly emptied their prisons of their homegrown troublemakers and sent them off to the Afghan jihad with the hope that they might not return. By the end of the war, we had estimated that as many as twenty thousand Arabs may have passed through Pakistan and Afghanistan.

The Afghan Arabs occasionally saw combat against Soviet and DRA forces, but their military role in the war would be greatly inflated after the Soviets withdrew. As fund-raisers, however, the Arabs played a positive, often critical, role in the rear areas. By 1989, the CIA estimated that Gulf Arabs raised as much as $20 million to $25 million each month for their humanitarian and construction projects. There was little concern at the time over the role of the Afghan Arabs in Pakistan or Afghanistan, with the exception of localized criticism by Western nongovernmental organizations of the harsh fundamentalism of the Saudi Wahhabis, whose influence in the refugee camps in Pakistan was pervasive. It was in these squalid camps that a generation of young Afghan males would be born into and raised in the strictest fundamentalism of the Deobandi and Wahhabi Islamic schools, the *madrassas,* setting the stage for new problems a decade later.

Thus, after the Soviet withdrawal from Afghanistan, the interests of Western governments turned to East-Central Europe as the drama of 1989 began to play out. Pretty soon the world would lose interest in Afghanistan. And the Pakistan government, now bringing to an end another of its experiments with democracy, would rapidly discover that it could no longer escape the mood swings of the U.S. Congress. As soon as Benazir Bhutto was dismissed on charges of gross corruption in 1990, the United States would impose new sanctions on Pakistan as a nuclear proliferator, a program even Benazir endorsed. After Boris Gromov crossed the Amu Dar'ya, less than two years passed before the old friends, Pakistan and the United States, went their separate ways as the United States directed its attention elsewhere.

In my last meeting with Hamid Gul, the plucky little general had high hopes for both Pakistan and the United States jointly building a new Afghanistan, adding stability and strategic depth to Pakistan's rear area as the Islamic republic turned its attention once again to India, its permanent foe to the east. As a parting gift, I would present Gul with a U.S. cavalry sword, and during my last days in Islamabad, I would help him choose an American university for his oldest son. Together we decided on Texas A&M University. It would be just right for the boy, I thought. But it wouldn't happen. The man Arnie Raphel dubbed "the PLG" would soon turn against us, convinced that we had used and then betrayed Pakistan and its people. In a way, he would be right. And some years later, the CIA would describe the plucky little general as "the most dangerous man in Pakistan." And that, too, would be right.

But for now, the time and place for the endgame of the contest with the USSR had shifted far to the west of the Eastern Mountains. The action now was closer to home for the Soviets.

PART THREE

ENDGAME

1

Vienna, Austria, April 27, 1989

Patience is sometimes rewarded, Ted Price thought with satisfaction. The quiet little Austrian home, complete with hausfrau, looked innocent enough. But every so often, unnoticed by neighbors, the little house had a strange visitor who would make an important telephone call and then leave again. The stranger was a man named Reino Gikman, a KGB "illegal," or deep cover operator, and once the CIA discovered this pattern, they began to watch the house and listen to the telephone—and, with great patience, to wait.

When Gikman arrived on April 27, he dialed a telephone number in the United States—in the 202 area code for Washington, D.C.—and Ted Price, deputy chief of the counterintelligence center at CIA, knew that he finally had his man. A quick check revealed that Gikman had dialed the home telephone number of Felix Bloch, the State Department's director of European and Canadian affairs and the former deputy chief of mission in the American embassy in Vienna. Price was not a Soviet expert—he had learned the craft of intelligence along the streets of Hong Kong and Beijing and in Third World postings like Addis Ababa—but he recognized instantly that he had a bombshell on his hands.

An arrogant and stiff man who affected old-world European mannerisms as he moved smoothly through diplomatic circles, Bloch was, on the surface at least, the embodiment of the State Department's tradition-bound culture. He was a man to whom custom and position were all important and hardly seemed to be the type to take the risk of leading a double life as a Russian spy. But the phone call from Gikman suddenly changed everything; Bloch was about to become one of the highest-ranking State Department officials ever to be investigated for espionage. Price knew his spy hunters would have to proceed carefully—and quietly.

Once Bloch was in their sights, the CIA and FBI moved quickly. After opening their investigation, they gained the help of French intelligence, which tracked Bloch to a meeting in Paris with Gikman on May 14. By now there was little doubt at Langley that Bloch was working for the Soviets. As counterintelligence teams handling the case dug into Bloch's background, they discovered that the outwardly dignified diplomat had a hidden penchant for S&M and had even gone so far as to hire his own dominatrix in Vienna. He seemed to have been working for the Soviets since at least 1974. He did it, by all appearances, for the money. His wife was totally oblivious to his secret life.

Yet there was still little hard evidence to take to court. The FBI didn't have absolute proof that Bloch had passed classified materials to Gikman and the Soviets. John Martin, the Justice Department's unsparing chief attorney on espionage cases, would demand a better case. Ted Price and his colleagues at the counterintelligence center would have to keep watching.

Idylwood Park, Fairfax, Virginia, May 22, 1989

Felix Bloch meant nothing to Robert Hanssen—less than nothing, really. Bloch was a State Department dandy who had sullied himself and deserved to be arrested. From what Hanssen had seen of the Bloch file, the diplomat was an urbane Europhile, just the sort of man the FBI special agent would love to put in handcuffs. Yet the other Robert Hanssen, the Soviet spy code-named B, could understand this other man with a secret life. What's more, he believed that he owed it to the KGB to warn them one of their agents was in trouble. Gikman was a KGB professional, operating without diplomatic immunity; if caught, he would face serious prison time. "Bloch was such a schnook," Hanssen later wrote to the KGB. "I almost hated protecting him, but then he was your friend, and there was your illegal I wanted to protect."

So Hanssen set aside his qualms about Bloch. He laid down

a "call-out" signal for an exchange, this time at the "Bob" dead drop under a footbridge in Idylwood Park, not far from his home. He left a package for his KGB handlers, and in the package was information revealing the existence of the FBI's investigation of Bloch and warning that Reino Gikman had been compromised. Hanssen also left a diamond that the KGB had previously given him for services rendered; he wanted the Russians to reimburse him with cash. For good measure, he threw in a computer diskette containing classified information about several FBI technical intelligence programs, along with a note suggesting an account in Switzerland where the KGB could send him more money.

After taking care of his business with the KGB, Hanssen eventually made his way home to his family. Over the years since she had stumbled onto his involvement with Russian intelligence in 1980, Bonnie Hanssen had repeatedly and pointedly questioned Bob as to whether he had fallen back on his old ways. He always acted hurt when she questioned him, hurt that she didn't trust him to uphold his promise. Their growing family was living on a shoestring, so she came to believe that Bob was living up to his pledge never to deal with the Russians again. After all, she had no real evidence of unexplained cash; her brother and sister-in-law would later claim that they knew she had found a large amount of money in the house, but she would respond that she didn't know what they were talking about.

Of course, there had been those odd moments when Bob had engaged in one of his many fantasies. There were the times when he had insisted on taking Bonnie out to expensive stores to try on ball gowns. Bonnie thought it was all so silly, a mother of six being treated like Cinderella, and she made it clear to Bob that she wasn't interested in buying one. In exasperation, she finally asked him where on earth did he expect her to ever wear such a fancy gown?

Bob actually had an answer. Why, to a presidential inaugural ball, of course. He explained to her that he'd received invitations to Republican inaugural balls—apparently for the inaugural of the first George Bush, for one of the inaugurals of Ronald Reagan, or for both.

A review of records at the Federal Election Commission did

not turn up any evidence that Robert Hanssen ever made contributions to any presidential candidates or other campaigns. Still, inaugural invitations tend to be given to campaign supporters and contributors, so it is possible that he gave money to some organization or political entity. That raises an intriguing question: Did some of Bob Hanssen's KGB money end up in Republican Party coffers?

After her husband's arrest, Bonnie reported to government investigators her belief that her husband had contributed money to Republican campaigns and conservative causes. It is unclear whether Bonnie had firsthand knowledge that her husband had contributed to political campaigns, but there is also no evidence that the government investigators followed up on her information.

Washington, D.C., June 22, 1989

Once again, the telephone rang in the middle of the night in Felix Bloch's home. This time the caller identified himself as "Ferdinand Paul" and said he was calling for "Pierre," who "cannot see you in the near future." Pierre was "sick," Paul said. He added that "a contagious disease is suspected."

Then, before hanging up, Paul added, "I am worried about you. You have to take care of yourself."

As Bloch nervously laid down the receiver, he knew that he had to think fast. The call had been from the KGB. He knew that "Pierre" was Gikman and that the message meant that Gikman had been betrayed. The KGB was telling him that he was in deep trouble, too.

Thanks to the warning in May, Gikman had already fled to Moscow, but the KGB had waited a month to warn Bloch after receiving Hanssen's tip. For whatever reason, the Soviets had moved first to protect Gikman and only later Bloch. Felix Bloch was now on his own.

When he arrived at the State Department the next morning, Bloch learned just how alone he really was. Confronted by the FBI, whose agents had been listening in on the call and were furious that the diplomat had been tipped off the previous night, Bloch found his whole world crumbling around him. Still, the warning from the KGB had been just enough to steel him against the FBI's hostile questioning. He stood his ground, refusing to give the agents the self-incriminating statements they needed to make an arrest.

Frustrated—both with Bloch's refusal to talk and their own inability to obtain Justice Department approval to arrest and prosecute him—the FBI began tailing him openly everywhere around Washington. By July, the fact that there was a suspected spy at the State Department finally became public when ABC News broke the story. Now, the FBI agents following Bloch were joined by television news crews, and the investigation that Ted Price had wanted to keep secret had become a media circus. Footage of the bald-headed Bloch sitting forlornly on a Washington park bench surrounded by cameras and reporters almost engendered public sympathy for this very unsympathetic man.

The scrutiny only hampered the FBI's efforts to persuade the Justice Department to move against Bloch. Soon the case reached a stalemate, and a deep bitterness set in among the investigators at the CIA and FBI who thought they'd been so close to nailing Bloch and now had to watch him slip out of their grasp.

Of course, Bloch didn't escape punishment completely. He was forced out of the State Department for security violations and later moved to North Carolina, where he was reduced to working first as a clerk at a grocery store and later as a bus driver. His wife divorced him, and he spent his days mounting a last-ditch legal battle against the State Department for denying him his pension.

The Bloch case remained open for years afterward, but Bloch himself was never arrested or charged with espionage. In 1992, after the end of the Cold War, a retired KGB archivist, Vasili Mitrokhin, defected to Britain and provided British intelligence with a cache of notes and transcripts he'd copied from secret KGB files, primarily from the illegals section of the KGB's First Chief Directorate. Mitrokhin's stash included notes about the KGB's handling of the Felix Bloch case, according to sources familiar with the case. The Bloch fiasco quickly faded from the media's attention, but at least a few counterintelligence experts at the CIA and FBI continued to wonder how their case had been exposed so quickly to the KGB.

Must have been the French.

CIA Headquarters, July 10, 1989

After Boris Gromov's melodramatic crossing of the Amu Dar'ya in February, Dick Stolz decided it was time for me to come back to Langley to take over the Soviet/East European Division from Burton Gerber, who'd held the job for the last five years. By May it was official, and I began preparations for a change of scenery—I would swap the Indus for the Potomac.

When I arrived at headquarters after the July 4 break, the only small sign I saw that Gerber had hung on to anything associated with his old SE fiefdom was so subtle that it had attracted no attention at all.

By tradition, the chiefs of the line divisions and senior staffs in the DO were assigned to thirteen reserved parking places just outside the southwest entrance of the Old Headquarters Building, with slot number one assigned to Chief, SE, and number thirteen to Chief Europe. My first day back, I spotted Gerber's Toyota in C/SE's slot, so I pulled into the vacant number thirteen. In my office, I found the parking permit for slot number thirteen among the welcome home items on my desk. I would never know whether it was the attraction of being in slot number one that had prompted Gerber to hang on to his old parking place or the possibly ominous portent of number thirteen. Either way, it didn't matter much to me.

SE had moved from its traditional real estate in the Old Headquarters Building to a new building that had gone up behind it while I was away. The new building was touted as a state-of-the-art affair, specially shielded to prevent electromagnetic attack and designed in every way for the needs of America's intelligence services approaching the twenty-first century. There was a massive atrium with suspended models of U-2 and SR-71 reconnaissance aircraft, an airy court with a James Sanborn sculpture called *Kryptos* telling a story of information gathering and cryptography. The new building was linked to the old one with a gently curving tunnel called, ominously, a "wave guide," which was supposed to prevent electromagnetic emanations from passing through from either direction.

But with all the advanced technology, there were signs that it had been thrown up a little haphazardly. In my second-floor corner office, one of the outer walls just missed properly joining a connecting wall and had to be patched, much in the way a pair of pants might be expanded at the waist with a sewn-in strip of cloth. High-tech, low-tech, I thought. A pretty appropriate description of the agency.

Paul Redmond, the deputy division chief, was waiting when I checked in.

"Welcome back," he said, extending his hand. "You've been out there goofing off too long."

"You been goofing off, too? Or do we have some new business?" I hadn't had any detailed briefings on what had been going on in SE since I'd left in the midst of the "1985 troubles"; I'd made a point of not overlapping with Gerber and hadn't asked for a briefing from him.

"We've got business," Redmond said.

That first morning back, Redmond brought me up to date on the cases that had been compromised after I'd left—FITNESS, MILLION, ACCORD, TOP HAT, JOGGER from Jakarta . . . the casualty list was long. The cause of the losses was still a mystery. Edward Lee Howard could account for some, but not all; and the Marine guard scandal in Moscow, though it had looked as if it might be the answer at the time, turned out not to be. Internal investigations at the CIA and FBI had turned up nothing, and our two probes had run dry. The fact that most of the losses seemed to have occurred in one brief but intense burst had prompted a review of obituaries of CIA employees, to see if someone who'd had access to the blown cases had died. The FBI had tried cold pitches of KGB officers in an effort to recruit a source who could tell them what had happened. But nothing worked—the investigation had gone cold. Redmond told me that Jeanne Vertefeuille was still looking at the problem in the counterintelligence center.

But Vertefeuille, an experienced SE Division hand, had been looking at the 1985 losses since late 1986, and had not had any success in solving the mystery. Gus Hathaway, then the counterintelligence chief, had asked Vertefeuille, who had been serving as a station chief in West Africa, to return to headquarters to analyze the damage and try to solve the puzzle of why the CIA was losing its Russian agents. When she arrived back at Langley in the fall of 1986, Vertefeuille began a lonely and painstaking effort to find out if the damaged cases had anything in common. Working in such secrecy that she even refused to tell Redmond exactly what she was doing, Vertefeuille and her small staff spent months sorting through old files and interviewing key SE Division employees who had had access to the cases. It was all in a vain attempt to develop a cross-referencing matrix that might reveal a common denominator and unlock the mystery. With limited resources and virtually no high-level interest in the investigation, she was unable to determine conclusively whether there was a mole or simply a compromise in the agency's communications. The best that Vertefeuille could offer was that Moscow Station had access to all but one or two of the cases. The FBI, concerned about the losses of its own Soviet agents, including Martynov and Motorin, consulted with the CIA and began its own probe as well in 1986, code-named ANLACE. But the bureau had no more luck than Vertefeuille, and both reviews had soon lost steam.

The Vertefeuille investigation continued for years, but it was crippled from the start by the fact that Hathaway had made it clear that he didn't want a full-fledged mole hunt, one that would have included polygraph examinations of all those who had had access to the blown cases. Instead, Vertefeuille worked her matrices and lists of names, but she lacked the evidence—or the bureaucratic power—to make much progress. Her inquiry was conducted at such a low level that top CIA officials were not aware that it had all but petered out.

Redmond told me that he hadn't been following what she was doing too closely since he was still on the short list of suspects.

I smiled when he said that, until he quipped, "Don't smile, you're on the list."

I quickly got a feel for how Gerber's security measures had changed the old routines. Back when I'd left in 1985, there had been one morning staff meeting, attended by all of the division's seven or eight senior officers. Each one would be able to hear what was going on in other areas—counterintelligence, external operations, Eastern Europe, Moscow operations, intelligence production, personnel matters. All that was history. My first morning staff meeting was actually a series of small sessions. Along with Redmond, who continued as my deputy, and Steve Weber, the division's chief of operations, or COPS, I met with each group chief one at a time. That way, the Eastern European group chief never knew what was going on in the Soviet Union, and vice versa. The only officers in the division aware of the full scope of our activities were the chief, the deputy chief, and the chief of operations. It was not the most efficient way to manage things, but it seemed to be keeping our agents alive, and that was undoubtedly a good thing.

After the endless compartmented staff meetings that first morning back on the job, I shuffled back to my new corner office and took in the lay of the land. Though the surroundings were different—modern steel and blue glass as opposed to the more Gothic architecture of the old building—the props were much the same: the same Federalist furniture, the couches arranged for small meetings, the secure STU-III phone on the credenza. But on the two-drawer safe behind my desk was something I'd never had before—a plain black telephone that linked me to KGB headquarters in Moscow—the Gavrilov channel. Inside the safe was Gerber's file on the link with Lubyanka, explaining in great detail how the communications pipeline had been opened in the early 1980s. Over the coming two years, Gavrilov would be used more than ever before.

I looked over the briefing papers that had been prepared for me, each sealed in a separate envelope. We were in the process of vetting about a dozen new volunteers from a wide variety of ministries and technical institutes. Business looked pretty good. Whatever had happened to us in the past was clearly not at work now.

As I settled into my new job in the summer of 1989, I had to take stock not only of the new surroundings in SE Division, where, as Redmond put it, nothing really ever changed, to the world in which we operated, where changes were happening faster than they could be assimilated. By the time I arrived at Langley, the real beneficiaries of the end of the Soviet war in

Afghanistan were emerging—not the people of Afghanistan, but the people of East-Central Europe.

The first word of looming change came in May, a scant ninety days after the Soviet withdrawal from Afghanistan, when the German chancellor was told by Gorbachev on the Soviet leader's first visit to West Germany that force was no longer a viable means for holding the Warsaw Pact together. Gorbachev reaffirmed his policy, first hinted at late the previous year, that in effect the Brezhnev Doctrine had been scrapped.

That same month, the Hungarians made an overt move that would send tremors through the Soviet empire in East-Central Europe—they began dismantling the barbed-wire span of the Iron Curtain on their frontier with Austria. The stringing of that barbed wire tripped off the Cold War, prompting Winston Churchill in May 1946 in Fulton, Missouri, to declare, "From Stettin in the Baltic to Trieste in the Adriatic, an iron curtain has descended across the Continent." For over half a century the world had accepted this shaky demarcation as a boundary between East and West—between the Communist sphere and Western Europe—and now, with a few snips, the landscape of the Cold War had changed overnight. Since then, people had begun to stream across that old line in growing numbers, and nobody seemed to be prepared to stand in their way.

Convinced that the Soviets had neither the stomach nor the means to do anything about it, Budapest took another fateful step in June. The Hungarian government rehabilitated the hero of the 1956 revolution, Imre Nagy, hung two years after the revolt was crushed by Soviet tanks, and reinterred him as a national hero. The probes in Hungary were the first acts of defiance by a member of the Warsaw Pact. But others would follow in breathtaking succession.

On June 5 the people of Poland elected Lech Walesa's Solidarity Party to a stunning majority in the Polish parliament. Communism was dealt a body blow at the very core of the Warsaw Pact, though most of America was transfixed by the images coming in from Tiananmen Square of the revolution that had exploded one day earlier.

And all through the summer of 1989, small knots of activists in the German Democratic Republic began gathering in the churches and coffeehouses of Leipzig, Dresden, and Berlin to talk of change and demand more travel rights. Their numbers were tiny at first, but then they grew, and by the time I checked in at headquarters, there was no longer any doubt that something truly historic was afoot in the Soviet Union's Eastern European empire.

First Chief Directorate Headquarters, Yasenevo, July 10, 1989

Leonid Shebarshin ought to have felt at the top of his game. Comfortably settled in his corner office on the second floor in the leadership suite at Yasenevo, he took stock of his career and his world and decided they were heading in opposite directions. His promotion to head of the First Chief Directorate, a job that put him in charge of KGB foreign intelligence operations worldwide, had been the source of some solace. He was more than a little relieved to finally be done with the betrayals and false promises of the Afghan enterprise that had consumed his professional and, in some ways, his personal life for the last five years. The fact that his old boss, Vladimir Kryuchkov, had moved downtown to take over as Chairman of the KGB made his position all the more secure. An ordinary general officer in the KGB might have just settled into this snug perch to mark time until he could start thinking about the corner suite at Lubyanka and maybe a seat on the Politburo. But Shebarshin felt no such satisfaction. On the contrary, in the five months since he had been on the job, he had become convinced that the world he had lived and worked in over the last three decades was coming to a crashing end.

It all began with the march out of Afghanistan on February 15, a fateful end to an adventure that, to his mind, had been doomed from the start. The troika of Gorbachev, Shevardnadze, and Aleksandr Yakovlev, the old Party propagandist who'd gone liberal and was now glued to Gorbachev's side, had in a few short years undermined the foundation of socialist unity that had been so carefully reinforced over the previous forty years. Gorbachev and his cohorts had almost flippantly declared that the USSR should abandon its paternalistic responsibility for the socialist countries of Eastern Europe. From now on, they'd have to stand on their own. It was every man for himself, the new policy troika had decided, and it didn't take long for things to start coming apart at the seams.

Shebarshin had seen it coming even before he'd moved to the top job at Yasenevo. The Afghan calamity had been the first breach of the Brezhnev Doctrine, the long-standing principle that Moscow would never abandon a fraternal socialist country. Before General Gromov marched his last column across Friendship Bridge, a telegram had been sent to all diplomatic posts and KGB *Rezidentura* abroad announcing the new policies of noninterference.

Shebarshin had been tracking the first whispers of rebellion in the Soviet Union's "near abroad" since early spring: the defiant moves in Hungary, the devastating elections in Poland, and, even more ominous, the growing restlessness in the German Democratic Republic. The stage was set for a total breakdown, he concluded darkly, and he decided he'd better call home his *Rezidents* from Eastern Europe. He'd need their assessments to draw a new road map for Eastern Europe, and a quick conference should help.

He may not have bargained for the frankness he got. The gathered KGB chiefs drew a dismal picture of events in their countries. Their collective judgment was that socialist unity was coming to an end, and rapidly. The economic position of the USSR, it was reluctantly agreed, was so weak that meaningful aid to the countries of Eastern Europe was no longer possible. They would have to tailor their activities accordingly.

A consensus was reached early in the conference that the ideological commitment in the fraternal socialist countries, never strong, was weakening to the point at which the collapse of socialism throughout the Warsaw Pact was likely, if not imminent. In Poland, over forty years of socialism had been wiped away at the polling stations just a month earlier. Less sensational, but equally irreversible, was the shift away from the principles of socialism in Hungary; and in Czechoslovakia, there was talk of a return to the Prague Spring of a generation ago. The key, of course, would be the German Democratic Republic. If the troubles took root in Germany, the results could be disastrous.

The belief in the common threat from the United States that had held the alliance together for forty years had suddenly given way to a race for rapprochement with the Americans. Shebarshin placed an equal share of the blame on Gorbachev and his two key political advisers, though his deepest distaste was reserved for Shevardnadze. It seemed that the Georgian Foreign Minister spent hours on end alone with his American counterparts, first George Shultz and now James Baker, without interpreters or note takers watching over the proceedings. There was no telling what sort of devil's deals he was cutting with the Americans when nobody was watching.

Shebarshin's last job had been cauterizing what Gorbachev had described as the "bleeding wound" of Afghanistan. This new job involved greater stakes, and he was afraid the outcome had already been decided.

Langley, 0900 Hours, July 12, 1989

I arrived a few minutes early for my first DDO staff meeting. Standing alone in the sixth-floor conference room where the DDO had been holding his weekly meetings for as long as I could remember, I felt surrounded, as I always had in that room, by the history of the Directorate of Operations. Punctuating the gray, sound-absorbing walls were the photographs of the men who had charted the history of the directorate for the forty years of its existence. At one end were the fading but somehow still dashing black-and-white snapshots of Allen Dulles and Frank Wisner, the establishment men who'd run the directorate from 1951 to 1959, when it was more mysteriously known as the Deputy Directorate for Plans. At the other end were the posed and somber color shots of the "citizen DDOs," ending with John Stein and Clair George, the Stars and Stripes hanging proudly in the background. In between were the directorate's icons—Dick Helms, Des FitzGerald, and Bill Colby—and its oddities like Max Hugel, who lasted just two turbulent months in 1981.

There were thirteen photos on the wall—that dangerous number again—and whenever I scanned them I would note the unsettling proportion of them who had come to grief. Dulles had been fired by JFK over the Bay of Pigs fiasco; Wisner had died by his own hand, tormented by demons; Helms had pleaded "no contest" to charges of failing to testify fully to

Congress regarding CIA activities in Salvador Allende's Chile. He was fined a few thousand dollars, a token sum paid in full by loyal colleagues who passed the hat, and then confirmed by Congress as ambassador to Iran. The last photo was of Clair George, Dick Stolz's predecessor, who had retired under the pressure of the Iran-contra affair two years earlier and was now under federal indictment.

As I waited for the meeting to begin, I wondered how many of the men who would be here this morning would want the DDO's job. Probably all of them, I decided.

"Welcome back, Milton."

I turned to find Burton Gerber walking toward me, hand extended.

"Settled in?" he asked.

"You left it all nice and tidy," I said. "And yes, thank you, I'm settling in fine."

Before the moment could become awkward, the other DO chiefs filed in, followed by Stolz and Tom Twetten. Stolz and his deputy took their seats at the end of the table nearest the entrance; the opposite end was occupied by the counterintelligence chief, Gus Hathaway. The rest of us fanned out along both sides of the table, according to a rigid territoriality—I took the seat that had been occupied by SE chiefs ever since the DDO staff meetings had been taking place in the room. The dozen chiefs at the table were known as the "barons." The chiefs of the smaller staffs took straight chairs along the wall.

Today's staff meeting was the season opener for those of us who'd just returned from the field. I spotted Bill Moseby, who controlled Africa, a man I hadn't seen since we'd run our probe involving the phony recruitment of the GRU *Rezident* when he was chief in Nairobi in 1986. Jim Higham ran the Near East, and I'd worked with him closely in Islamabad. A professorial man with a faint British accent, Higham had spent much of his career in the Middle East. Jack Downing had returned from Moscow earlier in the year to take over East Asia, which was his original home division. After spending the last three years as Moscow station chief, Downing had been astounded when he'd returned to headquarters that so little was being done to investigate the 1985 losses. But now that he was out of Soviet operations and was East Asia Division chief, he no longer felt it was his place to push for more action.

John MacGaffin was just in from Turkey and had taken over the powerful operational review and resource management staff of the directorate. I hadn't met John before, but we'd be spending much time together in the next few years. Terry Ward was another senior who was new to me—he was the new Latin America chief.

The half-hour meeting was taken up with a welcome back talk by Stolz, the renewal of acquaintances, and little else, except that Burton Gerber and I had managed our handover of SE Division.

2

East Berlin, July 20, 1989

David Rolph had come a long way in his twelve years at the CIA. On his first overseas tour, in Moscow, he'd been lucky enough to handle some of the agency's most important Soviet cases, including Adolf Tolkachev. Now, at forty-one, Rolph was back on the front lines of the Cold War, and this time he had been given his first command on the wrong side of Checkpoint Charlie in Berlin.

In many ways, the small East Berlin Station was a more difficult assignment for a CIA officer than Moscow. It wasn't that the surveillance by the East Germans was any better or more effective. In fact, it was less comprehensive than the blanket coverage one had to deal with inside the Soviet Union. In Moscow, the KGB could put twenty cars out onto the streets to trail one CIA officer. The East Germans never went to that kind of trouble.

The problem was the Ministerium für Staatssicherheit, the

MfS—infamously known as the Stasi. East Germany's ubiquitous security service had such an iron grip on its people that almost no one dared spy for the Americans. The Stasi had, by one conservative estimate, 174,000 *inoffizielle Mitarbeiter*—agents or full-time informants—and many more snitches in a country of just 17 million. With those odds, few people truly believed they could steal secrets and get away with it. The Stasi didn't follow CIA officers as diligently as the KGB, but then again, maybe they didn't need to.

By the 1980s, Berlin had lost some of its early Cold War status as a major hub of espionage operations. After the Berlin Wall went up in 1961, the ability of CIA officers based in West Berlin to conduct operations in the eastern sector plunged. West Berlin came to be known as a training ground, rather than a real hotbed of active operations. It was mockingly called "Brandenburg's School for Boys," since it was now little more than a place to hone skills before being sent off to the new hot spots where real espionage was being conducted. The East Berlin Station, meanwhile, had never quite been able to establish itself as a major operational hub over the years; it too had come to be regarded as little more than a training assignment for the other capitals in the Warsaw Pact, where real business was being carried out.

Some thought the problems with East Berlin might stem from its movie set atmosphere. A CIA officer operating under the watchful eye of the Stasi, unlike his colleagues in Moscow, could always call time out and slip through Checkpoint Charlie to the west a few hundred yards away for a break. Whatever the reason, the small East Berlin Station that opened for business a dozen years after the Wall went up had remained something of a backwater.

When Rolph arrived in East Berlin in the summer of 1988, the CIA had no agents inside the internal security apparatus of the MfS, or in the HVA, the Hauptverwaltung Aufklarung, its foreign intelligence arm. It wasn't for lack of trying. But every one of the men who seemed ready to change sides turned out to be a double agent; the CIA had had no luck in recruiting even the dullest functionaries.

Even so, there was plenty to keep Rolph busy. For some time, officers in East Germany had been secretly planting ground sensors near military bases. The sensors would measure the volume of traffic passing by a military installation and relay the data to a spy satellite in space. If the sensors suddenly detected spikes in traffic outside several military bases all at the same time, it might mean that the East Germans—and their Soviet allies—were mobilizing troops and preparing for war.

CIA officers were trained to install the shoebox-size sensors both at the Farm and in West Germany before they attempted to mount the operations in the East German woods. After making sure he was "black," the CIA officer would slip on nightvision goggles and plunge into the underbrush closest to the military base. His job was to bury the sensor, leaving only its antenna above ground so that it could regularly signal a passing satellite.

It was such an exciting and productive operation that the U.S. Army decided it wanted to get in on it, too. And that was where the trouble began. The Army didn't let its West German–based intelligence officers work in East Germany—it turned the task of planting the sensors over to German agents. One of the Germans turned out to be a double agent, and he immediately gave his sensor to the Stasi to examine. A flaw in the design quickly became apparent to the East Germans: All of the sensors had been assigned the same frequency. When they dialed in the frequency, they were able to intercept the transmissions from all of the sensors that had been planted at military bases throughout the country. In order to protect their spy, the Stasi left the sensors in place for a time. But the operation was blown.

Another technical operation was designed in response to recent agreements between the United States and the Soviet Union to gradually reduce the nuclear weapons both nations kept in Germany. To verify that Moscow was honoring the treaty, the CIA hit on the idea of hiding gamma radiation sensors next to the East German rail lines heading toward the Soviet Union. The Russians would have to ship their nuclear weapons back home on those rail lines, and the sensors could detect their radiation as they passed by. The CIA could then determine whether the Soviets were sending the missiles home, in compliance with their treaty obligations. It was valuable stuff, but still, technical operations couldn't make up for the lack of spies.

East Berlin, July 1989

They called him Curly. The fuzzy-haired German was a member of one of the MfS surveillance teams that followed David Rolph and his case officers in East Berlin, day and night, from home to work and back again.

For CIA officers serving in the Soviet bloc, being under surveillance was such a constant part of life that it sometimes helped to humanize their ever-present shadows. So they came up with nicknames for their followers, like Curly. Occasionally, there were even opportunities for small exchanges of professional courtesy between the hunters and the hunted. At the end of his tour of duty in Eastern Europe, one CIA officer stopped on his way to the airport and left a package by the side of the road. Inside was a case of beer, a going-away present for the surveillance team that he knew would shortly stop to examine his last dead drop.

Curly had one distinct habit: He usually drove the same car. Even in a country with such nondescript automobiles, the team in East Berlin could eventually recognize Curly and his car on first sight. One day while taking a walk near his East Berlin home, Rolph's predecessor as East Berlin station chief noticed a car parked outside an apartment building in his neighborhood. It was Curly's car, he was certain.

From then on, the CIA station chief made a point of looking for Curly's car each time he went out for a walk, and he saw it parked at the apartment complex in his neighborhood several more times before he transferred to a new assignment. The station chief left behind a report for Rolph, his successor, about his discovery. It wasn't much, but it was the only shred of information about the Stasi surveillance teams that the CIA had to go on.

At first, Rolph thought Curly might park his car at the apartment complex because it was the site of a hidden Stasi observation post, since it was so close to the CIA chief's home. Rolph was now living in the same house and frequently took walks to see Curly's car for himself. But eventually he started to think that Curly might actually live in the apartment building. He probably parked his car there when he drove home at night.

Rolph decided he had to make sure. Early one morning, a CIA officer dressed like an East German worker mingled with the other commuters waiting at the bus stop right outside the apartment complex, hoping to catch sight of Curly emerging from the building on his way to work. Sure enough, Curly eventually walked out, got in his car, and drove off, confirming Rolph's suspicion and giving the CIA the lead it needed.

The discovery of Curly's home address offered the CIA a rare chance to approach an East German surveillance officer away from work—and the prying eyes of his supervisors and other MfS officers. Rolph had to consider the best way to approach Curly without spooking him. If the pitch wasn't handled just right, Curly might suspect that it was a provocation by his bosses to test his loyalty. It was decided that Rolph's predecessor as station chief, whom Curly knew on sight, should come back from West Berlin to carry the message.

At about 6:00 A.M. on a workday, just before Curly left the apartment building, the former station chief left an envelope under the windshield wiper on Curly's car. Inside the envelope was a letter with a lucrative proposal for him to become a spy for the United States. The American then stood across the street and waited for Curly to come out of the apartment complex to drive to work. The former East Berlin station chief took the extraordinary measure of waiting around after leaving the letter because he wanted to make certain that Curly saw him when he picked up the note. The whole point of the former chief's involvement in the operation was to make sure Curly saw a man he knew to be a CIA officer—he'd then know that the letter wasn't part of a ruse engineered by the Stasi.

When Curly came out to his car, he found the envelope and looked across the street at the American. As Curly read the instructions that had been left for him to contact the CIA if he wanted to become a spy, the former station chief quietly disappeared.

Two days later, David Rolph drove past the site where Curly was supposed to leave a sign if he wanted to work for the CIA. He was ecstatic when he saw a chalk mark that signaled Curly was ready to spy. Over the next few months, Rolph's deputy and Curly met repeatedly in hotels around West Berlin, as the German poured out everything he knew about Stasi surveillance. The case marked the first time the CIA had recruited an active duty surveillance officer in East Germany. The excitement in Langley was palpable. Lonely, backwater East Berlin might finally begin to pay off.

Curly became such an important agent that Rolph grew worried when he was out of touch for very long. After losing contact with him for a time, Rolph's deputy decided to wait for him at a bus stop across from his apartment early one morning, to make sure that everything was all right. When Curly showed up, the two had a long talk and then hugged like long-lost friends. The CIA officer wrote a cable to headquarters describing the meeting and explained how his talk with the German had convinced him that Curly was a legitimate agent.

"I looked into his eyes," the CIA officer wrote, "and I realized that he was good."

Warsaw, July 20, 1989

Gromoslaw Czempinski had seen it coming for months. As a professional intelligence officer, Gromek, as his friends called him, was an astute judge of politics and people, and he could tell that the regime he'd worked for since he'd joined the service in 1972 was finished. Beset by economic stagnation and increasingly militant strikes, Poland's Communist rulers had grudgingly opened roundtable negotiations with Poland's burgeoning democratic movement—Solidarity—and had finally agreed to hold elections in June. The Party seemed to think it could manage the outcome and limit Solidarity's political influence. The fix, they thought, was in.

But Czempinski knew better. Poland's foreign intelligence service had well-placed spies inside Solidarity—better than those reporting to the SB, the internal security service—so Czempinski and his colleagues had a pretty good inkling that Solidarity was on the verge of a sweeping victory. The Communists were in for a surprise.

The foreign intelligence service decided not to wait for the final results. Months before the elections, officials throughout the Intelligence and Counterintelligence Bureau, where Czempinski worked, started to destroy documents in anticipation of the end of Communist rule. The destruction of the files, mainly those involving individual agents and informants, started in January and was conducted on a massive scale before the first vote was cast in June.

Among the most sensitive files were those dealing with Solidarity. When the trade union movement first burst onto the scene in the early 1980s, the foreign intelligence service had created a special branch to monitor ties between Solidarity and the CIA and other Western organizations. They had developed a network of agents inside Solidarity to help gather information about financial connections with the CIA, and by 1989, Polish intelligence was convinced that the links between Langley and Solidarity were extensive. The problem was, they overstated the case. While the CIA had provided covert assistance—printing presses, money, and some specialized equipment—so did the AFL-CIO and the Catholic Church. In any event, Western support was not the crucial factor in Solidarity's ultimate triumph.

Still, key Polish intelligence officials were convinced that the CIA would continue its covert actions for as long as it took to topple the regime, and they didn't think there was anything their government could do to stop it. Their belief in the intimidating power of the CIA sapped their confidence and played into their fatalistic conclusion that the downfall of the regime was inevitable. So by the time of Solidarity's stunning and sweeping victory in June, Polish intelligence had destroyed virtually all of the files of the special branch devoted to spying on Solidarity. Aleksandr Makowski, one of the officers running the special branch, wanted to be able to say truthfully, when the new Solidarity government took over, that "the files were apparently gone."

Even with the most sensitive and incriminating files now destroyed, Czempinski and his colleagues had no idea what their fate would be under the new government. A tall, hawk-nosed man with a piercing stare, Czempinski had, until this revolution, enjoyed a rapid rise through the ranks of Polish intelligence. He'd studied economics in college before he was recruited to join Polish intelligence in 1972. He took some pride in the fact that he was one of the first graduates of Poland's new espionage training school and that his first assignment, a tribute to his performance in school, had been to Chicago, at the heart of the American empire. In 1976, a defector gave the CIA and FBI the identities of the Polish intelligence officers stationed in the United States, so Czempinski was recalled to Warsaw before the Americans had a chance to kick him out. He then moved into counterintelligence and by 1989 had become chief of the counterintelligence branch of the foreign intelligence service. He had always been praised for his boldness and imagination, but now his career was in the hands of the steelworkers, union leaders, and former lawyers who had spent time underground or in prison for their defiance of the regime he had served. Czempinski was an optimist and a survivor, but even he had doubts about the future.

Langley, September 18, 1989

"What's going on in Leipzig?" I said to no one in particular at the morning staff meeting with the group managing Eastern Europe. It was the third week in a row that the East Germans had held their Monday demonstrations setting off from the twelfth-century St. Nicholas Church in the old city. They'd kicked off the demonstrations on September 4 with fewer than a thousand marchers chanting, "Down with the Stasi"; three weeks later, their numbers had swollen to around ten thousand. The Stasi had tried to crack down, but they'd been too timid and it didn't seem to be having any effect.

"Who knows," Redmond answered curtly. "But it's pretty clear Honecker's losing control."

The harsh truth was that we didn't have any spies in place who could give us much insight into the plans of the East German government or, for that matter, the intentions of the Soviet leadership in the Kremlin. Still, it was pretty clear that Eric Honecker, secretary general of the German Democratic Republic, was in a bind. When the Hungarians snipped the barbed wire and opened a route to the West, thousands of East Germans made their way to Hungary and streamed across the border into Austria. Honecker had blocked travel to Hungary, but that had only convinced the desperate East Germans to try to get out through Czechoslovakia. The West German embassy in Prague was now swamped with asylum seekers.

"Honecker knows Gorbachev won't bail him out," said Steve Weber, the division COPS, or chief of operations. "Sees him as worse than Brezhnev—part of the problem, not the solution."

The Soviet Union still had more than half a million troops in Eastern Europe, including about four hundred thousand in East Germany, the rest mostly in Hungary. But Gorbachev didn't seem to want to use his troops to restore order. Honecker had apparently told him that if it was up to him, the Berlin Wall would still be standing in a hundred years. Gorbachev let him know he wanted no part of that. He was on his own.

"The White House is playing its cards pretty close," I said, thinking back to my last meeting at the NSC a week earlier. "They think—actually, they hope—they've been able to convince Gorbachev and Shevardnadze that we're not trying to steamroll them in Eastern Europe. What they're angling for now is that no one overreacts and tries to stop whatever's happening."

The White House, like everyone else, was trying to develop a strategy on the fly, reacting to the fast-moving events day by day. No one in Washington had any sense of control or even of what the options would be in a month. What I did know was that the policy makers would soon be turning to us for answers, and we didn't have them. Things were moving so fast that it was hard even to know the right questions to ask.

That morning's session ended with a sense of expectation. Something was about to explode in East Germany, but nobody at Langley or across the river in Washington had a clue what it was. One thing I did know was that we'd have to find a way to get a handle on things, to get ahead of the daily rush of events. We'd have to turn things around pretty quickly if we wanted to have a prayer of giving the NSC what they wanted. "Let's understand what we're about from here on out," I'd said in closing. "And that's trying to be relevant."

I'd had a few months to take a close look at the division and now had a good idea where the strengths were, as well as the weaknesses.

In the front office, Redmond, the deputy division chief, was the operational continuity. He quite literally knew where the bodies were buried, but that was part of the problem. He was smart, no mistake about that, but he was so caught up in the 1985 problems that I wasn't sure I'd have him with me for the long haul.

Steve Weber was another matter. Weber had been born in Hungary before World War II and had been a kid when the war ended and the Communists took over. He'd ended up on the wrong side of the Hungarian security services and found himself in a forced labor battalion in the late 1950s. Somehow he'd forged a travel document and made his way to the West, where he was picked up by U.S. Army intelligence. After a few years working on the margins of the espionage world, Weber was recruited by the CIA, and now, a quarter century later, this Hungarian refugee was my COPS, with the equivalent rank of a two-star general. Only in America, I thought every time I looked at Weber. I'd decided I could rely on the smooth, gray-haired Hungarian operator for unvarnished counsel.

My counterintelligence chief, John O'Reilly, was a total iconoclast. Nothing was sacred to O'R, as we called him, and nobody was safe from his sharp wit. In his rabbit warren of SE counterintelligence, he surrounded himself with the quirky vestiges of espionage history, including an eight-by-twelve glossy of James Jesus Angleton staring through his horn-rimmed glasses. On a table below the photograph was a Buddhist prayer wheel that visitors couldn't resist picking up and spinning as they sought counsel from the counterintelligence chief. O'Reilly had been in SE counterintelligence for years. He had the history of the division down cold and the scuttlebutt even better. He'd already sensed that the center of gravity was shifting and that SE had a new role to play. I decided I'd bring O'R up to the front office. I wanted him closer when things started getting interesting.

East Berlin, October 1989

David Rolph's deputy walked into the CIA's East Berlin Station on a Saturday afternoon with a pale and stunned face.

"What's wrong?"

"Curly's bad. He's been controlled since the beginning."

The CIA officer had just returned from West Berlin, where he'd held his first meeting with another Stasi officer, who'd volunteered by dropping a letter into his car. The Stasi man had started off the meeting by saying that he knew Curly was working for the Americans, and he also knew when and where they met. Curly had reported the initial approach and had been working as a double ever since. After hearing of the CIA's approach to Curly, this second Stasi man decided that he would step in and become a legitimate agent.

While Curly turned out to be a Stasi-controlled operation, this second Stasi volunteer was genuine. The recruitment pitch to Curly hadn't worked, but his report of the contact—complete with the amount of money the Americans were offering—planted the seeds of espionage in this second Stasi officer's mind. He in turn would soon become the most important American spy in East Germany, turning over thousands of pages of documents from inside the Stasi, including organization charts and rosters of MfS and HVA officers. Those rosters would come in handy within a few weeks, when the East German nation began to crumble.

Langley, October 18, 1989

Steve Weber stuck his head in my office and said, "Honecker just resigned."

"What!"

"Yeah. Reasons of health, is what they're saying."

"Who's taking over?" I asked.

"Egon Krenz, his deputy."

"What's next?" I asked, knowing there was no ready answer.

"No telling," Weber said.

East Berlin, 1900 Hours, November 9, 1989

David Rolph was still at work in the early evening when he heard that a spokesman for the East German government had just said something on the radio that caught him—and the entire East German nation—by surprise. It was a statement, made casually and off the cuff, that helped bring down the Soviet empire in Eastern Europe.

For weeks, protests in the streets of East Germany's major cities had been growing, and the new East German leader, Egon Krenz, found that none of the regime's tried-and-true tactics were working to stem the tide of discontent. The mass exodus of East Germans through Hungary and Czechoslovakia over the proceeding months had been stanched only by draconian new travel restrictions; now East Germans were not only prevented from traveling to the West, they were barred from much of Eastern Europe as well. Anger welled up as a result. Between October 30 and November 4, an estimated 1.4 million people marched in 210 separate demonstrations around the country, according to the cold calculations of the ever watchful MfS.

And as the ranks of the protesters swelled, so did their demands. In addition to freedom to travel, they now wanted freedom at home. They wanted free elections and official recognition of the growing opposition groups.

Krenz had promised to ease the travel restrictions, but Party and government bureaucrats feared that a mass exodus would result, one that would threaten East Germany's continued existence. Krenz talked with Gorbachev about the situation on November 1. Like Honecker before him, he was told that Moscow wasn't going to provide economic or military support to keep the regime afloat.

Krenz's halfway measures for limited changes in travel rules served only to further incite the demonstrators. He was running out of maneuvering room. Under intense political and time constraints, the East German Politburo once again tried to hammer out new travel regulations in early November. The new regulations were designed to ease the pressure on the regime, but they were definitely not intended to provide unlimited freedom to travel to the West for East German citizens.

It was at this point that confusion stepped in to play a critical role. Krenz asked Politburo member Gunter Schabowski, then serving as Party spokesman, to announce the new rules. Schabowski was an unfortunate choice. He hadn't been adequately briefed on the details of the new regulations and hadn't even carefully read the text of the government's proposals before he spoke to the press at about 7:00 P.M. on November 9.

Speaking almost off the cuff, he vastly oversimplified the new rules. He made it sound as if the East German government were now going to allow East Germans to travel directly to West Germany—rather than going to a third country first—for both permanent exit and private travel, with virtually no restrictions. East German officials would approve the travel on short notice.

Schabowski was asked by surprised reporters when the new rules would go into effect. A flustered Schabowski said: Immediately.

The press conference was carried live on radio and television, and even though Schabowski badly misstated the regime's intentions, his words had the effect of changing policy on the spur of the moment. To everyone who had listened to Schabowski, it sounded as if East Germany had decided to open the Berlin Wall and let its citizens out, ending forty years of national isolation.

The televised press conference dumbfounded the border guards listening in as they manned the checkpoints on the Berlin Wall. Some East Germans who were near the checkpoints when they heard Schabowski's broadcast decided to test the new policy right away. The border guards, who had heard Schabowski and had no other instructions, decided to let them through to West Berlin. West German television—which could be seen in East Germany—reported the fact that people were being allowed through the Wall, and soon thousands of East Berliners were flooding through the newly opened checkpoints and into West Berlin.

Rolph was as surprised as anyone and, after listening to the press conference, went out into the night with his family, acting as tourists and eyewitnesses to history. That night, he sent a cable back to headquarters, just to confirm the news reports that the Wall had been opened and that East Berliners really were being allowed to cross into the West. But there was nothing poetic about the cable, despite its historic significance as the first CIA cable to report the fall of the Berlin Wall.

There was certainly nothing in the cable that was based on secret intelligence, either. Since the CIA did not have any high-level agents in the East German government, there was no one Rolph could turn to in order to gain special insights into the overnight collapse of East German discipline. East Germany's counterintelligence had done its job well; it had deprived the CIA of access to the political hierarchy of the government.

So it would be CNN rather than the CIA that would keep Washington informed of the fast-moving events in Berlin. In fact, the fall of the Berlin Wall was the first shot in an unspoken competition between CNN and the CIA that would continue throughout the closing years of the Cold War. With historic events occuring daily between 1989 and 1991, David Rolph and other CIA officers in the field, first in Eastern Europe and later in the Soviet Union, would begin to feel a subtle pressure to remain relevant by staying on top of events. Headquarters repeatedly told case officers not to try to match everything on the news and instead to focus on stealing secrets that the President couldn't find out about anywhere else. But it was hard for case officers to ignore the daily sweep of history taking place all around them.

At the same time, stealing secrets that could help the President better understand that daily history was also easier said than done. It's very difficult to get secret insights on rapidly moving events, even if you have well-placed spies. But in truth, the CIA didn't have spies with high-level political access who could provide important political insights. How then should CIA officers try to satisfy policy makers hungry for a continuous flow of information? Tell them to turn on CNN and hope for the best? That was the awkward situation facing the CIA in East Berlin in November 1989.

Warsaw, 2230 Hours, November 9, 1989

German Chancellor Helmut Kohl was on the first day of a five-day visit to Warsaw and, like everyone else, was caught off guard by Schabowski's astonishing statement and the news that the new East German travel regulations would take effect immediately. During a cocktail reception at the former palace of Count von Radzivill in Warsaw, Kohl spoke animatedly with his Polish hosts, including Lech Walesa, but he was distracted by events in Berlin and kept his ear cocked for the next fateful announcement.

When it came it was almost anticlimactic. An aide whispered in his ear, "The Wall is open!"

Later that night at Warsaw's Marriott Hotel, the German chancellor told the gathered press, "Now, world history will be written."

That evening in his hotel suite, Helmut Kohl, like the rest of the world, turned to the only functioning source of information on the most historical moment in the second half of the century: CNN.

Langley, November 9, 1989

Burton Gerber, now chief of the European Division, which was responsible for CIA operations in Western Europe, was in the midst of a quiet lunch with CIA Director William Webster and a small group of visiting West German intelligence officials in the Director's private dining room when he was told that he had an urgent message. Gerber excused himself from the table and went outside, where he was given electrifying news—the Berlin Wall had just been opened. Gerber went back into the dining room and broke the news to the CIA Director and his ecstatic German guests.

After lunch, Gerber went to see his counterparts in the Directorate of Intelligence to find out what the analysts could tell him about the situation, and then returned to his office to watch the latest news from Berlin. For Gerber, who had just spent five years running the SE Division and had devoted so much of his life doing quiet battle with the Soviet empire, it was a deeply emotional moment. As he sat and watched history unfold on television, Gerber exulted as he realized that Berlin, the original Cold War battlefield, had just been won.

Langley, 1830 Hours, November 9, 1989

I flipped back and forth between CNN and the CIA's satellite downlink of the East and West German channels covering events at the Berlin Wall. No one had predicted it would happen when and how it had. No one, not the CIA, not the State

Department, not the Bonn government. No one was prepared for the events of November 9 and 10. Where was the human intelligence? I would be repeatedly asked that question. What were our spies telling us would come next?

The CIA had no human intelligence on the events as they were unfolding. None of our human assets in the capitals of Eastern Europe and the Soviet Union were in a position to tell us what was going on; most were asking us what was happening. They were all watching the drama play out on television and wondering what the hell would happen next. Even the best agent couldn't tell what a government was going to do when no one in that government knew what it was going to do.

All of Washington had their television sets tuned to CNN. And as I watched the pieces of that despicable structure being pulled down, I thought back almost a quarter of a century when I had first seen the reinforced concrete barrier as a new CIA case officer in Germany. I had seen escapes to the West fail and a few succeed, but always the Wall seemed to get stronger, both as a physical barricade and as a symbol separating the minds of the human beings who lived on either side. More than any other structure, the Berlin Wall symbolized what had brought me to the CIA.

Now it was coming down, and I felt strangely dissociated from the process. I decided to send a cable to all hands in the field the next day to tell them to leave to the international media what it could best do, but to let us know if they saw things differently from the television coverage. Get out on the streets, I said, and keep the situation reports coming.

East Berlin, November 10, 1989

Thursday night had been crazy enough, but when Rolph and his wife went to Checkpoint Charlie the next day to see what was happening for themselves, it seemed as if all of Germany were there. Mixing in the crowd with the thousands of East Germans waiting to make the crossing, the CIA station chief found himself in the midst of the greatest party he had ever seen, the most indescribable, unforgettable moment of his life. Lost in a sea of champagne and open arms, Rolph was an elated Cold Warrior watching Germany come together. He made his way to the West Berlin side and saw that the East Berliners were being treated like returning heroes, lost in the wilderness for nearly thirty years.

Yet Rolph still wasn't sure he understood the dimensions of what was happening all around him. When he returned home to his East Berlin neighborhood of Pankow, there was a strange air of normalcy. Away from the massive block parties near the border checkpoints, Rolph was struck by how East German life was still grinding on. The Stasi is still here, he told himself, and they are still a fearsome intelligence service. The surveillance teams are still here, too.

The Kremlin, November 11, 1989

It was over. Of that, Anatoly Chernyaev, Gorbachev's foreign-policy guru, was certain. The entire seventy-year era of the socialist system was over. First Poland had gone over, then Hungary, then, suddenly, East Germany. All had gone peacefully. China's leader, Deng Xiaoping, and Bulgaria's Todor Zhivkov had announced their retirements. That left only Fidel Castro, Nicolae Ceauşescu, and Kim Il Sung. And they hated the Soviet Union's guts! Yes, it was over, Chernyaev decided.

The main thing had been the Berlin Wall. Its fall would have a profound effect not only on the final course of socialism, but also on the balance of world power. It meant the end of Yalta, the end of the legacy of Stalin, and the end of remembrance of the defeat of Hitler's Germany. It was all over.

And that, Chernyaev concluded with an ironic sense of pride, was all Gorbachev's doing. He had, indeed, turned out to be a great leader. Gorbachev had sensed the pace of history and had helped it find a natural channel. Gorbachev's loyal aide would never sway from the conviction that the dramatic historical shifts now under way in Eastern Europe were the result of Gorbachev's decision not to stand in the way.

3

Prague, November 17, 1989

Oldrich Cerny, a slight, sandy-haired writer, film translator, and dissident, had been following Václav Havel's lead since he was a star-struck teenager in the 1960s. Back then, Cerny had summoned up the courage to march into a Prague theater and had brazenly introduced himself to Czechoslovakia's brightest young playwright. Havel had agreed to the boy's simple request that he join him for coffee. Now, more than twenty years later, Oldrich Cerny was about to follow Havel's lead once more. This time, Cerny would help Havel foment a revolution.

But just now they were waiting, impatiently, for the revolution to begin.

In fact, both men had been waiting for at least twelve years. Havel had solidified his status as Czechoslovakia's most important anti-Communist dissident in 1977, with the creation of Charter 77, a group of intellectuals who signed a petition seeking freedom of speech and thought and, more broadly, freedom from the repression that had been imposed on the Czech people following the Soviet crackdown on the Prague Spring in 1968. Havel's reward for Charter 77 had been prison.

Throughout the late 1970s and early 1980s, meanwhile, Cerny had been ostracized for his refusal to become an informant and agent of the Czech secret services. First he rejected an overture from the internal security police and later a separate pitch from the foreign intelligence service, which was intrigued by his fluency in English and was eager to send him abroad as a spy. His defiance cost him his job at a Czech publishing house, and before long he was barely making ends meet unloading cargo on Prague's riverfront.

By mid-November 1989, Cerny could see that Havel was

worried that the new democratic spirit sweeping across Eastern Europe might pass Czechoslovakia by. Old regimes had tumbled in Poland through elections, and in Hungary through negotiations. The Berlin Wall had just come down, and the government of East Germany seemed to be on its last legs. Yet demonstrations in Prague had so far been modest, hardly enough to shake the Communists out of Prague Castle. Protests in late October on Czech National Day had been so unimpressive that Havel had become depressed. He spent several days in early November recovering from an illness—and frustration. He feared that Czechoslovakia was destined to remain an island of tyranny surrounded by democracy, the Cuba of Eastern Europe.

Havel thought that November 17 would just bring more of the same, so he didn't join that day's demonstrations marking the fiftieth anniversary of an infamous Nazi murder of a Czech student. But the students and others who did march peacefully that day through Prague and into Wenceslas Square, the city's long, narrow, and sloping centerpiece, to commemorate the anniversary were met by riot police eager for a confrontation. The police waded into the crowds, brutally wielding truncheons, beating men, women, and children. The incident outraged the Czech people and electrified the nation overnight. Through its own heavy-handed stupidity, the regime had finally managed to turn the Czechs into revolutionaries.

Suddenly energized, Havel moved to capitalize on the massive protests that were immediately sparked by November 17. He called together key dissidents from all over Prague, including many of the old Charter 77 members, and that weekend they crowded into the Actor's Studio Theater. In the midst of their heated talks, someone pointed out that they were meeting in a building that was easily accessible to the authorities, so they soon moved to the basement of Laterna Magika, the Magic Lantern Theater, to plot their next move. The Magic Lantern was to become their informal headquarters and the iconic symbol of the sudden and miraculous success of their peaceful "Velvet Revolution."

No one had elected or appointed Havel and his new dissident group, Civic Forum, to take charge and represent the people, but there had also never been any question among the people crowding into Wenceslas Square that anyone other than Havel would lead them. Within days, Civic Forum opened negotiations with the regime, even as the Communists grumbled that they would never sit down with Havel himself. Meanwhile, the protests grew exponentially, providing fuel to the revolution and sapping the strength of the regime. One local Communist leader in Prague belatedly sought to whip up blue-collar support, but when he went to a working-class district, he was jeered by restive workers who shouted, "We are not little children." Throughout the revolution, Cerny thought with some amusement, the Communists were always two days late.

Prague, Czechoslovakia, November 1989

Inside the cramped CIA space in the old American embassy, the CIA communicator, a young man with a keen technical mind, patiently worked the video equipment, searching the dial for just the right frequency.

"There!" he called over to David Manners, the CIA's chief in Prague, and proudly displayed his achievement. It had taken time, but the technician had finally plugged into a very special television show. He had just captured the video feeds from the surveillance cameras that the Czech security service had placed strategically all over Prague to watch their own people, who just now happened to be in the midst of a revolution. The television set in the CIA's station in the old mansion now filled with images of massive crowds of protesters surging through the streets of Prague. Suddenly, the video feed switched to a different camera and then another; Manners realized his communicator had stumbled across the entire Czech surveillance network, and he was now viewing the same live pictures from all over the city as the "watchers" of the Czech security service. As he watched the video feed cut from one protest to another, and then zoom in on individual protesters being confronted by undercover agents and by police, he realized with a jolt that he was watching, in real time, how Czech security was responding to the revolution.

The shifting camera angles and feeds from around the city suggested which protests and protesters the Czechs most feared, while close-ups of agents hidden in the crowds revealed how the Czech government was scrambling to try to respond in an effort to disrupt the demonstrations.

"Start taping," Manners told his communicator.

It was the best live coverage that the CIA had obtained in any of the revolutions sweeping across Eastern Europe that fall and winter. After recording a few hours' worth of video, Manners went to see his boss, American ambassador Shirley Temple Black. He thought the former child star might enjoy a good show, so he asked her to come to the CIA station and sat her down for a front-row seat to watch the Velvet Revolution unfold.

Langley, November 29, 1989

Redmond stuck his head in my office. "The bureau's got a guy from the Second Chief Directorate in New York," he said.

Actually, it turned out to be an *ex*-KGB man, Sergei Papushin, who'd quit his job and moved into Russia's new economy. Papushin had taken a job with an oil company. He'd come to New York on business, promptly got seriously drunk, and washed up in a hospital in New Jersey, where the police, and later the FBI, found him. As he sobered up, the FBI learned from him that he'd been in the Second Chief Directorate and decided to pitch him to see if he would work for them. The FBI knew that officers from the Second Chief Directorate, the KGB's secretive counterintelligence arm, were hard to come by.

Frightened by the experience, Papushin rushed back to New York, where he went to the Soviet mission to report the approach. Incredibly, the security officer at the mission told him to forget about it and get on with his business.

Instead, Papushin changed his mind. He called the FBI back and asked for asylum.

"When do we get a shot at him?" I asked Redmond.

"We're setting it up with the bureau now."

We were back to business—but somehow, in the midst of the revolutions sweeping Eastern Europe, I couldn't get too excited over this defector.

Moscow, November 29, 1989

Rem Krassilnikov dialed the home number of Mike Cline, our new Moscow chief, and waited.

"Hello?" a man's voice answered.

"Oh, hello, Michael," Krassilnikov said in his unmistakable accent, stretching out Cline's name. "This is Gavrilov. I was wondering if we could meet for a few moments tomorrow to discuss a matter of some importance."

Cline knew what Krassilnikov wanted. "Yes, I can do that," he said quickly. "What time?"

"Will noon be satisfactory?"

"Noon will be fine," Cline said in the same guarded language he always used on a phone he knew was live-monitored by the KGB. Never mind that it was the KGB who was actually calling—old habits were hard to break.

"Then noon it is, tomorrow," the KGB counterintelligence chief said, and rang off.

The next day at noon sharp, Mike Cline walked along the ring road toward the Chinese restaurant that had been preselected as the site for these furtive meetings. Cline had made his first call to activate the Gavrilov channel when he'd arrived in Moscow eight months earlier as Jack Downing's replacement, and he and Krassilnikov had agreed then that the Chinese restaurant would be their established rendezvous point. But since then they'd had almost no contact—it was as if the CIA-KGB hot line had gone cold.

Nearing the site, Cline spotted the black Volga pulled up against the curb, its engine running, spewing exhaust fumes into the cold air. Krassilnikov was huddled in the backseat, a woolen muffler around his throat and his hat pulled just above his ears. As Cline approached the car, both Krassilnikov and his driver got out. Krassilnikov offered his hand and drew the CIA man into the backseat of the overheated Volga.

With the driver standing dutifully out of earshot and smoking a cigarette, Krassilnikov told Cline that he thought it was time for a meeting at a higher level. The KGB side would be represented by himself and Leonid Nikitenko, chief of Directorate K, counterintelligence, of the First Chief Directorate. They would be able to meet their American counterparts in either Tokyo or Helsinki in the next month. The American side could take their pick, Krassilnikov offered.

Cline wrote down three words—"Tokyo, Helsinki, December"—and turned to Krassilnikov. "Is there anything special you'd like to talk about?" he asked.

"Nothing special," Krassilnikov said. "It's just been too long since we've gotten together."

Cline added a fourth word to his notes, "agenda," and underlined it. He told Krassilnikov he'd get back to him and stepped out of the car. He had no inclination to be chatty. It was not Cline's nature to hang out with the opposition on their own turf.

Langley, November 29, 1989

Stolz called down to tell me that he'd already talked to Gus Hathaway and that Gus would be accompanying me on the Gavrilov outing. "What do you think it's about?" he asked.

"Don't know," I said truthfully. "But it's been two years since we had an offshore Gavrilov meeting—they broke off contact in 1987. Maybe their new team wants to see our new team."

The CIA and KGB had always sent two senior officials apiece to Gavrilov meetings, except for the brief and infrequent encounters between the CIA's Moscow station chief and Krassilnikov. With two officers from each side present, the possibility of misadventure was greatly reduced. It eliminated the suspicions that one officer had been pitched by the other side and hadn't reported it fully. In the world of espionage, doubts, once raised, always lingered. So we went into the Gavrilov meetings two by two.

Gus and I met with Stolz later that morning, and we decided that we'd go to the meeting mostly just to listen. Since the KGB asked for the meeting, we'd hear them out and see what was on their minds. The only issues we might raise would be the perennials: the status of our embassy building in Moscow and the fate of Oleg Gordievsky's family.

I decided that Helsinki should be the meeting site and cabled Mike Cline to pass the decision along to the KGB. I then began to review our file holdings on both of the men I would meet at my first Gavrilov session. We'd had plenty of contact with Krassilnikov over the years, but Nikitenko was less known to us. He'd come up on our screen while he was *Rezident* in London, where he'd been Oleg Gordievsky's chief, but we hadn't had much firsthand experience with the man. It should be interesting, I thought as I prepared for the first Gavrilov meeting. Their empire was cracking; they must be feeling the aftershocks all the way to Moscow.

Prague, December 10, 1989

With hundreds of thousands of Czechs packing into central Prague each night, chanting and ringing their keys in the air, change came with astonishing speed. On December 10, Communist president Gustav Husák resigned, and by acclamation, Havel and Civic Forum took over. Though it would take until the end of the month for Havel to be formally elected president, a band of playwrights, stagehands, and poets suddenly had a country to run.

One of the most vexing questions as Havel and his motley band of ministers assumed their new posts was the fate of the Czech security and intelligence services. The Communists had been ousted so quickly that the intelligence services had no time to reform themselves or prepare for a smooth handover. In December, the government was still a strange amalgam of dissidents and Communists who had not yet been replaced. The domestic security service, known as the StB, and the foreign intelligence service, which was under the StB umbrella and was known as Sprava One, were still intact, and their seventeen thousand employees were reporting to work each day as if nothing had changed, even after Havel was sworn into office.

The Soviets, of course, knew that it was only a matter of time. The KGB had six officers who worked on a full-time basis inside Sprava One headquarters in Prague. Just before Christmas, the six KGB officers were called home to Moscow, and they never returned.

StB's direct links to the KGB were being cut, but Czech intelligence was still being run by Communists with no allegiance to Havel or democracy.

After the frantic days of November and December, Oldrich Cerny was about to return to his film studio job, but Václav Havel had other ideas. The new president decided in early 1990 that he wanted Cerny, the man who had twice rejected demands that he become a Communist spy, to help lead Czechoslovakia's spy service into the new world.

Frankfurt, December 1989

Dave Manners sat down for a hurried meeting with a key SE Division manager who had just flown into Frankfurt from headquarters. Manners and the other chiefs of station from the capitals of Eastern Europe had been summoned to Germany to talk through the remarkable changes sweeping the region.

It was hard to know where to start—all the old assumptions had to be thrown out the window. The United States had once worried about dominoes in Southeast Asia; now it was the Soviets who were watching their dominoes fall—Poland, Hungary, East Germany, and now Czechoslovakia.

So much was happening that Manners couldn't afford to spend much time away from his post. "You should know that you're getting somebody new to run the Czech desk at headquarters," Manners was told in quiet confidence. "Rick Ames. He's smart. If you had to pick the three or four people at the agency who understand the KGB the best, he would be one of them."

Helsinki, Finland, 1955 Hours, December 12, 1989

It was bitterly cold and slippery going as Gus Hathaway and I trudged along the icy sidewalks in a residential section of Helsinki. The meeting was to be held at the Soviet embassy promptly at 8:00 P.M., and as we came up to the gate of the embassy not far from Helsinki's waterfront five minutes early, Hathaway rang the bell and waited. A moment later a voice crackled over a speaker, asking who was there.

"We're here to see Rem Sergeyevich Krassilnikov," Hathaway announced in Russian.

"Never heard of him," the voice crackled back with curt dismissal.

I looked at my watch. "We're early. Let's walk for a few minutes."

Five minutes later, we approached the gate again and pushed the button. This time the latch buzzed and the iron gate popped open. My mind flashed back four years to the moment Edward Lee Howard had passed through this same gate as he made good his long escape from the FBI in Albuquerque to the Soviet Union.

Gus and I went twenty yards down the shoveled walkway to the embassy's front door, where we were met by a Soviet officer who ushered us into a secure room on the ground floor. There we met Krassilnikov and Nikitenko and a third KGB man who introduced himself as Viktor, a counterintelligence officer from the First Chief Directorate.

Their secure room was really a room within a room. It had the touch of the handyman; the walls and ceiling were covered with acoustic tiles and with heavy drapes hung slightly haphazardly on the walls. I thought there might be electronic white noise generated around the enclosure once the heavy door was closed, but I had no way of knowing for sure. Inside were a couple of couches, and some chairs had been arranged around a low table, where we found a spread of *zakuski,* Russian snacks ranging from salami and pickles to salads to cheeses. On a small end table were four half-liter bottles of Stolichnaya.

The Soviets seemed interested in sizing up the new team, and we were equally interested in sizing them up. As I settled into one of the couches, I thought about the secrets that must be running through the minds of the two men seated across from us in those cramped quarters.

Krassilnikov was the closest thing to a real-life Karla, the master spy of John le Carré's Cold War espionage series. He had an almost mythic status at Langley, as at the end of each disastrous compromise he would walk into the holding room and have his little chat with our ambushed case officer. I'd seen his photograph in the files, but it was an old one and looked nothing like the man before me. Krassilnikov seemed more like a kindly Russian grandfather than a man who spent his days and nights leading our agents to the executioner and trying to keep us off balance with a steady string of bogus volunteers.

As I looked at Krassilnikov's soft, lined face, set off by a mane of thick white hair, it was hard to picture him as the man who had rolled up so many of our operations over the last four years. I had to force the image into my head of him interrogating our agents, Tolkachev, Vorontsov, Polyshchuk, Varennik, and all the others, before they were led down to the dark basement and the KGB executioner.

Leonid Nikitenko was a barrel-chested bear of a man, full of life. From the moment he extended his hand, it was clear that he loved the drama of the spy game, and there was no question that he was good at it. He was at home in this secret universe and relished every moment we spent crowded together in the secure room with the *zakuski* and Stolichnaya. He was an actor on a stage that he had set for himself, playing a role he had scripted.

As chief of Directorate K, First Department, First Chief Directorate, Nikitenko was responsible for the KGB's counterintelligence operations against the American target worldwide. He had last been posted abroad as KGB *Rezident* in London, until he was expelled by the British in a series of carefully planned moves in 1984 that left Nikitenko's deputy and MI6's long-term asset Oleg Gordievsky in charge of the London *Rezidentura*. Gordievsky still thought Nikitenko had been behind his compromise in May 1985, when he was called back, interrogated, and then inexplicably set free. I wondered how much heat Krassilnikov had taken for Gordievsky's escape.

The Soviets didn't seem to have a specific agenda for the meeting. In fact, what was most remarkable was the topic that wasn't brought up—the ongoing rollback of the Soviet empire in Eastern Europe. It was the elephant in the room that no one dared talk about. No one mentioned the Polish election, the Berlin Wall, or events under way in Prague at that very moment. The KGB officers sitting across from us were probably as stunned as we were by what had been happening throughout Eastern Europe over the past weeks and months, but they weren't about to share their emotions with the CIA.

The KGB side got right to business, asking about a Soviet defector who had come across in the last year. Our response was the standard: "Your Mr. X is well and is living outside the country where he was last posted. He enjoys total freedom of movement and is acting on his own. He has expressed no interest in meeting with officials of the Soviet Union." The translation was always the same: "He's come to us but doesn't want it out in the open. And he doesn't want to meet your guys."

After a few rounds of drinks, I broached a long stalled but politically sensitive topic: How were we ever going to get beyond the stalemate on our new Moscow embassy building? Work on the project had been tied up for years as special American security teams sought to determine the extent to which the KGB had embedded listening devices in the building as it was going up. By now it was on its way to becoming the most expensive structure in the world for its size. If you took into account the cost of the original construction, and added to it the cost of the KGB's high-tech assault and of our defensive measures, the building's price tag was phenomenal. Large portions of the structure had been dismantled and sent back to the United States as diplomatic cargo for examination. The embassy remained unoccupied, and it looked like a never-ending standoff.

Krassilnikov leaned into the question. "Your embassy building is perfectly safe as it now stands," he said carefully. "You could occupy it right away without any concerns for matters of security."

"Are you saying that there are no devices in our embassy?" I asked.

"I am saying that there is nothing in the building that should cause you concern."

"Let me get this straight. I think I hear you saying that while there may have been some earlier intentions to attack our embassy, no such plans have been fully carried out. Is that what I'm hearing?"

"I think you have drawn a correct conclusion. The most important point is that your new embassy building is secure as it now stands."

"And we should just move into it, right?" I asked, half joking.

Krassilnikov smiled and said, "That would have to be your decision, but it would also be the right one."

"We'll pass along your comments," I said noncommittally. My instinct was to dismiss what Krassilnikov was saying, but deep down I knew that he was probably telling the truth. Somewhere between the mounting of the attack on the embassy and now, the decision may have been made at Lubyanka, or maybe in the Politburo, to call it off. But it was too late for trust to enter the game. Nevertheless, I saw something in Krassilnikov's eyes as he made his careful statement about the embassy that told me this man was trying to navigate his way out of troubled waters.

Hathaway changed the subject to the family of Oleg Gordievsky, an outstanding issue that was routinely raised at all levels of contact with the Soviets.

Nikitenko didn't react as emotionally as I'd expected—Gordievsky was working for him, after all, while he was spying for the British. He simply eased back a little deeper into the couch and concentrated on keeping his face as unreadable as possible.

Krassilnikov's expression was impassive. An awkward silence descended between us, but in the end he did respond. "Now that you raise the question of Gordievsky's wife and daughters," he observed at last with an ironic smile, "I am reminded once again of the mystery about our Mr. Gordievsky's disappearance from Moscow. I have always wondered why you Americans show such a strong interest in having this man's family leave the Soviet Union. Is it solely a humanitarian interest, or was there perhaps an American hand in getting Mr. Gordievsky out of the USSR?"

"Our interest is purely humanitarian," Hathaway said, ignoring Krassilnikov's probe. "We would like to see Gordievsky reunited with his family."

"And our position remains unchanged," Nikitenko interjected. For the first time that evening, his smile showed signs of brittleness.

At that point, Krassilnikov commented on the nature of our mutual engagement. "I would not suggest that spying against each other will ever cease," he said. "But at some point we should begin to look at what kinds of rules might be incorporated into the conduct of our business. I am speaking here of coercion. The use of drugs and, indeed, the use of violence. I think at some time, perhaps not today, we might examine certain, how should I say, provocative behavior."

"Are you actually referring to the allegations that we drugged, kidnapped, and used coercion against Yurchenko?" I asked.

"Yurchenko might not be the most appropriate example," Krassilnikov said. "I am talking about the conduct of our operations against each other in general, not in a specific case."

Hathaway leaned forward an extra few inches to signal that he, too, found Krassilnikov's statement provocative. "The Soviet side has chosen to cover the changing of sides of its officers over the years by accusing us, as well as the British, of using drugs, kidnapping, and violence. You know as well as I that these things have never happened, and to raise the issue, quite frankly, surprises me."

"What we are saying is that perhaps there would be some value to discussing certain ground rules to the way we carry out our business," Nikitenko interjected, attempting to defuse the issue. "This can be done over the course of some time, and I, too, think it would be of value."

"I think there is merit to keeping our agendas open," I said. "Though I think we should be careful not to bring certain themes to these meetings that might be more appropriately considered propaganda battles. But you can be certain that the CIA does not use drugs or violence against officers of your service. We have always thought it dangerous for your side to make such claims, as was done with Yurchenko, when we all know the truth in that case. But your points are taken."

With that exchange, it was clear that the substantive part of the meeting had come to an end. It was almost with relief that we turned the discussion to the harshness of the winter that had enveloped northern Europe at that moment. Within those few hours we'd gotten a look at our opposite numbers in the KGB, and they'd done the same with us. While nothing concrete had been accomplished, I felt that the Gavrilov channel, after two years of dormancy, had been resurrected. I wasn't certain what might come from it, but I was fairly sure it would do no harm. With the changes coming as rapidly as they were,

I was happy enough to have the option to call a temporary truce to talk things over from time to time.

After more than two hours of talk and vodka, Hathaway and I left for our hotel on the Helsinki waterfront. After we had been walking through a deserted park for about ten minutes, we heard a voice calling from the road fifty yards away. "Mister Gataway, Mister Gataway . . ." The Russian pronunciation of Hathaway's name was unmistakable. In a moment we were joined by the Soviet driver, who handed Gus his wallet. "Must fall out your pocket," he said, his breath streaming in the cold of the night, and quickly returned to his car.

Hathaway's look sent an unmistakable message: It wouldn't be good form for the new SE Division chief to spread the story around Langley about how the CIA's chief of counterintelligence had lost his wallet at a drinking party with a bunch of KGB hoods.

I stared at Hathaway's oversize and fully stuffed wallet. "Jeez, Gus, whatcha got in there?" I said. "Every phone number of every contact since you were in high school? Christ, the thing's probably radioactive from all the photocopying!"

Hathaway ignored my comment, and we walked the rest of the way in silence, both of us trying to make some sense out of the Alice in Wonderland evening we had just spent with our adversaries.

4

Langley, 1130 Hours, December 27, 1989

The revolution that swept through the northern tier of Eastern Europe had finally reached the Balkans, where it played out darkly in Romania. Over the course of the month of December, a rapidly spinning cycle of riots and government-fomented counterriots grew in intensity until all semblance of order simply evaporated. The U.S. embassy was forced to evacuate its personnel overland to Bulgaria, and for Washington the lights went out in Bucharest.

Romanian leader Nicolae Ceauşescu and his wife, Elena, escaped a step ahead of the mobs three days before Christmas, but they were soon captured, and on Christmas Day they were tried and executed by firing squad. Two days later, after a short Christmas break, I met with William Webster to bring him up to date on the Balkans.

"The Army went over to the opposition on the twenty-second," I said, "the same day the Ceauşescus escaped by helicopter. We're still not clear on the precise sequence and timing, but we think they were captured within a day or so. Over the next two days they were tried, and on Christmas they were executed."

Judge Webster perked up and, with a reflective expression on his face, said, "What does that tell us about the appeals process in Romania, Milt?"

I had gotten to know Webster from his visits to Pakistan and had witnessed his dry humor in action before. I didn't break a smile when I answered.

"I think that would be a good subject for the Directorate of Intelligence to check into, Judge Webster," I said. "And while they're at it, they might look into the reports that Ceauşescu had a hundred bullets in him after his execution. What does that tell us about Romanian firing squads?" For good measure, I threw in the final bizarre tidbit we had gleaned about the last hours of Nicolae and Elena Ceauşescu. "We've also heard reliably from London that Her Majesty's government was able to withdraw Nicolae's honorary knighthood, bestowed years ago for his staunch opposition to Moscow, a few hours before he stood before his firing squad. I'm sure there was great relief in Buckingham Palace."

Webster smiled and asked the real question that had been on his mind for the last several weeks. "What are you doing in Eastern Europe?"

"We're focusing on East Germany right now," I said. "That's where the opportunities are. I expect to see some results pretty soon, but to be completely frank, I'm not sure there's much we ought to do in the northern tier—in Warsaw, Prague, and Budapest."

"Why's that?" Webster asked, furrowing his brow. The DCI had been deeply interested in the region since he'd visited Europe a few weeks earlier and had called the collapse of the Wall ahead of most in the President's cabinet. Now he was following events in close to real time.

"Aggressive collection could backfire. I think we should plan to move in quickly with the new governments and see what we can do to shore them up and keep them on track." I'd been keeping a close eye on events in Prague and Warsaw and had come to the conclusion that stealing secrets might not make as much sense as linking up with the new intelligence services and helping them work with their new governments.

"What about East Germany?" Webster asked.

"We go after them hammer and tongs," I said, "whenever and wherever we can. They have nowhere to go. As the process moves along, we'll be all over them."

"You got a timetable for all this?"

"We're working the East German problem pretty hard now. And in the northern tier we're putting out our probes."

"Just keep me posted, Milt," Webster said. "There's a lot of interest in this downtown, I'm sure you know that."

"I do, Judge Webster. I'm on the phone with them most days."

The Kremlin, December 27, 1989

Val Aksilenko had seen events since the breach of the Berlin Wall through eyes sometimes blurred by tears of joy. A year earlier, the troubled KGB colonel had arranged to have himself seconded from Yasenevo to the office of the State Foreign Economic Committee in the Council of Ministers. It was his way of moving away from the KGB, one step at a time. The new post was pretty much a nothing job—his office was actually outside the Kremlin Wall—but it got him off the firing line.

Few of his colleagues in the Council of Ministers, and even

fewer at Yasenevo, appreciated the fact that socialism had been dealt a death blow. Poland, Hungary, Czechoslovakia, and the most Stalinist state of them all, the DDR, had fallen, all pretty much peacefully. And now, in the Balkans, the ruthless Ceauşescu had been toppled and killed. But those around him were too involved with their own increasingly desperate fates, Aksilenko thought, too preoccupied with what was happening inside Mother Russia, to become energized one way or another by events on the perimeter, or even to take much note of them.

The ideological and moral reevaluations under way inside every structure of the Soviet establishment were overwhelming; they were setting in motion nothing less than the collapse of the authority of the Communist Party and of the Soviet system. Better to look around for a soft landing, most of his colleagues thought, than to fret over what was happening in Berlin or Bucharest. And they had the best of it, the guys in the Kremlin and the KGB. For the poor slob in the streets of Moscow it was a different matter—the daily distress of scratching out a subsistence living was simply crushing.

Events were proceeding according to a grand scheme Aksilenko had decided was essential, despite the pain it caused around him. And that temporary pain Mother Russia felt was the source of his tears of joy. The fall of the Berlin Wall was the indispensable spark that had allowed change finally to come to the USSR. It had to happen this way, Aksilenko concluded; the world-shaking changes had to start in the satellites of Eastern Europe and roll inward, toward the center of socialism, toward Moscow itself. He knew that no change of any consequence would ever originate in Moscow. It had to come from the outside.

Aksilenko's frequent visits to FCD headquarters to measure the mood of his KGB colleagues were always enlightening. The temper at Yasenevo was dark, with opinion divided between the so-called liberals, like himself, who welcomed the coming changes and the conservatives who were scrambling to hold them back. Yasenevo was splitting between the hopeful and the fearful. He was in no doubt that trouble was brewing for the men of the KGB. Sooner or later there would be a showdown. And that conclusion made him all the more grateful that he was away from Yasenevo, off in his snug cubbyhole in the Council of Ministers.

East Berlin, January 15, 1990

The atmosphere was festive, at least at first. Then it became tinged with the fury of revenge as Berliners tore into Stasi headquarters in the vast Normannenstrasse complex and began ripping the place apart, spraying secret documents out of windows and onto the streets below. Others broke into a more valuable secret cache of imported wines and gourmet food reserved for Stasi officers. Forty years of pent-up hatred of the secret police—a security service that for generations had silenced all dissent—suddenly erupted into the streets of East Berlin.

For the people of East Germany, looting Normannenstrasse was an act of political catharsis, as if throwing the files out the windows would somehow purge the national bloodstream of its culture of suspicion and paranoia. They were turning on the security police with a vengeance born of resentment at being forced to spy on neighbors, on husbands and wives, on mothers and fathers.

It was one of the most dramatic moments of a frenzied few weeks that had transformed East Berlin from a Communist backwater to the hub of a historic revolution. And, as with so many of the other history-defying events since the Berlin Wall had come down, footage from Normannenstrasse was broadcast on CNN and the other networks back into American homes. The television coverage of the storming of Normannenstrasse caught the eye of the President, and he apparently made a casual, offhand remark to his daily CIA briefer about the incident. President Bush wondered aloud whether the CIA was getting its share of the documents floating down onto East Berlin's streets. Judge Webster heard about the President's interest, and soon what had started as an off-the-cuff remark at the White House turned into a scramble at the CIA.

Webster asked if the CIA was getting its hands on any of these Stasi documents. The answer was no, and the CIA Director then asked whether we needed new people in Berlin.

Webster's message was clear. After that, I put Redmond on a plane for Germany to light a fire under Rolph.

West Berlin, Late January 1990

Paul Redmond looked across the table and saw two angry case officers. Redmond had come to Berlin to pass on an unpalatable message to David Rolph and the East German station. And as Rolph and his deputy sat in a West Berlin restaurant listening to what Redmond had to say, they didn't like it one bit.

In all bureaucracies, bad news tends to start at the top and flow downhill, and the CIA was no exception. It just so happened that in this case, David Rolph was at the receiving end of a message that had started at the White House with the President of the United States.

President Bush had seen the looting of Normannenstrasse on CNN and had asked whether the CIA was getting its hands on the documents floating out onto the streets of East Berlin. The answer was no, and Langley realized that was a bad answer to have to give to the White House. So that meant the East Berlin Station had to be put on notice, and Paul Redmond was the one to do it.

Redmond tried to be polite and collegial, but there was no mistaking the message from headquarters: You are on notice that Washington is watching the revolution and wants results. For Rolph's part, he didn't believe Redmond was there to scold him for past mistakes, but rather to make it clear that the attitude in Washington about what a CIA station in Eastern Europe should be doing was changing—and changing fast. Overnight, the rules on how to run a bloc station were being rewritten. And whether Rolph and other case officers trained in the traditional clandestine arts of the SE Division liked it or not, they had to change the way they operated, use more openly aggressive tactics, or risk becoming irrelevant.

Rolph resisted. He didn't like headquarters telling him that he wasn't being aggressive enough and didn't think that Langley understood the realities facing CIA case officers in East Berlin. The Stasi wasn't dead, Rolph told Redmond insistently. We still have to be careful and prudent, or the Stasi will eat our lunch.

His caution was a reflection of his Cold War training and experience. Like many SE Division officers, he had grown up fighting the KGB and the Eastern European intelligence services when they were at their peak, and he had learned to respect their power. Although he had seen the fall of the Berlin Wall with his own eyes, Rolph wasn't convinced that the old order in East Germany was dead. The MfS, he believed, still might be able to ride out the political turmoil. If CIA officers abandoned their traditional stealthy "denied area" tactics and began to operate more openly, the MfS might strike back. The CIA would then find itself in an even smaller box in East Germany.

So for weeks after November 9, Rolph and his deputy were uncertain whether they could operate more boldly in East Germany. True, Stasi surveillance was beginning to ease up; there were now times when there was no one following them at all. But could it last? Rolph still didn't know. When the crowds stormed Normannenstrasse, Rolph suspected that the whole thing had been staged by the Stasi. He didn't believe that it was part of a popular uprising. He thought it was street theater concocted by the Stasi in a last-ditch effort to prompt an outcry from the East German people for a restoration of order and stability. It was, he believed, a modern-day equivalent of the burning of the Reichstag. People back in Washington were watching too much television if they thought that any real secrets had been tossed out of the Stasi windows. So over lunch at a restaurant in Mexico Platz in West Berlin, Rolph told Redmond that the Stasi wasn't dead.

Sitting in the Berlin restaurant that January, Paul Redmond didn't argue with Rolph. He tried to be understanding. He said he knew that perceptions in Washington weren't always the same as reality on the ground.

"But sometimes perception is reality," he said. "And the perception is that we are missing out."

Redmond then made it painfully clear that East Berlin Station was going to have to start taking risks, get some new cases going—or else.

Rolph and his deputy didn't like it, but they got the message. Almost immediately, they responded by launching a campaign to pick over the remnants of the Ministerium für Staatssicherheit. To their surprise, the CIA officers would quickly discover that, beneath the surface, there was little left of the once mighty MfS. As in Warsaw and Prague, the old order in East Berlin was beginning to crack.

Warsaw, 1990

Andrzej Milczanowski, a rough-hewn and tough-minded provincial lawyer and longtime dissident, had paid his dues to Solidarity. Born in 1939 in a section of eastern Poland that was later absorbed into the Ukraine, Milczanowski came by his hatred for the Communists early on. Soon after the Soviets invaded eastern Poland following Stalin's disastrous pact with Hitler, Milczanowski's father, a local prosecutor known for his anti-Communist beliefs, was dragged away by the NKVD, the predecessor to the KGB. His family later learned that he had been taken to Kiev and executed, along with other local Polish government and military leaders.

His mother took Andrzej and his sister and fled to Lvov and then to the countryside, and finally after the war they were able to settle in western Poland. Milczanowski studied law in Poznan and like his father became a local prosecutor, working, and chafing, under the Communist regime.

Milczanowski eventually left the prosecutor's office in Stettin to become a defense lawyer, and in 1978 he took on the case of a pair of local dissidents. The case had a major influence on Milczanowski, so when Solidarity emerged in 1980, he was ready to take on a leadership role in the local movement in Stettin. He served as a member of the Solidarity strike committee in the city. At the beginning of martial law in Poland in 1981, Milczanowski was leading a strike committee at Stettin's dockyards, and he was arrested and sentenced to five years in prison. An amnesty decree cut his sentence to two and a half years, and when he emerged from prison in 1984, Milczanowski went right back into dissident work, becoming head of the underground Solidarity movement in Stettin. In August 1988, he led a strike against the local public transit company, one of the many labor actions around the country that so bedeviled the Communist regime in the months before it finally agreed to roundtable talks with Solidarity.

After Solidarity took control of the government, Milczanowski was put in charge of intelligence matters and soon had to decide what to do with the Communist-era service.

Initially, Milczanowski was frustrated by the fact that so many files had been destroyed. When he asked to see the files from one particular department, an officer came and laid a few pieces of paper on his desk. "Is that your whole file?" Milczanowski asked in exasperation.

"Yes," the officer said matter-of-factly and with little embarrassment.

Despite his own tragic personal history with the Communists, Milczanowski approached the issue of what to do with Poland's foreign intelligence officers with hardheaded pragmatism. Poland had undergone a sudden and radical political transformation, but the Soviet Union still lurked next door. The new democracy, Milczanowski believed, was still vulnerable to external threats. He decided that Poland couldn't afford the wholesale dismissal of its most experienced spies. Milczanowski later watched in disgust as the new government of Václav Havel fired its intelligence service and started with greenhorns. It was nothing less than unilateral disarmament, Milczanowski believed, and he eventually told the Czechs so in what the Czechs recalled as a very unpleasant meeting.

One of Milczanowski's new duties was to head a special vetting committee to determine which foreign intelligence officers should be kept and which ones let go. Gromoslaw Czempinski was chosen by the foreign service to serve as an advocate for its officers in front of the vetting committee, and soon the ex-Communist spy had developed a close relationship with Milczanowski, the ex-dissident who was now his boss. Czempinski was eventually named deputy chief of the foreign intelligence service and became, in effect, Poland's DDO.

But they sometimes fought fiercely over which officers should be retained. The vetting committee was particularly suspicious of officers who had been extremely active under the Communists and often let those who lacked much of an operational track record slip through. In the end, the committee agreed to keep about six hundred of the approximately one thousand officers from the foreign intelligence service, although Milczanowski later regretted some of the individual selections. He discovered that many of those who had been the most active—and who thus came under the most scrutiny from the vetting panel—were also the best and most efficient. The officers who had done little under the Communists were not closet dissidents or secret Polish heroes, but simply lazy.

Among the most effective of the foreign intelligence officers to be fired was Aleksandr Makowski, the officer who had been in charge of the special branch spying on Solidarity and its ties to the CIA. Czempinski made a special plea to the vetting committee on Makowski's behalf, but his work against Solidarity was simply too much for the new government to swallow.

Prague, March 1990

Oldrich Cerny was surprised when Jiri Krizan, Havel's first national security adviser, asked him to walk with him in the gardens around Prague Castle, the seat of government. "We have to get rid of the intelligence service, and we need your help," Krizan told Cerny quietly. "We have all of these old Communists and we have to move them out. Havel wants you to do it," Krizan added.

"All right," Cerny said. "When do you want me to start?"

"Right now," Krizan said. "We are five minutes late for a meeting with British intelligence."

The first halting efforts by the new Havel government to reform the security services had been a failure, and now Havel was turning to Cerny to help clean up the mess.

The StB had been formally dismantled in February and its officers told not to report for work until they could be vetted by a commission set up by the new government. A counterterrorism unit was virtually the only branch of the foreign intelligence service that was kept intact. But something was needed in place of the old security services, so the Havel government had initially created an organization called the Office for the Protection of the Constitution and Democracy. To staff the new office, the government brought back officers who had been purged by the regime after the crackdown in 1968, on the assumption that if the Communists had gotten rid of them, they must not be all bad.

But the new organization quickly proved to be a mess. Given a new lease on life, these old hands started doing what they knew best from the 1960s—targeting the Americans and the British. What was worse, some units, most notably surveillance teams, hadn't gotten the word yet that they were supposed to be out of business. So StB surveillance teams were still trailing CIA and MI6 officers around Prague in early 1990, as if there hadn't been a revolution.

Krizan wanted Cerny to come in and start over. He would take the lead in creating a new intelligence service, one suited to a new, pro-Western democracy. Cerny would be joined in this daunting task by Jan Ruml, a ponytailed dissident appointed by Havel to be deputy interior minister in charge of intelligence. They would create a much smaller organization than had existed under the Communists and staff it with fresh blood, young people with no background in intelligence matters. Czechoslovakia was going to start again with a blank slate.

Before they could start fresh, however, the new government had to figure out what to do with the old files of the StB and Sprava One. While some of the files had been destroyed by the Communists on their way out, much of the archives was still intact, including an index card system that provided reference points to registry books identifying agents, their contacts within the intelligence services, and their operational targets dating back as much as forty years. The files showed that StB had had some ten thousand active informants and agents at one time and had thoroughly penetrated every branch of federal and local government. To avoid a witch-hunt within the ranks of the new government, files that were still active at the time of the Velvet Revolution were destroyed. Only old, closed files were retained and scrutinized.

Rumors abounded through Prague in the early days of the Havel government that former StB officers were planning a comeback and that they might plan a coup to topple Havel and reinstate the Communist regime. But closer scrutiny showed that the rumors had been fueled by the simple fact that a few old StB officers were getting together regularly in taverns around Prague to drink, swap stories, and get out of the house. To the relief of Cerny and others around Havel, it quickly became apparent that the StB was dead and that there was no chance that a Czech version of the Odessa network—the near mythical organization of former SS officers that faded into the fabric of postwar Germany—would emerge to threaten the new democracy.

Once they began to dismantle the old apparatus, Cerny and Ruml turned their attention to developing new relations with the British and the Americans. The CIA had not played any role with the dissidents during the Velvet Revolution, but now the Czechs wanted the CIA to help ensure that their communications were secure and that President Havel was adequately protected. So the CIA provided new communications gear and helped train Havel's bodyguards; Britain's MI6, meanwhile, agreed to provide field training for the new Czech intelligence officers.

The Czechs also worked with the Americans and British to clear their books of old sleeper agents burrowed deep into Western society. The FBI and CIA asked the new Havel government and its slimmed-down foreign intelligence service to recall longtime "illegal" agents who had been sent to the United States by the Communists years earlier. At the end of the Cold War, the Czechs had about twenty sleeper agents in place around the world, including several in the United States and Britain. They had never been activated; the Communists had planned to turn these illegals loose in case of a major crisis or war with the West.

But these illegals had been in place in their new "cover" lives for so long that some seemed to have forgotten they were spies, not Little League coaches. When the new Czech officials tried to recall them, two or three of the sleeper agents in the United States simply refused, saying that they were Americans now, with families and lives they didn't want to abandon. In Britain, one or two also refused to come home. The Havel government decided that they should be left alone to live their new lives, especially since none of them had ever really done any damage against the Americans or the British.

CIA Headquarters, Langley, Early 1990

Ever since the earliest days of the Cold War, the CIA had covertly provided funding for magazines, academic journals, and books published in Western Europe by expatriates from the Soviet empire.

Those émigré publications had told the truth to generations of Eastern Europeans and Soviets starved for real information. They had provided glimpses of banned literature and in many cases kept history alive for persecuted minorities. The CIA-backed publications had never had to publish false propaganda; all they had to do was tell the truth to people who lived under regimes built on lies and fabrications. The covert program to smuggle news and literature to people inside the Soviet bloc was one of the CIA's greatest—and noblest—success stories of the Cold War.

Poland had served as a case study in the power of information. Along with the AFL-CIO and the Catholic Church, the CIA had helped provide the Solidarity movement with the resources it needed to get its message out during the dark days of martial law, when it was forced underground.

For persecuted minority groups inside the Soviet Union, meanwhile, literature and other works funded by the CIA provided objective national histories. Over the years, the CIA had perfected the art of smuggling books to those groups. The agency seeded Eastern Europe and the Soviet Union with copies of the Bible, *The Gulag Archipelago,* and other great works, sometimes in the form of tiny books that could easily be hidden from the authorities.

Émigré publishers in Paris and other Western cities, with the quiet backing of the CIA, had fervently kept alive dreams of freedom for Russia, Poland, and Czechoslovakia. By the 1980s, some had added videos to their lineup, producing documentaries, music videos, and other programs that could be purchased in stores in Western Europe and then smuggled back into the East.

Many of the émigrés working with the CIA had turned gray-haired waiting, patiently, in exile. But now, suddenly, freedom had come. Overnight, their once banned publications could be purchased openly at newsstands in Prague, Warsaw, and Budapest.

By early 1990, the CIA realized that it was time to end its financial support for the émigrés. For the people in the agency who had provided the support for the émigré publishers, this would be a bittersweet parting. They would have to say goodbye to men and women who had endured through long, lean years when there was little evidence that their publications were having any impact.

For the Eastern Europeans, ending their secret relationships with the CIA was relatively easy. Many of them were already planning to move back home and set up shop as open and legitimate publishers. They no longer needed the agency.

It was harder for the émigrés from the Soviet Union, however. Revolution had not yet swept through Moscow. Even some officials in the CIA's Propaganda and Political Action Staff, which handled the covert support for the expatriate publications, were reluctant to shut down the Soviet programs so quickly. The ideological battle against Communism had gone on for so long that it was difficult just to declare victory suddenly and turn out the lights. But the programs cost the CIA millions and the agency could no longer justify the expense.

Soon, CIA officers all over Western Europe were quietly seeking out their contacts with the émigré publishers, passing along the message many of them had been waiting forty years to hear: Time to go home.

Lisbon, March 1, 1990

Ryszard Tomaszewski, the Polish *Rezident* in Lisbon, had handled important American operations during his career in the Polish foreign intelligence service, which was precisely why John Palevich, the officer known as "Mr. Poland" within the DO, had identified him as the right man to approach to see if the Poles were ready for a new relationship with the CIA.

The sweeping changes across Eastern Europe in late 1989 had convinced the CIA—and officials in SE Division in particular—that it was time to establish contact with the intelligence services of the newly democratic governments just then breaking free of the Soviet orbit. Hungary had come first, with an initial meeting in Vienna between CIA and Hungarian intelligence officers. The CIA now wanted to build on its new ties with Budapest by developing liaison relationships in other capitals, including Warsaw and Prague.

An approach in Washington was ruled out, in part because that would force the CIA to include the FBI, and the agency wanted this contact to be unilateral—and discreet. A direct contact in Poland was also rejected, for fear of exposing CIA officers serving in the Warsaw Station if the approach was rebuffed.

Paul Redmond, the deputy chief of SE Division who was helping to coordinate the efforts to contact the Eastern Europeans, decided to try to use the Hungarian model with the Poles, contacting them through one of their foreign residencies on neutral ground.

But which one? The CIA had over the years obtained a wealth of detailed information about the Polish foreign intelligence service—Department I of the Ministerstwo Spraw Wewnetrzynych, Ministry of Internal Affairs—and so knew plenty about the personalities and backgrounds of many of the Polish officers serving around the world.

The *Rezidents* in Rome and Lisbon seemed like good candidates. The Rome *Rezident* had actually studied at Harvard and was quite familiar with Americans. But he was more likely to be under heavy surveillance from the local internal security service, and the CIA didn't want any other country, even the Italians, to find out about the approach. So Palevich flew to Lisbon to personally knock on Ryszard Tomaszewski's door.

But when Palevich went to the Polish embassy and introduced himself to Tomaszewski as a representative of the Director of Central Intelligence, the Polish intelligence officer immediately went on the defensive. Palevich told him that he had come with instructions to open an intelligence dialogue with the Polish service and that Tomaszewski had been selected as the intermediary to pass this message to Warsaw. Convinced this was some sort of American provocation, Tomaszewski maintained that he was a diplomat, a representative of the Ministerstwo Spraw Zagranicznych, the Ministry of Foreign Affairs, and thus was in no position to talk to Palevich about anything of the kind. It was clear that Tomaszewski had not yet received any guidance from the new government in Warsaw about whether to consider the Americans friends or adversaries.

Palevich realized that Tomaszewski suspected he was wearing a wire, making him even more guarded and tense. Getting nowhere with the Pole, Palevich tried a new tack. "Do you have a camera?" he asked.

Tomaszewski took a step backward, bristling, and almost shouted, "No! Why should I have a camera? I am a diplomat!"

In his most soothing voice, Palevich said, "Because you might want a copy of my passport, so that when you report this to the Center they will be able to do a proper trace to confirm my identity and affiliation. Now why don't you at least photocopy this." Palevich then handed the man his diplomatic passport, which contained his name and contact information, including his home address and telephone number in Maryland. Tomaszewski took the passport and disappeared briefly. When he returned, he simply handed the passport back to Palevich and told him to leave.

"Would you be so kind as to have your secretary call me a cab?" Palevich asked the badly rattled intelligence officer, trying one last gambit to buy another few minutes.

"No!" Tomaszewski shouted. "Catch a ride with your backup team." The Polish officer believed that Palevich was only the front man for an elaborate operation to entrap him, and he wasn't going to fall for this American ambush.

Palevich flew back to Washington the next day, and when he reported in, he had to endure some jokes about the apparent failure of his mission. "It was a good plan, we just sent the wrong man." Redmond, a Harvard graduate himself, good-naturedly said that he might make the next approach, this time in Rome. He was sure that two Harvard men could sort things out.

Two days later, as Palevich stepped out of the shower in his Maryland home, his telephone rang. It was Tomaszewski, calling from a pay phone in Lisbon. He had been careful not to call from the Polish embassy, in case eavesdroppers from the Portuguese security service overheard the conversation.

Speaking in "commercial terms," Tomaszewski said he was

terribly sorry for the misunderstanding of the previous week and that in fact his home office was very much interested in accepting the proposal. Could further discussions be arranged? It was obvious to Palevich that Tomaszewski had reported the contact to headquarters and had then been thoroughly chewed out for abruptly dismissing the CIA approach.

The opportunity would come quickly, and when it did, Gromoslaw Czempinski and Andrzej Milczanowski would make the most of it.

5

Langley, April 5, 1990

"We're in the final stages of planning the PROLOGUE exfil," I said. I was sitting with Dick Stolz in his seventh-floor office. Tom Twetten, the ADDO, was with us.

The case of the mysterious KGB volunteer who had approached Jack Downing on the *Red Arrow* so long ago had continued to plod along without any resolution of the doubts over whether it was a KGB double agent operation. We had, however, finally confirmed PROLOGUE's identity, thanks to Sergei Papushin, the defector from the Second Chief Directorate who had been hauled in by the FBI in New Jersey. After he was shown a mug book, he gave us PROLOGUE's name and position.

It was Aleksandr "Sasha" Zhomov, Papushin said. Zhomov was an officer in the First Department of the Second Chief Directorate, working under Rem Krassilnikov and his deputy, Valentin Klimenko. We decided to give Zhomov a small jolt by letting him know we knew his name. In one of our letters we passed to him on the *Red Arrow* we opened with "Dear Sasha." But he was a cool customer and didn't react.

By the spring of 1990, the handful of CIA officers involved in the case agreed that PROLOGUE was either the CIA's most important spy in Moscow or an amazingly good KGB dangle. We would have to bring him in from the cold if we were ever to find out which one he was. So several weeks earlier we had told him we were beginning the necessary preparations for an exfiltration, and as part of the process he should give us a handful of passport-size photographs we could use to create an identity for his escape. Within two weeks we had our photographs and a face to go with a name. We could now start working on a detailed plan. But there was a catch. We couldn't use any really elaborate methods of getting PROLOGUE out because of the likelihood it was a controlled operation with the specific goal of smoking out our exfiltration methods. We'd have to come up with a way of getting him out without revealing too much about how we did this kind of thing. It was against that backdrop that I decided to brief the seventh floor. I was still hopeful that the PROLOGUE operation was real, but I also had to share with Stolz and Twetten the doubts that many in the SE Division still harbored.

"What has he really given us?" Stolz asked.

"He's confirmed a lot about the 1985 trouble. And he's tipped us to some controlled cases they were going to dangle in front of us. And he's given us some internal documents that tell us what they think of our last few Moscow chiefs."

"Anything we know for certain would hurt them?" Twetten asked.

"No," I said.

"Do you think he's controlled?" Dick Stolz was being the case officer now, the old street man who'd been kicked out of Moscow in the early days and had been running operations against the KGB ever since. He knew how difficult it was to quantify an operation like PROLOGUE.

"Every time we make an exchange with him, I call a meeting of the small compartment of people who know about the case—that's about five of us. I take a poll on two questions. First, I ask if he's controlled. About fifty percent of the time we vote that he's controlled, the other half of the time it goes the other way. And there's always some changing of positions between polls."

"What's the second question?" Twetten asked.

"Whether we should go through with the exfil despite our doubts. The vote is always four to one that we go ahead."

"What do we lose if he's bad?" Stolz asked.

"A passport, an unspectacular method of getting him out. That's about it."

"What's Redmond think?"

I paused for a second before answering Stolz's question. "Like me. Depends on the day. But whatever he says, I believe deep down he thinks the operation is good. And he has no doubts that we should go ahead with the exfil. That's my position, too. If PROLOGUE is bad, there's got to be a reason why they've been running him at us for two years. If he's good, he'll be pure gold."

"Can't we insist that he give us the answer to one hard question before we pull him out?" Twetten asked.

"We've tried that for two years. Every time we push him he says he's holding out till we get him out. Then he's ours, he says. Who can argue with that? This guy is a KGB counterintelligence officer. We've got that confirmed. If we were in his shoes, we'd hold out till we'd been sprung."

"What did Gerber think of the guy?" Stolz fidgeted a little when he asked the question.

"You tell me," I said. "Burton and I haven't talked. And he doesn't vote in my straw polls. But my spies tell me that he had his doubts. Like everybody."

"Your recommendation?" Stolz asked. He liked consensus.

"Let's do it."

Turning to Twetten: "Tom?"

"What do we have to lose?"

"Then let's do it." Stolz showed no reluctance at the decision. "When do we brief the judge?" CIA Director William Webster would have to approve the plan to exfiltrate PROLOGUE. If anything went wrong, it could spark a diplomatic incident.

"Next week, when we get him to sign off on the U.S. passport. He'll have to take that to Larry Eagleburger." The CIA could falsify Soviet identity documents, but it couldn't issue a false American passport for one of its spies without the State Department's approval.

"Get the package together," said Stolz, signaling that the meeting was over.

East Berlin, April 15, 1990

Where was that damn colonel?

That was the question that CIA officers in both West and East Berlin were asking. The missing colonel from the American Department of the HVA, East Germany's foreign intelligence service, was one of the top-priority targets of the CIA's aggressive new campaign to recruit agents from what was left of East Germany's security services. He had once been stationed in New York, and the CIA believed that he almost certainly knew the identities of American spies who had worked for East Germany. Like thousands of other officers from the disintegrating HVA and MfS, he had just been fired, and as far as the CIA was concerned, he was now one of the most important unemployed men in East Germany. If the CIA could entice him to talk, he might be able to help roll up long-running spy operations against the United States. But the colonel seemed to have disappeared. Finding him was a major operation.

Paul Redmond's January visit had shaken up the East Berlin Station, and David Rolph had gotten the message that it was time to become more aggressive. It didn't take him long to figure out how. Rolph and the East Berlin Station came up with a plan to launch a brutally simple frontal assault on the crumbling Stasi, beginning with a series of cold pitches to as many HVA and MfS officers as possible. Case officers were told to dispense with the usual operational foreplay of spotting, assessing, and gaining access to their targets. Instead, they'd track them down and bluntly ask them if they wanted a last-minute insurance policy against uncertainty. There were few subtleties involved. The idea was to be up front and in their faces, offering a simple bargain: information for cash. More and more HVA and MfS officers were being laid off each day. If the CIA didn't act now, they might all simply go home and forget the secrets they were carrying around in their heads.

Armed with organizational charts and rosters provided by

their Stasi source, as well as other information about the identities of MfS and HVA officers collected over the years, Rolph and his case officers started calling East German intelligence officers at night at their homes. First calling from pay phones in West Berlin and later from East Berlin, the CIA officers reminded each East German intelligence officer of his current plight. "I represent the Western services," they'd then say. "Would you be interested in working with us?"

The telephone pitches were blunt and bold—and they didn't work. Invariably, the East Germans would hang up on the Americans, perhaps suspecting that it was a hoax or even a provocation by the Stasi to test the loyalty of its remaining officer corps. East Germany's culture of suspicion was dying hard. After two or three luckless weeks, the CIA scrapped its telephone campaign and decided to start knocking on doors. In order to reinforce the small East Berlin Station, officers from the West Berlin base joined in as well.

CIA case officers based in West Berlin had only rarely been involved in operations in the East in the recent past. The West Berlin base was subordinate to the CIA's Bonn Station and focused on intelligence targets on its own turf. But there were so many potential recruitment targets in East Berlin now that David Rolph needed help, which explained why a CIA officer from West Berlin was now looking for that elusive HVA colonel.

Finally, a source in West Berlin was able to help the CIA track the colonel down. It turned out that the man who five months earlier had been a senior colonel in the HVA was now working as a doorman in Berlin, a downward slide symbolic of what was happening to the Stasi—and to East Germany. A case officer approached him, sat him down, and made his pitch. If he would tell the case officer about the American spies he had handled during his long career, the CIA would be generous. The colonel obviously needed money, and now he was being offered more than he could ever make in his new line of work.

The former HVA colonel looked at the American in disgust and responded with the only rebuke he could make. "You obviously know who I was," he said. "And you now know what I have become. The only thing I have left is my honor. I have no intention of giving that up. Please do not come back again."

The CIA officer was taken aback and suddenly felt a deep sense of professional respect for the man. No matter that he had served a corrupt and tyrannical regime that was now vanishing around him. The German would be a loyal officer until the end and would do his best to retain his dignity. The CIA officer said good-bye and then took him at his word. From then on, the CIA would leave him alone to fade away into the new Germany.

East Berlin, April 25, 1990

After years of failure and frustration, the CIA suddenly had a new and burgeoning network of spies in East Berlin, all brought on board over the space of just a few weeks. The telephone pitches hadn't worked, but when the CIA switched tactics and decided to start going directly to the homes of current and former HVA and MfS officers to talk to them in person, the results improved almost immediately.

Not every man was like the HVA colonel, willing to put a dying country before his own future, and soon so many East Germans had agreed to cooperate that we were starting to wonder back at Langley how we could keep up with all of our new East German agents. We had to create a special East German Task Force just to keep up with the flow of intelligence from East Berlin.

To be sure, most were short-term agents. The Stasi officer who had revealed that Curly was a double agent was the only one who seemed destined to become a long-term asset. But the logistics of processing all the new intelligence was becoming difficult. The payments we were willing to make to former Stasi officers were also starting to decline, now that their information was becoming less valuable as East Germany edged closer to political oblivion.

Still, some of our new spies continued to bring unexpected intelligence windfalls when they walked off their jobs laden with secret Stasi documents. One agent outdid the rest: He looted an entire file room before leaving his job and volunteering to work for the West.

Early in the spring of 1990, West German counterintelligence officers based in Bavaria contacted the CIA's base in Munich, seeking help with a new case. An East German had contacted them and told them he had a friend in the East who wanted to sell documents. Could the CIA, the West Germans asked, arrange to meet the man in the East? At the time, West German intelligence was still reluctant to conduct operations on its own in East Germany.

The request was routed to the CIA's East Berlin Station, and the station's most junior case officer was assigned to handle the case. The young American officer drove to a small village not far from East Berlin, called a phone number, and gave a "parole" to identify himself. The East German agreed to meet him.

That night, the CIA officer and the German drove separately out to some woods beyond the village, and then pulled their cars over into the dark. As the American walked over, the East German opened the trunk of his car, and the CIA officer saw that it was packed with bundles of documents wrapped in newspapers. As quickly as he could, he began transferring them to his own car. Before long, the CIA had the files in West Berlin ready for inspection.

The bundles turned out to be a vast compendium of the Stasi's logs of thousands upon thousands of telephone wiretaps that the East Germans had conducted against individuals in West Berlin and West Germany. The files, which included some seventeen thousand index cards, showed the telephone numbers that the East Germans had tapped, cataloged how often their conversations had been recorded, and in some cases included the transcripts of individual calls. The records provided a road map to many of the Stasi's operations in West Germany. They showed who had been targets of East German surveillance and investigation and so could help reveal how the East Germans had tried to penetrate its main target, the West German government. After sorting through and analyzing the files, the CIA turned them over to West German intelligence to examine.

Yet the records that the CIA really wanted—files from the most sensitive espionage cases of the HVA and MfS, including their joint operations with the KGB—were still out of reach. The crowds that had surged into Normannenstrasse in January hadn't gotten them, either. Instead, the protesters had ripped open file drawers filled with the records of the banal, neighborly betrayals that had sadly been so commonplace under the Communist regime.

Only later did the CIA pick up hints that a few handpicked Stasi officers had already trucked the most sensitive files to East Berlin's Schoenefeld Airport. From there, the boxed files were to be transported to Moscow. The Stasi was turning over its crown jewels to the KGB for safekeeping.

The most sensitive Stasi files were out of the CIA's reach—for now.

It would take years for the CIA to obtain those sensitive files after they were in KGB custody, and when the agency did, it would find a wealth of information about East German intelligence operations against the West.

The political wheels were now grinding inevitably toward the eventual absorption of East Germany into West Germany, but the CIA was still very interested in recruiting high-ranking HVA and MfS officers, particularly those who could reveal the identities of any additional American spies. So the most attractive targets of the cold pitch campaign were always the HVA and MfS officers who had been involved in operations against the United States. At the top of the target list was HVA Colonel Jürgen Rogalla, chief of the American Department of the HVA.

David Rolph had never held out much hope that he would be able to convince Rogalla to spy for his old adversary. Like the HVA colonel, Rogalla was a hard-core Stasi man. But the agency was determined to give it a try, and Rogalla was tentatively given the code name GTPULSAR.

Rolph was surprised when, on his second attempt to contact Rogalla, the burly colonel invited him into his apartment in downtown East Berlin. Rogalla ushered him into his living room, and after the two sat down to chat, Rolph outlined his pitch. The CIA, Rolph told Rogalla, would be very generous if he agreed to help. Rolph tried to make it clear that a high-ranking officer like himself would be treated well by the CIA. While lower-level Stasi officers had received only modest cash payments, Rogalla's cooperation would qualify him for resettlement in the United States.

Rogalla asked a few questions, saying he wanted to make certain he understood what Rolph was offering. Finally, he told Rolph he needed time to think about the offer and asked the CIA officer to come back to his apartment in two days. Rolph was wary of coming back; he knew that Rogalla could be setting him up for an ambush arrest or even for a roughing up by the KGB. But he agreed, and two days later he was back in the East German intelligence officer's living room. Rogalla asked Rolph to go over his offer once more. Once he had finished, Rogalla told him that he had decided not to accept the CIA offer. Rolph thanked him for his time and was preparing to leave when Rogalla asked him to stay.

"I have someone here that I would like you to meet," he said.

"No, thank you, that's okay," Rolph said. "I should be on my way."

"I have been patient with you," Rogalla said. "Now I would like you to please be patient with me." Then he turned to the curtain separating the apartment's living room from its small kitchen. "Herr General," he called. "Please come in."

With dramatic flair, the curtain was then swept aside and out stepped a silver-haired and impeccably dressed General Werner Grossman, chief of the HVA and successor to the retired legend, Markus Wolf.

Grossman shook hands with Rolph, and as they sat down to talk, Rolph felt a sense of relief that he hadn't been arrested or that a squad of Stasi goons hadn't stepped from behind the curtain.

"We know what you and your officers are doing," Grossman told Rolph. "We know that you are harassing our officers and our retirees, and you are embarrassing them in front of their families."

So the cold pitches were starting to bother them, Rolph thought. Probably because they are working. His mind was racing.

"We know that your service is better than this," Grossman lectured Rolph with Teutonic bluntness. "This kind of activity is unprofessional. You must stop this at once." He looked sternly at Rolph. "If you do not stop this harassment, we will go to the police. And if you persist after that, we will take this to the press."

Rolph looked at Grossman, dumbfounded. How sad, he thought. A year ago, this man could order men to their deaths. Now, the worst threat that the chief of the Hauptverwaltung Aufklarung could level against the CIA was that he would talk to a newspaper reporter.

"General Grossman, it was a pleasure to meet you, but I have to tell you I have a job to do. You can do what you feel you have to do." With that, Rolph stood, shook hands with Grossman and Rogalla, and walked out.

Rolph's cable arrived on my desk the following morning. I shared it with the DCI, who had long since forgotten his statement a few months earlier that my team in East Berlin could be replaced if that was what was needed to exploit the situation.

I cabled David Rolph, telling him that his meeting with Rogalla and Grossman was clearly a unique event in the annals of CIA history and in any case officer's career. I then followed up with a private channel cable, ending it with a historical perspective:

1. IN ADDITION TO OUR OFFICIAL RESPONSES TO YOUR SUPERB REPORT ON YOUR MEETING WITH ROGALLA AND THE GENERAL, I WOULD ONLY ADD THAT YOUR ACCOUNT WAS TREMENDOUSLY MOVING AND ALMOST REMINISCENT OF THE MIXTURE OF HONOR AND FATALISM SHOWN BY ANOTHER GENERATION OF GERMANS AT STALINGRAD. YOUR GENERAL GROSSMAN COULD HAVE EASILY BEEN VON PAULUS. ABOUT ALL WE NEEDED WAS A FINAL MESSAGE FROM THE FUHRER SAYING SOMETHING ALONG THE LINES OF HIS LAST MESSAGE TO PAULUS. "HUENDE WOLLT IHR EWIG LEBEN?"*
2. THIS IS HISTORY AND YOU ARE PART OF IT.

*"Dogs, do you want to live forever?"

East Berlin, Late May 1990

With German reunification just four months away, it was time, we decided, for the CIA to have a little chat with Markus Wolf, the one man who embodied East German intelligence. A mythic figure in the world of espionage, Markus Wolf had run the HVA for most of its existence until his retirement in 1986.

His circumstances and stature had taken a turn for the worse in the last six months, and in the current climate he seemed likely to face a tough investigation not only of his involvement in the suppression of the citizens of East Germany, but also of his contacts with international terrorist groups. Arrest and imprisonment were now very real threats for East Germany's legendary spymaster, which meant that it was a good time for the CIA to make him an offer.

An American businessman with commercial interests in East Berlin had been in contact with one of his friends, and we'd asked the businessman to serve as the go-between. Wolf was asked if he would be willing to meet with the CIA, and he said yes, he would be willing to hear what we had to say. By now Wolf was familiar with the process. Earlier in May he'd received a similar offer from the West Germans—"Give us your top sources in West Germany and you'll be free from prosecution and a considerably richer man," they had told him, hoping to tempt him with the lure of material and personal security. Wolf had listened patiently and turned them down. Now it was time, he decided, to hear out the Americans and close the loop.

Gus Hathaway came out of retirement to make the approach. Hathaway and Rolph's deputy met Wolf at his dacha in Prenden, outside of Berlin. Hathaway identified himself as the representative of the Director of the CIA, William Webster, and wasted no time in getting to the substance of his visit. Wolf's wife, Andrea, would later dismiss Hathaway as a "typical bureaucrat."

Hathaway found Wolf willing to listen, but not interested in coming over to the CIA. He treated the exchange as an entertainment—countering Hathaway's offer of resettlement in California with the statement that life in Siberia wasn't too bad, either. Wolf was all elusive affability and still a master of his game. He would later describe Hathaway as deadly serious in his efforts to get him to shed light on the terrible losses the CIA had suffered five years earlier.

After that brief meeting, no one ever returned to see if Markus Wolf had changed his mind. Hathaway left a typed card with a contact number in New York and a parole for Wolf to use should he ever want to get in touch, but we never heard from him again.

6

East Berlin, June 1990

David Rolph had been through this routine at least a dozen times over the last few weeks, and it was starting to get a little tedious. It seemed that every Soviet who had managed to buy a ticket for a bus vacation in East Germany now wanted to defect to the West. Over the years there had always been a small handful of Soviet walk-ins, but now the floodgates had opened. Rolph was screening as many as four a week, all seeking political asylum. Most were simple tourists, with no special knowledge of interest to the CIA. Rolph and other officers took turns with the screening and politely directed them to seek refugee status through the normal immigration channels. One look at the young Soviet in the waiting room and Rolph sighed and began to think about how soon he could send him on his way. He was wearing a T-shirt, shorts, and a baseball cap and had approached one of the Marine guards, who called to tell Rolph that another walk-in was in the waiting room. As he took him in, Rolph saw a young man in his early thirties and quickly dismissed him as a Russian tourist, just another unhappy factory worker from Leningrad or Moscow.

Rolph was too tired of these sessions to go through the standard, highly structured debriefing process with yet another tourist. He figured he would cut it short and have the guy out the door in a couple of minutes.

"What can I do for you?" he asked far too casually. He didn't even bother to sit down.

"I want to go to America," the man answered.

How many times had he heard that line? "Well, that's very difficult," Rolph said. "There is a lot of paperwork, and we really can't help you here." Time to get rid of this stiff, he thought.

"Oh, I thought it might be possible, because I am a Soviet officer."

Rolph stopped short. "What did you say?"

"I am a fighter pilot."

Rolph eased into a chair across from the young man, realizing with a jolt that he had nearly managed to throw a good prospect out on his ear.

Rolph's Russian tourist turned out to be a major in the Soviet Air Force, a decorated veteran of the Afghan War and now a flight instructor teaching new Soviet pilots how to fly the latest, nonexport version of the Soviet Union's most advanced fighter, the MiG-29. He was stationed at a Soviet air base not far from Leipzig, deep in East Germany, and had come to East Berlin on his day off in order to contact the Americans.

Quickly trying to make amends for his earlier casual approach, Rolph asked the Soviet how long he could spend before he had to leave. About forty-five minutes, he replied. Rolph handed him a legal notepad and told him to write down as much as he could remember about the MiG-29 that he believed was considered secret. "I don't know anything about MiGs," Rolph said. "But we have people in Washington who do. If they are interested in what you write down, then we can work with you."

Rolph left the Soviet alone for the full forty-five minutes, and when he returned, he found that the Soviet had filled a dozen pages with notes and drawings. He took the notes and told the pilot that if Washington was interested in what he had provided, he would meet him in an East Berlin park the following Saturday. He also told him never to come back to the embassy.

Rolph sent the Soviet's handwritten notes to CIA headquarters by a secure fax, and the next day Langley cabled back that the pilot was the real thing. His notes had already revealed details about the MiG-29 that American military experts hadn't known and were very much worth pursuing.

When the two men met as scheduled in an East Berlin park the next Saturday, the pilot agreed to stay in place and spy until the CIA could arrange for his escape. Rolph told him they could meet in a park in Leipzig, which was only a half-hour bus ride away from the Soviet air base where he was stationed. Rolph gave him a camera so that he could secretly take photographs of MiG-29 manuals and other classified materials stored at the base. If he ever missed a meeting, the fallback plan called for Rolph to wait for him two nights later in a small German village about three kilometers from his base.

The MiG pilot took to espionage with relish and began to hand over dozens of photographs of Soviet Air Force manuals. Soon he started asking Rolph to tell him what his CIA code name was. Revealing a crypt to an agent was frowned upon, but the pilot kept asking, and in the end Rolph gave in.

"You are SPANIEL."

"Spaniel, like a dog?" asked the incredulous pilot. "You call me a dog!"

Rolph tried to explain that the code names were generated randomly by computers and that the name was not a reflection of what the CIA thought of him. That didn't soothe the infuriated Soviet, who demanded that his code name be changed immediately. Soon, GTSPANIEL became GTMACRAME.

The MiG pilot's pique over his cryptonym didn't deter him from becoming a major league spy. His bitterness toward the Soviet system—and the hierarchy of the Soviet Air Force in particular—drove him on. He was soon photographing thousands of pages of Soviet Air Force documents, virtually everything of value in the classified library at his base.

He worked so fast that he complained that the CIA's tiny cameras, built to look like Bic cigarette lighters, slowed him down. Rolph gave in and gave him the money to go to Leipzig and buy a 35 mm camera on his own. The pilot's photographic production surged. Ingeniously, the Soviet made a big show of his fancy new camera and soon became the base's unofficial photographer, taking photos of his fellow pilots—and even his commander—so they could send them back home to their families.

Langley, July 10, 1990

The tension had finally begun to subside. The PROLOGUE exfiltration had been launched.

Technical Services had created an elaborate American identity for Sasha Zhomov—a passport and travel history, along with the usual pocket litter, had been painstakingly assembled and sent off to Moscow. It would be dead dropped to Sasha Zhomov, and then it would be up to him to get out of the USSR using the identity of a West Coast professional traveling from Moscow to the Baltic states.

Zhomov's American passport would show prior travel, entries, and exits from a variety of countries that backed up his new identity as an American on private travel. After the usual tours in Moscow and Leningrad, the traveler would proceed to the Baltics and eventually board a ferry in Tallinn, the capital of Estonia, for the run to Helsinki. The package was dropped in Moscow, and the rest was up to Zhomov. I dispatched my team to Helsinki to wait for the ferry from Tallinn. There was no turning back. Now we'd have our answer.

Helsinki, July 12, 1990

The ferry from Tallinn docked on schedule in Helsinki, but there was no sign of PROLOGUE. The team waited another day. Then another. Still, it was no show. By day four I called them home. We asked Mike Cline and his wife, Jill, to book a compartment on the *Red Arrow* to Leningrad, to see if PROLOGUE might show up, and if he did, to get his explanation.

On the *Red Arrow,* July 14, 1990

Mike and Jill Cline had slept fitfully on the overnight run to Leningrad, but then they never slept well on these runs—never more than ten-minute catnaps. Mike was always concerned that he'd oversleep and miss the early morning brush pass with PROLOGUE.

At 0640 hours, Cline quietly left the sleeping compartment and made his way down the passageway of the rocking train to the smoking vestibule between cars. He lit up and waited. Each time he took a drag of his cigarette, he checked his watch. Ten, then fifteen minutes passed. No sign of him. Cline decided it was a no-show and returned to his compartment. He just shook his head to Jill, indicating that there had been no contact, and said nothing. Then Jill cheerily announced to Mike and the microphones that it was her turn to take a smoke and made her way to the smoking vestibule.

While she was standing there smoking her cigarette, she saw a young man she thought was PROLOGUE pass between cars and then go by again in the opposite direction. Odd, she thought, and decided to return to the compartment to tell Mike what she had seen. But in the passageway of the sleeper she got caught up in conversation with some American tourists traveling to Leningrad. She was still speaking to them when out of the corner of her eye, she saw the man she thought might be PROLOGUE enter the sleeping car from the rear of the train and walk briskly toward her along the passageway. As he passed behind her, while she was still talking to the American tourists, the man thrust an envelope into her hand and proceeded forward into the next car. Jill Cline turned her head to watch him as he disappeared into the next car. The tourists kept chatting, never noticing the brush pass that had taken place right under their noses.

Langley, July 14, 1990

"Fuck!" I exclaimed in exasperation as Redmond and I read our copies of Cline's cable. The note PROLOGUE had passed to Jill Cline was written with a combination of exasperation and rage. He said that we had been dangerous and foolhardy in preparing the identity switch—for him to try to exit on that identity would have been suicide. Now, he declared, he would have to lie low for a while. He'd get back in touch when the time was right.

"We've got our answer, don't we?" Redmond was matter-of-fact.

"Yeah," I said. "We've got our answer."

"You win some, you lose some," said Redmond. I could see his disappointment equaled mine.

Neither of us believed PROLOGUE's plaintive cry. He was protesting too much. The KGB was good, but there had been no mistakes in the documentation package. The story just didn't fly. And that meant PROLOGUE was controlled.

Cline also reported that he and Jill had taken a walk through Leningrad and had noticed that they were under particularly heavy surveillance, something a little out of the ordinary for their visits to Leningrad. They understood a few minutes later when they spotted PROLOGUE with the surveillance team. Nice trick, they thought.

"No guts, no glory," I said without conviction, and picked up the phone to call the DDO before he called me. Neither Redmond nor I did a very good job of hiding our disappointment. I would admit later that the odds of the PROLOGUE operation were never better than trying to fill an inside straight, but that was what all but the most cautious poker players always tried to do. They got our passport and a pretty good plan that we wouldn't be using again, at least not there.

Now we were going to have to come to grips with what kind of game the KGB was playing. They had broken their cardinal rule: Never dangle KGB staff officers. We'd have to figure out what it meant for our other operations against them.

Berlin, August 1990

Interest in the Soviet MiG-29 pilot suddenly intensified in August, when the Iraqi Army of Saddam Hussein invaded Kuwait, setting the stage for war in the Persian Gulf.

Iraq's Air Force was equipped with Soviet-built fighter jets, and its pilots had been trained by the Soviets. The Pentagon's desire for more information about the MiG-29 was no longer academic.

The Soviet pilot upped the ante—he was photographing not only documents about the MiG-29's design specifications, but also air combat tactical manuals, giving the U.S. Air Force timely insights into the methods the Soviets had taught the Iraqis.

As he was examining the Soviet pilot's latest batch of photographs in early August, Rolph noticed that another pair of hands could be seen on the edges of some of the pictures. They appeared to be a woman's hands, holding open the pages of the manuals as they were being photographed. Someone else obviously knew about the pilot's espionage, and that was something he had never mentioned to the CIA. Who else was in the operation? At their next meeting in the Leipzig park, Rolph asked the Soviet about the hands on the pictures.

"That's my wife," he said. "I take the manuals home and she helps me photograph them."

"So she knows what you're doing?" Rolph's mind was racing. He thought for a second and then said, "Why don't you bring her to our next meeting?"

At their next scheduled meeting in the park, the pilot brought his wife for Rolph to meet. She was a lovely young brunette, and while they sat in the park, she convinced Rolph that she fully supported her husband's decision to work for the CIA. She said that they were both eager to move to the West with their two young children, and she would help her husband commit espionage if that's what it took to start a new life in America.

Langley, August 16, 1990

Sergei Papushin, who'd been picked up by the FBI after a drunken spree in New Jersey in late 1989, was still living in a CIA safe house, but interest in his case had gradually waned. Initially, the KGB had been so concerned about his defection that the Soviets had sent his father, the *Rezident* in Sofia, Bulgaria, to the United States to try to talk his son into returning home. But Papushin had stayed put. Now, nine months later, Papushin had been fully debriefed by the CIA and FBI, and it had become obvious that his knowledge of KGB counterintelligence operations against the United States was limited. He had worked in the unit that targeted British intelligence officers working in Moscow, so London had been interested in what he had to say. But he didn't have much for us, and the tedium of day-to-day life as a talked-out defector was starting to get to Papushin. He'd turned again to heavy drinking.

The CIA had tried counseling, but he wasn't much interested, and in the end he just settled into the routine of an on-again, off-again drunk, a former KGB officer who found himself of little value in his new setting.

During his sober moments, Papushin was clearly frustrated by the fact that he was largely being ignored by the CIA and FBI. So he did something he knew was guaranteed to once again grab attention: He gave one of his handlers an urgent message to be taken immediately to the top levels of the CIA. There is a mole in the agency, Papushin declared. The KGB has one of your people.

The CIA now gave Papushin their full attention and listened carefully to his story. He said that the KGB had a penetration of the CIA in Moscow. He had friends in the American Department of the Second Chief Directorate, and he'd overheard enough from his colleagues to conclude that they had an agent in the CIA station.

But as he was questioned further, it became apparent that he was scrambling with a fabricated story. Nothing he told his debriefers checked out, and eventually we concluded that he had come up with his story out of desperation. Another dead end in the search for an answer, any answer, to the problems five years earlier.

Warsaw, August 1990

When Saddam Hussein invaded Kuwait, a handful of CIA and American military officers stationed in Kuwait City were forced to move to Baghdad and into hiding without diplomatic immunity. With the very real possibility that the men could become hostages, the CIA began to look for help in arranging a rescue. After being turned down by other allies, the agency turned to the Poles.

General Henrik Jasik, Gromek Czempinski's immediate chief in the foreign intelligence service, thought that any attempt at a rescue was too risky. There were still about four thousand Polish citizens in Iraq, and if Poland's assistance to the CIA was exposed, they could be targeted by the Iraqi regime. But Czempinski realized that this was an opportunity for the Poles to prove to the CIA that they could become trusted partners and wanted badly to give it a try. Andrzej Milczanowski, the minister overseeing the intelligence service, overruled Jasik and approved the operation. But he decided not to inform his political superiors, including the prime minister, about the plan. He feared the operation might be vetoed, so he decided that he and Czempinski would sink or swim with the Americans.

By the end of August, the six Americans were still in Baghdad, staying in communication with Langley and a step ahead of Iraqi security. Warsaw and Langley were in constant contact, as Czempinski and his officers tried to figure out ways around the Iraqi domestic security apparatus, which was now assumed to be hunting for the Americans.

It wasn't going to be easy.

7

Langley, September 25, 1990

The meeting was a setup, but I was probably the only person who knew it. Over the last few weeks, there had been rumblings about what to do with East Germany once it was reunified with the Federal Republic of Germany. Politically, the Bush administration had made the cold calculation that it would drive for the absorption of East Germany into West Germany—with the new Germany solidly in NATO—even if it harmed Gorbachev's standing at home. If hard-liners returned to power in Moscow, at least German reunification would already be a fact of life. Now we were faced with the administrative challenge of working out a division of labor in a reunified Germany.

Now that a final agreement had been reached and the date for formal reunification was set for October 3, just days away, bureaucracies all over the Western world were scrambling to catch up with the new reality in Germany, and the CIA's Directorate of Operations was no exception. Throughout the Cold War, East Germany had been SE Division's turf, and West Germany had always been handled by the DO's European Division. Reunification raised a bureaucratic dilemma: Which division should be in charge of intelligence operations in the new Germany?

There was, in fact, no solid rationale for keeping East Germany under my purview, beyond the fact that the Soviet Western Group of Forces still had almost four hundred thousand troops on East German soil. But few people in SE saw it that way—especially the ones working on East Berlin.

Burton Gerber was known to be the most fastidious of DO barons when it came to matters of turf and responsibility. He neither encroached on another's turf nor allowed encroachment on his. He and I hadn't spoken much since I'd taken over the SE Division, though we'd had cordial, if stiff, exchanges at the weekly DDO staff meetings. He'd shared with me the deep emotional impact November 9 had had on him as he'd seen the Wall coming down, and I'd shared my own, similar feelings about that night in Berlin. Now he'd called a meeting to discuss how he and I could pursue our separate and legitimate tasks in East Germany after reunification less than ten days off.

Gerber had about four European Division officers with him, including line operations officers and administrative specialists. I brought John O'Reilly, whom I'd moved into the front office to manage division resources and plans. The atmosphere was expectant rather than tense as we exchanged cordialities and took our seats across from one another.

Gerber seemed to want to avoid confrontation. He opened the meeting with a statement on the parallel nature of our interests and the fact that we all worked for the same leader, the DDO. He was certain that we could work something out, perhaps move incrementally toward a realignment of responsibilities.

"Burton," I said after listening for a few moments, "why

screw around with all this? In eight days there will be one Germany. It will be in Europe and in NATO. It belongs in Europe Division. If you want it, it's yours. Have your personnel people talk to mine and let's work out a handover without any silliness."

There was a prolonged silence as my words sank in. Then Gerber, always the gentleman, thanked me for my suggestion and said he would check with the DDO and set things in motion. I didn't tell him I'd already told Dick Stolz that I planned to hand over East Germany. He would be responsible for a united Germany while I'd be watching over the Soviet Western Group of Forces still garrisoned in the eastern zones.

Paul Redmond was traveling when the meeting took place, and I hadn't briefed him on my plans before he left. When he learned what I'd done, he exploded. "Why the fuck did you give Burton East Germany?" he said. "We've got a lot to do over there."

"Because it was the right thing to do," I snapped. "For chrissakes, Paul, in a week it'll be part of the Federal Republic. Why do you want to hang on to it?"

"Because it's fun, that's why."

I could see that Redmond meant it. He wasn't just being his usual prickly self, this was deeply important to him. That exchange summed up the growing rift between me and my deputy. In the year since I had returned to the SE Division, I had begun to worry that Redmond and some others on the division staff were stuck in a time warp. Couldn't they see that the revolutions that had swept across Eastern Europe would inevitably change the CIA's mission? The sad truth was that the SE Division's insular subculture didn't want to let go of the Cold War. As Redmond said, it had been too much fun.

My problems weren't limited to Paul Redmond. I'd picked up enough of the rumblings from Steve Weber and John O'Reilly to know that not everyone had been happy to see me take over from Gerber. The hard-liners in the division were dug in, Weber told me. They didn't believe the changes in Eastern Europe would hold, and when the pendulum swung back, they were convinced we'd be caught off base. Weber counseled patience with the East Europe group. Most of them were feeling that the world they'd lived in for so many years had ended—they were sitting next to a safe full of dead drop site diagrams for Prague, Budapest, and Warsaw, and I was telling them those folks were our new friends. They'd come around, he said, just give them time.

O'Reilly was less sanguine about the hard-liners handling the Soviet Union. Get rid of them, had been his summary advice. Send them off to counterintelligence, where they'd be happier.

Both men were right. And I decided I'd have to start with Redmond.

Karlshorst, East Berlin, October 2, 1990

The leaves, caught in an eddy, swirled over the cobblestones and into the courtyard beyond the sullen Red Army soldier standing guard at the entrance to the Museum of Capitulation in Karlshorst, the heart of the huge KGB detachment in East Berlin. Once a fashionable residential district, Karlshorst found its place in history when the German Wehrmacht signed the documents of surrender in May 1945. The museum building itself, the site of the historic unconditional capitulation by Field Marshal Keitel, Admiral von Friedenburg, and General Stumpf, had in the early days of the Third Reich served as a Wehrmacht officers club, but for the last forty-five years the word *Karlshorst* had become synonymous with the Soviet Committee for State Security. And now I was walking along the quiet Rheinsteinstrasse with Rem Krassilnikov on a brilliant fall day in Berlin forty-five years after the German surrender and one day before the reunification of East and West Germany. Ted Price, who had succeeded Hathaway as counterintelligence chief, was with me for the Gavrilov meetings, as was Moscow chief Mike Cline. I had left my colleagues back in the KGB safe house with Leonid Nikitenko, the First Directorate counterintelligence chief, while I took a walk with Krassilnikov.

"Milton, do you know how many people died in the Great Patriotic War?" Krassilnikov said, inspired, I assumed, by the solemnity of the setting and the historical shift that was just a day away.

"Russians or total?" I asked, wondering where he was headed with his question. I did not yet know the man well, but each time we had met he had revealed a little more of himself. I had been surprised to learn earlier that he was an admirer of Elizabeth Barrett Browning, but not necessarily Robert Browning, he'd insisted with a smile. Now, I sensed, I would be catching another glimpse of this complex man, something less poetic than either Elizabeth or Robert Browning, something closer to the suffering Russian soul.

"I'll give you both numbers. It was more than twenty-one million Russians, and about fifty million people worldwide. All because of what started here in Germany before you were born." Krassilnikov, always careful with his choice of words, seemed preoccupied. Something was clearly bothering him, something beyond the casualty figures for the Second World War.

"How many troops did you lose in the battle of Berlin, Rem?" I asked, probing.

"More than you lost in the whole war. You Americans were clever, as usual, to let us take Berlin. For every German we killed, Marshal Zhukov lost four men. And do you know what happens tomorrow? Do you know why I wanted to have the meetings here start before tomorrow?"

"No, but I have a feeling you're going to tell me."

"Yes. Because even though we fought our way into Berlin forty-five years ago at great human cost, and even though we have been one of the four powers occupying Berlin since 1945, after tomorrow, I am told, I will need to apply for a visa to come to Berlin. Our military will have some arrangement until they formally withdraw, but my colleagues and I will need visas after tomorrow. Do you find irony in this?"

The truth was, I did. This was my third meeting with Krassilnikov in less than a year, and I had seen our personal relationship evolve from that of archadversaries ever wary of the other's motivations to opponents being drawn by events into areas of common concern. The evolution was incremental, extremely hesitant on both sides, and nothing even approaching trust had yet developed. But there was a realization that our world was changing. The changing world was a new element in the relationship with this man so consumed by the counterintelligence challenge he faced from the CIA that he could spare no time to contemplate another reality—that his system was faltering. Rem Krassilnikov, the man whose first name was an acronym for "World Revolution"—*Revolutsky Mir*—could not see that it was over, except perhaps in fleeting moments that he could as quickly subordinate. He still seemed convinced that if only the CIA would stop undermining socialist unity and the USSR at every point of contact, the crisis would pass. In that moment, I thought Krassilnikov was trapped in the same time warp that had captured Paul Redmond. The two men ought to meet, I thought. They had much in common.

Krassilnikov and I had taken this little walk at his suggestion. I always kept in the back of my mind the possibility that, depending on the circumstances, I might one day offer him an alternative to his KGB pension. I was certain that he had the same thoughts about me. It was what we did for a living. So when he suggested a walk during a break in our Gavrilov meetings in the KGB safe house two hundred yards behind us, I agreed. Now, walking down the Rheinsteinstrasse with this white-haired KGB major general, I saw a man opening up for just a moment. With Germany about to be reunited in less than twenty-four hours inside the NATO structure, it was all but over for the Warsaw Pact. The Soviet Western Group of Forces was still in place in East Germany, but that seemed as much because there were growing fears that the Soviet government wouldn't be able to provide the returning soldiers and their families housing and support if they all returned at once. Here in Germany, where the Soviets had made the Western Group a way of life, things were predictable, at least. Back in Moscow the future was a wide-open field of uncertainties.

"Yes," I said. "Of course there's irony in this. Would you have predicted it?"

"Would anybody?" Rem asked without sarcasm.

"Probably not. Germany is reunited tomorrow. The Warsaw Pact can't last. It's over. Now we're both faced with trying to figure how we adjust to each other in the changed world. Maybe it was easier before all this change. Have you ever thought about that?"

"Who has time? I have a job to do, as I am certain you do. But we will have to start working toward a more rational relationship," Krassilnikov said.

"You've said that before, Rem. I think I agree. I'm still not certain what is meant by a 'more rational' relationship," I said. "But I'm willing to explore it."

I didn't try to recruit Krassilnikov during our little walk, and he didn't try to recruit me, though we both had such thoughts as we walked through the streets of Karlshorst. I also wondered if he'd been thinking of how Lubyanka had aced Langley in the PROLOGUE operation a few months back, but if he had, he gave no hint of it.

Back in the KGB safe house, we got down to business. Leonid Nikitenko, the counterintelligence chief from the First Directorate, was gregarious and voluble and seemed to have loosened up even more since our first meeting in Helsinki. At one point during our lunch break I said to Nikitenko, "Leonid, you like this business of intelligence, don't you?"

He smiled and thought for a minute, and then he said, "Milton, there is no business like it. We are politicians. We are soldiers. And, above all, we are actors on a wonderful stage. I cannot think of a better business than the intelligence business. But now that we are talking the philosophy of the intelligence business, I have a question for you."

Here it comes, I thought.

"Why, Milton, are so many of our First Directorate officers going over to your side these days? I have looked into each case, and none of them, not one of them, demonstrated antisocial vulnerabilities before they went over to you. Most of them had honors diplomas from our universities—red diplomas with gold letters. They were our best officers, with good prospects. Was it their wives? Were the wives unhappy? What is happening to them?"

I thought before answering. We had indeed been bringing in a large number of young KGB majors and lieutenant colonels in recent months. Earlier in the morning, I had made my usual statement to our KGB hosts about the latest string of defections—they were safe and well and free, and if they wanted to talk to their old bosses, we'd be in touch. It was no longer what we used to call the "rummy rejects" of the system who were turning to us; we were getting their top officers now, who were coming to us with their own plans for making it in the West. We were delighted with the new quality of the defectors, and the KGB, not surprisingly, was troubled by it—and puzzled. Nikitenko, with his question, had given me an extremely informative window into the state of affairs in the KGB in those turbulent times. They were worried that their best officers were running for the door.

"Leonid," I said at last, "let me answer your question with a story. Picture this. The scene is a boardroom of a large American dog food company. The CEO is haranguing his staff about the poor sales performance over the last quarter. He states with pride that his company's product has the best nutritional values of all American brands. He says that the texture is the best and directs his staff to take a look inside the open dog food cans that have been set before each of them. He takes his own can and draws it to him. It even smells good, the CEO exclaims." I paused for a moment to check the nearly blank faces of Nikitenko and Krassilnikov, both of whom were wondering where in the world I was leading them. Then I continued.

" 'So why,' the CEO asks with great emotion, 'are sales going down, down, down?' There's a nervous shuffle around the boardroom, and finally the vice president for sales raises his hand and utters just five words. 'The dogs don't like it!' "

Nikitenko looked at me for a moment, the reluctantly polite expression gone, and repeated the punch line incredulously. "Dogs don't like it? Dogs don't like it? What can this mean?"

Ted Price interjected, "It means that the dogs just don't like it, Leonid. They're looking for something at least different."

Price, Cline, and I wondered if Leonid ever did get it. His foreign intelligence directorate had taken most of the heat over the last several months, with defections of First Directorate officers running one about every six weeks. The trickle had turned into a torrent, to the point that my budget for defectors needed constant reprogramming. Old averages were thrown out the window as the young KGB officers continued to come over to our side. As Nikitenko was making his representations about his officers gone missing, I would glance over at Rem Krassilnikov to see his reaction. Nothing. There was no sign of smugness that the First Directorate was taking so many hits; nor was there any sign that he thought this was his problem.

We would not meet with Leonid Nikitenko again. Some weeks later I would receive a message from Krassilnikov, relayed through Mike Cline in Moscow, advising us that Nikitenko had died suddenly in a Latin American country. It seemed there had been no foul play, but Rem asked if we could discreetly check on it for him and for the First Directorate. We did, and to the best of our understanding Nikitenko had died of a heart attack. I sent this to Mike Cline, who passed it on to Krassilnikov. I would wonder much later what the English-speaking counterintelligence chief had been doing down in Latin America when he died. Could he have been off to see one of the men who was betraying us from within?

Berlin, October 3, 1990

Ted Price, Mike Cline, and I had spent the final hours of October 2 among the crowds thronging East Berlin's main avenue, Unter den Linden. When the clocks finally struck midnight, shifting the center of gravity of postwar Europe from a small town near the German border with France to the reborn colossus of an undivided Berlin, I felt a lingering sense of discomfort, something I couldn't quite pin down. I thought of Krassilnikov's words earlier that morning and wondered where he might be walking in this new Berlin.

The next morning, a German tabloid ran a photograph of one of the previous night's revelers holding a placard high above him. It read, *"Und nun, Österreich?"*—"And now, Austria?"—a thinly veiled reference to Hitler's ambitions.

In the cold light of day, I still couldn't shake the odd sense of discomfort that had nagged at me since I'd walked through Karlshorst the previous morning. We were winding down a century that was widely thought to be the "American century," but the reality was that most of what had befallen mankind since 1914 had its origins in Germany. Would historians even think of calling the twentieth century the "German century"? I doubted it.

Baghdad, October 25, 1990

Czempinski had decided to run the rescue operation himself. He'd slipped into Baghdad with a team of Polish intelligence officers and was developing his plan on the fly, right there under the noses of Saddam Hussein's security apparatus. Initially, he nearly despaired of finding a way to beat Iraqi surveillance. But finally, on October 25—two months after he had been approached by the CIA for help—Czempinski and his team, using false documents, were able to slip the Americans quietly out of Iraq before the Iraqis could find them.

Interior Minister Andrzej Milczanowski was greatly relieved by the success of the operation. He had taken a great personal risk in keeping it secret from his prime minister and gladly greeted the CIA officers with evident pride as they passed through Warsaw on their way home to the United States. Milczanowski's decision not to keep his bosses in the loop was easily forgotten in the elation in Warsaw over the dramatic impact the Iraq operation had on relations with the United States. Suddenly, debt relief negotiations were far more positive, and Poland was now seen in Washington as a partner and reliable ally. The operation came at a time when many leading officials in the Solidarity government were still wary of the intelligence agency and had voiced criticism over Milczanowski's willingness to keep so many of the old officers. It effectively ended the debate within the Polish government over the fate of the service, and afterward few of Czempinski's requests for resources were denied.

The American Consulate General, West Berlin, November 1990

The security officer at the American consulate in West Berlin wasn't sure who the man in the waiting room was or what he wanted, but he'd said something about the Soviet military, so he figured he should notify the CIA.

By the time a CIA officer arrived to question the man, the walk-in had walked out. Undeterred, the CIA case officer ran out onto the street to catch him before he got away and asked him to come back inside to talk. If this man really had something to say about the Soviet military, the CIA was interested. You could never have too many Soviet military agents.

Once he sat the man down and began the debrief, the CIA officer discovered that he was not in the Soviet military at all. He was instead an unusual messenger. The man owned a sandwich and snack truck that served Soviet military bases in East Germany, and he had befriended a number of Soviet officers and soldiers over the years. One high-ranking Army officer had decided he could trust the snack truck driver and asked him if he ever traveled to the West. When the driver said yes, the officer asked him to take a message to the Americans. "Tell them I want to provide them with information and volunteer my services."

The CIA officer arranged to meet the snack truck driver again, this time away from the consulate. By then he had a list of questions for the Soviet officer. He explained that the CIA might be interested in working with him, depending on his answers.

When the snack truck operator returned a week or two later with the answers to the initial vetting questions, the CIA snapped to attention. The new volunteer belonged to a front-line unit of the Western Group of Forces stationed at Schlottheim, southwest of Berlin. The battalion would be at the point of any Soviet thrust into the infamous Fulda Gap, the invasion route that had been war-gamed as the kickoff point for World War III for the last half century. It was a combat unit that would have been among the first to engage NATO if war had ever broken out between the United States and the Soviet Union on the plains of central Germany.

At this point, the CIA officer arranged to meet the volunteer in person and quietly cut the snack truck driver out of the equation. The volunteer turned out to be a colonel, the commander of a motorized rifle battalion, and he quickly pledged that he was ready to do anything he could to get out to the West. He said he was scheduled to be transferred back to the Soviet Union and that he was eager to make a break for America as soon as possible, along with his wife and two children. Not every Soviet officer was looking forward to going home.

The colonel was an appealing prospect, but he wasn't in this alone. He said that his battalion adjutant, a captain, was also part of his plot to defect, along with the captain's girlfriend, who was the regimental code clerk. The operation was expanding. Now we were going to have to plot out escape plans for six instead of just one. The colonel was given the cryptonym GTROSETTA and the captain GTSTONE, and we began to try to figure out the best way to exploit this intelligence break.

At their next meeting, the CIA case officer told the colonel that his value would be enhanced dramatically if he could bring some Soviet weapons with him when he defected. The colonel readily agreed to try and asked for a wish list.

The Pentagon regularly publishes a classified list of foreign weapons that it would like to obtain and examine to keep its equipment a step ahead of the competition. Near the top of its list was the Soviet SA-19 surface-to-air antiaircraft missile. At approximately fourteen feet long, the SA-19 wasn't exactly something that a man could carry on his back on his way across the border, but the CIA decided to ask GTROSETTA if he could get his hands on one anyway.

Yes, the colonel said, his unit was equipped with SA-19s, and yes, he could try to steal one and bring it with him.

"But when I get it to you, you will need a truck to carry it away."

Near Schlottheim, Eastern Germany, November 1990

The night before the colonel and his crew were planning to make their escape, David Rolph and the case officer in charge of handling the Soviet officer met the colonel in a parking lot along the old border between East and West Germany to go over last-minute arrangements. The colonel blanched when he saw the size of the van they'd brought to haul away the SA-19.

"You're going to need a bigger truck," he said in a deadpan voice.

Rolph turned to a young CIA officer from Frankfurt who had brought the van. "I don't care how you do it," he said, "but get a heavy, over-the-road truck and have it back here by noon tomorrow."

At exactly noon the next day, the CIA officer and a driver pulled in with a semi that they'd picked up at a U.S. Army depot in Frankfurt. The CIA men scouted out the secluded rendezvous points on the eastern side of the old border between East and West Germany—one on the outskirts of a village near the Soviet base where they would pick up the colonel's family, and another in the nearby woods where they'd meet up with the officers and their missile at about 6:00 that night. The colonel was counting on the Soviet soldier's rigid obedience to higher authority in order to pull off this crazy scheme. Late that afternoon, the colonel ordered a surprise muster of his entire battalion. Following orders, his soldiers assembled on the parade grounds near the base's front gate.

While his men were forming up, the colonel drove a large Soviet Army GAZ truck up to the regimental arms depot and walked in to see the supply clerks. With his regiment standing in formation on the other side of the base, the colonel waved a requisition form at the clerks and ordered them to load an SA-19 into the truck. Once the missile was on board, he gave them a list of a few other choice pieces of equipment to load as well. When they were finished, he bounded back behind the driver's wheel and took off.

With virtually all of the base's personnel now standing in formation near the front gate, the colonel gunned the truck engine and barreled to the back of the base, crashing through the perimeter fence and out into the farmland beyond.

It was already dark when his CIA case officer, waiting at the rendezvous point a few kilometers away from the base, began to hear a grinding engine and the crashing sounds of a truck bowling through the woods. Suddenly the truck pushed through the brush and came to a stop in the clearing, and the colonel jumped out, shouting for the CIA officers to hurry up.

"Bystro! Bystro!" he shouted. "Hurry!"

Moving as fast as they could, the three men helped the colonel transfer the crated SA-19 and other weapons into the Army truck and took off, leaving the Soviet truck abandoned in the woods. As they sped down the narrow road leading to the old border, they passed Rolph, who pulled in behind them with the colonel's wife and children and the captain and his girlfriend packed into his car.

After a hectic fifteen-minute race they were across the border, and the strange little convoy pulled over. The colonel got out, pulled off his Soviet Army greatcoat, threw it on the ground, and angrily stomped all over it in his Army boots. He then got back in the truck and they sped on, making only one more stop before arriving at a U.S. Army base near Frankfurt: dinner at McDonald's, for the kids.

The SA-19 was soon on its way to an American exploitation team, which would have time to devise countermeasures against the weapon before the first fighters were launched against Iraq a few months later.

Moscow was not amused. General Boris Snetkov, the commander in chief of the Western Group of Forces in East Germany, and three senior generals of the Western Group were all sacked thanks to ROSETTA and STONE.

Berlin, December 12, 1990

By December, MACRAME was running out of documents to photograph. He had taken great risk to help us, and we decided it was time to pull him out. Rolph waited in the Leipzig park to tell him, but for the first time in six months, the young pilot didn't show up. Rolph would have to go to the fallback plan.

Two days later, Rolph drove through a cold, rain-soaked night to the small village near the Soviet pilot's air base. He parked his car and then made his way through the empty lanes to the alternate meeting site, a cemetery on the outskirts of the village. He shivered as he tried to remain inconspicuous, but he knew he couldn't stay long. If someone passed by, he'd have a hard time explaining why he was standing in the rain in the village cemetery at 10:00 P.M. Maybe he's been compromised, Rolph thought. Maybe he's already been dragged back to Moscow. . . .

He was about to leave the cemetery when, in the distance, he saw someone riding a bicycle toward him through the rain. As he peered into the darkness, he realized the figure was too slight to be the pilot. He began to hurry away, back to his car and safety. But as he glanced at the bicyclist one last time, he just barely made out the figure of a woman. He stopped and stared again. It was the pilot's wife. She had bicycled the three kilometers from the air base in the cold rain and was freezing, her hair matted and her flimsy Russian coat soaked through. Rolph took her to his car and turned on the heater while she assured him that her husband was safe. His mother had died, and he'd returned to the Soviet Union for her funeral. His wife had remembered the backup meeting site and had slipped away from the base on her own, determined to make the meeting in her husband's place. As she sat shivering in his car, Rolph vowed to himself that once the pilot and his wife were safely in the United States, he'd make sure she got a decent winter coat.

With Germany reunified, it was no longer difficult for a Soviet Air Force officer based in what had been East Germany to travel to West Berlin. Before long, the MiG pilot and his family were heading to the United States on a C-5 that had stopped in Germany to pick them up on its way back from the Persian Gulf. Intrigued by the American aircraft, the Soviet fighter pilot sat in the cockpit with the pilots as they landed at Andrews Air Force Base outside Washington.

At headquarters, Rolph checked in with NROC—the National Resettlement Operations Center, the arm of the CIA that handles defector resettlement—to hand over his charges. But a harried NROC official tried to fend him off.

"We're stretched thin," he said. "We're getting too many Soviets. Can you stay with them for a while and get them settled?"

Rolph hadn't realized that the CIA was quite so overburdened with Soviet defectors. He'd planned to head straight back to Germany, but he agreed nonetheless and ferried the family to a safe house in Virginia. The Soviet fighter pilot had arrived in time to consult with the U.S. Air Force just as the war against Iraq was about to begin. He was soon helping the Air Force teach American fighter pilots headed for the Persian Gulf how to deal with Soviet-style air combat tactics. And Rolph stayed with the family long enough to take the pilot's wife to an American department store, where the CIA bought her a good winter coat.

Langley, February 13, 1991

Not long after the brief intensity of the Gulf War, I was asked by NROC to pay a visit to Sergei Papushin in his apartment in Maryland. It would be a shot in the arm for him to get some high-level attention, his handler told me. Papushin was still fighting a losing battle with alcohol, and maybe a meeting with me would help. I was paired up for the trip with Rod Carlson, long since retired but now back on contract to handle Soviet defectors, of which there were more than enough trickling in every month.

Papushin's apartment was spotless. He himself was neatly dressed and looked clean and sober—more like a young Mormon missionary, I thought, than a rummy burnout from the KGB. We had a good talk about his getting acclimated to life in America. He said he was working on a possible girlfriend, and I wished him luck. I left the meeting telling Carlson I thought Papushin might actually turn the corner, that he might make it.

I was dead wrong.

Two weeks later, one of his handlers went in to check on him and found the young KGB defector's body lying underneath his bed, an empty bourbon bottle on the floor beside him. We went on full alert—a defector who had warned that there was a mole inside the agency had just been found dead. We wanted an autopsy to make certain that Papushin had not been murdered.

The autopsy results were clear—he had died of alcohol poisoning. This was of his own doing. Papushin's body was flown back to Moscow for a quiet funeral. An old friend from the KGB who attended the funeral later said that his face was so swollen that he was almost unrecognizable. The only way he could tell it was his friend was from a familiar scar on his hand.

8

Tyson's Corner, Virginia, April 12, 1991

Aldrich Ames's return to CIA headquarters in the summer of 1989 after three years in Rome was filled with uncertainty. His tour in Rome had been rocky at best. Ames was about to become a father for the first time, a fact that would dramatically alter his relationship with Rosario, his demanding Colombian wife. At work, meanwhile, he was drifting through what was left of his career. He bounced from one desk job to another and had to wonder whether his career had stalled so badly because he was now suspected of being a spy.

But that wasn't the problem—what was holding him back was much more mundane. Ames had developed a reputation as a clever but uninspired midlevel CIA officer, a "terminal GS-14." He was a smooth writer and astute analyst of Soviet intelligence, but many inside the agency considered him lazy and arrogant, and that was a poisonous combination. He was one of those people who don't get fired but whom managers tend to pass around.

When he returned from Rome, Ames was first sent back to his home division—SE—but he was given a lackluster assignment in the Western European branch. In December, a month after the Berlin Wall fell, he was moved to the Czech desk, but he promptly went on vacation, traveling to Colombia just as the Velvet Revolution swept through Prague.

When he returned in January, he apologized to David Manners, the Prague chief, for having been absent just as Václav Havel and the dissidents were swept into power. What he didn't tell Manners was that he had met his KGB contacts during his Christmas holiday in Bogotá. Ames stayed on the Czech desk through the summer of 1990 but by October was moved out of the division to a job in the analytical branch of the counterintelligence center.

One of the sources of tension in his life during this period was the polygraph examination he knew he'd have to take sometime after his return from Rome. He'd passed his last polygraph test in 1986—one year after he began working for the KGB—and CIA officers were routinely reexamined every five years. He was able to delay the polygraph test for several months, but by April of 1991 he could no longer avoid it. As he prepared for the test, which was now scheduled for April 12, he knew he had a lot to conceal and had to give serious thought to how he could beat the machine.

As a longtime operations officer, Ames had experience in administering polygraphs and had a good sense of the limits of their capabilities. He had been on the other side of the tests and knew what the examiners looked for. He also knew that polygraph results consistently reflect the expectations of the technicians. So his ability to pass the polygraph would depend on whether he could establish a good rapport with the examiner.

Ames was doing fine on the test until he hit a snag on questions related to money. When the examiner came back to the issue, he figured out that there was a problem. He began to talk about his plans for a career after the CIA. "We discussed at considerable length my nascent plans to do some import-export business with friends in New York and Colombia," he later recalled. "They had been, and remained, merely plans, but it took a lot of discussion to assure the examiner that I had not yet violated and didn't intend to violate any regulations about preretirement business planning and activities." Clever misdirection had carried him through.

The examiner called a break for the day but said he wanted him to come back the next morning. Ames was concerned, but he'd studied the examiner's behavior and methods during the test, and he was convinced that the man was showing no signs of trying to conceal hostility.

The next day they continued the examination, and Ames added more details to his thoughts about a future business career. He cruised through the rest of the test.

He had a great sense of relief—so great that it surprised him a bit. He seemed to be nowhere near so calm in his heart as he thought he'd been in his mind.

Canterbury Park, Springfield, Virginia, April 15, 1991

Three days after Aldrich Ames faced off against the polygraph machine at Tyson's Corner, Robert Hanssen was a few miles away, scrambling to make an exchange with the KGB. At Doris, a dead drop site under a footbridge in Canterbury Park, Hanssen left a computer diskette—the twenty-second diskette filled with classified information that he had turned over to the KGB since 1985. It included details of an FBI recruitment operation that the KGB had previously asked him about.

The KGB left a package for Hanssen at Doris as well, one that included $10,000 and a note filled with Russian sentiment.

> Dear Friend:
>
> Time is flying. As a poet said:
>
> *What's our life*
> *If full of care*
> *You have no time*
> *To stop and stare?*
>
> You've managed to slow down the speed of your running life to send us a message. And we appreciate it.

The KGB then tasked Hanssen with a series of specific requests for information. Among other things, they wanted information on how the U.S. intelligence community was planning to respond to the political upheaval in the Soviet Union. The KGB was worried that the CIA was going to try to exploit the situation. And if they could prove that the CIA was becoming more active behind the scenes inside the Soviet Union, maybe they could use that information against the reformers in Moscow. Maybe Gorbachev could still be stopped before he destroyed what was left of the empire.

Langley, May 15, 1991

Richard Kerr was a levelheaded officer, and it was reassuring to see that someone like him could rise through the CIA ranks from line analyst to Deputy Director of Central Intelligence. I'd known Dick fairly well over the years, as he occupied a number of important jobs in the intelligence and administration directorates on his way to becoming the number two. I'd always found that when he spoke it was wise to listen, even if what he said seemed cloaked in humor. One time in a conversation with the new Pakistani prime minister, Benazir Bhutto, in Islamabad, Kerr had concluded his description of a particular facet of developments in Afghanistan by saying, "If it looks like a duck, and walks like a duck, and quacks like a duck, CIA will probably call it a duck." The Radcliffe-educated Bhutto got Kerr's point, but her note takers clearly had to scramble.

A conversation I'd had with Kerr summed up what seemed to be wrong with the direction the DO had instinctively taken as it pursued the Soviet target after 1989.

"All you guys do is take in each other's laundry, don't you?" Kerr said with his disarming smile. "You just go after KGB guys." And the truth was I had no answer to that. Kerr's message was punchy but clear—SE Division was stuck in another era. I agreed with him and began making adjustments to the way we were doing business.

Too much of the CIA's clandestine collection effort had too little relevance in the fast-moving new world. Landing a Soviet defector had been our bread and butter in the old days, but now we found ourselves simply in the resettlement game, with no real evidence that we were getting much of anything useful in return. I'd raised the issue a few times and asked if we should really be taking so many of these defectors, but Redmond and the old guard were convinced that the next KGB officer coming over the hill would bring the goods. Only it just wasn't working out that way. Not only were we not getting important counterintelligence from the stream of young KGB officers defecting to us, we were still coming up short on collecting crucial intelligence the NSC needed for the tricky endgame in the USSR. Getting that kind of intelligence was now our most pressing mission.

Redmond had been stunned early in 1991 when I refused to accept a low-level KGB officer into the CIA's defector resettlement program. Instead, I ordered that the KGB officer, with our help behind the scenes, apply for immigration through normal refugee channels. He did so and joined the growing flood of Soviet immigrants to the United States. If he'd had something important to tell us, I'd have had no trouble resettling him myself. But to Redmond and others in the SE Division, that decision was unforgivable. He thought I had gone soft on the Soviets.

I'd decided by now that Redmond was blinded by the minutiae of espionage and had no interest in the big picture. He didn't seem to want to acknowledge that the Berlin Wall had fallen for good and that the Soviet Union was on the verge of collapse.

During one heated discussion with Paul, I flared.

"Jesus, Redmond, you're becoming precisely like the people I came here to fight," I said, thinking of the paranoia of the KGB and of James Jesus Angleton. "You are becoming like our enemy."

Redmond was still consumed by the 1985 losses. I decided I had to move him out of the division, and the seventh floor agreed to assign him as the deputy in the counterintelligence center, where he could concentrate full-time on catching spies.

He'd be happy; I'd be happy.

The Kremlin, May 1991

The first ominous indicators of the showdown in the KGB that Colonel Valentin Aksilenko felt so certain was coming came in the spring of 1991.

First, early in the year KGB Chairman Kryuchkov created a new central entity for internal propaganda within the KGB. The new unit, described as an "analytical center," operated independently from the First and Second Chief Directorates and reported directly to the KGB Chairman at Lubyanka. Kryuchkov pulled Nikolai Sergeyevich Leonov away from his job of supervising KGB operations in North and South America and assigned him to head up the new propaganda center. Leonov's orders were clear enough: bring about a reversal of the growing and dangerous mood of liberalism and defeatism in the KGB.

Leonov decided to reach down into the core of the organization for a solution. He would rekindle the KGB's patriotic pride, finding in its historical roots the sense of meaning and energy the Chairman required to prepare the KGB for a last great battle—not for socialism, but for the survival of the Soviet Union.

Leonov, who as a KGB wunderkind in his thirties had become a close confidant of Fidel Castro in Cuba's revolutionary days, took to the job with a passion. Immediately, flyers and leaflets began to appear on KGB desks everywhere, all stoking the patriotic nationalism believed to lie deep in every Russian soul, even the souls of the cynical and urbane officers of the Committee for State Security. "Russian greatness" was the slogan—the flyers did not extol the virtues of Marxism so much as sound the alarm against dangerous conspiracies cloaked in the guise of change.

Leonov relentlessly advanced the proposition that America's goal was to destroy the Soviet Union. Countless mutations of this theme were woven into the anti-Western propaganda that emerged with great fanfare from his agency. It was all supposed to stir a patriotic response among the rank-and-file KGB.

Aksilenko concluded that it was, in the end, mostly bullshit. He and others at the KGB might have dismissed the propaganda as useless rhetoric had it not been accompanied by more troubling orders. In April, Kryuchkov demanded that all officers of the KGB once again be issued personal weapons, and ordered that they begin carrying them immediately.

Almost two decades earlier, Leonid Brezhnev had declared that class struggle within the USSR had come to a peaceful end and that socialism had been victorious. The Soviet Union no longer had internal enemies. Thus, the KGB was quietly disarmed. Its officers were told to turn in their service weapons. With the issuance of Makarov automatics and even Kalashnikovs to some, Kryuchkov was preparing the KGB for an as yet undefined last battle, Aksilenko concluded.

Kryuchkov was gearing up for a showdown, and he wanted his officers armed and ready to follow. What the KGB Chairman apparently didn't realize was that the order to rearm served only to harden the positions of the KGB officers who believed that change was the Soviet Union's only possible salvation.

Val Aksilenko, along with many other officers, quietly decided to retire from the KGB rather than be drawn into Kryuchkov's patriotic struggle.

Langley, May 1991

Aldrich Ames breezed by Dottie, my executive assistant, and marched right up to my desk.

"Milt, I've decided it's time to come back to SE. What I want to do is run cases. I want to come back and work in the 'back room' on your internal cases."

I was more than a little taken aback. Here was Ames, a man some put on a short list of officers who ought to be watched, coming in and almost demanding I take him back in the division after I'd just cleared him out. But what caught my attention as much as his demand was his transformation. The Aldrich Ames I'd met briefly before his departure for Rome in 1985 was a shoddy-looking guy with bad teeth. He had been replaced by a new Ames in a $1,500 sport-coat-and-slacks outfit, and the teeth that had been so hopelessly discolored had now been beautifully capped at what I guessed was a cost of around $1,000 a cap.

I told Ames I would get back to him. After he left, I went over to Redmond's office.

"Rick Ames just barged into my office and told me I'd better bring him back to the division now and put him in the back room working the sensitive cases. What do you make of that?"

Redmond, who was packing out and transferring to the counterintelligence center, had no flip answer this time. He just stared at me, taking in what I had said.

A few security questions over Ames's sudden show of wealth had been raised after his return from Rome. Redmond had followed the counterintelligence center search for the source of our 1985 problem, and he'd told me they had noticed that Ames had bought a $500,000 home in Arlington without taking out a mortgage.

Credit checks had been run on Ames, and a CIA officer was sent to Colombia to investigate whether his sudden wealth came from his wife's family in Bogotá, as Ames had told colleagues. The reports that came back showed that Ames's story seemed plausible. His finances looked to be okay, and his wife's family did appear to be wealthy.

In passing, Redmond had told me that there were a couple of other DO officers who had also bought expensive homes, but unlike Ames, each had taken out mortgages.

"You find my mortgage?" I asked Redmond.

"Haven't even looked . . . yet." Redmond didn't smile.

Ames came back later that summer for a study on the KGB, but he was never granted his wish to get back into the division's sensitive cases. A few months after that I moved him out again, this time to the counternarcotics center.

CIA Headquarters, July 1991

Paul Redmond had mixed feelings about being moved out of the SE Division to his new home in the counterintelligence center. Soviet operations were all he had ever done, and it was going to be hard for him to leave that part of his life behind. But most of all he was deeply bothered because he disagreed with the way the SE Division was now being managed—by me.

Redmond and other old-school Soviet hands were especially angry over my decisions to downgrade the SE Division's traditional bread and butter—the more or less unlimited recruitment operations against KGB officers around the world. Over the signatures of Dick Stolz and Tom Twetten, I had sent out cables aimed at the CIA's field stations in Africa and Latin America that had made it clear the SE Division was no longer interested in targeting every Soviet intelligence officer posted in every remote embassy in the Third World, particularly if the operation ended up inducing a defection. From now on, we'd look at the cases more carefully.

I saw the collapse of the Soviet empire as a moment that called for new ideas. On the one hand, we needed all the policy-relevant intelligence we could get, but on the other, we were beginning to find common ground with the Soviets on issues such as international terrorism, narcotics, and control of their arsenal of tens of thousands of nuclear warheads. We were making the first steps toward cooperation in these areas, and we needed to change the way we dealt with the Soviets.

This included easing back on the provocative pressures we had maintained on them for the last thirty years in literally every backwater capital in the Third World. In short, I thought that the USSR was going to become a more classical intelligence target now that we were having to deal with them directly on a number of important issues. It didn't make sense for the left hand to provoke them in one capital and the right hand to try to cajole them into helping out in another capital at the same moment. I was determined to introduce a little more finesse into the targeting equation.

I also decided that any new defectors had to earn their passage to the United States up front and issued the order to start screening Soviet defectors carefully before committing to resettlement in the United States. Over the previous two years, we had resettled more than a dozen defectors, each new one more or less like the previous one. I had been assured in each case that the most recent defector had been a "gold mine" of counterintelligence, but the claims never lived up to the hype. The reality was that KGB officers were becoming part of a massive flow of Soviet citizens trying to find a new life in the West and were turning to us for what they still believed was the old reliable CIA million-dollar sure thing. In the process, their growing numbers had become a costly liability, as each defector and his family would cost the U.S. taxpayers close to $1 million over the long haul.

Redmond and the other old SE hands considered my actions heresy. Generations of CIA officers had spent their careers trying to recruit the KGB and GRU officers stationed in Soviet embassies in the Third World. There was no doubt that some of the CIA's most productive spies had originally been recruited while they were working in remote embassies, but times were changing. Redmond feared that, once abandoned, it would be difficult for the CIA to reestablish its worldwide targeting mechanisms to recruit Soviet intelligence officers.

From his new post in the counterintelligence center, Redmond kept in close touch with old friends in the SE Division, and almost every day they complained bitterly to him about the direction I was taking the division. Redmond was frustrated that he was helpless to prevent me from overhauling the division—actions that he believed were tantamount to the dismantling of traditional Soviet operations. So he and Robert Wade, a senior FBI representative at the counterintelligence center who shared Redmond's views, decided to try to draw wider attention within the CIA to the dispute over the future direction of Soviet operations.

In July, they challenged me and the rest of the SE Division leadership to a debate. Redmond printed up flyers advertising a showdown and circulated them throughout the SE Division's offices.

"There appears to be a growing tendency in some quarters to establish a politically correct policy that the KGB is no longer an effective organization," the flyer read.

"With this tendency in mind, Paul Redmond, DC/CIC, and Robert Wade, FBI, challenge the senior management of the Soviet/East European Division to a debate. Resolved: 'The KGB Is No Longer a Threat to United States National Security.' The challengers, of course, will support the negative side. CIC/FBI will supply the vodka, SE will supply the Brie."

Counterintelligence may have had its point about the KGB still being able to run spies against us, but in the cosmic view I saw the KGB as one of the three pillars that propped up the Soviet Union as a whole—the Red Army, the Party, and the KGB. The Army had fallen on hard times, the Party was being torn apart, and the KGB, in my opinion, was no longer the element that would hold together the creaking empire. The threat from the KGB for the last forty years was always part of the whole, and that whole included the Red Army and the tens of thousands of nuclear warheads aimed at us. Whether or not it could penetrate the CIA or the FBI with spies was not really in doubt, but it was also not the most important part of the new equation. But I had no confidence that either Redmond or Bob Wade could discuss the matter outside their narrow counterintelligence world, so I flipped Redmond's challenge into a burn bag and went back to dealing with the final six months of Soviet history.

Langley, July 10, 1991

Not long after he'd vacated his office next to mine in SE, Redmond got an unexpected call on his STU-III secure phone in the counterintelligence center, where he was still settling in. A European station chief was on the line. He was calling to say that one of his case officers had picked up something about a KGB penetration of SE Division. It was a very detailed and sensitive report, and the station chief said he didn't want to put it in the normal cable traffic. So he had called Redmond personally.

Redmond told the station chief to send the case officer back to Washington, have him check into a hotel in the Virginia suburbs, and then have him call him directly. The case officer was to say he was "Bobby," who was passing through town. Redmond would come out to his hotel to meet him. The case officer was to stay away from CIA headquarters.

The station chief assured Redmond that the case officer would be in Washington by the next day.

Redmond came down the flight of stairs that separated our offices, walked in, and closed the door. "We've got something coming in. It might be what we've been looking for," he said. There was a deadly serious look on his face that told me he was on to something directly related to his passion—the search for the mole. Then he told me about the call from the European station chief.

"Oh, shit!" was about all I could muster.

I knew the case officer who had turned in the report. And I knew he couldn't be trusted. He had a track record that convinced me he played fast and loose with his intelligence reports. I'd already had to clean up after him on a couple of Eastern European operations, and I'd come to believe that he'd fabricated his reports on those operations. "Paul," I said, "I'd feel a hell of a lot better if this was coming from somebody else. This guy's got a real problem with the truth. His stuff always seems too good to be true. And guess what? It probably isn't."

I could see Redmond deflate just a bit when he heard my assessment of the case officer with the story. "I'll keep that in mind," he said. "And I'll be in touch as soon as I've met him."

As bad as I felt about shooting down Redmond's new lead, I felt pretty good about how we were getting on together. But for his challenge to a debate, we'd been able to put aside our differences and get on with the job. After he left, I thought that at least Redmond could now find satisfaction in his new job at the counterintelligence center, where he was in a position to focus full-time on the unsolved spy cases that had burdened him for so long. After moving to the center, he was shocked to learn that the investigation of the 1985 losses had been all but abandoned. Since he had always been on the possible list of suspects, he had been reluctant to ask many detailed questions about the progress of the investigation over the last few years. But now that he was deputy chief of the center, Redmond found to his dismay that Jeanne Vertefeuille and her small team had made virtually no progress. The probe that had been started back in 1986 by Gus Hathaway was now firmly relegated to the back burner inside the center. Gus Hathaway had retired, and no one else in the CIA's management was paying any attention to what Vertefeuille was doing. Redmond was determined to change that. He owed it to the agents who'd been executed.

Langley, July 12, 1991

Redmond checked in with me again a day later. He said he'd met with the case officer. It turned out that a KGB informant had told him about the penetration of SE. After their first extended conversation, Redmond asked the case officer to write down the details of what the KGB officer had told him. The next day, Redmond compared the case officer's new notes with his original report, which had finally been sent over from Europe.

When he looked at the two reports side by side, Redmond found that the case officer had included much more detail in the notes he'd written in his hotel the previous night than in his first report, written right after he'd met the KGB officer. What bothered Redmond most was that he'd added detailed answers to questions that Redmond had asked him in the hotel, and he'd attributed the new details to what the KGB officer had told him. He said his talk with Redmond had jogged his memory.

His claim was that the KGB had recruited an ethnic Russian CIA case officer who was working in the SE Division. Redmond wasn't sure he could believe the case officer's report, but he knew he had to follow the lead. And he didn't want to let the case officer know that he had doubts about the credibility of his report.

I was about to leave for Africa to meet with our stations there to explain the new Soviet targeting rules, and then I planned to transit Europe. I'd stop in on the station and have a little talk with the case officer myself to see if I could make sense of all this.

At a European Station, July 20, 1991

We were seated across from each other in an acoustic conference room, which was both secure and claustrophobic. The station chief had arranged for my meeting with the case officer on a ruse, saying that I'd been traveling when he'd come back to Washington to meet Redmond and needed a briefing on the sensitive case.

"I hear you've got a live one," I said.

"Yeah. I hope so," he said, his eyes never locking on mine.

"Tell me about it," I said.

"My KGB guy I'm working told me that he'd picked up something about a penetration of your division. He said there'd been a recruitment. An ethnic Russian."

"Did he have a name?" I asked, leaning forward to show my deep interest.

"No name," he said, "but he said he thought the guy's name began with the letter *K*." The man sitting across from me was still reluctant to make lasting eye contact, though he didn't seem otherwise overly nervous.

"Do you think the K is for his true name or his code name?" I asked.

"You know, I didn't even think to ask," he said, livening up a little. He then set off on a rambling but rich and informative yarn full of color and detail.

The trouble was, I'd heard his stories before. The CIA had never been able to catch him in an outright fabrication, but he'd come damn close one too many times. In one of those earlier cases, we'd tried to get him to let another case officer meet with his foreign agent to verify his information, but something always seemed to get in the way, and no one ever managed to meet him. Now, sitting across from him in the soundproof room, I decided that I still didn't trust him one bit.

When he had finished his long and elaborate story about the KGB penetration of SE Division, I kept quiet, saying nothing, but with what I hoped was a friendly if expectant look on my face. The painful silence lasted about half a minute, until he started telling more of the story. This time there were new details that he hadn't included in his original report or in his follow-up report to Redmond.

When I returned to Washington a week later, I met with Burton Gerber and his station chief at the Farm for a private talk about the case officer and his sensational reporting.

I made it clear that I thought he was making up the whole thing.

"Have you written it up?" Gerber asked, always one to focus on procedural protocol.

"Yes, I have."

"I haven't seen it," he said with a touch of irritation in his voice.

"It's a memo for the record right now," I said. "I haven't sent it forward. But I will now that we've talked."

"Now what?" came the third voice in the room, bringing our tense exchange to a merciful end. "You're saying that there's nothing there? That this guy's sitting on the curb and making this stuff up?" The station chief was incredulous.

"Yes," I said. "That about sums it up. But we're going to need more than my gut reaction to this guy. We need to talk to the KGB officer."

Gerber suggested using the former deputy in Moscow, whose pseudonym was KLETTERING. (The CIA makes an important, if little understood, distinction between a *pseudonym* and an *alias*. A CIA officer is assigned one *pseudonym* for use in internal agency cable traffic and usually keeps the same one throughout his or her career. CIA officers use their pseudonyms to sign cables sent back to headquarters and are sometimes even referred to by their pseudonyms in internal discussions. By contrast, CIA case officers use many *aliases* during operations in the field to mask their true identities. A case officer never uses a CIA pseudonym as one of his or her aliases.) KLETTERING had the expertise needed to talk to the KGB officer and figure out whether there was anything to the story we had been told.

In a European Capital, August 1, 1991

KLETTERING had a doctorate in Russian studies and was counted among a handful of the best operations officers in his generation at SE. He'd served as Mike Cline's deputy in Moscow and was now back at Langley handling our internal operations; but at the moment he was sitting on the verandah of a riverside restaurant in Europe, engaged in one of the more bizarre conversations of his career. It had taken him several days to arrange the meeting, but in the end he had succeeded. Across from him was a smooth, urbane Soviet intelligence officer, the source to which the case officer had attributed the counterintelligence yarn that had gotten Redmond so spun up, at least initially. KLETTERING had explained to him in detail the information he had supposedly passed on to us about a penetration of SE Division. The Soviet took it all in, registering deep interest. "There is, indeed, a serious problem," he said at last. "But it has very little to do with me. It has everything to do with your own officer. I have met this man, but I am saddened to say that everything he has told you is sheer fantasy. But excellent fantasy!"

The case officer had already been transferred back to Washington, and when he was confronted with a more hostile interrogation, both he and his story began to fall apart. But the case officer still scrambled to explain himself, never admitting that he had fabricated the whole story. In the end, the errant case officer decided he'd had enough with the CIA and simply resigned. It was another chapter closed in the search for the truth, and it had itself involved nothing but lies.

Like the alarm raised earlier by Sergei Papushin, the drunken defector who'd said he knew the CIA had been penetrated in Moscow, the case officer's story had been debunked. It was just the latest in a series of dead ends in the hunt for a solution to the 1985 losses over the past few years. Nothing had come of the mysterious case of "Mr. X," the anonymous volunteer in Germany who had warned earlier that the CIA's communications had been compromised, and nothing had come of our gambit to test those communications by conducting phony recruitment operations of KGB officers, including my effort in Nairobi. There was no sign that the KGB was reading our mail, since the Soviets never moved against the KGB officers we had set up in our cable traffic. The investigation was back to square one.

9

Moscow, August 1, 1991

It was still hard for David Rolph to comprehend. When he'd read the cable back in December notifying him that he was being reassigned as Moscow chief, he'd thought it was a joke. As chief of the small East Berlin operation, Rolph was only a GS-14 and too junior to be considered for the flagship field assignment in the Soviet Division. Moscow was a post that had always been reserved for a Senior Intelligence Service officer—the CIA equivalent of a general.

But his assignment was no joke. Rolph had responded well to the stern message he had received from Paul Redmond, and now he was being rewarded for the remarkable success of the Berlin cold-pitch campaign. Promoting Rolph to Moscow was part of my effort to revitalize SE Division with young blood. For Rolph, it was a dream come true.

Rolph knew that his promotion had irritated a number of more senior officers in the division who thought they deserved Moscow. But he was determined to prove them wrong. Still, he knew that Berlin would be a tough act to follow. "At least I'm going someplace that's stable," he'd joked at his good-bye party in Berlin in June.

But just beneath the surface, Moscow in the spring of 1991 was anything but stable. By now, Gorbachev was walking a tightrope between the reformers he had once empowered and the Communist hard-liners who were convinced he was responsible for the collapse of the old order in Eastern Europe and their own diminishing powers. The Soviet leader had long since lost control over the pace of change, and his perestroika campaign now seemed quaint and outmoded even to many of his supporters. He had calculated that if he slipped the knots with Eastern Europe, a weight would be lifted from the Soviet Union. And he was convinced that the chaos would stop at the Soviet border.

He was soon proved wrong. By 1991, powerful independence movements had sprung up in the three most western Soviet republics in the Baltics, finally forcing Moscow to crack down. In Lithuania, in January, fear made a fleeting comeback. In order to quash the growing independence movement, KGB and Soviet military units had moved into the capital of Vilnius in force, sending tanks against dissident crowds, killing fourteen protesters, and wounding many others as the military seized the city's main television tower. The Soviets had moved into Lithuania just as the world was focused on the Persian Gulf crisis, so the incident received relatively little attention in the West.

Yet Moscow's attempt to turn back the clock failed miserably. Soviet troops failed to curb the independence movement in Lithuania, and their violent assault backfired at home, prompting a bitter outcry in Moscow among Russians who had come to believe that the time for such ruthless actions had long since passed. Journalists resigned from the Communist Party, Soviet radio and television broadcast the attacks and aired the angry recriminations of citizens, and members of the Soviet legislature marched in the streets of Moscow. The Supreme Soviet demanded to know how many protesters had been killed in Vilnius—it called for an investigation and demanded answers.

Gorbachev was forced to distance himself from the military action, although few believed him. Shevardnadze had resigned as Foreign Minister in December 1990, warning darkly that a dictatorship was coming and telling those who would listen that the hard-liners were back in charge. Gorbachev had dismissed his old adviser's fears, but the truth was that he was so close to the hard-liners that he didn't recognize the contempt they had for him and his policies.

Now, even in remote areas of the Soviet Union, far from the volatile and impatient Baltics, new nationalist and democratic tides were surging in. In June, Boris Yeltsin became Russia's first popularly elected President, and the white, blue, and red flag of Russia began to appear at official functions. The emergence of an independent-minded Russian leader and government posed grave threats to Gorbachev and the Soviet order. By the time David Rolph arrived in Moscow, it was clear that something would have to give.

Langley had been watching the warning signs for months. A source inside the Soviet military in Germany had told the CIA six months earlier that volunteers were being sought among Soviet Army officers for some sort of contingency operation in Moscow. Marshal Dmitri Yazov, the Defense Minister, was reported to have ordered the Soviet Western Group of Forces based in Germany to form units of reliable troops prepared to do whatever was necessary to preserve the union. The CIA had not seen any evidence that volunteers had actually been sent back to the Soviet Union, but the threat that the Soviet military might be used to deal with civil unrest hung in the air throughout the spring and summer of 1991.

In June, Secretary of State James Baker passed on a specific warning to Soviet Foreign Minister Aleksandr Bessmertnykh that a coup was in the works, and he identified some of the key leaders of the plot. The information had originated with Moscow Mayor Gavril Popov, who had warned American ambassador Jack Matlock about the threat. When Gorbachev heard about the American warning, however, he dismissed it as fantasy.

By mid-August, though, it was becoming clear to the CIA's analysts that Gorbachev's decision to sign the All-Union Treaty that month could prompt the hard-liners to act. In the President's Daily Brief for August 17, the CIA warned President Bush that the scheduled treaty signing had created a deadline for the conservatives in Moscow. There was a strong chance that they would act within the next few days, before the treaty was signed.

Termez, Uzbekistan, August 6, 1991

Stepping out on Friendship Bridge was an eerie experience. I had spent three years assisting the men on the other side of the river in their fight against those on this side of the river, and now here I was looking across the bridge in what seemed like the wrong direction. With me was Jack Devine, who was now chief of the CIA's counternarcotics center, and the purpose of our visit to Central Asia was to talk with the Soviets about ways to cooperate on the international war on drugs. Devine had been chief of the Afghan Task Force when I first arrived in Islamabad, and we both found it strangely unsettling to stand on Friendship Bridge looking into Afghanistan with our KGB escorts.

We'd flown along the border between the Soviet Union and Afghanistan in a Soviet MI-8 helicopter, exactly the same chopper that the Afghan rebels had so frequently shot down with Stinger missiles that I'd helped supply them with during the war. As we flew low and slow along the north bank of the Amu Dar'ya, the pilot spoke into his intercom. Across from me, a KGB colonel became alert as he listened to his headset. Then he barked back a brief answer.

"What did he say?" I asked the colonel.

"He said to tell you that we are flying so low because the Afghan bandits across the river still have Stinger missiles. They are not supposed to work so well if you fly below three hundred meters. The pilot wanted me to tell you that."

"And what did you say to him?" I asked.

The colonel held my gaze for a couple of seconds, then answered. "I told him you already knew all about that," he said coldly.

Moscow, August 7, 1991

I was riding along in a rattling KGB Volga that smelled as if it had a leak in its fuel system. With me in the backseat was Rem Krassilnikov, who despite the changes and upheavals in Moscow over the last twenty-four months was still chief of the First Department of the Second Chief Directorate. His perch, as far as he was concerned, was unchanged and secure. For the last twenty minutes I had been watching the street pattern around us, and I thought I had detected surveillance teams following us.

"Rem, do you think it's possible that your boys are following us around town?"

Krassilnikov glanced at me quizzically. "No," he said, "that would not be possible." His answer was definitive. One just did not argue with Rem Krassilnikov on his turf.

But as we drove on, Krassilnikov began to look more carefully at the rhythm of the street. About two minutes later he said, "Perhaps it is, Milton." He stared at a beige Zhiguli beside us. "Yes, it is possible." He looked puzzled for a minute, then recovered without commenting further on the oddity of having KGB surveillance units trailing the guest of a KGB general in his own car.

It was early August, and we had spent several days in Moscow trying to find areas where the CIA and the KGB could work together. The drug war and the spread of weapons of mass destruction were two seemingly fruitful options. Poppy cultivation in Afghanistan and the republics of Soviet Central Asia meant the region was a leading source of heroin, and the Soviets had a growing drug problem in their cities. Meanwhile, the breakup of the Soviet empire in Eastern Europe was creating new fears in Washington about the security of nuclear, chemical, and biological weapons. We approached these topics with our KGB counterparts in the abstract, discussing them as looming problems but never tracing their origins to the breakup of the old order.

We met in a KGB safe house in a residential section of Moscow not far from Communist Party headquarters. The house had once been used by Lavrenti Beria, Stalin's ruthless and perverse henchman and intelligence chief. We held our meetings on the second floor, and during the breaks I was able to look around. I came upon a very large tiled bathroom with ancient fixtures and, inexplicably, a gynecologist's examination table, complete with stirrups. I could only imagine what amusements Beria had found in that room.

While in Moscow, I had a chance to glimpse anecdotal evidence of the diminished power of the KGB in Soviet society. My traveling companions and I, accompanied by a lively KGB colonel by the name of Kuzmin, attempted to get into the Kremlin courtyard to view the czar's cannon. We were stopped at the entrance by a guard, who with great aplomb pointed to his watch and told us we had come too late. The courtyard had closed three minutes earlier. Kuzmin tried to sweet-talk the guard, saying we were an important American delegation, but the man would have none of it. Finally, Kuzmin winked at me and said, "Watch this."

With practiced flair, he whipped out his red KGB identity book, flipped it open, and eased it in front of the guard's eyes. "Committee for State Security," Kuzmin said. "Now please let us through."

The guard took the identity book, looked at it carefully, then folded it shut and handed it back to the KGB colonel. "I don't care if you're Vladimir Kryuchkov," he said. "You're not getting in here after closing time." With those words he wheeled around and walked away. End of discussion. I would have to wait until my next visit to get a good look at the czar's cannon, though watching the look of surprise on Colonel Kuzmin's face had been a worthy trade-off.

We left the Soviet Union on the morning of August 8. Although we could see that the Soviet system was under great stress, we saw nothing to alert us to what would follow only ten days later. The fact that we had been invited to Moscow by the KGB at that precise time would later convince me that our hosts had no inkling of what was coming either.

Langley, August 12, 1991

As Soviet intelligence officers continued to volunteer to the CIA in growing numbers, there came the inevitable requests for the means to commit suicide to avoid arrest and interrogation. One such request had crossed my desk, and now I found myself sitting across the conference table from the chief chemist in Technical Services, who was explaining in more detail than one might ever want to know the inner workings of the L-pill, euphemistically called "special preparations."

He explained that cyanide was hands down the historically preferred means of exit. It was reliable, and it was quick—most of the dead in Hitler's bunker had bitten down on the glass-encased cyanide capsules. The downside was that it took a large pill to hold a lethal dose, something that might not be easy for a spy to conceal in an everyday object he could carry about without attracting attention. There were other options nowadays in more discreet preparations, but they generally took longer to take effect, which could be quite inconvenient! If concealment size was not an issue, it was always best to go with the cyanide, because it was neat and quick.

The chemist had a couple of demonstrator L-pills with him, inert gas capsules concealed in small trinkets. All you had to do was bite down on the concealment, break the capsule, and take a couple of deep breaths. It would be over in a matter of seconds. He slid one across the table to me. "Want to try it?" he asked, deadly serious.

I picked up one of the concealment devices and felt its weight. "You're sure this is a practice one?" I asked.

"Sure it is. . . . No, wait a minute . . . I think it's . . ." The chemist smiled for the first time as I dropped the device back on the table pretty quickly.

I had asked for this meeting so that I'd be able to provide a detailed justification to Bill Webster when I hand-carried the memo requesting L-pills to him for his authorizing signature. Judge Webster was a cautious, thoughtful man, and I had voiced my concern to Dick Stolz, who thought Webster's only problem with this would be the usual revulsion toward the concept, plus a recognition of the need for safeguards. He'd want to know that the special preparations were not being requested frivolously or for the purpose of killing another person. Stolz was in an expansive mood and told me the story of how he'd authorized the L-pill for TRIGON. In those less complicated days, he'd signed the authorizing memorandum himself to keep the DCI out of the process—to protect him.

Those days were long past, Stolz said wistfully. Take it to the judge and tell him what he needs to know.

A week later, I presented the memo to Bill Webster. He asked me if we had denied the Soviet agent's request the requisite three times. I told him yes, we had. Can the man use the device on another person? he asked. I assured him that anything was possible, but that the delivery system did not easily lend itself to murder. Without hesitation, and without further question, Judge Webster signed the memo.

Foros, Crimea, Sunday, August 18, 1991

Mikhail Gorbachev was ready to wrap up his vacation at the picturesque resort town of Foros on the Crimean coast of the Black Sea, where he'd gone for his August break and a much needed rest with his wife, and return to the political intrigue of Moscow. Despite his earlier misgivings, he was planning to sign the All-Union Treaty as soon as he returned to the capital. The treaty represented a historic devolution of power from the Soviet central government to Russia and the other republics. Despite his agreement to sign the treaty, Gorbachev knew that he had not yet developed a clear political accommodation with Russia's new President, Boris Yeltsin. The pugnacious former Party boss from Sverdlovsk clearly had political momentum behind him, thanks to his sweeping victory in Russia's June elections, but Gorbachev still controlled the national security apparatus of the Soviet Union, so the battle for political dominance between the Soviet Union and the republics remained unresolved.

Gorbachev's vacation was shattered just before 5:00 P.M. on August 18, a quiet Sunday afternoon, when surprise visitors arrived from Moscow. The delegation included Oleg Baklanov, head of the Soviet Union's Military Industrial Commission; General Valentin Varennikov, chief of Soviet Ground Forces; Oleg Shenin, a Central Committee and Politburo apparatchik; and Valery Boldin, Gorbachev's own chief of staff. They were backed up by Yuri Plekhanov, chief of the KGB's Ninth Chief Directorate, in charge of the security of the Soviet leadership.

Gorbachev's unexpected visitors told him that they were

representatives of an emergency committee that had taken control of the Soviet government. Just as they arrived, the phone lines into the vacation compound went dead, including the communications link that allowed the Soviet leader to command his country's nuclear forces. Gorbachev was now cut off from the outside world.

It soon became apparent that the delegation that had traveled to Foros was actually made up of backbenchers. The real driving force behind the coup was KGB Chief Vladimir Kryuchkov, whom Gorbachev had disastrously considered an ally.

Gorbachev angrily rejected the delegation's request that he endorse the emergency committee and join their effort to turn back the clock. Early Monday morning, Soviet television and radio announced the creation of a new emergency committee, which claimed that it had acted in part because Gorbachev was suddenly ill. Gorbachev, along with his family and a few close aides, remained isolated at Foros, uncertain whether they were to be executed, sharing the fate of the Romanovs at the beginning of the Soviet experiment.

Moscow, 0700 Hours, Monday, August 19, 1991

Dave Rolph's drive into work at the U.S. embassy from his southern Moscow apartment seemed no different from any other early Monday morning commute. As he guided his BMW through Moscow's streets, he saw nothing that would alert him to the events that were already under way. He had gone to sleep early the night before and hadn't listened to the news before leaving for the office. As far as he was concerned, it was just another sultry August morning in the Soviet capital.

Walking into the office at 7:00 A.M., he ran into other embassy officials who told him that some kind of an emergency had just been announced on the radio and that there were reports that the military had been called into Moscow. That's how the CIA's Moscow station chief found out about the coup that changed the twentieth century. The CIA simply did not have any assets inside the Kremlin who were in a position to give the Americans detailed and timely information about when or where a coup might take place. So when David Rolph walked into the embassy Monday morning, he did not realize that the coup had actually been under way since the day before, did not know that Mikhail Gorbachev and his family had been surrounded and cut off from all communications.

But Rolph moved quickly to catch up and scrambled his case officers out onto the streets; it was still the middle of the night in Washington, so he could wait until about noon to have his first cable waiting on the desks of senior CIA officials when they arrived at work. Rolph realized that he would once again be in a race with CNN, just as he had been in Berlin. He was, in fact, already playing catch-up with the media. At 11:30 Sunday night in Washington, National Security Adviser Brent Scowcroft learned from CNN reports that a coup might be in the works in Moscow.

As Rolph began to hear back from the case officers fanned out across the city, something quite remarkable was becoming clear. There were no roadblocks, no checkpoints established to restrict movement around the city. In fact, after driving out to Moscow's Sheremetyevo Airport, one officer reported that not only was the road to the airport open, but the airport itself had not been closed down. Meanwhile, the television and radio stations didn't appear to have been commandeered by the leaders of the coup, at least not effectively. They were still reporting on what was going on. There were Army units in the streets, mostly armored units with tanks and armored personnel carriers, but they didn't seem to be taking any action.

As the morning wore on, a question formed in Dave Rolph's head: What the hell kind of a coup is this?

After dashing off his first cables, Rolph picked up a phone and dialed a number at Lubyanka.

"May I speak with Gavrilov?" he asked the anonymous KGB officer who answered his call. When he heard the smooth and familiar voice of Rem Krassilnikov, Rolph didn't mince words. "How soon can we meet?"

First Chief Directorate Headquarters, Yasenevo,
0900 Hours, Monday, August 19, 1991

Leonid Shebarshin saw it all coming together now. As he sat in his corner office in the First Chief Directorate's leadership suite, reading the announcement of the new "emergency committee," he had a sense of foreboding. All through the summer he had picked up murmurings that something was brewing, some bold move would make things right again, and he had studiously avoided getting drawn in. He knew enough to know he didn't want to know more.

It had begun in June, when Yeltsin won the presidential elections in Russia. At that moment it was clear to Shebarshin that the die was cast for the Soviet Union. The idea of the putsch now unfolding had begun even before Yeltsin's victory, and he had picked up on it then. But his personal decision to distance himself from such an ill-fated enterprise had been easy. Now, looking down at the text of the emergency committee's announcement, he saw that there was not a single new idea in it—it was a hodgepodge of fuzzy ideas about going back to the way things were. Shebarshin thought it would fail. And he suspected that the costs of that failure would be high.

Moscow, 1200 Hours, August 19, 1991

As tanks from the Taman Guards Division and other units lined the streets of Moscow, Rolph drove out of the American embassy compound. He headed north along the Garden Ring Road and then parked just off Mayakovskaya Square. He walked to a black Volga parked nearby and slid into the backseat next to the white-haired Krassilnikov. As he got in, the KGB driver quietly opened his door, got out, and walked across the square for a cigarette, leaving Rolph and Krassilnikov alone. On the first full day of the coup, the CIA and the KGB had a lot to talk about.

Rolph tried to probe Krassilnikov to find out what he knew about the situation, particularly about the KGB's role in the putsch.

Krassilnikov responded defensively, arguing that the actions of the emergency committee were lawful and constitutional. Gorbachev was sick and unable to act, Krassilnikov insisted, but the Supreme Soviet would soon meet to review the actions of the emergency committee to make sure they complied with the law. Without providing any real information about the KGB's involvement, Krassilnikov sounded a tone of support. It is a mistake for Yeltsin to defy the emergency committee, Krassilnikov said. But if Yeltsin wants a confrontation, the KGB general added in a slightly menacing tone, he's going to get one.

Krassilnikov stressed that there was no reason why the coup should harm relations between the KGB and the CIA, which had been improving in recent months. The SE chief and a delegation of senior officers had just been to Moscow to meet with the KGB, and now a meeting between the two agencies was scheduled for October in Helsinki, Krassilnikov reminded Rolph. He insisted that the Helsinki meeting go on as planned. After all, the coup was purely an internal matter, he noted dryly.

While the aging spymaster hadn't shed much light on the degree of KGB complicity in the coup, he had certainly made clear his own position of support. As Rolph stepped out of the Volga and headed back to the office, he toyed with a difficult but essential question: Was Krassilnikov speaking for himself or for the entire officer corps of the KGB?

Rolph sat in his office that night firing cables back to Langley as thousands of Russians stood vigil outside the White House, guarding the man they now viewed as their salvation—Boris Yeltsin. There was still no sign that the plotters were prepared to wade through the crowds and their handmade barricades and move against Yeltsin. And every hour they waited gave the democrats more time to gain strength and confidence. While Yeltsin and his band of Russian reformers stood at the ramparts, Mikhail Gorbachev, still trapped and isolated in his villa on the Black Sea, was rapidly becoming irrelevant.

Lewinsville Park, McLean, Virginia, Monday, August 19, 1991

While the CIA was scrambling to try to make sense of the crisis unfolding in Moscow, the KGB was conducting a secret operation just a few miles from CIA headquarters.

Robert Hanssen made his way on August 19 to a dead drop site code-named FLO, which was the space underneath a footbridge on the wooded edge of Lewinsville Park, a few steps from a residential street in the upscale suburb of McLean. That Hanssen and his KGB handlers were willing to carry out an exchange almost in the shadow of CIA headquarters also revealed the level of confidence they had in their ability to counter American counterintelligence efforts at the time. Of course, Hanssen had over the years helped the KGB learn how to defeat FBI surveillance, since he had betrayed many of the techniques the FBI used to monitor the Soviets.

In fact, at the FLO dead drop that day, Hanssen left a package that contained a new FBI memorandum about the methods the bureau was using to conduct surveillance of a particular Soviet intelligence officer. In addition to other classified documents crammed onto a computer diskette, Hanssen included an essay that he had crafted for the private benefit of his Soviet handlers.

Given the political instability that the Soviet Union was experiencing, he suggested that the KGB review the history of Chicago. In particular, he wrote that the Soviets could benefit from a thorough study of Chicago's legendary mayor Richard J. Daley and how he had used an iron fist and a well-oiled political machine to turn Chicago into the "city that works." Maybe the Soviets needed a little infusion of Chicago-style politics to regain order and stability.

In October, the KGB responded with thanks to "B," marveling that the "magical history tour" to Chicago was mysteriously well timed.

"Have you ever thought of foretelling the things?" they wrote. "After your rctircmcnt, for instance, in some sort of your own cristall ball and intelligence agency (CBIA)? There are always so many people in this world eager to get a glimpse of the future."

Cairo, 2000 Hours, Monday, August 19, 1991

I had just arrived in Cairo from Tel Aviv for a series of meetings. The telephone was ringing as I stepped into my hotel room.

"Milt? Bill Piekney." Piekney was now chief in Cairo. "It looks like things have come unstuck in Moscow," he said. "A gang of the old guard have seized power from Gorbachev. I'm sending an officer with a reading file and have already booked you on the next plane to Washington if you want to head back tonight."

"Oh, shit," I said, flipping to CNN.

Two hours later I was on a flight to Washington.

10

Langley, 0800 Hours, Tuesday, August 20, 1991

There was a buzz of excitement in SE Division and throughout the Directorate of Operations when I arrived home from Cairo the next morning. Some of the old guard felt a delicious sense of vindication, particularly those I had moved out of the division. They had been right—and I had been wrong. So much for Bearden's ideas of historic change in the Soviet Union. And so much for his notions about overhauling the division to adapt to the new realities. Happy days were here again!

"You're fucked, chief," O'Reilly said as I passed his office.

I turned back and slumped into a chair across from his desk. I picked up his Buddhist prayer wheel and began to twirl it. "Tell me about it," I said.

"There were whispers all yesterday," O'Reilly said. "Bearden furled his colors too soon, they said. Some of them were pretty happy about it."

"What do you think?" I asked.

"They're wrong," he said, handing me a stack of cable traffic. "Look at this stuff, and you'll see the ones who're really fucked are Kryuchkov and his gang."

By the afternoon of August 20, the heady feelings of vindication had dissolved. As the intelligence and overt reporting flowed in, the coup appeared to be bogged down and was looking more and more like a slapdash affair. Something was definitely going wrong.

The intelligence on the specially screened cadre of volunteers in the Red Army's Western Group of Forces in Germany bore out that assessment. The Army volunteers had been handpicked months earlier for possible action, and now we learned that though they had been alerted, they were still sitting in their barracks as confused as the rest of the world. Stand by, they had been ordered. A little later, almost as an afterthought, they were told that instead of leaving immediately, they might be asked on short notice to report to their assigned train stations. After waiting for orders that never came, most of the personnel simply went back into the routine of spreading rumors like everybody else.

Moscow, 0900 Hours, Wednesday, August 21, 1991

Like the Red Army volunteers in Germany, Leonid Shebarshin had been sitting by the telephone since Monday, waiting for orders to act that had never come. Early on Monday morning, KGB Chairman Vladimir Kryuchkov had called him and asked him to put all of his directorate's resources at the disposal of the emergency committee. Shebarshin had agreed and had then ordered the nation's foreign intelligence service to begin spying on Moscow.

Over the course of the rest of that day, he had passed on reports from his officers to Kryuchkov. Shebarshin had also agreed to order the First Chief Directorate's paramilitary team to gather at the KGB's central club in downtown Moscow. Kryuchkov, a former chief of the First Directorate himself, wanted a loyal unit in place when the time came to storm the White House and crush the ragtag forces now protecting the defiant Boris Yeltsin. But since that initial flurry of activity on Monday, Shebarshin had done little but wait patiently through an odd silence. Kryuchkov never called back.

That silence was the best evidence Shebarshin had that something was very wrong. Shebarshin was a man of the KGB, and if Kryuchkov had told him to send in the paramilitary unit on Monday, he would have followed the Chairman's orders. But obedience had its limits. By Wednesday morning, it was clear to him that the coup was collapsing into a farce; and he told himself that if Kryuchkov called him into action now, he would not obey the chairman's orders.

So he called the commanding officer of the paramilitary unit still standing by at the KGB club and told him not to accept any orders from anyone except himself. And he had decided that he wasn't going to be issuing any orders. It had become obvious to Shebarshin that Kryuchkov and his cohorts had suffered from a fatal lack of will.

Across Moscow, other military, intelligence, and political leaders were all coming to the same conclusion. The plotters had lacked the conviction to follow up their drunken grab for power with an immediate show of ruthless action and instead had bumbled at every turn. Men like Leonid Shebarshin—the people in the upper tiers of the bureaucracy who really controlled the levers of power in the Soviet system—calculated the odds and in the end simply stopped returning calls.

Moscow, 1200 Hours, Wednesday, August 21, 1991

As he slid into the backseat of the black Volga for another meeting with Rem Krassilnikov, David Rolph saw that the KGB general looked exhausted and disheveled, as if he hadn't slept since the coup began. The confidence and bravado that Krassilnikov had displayed in their meeting on Monday was gone, replaced by a more tentative attitude toward the crisis that was now moving to its whimpering conclusion. This time it was Rolph who had a message to deliver from the CIA to the KGB.

The Helsinki meeting, planned for October, was being postponed, Rolph told Krassilnikov. So was a proposed visit by a KGB delegation to the United States. The CIA was sending a message to the KGB—the new relationship between the two intelligence services, which had seemed so promising just a few weeks earlier, was being put on hold. With Kryuchkov's coup failing, the KGB that he led was now on the wrong side of history. The CIA was looking to the new leaders of Russia.

Langley, 1900 Hours, Wednesday, August 21, 1991

By Wednesday, we'd concluded that the coup was in serious trouble and chances were it would fail. That analysis was carried by Deputy National Security Adviser Robert Gates to President Bush's vacation headquarters in Kennebunkport, Maine.

The CIA assessment was based on the continued lack of signs that the coup plotters were actually in control. None of the usual indicators were being picked up—there were no widespread arrests, no communications blackouts, and telephone and fax traffic between university students in the United States and the Soviet Union were operating and were full of defiance.

By the end of the day, the President would observe on national television that sometimes coups failed, making the United States the first among the Western allies to suggest that perhaps the clock couldn't be turned back in the USSR by a handful of old guard plotters. The President's observation was then flashed across the world by CNN to Moscow, where the men who ran the USSR sat transfixed by the television coverage.

First Chief Directorate Headquarters, Yasenevo, 0630 Hours, Thursday, August 22, 1991

To Leonid Shebarshin, it seemed the slide down the slippery slope had accelerated. The emergency committee was in free fall. Gorbachev's return from the Crimea in the early hours of the morning had been a dreamlike affair. The President was greeted at Vnukovo-2 airport, but not by the usual crowd. There were no Politburo members, no Vice President or members of the presidential council. Members of the KGB's Ninth Directorate bodyguards were lost in the colorful sea of men in uniforms and in civilian clothes, all armed with automatics and pistols. The crowd was animated, maybe even a little drunk.

Descending the steps from his plane, Gorbachev waved to those greeting him, his manner friendly but lethargic. His smile was uncertain—maybe he was tired, or maybe guilty, Shebarshin didn't know which. The huge armored presidential

Zil limo wheeled up to the aircraft stairs, and its heavy door swung open.

"Whose car is this?" the President demanded unexpectedly. "The Ninth's?"

Upon hearing the response—"Yes, Mikhail Sergeyevich, the Ninth's"—Gorbachev gestured, as if to brush away the Zil and his Ninth Directorate KGB bodyguards. He declared, "I will not go with the Ninth!"

Most of the onlookers could not have known that the head of the Ninth Directorate, Yuri Plekhanov, had been one of the members of the emergency committee delegation that had placed Gorbachev under house arrest in Foros or that Plekanov himself was now under arrest.

The crowd of greeters reacted approvingly. The guards, their composure still intact, immediately brought in a Volga, and the President slid into the rear seat of the ordinary sedan as the disorganized, confused cortege, with a wail of sirens and flashing red and blue lights, sped off in the direction of the Kremlin.

At that same moment, but on a different road, KGB Chairman Vladimir Kryuchkov, Oleg Baklanov, the head of the Soviet Union's Military Industrial Commission, and Defense Minister Dmitri Yazov—Gorbachev's closest colleagues until their arrest on the tarmac by Moscow prosecutors—were being driven away for interrogation.

Shebarshin reflected on the irony of Gorbachev's statement on arrival that, having returned to Moscow, he seemed to have come home to a different country. It may have been sincere, he decided. These were strange and unusual times.

Langley, 2330 Hours, Wednesday, August 21, 1991

There was no longer any doubt that the old guard in Moscow had failed. The old guard in Langley had retreated into a corresponding silence. Closing up late that evening, I began to plan a strategy to deal with the even more rapid change brought about by the cataclysmic failure of the Moscow hard-liners.

I had relayed to Rolph an order from the seventh floor to tell Krassilnikov that all cooperation with the KGB was suspended until the situation had clarified and a new leadership surfaced. There was nothing to lose by playing it cool with the KGB over the next week or so. On the contrary, now was the time to see if there were any new openings at Lubyanka we might be able to exploit.

I also began planning a return visit to Moscow as soon as the dust cleared.

I continued to work in a split-screen world, keeping one eye on the satellite feed from Moscow and the other on the official reporting. It was all pointing to the same conclusion. Even the race to reach Gorbachev in Foros by the old guard led by Vladimir Kryuchkov in one plane and the Russian group in a second plane led by Boris Yeltsin's Vice President, Aleksandr Rutskoi, had been slapstick comedy.

But as I read the reports of Gorbachev's departure from Foros with Rutskoi, as Kryuchkov and the other plotters stood under guard in the rear of the plane, I focused for the first time on the photographs and biographical sketch of Yeltsin's Vice President that came with the report. Aleksandr Rutskoi, a much decorated fighter pilot and Afghan War veteran, had been shot down in eastern Afghanistan in August 1988, the report said. He'd been a colonel at the time and later made his way to safety with the help of the "competent organs"—the euphemism for the KGB. After the Afghan War, Rutskoi had swapped his Air Force wings for the rough-and-tumble of Russian politics, aligning himself with Boris Yeltsin.

History was wonderful! I thought as it all came together. Rutskoi was the Soviet colonel who'd been captured in Paktia Province in Afghanistan in the last year of the war. He was the colonel who'd been released after I'd paid the prescribed ransom of Toyotas and rocket launchers.

I began to enjoy the final days of the August coup even more and hoped one day to sit down with Rutskoi to talk over old times.

Moscow, 0700 Hours, Thursday, August 22, 1991

For a fleeting moment, Leonid Shebarshin thought himself lucky for having avoided either joining in the conspiracy against Gorbachev or playing a role in its suppression. But then he thought of Pascal's dictum: Don't call a man lucky while he's still alive; in the best of cases things are just going his way.

Luck aside, Shebarshin had dodged both bullets. Now all he had to do was deal with the aftermath—the hypocrisy and denial he knew was coming. Arriving at Yasenevo early, he found the few officers already at work excited and alert the morning Gorbachev returned to Moscow. They studied him closely, and he felt himself unconsciously assuming a brave, businesslike attitude, cheerfully greeting the guards and the others he met as he entered the First Chief Directorate compound. Shebarshin was relieved that there were few seniors around at the early hour.

The newspapers were delayed, but there was no shortage of sensational coverage by the broadcast media. Shebarshin reviewed the world reaction to events in Moscow. Foreign capitals uniformly welcomed the great victory of democracy, he thought wryly. German Chancellor Helmut Kohl declared that the defeat of the putsch would open a new chapter in the history of Russia and the Soviet Union. British Prime Minister John Major announced the renewal of British aid to the USSR, which had been frozen in conjunction with the coup attempt. France's foreign minister, Roland Dumas, proposed that the European Community invite Gorbachev for a joint discussion of the future of the Soviet Union in Europe. NATO Secretary General Manfred Woerner declared that the leadership of the Soviet Union had now attained greater stability and democracy.

Moscow simmers and democracy celebrates, Shebarshin said to himself. Those who didn't have time to do so yesterday were rushing today to separate themselves from the plotters and align themselves with the ranks of the victors. The time had come to betray yesterday's friends and find witnesses to one's loyalty to the new regime. Gorbachev now appeared before the world and the people of the USSR as an innocent victim of the coup, a person betrayed by those he'd trusted.

But Gorbachev hadn't even had time to recover from his long flight from the Crimea when the first whispers were heard that the President might not have been simply a helpless, captive witness to what was happening. Perhaps he had found himself in a complex situation, one that begged a complex solution. Perhaps he was a little lucky after all to have dodged the bullets, Shebarshin concluded with deep irony. There was more play left in the game.

Later, rifling through his safe, Shebarshin put all registered documents on one side—they should be given to his assistants. Records of Kryuchkov's orders, drafts, and rough notes came next. They should all go immediately into the incinerator. But some documents—for instance, an anonymous paper sourced to one of the new "democrats," which reported in detail on Russian President Boris Yeltsin—could not, he decided, be entrusted to anyone. Shebarshin tore the document himself into small pieces and flushed them down the toilet.

When he finished, Shebarshin checked his safe again and decided that should any new authority become interested in the contents of the safe of the chief of the First Chief Directorate, the man propelled into the KGB's top ranks by Vladimir Kryuchkov, they would find a box with personal documents and a pistol with sixteen rounds. Nothing more.

The pistol was carefully cleaned and oiled, the clip inserted, but no round chambered. The Makarov, Shebarshin thought as he looked at his service automatic, is a simple, dependable item whose mass fits nicely into the palm of one's hand. The lead content of a single round of ammunition was the equivalent of a person's life, any life, whether worthy or pitiful.

After he had finished reordering his safe, he heard the old Vietnamese clock outside his door strike nine, and as if on cue, the duty officer appeared. Everything was in order, the officer reported, there were no incidents, either in Moscow or abroad. The foreign intelligence service had hunkered down again.

First Chief Directorate Headquarters, Yasenevo, 0900 Hours, Thursday, August 22, 1991

The leadership telephone on the table by his desk rang insistently. Shebarshin lifted the receiver cautiously, knowing the system was limited to some thirty top officials in the USSR, including the head of the First Directorate. He wondered who might be at the other end.

A woman's voice came across the line. "Leonid Vladimirovich? This is the office of Gorbachev. Mikhail Sergeyevich asks that you be at this office at twelve o'clock."

Hesitant, Shebarshin asked a question that might not have been necessary a week earlier: "Where is that?"

The woman, without any hint of surprise, said politely, "Third floor, the Council of Ministers Building in the Kremlin. The Walnut Room."

"Fine, I'll be there," Shebarshin said, and then hung up, thinking there must have been some new turn of events.

Shebarshin decided to move from Yasenevo to Lubyanka in order to be closer to the Kremlin, so as not to be late for his appointment with Gorbachev. As he was driven into central Moscow, he found the city completely calm, no crowds, no flags, no excited faces in the streets. As his car pulled into Dzerzhinsky Square, the landmark toy store, Children's World, opposite the KGB's Lubyanka headquarters was thronged with people as usual. Children's World and Lubyanka, both looking out on the same square, had always fueled Moscow humor, but today there was little room for it. There was a crowd around the statue of Felix Dzerzhinsky, standing tall in front of the Lubyanka. The pedestal of the memorial was defaced with crudely written slogans, including "Down with the KGB." The same letters also appeared on the facade of the KGB buildings—even, oddly, English slogans such as "Fuck this KGB!" It is all for the benefit of the international press, Shebarshin thought with irritation, whose cameras are capturing every twist in our fate.

Shebarshin was angered by what he saw, thinking that these new slogans were probably written by the same small people who scribbled their dirty little jokes on the walls of public toilets. They have now turned to politics, he mused, shrugging. The thought was not a calming one.

The Kremlin, 1145 Hours, Thursday, August 22, 1991

Identity documents were being carefully checked at the Kremlin's Borovitsky gate; the number of guards was greater than usual, and they were serious and alert. Shebarshin saw two huge Zils parked at the entrance and spotted the chairman of the general staff, General Moiseyev, heading toward the Walnut Room, which had already begun to fill with somber, serious-looking men. The two men greeted each other briefly but were unable to speak before Gorbachev entered the room. After shaking a few hands, the President drew Shebarshin into an adjoining room.

The conversation was brief and animated. "What was Kryuchkov after?" Gorbachev asked. "What orders were given to the KGB? Did Grushko know about the coup?"

Shebarshin felt uncomfortable with his answers; it was as if they were some sort of confession. He had bumped into Viktor Grushko, who was now the senior KGB official after Kryuchkov's arrest. He'd seen the fear in his eyes when he'd told him he had been called in to meet Gorbachev.

Shebarshin would also feel disappointed with himself, but only later, because his intense dislike of Gorbachev had somehow disappeared when he was face-to-face with him. When he described his meeting with Kryuchkov on August 19, Gorbachev exclaimed, "That bastard! I believed him more than anyone else, him and Yazov. You know that."

Shebarshin nodded in assent. When he was asked again by Gorbachev whether Viktor Grushko had been part of the plot, he said, "I don't know. Perhaps he knew about it." Shebarshin wondered momentarily why the President seemed so certain that he himself hadn't been involved in the plot. But the grilling continued.

"Who is your border guard chief?"

"Ilya Yakovlevich Kalinichenko," Shebarshin answered.

"The way they surrounded me, stood guard over me," the President mused, "the order was given to fire should anyone attempt to get through."

Shebarshin tried to say something in defense of Kalinichenko, a man he considered incapable of evil. But the President ignored him.

Then Gorbachev said he was appointing Shebarshin temporary Chairman of the KGB. "Go now and assemble the deputy chiefs and advise them of this decision," he ordered. "And issue the order for your colleagues to prepare reports on their actions during August 19 to 21. Send them personally to me in a sealed envelope."

As he returned to the Walnut Room, the brand-new KGB chairman, instead of suspicion, found symbolic handshakes and friendly, warm smiles. *Just in case,* he thought dryly.

The Lubyanka, 1300 Hours, Thursday, August 22, 1991

Shebarshin returned to KGB headquarters and announced the President's decision to the few colleagues gathered there. There were no immediate questions, and he found instant agreement to his order that the senior leadership cadre be gathered the following day to decide on the next steps. Shebarshin called for the creation of a commission to investigate the activity of the KGB during the coup and appointed Gennady Titov to head it. He thought Titov would be a good investigator but wondered whether they would let him remain head of the commission. Titov was a controversial old-line KGB officer who had as many enemies as friends. He could handle the job, but perhaps not the politics, Shebarshin thought.

After the brief meeting, Shebarshin walked the long corridor to his new office. Along the way, he was stopped by a friend from the Ninth who reported that Boris Pugo, former member of the Ministry of the Interior and one of the coup plotters, had killed himself with his own gun. Shebarshin knew Pugo and wondered why the honest and dedicated man had to take his own life. Were he and his co-conspirators so sure of the success of their enterprise that failure was tantamount to death?

Eternal memory to Boris Karlovich Pugo, Shebarshin thought dryly. He would have the same feeling later when he learned that Marshal Akhromeyev, another of the coup plotters and, yes, another honorable man, had hanged himself.

11

Moscow, 1530 Hours, Thursday, August 22, 1991

Dave Rolph had kept his team fanned out across Moscow since Monday, and as the mood in Moscow shifted from fear to jubilation, his officers were out there in the crowd capturing the images of a failed counterrevolution that had by now caught the imagination of the world.

One of Rolph's officers was mingling with the growing crowd around Dzerzhinsky Square, noting that some had begun to paint slogans on the wall of the Lubyanka, while others were gathering around the statue of Felix Dzerzhinsky, Moscow's cast-bronze symbol of repression. He began snapping pictures like everybody else, thinking that before it was over, he might get lucky and get that one photograph that summed up the history of what was happening in the square.

The Lubyanka, 1530 Hours, Thursday, August 22, 1991

The chief of physical security for the KGB's Dzerzhinsky complex reported to the new Chairman of the KGB that the crowd in the square outside had grown and that it might be getting ready to storm the building. What were his orders?

"Close and block all doors and gates, check the gratings," said Shebarshin. "Under no circumstances, no matter what the situation, are firearms to be used. I'll order the Moscow authorities to contact the militia."

With great difficulty, the security department at the KGB headquarters was able to find someone from the militia leadership who promised to send help. But they never showed up. Shebarshin dismissed it as another sign of confusion and uncertainty in all of Moscow's institutions. Not long after that, he received a call from the Soviet prosecutor's office advising him that criminal charges had been filed against Kryuchkov. He was further advised that a team was ready to head over to search Kryuchkov's office.

"All right, let them come," he said without hesitation. The call was followed immediately by another from the Russian Federation's prosecutor's office, advising the new KGB Chairman that the Russian Federation had also initiated criminal charges against Kryuchkov. They were sending a team of investigators to search Kryuchkov's office and would be accompanied by a team from Central Television.

Television! Shebarshin reacted in a flash. But he immediately resigned himself to the new way of things. What's the difference? he thought. He told the Russian Federation prosecutor to send over his investigators and to let them know that there would also be a team from the Soviet Union prosecutor's office.

In ten minutes, there were a dozen justice investigators led by the general prosecutor of the Russian Federation. Their appearance was sharply different from what Shebarshin and his colleagues were used to seeing within the confines of the Lubyanka—few wore coats and ties, and they all look rumpled somehow. Shebarshin found them polite but slightly agitated. To his surprise, they seemed to make decisions quickly and sensibly. They divided into groups, and one tackled Kryuchkov's office while another set off for Kryuchkov's dacha, where the former KGB Chairman's wife, Ekaterina Petrovna, had been weeping for the last two days. A third group was dispatched to Kryuchkov's Moscow apartment to begin its search.

Shebarshin took in the activity about him and asked his aide for a strong cup of tea. Then he began to write his report for Gorbachev. As he was writing, the leadership telephone rang. He picked up the receiver and heard Gorbachev's voice: "I have signed your temporary appointment as acting KGB Chairman," he said. "Get to work!"

Sitting there in the Chairman's office, Shebarshin wondered why it was that three hours ago, or even now, for that matter, he never had the thought of declining this appointment. Was it force of habit that he should never refuse? Was it discipline?

Perhaps it was his training to always obey his seniors, particularly since in this instance it had been the President himself who commanded his fate. But Shebarshin made an unpleasant discovery, which he tried to suppress. It was simply vanity, he decided. Leonid Shebarshin, the son of a shoemaker from Marina Woods, most recently a common intelligence officer, has become the head of the Committee for State Security.

People are weak, he decided. It is all about vanity.

Langley, 0745 Hours, Thursday, August 22, 1991

The pile of cable traffic on my desk seemed to grow each morning after the coup collapsed. As I flipped through the reports, I was able to keep track of the new trajectory of the Soviet Union about as well as anyone else in Washington, Moscow, or other world capitals, which still wasn't very good.

This morning I had a situation report stating that the crowds building in central Moscow were becoming more brazen and that it might not take much to spark a real riot. The most volatile crowds seemed to be forming up at the Lubyanka, and many seemed to be spurred on by that old Russian standby, free-flowing vodka. In short, fear had changed sides.

Dzerzhinsky Square, 2130 Hours, Thursday, August 22, 1991

The crowd of some twenty thousand packed into Dzerzhinsky Square cheered the prospect of toppling the statue of "Iron" Felix. All over Moscow, crowds had been pulling down the bronze testaments to Bolshevism and hauling them off to a temporary graveyard next to the Tretyakov Gallery. Now it was Dzerzhinsky's turn.

Under the watchful eye of the Russian militia, the Moscow city government had assumed charge of the operation, and it had taken most of Saturday to find a crane big enough for the task. As the crane eased into position next to the statue, the crowd began to sing a song about Magadan, the western Siberian city most famously known for its role as a key part of Stalin's disposal system—the Gulag. Sergei Stankevich, the young deputy mayor of Moscow, leaned into the microphone to lead the chorus. Stankevich was a poor conductor, and the singing was ragged, but the crowd seemed unwilling to abandon the mournful lyrics.

Inside the Lubyanka, looking out on the square from behind a fifth-floor window, Leonid Shebarshin stood back in the shadows. He watched the crane by the statue, the volunteer "executioner" climbing atop Dzerzhinsky's shoulders, encircling the neck and torso of the first head of the Soviet secret intelligence service with the crane's iron cable. The "executioner" straightened up, hitched up his falling pants, and gestured with his hand. "Ready! Proceed with the hanging."

He is probably a rigger, Shebarshin thought. Naturally, Moscow Deputy Mayor Sergei Stankevich himself couldn't put on the noose. No, there were always those who gave orders and those who followed them.

Finally, the statue lifted off its pedestal, and the symbol of repression that had towered over the square since 1926 was laid on its side. In a few more days, it would be hauled off to the field near Gorky Park to join the corpses of Lenin that had already begun piling up in the makeshift graveyard.

Few in the crowd seemed to notice the letters and logo emblazoned across the counterweight of the giant crane—KRUPP. But David Rolph's officer in the crowd at Dzerzhinsky Square brought his camera up at just that moment and snapped the picture he'd been waiting most of the day to get.

Only after the photographs were developed overnight would the irony of a German crane lifting the bronze statue of Dzerzhinsky become the subject of whispers. Many would later opine that some sort of historical irony had just played itself out—that Dzerzhinsky's statue, itself thought to be cast from the bronze barrels of Krupp cannon forged for wars long since past, was finally hauled off its perch by a crane built by the same German conglomerate.

An exhausted Leonid Shebarshin returned to his dacha in the early hours of the morning. His wife, Nina, was waiting for him, worried. She had heard about his appointment. "Do you think it's for long?" she asked.

"I think it will be for just a few days," he answered.

Moments later, Shebarshin fell into a deep sleep, his last thought not to forget to ask the *Rezidents* the next day about the state of mind of their personal staffs and, more important, of their intelligence agents. It was essential that the helpers be reassured.

The Lubyanka, 0300 Hours, Friday, August 23, 1991

Dzerzhinsky Square was deserted three hours after midnight when a small group of KGB officers, unaccustomed to looking over their own shoulders, furtively made their way through the clutter and trash littering the square to the fallen statue of their founder. In dark paint they printed out the words on the pedestal that Iron Felix would carry with him into his uncertain future:

DEAR FELIX, WE ARE SORRY THAT
WE COULDN'T SAVE YOU
BUT YOU WILL REMAIN WITH US.

Then they disappeared into the night.

Moscow, 0600 Hours, Friday, August 23, 1991

Shebarshin woke with a start. For a few moments he wasn't sure it hadn't all been a bad dream—the emergency committee, Kryuchkov's arrest, Dzerzhinsky's "execution." The events of the previous day seemed like fragments of a film—the meeting with Gorbachev, the investigators in Kryuchkov's office, it was all a disjointed jumble.

Awake now, he wondered what the day would bring. He knew trouble would be coming. But he also knew that the new democrats would eventually realize that no government can rule without state security. Unfortunately, in the exuberance of victory, in vengeful celebration, they would not think of the future. Yes, there would be trouble, and soon, he decided.

Two hours later he was back at Lubyanka, already caught in a struggle with tradition. An acting chief was never supposed to sit in the office of the Chairman of the KGB. It was not just a matter of appropriate reticence, but one of deep Russian superstition. To sit in a chair prematurely would frighten off success. But Shebarshin decided that the drama of the situation demanded he dispense with tradition and ignore superstition. He took over at Kryuchkov's desk.

The Chairman's office was huge, somber, and now free of any lingering trace of its previous occupant. Kryuchkov had been a man indifferent to his surroundings; he simply did not notice them. All he'd needed was a well-lit desk, his telephones, and any kind of ballpoint pen, no matter how cheap. The pens stood fanlike in a tumbler. As soon as he sat down, Shebarshin was assaulted by a flood of calls on the bank of nearby telephones: internal calls from the special Kremlin phones, calls on the supreme command link, and calls on lines he simply could not identify. He decided to switch the telephones to his assistants, leaving only the leadership and supreme command phones to himself.

The reports coming in were familiar: The KGB was under threat; some forces were preparing to storm the building; all the chiefs were awaiting orders. Shebarshin decided that he must reinforce his rule of the previous day: The KGB cannot allow itself to be drawn into any confrontation with the crowd.

The phone rang again. This time it was the chief of the investigative directorate, reporting that the supporters of Moscow dissident Valeria Novodvorskaya were preparing to storm the Lefortovo Prison to free their leader. Shebarshin was familiar with Novodvorskaya and had always dismissed her as part of what he considered the hysterical end of the political spectrum. But he also understood that it was precisely that end of the political spectrum that was now in charge.

Almost wearily he asked, "Do we have her?"

"We do," the chief of investigations answered.

"What should we do?"

"Release her."

"Who can authorize that?" Shebarshin asked.

"You can."

"Then release her," Shebarshin said with finality.

Langley, 2345 Hours, Thursday, August 22, 1991

It had been a long day, I thought as I drafted a cable to Rolph telling him that at his next meeting with Krassilnikov he might see if the general was interested in "reinsuring with us." But gently, I instructed my Moscow chief. Do it with finesse.

Before I closed up, I just sat there alone in my office, trying to come to grips with the drama that now seemed to have played out with such finality. Was this it? I wondered. Was history really going to play another of its anticlimactic tricks, dragging us along for almost half a century in a struggle that seemed so endless that it had defined generations—it had certainly defined mine—and then just get tired and call it quits? Was I missing something? Were the hard-liners like Redmond right? Would we all arrive in Langley some Monday morning and find the Berlin Wall neatly restored and propping up the Humpty-Dumpty of the Warsaw Pact?

None of this really made any sense at the end of two turbulent weeks. Maybe it would take a little more time to sink in, I decided, and pulled the vault door closed and initialed the sign-out sheet.

Lubyanka, 1400 Hours, August 23, 1991

Shebarshin had not been wrong when he'd told his wife that he'd probably hold the acting chairmanship of the KGB for only a couple of days. In the afternoon after the festivities at Dzerzhinsky Square, he was advised by the President's office that Vadim Bakatin, the minister of the interior and a liberal oppositionist, had been appointed Chairman of the KGB, effective immediately. Shebarshin would continue on concurrently as Vice Chairman of the KGB and as head of the First Chief Directorate's foreign intelligence service.

Shebarshin understood that he would hold an important record in the annals of the Soviet Union—he had been chairman of the Committee for State Security, the twenty-first in the line of succession that began with Felix Edmundovich Dzerzhinsky in 1917, but only for a single day.

Moscow, 1230 Hours, Monday, August 25, 1991

The two men didn't have to huddle in the backseat of a KGB Volga this time. Moscow was suddenly an open city, and they could talk more comfortably over lunch in a Chinese restaurant inside the Peking Hotel.

As Rolph ate the Russian-Chinese food and talked about the coup and its stunning aftermath, he could see that Krassilnikov was a changed man. For one thing, Krassilnikov observed that Boris Yeltsin had shown great courage by standing up to the coup plotters. When Rolph reminded him of his earlier words—that if Yeltsin wanted a confrontation, he'd get one—the old man shrugged. I didn't mean a military confrontation, the KGB general explained. I meant an ideological one. We were misled and misinformed by the emergency committee. Fortunately, the Second Chief Directorate never got its hands dirty with the plotters. It had no involvement in the coup, he stressed.

As Rolph listened and studied Krassilnikov's deeply lined face, he finally eased into his pitch.

"You know, Rem, I have really come to enjoy the time we spend together. These meetings have been very useful for me. Of course, we don't know which way things are going to end up now. But as a friend, if there is anything I can do to help you, I would be happy to. I have no authority to say this, of course, I'm speaking just as a friend, but if you need anything . . ."

A stern look crossed Krassilnikov's face, and he raised his hand and held it in front of Rolph. "Stop. Don't do this."

Rolph brought his pitch to a halt. Rem Krassilnikov, the professor of counterintelligence, was not interested in working for the CIA, no matter how bleak the outlook for the KGB.

Rolph abandoned his recruitment efforts, and Rem Krassilnikov refused to let the incident interrupt their meeting. He went right back to explaining the KGB's new realities.

With Yeltsin now calling the shots, the KGB was to be broken up, Krassilnikov revealed. The First Chief Directorate was to become independent, as were the signal intelligence units of the Eighth and Sixteenth Directorates—the KGB's version of the NSA. The border guards and VIP security units would also be split off. Vadim Bakatin, a liberal former interior minister who had already proposed ways to reform the intelligence service, was to run the KGB. And guess who would be a member of an "advisory" panel, helping Bakatin "reform" the KGB? Why, Rem Krassilnikov's boss, Gennady Titov, the current head of the Second Chief Directorate.

And that's when Rolph realized: *These guys won't give up easily.*

But Bakatin moved quickly to break up the KGB. He summed up his view of the organization in the immediate aftermath of the coup: *You see, the most terrible thing is that the KGB in its old form had an absolute monopoly on government communications, total surveillance, secrecy, the encrypting and decrypting of documents, the protection of the USSR's borders, and even the protection of the president. That, I am sure, played the decisive role in the coup. The danger for the Soviet Union was precisely in the very structure of its security organs—that's the paradox!*

12

The Lubyanka, Moscow, Mid-September 1991

Robert Strauss was as smooth an operator as I had seen in over a quarter century of dealing with smooth operators and trying, sometimes with grave self-doubt, to be one myself. Though I had made that decision in my first meeting with Strauss, the high-stakes poker player from Texas, the Democratic Party healer, and one of the shrewdest lawyers to work Washington's K Street, watching him here in the Lubyanka, not more than a hundred feet from Yuri Andropov's museum office overlooking Dzerzhinsky Square, I knew I had been right about America's new ambassador to Moscow from the moment we first met.

I had briefed Strauss on the USSR, from the CIA's perspective, as soon as he was confirmed as President George H. W. Bush's envoy to the Kremlin. He'd put me at ease with a couple of old J. Edgar Hoover stories from his days as an FBI agent in Dallas to set the mood and probably to let me know that he knew a little something about my world.

"I was a young agent in the Dallas Field Office when J. Edgar made one of his imperial visits," Strauss told me in that down-home Texas drawl I'd grown up with. "I was picked as the guy to drive him around, but there was one catch. J. Edgar didn't like his drivers to make left turns. I guessed it was because he never wanted to be broadsided, but anyway it was a pretty big thing back then. So I'd have to figure a way to drive him all over Dallas without making any left turns!"

I guessed Bob Strauss was telling me how he navigated his way through the tricky intersections of life, not just how he'd gotten the FBI Director through Dallas traffic. He also told me how he took the job of ambassador to Moscow when it was offered by a Republican President.

"I was sitting there in front of George Bush's desk in the oval office as he asked me to go to Moscow for him. I said that I had not voted for him the last time and that I'd probably never vote for him. But the President said that didn't matter and that the man he wanted in Moscow was me."

While I was briefing him on what was going on, Strauss cut to the chase.

"What do I tell the Soviets when they ask why I'm the President's man in Moscow?"

"It's easy," I told him. "Tell them that the President sent you to Moscow not because you know a damn thing about Russia or how the Soviet Union works. He sent you because you know everything about how Washington works."

Strauss looked at me like a guy who has just filled in a straight flush and said, "I'm gonna like you, Milt."

Now, sitting with this old fox and watching him handle Boris Yeltsin's new KGB Chairman, Vadim Bakatin, the former minister of the interior fired by Gorbachev as he scrambled to distance himself from the liberals in the summer of 1991, I knew that George Bush had sent the right man to Moscow.

Bakatin asked Strauss a number of questions, and then the new KGB Chairman turned to me.

"How many analysts do you have in CIA?"

"Around two thousand," I answered.

Bakatin called an aide over to the table and asked him how many analysts the KGB had. After hearing the man's answer, he turned back to me. "He says we have less than a dozen!" His tone was one of exasperation. The KGB had never put much stock in analysis, since for generations the Kremlin had not wanted to hear bad news.

Bakatin said that the time had come to end the Cold War contest between our agencies. He complained about all the money and resources spent just on spying against our respective embassies in Moscow and Washington. Pointing to his safe in the corner of his large office, Bakatin said, "In that safe are the complete plans of the efforts to put listening devices in your embassy. Now your embassy stands empty and we are at an impasse!"

Strauss perked up. He and I had talked earlier about ways to get the Soviets to move on the issue of the bugging of our embassy. I had briefed him on the claims by the KGB, made to me in Helsinki more than a year earlier, that the embassy was now "safe." But Strauss would need solid proof that the embassy was actually safe for occupation. As the ambassador talked with Bakatin about the need to get the embassy problem behind us, I slipped him a note.

"Ask him to give you the blueprints."

Without casting more than a sideways glance at the note, Strauss continued his statement about getting on with the important work and getting the problem of the bugged embassy resolved once and for all. Then he dropped the bomb.

"Mr. Chairman, there is one way you could help us get over this hurdle of the status of my embassy. Why don't you just give me those blueprints in your safe. I'm sure that would set us on the right course."

I watched the other KGB officers in the room as they leaned forward in their chairs at this point in the conversation. There was something close to shock in their faces as Bakatin's interpreter translated Strauss's suggestion.

Bakatin thought for a moment, then said, "I will be back to you on this, Mr. Ambassador."

Strauss had made his point very smoothly, and I thought Bakatin had been intrigued by the ambassador's suggestion. I then took my turn at speaking and passed along the greetings of our new acting Director of Central Intelligence to the new KGB Chairman. Bill Webster had retired at the end of August, and Dick Kerr was acting DCI, while Robert Gates, the President's nominee to take over at Langley, was working through the confirmation process.

"Mr. Chairman," I said, "our acting Director, Mr. Richard Kerr, sends you his compliments and as an accomplished historian in his own right wanted you to know his view of the events that you have been so personally associated with here in Moscow in the last forty days. Mr. Kerr places the beginning of the twentieth century at August 1914, in the Balkans. And he places the beginning of the twenty-first century at August 1991, in Moscow."

As Bakatin smiled, I felt Strauss turn to look at me twice.

A few moments later, we ended our visit with Bakatin and took a short tour of Yuri Andropov's museum office overlooking Dzerzhinsky, now denuded of the once proud statue of Iron Felix. Then, as Strauss and I were walking down a broad staircase to the parade entrance of the Lubyanka, the ambassador turned to me.

"Milt, how does that 1914 thing you said to Bakatin go again?"

I told him, wondering where the old fox was headed. Strauss thought for a moment and then said, "Milt, I don't want to hear you ever say that again. Not in this town. Not in any other town. You understand me?"

"Sure, Mr. Ambassador. But are you going to tell me why?"

"Yes, I am. That is so goddamn good that it now belongs to me. I'm stealing that from you, and I don't want to hear you say it again." Then he smiled.

I saw the "1914 thing" appear in an interview Bob Strauss gave to *The Washington Post* a few weeks later.

Vadim Bakatin did indeed hand over the blueprints to the KGB's bugging scheme against our embassy in Moscow. No one in Washington really believed that the blueprints were complete, however, so it didn't resolve the debate over what to do with the embassy building.

The action did, however, help get Bakatin fired and earned

him a place in KGB history as the most reviled Chairman the organization had ever had.

Moscow, Mid-September 1991

I later met with a group of the new KGB leadership, one of whom provided me with an animated description of the role CNN had played on KGB thinking during the crucial moments of the putsch. The KGB officer staff, uncertain whether to throw in with the supporters of the new emergency committee or the resisters backing Yeltsin, found themselves in an information blackout. Lacking any other source of information on what Kryuchkov and his cohorts were up to, the men in the Lubyanka had tuned in to CNN to watch events in Moscow unfold.

The general summed it up for me, his voice full of irony and amusement. "We are sitting here in KGB headquarters watching CNN like probably you were, Milton, and we see Boris Yeltsin come out of the parliament building and get up on the tank. But we see on CNN that the turrets on the tanks lined up in front are turned in the wrong direction—they are no longer pointed at the parliament. Then the American President, who is on vacation, comes on CNN saying that coups sometimes fail. And by then there are whispers all over Dzerzhinsky that CIA knows more about what is happening right now in Moscow than we do in the KGB. And I even have reports that President Bush has called Boris Yeltsin while he is surrounded by tanks and tells him to be strong! And so we just turn off our phones and go home or to our dachas."

Moscow, September 18, 1991

Vanity had its limits, Shebarshin decided after less than a month on the job as deputy to the new and reform-minded KGB Chairman, Vadim Bakatin. He submitted his resignation on Wednesday, September 18, and it was accepted on Friday. He had spent almost thirty years in the KGB, and now he would retire to his dacha to reflect on what it had really meant. It would take a few years for him to sort through those years, but then he would begin to write it all down.

Moscow, October 1991

David Rolph didn't wait this time for headquarters to tell him to get moving; he decided to take advantage of the revolutionary climate in Moscow by launching an aggressive new campaign to recruit Russian agents. In the upheaval after the failed coup, KGB surveillance in Moscow had all but vanished. For the first time since the start of the Cold War, CIA officers could walk or drive around Moscow without being followed and could meet Russian officials without fear of exposure or arrest. Moscow was no longer a "denied area."

Five months earlier, CIA case officers still feared the KGB's mythical power to follow them everywhere, using what some called "ultradiscreet surveillance." Now, case officers in Moscow trained in the clandestine arts of "sticks and bricks"—dead drops, chalk marks on walls, burst transmissions—could simply call up a Russian and ask him to lunch.

Moscow Station prepared a list of Soviet and Russian officials who were worth the time and energy to get to know, divided up the names, and started calling them to see if they'd be interested in talking. It was the kind of routine meet-and-greet activity that diplomats conduct the world over, yet it was something that had never been done before by the CIA in Moscow. And it worked. The case officers found that in the wake of the coup, government officials all over Moscow were eager to talk to them, to make their observations and opinions heard in Washington—particularly if it meant a free lunch.

The end of the Soviet Union, like so many upheavals, stirred things up and brought a few old ghosts out of hiding. Long-lost agents, people who had spied for the CIA and then either been arrested or had simply gone underground, now began to come forward, demanding payment for services rendered during the Cold War. One of these was a former GRU officer who'd gone to extraordinary lengths to try to spy for the CIA a decade earlier. Back in 1981, he'd swum down the Moscow River until he'd reached a beach reserved for foreign diplomats. Coming ashore, he had found an American embassy official having a picnic with his family and handed him a note volunteering his services. The note had been turned over to the

CIA, and a case officer had been sent out to meet him, but the GRU officer had been quickly caught and arrested.

He was out of prison now, however, and he came to the embassy looking for help, and so the CIA agreed to give him some assistance.

Throughout the fall of 1991, the KGB was a confused mess. Kryuchkov was under arrest, and Boris Yeltsin was determined to defang the intelligence and security apparatus. Not only was the KGB broken up under new chief Vadim Bakatin, as Rem Krassilnikov had predicted, but massive budget cuts were forcing wholesale firings and layoffs. Krassilnikov had survived, but he was no longer the KGB's only contact with the CIA. Now the CIA was meeting representatives from the SVRR, the successor to the First Chief Directorate; the FSB, the successor to the Second Chief Directorate; and even the new Russian republic KGB, which reported directly to Russian President Yeltsin.

Still, there were already signs that the old KGB wasn't going to simply disappear as easily as the East German Stasi.

CIA Headquarters, Langley, Virginia, October 1991

Dottie didn't know the purpose of the meeting, only that it was an interview in the counterintelligence center. I was expected, she had said. And I found myself in a small room at a conference table with Sandy Grimes, Jeanne Vertefeuille, Jim Milburn, and Jim Holt, the latter two FBI officers attached to the CIA to help with the investigation of the 1985 losses that had been given new life when Redmond was transferred to the counterintelligence center.

No one made any effort to conceal what was going on: The panel was looking over the list of possible suspects, and I had been on the list from the start. We went over a number of questions about where and when I became aware of certain compromised operations. Most of them in 1985, I answered. Then came a slightly offbeat question.

"If you were going to spy for the KGB, how would you pull it off?"

I thought only briefly before I responded. "It wouldn't be

hard at all," I said. "I have a very quiet but sanctioned contact with the top levels of the KGB, and disappear every so often to have a little talk with them about matters of mutual interest. If I were interested in spying for the KGB, I'd easily be able to roll it into my official contact with them. What would it take?" I said. "A couple pieces of paper passed at one of these meetings and we've got another disaster in SE."

I would learn much later that of all forty-four people interviewed by the counterintelligence panel, only Aldrich Ames would stumble over that question.

Idylwood Park, Vienna, Virginia, Monday, December 16, 1991

Bob Hanssen left one last package for the KGB under a footbridge, this one containing a classified paper entitled "The KGB's First Chief Directorate: Structure, Functions, and Methods." It was something that the KGB's First Chief Directorate might want to see.

In a note that Hanssen left for his KGB handlers, he said that he had been promoted to a new position that was not directly involved in Soviet matters.

Hanssen would soon break contact with Moscow. On a business trip to Indianapolis, apparently in late 1991 or early 1992, he walked into a Catholic church and once again confessed to a priest that he had been spying for the Soviets. Just as he had done after his wife had caught him in 1980, Bob Hanssen had turned to his church to help him purge his sins. Now he was determined to end his double life.

But perhaps Hanssen's change of heart was not the result just of his religious convictions. Perhaps the collapse of the Soviet Union and the turmoil inside the KGB had something to do with convincing him that spying for Moscow was no longer a good idea. In the end, he would find it impossible to really stop. Eight years later, he would start up with the Soviets one last time.

Langley, December 31, 1991

The Soviet Union had ceased to exist. With little fanfare, a detachment of Red Army soldiers had marched out on the

Kremlin wall and had for the last time lowered the Hammer and Sickle, raising in its place the Russian tricolor.

It's over, I thought. The whole thing we called the Cold War was over. And it felt pretty good. We hadn't beat them in straight sets, not by any stretch of the imagination. But beat them we had. Our KGB adversaries had been gifted. We might not have been more gifted, but our system was, and in the end we were probably just good enough.

I remember the reaction of the many visitors to the Christmas party we held in our corridor at headquarters when we handed out a party favor unique to our efforts that year and for many years before. It was a white campaign-style button with a red hammer and sickle and star and the words in red across the top, *SE Division Christmas Party 1991.* Below and to the right of the symbol of the USSR were the words

The Party's Over

But it wasn't over—not quite yet.

EPILOGUE

As the Hammer and Sickle was lowered for the last time over the Kremlin at the close of 1991, marking the end of the Soviet Union, the CIA's SE Division disappeared too. Replacing it at Langley was the Central Eurasian Task Force, later to become the Central Eurasian Division, whose new role was more closely linked to monitoring and managing a disintegrating Soviet empire than assaulting it from all quarters. From the Baltics to the Caucasus and Central Asia, the CIA moved quickly to open up new ties to the security and intelligence services of the nations rising from the ashes of the Soviet Union.

Many of the newly independent countries were eager for relationships with the CIA, partly to counterbalance the power of Soviet intelligence. John MacGaffin, who took over the division in January 1992, was rather startled by his first meeting with the new president of Turkmenistan; he was happy to have a visit from a senior CIA official who might be able to tell him about Moscow's attempts to spy on his new government. As they sat in the president's office, the leader's first question for MacGaffin came in a whisper: "Is it safe to talk in here?"

For a time, newly opened CIA stations across Central Asia were lightly staffed and received little interest back at headquarters. It was difficult to imagine in the early and mid-1990s what intelligence could possibly come out of Uzbekistan that would be of much interest to the President of the United States. Washington was reveling in a new world order, and Langley was earnestly in search of a new identity, a new rationale for its existence. Yet even as the agency attempted to reorder and redesign itself, the effort to solve the lingering mystery surrounding the 1985 losses ground on, until February 1994, when an FBI team forced Aldrich Ames's Jaguar to the curb and arrested him on charges of espionage.

Ever since his arrest, the CIA has insisted that Ames was uncovered purely through painstaking analysis, but there is more to the story, a piece of the puzzle that has remained hidden for nearly a decade. In solving the Ames case, the CIA had help from a Russian agent. The agent didn't identify Ames by name, but he did provide information, such as times, dates, and places, that meshed with the background of one suspect—Aldrich Ames.

At first, it seemed that Ames's arrest would allow the mole hunters to close the books on 1985. But their relief was short-lived. Paul Redmond and his team knew within weeks of the arrest that there was at least one other mole still at large. Ames couldn't possibly have known about all of the cases and operations that had been blown over the years—including the investigation of Felix Bloch and several highly sensitive technical intelligence probes. Redmond soon established a new mole hunt unit to track down yet another spy.

In time, Redmond began to suspect that the new mole might be at the FBI, but he was rebuffed by bureau officials who seemed intent on ignoring the warning signs. Determined to take advantage of a weakened and exposed CIA, under fire for having allowed Ames to go undetected for so long, the FBI demanded and won from Congress new powers to take the lead on counterintelligence investigations. In the wake of the Ames case, a senior FBI agent was dispatched to CIA headquarters to take control of the counterespionage group, the spy-hunting unit within the CIA's counterintelligence center. FBI investigators agreed with Redmond that there was another spy—but they were determined to look for the mole inside the CIA. And now they were calling the shots.

Redmond bristled as the FBI trampled on his turf, and he ominously told colleagues that "people who live in glass houses shouldn't throw stones." Undeterred, FBI officials lorded it over their CIA counterparts, setting counterintelligence policy on their own terms. With the FBI now in charge and eager to consolidate its bureaucratic gains over the CIA, the last thing it wanted to do was launch an investigation that would target its own agents.

And so Robert Hanssen went undiscovered for another seven years, until he was finally arrested in February 2001. Hanssen's arrest blindsided the FBI, and his case would ultimately prove every bit as traumatic for the bureau as the Ames case had been for the CIA. Like Ames before him, Hanssen was discovered with help from a Russian agent—but not the same one.

The Hanssen case seemed to answer many of the questions that had been left unresolved by the arrest of Aldrich Ames: It was Hanssen who had tipped off the KGB that Felix Bloch was under investigation; it was Hanssen who had revealed the existence of the tunnel built under the Soviet embassy in Washington; and it was Hanssen who had betrayed dozens of other FBI technical operations. But maddeningly, even Hanssen couldn't account for everything.

The more investigators kept digging, the more they found that Hanssen, Ames, and Edward Lee Howard—the spies thought to be responsible for the 1985 losses—could not account for all of them. Gradually it became clear that there could be a fourth man, still undiscovered, who was behind at least some of the betrayals.

For starters, there was the case of Sergei Bokhan, the GRU colonel in Athens who defected in May 1985 after receiving a suspicious order to return home. Bokhan received his summons a full month before Ames identified him and five months before Hanssen volunteered his services to the KGB. Edward Lee Howard, who was preparing for an assignment in Moscow when he was fired in 1983, knew only about operations that required internal handling in Moscow. Bokhan was being handled with rigid compartmentalization by Athens, so Howard was eliminated as the source of compromise.

And Bokhan was not the only anomaly. There was also Leonid Polyshchuk, the KGB officer posted to Lagos who'd been arrested unloading a dead drop in Moscow in August. After his arrest, the KGB put out the word that Polyshchuk had been caught because of the vigilant surveillance conducted by the Second and Seventh Chief Directorates. But a careful review of the case strongly suggests that the KGB was tipped off in the spring of 1985, shortly after Polyshchuk arrived in Lagos. The KGB, aware that Polyshchuk had been in the market for an apartment near his parents in Moscow, almost certainly arranged for one to come on the market in order to lure him back to Moscow. Polyshchuk's father sent word to him in Lagos about the good fortune of finding an apartment in early April—well before Ames betrayed him on June 13.

Oleg Gordievsky was another unresolved case. He was recalled to Moscow in May 1985, before Hanssen went to the KGB and before Ames's fateful meeting at Chadwicks. The fact that the KGB questioned but did not immediately arrest Gordievsky suggests that they lacked the hard evidence they had against the other compromised agents. Ames has been held responsible for betraying Gordievsky, and there is no doubt that he identified him to the KGB. But he did so on June 13, by which time Gordievsky was already back in Moscow and under hostile interrogation. Since his arrest, Ames has consistently told the CIA and FBI that he betrayed Gordievsky at Chadwicks in June, when he first gave the KGB his long list of Soviet agents. Both agencies are convinced he is telling the truth. Neither Howard nor Hanssen could have known about Gordievsky.

Finally, there was the case of FAREWELL, the French spy Vladimir Vetrov, arrested in a sensational but highly suspect Moscow murder case in 1982 and then supposedly uncovered as a spy in prison two years later. While the CIA did not know Vetrov by name, the agency had been briefed on his intelligence by the French as early as 1982. This means that someone at the CIA was in a position to report to the KGB that one of its science and technology collection officers was working for French intelligence. Any list of suspects in the KGB's S&T collection directorate would have quickly narrowed to Vetrov. FAREWELL was executed in 1984, at least a year before Howard, Ames, and Hanssen volunteered to the KGB. (It is true, of course, that Hanssen spied for a year or two for the GRU beginning in 1979 and then resumed his espionage career with the KGB in October 1985, but it doesn't appear that he betrayed any of these unresolved cases during his earlier stint as a GRU agent.) Viewed against the pattern of betrayal and misdirection, it is possible, if not probable, that Vetrov was betrayed—like Bokhan, Polyshchuk, and possibly Gordievsky—by an American who has still not been identified.

Could the KGB have caught some or all of these men as a result of its own extensive counterintelligence efforts? Possibly, but then there would not have been any reason for the Soviets to create elaborate cover stories to lure Bokhan and Polyshchuk back home. There also would not have been any reason for the Soviets to create the even more elaborate murder story to cover Vetrov's demise. Gordievsky could have been compromised by his own operational mistakes, but the prospect of betrayal still looms large. The conclusion is almost inescapable that there was a fourth man—an as yet unidentified traitor who may have left Langley or simply stopped spying by 1986.

It is because of suspicions that there are further spies to be uncovered on both sides that mole hunts still quietly grind on in Washington and Moscow, more than a decade after the Soviet Union ceased to exist.

Aldrich Ames's betrayal and arrest played a major role in the evolution of the CIA in the post–Cold War era. The initial after-action investigations, which revealed the shocking ease with which Ames had eluded detection for nine years, prompted bitter recriminations at Langley, and the CIA's inept security soon became fodder for late-night comedians. Just about everyone who'd had a hand in running the show at SE and in the counterintelligence center received letters of reprimand from CIA Director R. James Woolsey, which unnerved an already rattled agency. The finger-pointing erupted just as the CIA was trying to deal with budget cuts, an exodus of experienced officers, and a post–Cold War identity crisis. Woolsey would soon be gone, too, and by the mid-1990s, turnover at the top of the agency was so bad that each new DCI seemed to come in and out through a revolving door.

Though it had long been suspected in counterintelligence circles that Langley had been penetrated by Moscow, investigators had been hampered by a deep resistance within the agency to a return to the witch-hunting days of the Angleton era. After Ames's arrest, the pendulum swung hard in the other direction. Hundreds of officers were made to endure torturous polygraph reexaminations. Some were forced to stand idle, unable to perform their jobs, while awaiting the resolution of phantom security issues that prevented them from taking part in classified activities. Senior officers with long records of successful clandestine operations were subjected to wasteful and demeaning scrutiny based on the flimsiest of evidence. Since Ames had skated through his last polygraph examination so easily, the CIA's Office of Security became wary of giving its seal of approval to any polygraph. Security officials even reopened scores of old investigations after reviewing past polygraph examinations. If Ames had beaten the machine, how many others might also have defeated it in years past?

Pressure from the outside was building, too. With the Cold War's end, public and congressional scrutiny of the agency's operations increased, and the nation's tolerance for expensive and dangerous intelligence activities waned. New political considerations intruded at Langley as a result, and a cautious, risk-averse climate took hold. The CIA sought desperately to be "correct"—to look like the rest of America. Convinced that the agency was lost and drifting, many of the CIA's best managers and field officers, the people who had fought the Cold War, headed for the exits. The CIA of the late 1990s had become like the U.S. Army of the 1930s: a peacetime service mired in petty bureaucratic battles and drifting without a clear mission.

September 11, 2001, changed everything. When the terrorists struck, the CIA did, indeed, look like America. The percentage of DO officers with prior military service was only a tiny fraction of the organization, and its WASPish adventurers had disappeared. Officers and their families, like most Americans, were in no hurry to rush off to places where you had to boil your drinking water and check under the car for bombs—let alone keep an eye in the rearview mirror not for local surveillance teams, but for the guy back there on the motorcycle who might want to kill you. Risk aversion had replaced the boldness and romanticism of the old guard. The DO had no bench to draw from when things heated up.

But ready or not, the CIA was thrown back into the game. Less than a month after the twin towers collapsed, the CIA, in tandem with the United States military, was in Afghanistan. Its mission this time was to capture or kill Osama bin Laden and his cohorts—and to neutralize and punish those who protected them.

To meet the immediate challenge, the agency began making badly needed changes. It brought in new officers from the military, cross-training them in the trade and craft of human intelligence and the languages needed, and tried to get them out to the field as soon as possible. The agency got off to a reasonable start, but the challenges in Afghanistan are far from squarely met. Afghanistan is an unforgiving land, a graveyard of empires, and it will be there that a reinvigorated CIA will pass or fail its most difficult test.

To observers unfamiliar with the martial history of the land between the Indus and the Oxus, America's foray into Afghanistan—Operation Enduring Freedom—seemed to be a textbook example of how to mount an insurgency using indigenous forces. CIA officers, along with U.S. and allied special operations forces, moved quickly and quietly into Afghanistan, where they reestablished old contacts and linked up with the Northern Alliance, the anti-Taliban force that had shrewdly been cobbled together by the late Ahmed Shah Massoud. With U.S. airpower clearing the way, they raced to Kabul. In less than five weeks, the Taliban had been routed and the Afghan capital liberated—with more casualties among journalists covering the war than in the U.S. military in that first blitz. It wasn't until November that American forces took their first casualty, CIA officer Johnny Micheal Spann, killed during the revolt at Qala-i-Jangi prison fortress.

Enduring Freedom looked easy—maybe a little too easy, like the British march on Kabul in 1839 or the Soviet Christmas invasion in 1979. All three enterprises had a common thread—getting in was almost painless. Then Afghan history always kicks in. The British would founder and be forced into retreat in January 1842, three years after their fluid entry. They marched out of Kabul with a column of 16,500 souls, headed east to their garrison at Jalalabad, a distance of 110 miles. A single British officer made it to safety. Almost a century and a half later, the Soviets faced a similar fate. After a flawless invasion, the Red Army bogged down, and a decade later it limped home across the Oxus after giving up almost 15,000 dead. Their Afghan misadventure would also cost the Soviets an empire.

Now, in the second year of America's Afghan enterprise, there is less talk of things being easy. The accounts of Operation Enduring Freedom and Leonid Shebarshin's sobering analysis of Soviet operations in the Panjshir in 1984 have begun to sound hauntingly familiar: crisp military briefers giving cheerily optimistic but unconvincing accounts of a beaten enemy, of high enemy body counts, but again without the bodies. "How can thirteen hundred rebels carry off seventeen hundred of their dead—and their weapons?" Shebarshin naively asked the 40th Army briefing officer in Ahmad Shah Massoud's Panjshir Valley in 1984. Those same questions have already been asked by journalists briefed on the battles of Tora Bora and Shah-i-Kot. And more are now asking how it is that those we have liberated seem to shell and rocket our troops with such regularity.

According to the premier historian on Afghanistan, the late Louis Dupree, four factors contributed to the British disasters in Afghanistan: having troops there in the first place; installing an unpopular emir on the Afghan throne; allowing "your" Afghans to mistreat other Afghans; and reducing the subsidies paid to the tribal chiefs. These fatal miscalculations, barely altered in form, were committed by the British in 1839 and again in 1878, and a century later by the Soviets. They are being committed today, and how we deal with them will determine the ultimate outcome of the American undertaking in Afghanistan.

The United States may not have placed a wildly unpopular emir on the throne—indeed, America's choice for an Afghan leader, Hamid Karzai, was the least objectionable of the possible candidates—but Afghan politics, always murky, is as much defined by the contenders to the throne as by the occupant. The real power in Kabul after the rout of the Taliban is not Hamid Karzai but Marshal Mohammad Qasim Fahim, the successor to the murdered Ahmad Shah Massoud. Fahim is a Tajik, a Panjshiri with a reputation for ruthlessness. He has, to be sure, violated Dupree's third dictum by grossly mistreating other segments of the Afghan population, notably and most dangerously the majority Pashtuns. As each day passes, Fahim is increasingly viewed by the Pashtun population and some other ethnic groups as the unpopular emir America has placed on the throne. Finally, the continued failure of the United States and its allies to make good on the pledges of massive reconstruction assistance—more than $4 billion pledged but undelivered—amounts to the same as the reduction of tribute paid by the nineteenth-century British to the tribal chiefs. This failure of the United States and its allies to engage in nation building is behind much of the unrest in the provinces.

Afghanistan, a year into its "American era," is troubled and dangerous, but it is not hopeless. The success or failure of the Afghan enterprise will depend in large measure on how the United States manages to build alliances with the inhabitants of all of Afghanistan, not just the Tajiks from the Panjshir Valley. The CIA will have to rekindle and nurture old relationships with the dominant Pashtuns of eastern Afghanistan and undertake measures to convince the broader population to take a stake in a new Afghanistan and join in its reconstruction. It is a daunting task and the learning curve is short. But failure could allow the country to become a haven for international terrorists once again. Afghanistan will thus be the ultimate testing ground for the new CIA as it seeks to remake itself for the global war on terrorism.

More than ten years have passed since we left off this story, and a vastly different set of struggles consumes our protagonists these days.

Of the Russians, Rem Krassilnikov died in March 2003. He had retired from the KGB with the Order of the October Revolution for his brilliant work against the Americans. During his retirement, he lived in Moscow with his wife, Nellie, and wrote two books covering his years in counterintelligence. One is about his CIA adversaries, *The Phantoms of Tchaikovsky Street,* and the second deals with his years of tracking British intelligence.

Leonid Shebarshin lives in Moscow, where he heads the private Russian National Economic Security Service with its offices in Dynamo Stadium, home of the old KGB soccer team. He has written his memoirs and remains philosophical about the collapse of the Soviet Union. A mural on his office wall hints at his lingering sentiments, with its heroic scenes of Stalingrad and the Bolshevik revolution. He has traveled in Eastern Europe, but has politely declined invitations to visit the United States for what he terms "obvious reasons."

Viktor Cherkashin retired in 1995 and settled down in Moscow. He is a proud grandfather, whose most recent progeny is a grandson born to his daughter and the American husband she met while studying in California. Cherkashin has traveled to the United States on several occasions but has steadfastly resisted approaches by the FBI. He now splits his time between international consulting and relaxing with his growing family at his dacha outside Moscow.

Vitaly Yurchenko miraculously survived his defection and redefection and has since worked in Moscow as a bank security officer. He refused all requests for an interview. He is uniformly despised as a traitor by his former KGB colleagues, some of whom believe that at an appropriate moment "justice" will be meted out to the traitor Yurchenko somewhere along the Moscow River.

Valentin Klimenko rose to be head of the American Department of the new Russian internal security service, the FSB. He is now its representative in Tel Aviv.

Aleksandr "Sasha" Zhomov, whom Klimenko launched against Jack Downing as PROLOGUE, is chief of the FSB's American Department. He admits he is obsessed with finding the man or men who he is convinced betrayed Aldrich Ames and Robert Hanssen and has pledged to stay with the hunt until he has found his man.

Oleg Gordievsky lives in the United Kingdom. He and his wife, Leila, have divorced, though she and their daughters, Anna and Maria, were finally allowed to resettle in England. Gordievsky has written two books with British author Christopher Andrew detailing his life working for Moscow Center: *KGB* and *Next Stop Execution.* He is mulling over the idea of a Russian cookbook.

Gennady Vasilenko survived his interrogation at Lefortovo Prison from January to June 1988, though he was reduced in rank and fired without pension for misconduct in his association with Jack Platt. He and Platt remain close friends, and

Vasilenko now works on private security investigations in Moscow when he is not hunting in Russia's birch forests.

Valentin Aksilenko broke with Moscow and resettled in Virginia, where he lectures on the Soviet Union and the KGB and engages in business consulting. Sasha Zhomov considers Aksilenko a short-list suspect in the betrayal of Aldrich Ames, but he is wrong.

Among the Afghans, Ahmad Shah Massoud, the legendary "Lion of Panjshir," the man who was to strike a delicate balance between the Soviet occupiers of Afghanistan and the Americans supplying the rebels, was assassinated on September 9, 2001. The CIA believes he was murdered by al-Qaeda, linking his killing to the perpetrators of the terrorist attacks against America two days later. Osama bin Laden almost certainly ordered his death because he knew that an American retaliation for the attacks on New York and Washington would rely on Massoud and his Northern Alliance.

Abdul Haq was executed by the Taliban in Afghanistan in October 2001 as he sought to rally anti-Taliban forces to his side, just weeks before American-backed Northern Alliance forces surged to victory.

Jalaluddin Haqqani, the fierce mujahideen commander of Paktia Province, reached an accord with the Taliban after their 1994 victory. By the time the United States attacked Afghanistan in 2001, Haqqani was on the U.S. wanted list. He is still at large.

Gulbuddin Hekmatyar was driven into exile in Iran by the Taliban in 1995. He returned to Afghanistan in 2001 to rally Pashtun resistance against American forces. The CIA launched a Hellfire missile from an unmanned Predator drone in Afghanistan in 2002 in an unsuccessful attempt to kill Hekmatyar. He is now a hunted man.

Engineer Ghaffar, the team leader in the first stunning Stinger attack against Soviet helicopter gunships outside Jalalabad in September 1986, was killed late in the war when he stepped on a land mine.

In Pakistan, Lieutenant General Hamid Gul retired from the Pakistani Army and went into politics. According to U.S. government sources, he has become linked to extremist groups both in Pakistan and in Afghanistan, and after September 11,

2001, he was characterized by officials at the CIA as "the most dangerous man in Pakistan." Hamid Gul described the September 11 attacks as an "Israeli conspiracy."

On the American side, Clair George was convicted in 1992 of giving false testimony before two congressional committees in 1986, during the Iran-contra investigation. He received a pardon from President George H. W. Bush on Christmas Eve 1992. Later, he did consulting work for Ringling Brothers. He is now retired and lives in the Washington area.

Richard Stolz retired for a second time from the CIA in 1991 and now lives in Williamsburg, Virginia. He has been engaged in a number of consulting activities involving political and economic developments in Eastern Europe, in particular Bulgaria.

Tom Twetten retired in 1996 and moved with his wife, Kay, to the "Northeast Kingdom" in Vermont, where he has become an award-winning bookbinder and successful seller of rare antiquarian books. He is also making the rounds on the lecture circuit.

Jack Downing retired from the CIA in 1996 but was called back to serve as DDO from 1997 to 1999 to try to restore flagging morale in the clandestine services. He has since done work for both Congress and the Pentagon.

Ted Price succeeded Tom Twetten as DDO and retired in 1996. He has since served at the executive level at several corporations involved in international security and risk assessment.

After spending much of his career on the front lines of the Cold War battling the KGB, Burton Gerber retired from the CIA in 1995, four years after the collapse of the Soviet Union. He now does volunteer work in the Washington area and speaks publicly on the ethics of espionage.

During a liaison visit between the CIA and Russian intelligence in Moscow after the collapse of the Soviet Union, David Rolph mischievously locked his new boss, John MacGaffin, out of a sauna at a KGB dacha, after MacGaffin had gone outside to experience the bracing effects of the Russian winter and snow. After Rolph finally let him back in, an unamused MacGaffin told Rolph, "You're going to Botswana." Rolph left Moscow in 1993 and returned to CIA headquarters for an assignment in the DO's Africa Division. Rolph later served in Turkey and Bosnia and held other posts before retiring in 2000. For a time he worked with former KGB officer and defector Viktor Sheymov in a computer security venture; he now works with a Washington-area high-tech company.

Paul Redmond retired from the CIA in 1999, but was called back in 2001 to assess the damage to national security from the Hanssen case.

Jack Platt retired with predictable flair on "International Workers Day"—May 1—in 1987. He is a partner in an international security company and works closely with his old adversaries assisting American businesses in Moscow.

Paul Stombaugh left the CIA in the mid-1990s to take over as CEO of York Barbell, an international sports equipment enterprise, and a Pennsylvania investment group, Susquehanna Investment.

Steve Weber died of a heart attack while visiting his native Budapest in 1994.

Edward Lee Howard, according to Russian police authorities, died in Moscow on July 12, 2002, as a result of an accidental fall in his residence. His body was cremated privately at the instructions of his next of kin.

Aldrich Ames and Robert Hanssen are in federal prison and will remain there for the rest of their lives.

A NOTE ON SOURCES

The Main Enemy is an oral history based on hundreds of interviews with dozens of intelligence officers who played critical, hands-on roles on both sides of the Cold War competition between the CIA and KGB. In many cases, our sources asked that they not be identified. In the cases of the KGB sources, the coauthors used both the interview method and written responses to specific questions or written materials provided by the former KGB officers themselves.

The written answers to questions posed to General Leonid Shebarshin, as well as excerpts from his memoirs published in Russian that he graciously provided, added critical texture to the characterization of the Soviet side of the Afghan period as well as the tumultuous days of August 1991 at Lubyanka and Yasenevo. We are greatly appreciative of his assistance. Similarly, Rem Krassilnikov's patient cooperation and his writings, particularly his account of CIA operations and activities in Moscow cited in the bibliography, provided unique insight into the workings of the KGB's Second Chief Directorate as it tracked its main adversary. We are deeply in Krassilnikov's debt for his help.

The minutes of Politburo meetings and records of conversations between Soviet Politburo members made available by the Gorbachev Foundation and Anatoly Chernyaev and the Woodrow Wilson Cold War International History Project provided valuable insight into Soviet thinking not only about the decision-making process of intervening in Afghanistan, but about the debate on how to withdraw from the war. Chernyaev's presentations and participation in the discussions during the April 2002 conference "Toward an International History of the War in Afghanistan, 1979–1989," hosted by the

Cold War International History Project at the Woodrow Wilson Center, in cooperation with the Asia Program and the Kennan Institute for Advanced Russian Studies at the Woodrow Wilson Center, the George Washington Cold War Group at the George Washington University, and the National Security Archive, provided rich insight into the thinking in the Kremlin as Gorbachev brought the Politburo around to the decision to withdraw from Afghanistan.

Finally, of all the books used as references, David Wise's work on the Edward Lee Howard story is the definitive account of that strange twist of the Cold War. It proved immensely valuable in constructing a timeline for merging the various elements and other firsthand accounts of Howard's defection.

SELECT BIBLIOGRAPHY

DOCUMENTS

CIA's Analysis of the Soviet Union 1947–1991. Editors Gerald K. Haines and Robert E. Leggett, Center for the Study of Intelligence, Central Intelligence Agency, 2001.

The Cold War International History Project Working Paper Series. Cold War International History Project, the Woodrow Wilson Center, senior editor Christian F. Ostermann, Washington, D.C., 2002.

Lundberg, Kirsten. *Politics of a Covert Action: The U.S., the Mujahideen, and the Stinger Missile.* Kennedy School of Government Case Study. Cambridge, Mass., 1999.

Minutes of Politburo Meetings and Records of Conversations between Soviet Politburo Members. Courtesy of the Gorbachev Foundation and Anatoly Chernyaev and the Woodrow Wilson Cold War International History Project, Washington, D.C., April 2002.

On the Front Lines of the Cold War. Documents on the intelligence war in Berlin, 1946–1961, editor Donald P. Steury, CIA History Staff. Center for the Study of Intelligence, Central Intelligence Agency, 1999.

BOOKS

Adams, James. *Sellout.* New York, 1995.

Andrew, Christopher, and Oleg Gordievsky. *Instructions from Center.* London, 1991.

———. *KGB: The Inside Story.* London, 1990.

Andrew, Christopher, and Valili Mitrokhin. *The Sword and the Shield.* New York, 1999.

Ash, Timothy Garton. *The Magic Lantern.* New York, 1990.

Bamford, James. *Body of Secrets.* New York, 2001.

———. *The Puzzle Palace.* New York, 1983.

Barker, Rodney. *Dancing with the Devil.* New York, 1996.

Behr, Edward. *Kiss the Hand You Cannot Bite.* New York, 1991.

Benson, Robert Louis, and Michael Warner. *Venona.* Washington, D.C., 1996.

Chernyaev, Anatoly. *My Six Years with Gorbachev.* English translated version. University Park, Pa., 2000.

Claridge, Duane R., with Digby Diehl. *A Spy for All Seasons.* New York, 1997.

Coleman, Fred. *The Decline and Fall of the Soviet Empire.* New York, 1996.

Crozier, Brian. *The Rise and Fall of the Soviet Empire.* Roseville, Calif., 1999.

Daniloff, Nicholas. *Two Lives, One Russia.* New York, 1988.

Dunloop, John B. *The Rise of Russia and the Fall of the Soviet Union.* Princeton, 1993.

Dupree, Louis. *Afghanistan.* Princeton, 1980.

Early, Pete. *Confessions of a Spy.* New York, 1997.

Echikson, William. *Lighting the Night.* New York, 1990.

Fischer, Benjamin. *At Cold War's End.* CIA, Washington, D.C., 1999.

Gates, Robert M. *From the Shadows.* New York, 1996.

Gordievsky, Oleg. *Next Stop Execution.* London, 1995.

Grau, Lester, and Michael Gress. *The Soviet Afghan War.* Lawrence, Kans., 2002.

Herrington, Stuart A. *Traitors Among Us.* Novato, Calif., 1999.

Hough, Jerry F. *Democratization and Revolution in the USSR.* Washington, D.C., 1997.

Howard, Edward Lee. *Safe House.* Bethesda, Md., *1995.*

Hunter, Robert W. *Spy Hunter.* Annapolis, Md., 1999.

Jalali, A. A., and Lester Grau. *The Other Side of the Mountain.* USMC, Quantico, Va., 1995.

Kalugin, Oleg. *The First Directorate.* New York, 1994.

Kessler, Ronald. *Escape from the CIA.* New York, 1991.

Klass, Rosanne. *Afghanistan: The Great Game Revisited.* Freedom House, Washington, D.C., 1987.

Koehler, John O. *Stasi.* Boulder, Colo., 1999.

Krassilnikov, Rem S. *The Phantoms of Tchaikovsky Street.* Moscow, 1999.

Maas, Peter. *Killer Spy.* New York, 1995.

Mangold, Tom. *Cold Warrior.* New York, 1991.

Murphy, David, and Sergei A. Kondrashev. *Battleground Berlin.* New Haven, 1997.

Persico, Joseph E. *Casey.* New York, 1990.

Polmar, Norman, and Thomas B. Allen. *The Encyclopedia of Espionage.* New York, 1997.

Pryce-Jones, David. *The War That Never Was.* London, 1995.

Remnick, David. *Lenin's Tomb.* New York, 1993.

Richelson, Jeffrey T. *A Century of Spies.* Oxford and New York, 1995.

———. *The U.S. Intelligence Community,* 4th ed. Boulder, Colo., 1999.

Roberts, Jeffrey. *The Soviet Union in World Politics.* London, 1999.

Schecter, Jerrold L., and Peter S. Deriabin. *The Spy Who Saved the World.* New York, 1992.

Shannon, Elaine, and Ann Blackman. *The Spy Next Door.* New York, 2002.

Shebarshin, Leonid V. *The Hand of Moscow.* Moscow, 1992.

———. *The Life of the Intelligence Chief.* Moscow, 1994.

Shvets, Yuri B. *Washington Station.* New York, 1994.

Singh, Simon. *The Code Book.* New York, 1999.

Sontag, Sherry, and Christopher Drew. *Blind Man's Bluff.* New York, 1998.

Teltschick, Horst. *329 Tage.* Hamburg, 1991.

Thomas, Evan. *The Very Best Men.* New York, 1995.

Vise, David A. *The Bureau and the Mole.* New York, 2002.

Weiner, Tim, David Johnston, and Neil A. Lewis. *Betrayal.* New York, 1995.

Weinstein, Allen, and Alexander Vassilicv. *The Haunted Wood.* New York, 1999.

Wise, David. *The Spy Who Got Away.* New York, 1988.

———. *Nightmover.* New York, 1995.

———. *Spy.* New York, 2002.

Wolf, Markus. *Spionage Chef im Gehimen Krieg.* Düsseldorf, 1997.

———. *The Man Without a Face.* New York, 1997.

Woodward, Bob. *Veil.* New York, 1987.

Yousaf, Mohammad. *Silent Soldier.* Lahore, Pakistan, 1991.

Yousaf, Mohammad, and Mark Adkin. *The Bear Trap.* Lahore, Pakistan, 1992.

Zelikov, Philip, and Condoleezza Rice. *Germany Unified and Europe Transformed.* Cambridge, Mass., 1995.

ARTICLES

Shannon, Elaine. "Death of a Perfect Spy," *Time Magazine International Edition,* no. 32 (August 8, 1994).

Wise, David. "The Spy Who Wouldn't Die," *GQ,* July 1998.

———. "Spy on a Tightrope," *GQ,* November 2000.

NEWSPAPERS

Los Angeles Times

The New York Times

The Washington Post

INDEX

Able Archer nuclear exercise, 46
ABSORB, 163
ACCORD, *see* Vasilliev, Vladimir Mikhailovich
Afghanistan, 201–89
  Afghan casualties in, 211, 226–28, 308–9, 324–25, 353
  Afghan intelligence service in, 250, 325
  Afghan morale in, 248, 269–72, 310
  air operations in, 236, 239–40, 244, 246–48, 252, 270, 280–81, 331–33, 335–37, 350, 433, 489
  April Revolution in (1978), 215
  Arab legions in, 237, 357
  borders of, 253, 254–55, 256
  British garrison in (1842), 240, 334, 519, 520
  Chagasaray garrison in, 307–10
  CIA covert operations in, 174, 201, 204–10, 213, 214–15, 225, 229, 232, 244–45, 248, 249–52, 258–59, 268–89, 300–310, 322–58, 489, 518–19, 521
  drug trade in, 336
  Friendship Bridge in, 347, 348–49, 372, 474
  Hazaras in, 235, 274
  helicopter gunship assaults in, 224, 240–48
  Indian-Pakistani conflict and, 260–65, 284, 327, 340, 343
  intelligence on, 216–17, 218–21, 225–28
  Islamic militants in, 212–13, 231, 235, 272–76, 343, 357–58
  Jalalabad Airport ambush in (1986), 240–48, 523
  Jowzjanis in, 274
  KGB covert operations in, 214–18, 231, 252, 325, 327, 341, 351
  Kharga facility in, 221–26, 244, 309
  leadership of, 215–17
  media coverage of, 182, 222–23, 224, 225, 282, 348–49, 351, 357, 519
  mortars used in, 306–10
  mujahideen in, 204, 220, 222, 223, 228–40, 248, 250, 259, 307–8, 332, 333, 336, 342, 344–45, 353
  mules used in, 302–6, 308, 309
  Nangarhar Province of, 233, 234, 244, 271, 332, 333, 357
  Ojhri camp explosion in, 324–28, 338, 342, 346
  pacification efforts in, 201
  Pakistan's support for, 202, 203, 206, 236–40, 248, 256, 268, 282–89, 307–10, 325–28, 352–53

Paktia Province of, 234, 271, 280–82, 332, 335–36, 347, 350, 357, 523
Panjshir Valley of, 226–27, 231, 251, 520, 521
Pashtuns in, 230, 233, 273, 346, 520–21
peace negotiations on, 268, 269, 271–72, 300, 322–23, 325, 327–28, 346
peasantry of, 256–57
Politburo resolutions on, 215–21, 252–58, 265–68
political conditions in, 254–57, 265–68
poppy cultivation in, 475
post-Soviet situation in, 345–58
prisoners-of-war (POWs) in, 332–33, 335–37, 489
propaganda operations in, 215, 226, 231, 272, 350
"silver bullets" in, 269–71, 306–7
Soviet-backed government of, 226, 236, 247, 248, 252, 254–58, 265–68, 270, 271, 280, 282, 325, 333–35, 345–47, 350, 351–52, 356, 357
Soviet casualties in, 246, 310, 344–45, 348
Soviet invasion of, 63, 64, 174, 182, 201–89, 519–20
Soviet territory attacked from, 282–89, 301–2
Soviet withdrawal from, 211, 214, 218, 221, 224, 228, 252–58, 265–68, 269, 271–72, 282, 302, 310, 322–53, 357, 358, 366, 369–70, 371, 373, 474
special operations teams in, 204, 216–17, 307–10
Stinger missiles used in, 202, 204–6, 209, 221–26, 232, 235, 236–48, 269–70, 275, 280, 325, 333, 474, 523
strategic interest of, 212–13, 217–18, 228–29, 518–21
Tajiks in, 230, 346, 520–21
Taliban regime of, 519, 523
tank warfare in, 250, 270–71
Tora Bora cave complexes in, 520
tribal factions in, 228–36, 271–72, 346–47, 352–53, 356, 520–21
U.S. intervention in, 518–21
U.S. policy on, 201–6, 208–9, 211–12, 216, 217, 221, 229, 235, 239–40, 254, 257, 258–59, 272–89, 346–47, 352–53
U.S.-Soviet relations and, 203–4, 267, 275–76, 282–89, 327–28, 342–43, 344–47
Uzbeks in, 346
women in, 231, 274
see also Democratic Republic of Afghanistan
Afghan Task Force, 270, 304–6, 474
AFL-CIO, 381, 417
Africa, 64, 65, 268
agents:
arrests of, 4, 14–15, 30, 65–66, 181–90, 297, 476–77, 515–17
bona fides of, 69, 169
cash payments to, 105, 123, 149–50, 164, 169–70, 189, 362, 425, 429
code names of, 6, 9, 83–84, 106, 434
communications schemes of, 5, 9, 10, 36, 37, 164, 319, 321
controlled, 421–24, 437
as "dangles," 70, 99, 295, 421–24, 435–37
debriefings of, 432–35, 438–39
as "developmentals," 316
double, 16, 21–23, 35, 123, 134,

179, 181, 186, 289–92, 298–99, 376, 377, 385, 426
drugging of, 76, 132–35, 141–42, 144, 168, 404
entrapment of, 192–94
executions of, 132, 151, 179–81, 197, 295–96, 320, 321, 401, 516
exfiltration plans for, 30, 66–68, 421–24, 435–37
fabrications by, 439, 466–71
handlers for, 32, 38–41, 45
"illegal," 361, 362, 416
interrogation of, 9, 31–32, 46–47, 71, 188–89, 197, 320–21, 354, 395, 401, 476–77
kidnapping of, 141–42
as "moles," 29, 31, 46, 367–68, 439, 455, 466–71, 513–17
motivation of, 150–51, 188–89, 425–26
pay phones used by, 33, 35, 55–56
provocateur, 49–60, 77, 99
recall of, 14–15, 30, 45, 124–25, 145, 151
recruitment of, 13, 21–24, 26, 160–61, 170–71, 174–77, 314–18, 379–80, 385, 424–35, 446, 502, 508–9
resettlement of, 429, 438–39, 509
roll-up of, 145–61
secret writing techniques used by, 35
"sign of life" given by, 95
sleeper, 416
suicide by, 10–11, 32, 40, 41, 188, 476–78
traps set for, 153–56, 192, 374, 471
volunteer, 24, 31–35, 54, 104–5, 122–24, 295–97, 369, 401, 421–24, 432–35, 449–55
see also specific agents

Air Force, U.S., 36–37, 281, 331, 454, 519
AK-47 assault rifle, 202
Akhromeyev, Sergei, 255–56, 257, 494
Akhtar Abdur Rahman Khan, 279–89
Bearden's meetings with, 260–65, 272, 287–88, 337–39
death of, 340
Indian-Pakistani confrontation and, 260–65
as ISI chief, 208, 228–30, 232–33, 234–35, 244, 327, 337
as JSC chief, 327, 337–39, 342
Wilson's visit arranged by, 279–82
Zia's relationship with, 208–9, 279–80, 284, 287–88, 338
Aksilenko, Valentin, 166–69, 177–81, 186–87, 407–9, 460–62, 523
Alexander the Great, 229, 240
Allen, Lew, Jr., 37
Allende, Salvador, 223, 374
Alliluyeva, Svetlana, 23
All-Union Treaty, 474, 478
al-Qaeda, 523
American Chemical Society, 100
American International School, 325
Ames, Aldrich, 514–18
arrest of, 514, 517–18, 522, 523, 525
Bearden's encounters with, 80–81, 462–63
cash payments to, 15
as CIA agent, 15–16, 399, 456–58, 462–63, 510
in Colombia, 456–57
as counterintelligence officer, 77, 79, 456–58, 462–63
in counternarcotics center, 463
Czech desk assignment of, 456–57

Ames, Aldrich (*cont'd*)
espionage activities of, 15–16, 79, 123–24, 126, 456, 457, 510, 515–16
FBI investigation of, 514–15
financial situation of, 457, 462–63
Gordievsky investigated by, 46, 67
Hanssen compared with, 129, 515
as KGB agent, 78–79, 123–24, 456, 457, 510, 515–16
marriage of, 456, 463
polygraph tests taken by, 457–58, 517–18
Rome assignment of, 456, 457, 462
as Soviet mole, 15–16, 78–80, 123–24, 129, 157–58
Walker's arrest and, 16
Yurchenko's defection and, 77–81
Ames, Bruce, 100
Ames, Rosario, 456, 463
Amin, Hafizullah, 215, 216, 217–18
AMTORG, 125
Anderson, Frank, 269–70
Anderson, Mike, 109
Andrew, Christopher, 522
Andropov, Yuri, 45, 158, 214–15, 216, 217, 220, 503, 506
Androsov, Stanislov, 79–80, 106–7, 123–24, 139–40
Angleton, James Jesus:
as Counterintelligence Staff chief, 19–24, 31, 384
Helms's relationship with, 21, 23
"sick-think" mentality of, 19–24, 25, 26, 31, 296, 460, 517
ANLACE probe, 368
Antonov AN-26 transport plane, 334
Armacost, Mike, 323
armored personnel carriers (APCs), 270
Army, U.S., 306, 331, 377, 384, 518
Artamonov, Nikolai F. (Nicholas George Shadrin), 132–35, 137, 140
Asquith, Raymond Lord, 66
Association of Russian Orthodox Youth, 52
AT-4 antitank missile, 249
Austria, 170–71, 370, 382, 448
Avtomotora Institute, 313

Baader Meinhof gang, 148
Baca, Phil, 111–12, 115
"Bacha" (interpreter), 229, 233, 234–35, 272, 346
Bahawalpur plane crash (1988), 339–44
Bakatin, Vadim, 501, 502–3, 504–7, 509
Baker, James, 351, 373, 473
Baklanov, Oleg, 478, 488
Bay of Pigs invasion, 373
Bearden, Marie-Catherine, 174, 260, 302, 323–24
Beg, Mirza Aslam, 340–41
Benson, Ray, 51, 52
Beria, Lavrenti, 475–76
Berlin, Battle of, 444
Berlin, East, 148–50, 169–70, 375–80, 387–91, 421–35, 441, 448
Berlin, West, 62, 375–80, 387–91, 407–12, 424–25, 448
Berlin Brigade, 39
Berlin Tunnel, 29
Berlin Wall, 62, 376, 383, 387–91, 393, 401, 407–9, 441, 456, 460, 501
Bessmertnykh, Aleksandr, 473
Bhutto, Benazir, 353, 358, 459
Bhutto, Zulfiqar Ali, 202, 301, 342, 353
bin Laden, Osama, 357, 518–19, 523
Bitov, Oleg, 141–42
Black, Shirley Temple, 395

blackmail, 170–71, 317
black propaganda, 178, 179, 215, 272
Blake, George, 13–14
Blee, David, 23–25, 26, 85
BLIP, *see* Filatov, Anatoli
BLIZZARD, *see* Bokhan, Sergei
Bloch, Felix, 361–66, 514, 515
Blowpipe missile, 239
BM-12 rocket launchers, 332–33, 337
Bokhan, Alex, 30, 104
Bokhan, Sergei (BLIZZARD), 15, 29–30, 151, 240, 515, 516–17
Boldin, Valery, 478
Bolshevik Revolution, 522
Bonn Station, 425
Bosch, William, 109–10, 111, 114–15
Botshan-Kharchenko (Soviet minister), 345
Bracy, Arnold, 293, 294
"Brandenburg's School for Boys," 376
Brasstacks, Operation, 252, 260–65
"bren," 11
Brezhnev, Leonid, 135, 217, 220, 224, 461
Brezhnev Doctrine, 224, 370, 372
Broce, Reid, 86, 145
Brodine, James, 101
Brown, Jerry, 110, 112
Browning, Elizabeth Barrett, 444
Browning, Robert, 444
"brush pass," 25, 66, 436
Brzezinski, Zbigniew, 202–3, 213
Bucciarelli, Robert, 126
Buckley, William, 184
Bulgaria, 406
Burma, 189
burn bags, 64, 339, 465–66
burst transmission equipment, 5, 36
Bush, George H. W., 363, 388, 409, 440, 474, 487, 503, 504, 507, 524

C-5 transport plane, 454
C-130 transport plane, 340–43
cables, intelligence:
- on Afghanistan operations, 244, 248–49, 305–6, 324, 349–50
- circumvention of, 157, 160–61
- "critic," 339–40
- distribution list for, 153–56, 157
- on Eastern European liberation, 390, 430
- encryption of, 160–61
- internal, 470
- on Kharga attack, 221–26, 244
- on Ojhri camp explosion, 324
- operational details in, 4, 172
- phony, 153 56, 192
- on post–Cold War conditions, 463–64
- on Soviet collapse, 480, 482, 484, 497, 500–501
- on Soviet withdrawal from Afghanistan, 349–50
- on Stombaugh arrest, 6–7, 17–18, 26–28
- traffic of, 65, 153–56
- on Yurchenko, 74–76

Canada, 116–18
Carlson, Rod, 106–7, 145, 455
Carter, Jimmy, 26, 63, 135, 202, 204, 213, 229
case officers:
- agents recruited by, 21–23, 160–61, 174–77, 314–18, 354, 424–35
- aliases vs. pseudonyms of, 469–70
- background of, 4, 62, 294, 299
- CIA, 4, 293–94, 298–99, 466–71, 480, 508–9
- debriefing of, 6, 47–49, 59–60
- disguises used by, 39–40, 56–57, 165, 166
- female, 170–71
- "inside work" by, 5, 289, 411, 508

case officers (*cont'd*)
interrogation of, 6, 48–49, 163–66
KGB, 23, 290–91, 295–97, 437, 460–62, 508–9
messages relayed by, 5, 10, 24–25, 35–36, 66, 435–36
miniature tape recorders used by, 12, 55–56
official covers for, 83, 361
operational travel by, 174–77
spouses of, 19, 297
surveillance of, 5–6, 11–12, 25, 33, 39–40, 53, 58–59, 165, 172, 173
training of, 4–7, 83–84, 86, 103, 108–9, 113, 136, 318
weapons carried by, 275, 461–62, 491, 494, 495
see also specific case officers
Casey, William J., 204–10
Afghan operations as viewed by, 204–10, 213, 224, 244–45, 248, 287–88
Bearden's meetings with, 89–90, 151–53, 206–10, 269, 287–88
as CIA director, 51, 57, 61, 64, 89, 119, 142, 174, 206–7, 277, 354–55
congressional relations of, 204–6, 208, 209, 248, 258–59
death of, 268–69
Gavrilov line approved by, 183
Gerber's briefing of, 151–53
Hatch's phone call to, 206
health problems of, 258, 259, 260, 261–62, 265, 268–69
Iran-contra scandal and, 248, 258–59
media coverage of, 119
Nigeria visited by, 206–8
Soviet Union as viewed by, 148–49, 150, 208
Stein's report to, 158–60
Yurchenko's defection and, 80–81, 87–88, 89–90, 119, 142, 151, 152
Castro, Fidel, 391, 461
Catherine II, Empress of Russia, 52, 91
Catholic Church, 126, 311, 381, 417, 510
Ceauşescu, Elena, 406
Ceauşescu, Nicolae, 391, 406
Central America, 119, 209, 258–59, 276–78
Central Intelligence Agency (CIA):
analytical vs. operational elements of, 148, 160–61, 369
"barons" in, 374, 441
budget of, 36
bureaucracy of, 17, 368–69, 441–43, 471–72
case officers of, 4, 293–94, 298–99, 466–71, 480, 508–9
Central American operations of, 209, 258–59, 276, 278
Central Eurasian Division, 513
Cold War mentality in, 395, 410–12, 442–43, 459–60, 462–66, 484–85
congressional oversight of, 63, 258–59, 270, 272, 276–82, 355
Counterintelligence Staff, 18–24, 31, 296, 361–62, 367–68, 384, 456–58, 462–63
counternarcotics operations of, 463, 474, 475
Defector Resettlement Staff, 77
Deputy Directorate for Plans (DDP), 62, 63, 373
Directorate of Intelligence, 315, 389, 406
Directorate of Operations (DO), 50, 60–61, 63, 201, 354–55, 373–75, 441–43, 484, 518
FBI cooperation with, 5–6, 81–82, 108–10, 128, 174–77,

315–16, 319, 395, 438–39, 514
field offices of, 160–61
headquarters of, 3, 160–61, 173–74, 366
KGB penetrated by, 72–74, 438–39, 446–48, 455, 459–60, 462–66, 476–77, 508–9
KGB penetration of, 20–24, 25, 31, 124, 153–56, 158–60, 195–97, 292–99, 465–71, 513–17
KGB relations with, 3–4, 8, 13, 183–84, 313, 396–405, 446–48, 464–66, 475, 481–82, 486, 488–89, 504–7, 509–10, 511
Latin American Division, 175
morale in, 26, 33–34, 63, 105, 173–74, 322, 459–60, 517–18, 524
National Resettlement Operations Center (NROC), 454–55
Near East Division, 23, 71
"1985 losses" of, 145–61, 172, 192, 290, 297, 322, 367–68, 374–75, 422, 432, 439, 467, 471, 509, 513–18
Office of Scientific and Weapons Research, 50
Office of Security (OS), 82, 84, 85, 315, 518
Office of Technical Services, 221
in post–Cold War era, 513, 517–18
Propaganda and Political Action Staff, 418
reputation of, 63, 82, 119, 258–59
Soviet coup attempt monitored by, 474, 479–89, 507
Soviet/East European (SE) Division, 3–4, 17, 18–26, 145–49, 158–60, 169–70, 192, 293, 297, 322, 355–56, 366–71, 374–75, 382–84, 411, 418, 441–43, 459–60, 463–71, 510, 511, 513
Technical Services, 477
training programs of, 4–7, 83–84, 86, 102, 103, 108–9, 113, 136, 318
turnover in, 517–18
Vertefeuille internal investigation of, 367–68, 467, 509–10
wiretaps used by, 10, 28–29, 84, 85, 192, 361–62
Cerny, Oldrich, 392–93, 394, 399, 414–16
Chagasaray garrison, 307–10
Charter 77, 392, 393
Chebrikov, Viktor Mikhailovich, 158, 197, 253, 254–55
Checkpoint Charlie, 375, 376, 390
chemical tracking, 58, 99–101, 152
Cheney, Dick, 277
Chepil, Aleksandr, 69–70
Cherkashin, Viktor I., 79, 122–25, 139–40, 157–58, 522
Chernenko, Konstantin, 217, 220–21
Chernyaev, Anatoly, 214, 218, 253, 265, 391
chief of operations (COPS), 17, 369
Children's World, 492
Chile, 223, 374
China, 62, 212, 267, 331
Churchill, Winston S., 220, 370
Churkin, Vitaly, 141, 144
Chuvakhin, Sergey D., 15
Civic Forum, 393–94, 398
Clancy, Tom, 115
"clean slot" jobs, 83
Cline, Jill, 435–37
Cline, Michael, 396–97, 435–37, 443, 447–48, 470
CNN, 388, 389, 390, 409, 480, 484, 487, 507
Colby, William, 373

Cold War, 18, 61, 117, 162, 189, 229, 313, 355, 365
  end of, 370–71, 375, 388, 389, 411, 416, 417–18, 441, 505, 508–9, 513, 517–18
  U.S.-Soviet relations in, 94, 216–17, 319
Committee for State Security, Soviet, 135, 189–90, 325, 443, 461, 476, 497, 501
Communism, Communists:
  downfall of, 391, 393, 408, 412–13, 417–18, 445, 460–62, 472–74
  icons of, 497–99
  international movement of, 224, 370, 371–72
  Islamic activism against, 273
  world revolution as goal of, 13, 371–72
COWL, *see* Vorontsov, Sergey
Crile, George, 282
Crockett, Vincent, 26
Cuba, 22, 312–13
Cuban missile crisis, 22
Curly (Stasi agent), 378–80, 385, 426
Czechoslovakia, 133, 392–95, 398–99
  CIA intelligence on, 394–95, 399, 415, 416
  Communist downfall in, 393–94, 398–99, 408, 414–16
  East German exodus into, 386
  popular discontent in, 372, 392, 393–95
  Prague Spring in (1968), 372, 392
  security service of, 392, 393–95, 398–99, 413, 414–16
  Soviet occupation of, 372, 392–93, 398
  Velvet Revolution in, 392–95, 398–99, 414–16, 456–57
Czempinski, Gromoslaw, 380–82, 413, 421, 439–40, 449
Daley, Richard J., 483
Daniloff, Nicholas, 50–52, 57–58, 59, 60, 182–85, 292
Daniloff, Ruth, 51
dead drops, 10, 25–26, 136, 147, 190, 299, 378
defectors:
  acceptance of, 143, 150–51, 336, 401–2
  aliases used by, 133–35
  debriefings of, 20–21, 72–76, 88–89, 110–11, 117, 118, 123
  intelligence provided by, 20–21, 72–76, 382, 459–60
  from KGB, 72–74, 438–39, 446–48, 455, 459–60, 462–66, 476–77, 508–9
  kidnappings of, 132–35, 138
  rejection of, 20–21, 142–43, 459–60
  resettlement of, 454–55, 464
  from Soviet military, 432–35, 449–55
Defense Intelligence Agency, 37, 134
Degtyar, Viktor M., 122–25, 127
Democratic Party, 277, 503
Democratic Republic of Afghanistan (DRA), 226, 236, 247, 248, 252, 254–58, 265–68, 270, 271, 280, 282, 325, 333–35, 345–47, 350, 351–52, 356, 357
Deng Xiaoping, 391
"denied-area" work, 5, 61, 289, 411, 508
Desert One, Operation, 63
détente, 94, 216, 318
Devine, Jack, 223, 244–45, 247–48, 269–70, 474
Discus transmission system, 36
Dobrynin, Anatoly, 253, 255, 257, 283, 286
Dostum, Abdul Rashid, 352

Dottie (Bearden's secretary), 462, 509
Downing, Jack, 289–99
as East Asia chief, 374–75
Leningrad visited by, 290, 291, 292, 298
as Moscow station chief, 185–86, 289–99, 374, 396
"1985 losses" and, 374–75
Ogorodnik's contacts with, 10, 11, 185
Red Arrow trips of, 289–92, 298, 421
restaurant routine followed by, 291, 297–98
retirement of, 524
Zhomov's contacts with, 289–99, 421, 522
Downing, Suzie, 297
DRA, *see* Democratic Republic of Afghanistan
Dubs, Adolph, 215–16
Dudelcyzk, Michael, 111
Dulles, Allen, 373
Dumas, Roland, 490
Dunn, Bert, 205
Dupree, Louis, 520
Dynamo Sports Complex, 177, 314, 521
Dzerzhinsky, Felix, 492, 495, 497–99, 501, 506

Eagleburger, Lawrence S., 423
East Berlin Station, 375–80, 407–12, 424–35
EASTBOUND, 152, 172
East German Task Force, 426
Egypt, 212, 213, 326
8th Army, Afghan, 221–22, 225–26
Ely-Raphel, Nancy, 341
Enduring Freedom, Operation, 519–21
Engels, Friedrich, 314
espionage:
in Cold War, 62–63
human vs. technical penetration in, 153–56, 159, 161, 190–91
media coverage of, 100–101
"miracle laboratories" used for, 156–57, 162–63
morality of, 63
tradecraft of, 4, 25
see also agents
Ethiopia, 61
Europe, Eastern, 370–421
émigré publishers in, 417–18
Iron Curtain in, 370
liberation movements in, 355, 370–421, 472
Soviet occupation of, 19–20, 355, 370–71, 383, 401, 472, 475
U.S. relations with, 372–73
see also specific countries
Europe, Western:
military alliance of, 46, 240, 252, 331, 440, 442, 445, 450, 490
Soviet threat to, 450
European Community, 490
explosive ordnance disposal (EOD) teams, 327

F-15 fighter, 37
Fahim, Mohammad Qasim, 520–21
Falasha Jews, 61
FAREWELL (Vetrov), 131–32
Farm, the, 21, 29, 83, 84, 289, 377, 469
Federal Bureau of Investigation (FBI):
agents of, 315–16, 322
ANLACE probe of, 368
Bloch investigated by, 362, 364–66
CIA cooperation with, 5–6, 81–82, 108–10, 128, 174–77, 315–16, 319, 395, 438–39, 514
code names used by, 106

FBI (*cont'd*)
counterintelligence operations of, 124, 127–28, 296, 311, 316, 367, 483
KGB penetration of, 124, 367, 465, 515
"1985 losses" and, 509
Soviet agents interrogated by, 71, 354, 395
Soviet Analytical Unit of, 311
Soviet embassy tunnel of, 128, 515
in Vasilenko recruitment attempt, 315–16
Yurchenko defection and, 78
Zakharov arrested by, 181–85
Filatov, Anatoli (BLIP), 25–26, 151
FITNESS, *see* Varennik, Gennady
FitzGerald, Desmond, 373
Foley, Tom, 278
Ford, Gerald R., 135
Forden, David, 30, 83, 84, 85
40th Army, Soviet, 206, 226–28, 229, 246–47, 271, 310, 330, 333–34, 344, 350, 353, 520
France, 131, 179, 180, 362, 366
Friedenburg, Hans Georg von, 443
Front for the Rescue of Afghanistan, 230
FSB security service, 509, 522
Fulton, Robert, 33–34

G-2 Intelligence Directorate, 276
Gailani, Pir Sayed Ahmad, 233, 234, 235, 334–35
Gandhi, Rajiv, 263, 264
Gates, Robert, 323
as acting CIA director, 261, 265, 269, 487, 506
as deputy CIA director, 248, 258
Pakistan visited by, 248–52
Gavrilov channel, 183–84, 369, 396–405, 443–48, 480
Gebhardt, Carl, 85, 183
Geer, Jim, 81
GENTILE (PIMENTA), 106–8, 145, 147, 152
George, Clair:
Afghan policy and, 239, 245, 282–84
as Deputy Director for Operations (DDO), 7, 61, 151, 153, 158–59, 173–74, 191, 201, 208, 209, 292, 355, 373, 374
in Iran-contra scandal, 524
"1985 losses" and, 156, 158–59
Yurchenko's defection and, 74–75
Gerber, Burton, 59, 151–56
background of, 3–4, 18–20
case book of, 104–5
Casey briefed by, 151–53
at CIA training exercise, 4–7
Downing appointed Moscow station chief by, 289–90, 293
as European Division chief, 389, 441–42, 469
Father Potemkin affair as viewed by, 49, 59–60
Gavrilov line used by, 183–84
Howard case as viewed by, 81–82, 85–86, 143
as Moscow station chief, 4
"1985 losses" and, 151–53, 155–56, 160–61, 166, 296–97
personality of, 3–4, 61–62
Polyshchuk's arrest as viewed by, 106–7
retirement of, 524
as SE Division chief, 3–4, 46, 60, 61–62, 83, 102, 109, 171, 172–73, 174–77, 185, 355–56, 366, 368, 374–75, 389, 442
as "sticks and bricks" man, 61
Stombaugh's arrest and, 6–7, 26–28, 47–49, 59–60
Tolkachev's arrest and, 3–7
Yurchenko case and, 74–75, 89,

121–22, 137–38, 139, 140, 143
Zhomov as viewed by, 296–97, 298, 423
Gerber, Rosalie, 3
German Democratic Republic (East Germany), 375–91
CIA intelligence on, 375–80, 382–85, 387–90, 406–12, 441
CIA recruitment campaign in, 424–35
Communist downfall in, 382–91, 393, 399, 408, 427–28
media coverage of, 387–90, 409, 430
military sensors placed in, 376–78
popular demonstrations in, 370–71, 372, 386–91, 409–12
security service of, 375–80, 382, 385, 386, 391, 409–12, 424–32, 509
Soviet military forces in, 442, 445, 449–55, 473, 485
Soviet occupation of, 370–71, 383, 386, 443–48
surveillance in, 375–76, 378–80, 411
travel restrictions lifted in, 382–83, 385–91
West Germany reunited with, 428, 431, 440–48, 454
see also Berlin, East
Germany, Federal Republic of (West Germany):
CIA operations in, 376–78, 425, 441
East German exodus into, 387–91
East Germany reunited with, 428, 431, 440–48, 454
terror campaign planned for, 148–50, 152
see also Berlin, West
Germany, Nazi, 391, 416, 430, 443–44, 448, 477
"get black," 6, 12, 114, 165, 173, 377
Ghaffar, Engineer, 237–43, 245–46, 523
Gikman, Reino, 361–63, 364
global positioning satellite (GPS) system, 307–8, 309
Golden Temple (Amritsar), 261
Golitsyn, Anatoliy, 21, 22
Golubev, Sergei M., 46, 131–32
Gora, Blanka Ewa (Ewa Shadrin), 133, 134–35
Gorbachev, Mikhail, 478–94
Afghan policy of, 204, 211, 214, 218, 221, 252–58, 265–68, 322–23, 371, 373
coup attempt against, 373–74, 478–94, 507–8
Eastern European policy of, 370, 371–72, 383, 386, 440
foreign policy of, 255
perestroika policy of, 472
Reagan's relationship with, 183, 292
as Soviet premier, 54, 186, 458, 472–74, 478–79, 504
Yeltsin's relationship with, 473, 478
Gordievsky, Oleg Antonovich, 14–15, 44–47, 66–68, 108, 111, 167, 397–98, 401, 403, 516, 517, 522
Great Britain:
Afghan interests of, 212, 213, 240, 334, 519, 520–21
agents exfiltrated by, 66–68
empire of, 211, 229, 240
intelligence services of, 167, 401, 404, 414, 416, 521
KGB agents in, 13, 14, 44–47
Grimes, Sandy, 94, 160, 171, 195, 509
Gromov, Boris, 344, 348–49, 350, 351, 358, 366, 372
Gromov, Maksim, 349
Gromyko, Andrei, 216, 217, 253–54, 256, 266

Grossman, Werner, 429–30
GRU:
  Afghan intelligence of, 217, 227–28
  CIA penetration of, 25, 29
  defectors from, 464, 508–9
  front organizations of, 125
  headquarters of, 188–89
  Nairobi *Rezident* of, 153–56, 374
  Stinger missile acquired by, 239–40, 252
Grushko, Viktor, 493
"Gs, the," 109, 136, 137
Guilsher, John, 35–36, 37, 38
Gul, Hamid, 284–88
  as ISI chief, 284–87, 288, 301–2, 327, 333, 337
  as "plucky little general" (PLG), 301–2, 358
  as U.S. adversary, 358, 523–24
  Zia's death as viewed by, 343
Gulag Archipelago, The (Solzhenitsyn), 38
Gulf War, 437–38, 439–40, 449, 454–55, 472
Guyana, 174–77

Hannah, Tom, 138–39
"Hans" (polygraph operator), 105
Hanssen, Bonnie, 126–27, 363–64
Hanssen, Robert, 122–29
  as agent "B," 124, 129, 311, 362, 483
  Ames compared with, 129, 515
  arrest of, 515, 522, 525
  background of, 128–29
  Bloch operation betrayed by, 362–66
  cash payments to, 123, 126–27, 129, 363, 458
  Catholic identity of, 126–27, 129, 311, 510
  classified information stolen by, 122–25, 363, 458
  communication plan of, 310–11, 362–63
  dead drops serviced by, 128, 310–12, 363, 458, 482–83, 510
  Degtyar letter of, 122–25, 127
  double agents betrayed by, 123, 124–26, 129
  espionage activities of, 122–29, 310–12, 482–83, 515, 516
  as FBI agent, 124–29, 311–12, 363–65, 458, 483, 510, 514–15
  as GRU agent, 125–27, 187, 516
  as KGB agent, 122–29, 310–12, 362–66, 458, 482–83, 510, 515, 516
  marriage of, 126–27, 129, 311, 363–64
  in New York Field Office, 125, 127–28, 129
  political campaign contributions by, 363–64
  Polyakov betrayed by, 187
  in Soviet Analytical Unit, 311
  Soviet collapse as viewed by, 483, 510
Haq, Abdul, 222–23, 523
Haqqani, Jalaluddin, 282, 523
Hartman, Arthur, 51
Hatch, Orrin, 201–2, 205–6, 208
Hathaway, Gardner "Gus":
  as counterintelligence chief, 155, 183–84, 367–68, 374, 405, 443
  at Helsinki meeting, 397–405
  as Moscow station chief, 34–35
  Wolf's meeting with, 431–32
Hauptverwaltung Aufklarung (HVA), 376, 385, 424–32
Havel, Václav, 392–94, 398–99, 413, 414–16
Hayden, Thomas, 68–70, 99
Hecht, Chic, 208
Hekmatyar, Gulbuddin, 223, 231–33, 234, 235, 236, 251, 272–76, 346, 523

Helms, Jesse, 208
Helms, Richard, 21, 23, 373–74
Helsinki meeting (1989), 396–405, 446, 505
Higham, Jim, 374
Hinton, Dean, 300
Hisb-e-Islami, 272, 273
Hitler, Adolf, 38, 391, 412, 430, 448, 477
Holt, Jim, 509
Honecker, Eric, 382–83, 385, 386
Hoover, J. Edgar, 503–4
House Permanent Select Committee on Intelligence (HPSCI), 277–78
Howard, Edward Lee, 81–86, 89, 90–91
  "angry colonel" mentioned by, 146–47
  background of, 82
  CIA investigation of, 81–86, 117, 130
  death of, 525
  defection of, 130, 151, 296, 400
  dismissal of, 75, 81–86, 89, 108–9, 149
  drug use by, 82, 84
  as economic analyst, 84–85, 90, 111–12
  espionage activities of, 83–84, 85–86, 89, 90–91, 109–10, 115, 137, 145, 159, 163, 168, 367, 515, 516
  FBI investigation of, 81–82, 86, 108–15, 117, 130, 136–37
  marriage of, 83, 111–15, 136–37
  Moscow assignment of, 83–84
  polygraphs taken by, 75, 82, 84, 111
  surveillance evaded by, 86, 103, 108–15, 130, 136–37
  training of, 83–84, 103, 108–9, 113, 136
  Vienna visited by, 75, 90–91
  wiretap of, 85, 110
  Yurchenko's identification of, 75, 76, 80, 86, 89, 98, 109, 111, 117, 142, 145
Howard, Lee, 85, 113, 137
Howard, Mary, 83, 111–15, 136–37, 149
Hugel, Max, 158, 354–55, 373
Humphrey, Gordon, 208
Hungarian Revolution (1956), 370
Hungary:
  barbed-wire border removed in, 370, 372, 382
  Communist downfall in, 391, 393, 399, 408
  East German exodus into, 382, 386
  security service of, 418–19
Hunt for Red October, The (Clancy), 115
Husák, Gustav, 398
Hussein, Saddam, 437, 439, 449
HVA (Hauptverwaltung Aufklarung), 376, 385, 424–32

Ilschenko, Annelise, 278, 344
India:
  air force of, 327
  army of, 260–65
  China's relations with, 212
  intelligence service of, 263
  military exercises of, 251–52, 260–65
  nuclear weapons of, 264–65
  Pakistan's confrontations with, 251–52, 260–65, 284, 327, 340, 343, 358
  Punjab Province of, 263, 284
  Soviet relations with, 262, 267–68
intelligence:
  analysis of, 148, 160–61, 368–69, 382–83, 504–5
  cables on, *see* cables, intelligence
  collection of, 62–63, 426–28

intelligence (*cont'd*)
communications, 10, 28–29, 84, 98–99, 128, 159, 160–61, 170–71, 190, 192, 316, 361–62, 369, 402–3, 427, 471
compartmentation of, 79, 160–61, 368–69, 515
counter-, 5–6, 73, 80, 98–99, 118, 129, 298–99, 312, 465
covert operations in, 61–62, 204–10
destruction of, 64, 339, 409–12, 491
efficiency vs. security in, 368–69
foreign policy and, 184
human, 519
leaks of, 119, 121, 132–33, 137
military, 29, 35, 36–37, 98–99, 105, 146–47, 377–78, 432–35, 449–55
paranoia in, 19–24, 25, 26, 31, 296, 460, 517–18
political, 178
relevance of, 382–83, 406–7, 410–12, 479–83, 487–89
research and development (R&D), 37
satellite, 28, 29, 225, 244–45, 247, 309, 346–47, 377
security measures for, 160–61, 293–94, 368–69
surveillance, 8, 39–40, 51, 55–59, 92–93, 97, 99–102, 106–7, 152, 290–92, 293–94, 299, 375–76, 402–3, 475, 508
tracing of, 122–25
see also espionage
Internal Operations (IO) course, 4–7, 83, 86, 103, 108–9, 113, 136, 318
Inter-Services Intelligence Directorate (ISI), 225, 228, 243, 262–63, 272, 279–81, 284–85, 301–2, 327, 353
Iran, 63, 204, 211, 214–15, 217, 219–20, 237, 253, 356, 374
Iran-contra scandal, 248, 258–59, 269, 277–78, 355, 374, 524
Iran hostage crisis (1979), 63–64, 217
Iran-Iraq War, 212
Iraq, 212, 437–38, 449, 454
Iron Curtain, 370
Isakov, Viktor, 141, 144
Islam, 202, 212–13, 228, 230, 231, 233, 234, 235, 287, 357–58
Islamabad, 202, 206, 210, 228, 281, 300–302, 322, 327
Islamic Movement, 273
Israel, 61, 92, 524
Ivy Bells, Operation, 98–99, 316

Jalalabad, 333–35, 353
Jalalabad Airport ambush (1986), 240–48, 523
Jamiat Islami, 231
Janjua, Brigadier, 325–26
Jasik, Henrik, 439–40
Jews, Falasha, 61
JIB ("jack-in-the-box" pop-up dummy), 113–14
jihad, 232, 235, 274, 275, 357
JOGGER, *see* Piguzov, Vladimir
John Paul II, Pope, 64, 149
Jones, Elizabeth, 340
Jones, Philippe, 326–27
Juchniewicz, Ed, 61, 74–75, 140–41, 152, 174
Junejo, Mohammed Khan, 263, 285, 327, 328–29
Justice Department, U.S., 362, 365

Kabul, 330, 345–47, 519, 520
Kabul University, 230, 231, 274
Kalashnikov rifle, 246, 250
Kalinichenko, Ilya Yakovlevich, 493
Kamman, Curt, 54

Kampiles, William, 29
Karmal, Barak, 218, 257, 351, 352
Karzai, Hamid, 520
Keitel, Wilhelm, 443
Kelly, Barry, 24
Kennedy, John F., 20–21, 22, 373
Kerr, Richard, 459, 506
KGB:
  arrest procedures of, 9–10, 17, 312–13
  budget of, 509
  bureaucracy of, 14, 30, 79, 88–89, 158, 166–69, 495–97
  case officers of, 23, 290–91, 295–97, 437, 460–62, 508–9
  Chief Directorates of, *see* KGB Chief Directorates
  CIA as "main enemy" of, 3–4, 8, 13
  CIA penetrated by, 20–24, 25, 31, 124, 153–56, 158–60, 195–97, 292–99, 465–71, 513–17
  CIA penetration of, 72–74, 438–39, 446–48, 455, 459–60, 462–66, 476–77, 508–9
  CIA relations with, 3–4, 8, 13, 183–84, 313, 396–405, 446–48, 464–66, 475, 481–82, 486, 488–89, 504–6, 509–10, 511
  counterintelligence operations of, 9, 17, 46–47, 58–59, 79, 99, 106–7, 122, 163–64, 295–97, 298–99, 314, 517
  deception operations of, 22, 49–60, 97, 178, 179, 190–92, 231
  dismemberment of, 502–3, 509
  duty phone lines of, 149, 164
  FBI penetrated by, 124, 367, 465
  Helsinki meeting arranged by (1989), 396–405
  internal propaganda operation in, 460–62
  interrogations by, 9, 31–32, 46–49, 131–32
  JFK assassination and, 20–21
  Karlshorst headquarters of, 148–50, 443
  Line officers of, 106, 122, 123, 145, 152, 167, 177–81, 318
  morale in, 318, 321, 408–9, 460–62
  Moscow Center, 72, 154–55, 157, 186–87, 317–18, 321, 408–9, 491, 508
  paramilitary units of, 485–86
  protest demonstrations against, 492, 495, 497–99
  reform of, 494, 502–3, 509
  replacement agencies for, 509
  Science and Technology (S&T) Directorate, 131–32, 516
  security department of, 495
  Soviet collapse and, 408–9, 460–62, 475–76
  Soviet coup attempt and, 478–79, 480–82, 485–94, 507–8
  terror campaigns sponsored by, 148–50, 152
  tracking substance used by, 58, 99–101, 152
  volleyball team of, 177, 314, 521
  Washington *Rezidentura* of, 79, 106–7, 116, 122–25, 138, 152, 166–69, 177–78, 314, 316
  Yasenevo headquarters of, 177, 180–81, 186
KGB (Gordievsky and Andrew), 522
KGB Chief Directorates:
  First, 13, 14, 68, 73, 79, 91, 157–58, 166–69, 172, 177, 179, 180, 184, 186, 218, 314, 319, 321, 365, 446–48, 460, 485–86, 490–92, 501, 502, 509, 510

KGB Chief Directorates (*cont'd*)
Second, 5, 11, 13–15, 32, 71, 91, 97, 106–7, 157, 164, 167, 173, 196, 197, 291, 295, 296, 395, 401, 421, 460, 475, 502–3, 509, 515, 522
Seventh, 5, 9, 71, 97, 107, 167
Ninth, 487–88
Sixteenth, 502, 515
Eighteenth, 502
"KGB's First Chief Directorate, The: Structure, Functions, and Methods" (Hanssen), 510
KH-11 spy satellite, 29, 309, 346–47
Khad, 250, 325
Khales, Maulvi Yunis, 233–35
Khan, Isma'il, 216
Kharga attack (1986), 221–26, 244, 309
Khomeini, Ayatollah Ruhollah, 212, 219
Khrushchev, Nikita, 22, 214, 230
Khyber Agency, 249–52, 278, 353–54
Kim Il Sung, 391
King, Stephen, 182
Kipling, Rudyard, 211
Kireyev, Anatoly Tikhonevich, 184
Kirilenko, Andrei, 216
Kirpichenko, Vadim, 168
KLETTERING, 469–70
Klimenko, Valentin, 97, 196–97, 421, 522
Kochnov, Igor, 134
Kohl, Helmut, 388–89, 490
Koran, 228, 234, 287
Korean War, 336
Kosygin, Alexei, 216
Krasnaya Pakha, 28
Krassilnikov, Rem Sergeyevich, 396–405
background of, 13–14, 30
Bearden's meetings with, 396–405, 443–48, 475–76
death of, 521
German reunification as viewed by, 443–48
at Helsinki meeting, 396–405
interrogations by, 9, 31–32, 48–49, 91, 92–94, 97, 165–66, 401
"miracle laboratory" discovered by, 156–57, 162–63
name of, 13, 445
personality of, 13, 396–405, 444
physical appearance of, 400–401, 486
Polyakov investigated by, 187
retirement of, 521
Rolph's meetings with, 486, 488–89, 500–503
as Second Directorate chief, 13–14, 197, 401, 421, 475, 502–3, 521
Seller's arrest planned by, 163–66, 172, 173
Soviet collapse as viewed by, 502–3, 509
Soviet coup attempt and, 481–82, 500–501
Stombaugh's arrest planned by, 8–9, 11, 13, 15, 17, 42–43, 48–49
Tolkachev investigated by, 9, 31–32, 91, 401
Krassilnikova, Ninel, 13, 521
Kremlin, 476
Krenz, Egon, 385–87
Krizan, Jiri, 414
Kryptos (Sanborn), 366
Kryuchkov, Vladimir:
arrest of, 493, 496, 499, 509
coup attempt supported by, 479, 484, 485–86, 488, 489, 493, 507
as First Directorate chief, 157–58, 168, 186, 255, 257, 334–35, 351–52, 371
Gorbachev's relationship with, 479, 493

internal propaganda operation of, 460–62
as KGB director, 371, 476, 479, 491, 500
Kryuchkova, Ekaterina Petrovna, 496
Kulagin, Vladimir, 141
Kunjerab Pass, 302–3, 304
Kuwait, 437, 439
Kuzmin, Colonel, 476

Lameroux, Dave, 154–55
Lauder, Ron, 192
le Carré, John, 400
Lefort, Franz, 91
Lefortovo prison, 9, 44, 91–94, 131–32, 156, 182, 320–22, 500
Lenin, V. I., 13, 498
Leningrad, 290, 291, 292, 298, 437
Leonov, Nikolai Sergeyevich, 460–61
Leven, Chuck, 149, 169, 191
Ligachev, Igor, 267
Lincoln, Abraham, 106
Lithuania, 472
Lonetree, Clayton, 192–95, 292–94
L-pill, 9–11, 32, 40, 41, 188, 476–78
Lubyanka Prison, 7, 165–66, 492, 495
Luzin, Mikhail, 182

MacGaffin, John, 13, 375, 513, 524
McMahon, Dennis, 83
MACRAME, 432–35, 453–55
madrassas (religious schools), 213, 358
Major, John, 490
Makarov pistol, 251, 275, 461
Makowski, Aleksandr, 381, 414
Manners, David, 394–95, 399, 456
Marine guard spy scandal, 192–95, 292–95, 367
Markov, Georgi, 132
Martin, John, 362
Martynov, Valeriy, 123, 125, 151, 168–69, 177–78, 190, 320, 368
Marvin, Lee, 115
Marx, Karl, 314
Massoud, Ahmad Shah, 226–28, 231–32, 251, 271–72, 273, 346, 352–53, 519, 523
Matlock, Jack, 473
Mazar-e-Sharif, 352
Medanich, Chuck, 77–78, 86–89, 90, 98, 115–22, 138
MEDIAN, *see* Potashov, Vladimir
Mein Kampf (Hitler), 38
Meir, Golda, 38
MI6, 401, 415
MI-8 helicopter, 474
MI-24D attack helicopters, 238, 239, 240–48, 252, 270–71, 275
Michni Point, 202
MiG-21 fighter, 280–81
MiG-23 fighter, 37
MiG-25 fighter (attack helicopter), 37, 331–32
MiG-29 fighter, 37, 432–35, 437–38, 453–55
Milan antitank missile, 270–71
Milburn, Jim, 509
Milczanowski, Andrzej, 412–14, 421, 440, 449
MILLION, *see* Smetanin, Gennady
Mills, Tom, 85, 110
Ministerium für Staatssicherheit (MfS), *see* Stasi
Mirage fighter, 327
Mitrokhin, Vasili, 365
Mohammedi, Nabi, 233
Moiseyev, General, 493
Mojaddedi, Sibghatullah, 230, 235, 347
M1 Abrams tank, 338
MONOLITE, *see* Vasilenko, Gennady
Moore, Edwin G., 76–77
Morris, Jim, 339, 342

Moscow:
apartment vacancies in, 96, 103, 516
CIA headquarters in, 25–26, 32–33, 102, 161, 292–95, 367, 439
CIA operational runs in, 3–7, 65, 95–97, 149, 151–53, 163–66, 299
Gorbachev's return to, 487–88, 489, 491–93
KGB surveillance in, 8, 39–40, 51, 55–59, 92–93, 97, 99–102, 106–7, 152, 290–92, 293–94, 299, 375, 402–3, 475, 508
"1985 losses" in, 145–61, 172, 192, 290, 297, 322, 367–68, 374–75, 422, 432, 439, 467, 471, 509, 513–18
operational stand-down in (1977–1978), 26, 34
popular demonstrations in, 492, 495, 497–99, 507
U.S. embassy in, 3, 26, 33, 37, 51, 54, 101–2, 161, 165, 185–86, 192–97, 292–93, 402–3, 505, 506–7
White House in, 482, 485
"Moscow Rules," 5, 161
Moseby. Bill, 154–55, 374
Mossad, 61
Motorin, Sergey, 123, 177, 178–79, 190, 320, 368
Movement for the Islamic Revolution of Afghanistan, 233
"moving through the gap," 25, 113–14
mug books, 98–99, 120
mules, 302–6, 308, 309
Muslim Brotherhood, 233, 234
Muslim Youth, 273

Nagy, Imre, 370
Nairobi, Kenya, 153–56
Najibullah, Fatan, 352
Najibullah, Muhammad:
downfall of, 325, 345–47, 350, 352, 353
Soviet support for, 254–58, 265, 268, 325, 334, 350, 351–52
Natifboff, Murat, 4, 53–55, 121, 185, 293, 297–98
National Islamic Front, 233
National Security Agency (NSA), 28–29, 55, 75–76, 98–99, 120, 128, 159, 316, 502
National Security Council (NSC), 184, 344, 383
National Security Decision Directive 166, 204
NATO, *see* North Atlantic Treaty Organization
Naval Investigative Service, 195
Navy, U.S., 29, 69, 98–99
Next Stop Execution (Gordievsky), 522
Nicaragua, 119, 209, 277
Nigeria, 61, 206–8
Nikitenko, Leonid, 45, 47, 396–405, 443, 446–48
nitrophenylpentadienal (NPPD), 100
Nixon, Richard M., 63
NKVD, 13, 412
Noonan, Bob, 109
North, Oliver, 259
North Atlantic Treaty Organization (NATO), 46, 240, 252, 331, 440, 442, 445, 450, 490
Northern Alliance, 272, 519, 523
Nosenko, Yuri, 20–21
Novodvorskaya, Valeria, 500
nuclear disarmament, 377–78
nuclear proliferation, 264, 358
nuclear war, 45–46, 264–65
Nunn, Sam, 239

Oak, Operation, 218
Oakley, Robert, 340, 344

Odessa network, 416
Office for the Protection of the Constitution and Democracy, 414–15
Office of Strategic Services (OSS), 19
Ogorodnik, Alexander (TRIGON), 10–11, 25, 32, 151, 185, 289, 477
Ojhri Camp, 236–40, 242, 324–28, 338, 342, 346
Olga (CIA "poet"), 11
Olson, Jim, 6, 29, 47, 192–94
Olson, Meredith, 192
O'Malley, Ed, 81
Opus Dei, 126, 311
Order of Lenin, 69
Order of the October Revolution, 521
O'Reilly, John, 384, 441, 442–43, 484
Organization of the Islamic Conference, 353
Oswald, Lee Harvey, 20–21

Pakistan, 260–65
  Afghan policy of, 202, 203, 206, 236–40, 248, 256, 268, 282–89, 307–10, 325–28, 352–53
  Afghan resistance leaders in, 222–23, 228–36, 275–76, 346–47, 353
  air force of, 340–43
  army of, 229–30, 260–65, 284, 302, 307–10, 327, 328, 337–44
  British influence in, 211
  Casey's proposed visit to, 248, 249
  democracy in, 353, 358
  Indian confrontations with, 251–52, 260–65, 284, 327, 340, 343, 358
  intelligence service of, 225, 228, 243, 262–63, 272, 279–81, 284–85, 301–2, 327, 353
  Islam in, 202
  Northern Territories of, 210
  North-West Frontier Province of, 249, 278–79, 357
  nuclear weapons program of, 264–65, 358
  Punjab province of, 210–11
  Soviet relations with, 253, 257–58, 267, 268, 286
  Stinger training program in, 236–40
  training camps in, 236–40, 242, 248–52, 259
  U.S. embassy in, 63, 326–27, 344
  U.S. relationship with, 202–6, 213, 264, 282–89, 327–28, 339–44, 353–54, 357–58
  U-2 flights flown from, 203
Pakistan Frontier Forces, 278
Palevich, John, 418–21
Papushin, Sergei, 395, 421, 438–39, 455, 471
Parker, Phillip, 110, 114
Parker, Stuart, 165
"paroles," 16, 427, 432
Pascal, Blaise, 489–90
Paulus, Friedrich von, 430
Pearl Harbor attack, 62
Pelton, Ronald, 120, 316–17
Penkovsky, Oleg, 22, 151
People's Democratic Party of Afghanistan, 215
Pershing missiles, 215
"Peshawar Seven," 228–36, 276, 346–47, 353
Peter I, Czar of Russia, 91
Peterson, Marty, 25
Pfister, Mike, 340
Phantoms of Tchaikovsky Street, The (Krassilnikov), 521
Philby, Kim, 13, 31
Piekney, Bill, 201–2, 204–6, 281, 483–84

Piguzov, Vladimir (JOGGER), 191, 367
Pillsbury, Michael, 205–6
PIMENTA (GENTILE), 106–8, 145, 147, 152
Platt, Jack:
  background of, 313–15
  Guyana trip of, 174–77, 311
  Howard investigation and, 108–9, 136–37
  intelligence report filed by, 311, 319
  Internal Operations (IO) course run by, 5, 83, 86, 318
  retirement of, 322, 525
Plekhanov, Yuri, 478, 488
PNG (persona non grata) war, 185–86, 292, 293
Poland:
  CIA intelligence on, 381–82, 418–21
  Communist downfall in, 267, 370, 372, 380–81, 391, 393, 399, 401, 408
  security service of, 380–82, 412–14, 418–21, 439–40
  Solidarity movement in, 370, 380–82, 412–14, 449
  Soviet occupation of, 370, 412–14
  U.S. relations with, 439–40, 449
Politburo, Soviet, 212, 215–21, 252–58, 265–68, 371, 403, 487
Polyakov, Dmitri Fedorovich (TOP HAT), 125–26, 153, 181, 187–89, 367
Polyakov, Peter, 187
polygraphs, 69, 75, 82, 84, 105, 111, 114, 137, 186–87, 368, 457–58, 517–18
Polyshchuk, Leonid Georgiyevich (WEIGH), 92–97
  arrest of, 92–97, 106–8, 151, 152, 515–17
  cash payments to, 94, 96–97
  CIA handlers for, 94–97
  communications plan of, 93
  as counterintelligence colonel, 92, 94–95
  Katmandu posting of, 94–95
  Krassilnikov's interrogation of, 92–94, 97, 401
  Lagos posting of, 92, 95, 152, 167, 515–16
  Moscow dead drop serviced by, 92–97, 107, 152, 167
Popov, Gavril, 473
Popov, Pyotr Semyonovich, 151
Portugal, 104–5, 418–21
Potashov, Vladimir (MEDIAN), 191
Potemkin, Roman, 49–60
  Daniloff's contacts with, 50–52, 57–58, 59–60, 183
  as KGB agent, 52, 57, 184
  letter supposedly written by, 50, 53–55, 60
  Stombaugh's meeting with, 49, 50, 53–60
Powers, Francis Gary, 203
Prague Spring (1968), 372, 392
Price, Ted, 361–62, 365, 443, 447, 524
PROLOGUE, *see* Zhomov, Alexander "Sasha"
propaganda, 226, 231, 350, 404, 417, 460–62
  black, 178, 179, 215, 272
Pugo, Boris Karlovich, 494
PULSAR, *see* Rogalla, Jürgen
Pushkin, Aleksandr, 38

Qala-i-Jangi prison uprising, 519

Rabbani, Burhanuddin, 230–31, 232, 235
radiation detection, 156–57, 162–63, 377–78
Radzivill, Count von, 388
Rankin (agent), 175, 176
Raphel, Arnie:
  death of, 339–41, 343, 344

as U.S. ambassador to Pakistan, 300–302, 322–23, 326–27, 328–30, 358
Rawalpindi, 211, 287, 326–27
Reagan, Ronald:
Afghan policy of, 174, 203, 204, 205, 206, 208, 224, 245, 248, 274, 323
Daniloff affair and, 183–85
foreign policy of, 45, 64, 87–88, 149
Gorbachev's relationship with, 183, 292
Hekmatyar's proposed meeting with, 274, 276
inaugurations of, 363
Iran-contra scandal and, 355
Pakistan nuclear capability as viewed by, 264
Reasoner, Harry, 282
Red Army, 187, 189, 221, 344, 465, 485, 510–11, 519–20
Red Army Faction, 148
Red Arrow express train, 289–92, 421, 435–36
Redmond, Kathy, 30
Redmond, Paul, 459–60, 462–68
Ames as viewed by, 462–63
background of, 30–31
Bearden's relationship with, 65–66, 107–8, 148–50, 367, 395, 442, 459–60, 462–68
as counterintelligence officer, 459–60, 463, 465–68, 470, 471, 509, 514
debate requested by, 465, 467
East European liberation as viewed by, 382, 384, 419, 420, 442–43, 445, 501
Lonetree case reviewed by, 194–95
"Mr. X" as viewed by, 190–91
"1985 losses" and, 145–46, 147, 148–50, 155–56, 159, 163, 166, 190–92, 296–97, 367, 467
Polyshchuk's arrest as viewed by, 106–8
retirement of, 525
Rolph's meeting with, 410–12, 424
as SE Division deputy chief, 356, 367, 369, 384, 442–43
Smetanin's recall as viewed by, 104–5, 108
Stombaugh's arrest and, 26–28, 47, 48, 108
transfer of, 443, 460
Vertefeuille investigation and, 367–68
Yurchenko case and, 145
Zhomov's exfiltration as viewed by, 423, 436–37
Reiser, Dick, 30
Republican Party, 363–64
Riaz, Colonel, 244, 263–64, 265
Ridgeway, Rosalyn, 144
Rochford, Michael, 86, 145
Rogalla, Jürgen (PULSAR), 428–29
Rolph, David:
as East Berlin station chief, 375–80, 384–85, 387–88, 390–91, 410–12, 424–35, 438, 471
Krassilnikov's meetings with, 486, 488–89, 500–503
MACRAME defection and, 432–35, 453–55
as Moscow station chief, 471–73, 479–82, 486, 495, 498, 500–501, 508, 524–25
Redmond's meeting with, 410–12, 424
ROSETTA defection and, 451–53
Soviet coup attempt and, 479–82, 486
Tolkachev's meetings with, 38–41, 375
Romania, 391, 405–6
Roosevelt, Franklin D., 220
ROSETTA, 449–53

Royden, Barry, 161
RPG-7 grenade launchers, 250, 270
Ruml, Jan, 415–16
Russia (Russian Federation), 473, 486, 509
Russian National Economic Security Service, 521
Russian Orthodox Church, 52
Rutskoi, Aleksandr, 332–33, 335–37, 489
RYAN, Operation, 45–46
Ryzhkov, Nikolay Ivanovich, 266–67

SA-7 missile (SAM-7), 236, 237, 239, 247
SA-19 missile, 449–53
safe houses, 30, 249, 251, 438, 443, 446
Salvo Bay, Battle of, 289
SAMs (surface-to-air missiles), 221–26, 449–53
Sanborn, James, 366
Saudi Arabia, 212–13, 234
Sayyaf, Abdul Rasul, 233–34, 235, 346–47
SB security service, 380–82
Schabowski, Gunter, 386–87, 388
Scowcroft, Brent, 480
SDR (surveillance detection route), 11–12, 25, 40, 43, 53
2nd Army Corps, Afghan, 333
secret agents, *see* agents
Secret Intelligence Service (SIS), 14, 44–47, 66
Seina, Violetta, 195
Sellers, Michael, 53, 58–59, 83, 163–66, 172, 173
Senate Armed Services Committee, 239
September 11 attacks, 518, 523–24
Shadrin, Ewa (Blanka Ewa Gora), 133, 134–35
Shadrin, Nicholas George (Nikolai F. Artamonov), 132–35, 137, 140
Shah of Iran (Mohammad Reza Pahlavi), 215
shalwar kameez, 231, 233, 237, 251, 344, 354
Sharansky, Natan, 92
Sharavatov, Vladimir, 9, 15, 43, 92, 93, 94
Shebarshin, Leonid Vladimirovich:
  as acting KGB director, 491–501
  Afghan situation as viewed by, 218–21, 226–28, 252, 325, 330, 333–36, 350–53, 371, 373, 520
  documents destroyed by, 491
  Eastern European liberation as viewed by, 371–73
  as First Directorate chief, 371–73, 485–86, 490–92
  India-Pakistan conflict as viewed by, 262
  retirement of, 507, 521–22
  Soviet collapse as viewed by, 489–97
  Soviet coup attempt as viewed by, 480–81, 485–94
  Zia's death as viewed by, 341–42
Shebarshina, Nina, 498
Shenin, Oleg, 478
Shevardnadze, Eduard, 163, 183, 211–12, 253, 255, 266, 267, 323, 351, 371, 373, 383, 473
Sheymov, Viktor, 525
Shia Muslims, 212, 235
Shorer, David, 71, 72–74
Shultz, George, 183, 211, 283, 286, 323, 340, 344, 351, 373
Sibelius, Jean, 67
Siberia Maru, 162
Sikhs, 260–61
Simon, Mort, 111
60 Minutes, 282
Slavnov, Anatoly, 178, 186
Smetanin, Gennady (MILLION), 103–5, 108, 151, 152, 367
Smith, Havilland, 24–25

Snetkov, Boris, 453
Snyder, Dutch, 304–6
Sokolov, S. L., 226–27, 253, 267
Solidarity movement, 370, 380–82, 412–14, 449
Solomatin, Boris, 72
Solzhenitsyn, Aleksandr, 38
Soviet Union:
- Afghanistan invaded by, *see* Afghanistan
- air force of, 36–37, 236, 239–40, 244, 280–81, 331–33, 335–37, 432–35, 474
- arms exports of, 213
- borders of, 67–68, 253, 254–55, 256, 282–89, 301–2
- collapse of, 372, 408, 460–62, 465–66, 472–74, 475–511, 513, 519–20, 521
- Communist Party of, 215–21, 252–58, 265–68, 371
- coup attempt in (1991), 473–74, 478–94, 507–8
- decline of, 64
- democratic reforms in, 490, 492
- economic conditions in, 372
- encirclement of, 215, 217
- as "Evil Empire," 64, 149
- expansionism of, 213, 224
- gulag prison system of, 497
- land-based communications in, 28–29
- media coverage of, 50–51, 182–85, 479–80, 484, 490, 492, 507
- navy of, 29, 98–99, 316
- nuclear weapons of, 22, 28, 50, 156–57, 162–63, 377–78, 465
- political repression in, 32–33, 38, 54, 91–92, 188–89, 497, 500
- popular discontent in, 472–74, 507
- as superpower, 262, 275, 344
- technical probes of, 156–57, 162–63
- U.S. relations with, 3–4, 8, 13–14, 94, 185–86, 203–4, 215, 216–17, 267, 275, 282–89, 292, 293, 319, 327–28, 342–43, 344–47, 358, 372–73, 445
- Western Group of Forces, 442, 445, 449–55, 473, 485

Spann, John Micheal, 519
Spaso House, 34, 57, 100–101
"special preparations," 9–11, 188, 476–78
Spetsnaz (special operations troops), 204, 307–10
SPG-9 recoilless rifle, 271
Sprava One, 398, 415
"spy dust," 58, 99–101, 152
SR-71 reconnaissance aircraft, 366
SS, 416
Stalin, Joseph, 23, 32, 91–92, 214, 220, 391, 412, 497
Stalingrad, Battle of, 430, 522
Stankevich, Sergei, 498
Stasi, 375–80, 382, 385, 391, 409–12, 424–32, 509
State Department, U.S.:
- CIA relations with, 205
- KGB penetration of, 361–66
- passports issued by, 423
- "spy dust" briefing by, 100–101
- Yurchenko redefection and, 141, 143–44

StB security service, 398–99, 414–16
Stein, John, 158–60, 355, 373
Stinger antiaircraft missiles, 29–30, 202, 204–6, 209, 221–26, 232, 235, 236–48, 269–70, 275, 280, 325, 333, 474, 523
Stolz, Richard:
- as Deputy Director for Operations (DDO), 353–56, 366, 374, 375, 442, 463, 477–78, 524
- Helsinki meeting and, 397
- Zhomov's exfiltration approved by, 421–24

Stombaugh, Betsy, 12, 43, 47
Stombaugh, Paul M.:
arrest of, 6–9, 11, 13, 15, 17–18, 26–28, 42–43, 47–49, 59–60, 108, 152
debriefing of, 47–49
expulsion of, 47, 112
retirement of, 525
Tolkachev's proposed meeting with, 11–12, 42–43, 47, 53
STONE, 449–53
Storm, Operation, 218
Strauss, Robert, 503–6
"stump broke," 305–6
Stumpf, Hans Jürgen, 443
Sudan, 61
Sufis, 230, 233
suicide pills, 9–11, 32, 40, 41, 188, 476–78
Sukhoi-25 fighter, 331–32, 335–36, 338, 342
Sukhoi-27 fighter, 37
Sundarji, Krishnaswami, 252, 260–61, 263, 264, 265
Supreme Council of the North, 272, 346
Supreme Soviet, 472–73, 481
surface-to-air missiles (SAMs), 221–26, 449–53
surveillance detection route (SDR), 11–12, 25, 40, 43, 53
SVRR, 509

Taman Guards Division, Soviet, 481
Taraki, Nur Muhammad, 215–17
Tass news agency, 112–13, 148, 168, 189–90
TAW, Operation, 28–29, 30, 84, 91, 108
Teheran Conference (1943), 220
Teresa, Mother, 126–27
terrorism, 148–50, 152, 184
Thailand, 323–24
Tharpe, Arvel, 259
Thatcher, Margaret, 46, 213
Third World, 61–62, 202, 463–64
Thompson, Colin, 117–18, 120, 139, 140
Tiananmen Square massacre, 370
Titov, Gennady, 150, 494, 503
Tolkachev, Adolf Grigoryevitch, 3–10
Ames's betrayal of, 16
arrest of, 7, 8–10, 30, 31–32, 38, 40–43, 60, 80, 84, 91, 105, 107, 108, 112–13, 151, 152, 167, 172
background of, 9, 32–33
cash payments to, 12, 17, 37–38, 41
CIA handlers for, 26, 31–41, 83, 112–13, 375
communications schemes of, 9, 37, 42
execution of, 189–90
imprisonment of, 9, 92
Krassilnikov's investigation of, 9, 31–32, 91, 401
motivation of, 32–33, 37–38
secret documents photographed by, 9, 12, 16–17, 36, 40–42, 50, 112–13
security probe and, 40–41, 91
Stombaugh's proposed meeting with, 11–12, 42–43, 47, 53
suicide pill possessed by, 32, 40, 41
ventilator-window signal of, 37, 43
Tolkachev, Oleg, 32, 37
Tolkacheva, Natalia, 32, 34, 37
Tomaszewski, Ryszard, 418–21
TOP HAT, *see* Polyakov, Dmitri Fedorovich
Treholt, Arne, 150
TRIGON, *see* Ogorodnik, Alexander
Tsymbal, Vladimir, 319
Turgenev, Ivan, 38
Turkmenistan, 513
Turner, Stansfield, 25–26, 34, 37, 63

Twetten, Kay, 524
Twetten, Tom, 245, 355–56, 374, 421–24, 463, 524

UH1 "Huey" helicopter, 249–50
ultradiscreet surveillance, 293–94, 299, 508
United Nations, 128, 181, 185–86
United States:
- Afghan policy of, *see* Afghanistan
- defense programs of, 36–37
- nuclear weapons of, 45–46, 377
- Pakistani relations with, 202–6, 213, 264, 282–89, 327–28, 339–44, 353–54, 357–58
- Polish relations with, 439–40, 449
- Soviet diplomats expelled by, 185–86, 292, 293
- Soviet relations with, 3–4, 8, 13, 94, 185–86, 203–4, 215, 216–17, 267, 275, 282–89, 292, 293, 319, 327–28, 342–43, 344–47, 358, 372–73, 445
- superpower status of, 275, 448

U.S. News & World Report, 50–51, 182
Ustinov, Dmitri, 214–15, 217
U-2 reconnaissance aircraft, 203, 366
Uzbekistan, 204, 282–89, 301–2, 348–49, 513

Varennik, Gennady (FITNESS), 148–51, 169, 191, 367, 401
Varennikov, Valentin, 478
Vasilenko, Gennady (MONOLITE), 312–22
- arrest of, 312–13
- background of, 176–77, 313–14
- dismissal of, 321–22
- Guyana assignment of, 174–77, 312–13, 317–19, 320
- hunting rifle acquired for, 174–77, 318, 322
- interrogation of, 320–21, 522
- loyalty of, 314–20
- Platt's friendship with, 174–77, 311, 313–22, 522–23
- volleyball played by, 176–77, 313–14

Vasilliev, Vladimir Mikhailovich (ACCORD), 146–47, 367
Vatican, 64, 71–72
Velvet Revolution, 392–95, 398–99, 414–16, 456–57
Vertefeuille, Jeanne, 367–68, 467, 509
Vetrov, Vladimir Mikhailovich, 131–32, 179–81, 516, 517
Vienna, 134–35, 183–84, 192–94, 361–62
Vietnam War, 38–39, 62–63, 69, 203, 214, 267, 323, 333, 336
Villa Abamelek, 71–72
Vilnius uprising (1991), 472–73
Vorontsov, Sergey (COWL), 58–59, 100, 152, 156, 163–66, 172, 173, 401
Vorontsov, Yuli, 255, 256–57, 323

Wade, Robert, 465
Waguespack, Michael, 110–11, 112
Walesa, Lech, 388
Walker, Arthur, 69
Walker, John:
- arrest of, 16, 69, 70, 124
- spy ring run by, 69, 99, 191

Walker, Michael, 69
Wallenberg, Raoul, 92
Ward, Terry, 375
Wardak, Rahim, 223, 282
Warren Commission, 20
Warsaw Pact, 213, 217, 271, 306, 370, 372, 376, 445, 501

Washington, D.C.:
diplomatic zone around, 88, 137–38
KGB *Rezidentura* in, 79, 106–7, 116, 122–25, 138, 152, 166–69, 177–78, 314, 316
Soviet embassy in, 120, 128, 141–43, 515
Washington Post, 111, 354, 506
Washington Times, 119
Wassom, Herb, 339–40, 343, 344
Watergate scandal, 63
weapons of mass destruction, 475
Weber, Steve, 369, 383, 384, 385, 442, 525
Webster, William, 269, 323, 355, 389, 406–7, 409–10, 423, 431, 477–78, 506
Wehrmacht, 443
WEIGH, *see* Polyshchuk, Leonid Georgiyevich
Whitehead, John, 144
Whitworth, Jerry, 69
Wilson, Charlie, 276–82, 344
Wisner, Frank, 373
Woerner, Manfred, 490
Wolf, Andrea, 431
Wolf, Markus, 429, 431–32
Wolfe, Alan D., 71
Woolsey, R. James, 517
World War II, 62, 188, 220, 289, 384, 391, 412, 430, 443–44
Worthen, Diana, 160, 195
Wright, Jim, 277–78

"X, Mr.," 169–70, 190–91, 471

Yakovlev, Aleksandr, 371
Yakushkin, Dimitri, 77, 157, 178–79, 181
Yaqub Khan, Sahabzada, 286, 301
Yazov, Dmitri, 473, 488
"yellow submarine," 102, 161
Yeltsin, Boris, 507, 509
Gorbachev's relationship with, 473, 478
KGB documents on, 491
KGB reformed by, 502–3, 509
media coverage of, 507
as Russian president, 473, 478, 482, 485, 489, 509
Soviet coup opposed by, 482, 485, 489
Yereskovsky, Valentina, 115–20
Yousaf, Mohammed, 284–85, 287, 288–89
Yurchenko, Vitaly Sergeyevich, 68–82
Artamonov (Shadrin) case and, 132–35, 137, 140
background of, 68, 76–77, 116, 121
Bearden's relationship with, 74–75, 80–81, 89–90, 131–33, 140–41, 143–44
cancer fear of, 72, 117, 131
CIA handlers for, 86–89, 120, 121–22, 137–38, 140–41, 311
debriefings of, 72–76, 77, 78–80, 88–89, 98–99, 116, 117, 141–42, 145–46, 311
defection of, 68–82, 115–22, 311
FBI involvement with, 86–87, 88–89, 120, 139, 311
Hayden interrogated by, 68–70, 99
Howard identified by, 75, 76, 80, 86, 89, 98, 109, 111, 117, 142, 145
in KGB First Chief Directorate, 68, 73
love affair of, 115–20
media coverage of, 119, 121, 132–33, 137, 141–45
moodiness of, 88–89, 116, 118–22, 131–33
mug shots examined by, 98–99, 120
Pelton identified by, 120

redefection of, 121, 137–45, 151, 152, 168–69, 177, 179, 311, 404, 522
in Rome, 68–74, 116
safe houses for, 77–78, 80–81, 86–89, 98, 116, 121, 131–33, 138
tracking agents confirmed by, 99, 100
U.S. arrival of, 77–80
Yuzhin, Boris, 123

Zakharov, Gennady, 181–85
Zenith, Operation, 217
Zhomov, Aleksandr "Sasha" (PROLOGUE), 196–97, 289–99, 421–24, 435–37, 522
Zhukov, Georgi K., 444
Zia ul-Haq, Mohammed, 260–65, 339–44
Afghan policy of, 202, 203, 204–6, 208–9, 229–30, 232–33, 235, 268, 287–88
Akhtar's relationship with, 208–9, 279–80, 284, 287–88, 338
Bhutto as rival of, 202, 301, 342, 353
death of, 339–44
Indian military exercise as viewed by, 251–52, 260–65
as president, 208–9, 260–65, 279–80, 284, 285, 328–30
U.S. support for, 208–9, 251–52, 268, 277, 282, 329–30